# The Handbook of
# Counselling Children and Young People

Sara Miller McCune founded SAGE Publishing in 1965 to support the dissemination of usable knowledge and educate a global community. SAGE publishes more than 1000 journals and over 800 new books each year, spanning a wide range of subject areas. Our growing selection of library products includes archives, data, case studies and video. SAGE remains majority owned by our founder and after her lifetime will become owned by a charitable trust that secures the company's continued independence.

Los Angeles | London | New Delhi | Singapore | Washington DC | Melbourne

# The Handbook of
# Counselling Children
# and Young People

Edited by

## Maggie Robson | Sue Pattison

**2nd Edition**

Los Angeles | London | New Delhi
Singapore | Washington DC | Melbourne

Los Angeles | London | New Delhi
Singapore | Washington DC | Melbourne

SAGE Publications Ltd
1 Oliver's Yard
55 City Road
London EC1Y 1SP

SAGE Publications Inc.
2455 Teller Road
Thousand Oaks, California 91320

SAGE Publications India Pvt Ltd
B 1/I 1 Mohan Cooperative Industrial Area
Mathura Road
New Delhi 110 044

SAGE Publications Asia-Pacific Pte Ltd
3 Church Street
#10-04 Samsung Hub
Singapore 049483

Editor: Susannah Trefgarne
Assistant editor: Talulah Hall
Production editor: Martin Fox
Copyeditor: Camille Bramall
Proofreader: Mary Dalton
Indexer: Martin Hargreaves
Marketing manager: Camille Richmond
Cover design: Sheila Tong
Typeset by: C&M Digitals (P) Ltd, Chennai, India
Printed in the UK

Preface © Mike Shooter 2018

Editors' Introduction © Maggie Robson and Sue Pattison 2018

Chapter 1 © Divine Charura 2018
Chapter 2 © Graham Bright 2018
Chapter 3 © Sue Kegerreis and Nick Midgley 2018
Chapter 4 © Paul Stallard 2018
Chapter 5 © Belinda Harris 2018
Chapter 6 © Niki Cooper and Kelli Swain-Cowper 2018
Chapter 7 © Lisa Gordon Clark 2018
Chapter 8 © Barbara Smith, Kaye Richards, Karen
      Lowe and Peter Lowe 2018
Chapter 9 © Ani de la Prida and Wendy Hay 2018
Chapter 10 © Edith Bell and Dave Stewart 2018
Chapter 11 © Sue Pattison and Sandra Bell 2018
Chapter 12 © Claire Harrison-Breed 2018
Chapter 13 © Penny Leake, Ann Beynon and Jenny Biancardi 2018
Chapter 14 © Peter Pearce, Gwen Proud and Ros Sewell 2018
Chapter 15 © Dee C. Ray 2018
Chapter 16 © Katie McArthur and Mick Cooper 2018
Chapters 17 and 18 © Peter Jenkins 2018
Chapter 19 © Divine Charura, Tom McAndrew and Sue Pattison 2018
Chapter 20 © Maggie Robson 2018
Chapter 21 © Jennifer Baggerly 2018
Chapter 22 © Sum Yu Pansy Yue and Dennis Ougrin 2018
Chapter 23 © Beverly Turner-Daly 2018
Chapter 24 © Rebecca Kirkbride 2018
Chapter 25 © Paul Nicholson, Divine Charura and
      Brian Charlesworth 2018
Chapter 26 © Barbara Smith, Sue Pattison and Cathy Bell 2018
Chapter 27 © Peter Pearce, Ros Sewell and Karen Cromarty 2018

First edition published 2014. Reprinted 2015 (three times),
2016 (twice), 2017
This second edition published 2018

**Library of Congress Control Number: 2018931031**

**British Library Cataloguing in Publication data**

A catalogue record for this book is available from the British Library

ISBN 978-1-5264-6116-2
ISBN 978-1-5264-1055-9 (pbk)

At SAGE we take sustainability seriously. Most of our products are printed in the UK using responsibly sourced papers and boards.
When we print overseas we ensure sustainable papers are used as measured by the PREPS grading system. We undertake an annual audit
to monitor our sustainability.

# CONTENTS

# LIST OF FIGURES AND TABLES

## FIGURES

## TABLES

# LIST OF ABBREVIATIONS

| | |
|---|---|
| AA | Alcoholics Anonymous |
| ADHD | attention deficit hyperactivity disorder |
| AN | anorexia nervosa |
| APA | American Psychiatric Association |
| ASA | adoption support agency |
| ASD | autistic spectrum disorder |
| ASLI | Association of Sign Language Interpreters |
| BACP | British Association for Counselling and Psychotherapy |
| BACPCYP | British Association for Counselling and Psychotherapy Children and Young People |
| BAPT | British Association of Play Therapists |
| BN | bulimia nervosa |
| BPS | British Psychological Society |
| BSL | British Sign Language |
| BTE | behind-the-ear |
| CAMHS | Child and Adolescent Mental Health Services |
| CBT | cognitive-behavioural therapy |
| CCS | Catholic Children's Society |
| CORC | CAMHS Outcome Research Consortium |
| CORE-OM | Clinical Outcomes in Routine Evaluation – Outcome Measure |
| CORS | Child Outcome Rating Scale |
| CPS | Crown Prosecution Service |
| CSRS | Child Session Rating Scale |
| CYP | children and young people |
| CYP IAPT | Children and Young People's Improving Access to Psychological Therapies |
| CYP PRN | Children and Young People Practitioner Research Network |
| DBT-A | Dialectical Behaviour Therapy for adolescents |
| DCHP | Deaf Children of Hearing Parents |
| DfE | Department for Education |
| DGP | Developmental Group Psychotherapy |

| | |
|---|---|
| DoH | Department of Health |
| DPM | Dual Process Model |
| DSM-5 | Diagnostic and Statistical Manual of Mental Disorders, Fifth Edition |
| EBD | emotional and behavioural difficulties |
| EBP | evidence-based practice |
| EDNOS | eating disorder not otherwise specified |
| EMDR | eye movement desensitisation and reprocessing |
| FBT | family-based treatment |
| GCSE | General Certificate of Secondary Education |
| GP | general practitioner |
| HCPC | Health and Care Professionals Council |
| HI | hearing impaired |
| IAPT | Improving Access to Psychological Therapies |
| IPT | interpersonal therapy |
| IQ | intelligence quotient |
| LA | local authority |
| LMS | Local Management of Schools |
| LSCB | Local Safeguarding Children Board |
| MBT-A | Mentalisation-Based Therapy for Adolescents |
| MCE | manually coded English |
| MHF | Mental Health Foundation |
| MI | motivational interviewing |
| NDPT | Non-directive play therapy |
| NHS | National Health Service |
| NICE | National Institute for Health and Clinical Excellence |
| NSPCC | National Society for the Prevention of Cruelty to Children |
| OCD | obsessive compulsive disorder |
| Ofsted | Office for Standards in Education, Children's Services and Skills |
| ORS | Outcome Rating Scale |
| PACE | Playfulness Acceptance Curiosity and Empathy |
| PBRN | practice-based research network |
| PCA | person-centred approach |
| PTSD | post-traumatic stress disorder |
| RCT | randomised controlled trial |
| SAN | sub-threshold anorexia nervosa |
| SATs | Standard Assessment Tests |
| SBN | Sub-threshold bulimia nervosa |
| SCIE | Social Care Institute for Excellence |
| SCoPReNet | School-Based Counselling Practice Research Network (now CYP PRN) |
| SDQ | Strengths and Difficulties Questionnaire |
| SE | Signed English |
| SEE | Seeing Exact English |

| | |
|---|---|
| SEL | social and emotional learning |
| SENCO | special educational needs coordinator |
| SIGN | Scottish Intercollegiate Guidelines Network |
| SSE | Sign Supported English |
| STPP | short-term psychodynamic psychotherapy |
| UKCP | United Kingdom Council for Psychotherapy |
| UNCRC | United Nations Convention on the Rights of the Child |
| UPR | unconditional positive regard |
| WAG | Welsh Assembly Government |
| WHO | World Health Organization |
| YCORS | Young Child Outcome Rating Scale |
| YP-CORE | Young Person's Clinical Outcomes in Routine Evaluation |
| ZPD | zone of proximal development |

# ABOUT THE EDITORS AND CONTRIBUTORS

**Dr Maggie Robson** is a senior teaching fellow at Keele University, where she supervises PhD students and the dissertations of Master's students. Before taking partial retirement, she was responsible for the professional counsellor training programme. She is also a qualified play therapist and has a special interest in working with, and researching, children's bereavement. She has taught play therapy training programmes in the UK, Kenya and the US, and trained the first play therapy supervisors in Kenya. She is currently joint Chair of the British Association for Counselling and Psychotherapy (BACP) Children, Young People and Families Division. In her free time she is a bit of a water baby and enjoys sailing, canoeing and swimming. She also loves walking with her beautiful dog, bike riding and the occasional glass of wine!

**Dr Sue Pattison** is a counsellor, supervisor and trainer with Sue Pattison Consulting. Sue was Director of a PhD programme at Newcastle University for many years and is now lecturer in psychology at Arden University. She teaches and researches counselling internationally, and has a busy counselling and supervision practice. She is a founder member of the BACP Counselling in Schools Research Consortium and joint Chair of the BACP Children, Young People and Families Division.

**Dr Jennifer Baggerly** is a professor in the Counseling programme in the School of Human Services at the University of North Texas at Dallas. Dr Baggerly is a licensed professional counsellor supervisor and a registered play therapist supervisor. She served as Chair of the Board of Directors for the Association for Play Therapy from 2013–2014 and was a member of the Board from 2009–2015. Dr Baggerly has taught and provided counselling for children for 18 years. Her published books include *Counseling Families: Play-Based Treatment* (2015, Rowman & Littlefield), *Group Play Therapy: A Dynamic Approach* (2014, Routledge) and *Child-Centered Play Therapy Research: The Evidence Base for Effective Practice* (2010, John Wiley and Sons). Dr Baggerly's multiple research projects and over 60 publications have led to her being recognised as a prominent expert in play therapy and children's counselling.

**Cathy Bell** has worked with children and young people in statutory social services settings, within a voluntary organisation and in a residential setting in the developing world. While working with the NSPCC, Cathy set up the school counselling services in Northern Ireland, now Independent Counselling Services for Schools (ICSS) funded by the Northern Ireland Department of Education. Cathy is currently the ICSS coordinator, committed to advocating for a rights-based approach to services for children. Since September 2012 Cathy has been chair of the BACP's Children and Young People's Executive and has recently been awarded a Fellowship with BACP.

**Edith Bell** is Director of Counselling for Familyworks NI. She currently leads the team that delivers community counselling for the company and schools counselling to every post-primary school in Northern Ireland. She is an accredited counsellor with BACP and works with children and young people (CYPs), adults and families. She is passionately committed to the idea of developmental theory informing her work with CYPs and families. She is also a Director of Summit Training, which offers specialist post-qualifying training to CYP counsellors and supervisors. She sits on the BACP CYP committee. She believes her clients have taught her most of what she knows!

**Sandra Bell**, MA, is a BACP accredited counsellor and the founding Director of Time 4 You Psychological Services CIC, an organisation specialising in delivering counselling and therapeutic play to children and young people in schools in the north-east UK. She is a counsellor, clinical supervisor and trainer specialising in attachment-informed practice, with a special interest in looked-after children and adoptive families within the local authority. Sandra has developed counselling services in over 25 schools. She is an eye movement desensitisation and reprocessing (EMDR) practitioner and is trained in dyadic development psychotherapy. Sandra is committed to promoting specialist training competencies for working with children and young people and has successfully developed and delivered training in this field. She welcomes the BACP's 'Essential Elements of Counselling Young People' Introductory modules. Sandra received a special invitation to a reception at Buckingham Palace on World Mental Health Day, where she met with TRH Duke and Duchess of Cambridge and HRH Prince Harry. Sandra is passionate about her family and has three grown up sons and two granddaughters.

**Ann Beynon** is an experienced teacher, school-based counsellor and supervisor. Her experience during the past 40 years has provided researched evidence for the introduction of structured time for self-reflection (STSR) into teachers' professional practice. The recognition of the parallel nature of learning relationships in education and counselling has provided the foundation for this person-centred approach to child development. The STSR model has a fundamental place in child-centred team work in schools. The work on establishing this initiative in education stood in the way of her continuing a co-editing role of this second edition of the handbook.

**Jenny Biancardi** is a person-centred psychotherapist, trainer, mentor and qualified psycho-dramatist. Jenny annually runs a Creative Supervision Certificate training course (now for over 20 years), and is a British Psychodrama Association (BPA) registered senior trainer, BACP senior registered practitioner and United Kingdom Council for Psychotherapy (UKCP) registered psychotherapist. She has a Lifetime Achievement Award for services to psychodrama. She set up the first psychodrama training in the north of England, and later co-founded the Northern School for Psychodrama. Early and enduring influences included working with both children and adults, the training she took at the Castle Hospital in London (which was based on a psychosocial model of psychotherapy) and embedding the core values of Carl Rogers' person-centred approach into the psychodrama process. Now, Jenny continues to work in private practice and is passionate about the importance of seeing each client as a unique individual.

**Graham Bright** is a senior lecturer in childhood and youth studies and youth and community work at York St John University, where he continues to teach counselling skills to undergraduate students. He was formerly a counsellor in a primary school and young offender institution.

**Brian Charlesworth** is a senior lecturer at Leeds Beckett University and Course Leader for the BACP accredited practitioners' course in relational therapy. He has 17 years' experience as a psychotherapist, trainer and clinical supervisor working from a relational perspective and is a senior accredited member of the BACP and a chartered psychologist. He has a special interest in how therapeutic relationships are formed and has worked in residential schools for excluded students with a wide range of presentations.

**Dr Divine Charura** is a chartered psychologist, counselling psychologist and psychotherapist registered with the Health and Care Professions Council and the United Kingdom Council for Psychotherapy (UKCP). He is also Course Director for postgraduate courses in psychotherapy and mental health at Leeds Beckett University. He has many years of work experience in diverse psychiatric/clinical and therapeutic settings. He is a practising psychologist and psychotherapist with individuals, couples and families. Divine has co-authored numerous books and book chapters. His latest books are *The Person-Centred Counselling and Psychotherapy Handbook: Origins, Developments and Current Applications, co-edited with Colin Lago (2014, Open University Press); and Love and Therapy*, co-edited with Stephen Paul (2015, Karnac Books). Divine is a lover of photography, art and outdoor pursuits.

**Mick Cooper** is professor of counselling psychology at the University of Roehampton, where he is Director of the Centre for Research in Social and Psychological Transformation (CREST). Mick is a chartered psychologist, a UKCP registered psychotherapist, and a Fellow of the BACP. Mick is author and editor of a range of texts on person-centred, existential and relational approaches to therapy; including *Working at Relational Depth in Counselling and Psychotherapy (2005, SAGE, with Dave Mearns), Pluralistic Counselling and Psychotherapy*

(2011, SAGE, with John McLeod) and *Existential Therapies* (2nd edn, 2017, SAGE). Mick has led a series of research studies exploring the processes and outcomes of humanistic counselling with young people. Mick is the father of four children and lives in Brighton on the south coast of England.

**Niki Cooper** is the Head of Learning at Place2Be, which is the leading UK provider of school-based emotional support services, reaching a school population of 135,000 children and young people. She is co-author of the Place2Be Postgraduate Diploma in Counselling Children and Young People in Schools, and has also overseen and developed a comprehensive professional pathway from beginner to Master's level child and young person counsellor.

**Karen Cromarty** is a freelance consultant in the field of children and young people's mental health, specialising in young people's counselling. Karen has made significant contributions to the counselling sector over 20 years – as a researcher, advisor, author, broadcaster, ambassador and advocate. She has worked with governments, opinion formers, academics and services (within the statutory, voluntary and private sectors) promoting and supporting evidence-based counselling for children and young people. Karen's main role recently has been as School Coordinator for the ETHOS study – the world's first fully powered randomised controlled trial researching the effectiveness and cost-effectiveness of school counselling.

**Ani de la Prida** is a counsellor, lecturer and supervisor, and co-authored the Counselling MindEd e-learning programme. She developed an MA and DipHE in counselling children and young people for Anglia Ruskin University. Ani has worked in schools, exclusion projects, foster care and drug treatment programmes. She currently teaches and maintains a varied private practice. Her special areas of interest and research include looked-after children, digital media and creative arts therapy.

**Lisa Gordon Clark** is the Programme Convener and a senior lecturer for the Play Therapy MA at the University of Roehampton, where she has been on the staff team for ten years, alongside a private play therapy practice based in Wiltshire. She also offers filial therapy and provides training in child–parent relationship therapy (CPRT). Having trained at Roehampton herself in the mid-1990s, following a previous career as a primary school teacher, Lisa was active on the Board of Directors of the British Association of Play Therapists (BAPT) for over a decade, including chairing the Communications and Public Relations subcommittee. She remains Editor of the annual peer-reviewed British Journal of Play Therapy.

**Belinda Harris**, PhD, is associate professor at the University of Nottingham, where she has undertaken research with head teachers, teachers and school counsellors over many years. She is a UKCP registered gestalt psychotherapist, ICF accredited gestalt coach, Chair of the UK Association for Gestalt Practitioners and serves on the Training Standards Committee for the Gestalt Psychotherapy Training Institute. Prior to training as a psychotherapist, Belinda worked as a teacher and pastoral leader in inner city secondary schools, where she promoted awareness of young people's personal, social and emotional well-being amongst head teachers, teachers, governors and parents.

**Claire Harrison-Breed** is a child psychotherapist and adult psychotherapist specialising in working with trauma and dissociation. Alongside therapeutic practice she is a senior lecturer in counselling for the University of Northampton. Claire has over 25 years' experience working therapeutically in a range of settings, as a registered gestalt psychotherapist, counsellor, cognitive-behavioural therapist, play therapist and social worker. In 2001 Claire founded Broad Horizons, a UK Midlands-based Therapy Centre that specialises in trauma-informed therapy. Claire lectures, researches and publishes both nationally and internationally in the field of trauma and dissociation.

**Wendy Hay** is an experienced counselling practitioner having worked within charitable and social care settings for over 15 years. Wendy also has worked for many years within the childcare system, working systemically to support professionals around looked-after children. Having established a school-based counselling service, she continues to practise as an adult and young persons' counsellor, clinical supervisor and tutor. Wendy is a member of the BACP Children, Young People and Families Division, and served as Deputy Chair from 2012–2018.

**Peter Jenkins** is a registered counsellor, trainer, supervisor and researcher. He has been a member of both the BACP Professional Conduct Committee and the UKCP Ethics Committee. He has written extensively on legal, ethical and professional aspects of counselling and psychotherapy, including *Counselling, Psychotherapy and the Law* (2007, 2nd edn, SAGE) and, with Debbie Daniels, *Therapy with Children: Children's Rights, Confidentiality and the Law* (2010, 2nd edn, SAGE). His most recent book is *Professional Practice in Counselling and Psychotherapy: Ethics and the Law* (2017, SAGE).

**Sue Kegerreis** is a senior lecturer at the Department of Psychosocial and Psychoanalytic Studies at the University of Essex. As a psychotherapist and counsellor (both child/adolescent and adult) she has practised in health, education and community settings as well as in private practice. She devised and ran the MSc in psychodynamic counselling with children and adolescents at Birkbeck and the MA in psychodynamic counselling at the University of Essex, and has taught on numerous other psychotherapy/counselling trainings. She has published widely in professional journals, is Managing Editor of the journal *Psychodynamic Practice and her book Psychodynamic Counselling with Children and Adolescents* appeared in 2010 (Palgrave).

**Rebecca Kirkbride** is a BACP senior accredited counsellor of adults, children and young people. Rebecca trained initially as a psychodynamic counsellor and clinical supervisor, and currently works in private practice with adults and young people. She previously worked for many years as a counsellor with children and young people in schools and the community. Rebecca is the author of *Counselling Children and Young People in Private Practice:*

*A Practical Guide* (Karnac, 2016) and *Counselling Young People: A Practitioner Manual* (SAGE/BACP, 2017).

**Penny Leake** started her professional life as a teacher, but later retrained as counsellor, social worker and clinical supervisor. She began counselling in 1980, and since 1992 has specialised in working with children and young people. She spent many years as practitioner, manager and clinical supervisor for therapeutic services in the north-east, in both the statutory and voluntary sectors. She is BACP senior accredited as both supervisor and counsellor, and now works freelance in Derbyshire. Her supervisees have included several Child and Adolescent Mental Health Services (CAMHS) workers and play therapists. She strongly believes that workers must feel well supported themselves if they are to support others.

**Karen Lowe,** MA, is Director and senior therapist at ABC Counselling, Play Therapy & Family Solutions located in Billingham, Stockton on Tees. Karen is a BACP accredited counsellor, PTUK accredited play therapist and qualified clinical supervisor. She has an MA in Play Therapy and is an EMDR therapist with a particular interest in working with trauma and attachment. As well as delivering play therapy to adopted and looked after children, Karen delivers training to schools, residential homes, foster carers and local authorities as part of an integrated family team that works across the Tees Valley. She works in schools with children aged between 4 and 16 years and has a clinical supervision practice for trainee and qualified counsellors and play therapists.

**Peter Lowe,** MBE, is a qualified social worker, family mediator, restorative facilitator and play therapist who received an MBE for his services to Youth Justice in the North East in 2011. Peter has successfully developed integrated family and counselling services to improve the quality, reach and access to therapy for vulnerable children and young people living in the North East of England. He is Director for ABC Counselling, Play Therapy & Family Solutions located in Billingham, Stockton on Tees, and delivers specialist therapeutic interventions as part of an integrated Family Therapy team. Peter retains a keen interest in supporting children and young people to access the benefits of therapy and creative therapeutic interventions.

**Tom McAndrew** has over 15 years' experience in education including British and international institutions, and has spent a significant part of his teaching career working with deaf children. He holds an MA in deaf education from Leeds University and is a qualified teacher of the deaf. Passionate about British Sign Language, he is a keen traveller and aspires to build bridges between the hearing and deaf cultures. He recently attended a Malaysian Sign Language course to help continue learning about deaf culture in other countries. He has two young children and he currently lives with his children in Kuala Lumpur.

**Katie McArthur** is a counsellor, supervisor, researcher and teaching associate. School-based counselling is her main research interest and the focus of her PhD from the University of Strathclyde. In 2013 she was awarded the BACP's Outstanding Research Award for a pilot randomised controlled trial of school-based counselling. Her previous research interests include the needs and rights of disabled children in the UK child protection system, and social inequalities in entry to higher education. She is a core group member of the Children and Young People Practice Research Network developed by the BACP. In 2012, she co-edited a school-based counselling symposium edition of the *British Journal of Guidance and Counselling*. Katie lives in Glasgow with her partner and their son.

**Nick Midgley** is a senior lecturer at University College London (UCL), and a child psycho-therapist at the Anna Freud National Centre for Children and Families, London. He is Co-director of the Child Attachment and Psychological Therapies Research Unit (ChAPTRe) at UCL/Anna Freud, where he has a particular interest in evaluating therapeutic interventions for children in foster care. Nick has been involved in the development of mentalisation-based treatments for children and families, and his latest book, *Mentalization-Based Treatment with Children: A Time-Limited Approach*, was published by the American Psychological Association in 2017. With SAGE, he is also the co-editor of *Essential Research Findings in Child and Adolescent Counselling and Psychotherapy* (2017).

**Paul E. Nicholson** is Course Director in Psychological Therapies and Mental Health at Leeds Beckett University. He is a BACP accredited relational therapist who has worked within a range of mental health settings since 1995, including forensic psychiatry, private practice and NHS counselling services. Originally trained as a schoolteacher, Paul has worked with children and young people in both educational and therapeutic contexts and is now involved in the delivery of relational integrative counsellor training at Leeds Beckett University. He has an enduring interest in relational perspectives in therapy, developing a cohesive language that accurately reflects the processes involved and has written about relational methodology and expertise in practice.

**Dr Dennis Ougrin** is a consultant child and adolescent psychiatrist at South London and Maudsley NHS Foundation Trust (SLaM). His research interests include prevention of borderline personality disorder and interventions for self-harm. He pioneered therapeutic assessment, a new assessment method for young people who present with self-harm in emergency. He is a Clinical Senior Lecturer at the Institute of Psychiatry.

**Peter Pearce** is Faculty Head at Metanoia Institute in London where he runs Master's, and Post Qualification Conversion training in adult and adolescent counselling. He has worked as a person-centred counsellor with adults and young people within NHS and secondary school settings since 1989, and has been conducting research for more than a decade on counselling in schools. He is author of several books and articles and has presented internationally on these and other issues. Together with Ros Sewell, he was Principal Researcher for the Align Randomised Controlled Trial: an Efficacy Study of Person-Centred/Humanistic School Based Counselling, which led to the development of Hear4You, the Metanoia school-based counselling service. He is currently Clinical Lead and a co-researcher, in collaboration with Professor Mick Cooper at University of Roehampton and colleagues at universities across the UK for the ETHOS Study, an Economic and Social Research Council (ESRC) funded study of humanistic school-based counselling.

**Gwen Proud** has been employed in educational organisations for the majority of her working life including being a secretary in local government and independent schools, counselling in secondary schools in the North East of England for a children's charity and later for the local education authority. She completed a Master's Degree in Counselling at Durham University, a Doctorate in Counselling Studies at the University of Manchester, and is a BACP Accredited Counsellor. Gwen has divided her working practice between primary care and school settings and is experienced in working therapeutically with groups of children of secondary school age.

**Dee C. Ray**, PhD, LPC-S, NCC, RPT-S, is Distinguished Teaching Professor in the counselling programme and Director of the Center for Play Therapy at the University of North Texas. Dr Ray has published over 100 articles, chapters and books in the field of play therapy, specialising in research specifically examining the process and effects of child-centred play therapy. Dr Ray is author of *A Therapist's Guide to Development: The Extraordinarily Normal Years* (2016 Routledge) and *Advanced Play Therapy: Essential Conditions, Knowledge, and Skills for Child Practice* (2011 Routledge), and co-author of *Group Play Therapy* (2014 Routledge). Dr Ray supervises counselling services to community clients at her university clinic and leads a school outreach programme providing play therapy to hundreds of children each year.

**Kaye Richards**, PhD, is senior lecturer in outdoor education at Liverpool John Moores University and a chartered psychologist of the British Psychological Society. She has worked in outdoor and higher education for over 20 years, with a specialist area in adventure therapy, and counselling and psychotherapy research. This has included working at the BACP, and being a long-standing member of the Adventure Therapy International Committee, having hosted a range of national and international events in adventure therapy. She has published across all these areas and her interests include the role of nature in promoting health and well-being, psychotherapy outdoors, mental health and sport, and expedition leadership.

**Ros Sewell** is Primary Tutor for the Post Qualification Conversion Diploma from Adult to Adolescent and School Counselling at Metanoia and a BACP Accreditation Assessor. She has provided person-centred counselling with young people within NHS and education settings since 1989 and worked as a school counsellor in secondary school settings since 1997. She is joint Lead and Supervisor to the Metanoia School Counselling Service.

**Barbara Smith**, PhD, is a psychotherapist in private practice and also works with children and young people at Alder Hey Children's Hospital Trust CAMHS. She is a senior accredited psychotherapist with BACP and a registered psychotherapist with UKCP. Barbara is also a registered child psychotherapist. She lectured for many years in counselling in Liverpool. She is published in the areas of diversity, children's self-esteem, working in the outdoors and working creatively. Her PhD is based on 2 years' work in counsellor training that she delivered in the Maldives islands. She is a volunteer with the British Red Cross undertaking urgent response work in international disasters. She has a keen sense of humour, which she shares with her clients, and a deep commitment to helping people find their way through life's many and varied challenges.

**Paul Stallard** is Professor of Child and Family Mental Health at the University of Bath and Head of Psychological Therapies (CAMHS) for Oxford Health NHS Foundation Trust. He trained as a clinical psychologist and works within a specialist child mental health team, where he leads a cognitive-behavioural therapy (CBT) clinic for children and young people with emotional disorders of anxiety, depression, obsessive compulsive disorder (OCD) and post-traumatic stress disorder (PTSD). He is registered with the Health and Care Professions Council (HCPC) and is a British Association for Behavioural and Cognitive Psychotherapies (BABCP) accredited CBT therapist. He is an active researcher and a leading figure in the development of CBT with children. He is the author of the much acclaimed *Think Good Feel Good: A Cognitive Behaviour Therapy Workbook for Children and Young People* (2002, Wiley-Blackwell).

**Dave Stewart** is a BACP accredited counsellor-psychotherapist and registered social worker. With over 20 years' experience in therapeutic work with children, young people and families, Dave first trained and worked as a music therapist. He later worked as a child therapist in a community setting before taking up the post of senior trauma counsellor in the children's charity Barnardo's. Dave currently leads a team of Barnardo's school-based counsellors which won the BACP award for 'Innovation in Counselling and Psychotherapy' in 2012. His special areas of interest include therapy with younger children, children and young people with special needs and outcome-informed practice. Dave has many years' experience as a trainer and has presented and published widely. The last 5 years have seen him develop a relational, outcome-informed model of counselling practice specific to younger children.

**Kelli Swain-Cowper** is co-author and Curriculum Lead on the Postgraduate Diploma for Counselling Children in Schools at Place2be, University of East London, a BACP accredited course. She has worked internationally in school counselling and child mental health for over 20 years, as a practitioner, educator, supervisor, advisor, author and advocate for children's mental health. Kelli has written the MindEd Curriculum for Counselling Children in Primary Schools. She currently consults in developing and delivering training for school counselling practitioners across the country and maintains a private consultancy practice.

**Beverly Turner-Daly** is a qualified social worker, counsellor and clinical supervisor with over 30 years' experience in the field of post-abuse counselling and therapy. Having for 20 years juggled the roles of Senior Lecturer and Clinician, Beverly now works exclusively as an independent supervisor, trainer and consultant providing services for a wide range of professionals who work with children and families. She can be found on Twitter @PeopleCentre.

**Sum Yu Pansy Yue** is a final year medical student at King's College London. She has co-authored a book called *Self-Harm in Young People* with Dr Dennis Ougrin (2016, iConcept Press).

# FOREWORD TO THE SECOND EDITION

## MIKE SHOOTER

When I was asked to write the foreword for this second edition, I assumed that what I had written for the first edition would just about do. It was a lazy assumption, and I should have known better.

For as Ricky, one of my most recalcitrant teenage patients said to me in a sudden flash of insight: 'The trouble with you, Shooter, is that you're old and getting set in your ways. I'm young and can still change. I've got the world in front of me.'

Just as we ask our patients to take risks and change their assumptions about themselves and the world, so we as therapists must take risks and change too. We must tackle old problems with new ideas and new problems with new wisdom. We have fresh research to take account of and a whole range of emerging disorders that are products of modern life or which we were simply unaware of before. And all of it is ground down under the burden of material poverty and emotional deprivation. We only have to ask the thirteen-year-old girl how it feels, sitting up all night in the loneliness of her bedroom, desperately seeking 'likes' on social media. Any sort of contact, in lieu of real friendships.

The first edition of this admirable handbook has sat next to my computer since the day I received it three years ago. I keep meaning to put it back on the shelf, but every day I have reason to consult it, for my practice, my writing, or just for the sheer joy of reading what other people are doing and thinking out there in the counselling world. It is becoming grimy and well-thumbed, page corners turned down at particular points of interest, passages underlined for quotation, exclamation marks scattered in the margin, and the occasional question mark in red. This is, after all, a controversial business and the editors are as unafraid of giving chapter authors their head as we must be of giving our patients room to experiment with their lives. Empowerment is the name of the game.

It all seems such a recent companion, born of the emerging field of counselling young people and BACP's establishment of the core competencies for its practitioners. And yet the knowledge of what is needed and the techniques to provide it, have moved on so fast. The arrival of this second edition, so soon after the first, is testament to the ability of the authors to keep pace with the demand; I will be as excited to read it as I was as a parent, marvelling each day at how my children mastered one developmental skill or another.

And there is the most important reason why I like this book. Amongst all the innovation, the editors and their authors have not forgotten that it is the individual child and young person that is at the centre of it all. It is their story, confided in us for the first time, through all their anxiety, guilt, fears and bewilderment, that matters. Their own experience, and we must give it the respect it deserves.

So, I ended my first foreword by saying that my test of the book was that I wished I had written it. I know now that I haven't the combination of perseverance and openness of ideas to do what the editors have done. I'm just grateful to have this new edition to guide me. I shall pension my old edition off and be appropriately surprised at what the new one will teach me. And editors, Ricky will love you!

# ACKNOWLEDGEMENTS

We would like to thank all the contributors in this book for their generosity in sharing their knowledge, skills and experience for the benefit of children and young people worldwide and their counsellors. In addition, we would like to thank David Smyth for his input.

We would like to acknowledge the professionalism and editorial help given by Rachel Burrows, Laura Walmsley, Talulah Hall and Susannah Trefgarne from SAGE and for their patience and expertise.

We are grateful to BACP, the MindEd team and, particularly, the Children and Young People and Families Committee for their ongoing support.

Finally, it is important to acknowledge the relationships forged through the process of writing this book, between the authors and the editorial team. We have learnt much from each other.

Maggie Robson

Sue Pattison

# EDITORS' INTRODUCTION
## MAGGIE ROBSON AND SUE PATTISON

Welcome to the second edition of this handbook. The ideas and impetus for the first edition of the book came together as a response to the growing need for high-quality training and reference resources in the expanding field of counselling children and young people. This book was waiting to be written – we had discussed producing a unique resource for counsellors of children and young people for some time. The opportunity to 'walk the walk' came when we were approached by SAGE as members of the British Association for Counselling and Psychotherapy's Children and Young People Committee (BACP CYC). The timing was key, as BACP was developing the Counselling Competences and the MindEd e-learning resources. BACP has developed a set of competencies for therapists who work with young people. These are available on its website (www.bacp.co.uk). These competencies were developed as humanistic competencies, but the further development of core and generic competencies, in our view, details the general therapeutic skills relevant to all practitioners working both with children and young people, regardless of theoretical orientation. Some of the issues identified in these core competencies are explored in detail within this handbook, reflecting the importance of these areas when working therapeutically with children and young people. Competencies identified by BACP (2014) include knowledge of child and family development and transitions, and knowledge and understanding of mental health issues. Knowledge of legal, professional and ethical frameworks is considered essential, including an ability to work with issues of confidentiality, consent and capacity. BACP (2014) suggests that therapists need to be able to work across and within agencies and respond to child protection issues. In addition, therapists need to be able to engage and work with young people of a variety of ages, developmental levels and backgrounds, as well as parents and carers, in a culturally competent manner. They also need to have knowledge of psychopharmacology as it relates to young people. The generic competencies relate to knowledge of specific models of intervention and practice, an ability to work with emotions, endings and service transitions, an ability to work with groups and measurement instruments and to be able to use supervision effectively. The ability to conduct a collaborative assessment and a risk assessment is paramount. Crucially, BACP (2014) suggests the therapist needs to be able to foster and maintain a relationship that builds a therapeutic alliance and understands the client's 'worldview'. In our experience most proficient therapists, irrespective of their modality, work to achieve this trusting relationship necessary for human change. BACP is also developing a children and young people specialist training curriculum based on the competencies. It is intended that this will be a postgraduate top-up for counsellors/psychotherapists who have a completed an 'adult' practitioner training and who want to develop knowledge and skills to work with children and young people.

In response to the success of the first edition we were invited by SAGE to edit a second edition. In this book we have updated the chapters and added sections on key learning, developing your skills and a series of discussion questions. Each chapter maintains its commitment case studies and suggestions for further reading. Each chapter also continues to provide references to research and the evidence base, further supplemented through links to the BACP/ NHS MindEd e-learning resources, which are indicated at the end of each chapter, where appropriate.

We use the term 'therapeutic work' as an overarching term for the range of therapies referred to loosely as 'counselling' or 'psychotherapy'. Although each professional body has its own definition of counselling and psychotherapy, they are all similar in nature. 'Counselling and psychotherapy are umbrella terms that cover a range of talking therapies. They are delivered by trained practitioners who work with people over a short or long term to help them bring about effective change or enhance their wellbeing' (BACP, www.bacp.co.uk). However, we would like to add to this definition, which refers to 'talking therapies', to include creative forms of communication including artwork and play to address the therapeutic needs of the wide age range of children and young people covered in this book (3–18 years and beyond, for young people with developmental delays).

This handbook is unique as the only comprehensive resource for counsellors, trainees and trainers working in the field of counselling children and young people that is linked to high-quality online resources developed by BACP. The book is designed to provide essential reading for all counselling trainees and a guide to curriculum for the trainers. Any counsellor working with children and young people, or aspiring to work with this client group, will be able to refer to the handbook and use it to contribute to their continuing professional development. There are challenges around improving the quality and provision of support for the mental health of children and young people. Statistics show that the suicide rate is rising and children and young people's levels of well-being are falling. The quality of counsellor training and the evidence base required to ensure effective provision are both issues addressed in this book. By far the most important aspects of this book are the unique contributions each author has made. Each is expert in their field and has their own approach to the chapter topics, which makes for overlap in places, but with a different perspective in each case. The handbook will invite you in as reader, hold your attention and entice you to read further, giving you flavours of approaches to counselling children and young people that may be new to you, and insights into topics that stimulate and leave you wanting more.

We intend this handbook to provide a comprehensive guide to the complex field of counselling children and young people in the UK and to serve as a resource in the international arena. As its intended audience, you may be a trainee, trainer, practitioner, a service provider or a commissioner of therapeutic work with children and young people. The level of your training programme may be introductory or more advanced. The book is based on a set of values and principles, the rights of the child, the need to keep the child at the centre of our therapeutic work, unconditional acceptance, trustworthiness and congruence. The book will help you as the reader to identify, clarify, reflect upon and work with the underpinning legislation, ethics and values; theoretical approaches; research evidence; and interventions and techniques that apply to the practice of counselling children and young people. You will be introduced to the diversity of working with children and young people at different developmental stages. In order to achieve this, the handbook follows a structured and logical approach that introduces you to a set of underpinning values related to legislation, policy and professional practice, demonstrating how these are used in practice by providing you with case study material. Although each case study represents the therapeutic way of working, the actual cases are amalgams in order to protect client confidentiality and identity. The handbook is presented in four major parts with 27 chapters. Throughout the book there is evidence of how therapeutic work with children and young people and the related services have developed historically. Although a range of theoretical approaches and different ways of working are explored in this book, the philosophical base when translated into underpinning values and principles of working with children and young people includes trustworthiness of the counsellor, acceptance, empowerment and a belief in the power of relationship. These values and principles will be woven throughout the book and are present in every chapter to enable theory, research and practice to be linked and consolidated for you, the reader.

As the field of counselling children and young people has rapidly developed over the past few years, the delivery, approaches to counselling and the nature of interventions have increased in number and range and been applied across an increasing range of contexts. Counselling practitioners come from a variety of backgrounds and professions. They bring new ideas into the field and also adapt concepts, ideas and tools developed in their own professions, including theoretical approaches. The diversity of the field creates increasing opportunities for interdisciplinary work and cross-fertilisation of ideas. However, there is also a sense of counsellors requiring help to position themselves professionally in relation to theoretical approach, methods, techniques and tools, bearing in mind the increasing demand for practice based on research evidence.

Questions that you may ask as a counselling practitioner, trainer, trainee or commissioner of therapeutic work with children and young people may include: Which is the best counselling approach for working with young children in primary schools? How is a therapeutic relationship with an adolescent who has problem behaviour established and maintained? Is it possible to provide complete confidentiality for a child in therapy? Should a child be 'sent' for counselling? Is parental permission needed to offer counselling to an adolescent? Although not all of your questions will be answered, this book provides the answers to a range of questions that the authors have been asked over their many years of experience.

The structure of the book has been designed to enable you to access any section independently of the others, yet they intrinsically link together. The book comprises four overarching sections: Theory and Practice Approaches; Counselling Practices and Processes; Practice Issues; and Practice Settings.

In Part 1 'Theory and Practice Approaches', the authors discuss a range of therapeutic approaches aimed at helping children and young people at different ages and stages. This includes child development and attachment, the child-centred approach, psychodynamic, cognitive-behavioural, gestalt, transactional analysis, play therapy and other creative therapeutic approaches. Where appropriate, the chapters will look at brief therapy where it is included within each approach. Age-appropriate interventions in relation to each theoretical approach are examined, for example, brief therapy, play therapy and its theoretical perspectives, cognitive-behavioural approaches such as problem-solving, and solution-focused therapy. Each chapter refers to the underlying principles fundamental to counselling work with children and young people and relevant research. Part 2 'Counselling Practices and Processes' examines the nature of the process that can take place when counselling children and young people and looks at referral and indications for therapy, including: assessment; preparation for therapy and beginnings; the therapeutic alliance and the middle part of therapy; counselling skills; supervision; group work; and endings. Part 3 on 'Practice Issues' looks at law and policy; ethics; diversity; bereavement; depression; suicide and self-harm; sexual abuse; and eating disorders. Finally, Part 4 on 'Practice Settings' identifies and examines working in a range of contexts: statutory health and social care services; and non-statutory services, for example, the third sector. The chapters in each major part of the handbook have an established common structure, and all case material used in the book is anonymised, to preserve confidentiality. This is the structure, which organises information and acts as a guide for you, the reader.

# PART I
## THEORY AND PRACTICE APPROACHES

# 1

# CHILD DEVELOPMENT AND ATTACHMENT

## DIVINE CHARURA

**This chapter will discuss:**

- The theoretical underpinnings and some conceptual frameworks of child development and attachment
- The centrality and importance of considering diversity
- Implications of child development and attachment for therapeutic practice when working with children and young people
- Case presentations of young people whose development and attachment is affected. These aid reflection on the key points

## INTRODUCTION

Theories on childhood development and attachment remain some of the most studied and central theories in helping us understand how as humans we develop physically and psychologically. There are numerous debates on attachment and development, which primarily hail from the nature–nurture question. In responding to these debates, I draw from research on epigenetics and environment interactions which states that it is not nature or nurture nor is it nature and nurture but that life emerges from the interaction between the two. That there are no genetic factors that can be studied independently of the environment, and there are no environmental factors that function independently of the genome (Meaney, 2001: 51; Meaney, 2010). Additionally, given the importance and centrality of diversity when exploring child development, in the context of counselling I also draw from cultural and relational neuroscience research that examines how psychological processes develop and are influenced and shaped by the interplay between culture, biological and physiological factors, genetic influences, patterns of neural activation and environmental processes (Schore, 1994; Siegel, 2010; Sasaki and Kim, 2017). Furthermore, I believe that human experience is organised physiologically, affectively, cognitively, biologically and experientially (Erskine and Moursund, 2011). Thus, whilst Bowlby and Ainsworth's attachment models, which primarily explain infant behaviour towards their attachment figure, will be explored, I will outline a wide range of other orientations in order to mirror the complexity of processes that make up child development and the plethora of theoretical perspectives that have already been published in the vast literature within developmental psychology, psychotherapy and counselling literature.

Given the magnitude of this subject area, it is impossible to cover any particular theories in enough depth to do them justice or to cover all theories that relate to attachment and child development. Thus, in order to contextualise, synthesise and integrate perspectives noted in this chapter, I will use a relational framework that asserts a range of considerations (see Erskine, 2015; Finlay, 2015; Paul and Charura, 2015). These include that what happens in the therapy room may well reflect developmental and phenomenological processes that are happening outside for the client. It also highlights the importance of the intersubjective space between two people, in the here-and-now, and the containing and psychologically holding presence of the therapist in a human-to-human, collaborative relationship within a safe space and working with whatever emerges (Erskine, 2015; Finlay, 2015; Paul and Charura, 2015). Hence past experiences that may have impacted the development, attachment and relational patterns of the child/young person require the therapist to be flexible enough to attune to each client's relational needs (Clarkson, 2003). Therefore, these relational principles will form the basis for the perspectives noted in this chapter, particularly when considering the implications for therapeutic practice on child development and attachment. To end the chapter a list of points for key learning is provided.

## UNDERPINNING THEORETICAL AND THERAPEUTIC CONCEPTS – BEGINNINGS

### Psychosexual development

Before focusing on attachment theory (Bowlby, 1969; 1988; Ainsworth et al., 1978), I will offer a few different theoretical perspectives of development in order to contextualise both the history and the diversity of thought within developmental and psychotherapy theory.

In this section I will offer a brief overview of the psychosexual stages, though it is impossible to do it justice in a few paragraphs, especially given that so much has been written about this in psychoanalytic literature. My intention, however, is to point to some of the theoretical conceptions around psychosexual development in children and young people in order to further the stimulus of practitioners' thinking and considerations on psychosexual development theory as one of the pillars of psychological theories on child development. In Sigmund Freud's writing from 1905 onwards to other contemporary writing that has followed he depicted the emergence of human development through psychosexual stages.

It is worth highlighting at this early stage in this chapter the historical context of two distinct and often contradictory schools of thought found in Freud's classical psychoanalytic school of thought. Shuttleworth (1989) described these as Freud's *mechanistic* model of emotional life, which Freud (1911) postulated as that of an organism dealing with different quantities of excitation. In later writings this was interwoven with more psychological development concepts which were hypothesised as being concerned with the relationship between instincts and internal drives as well as the capacity for contact with reality and rational thought (Shuttleworth, 1989).

Thus as Freud's writing and clinical practice developed, he shifted his model of development and hypothesised that consequently the capacity in later life to process emotion and relate to others or psychopathological presentations could not be simply translated as being linked to childhood sexuality and the relationship with primary caregivers – the 'past causing the present' – but rather experience accumulates and develops in indirect and multifaceted ways (Freud, 1911; Shuttleworth, 1989).

In relation to Freud's contribution to development on psychosexual stages, he hypothesised that in developing from infancy to adolescence, the individual develops through psychosexual stages and activities that consist of contending with libidinal tensions and their accompanying anxieties (Freud, 1905; Shuttleworth, 1989). These stages are notably the oral, anal, phallic (which also constitutes the Oedipus complex), latency and genital stages, all of which have been written about extensively elsewhere and thus I will not focus on their descriptions in this chapter (see Freud, 1905; 1924; Freud et al., 1953; Garcia, 1995).

Given the infant's dependency on its primary caregivers, its interpersonal struggles and anxieties are thus made relational and are manifested through overindulgence and overfrustration. His conceptual framework of the psychosexual stages is not one that is a linear, or unidimensional staged process in its progression but rather it is less sequential and is an oscillating evolvement of developmental patterns (Freud, 1933; Garcia, 1995). Freud used the term *polymorphously perverse* to mean that during the stages of development, which are manifested through undifferentiated impulses for sensual pleasure, because the child lacks knowledge that certain modes of gratification are forbidden, they seek gratification wherever it occurs. For example, in the earliest phase of life (the oral phase), the child forms a libidinal bond with the mother by gaining pleasure from (for example) sucking the breast. Thus, he argued that infantile development through the psychosexual stages is mostly in the form of perversion (*polymorphously perverse*), as they have not yet built up the capacity to focus their sexuality on their genitals, but they allow it to be experienced over the entire body. This means with the *pleasure principle* dominating, and without having matured to learn to constrain sexual drives to socially accepted norms, and without having yet matured to adult sexual behaviour/ capacity that focuses on the genitals, and/or reproductive functions, the infant/child seeks pleasure in whatever form. This includes initially from their primary caregiver as well as gaining pleasurable stimulation from their own body. It is only through these developmental stages that children learn to constrain sexual drives to socially accepted norms (Shuttleworth, 1989; Garcia, 1995).

Furthermore, apart from psychosexual development I would like to briefly make reference to the development of the psyche, which underpins and has influenced theories of interpersonal relationship, child development and early attachment (Klein, Winnicott and Bowlby), and latterly relational theory (Kohut).

The psyche, which is the basis of personality structure, is composed of the 'id', which is the home of our instinctual drives; the 'ego', which is the sense of our conscious (i.e. the 'I'), and it is the ego, according to this model, which regulates our inner drives and our social self; and the 'superego', which has a sort of parental quality and is concerned with how we behave in relation to social expectations (Freud, 1915).

Fig. 1.1 depicts the model of the psyche.

As can be seen in Fig. 1.1 the ego and superego are partly conscious and the id is wholly *unconscious* and below the surface of our awareness according to this model.

In relation to childhood development this model of the mind asserts that psychological problems emerge as a result of repressed childhood conflicts and the inadequate working through of developmental needs as the child grows (Freud, 1915; Paul and Charura, 2015). Thus, the importance and link to attachment is that a template is created based on early primary relationships that mould the capacity for future relational and cognitive patterns. If a child is raised in loving early relationships in which needs are met, a psychologically healthy development ensues. However, if the early relationships with primary caregivers are unfulfilling in a variety of ways this leads to unfulfillment and repression of experiences. If not worked

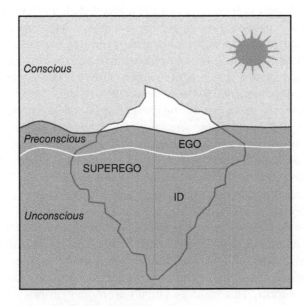

**Figure 1.1**  The Freudian model of the psyche

through as the young person develops into adulthood these experiences will be unresolved and contained in the unconscious, and will manifest through a range of psychopathological presentations. These could, for example, include difficulties in relational or attachment patterns in adulthood, or could manifest as behavioural, interpersonal or other psychological difficulties (Paul and Charura, 2015).

This contribution from the psychoanalytic/psychodynamic orientation and turn to focus more on the mind's experience of itself and of the world around it (phenomenological model of the mind) spurred further interest and development from others (Klein, Winnicott, Bion, etc.). They were interested in the interconnectedness of how we as humans experience the world and develop emotional states, as well as the capacity to relate to others, and think and generate meaning as we develop from infancy through to childhood and subsequently adulthood.

The evolution of this idea into object relations theory is based on the principle that infants primarily seek relationship, and that relationships with significant others are what is at the heart of personality development. This development of relational theory is a shift from one-person to two-person intersubjective psychology (Mitchell, 2000; Finlay, 2015).

An example can be given here of a contribution to the interconnection between development of the psyche, the nature of attachment in the primary relationship and developmental description of the origins of the self in the infant–caregiver relationship. In line with this, Winnicott (1953) argued that the initial building blocks of the ego were created through the child experiencing threats of annihilation that did not in reality lead to annihilation and from which, repeatedly, there was recovery. He stated that this was afforded by what he termed the *good-enough mother*, whose role he saw as that of allowing the child to project fears, anxieties, frustrations (bad objects) into her and then re-introject (the process by which the child unconsciously re-incorporates these project fears, anxieties, frustrations (bad objects) into his/her psyche) them when they can see how well she handles them (Winnicott, 1953). Thus, through the holding, caring and safe environment the child's fears and anxieties are contained, enabling the infant to have a personal existence, and consequently to build 'a continuity of being' (Winnicott, 1953; 1967). It is through this continuity of being that the ego develops and the individuality of the infant gradually develops. If, however, the child's care is not good enough then he hypothesised that there is no continuity of being and consequently personality development will be founded on reactions to environmental impingement and thus could result in a young person with psychological and relational difficulties (Winnicott, 1960).

Other contributions to child development from the object relations school include how societal and parental influences become internalised as the superego, which consequently imposes rules for living (Klein, 1975). Klein elaborated on the interplay between the conscious and unconscious (the psyche) of the infant and caregiver as well as with the environment. She asserted that the drive to be met and regulated by the other (primary caregiver), which is characterised as an 'object' emerges, and is relayed as love/hate and envy/gratitude (Klein, 1952). The relationship in which these emotions are regulated results in internalisation of the quality of the experience, thereby a healthy adult's internal objects are balanced and integrated (whole objects and not part objects). This allows for optimal object relations, whether internally (within one's self) or with others (Klein, 1975).

Similarly, we can also draw on understanding development from self-psychology perspectives and, in particular, the work of Kohut, who linked the development of the internal world with the influence of the environment through his concept of the self. Kohut (1977) argued that what drives development in the human infant is the need to be met emotionally by others and to have the self reflected back via other/significant relationships (through what he termed twinship, mirroring and idealisation) and 'transmuting idealisations' (Kohut, 1977). These mirroring, idealising and twinship experiences enable the development of the self-structure as well as the ability to regulate the self in moments of bearable frustration. Kohut (1984) also offered insight into how psychopathology develops and argued that excessive admiration by parents, lack of realistic feedback from parents, or inconsistent or neglectful parental caregiving during development resulted in narcissism and other personality deficits.

It is from within this school of object relations that from the 1930s onwards, Bowlby (attachment theory) radically transformed psychoanalysis (Greenberg and Mitchell, 1983; Paul and Charura, 2015). Larsson (2012) noted how Bowlby's (1958) attachment theory served as a catalyst for the shift from theory on libidinal drives to focusing more on infants as relation seeking, and to adopting a lifespan approach to understanding the influence of relationships on personality, relational patterns, social development and psychopathology.

The quote that follows encapsulates John Bowlby and Mary Ainsworth's work as contributors to the perspective that an infant's innate tendency is to move towards the exploration of new things. However, when moving proximity from the primary caregiver, the infant may become scared and the primary caregiver will be the infant's secure protection base (Paul and Charura, 2015). Thus, the experiment that Ainsworth developed (the Strange Situation) enabled this innate tendency to be manifested and the responses of different children to the *strange situation* indicated the nature of their attachment pattern.

> Observation of how a very young child behaves towards his mother, both in her presence and especially in her absence, can contribute greatly to our understanding of personality development. When removed from the mother by strangers, young children respond usually with great intensity: and after reunion with her, they show commonly either a heightened degree of separation anxiety or else an unusual detachment. (Bowlby, 1969: 3)

As so much has already been written in depth about attachment and attachment patterns hailing from the work of numerous researchers, with primarily John Bowlby and Mary Ainsworth, and later Mary Main, at the forefront (Bowlby 1969; 1988; 1973; 1980; Ainsworth, 1982; 1985; Ainsworth et al., 1978; Main et al., 1985), and also on child development and attachment (Gibbs et al., 2014), I will make only brief reference to the attachment patterns as identified by Ainsworth et al. (1970; 1978) as well as to other perspectives as noted by Bowlby (1969; 1988).

Attachment, as noted by Ainsworth (1963) is a 'secure base from which to explore', and this perspective and description continues to hold as a fundamental principle within attachment theory. Following from this Bowlby (1969) described attachment as a unique relationship between an infant and his caregiver and stated that it is this relationship and an attachment that is the foundation and basis for further healthy development.

Ainsworth et al. (1970; 1978) noted the following patterns:

- Secure attachment: In this style, the caregiver's qualities are usually hypothesised as affectionate, containing, loving and consistently providing care. In the Strange Situation, and when emotionally distressed, the infant thus seeks protection and comfort from the mother and is quick to settle to the mothers' comforting attempts.

*Insecure attachments* are briefly described as follows:

- Avoidant attachment: In this style of attachment, in the day-to-day relational encounter the mother is usually hypothesised as being rejecting of the child's attachment behaviour. In the Strange Situation, when united with the mother, the infant characteristically pulls away or ignores her.
- Resistant attachment style: In cases where the mother is hypothesised as being inconsistent in responding to the child's emotional needs and care, in the Strange Situation, the infant usually tends to stay close to their mother (Fraley and Spieker, 2003).
- Main and Solomon (1990) defined a fourth attachment style, which they termed the disorganised style. They hypothesised that this style of attachment had its roots in a primary caregiver who presented as emotionally erratic, or passive. Thus, in the Strange Situation the child was non-responsive.

One of the significant contributions to attachment theory is that of Bowlby (1988), who formulated the concept of an *internal working model* of self and relationships. He argued that this internal working model is a conceptual framework central to making sense of the world, self-appraisal and appraisal of others. It forms as a result of the nature of interaction between the child and the primary caregiver. It consequently foreshadows later psychological growth and governs how the child feels towards their parent/primary caregiver and towards their self, how the child expects to be treated, and is the prototype from which behaviour towards others and future relational patterns and choices emerge (Bowlby, 1969). It has been suggested that this development in infancy is placed within a matrix of two subjectivities, namely that of the caregiver and that of the infant, and thus a child becomes an independent subject only if they recognise the separateness and autonomy of their caregiver and this is what has been termed intersubjectivity (Finlay, 2015; Paul and Charura, 2015).

It is generally accepted that *good-enough* parenting (Winnicott, 1960) and consistent, positive attention from their caregiver are most likely to develop a positive internal working model. Elsewhere I have co-written examples of how an infant or young person who experiences neglect and rejection may develop a negative internal working model that informs them 'No-one cares about me', or 'I am unlovable', or 'I am not good enough'. If this 'internal model' of self and others remains unchanged through childhood development, low self-esteem, depression, being overly dependent or independent, and sabotage in relationships or jobs may ensue (Paul and Charura, 2015).

Attachment theories, however, are not without their criticisms. For example, critics argue that the correlation between parental sensitivity and the child's attachment as hypothesised by Bowlby and Ainsworth and others is weak, and that it places too much emphasis on the mother/primary caregiver and is reductionist in its hypothesis (Belsky, 2002). Meaney (2010) offered arguments that highlight the importance of considering environment interactions and thus asserted the importance of taking into consideration the roles and interactions that that both nature and nurture play in child development.

There are also arguments which emphasise that there are other explanations which may offer responses to criticisms on attachment as a lens to view developmental perspectives. For example, Fox's (1989) findings showed that infants with an 'easy' temperament (those who eat and sleep regularly and accept new experiences) are likely to develop secure attachments, whilst those with a 'slow to warm up' temperament (those whose development to get used to new experiences took time) are likely to have insecure-avoidant attachments. Furthermore, it was noted that babies with what Fox termed a 'difficult' temperament (those who eat and sleep irregularly and who reject new experiences) were likely to have insecure-ambivalent attachments (Fox, 1989). Thus, Fox concluded that an interactionist theory that factors in a combination of the child's innate temperament and their parent's sensitivity towards their needs offered an alternative perspective to attachment theory as proposed by Ainsworth et al. (1970; 1978) (Fox, 1989).

Another criticism of attachment models is that the conceptualisation of attachment behaviours is based on those that occur with the primary attachment figure, and typically the mother (Field, 1996). Furthermore, it has been argued that when considering the child's or parental behaviours, there is a lack of consideration of other attachments, for example, with the father or sibling, or of the role of others in cultures/families where there are multiple people involved in the care of a child (Field, 1996).

Despite these criticisms, the potency of attachment theories and their contributions cannot be ignored. Pickover (2002), for example, argued that insecure attachment patterns could be linked to psychiatric disorders, to which a child becomes vulnerable following the loss of an attachment figure. Furthermore, children and young people with insecure attachment patterns struggle to form secure attachments and react in a manner that may be hostile, rejecting or devaluing of others within their environment (Pickover, 2002).

When children or young people with severe attachment disorders, or who have undergone loss or trauma, are offered a close and secure relationship, if they become close to the attachment figure, they will often then withdraw from that relationship before they can be rejected, or they will react in ways that reflect their innermost feelings of being unworthy of love, and fearful of loss and of investing in a secure attachment. Furthermore, other writing and research has suggested that secure attachment is influential in supporting individuals through particularly major life stressors/traumas that may otherwise result in psychological distress (Paul and Charura, 2015).

Children with secure attachment patterns are capable of healthy relational patterns and can build other relationships whilst maintaining their primary relationship with their parents, not only in childhood and adolescence, but going into adulthood (Pickover, 2002).

## Psychosocial Development

With the focus so far having been on the psychodynamic, object relations, intersubjectivity and attachment perspectives, a shift to the work of Erikson (1950/1963) offers a different eight-stage developmental theory, which shifted away from drive theory and thus may be used as a conceptual base for psychosocial developmental theory (Knight, 2017). Erikson's use of the word 'stage' refers to a period of life such as childhood or adulthood, and he outlined that in each of the eight developmental stages he proposed, there is a pair of opposing psychological tendencies that need to be balanced (Knight, 2017). Furthermore, he clarified that the transition between the stages is not clear cut, nor is it an achievement grading where the crisis stages can be resolved permanently, but rather it is interconnected and fluid. Erikson argued that development starts with the first stage, which is trust vs. mistrust, in which the infant learns to trust the primary caregiver to meet their basic needs and consequently this relationship and experience contributes to the infant's feelings of security at times of uncertainty. He stated that if the adaptive strength (*virtue*) of hope is not established, then fear and mistrust will be the predominant experience of the infant and consequently the development of the other seven psychosocial stages will be impacted. Table 1.1 outlines the eight stages as hypothesised by Erikson (1950/1963). The first stage of *basic trust versus mistrust* mirrors Bowlby's theory of infant attachment, where experience with caregivers is crucial. The second to fourth stages of Erikson's theory parallel the possible outcomes of development and relational attachment in children, and the developmental context in which there is expansion from family to school and other contexts outside the home (Knight, 2017). In relation to development, the child's engagement in the attachment relationships and wider contexts in the first four stages enable the child to develop their ego, further cognitive, motor skills and language, and to obtain achievements or accomplishments.

Furthermore, Erikson's first four stages correspond to the development phase in Bowlby's attachment theory during which the formulation of the internal working model occurs (Bowlby, 1973). Given that the focus of this chapter is on children and young people, this section offers only a brief overview as noted and Table 1.1 will not elaborate on the descriptions and critique of each stage (for more detail, please see Erikson (1950/1963) and Knight (2017)).

Table 1.1   Erikson's eight stages of psychosocial development

| Stages | Age in years | Stage description | Adaptive strength or virtue | Maldevelopment (maladaptive tendency/malignant tendency) |
|---|---|---|---|---|
| Infancy | Birth – 1½ years | Basic trust vs. mistrust | Hope | Sensory maladjustment/withdrawal |
| Early childhood | 1½–3 years | Autonomy vs. shame and doubt | Will | Shameless wilfulness/compulsion |
| Play age | 3–5 years | Initiative vs. guilt | Purpose | Ruthlessness/inhibition |
| School age | 5–12 years | Industriousness vs. inferiority | Competence | Narrow virtuosity/inertia |
| Adolescence | 12–18 years | Identity cohesion vs. role confusion | Fidelity | Fanaticism/repudiation |
| Young adulthood | 18–40 years | Intimacy vs. isolation | Love | Promiscuity/exclusivity |
| Adulthood | 40–65 | Generativity vs. stagnation/ self-absorbtion | Care | Over-extension/rejectivity |
| Old age wisdom | 65+ | Integrity vs. despair | Wisdom | Presumption/disdain |

## CONSIDERATION OF WIDER SYSTEMIC THEORY

Having considered object relations, attachment and psychosocial perspectives to development, the link can then be made here between humanistic and systemic perspectives. Different authors have written on the impact of the family system. Human development across the lifespan is created and re-created, variously within each interaction, in the family and wider systems (Roy-Chowdhury, 2010). In line with this, Burns et al. (2015) highlight the importance of considering ecological systems theory (EST) (Bronfenbrenner, 1986; Bronfenbrenner and Morris, 1998; Dallos and Draper, 2010), which states that to understand the child, the environment in which the child lives must be fully examined. Others, like Sumontha et al. (2017), research associations between children's gender and sexuality development and their parents' gender – attitudes and behaviours could be linked to the impact of not only the family system but also the wider system as hypothesised by Bronfenbrenner (1986).

As noted in Fig. 1.2, Tudge et al. (2009) highlighted the wider systems as microsystem, mesosystem, exosystem and macrosystem frameworks, and stated that these proximal processes are a contemporary aspect of Bronfenbrenner's theory. Furthermore, they added that it is essential to consider them when conceptualising human development.

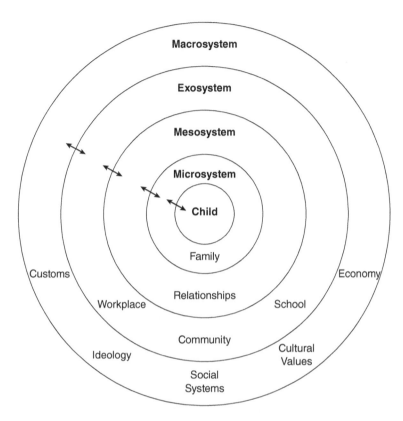

**Figure 1.2**   The context of human development – Bronfenbrenner's (1977) bio-ecological systems theory

## Importance of play

There have been numerous contributors who have highlighted the importance and centrality of play in child development (Klein, 1924; Rogers, 1939; Vygotsky, 1966; Else, 2009; Hughes, 2010). Furthermore, the importance of play has been identified as instrumental to physical, psychological, cognitive and social development by theorists of different orientations (Brown, 2014).

Vygotsky (1966) similarly highlighted how play contributes to mental development, and stated that in play a child deals with objects as having meaning and could, for example, take a stick to be horse. He argued that in play a child unconsciously and spontaneously makes use of the fact that meaning can be separated from an object without the cognitive recognition that this is happening and, thus, although superficially play bears little resemblance to what it leads to, profound internal analysis or examination of what presents makes it possible to determine its course of movement and its role. Thus, Vygotsky's arguments here highlighted that from the point of view of development, the creation of an imaginary situation is not a fortuitous fact in a child's life but can be regarded as a means of developing abstract thought and is the first step to a child's emancipation from situational constraints (Vygotsky, 1966). In other words, the ability to create imaginary situations and to use objects creatively enables freedom to explore unconscious and conscious material in relation to or in reaction to experiences.

More recently, Brown (2014) also identified how play contributes to development. He suggested that playing contributes to the ability to experience pleasure through fun, an experience of freedom gained through assessing risk and testing boundaries; flexibility through, for example, experimenting with possibilities and developing combinatorial thinking; that play helps to develop social interaction, and capacity for socialisation as well as creativity, problem-solving, self-discovery and so on. He further suggested that play contributes to muscular-skeletal development as some play utilises fine motor skills, gross motor skills and hand–eye coordination. With Brown's assertion of play contributing to psychological development, it is evident that it is therefore important that therapists working with children and young people be open to engaging with play within the therapy room and understand the essential contributions it offers to development.

## Neurological development, survival, and the centrality of love and attachment

I have co-written elsewhere about the centrality of love and attachment in development (please see Charura and Paul, 2015). However, there are many other sources and colleagues who have written on the importance of love and attachment, and how neurological development, experiencing love and secure attachments are all intricately interconnected to development and survival itself (please see Joseph, 1999; Fisher, 2004; Cozolino, 2010; Gerhardt, 2015).

I would like to make reference here to the brain's innate capacity for *neuroplasticity* (the ability to develop new neural pathways in line with what is stimulating in their environment); *neurogenesis*, which refers to the brain's capacity to generate new neurones; and, lastly, the importance of *neurotransmitters*, which are chemicals that are exchanged between neurones and carry messages that stimulate biological reactions in different parts of the brain (Siegel, 1999; Paul and Charura, 2015). Relational research and writing drawing from neuroscience have shown the positive effects of love and good early attachments, as well as the environmental influences on neuroplasticity and neurogenesis, social, emotional and relational development (Joseph, 1999; Fisher, 2004; Cozolino, 2010). Conversely, a lack of love, trauma, neglectful or abusive care have a negative effect on the development of the limbic system, and on the growth and survival of neurones in many other parts of the brain and the body, all of which severely impacts on all aspects of social and emotional functioning (Hughes, 2010; Charura and Paul, 2015; Gerhardt, 2015). Specific reference has been made to how the human baby without love experiences nuclei in the limbic system atrophying (weakening), or neurological/neurochemical impairment, or formation of abnormal neural interconnections, all of which consequently results in an inability to form normal emotional attachments, social/relational withdrawal and inability to interact appropriately (after Joseph, 1999; Cozolino, 2010; Gerhardt, 2015). Thus, in relation to the importance of love, attachment and neurone development, it has been continually asserted that they are important pinnacles as they can affect physical growth, attachment/relational patterns, play behaviour, and psychosexual and cognitive stages of development (Cozolino, 2010; Charura and Paul, 2015; Gerhardt, 2015). At worst neurological impairment, lack of growth and even death can result from neglect and a lack of love. For example, the work of Brown and Webb (2003), colleagues who worked with Romanian orphans rescued from what, in some cases, were called death rooms, who were tied in cots all day without much human love, describes how they started to develop and thrive as they were given positive care and love.

Piaget's (1971) theory on developmental stages and developmental processes stressed the innateness of equilibration about the world and consequent adaptation (harmony of organism and world). He also highlighted the importance of organisation (harmony within the organism). In order for adaptation to occur in development, he suggested that the child uses cognitive-affective structures (schemata). These are understood to be patterns of physical or mental action that underlie specific acts of intelligence and memory functions (Piaget, 1971). He then asserted that assimilation and accommodation were representations of maintenance and modification of these cognitive schemata (Piaget, 1971). Thus, it could be argued that in considering sensory and cognitive development, Paiget's postulation that cognitive development consists of a constant endeavour to adapt to the environment links well with attachment theory and neurobiological perspectives, as it highlights the importance of the primary caregiver providing a loving, safe and secure environment. This will provide the optimum conditions for sensory, neurological and cognitive development. However, a critical perspective on Piaget's developmental models is provided by the critique from Thelen and Smith, who argued that cognition is but one aspect of the entire developmental dynamic system (Thelen and Smith, 1994: 337). It is through this critique that we can link attachment and some humanistic perspectives. To mature and grow entails more than the need for homeostasis, but rather growth in a positive direction influenced by the innate actualising tendency (Rogers, 1959). If nurtured under the right conditions, then positive growth and authenticity ensue. If the conditions are not favourable, however, although the organism's/individual's actualising tendency still strives to grow towards a positive direction, incongruence and psychological maladjustment ensue (Rogers, 1959; Lago and Charura, 2016). Figure 1.3 that follows outlines a summary of some of the theoretical concepts discussed in this chapter so far.

## CENTRALITY OF DIVERSITY

With Ainsworth having conducted studies in Uganda, she and Bowlby contributed to the centrality of attachment theory and its utility in cross-cultural research and practice (Ainsworth, 1967). Competent practice in working with children, young people and their

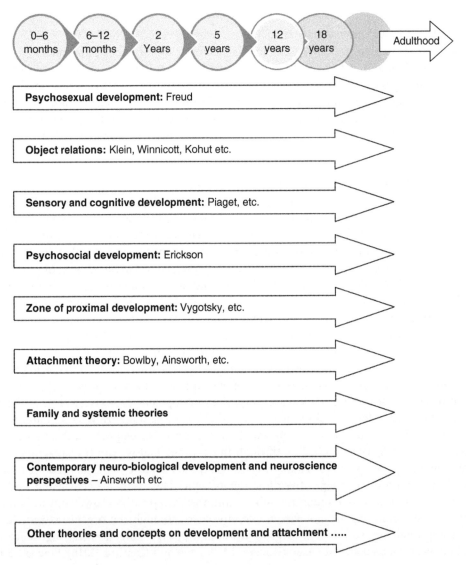

**Figure 1.3**   Theoretical concepts on development and attachment

Note: The arrows signify that each theory asserts development to a particular age stage: identify the accurate age stages for each and critique each one.

families can be informed by adhering to current local legislation (e.g. in the UK the Equality Act (2010), which promotes equality amongst protected characteristics of age, disability, gender reassignment, pregnancy and maternity, race, religion or belief, sex and sexual orientation). In line with this thinking about development amongst young people, the therapeutic approach of systemic therapy developed what is referred to as the social GRRAACCES (an acronym for gender, race, religion, age, abilities, culture, class, ethnicity and sexual orientation), and enables the therapist to take account of their own and the client's experiences of challenges from these perspectives (Burnham, 1992). Moodley's (2005) inclusive definition, which extends difference and diversity to seven major categories of race, gender, class, sexual orientation, disability, religion and age, also contributes to the dynamics of the relational encounter when considering working with difference and diversity with children and young people. Awareness of potentially marginalised children and young people and of difference in relation to attachment patterns and development therefore enables practitioners to explore not only their position but also those of the clients and colleagues with whom they work.

## IMPLICATIONS FOR PRACTICE

This chapter has contributed a wide range of perspectives that relate to attachment, multi-theoretical and intersubjective perspectives. I will now outline briefly how relational principles (Paul and Charura, 2015; Finlay, 2015) can enable therapists to draw parallels in practice from the integration of knowledge of child development in order to enhance and improve their work. Thus:

- A parallel can be drawn between the importance of love, care and secure attachment and the importance of a therapeutic relationship that offers the right conditions and environment for healing and transformation for the child or young person (through empathy, warmth, congruence and acceptance of the child or young person as hypothesised by Rogers (1959)).
- From a relational and developmental perspective, therapy can offer a relationship that helps to work through the attachment difficulties and experience the child or young person has in relation to the therapist (Erskine, 2015; Finlay, 2015; Paul and Charura, 2015). Working through the attachment difficulties or developmental problems with the child/young person or their parents/caregivers in the here-and-now could take different forms: dialogue, creative media or play, for example. This enables the child/young person to develop insight into the attachment difficulties or developmental impairment as well as enabling exploration of new and growthful ways of relating.
- Working with difference and diversity means to be open to encountering and working with the known as well as the unexpected. In many cases of working with diversity the therapist is open to working with issues of development, meeting the child or young person at whatever stage they are at and working with difference in race, identity, class, disability, religion, age and so on (Burnham, 1992; Moodley, 2005).
- The theoretical concepts of holding and containing, which in therapeutic process align with the parallel of how a mother allows a child to express emotion whilst keeping them safe. In therapeutic practice, the therapist thus provides a similar function in working with the child or young person's projections of painful, angry, unbearable feelings or experiencing, and returning them to the child in a modified, contained way. Through this way of working, the

client learns to think through and understand their feelings and emotional experience as well as learning to contain their own emotions (Finlay, 2015). The concepts of *holding* (Winnicott, 1953; 1971) and *containment* (Bion 1959; 1962) thus have immense value in relational work with children and young people, not only in providing a space where the individual can learn to emotionally regulate, but also in providing a reparative and facilitative environment.

- The section on love and neurological development aims to further the understanding of the link between neuroscience, neurobiology, child development and developing appropriate therapeutic interventions that facilitate therapeutic growth. In line with this it can be concluded that as a good loving relational attachment with primary caregivers can contribute to positive neurological development, therapy can also contribute to neurological development and change in the client and therapist (Joseph, 1999; Cozolino, 2010; Gerhardt, 2015; Paul and Charura, 2015).

- The importance of play and creativity is highly valued in considering the development of children and young people; thus, is to be also highly valued in therapeutic practice. For example, as drawn from the assertions of Klein, who postulated the importance of play in symbol formation in the development of the ego (Klein, 1930); or the arguments of Vygotsky (1966), which highlighted that from the point of view of development, the creation of an imaginary situation can be regarded as a means of developing abstract thought and is the first step to a child's ability to use objects creatively, thus enabling freedom to explore unconscious and conscious material in relation to or in reaction to experiences.

In considering the perspectives I have covered in this chapter, it is evident that the relationships between attachment experiences, intersubjectivity and development are incredibly complex, and warrant further exploration.

## Case Studies

Bella is a 15-year-old who presents referred from her class teacher. She is reported to be quiet, withdrawn and recently tearful when asked how she is. She has lost a lot of weight and states she feels she is 'fat and just doesn't feel hungry'. In the most recent contact she has had with the teacher, the teacher noticed some superficial scratches on her skin, which Bella stated she did with a pencil sharpener blade a few days ago. She stated she does 'not have a good relationship' with her mother, and her father, whom she has contact with, left when she was 3 years old.

James presents to your consulting room following a referral from the head teacher. He has recently transferred from a local school to the grammar school following being awarded a scholarship. He states that he has been bullied and feels different, saying his 'parents are working class and [my] upbringing is very different from all the other children's upbringing' in his class. He states that he has a very good relationship with his mother and father. He also explains that he is worried that his parents and others may not accept him because he feels that he is 'a girl in a boy's body'.

Ibrahim and Ashna present with their 7-year-old daughter Yana for therapy. They state that they arrived from Syria 2 years ago and were granted refugee status in the UK. It emerges that they adopted Yana when she was 4 years old. They explain that when they adopted her she had been in an orphanage, having lost both parents 'in the war'. They describe that at the time she was much smaller than the other children and she used to 'make strange shouting noises'. They also said that they believed that she had epilepsy, but recently having started having more seizures, she has been given a diagnosis of non-epiletic seizures, which the consultant believes are stress-induced.

# Key Learning

- Different theoretical and conceptual perspectives on child development and attachment have been presented.
- The impact and influence of attachment on physical, neurological, cognitive, behavioural, psychological, social, relational or emotional growth.
- The importance of attachment and its impact on development of an internal working model and capacity for relational patterns not just in childhood and adolescence but later in life.
- The importance and consideration of diversity.
- The parallels and learning that can be drawn between the child–primary caregiver relationship and the necessary conditions for development and the implications for the therapist–client relationship in practice.

# Summary

How a practitioner works therapeutically with children and young people whose life experience has impacted on their development or attachment patterns will depend upon their professional setting and theoretical orientation (see Chapters 2–8 in this handbook). In this chapter I have thus:

- Summarised how the traditional psychodynamic and humanistic approaches conceptualise the person as coming into the world prewired, with a predetermined instinctual nature. The individual then encounters an environment that might encourage, facilitate, suppress, repress or distort this innate drive. In these traditional approaches there is the assumption that the individuals' development is driven by, and is a response to, intra-psychic, innate

*(Continued)*

(Continued)

tendencies and environmental needs. However, within a relational and attachment approach it is accepted that there is still an inner drive but this drive is more focused towards fulfillment in relation to others (Erskine, 2015; Finlay, 2015; Paul and Charura, 2015).

- Primary attachment experiences are central to the development of internal security and influence the development of an internal model, personality, sense of self, the capacity to relate to others and identity development. Thus, it is generally accepted from a relational perspective that as humans we are motivated by a need to relate. From the moment we are born our phenomenological (subjective) worldview and sense of self are grounded in and developed through our relationship with others. This can be illustrated in relational psychoanalytic, intersubjective, object relations, cognitive, humanistic, existential, gestalt and transpersonal perspectives on human development.

Furthermore genetic dispositions and the socio-cultural environment in which we live influence further how we develop (Meaney, 2010). Thus, in relation to implications of attachment and development for therapeutic practice I note that:

- For those working with individual children/young persons or parents and family systems, understanding more about developmental concepts, attachment theory, the importance of love and diversity enables a number of things to occur. It enables them to explore how the family system or parent–child relationship could have contributed to psychological and emotional vulnerabilities the child or young person is presenting with. It also allows for curiosity and exploration of how the family and parent–child dynamics may be unintentionally supporting or maintaining the developmental, emotional or relational presenting difficulties. This will enable us as practitioners to be more competent in our work, thus minimising possibilities of unintentionally missing presentations that may require safeguarding protocols to be activated.

In addition:

- Understanding the centrality of attachment theory, developmental concepts and the importance of love in working with children and young people has further implications for practice. It opens therapists and practitioners up to an appreciation of how counselling and psychotherapy can offer a reparative space and process for working with often very distressed individuals.
- It can be difficult to witness pain and hear the experiences of children and young people who have been neglected, abused or traumatised, or whose life experiences have resulted in disrupted childhoods. Thus, it is important to ensure that when working with this client group we make sure we engage in support for ourselves, self-care and access regular good supervision.
- It is also important to ensure that we are aware of developmental and attachment impairments when working therapeutically with vulnerable children and young people. These may present in cognitive, behavioural, psychological, social, relational or emotional problems.

## Discussion Questions

Some of these discussion questions, as with all personal development work, may be upsetting, so make sure you are well supported if you choose to answer them.

1. Think about your own childhood experience; write down or reflect on your own account of your development. How would you describe your own attachment pattern?
2. How well do the descriptions of how development and attachment is conceptualised in the different theories noted in this chapter fit with your own experience? What is your critique?
3. Can you reflect on the case studies presented and explore your thoughts in relation to development and attachment? What feelings emerge in you? What were the challenges? What can the therapeutic relationship offer? Consider issues of difference and diversity.
4. What support do you have in working with children whose developmental process and attachment have been disrupted?

## Develop Your Skills

1. Write down your understanding of child development from the viewpoints of a couple of theoretical concepts different from your own orientation of practice/training.
2. When do you think it would be appropriate to refer a child or young person to a specialist service different from your own, or when is it not appropriate to offer a therapeutic intervention?

## Further Reading

Gerhardt, S. (2015) *Why Love Matters: How Affection Shapes a Baby's Brain* (2nd edn). London: Routledge.

Now in its second edition, this well written book is an accessible read and focuses on the power of love and attachment.

Charura, D. and Paul, S. (2015) *Love and Therapy: In Relationship.* London: Karnac.

*(Continued)*

---

(Continued)

This text, with contributions from a wide range of contributors interested in love and attachment, addresses critical themes of love, attachment and therapeutic process.

Cozolino, L. (2010) *The Neuroscience of Psychotherapy: Building and Rebuilding the Brain*. New York: W.W. Norton.

A useful text for learning more about the neurological impact of attachment as well exploring perspectives on the reparative power of psychotherapy.

### Online Resource

BACP website: www.bacp.co.uk, especially the BACP Children and Young People.

---

# REFERENCES

Ainsworth, M.D. (1963) The development of infant–mother interaction among the Ganda. In: Foss, B.M. (ed.) *Determinants of Infant Behavior*. New York: Wiley, pp. 67–112.

Ainsworth, M.D. (1967) *Infancy in Uganda: Infant Care and the Growth of Love*. Baltimore, MD: The Johns Hopkins University Press.

Ainsworth, M.D. (1982) Attachment: Retrospect and prospect. In: Parkes, C.M. and Stevenson-Hinde, J. (eds) *The Place of Attachment in Human Behavior*. New York: Basic Books, pp. 3–30.

Ainsworth, M.D. (1985) Patterns of attachment. *Clinical Psychologist* 38(2): 27–29.

Ainsworth, M.D. and Bell, S.M. (1970) Attachment, exploration, and separation: illustrated by the behavior of one-year-olds in a strange situation. *Child Development* 41: 49–67.

Ainsworth, M.D., Blehar, M.C., Waters, E. and Wall, S. (1978) *Patterns of Attachment: A Psychological Study of the Strange Situation*. Hillsdale, NJ: Erlbaum.

Belsky, J. (2002) Developmental origins of attachment styles. *Attachment and Human Development* 4(2): 166–170.

Bion, W.R. (1959). Attacks on Linking. *The international Journal of Psychoanalysis*, 40: 308–315.

Bion, W.R. (1962). *Learning from Experience*. London: Heinemann.

Bowlby, J. (1958) The nature of the child's tie to his mother. *International Journal of Psycho-Analysis* 39: 350–373.

Bowlby, J. (1969) *Attachment and Loss: Vol. 1. Attachment*. New York: Basic Books.

Bowlby, J. (1973) *Attachment and Loss: Vol. 2. Separation: Anxiety and Anger*. New York: Basic Books.

Bowlby, J. (1980) *Attachment and Loss: Vol. 3. Sadness and Depression*. New York: Basic Books.

Bowlby, J. (1988) *A Secure Base*. New York: Basic Books.

Bronfenbrenner, U. (1977) Toward an experimental ecology of human development. *American Psychologist 32*: 513–531.

Bronfenbrenner, U. (1986) Ecology of the family as a context for human development: research perspectives. *Developmental Psychology 22*: 723–742.

Bronfenbrenner, U. and Morris, P.A. (1998) The ecology of developmental processes. In: Damon, W. and Lerner, R.M. (eds) *Handbook of Child Psychology: Volume 1: Theoretical Models of Human Development* (5th edn). Hoboken, NJ: John Wiley & Sons, pp. 993–1028.

Brown, F. (2014) *Play and Playwork: 101 Stories of Children Playing.* Maidenhead: Open University Press.

Brown, F. and Webb, S. (2003) Playwork in adversity: working with abandoned children in Romania. In: Brown, F. (ed.) *Playwork Theory and Practice.* Buckingham: Open University Press, pp. 157–175.

Burnham, J. (1992) Approach–method–technique: making distinctions and creating connections. *Human Systems 3*: 3–27.

Burns, M.K., Warmbold-Brann, K. and Zaslofsky, A.F. (2015) Ecological systems theory in school psychology review. *School Psychology Review 44*(3): 249–261.

Charura, D. and Paul, S. (2015) *Love and Therapy: In Relationship.* London: Karnac.

Clarkson, P. (2003) *The Therapeutic Relationship* (2nd edn). London: Whurr Publishers.

Cozolino, L. (2010) *The Neuroscience of Psychotherapy: Building and Rebuilding the Brain.* New York: W.W. Norton.

Dallos, R. and Draper, R. (2010) *An Introduction to Family Therapy: Systemic Theory and Practice* (3rd edn). Maidenhead: Open University Press.

Else, P. (2009) *The Value of Play.* London: Continuum.

Erikson, E. (1950/1963) *Childhood and Society* (2nd edn). New York: W.W. Norton.

Erskine, R.G. (2015) *Relational Patterns, Therapeutic Presence: Concepts and Practice of Integrative Psychotherapy.* London: Karnac.

Erskine, R. G. and Moursund, J. P. (2011). *Integrative Psychotherapy in Action.* London: Karnac Books. Originally published 1988. Newbury Park, CA: Sage.

Field, T. (1996). Attachment and separation in young children. *Annual Review of Psychology, 47*, 541–562.

Finlay, L. (2015) *Relational Integrative Psychotherapy: Process and Theory in Practice.* Chichester: Wiley.

Fisher, H. (2004) Your brain in love. *Time* [serial online] *163*(3): 80–83.

Fox, N.A. (1989) Infant temperament and security of attachment: a new look. Paper presented at the International Society for Behavioral Development, Jyviiskylii, Finland, July, 1989.

Fraley, R.C. and Spieker, S.J. (2003) Are infant attachment patterns continuously or categorically distributed? A taxometric analysis of strange situation behavior. *Developmental Psychology 39*: 387–404.

Freud, S. (1905) *Three essays on sexuality.* In J. Strachey (ed. and trans.), *The Standard Edition of the Complete Psychological Works of* Sigmund Freud (1968) (Vol. 7, pp. 130–243). London: Hogarth Press.

Freud, S. (1911) Formulations on the two principles of mental functioning. In J. Strachey (ed. and trans.), *The Standard Edition of the Complete Psychological Works of Sigmund Freud* (1968) (Vol. 12, pp. 218–226). London: Hogarth Press.

Freud, S. (1915) *The Unconscious (Strachey, J., translator)*. London: Hogarth Press. Standard Edition.

Freud, S. (1924) *The Dissolution of the Oedipus Complex*. London: Hogarth Press. Standard Edition.

Freud, S. (1933) New introductory lectures on psychoanalysis. *Lecture 33: Femininity. Standard Edition*, v. 22. pp. 136–157. In S. Freud and J. Strachey (1964) *New Introductory Lectures on Psychoanalysis*. London: Hogarth Press.

Freud, S., Strachey, J., Freud, A., Rothgeb, C. and Richards, A. (1953) *The Standard Edition of the Complete Psychological Works of Sigmund Freud*. London: Hogarth Press.

Garcia, J.L. (1995) Freud's psychosexual stage conception: a developmental metaphor for counselors. *Journal of Counseling and Development 73*(5): 498–502.

Gerhardt, S. (2015) *Why Love Matters: How Affection Shapes a Baby's Brain* (2nd edn). London: Routledge.

Gibbs, S., Barrow, W. and Parker, R. (2014) Child development and attachment. In: Pattison, S. Robinson, M. and Beynon, A. (eds) *The Handbook of Counselling Children and Young People*. London: SAGE, pp. 7–18.

Greenberg, J. and Mitchell, S. (1983) *Object Relations in Psychoanalytic Theory*. Cambridge, MA: Harvard University Press.

Hughes, F.P. (2010) *Children, Play, and Development* (4th edn). London: SAGE.

Joseph, R. (1999) Environmental influences on neural plasticity, the limbic system, emotional development and attachment: a review. *Child Psychiatry and Human Development Journal, 29*(3): 189–208.

Klein, M. (1924) An obsessional neurosis in a six-year-old girl. In: *Psycho-analysis of Children*. London: Hogarth Press, 1975.

Klein, M. (1930) The importance of symbol-formation in the development of the ego. *International Journal of Psycho-Analysis 11*: 24–39.

Klein, M. (1952) Some theoretical conclusions regarding the emotional life of the infant. In: Klein, M., Heimann, P., Isaacs, S. and Riviera, J. (eds) *Developments in Psycho-analysis*. London: Hogarth Press, pp. 61–93.

Klein, M. (1975) A contribution to the psychogenesis of manic-depressive states. *Love, Guilt and Reparation and Other Works*, 1921–1945 (pp. 262–289). London: Hogarth Press

Knight, Z.G. (2017) A proposed model of psychodynamic psychotherapy linked to Erik Erikson's eight stages of psychosocial development. *Clinical Psychology and Psychotherapy 24*(5): 1047–1058.

Kohut, H. (1977) *The Restoration of the Self*. New York: International Universities Press.

Kohut, H. (1984) *How Does Analysis Cure?* Chicago, IL: University of Chicago Press.

Lago, C. and Charura, D. (2016) *The Person-centred Counselling and Psychotherapy Handbook: Origins, Developments, and Current Applications*. Maidenhead: Open University Press.

Larsson, P. (2012) How important is an understanding of the client's early attachment experience to the psychodynamic practice of counselling psychology? *Counselling Psychology Review 27*(1): 10–21, 104.

Main, M., Kaplan, N. and Cassidy, J. (1985) Security in infancy, childhood, and adulthood: a move to the level of representation. *Monographs of the Society for Research in Child Development* 50(1–2): 66–104.

Main, M. & Solomon, J. (1990) Procedures for identifying disorganized/disoriented infants during the Ainsworth Strange Situation. In M. Greenberg, D. Cicchetti and M. Cummings (Eds), *Attachment in the preschool years*. Chicago: University of Chicago Press, pp. 121–160.

Meaney, M.J. (2001) Nature, nurture, and the disunity of knowledge. *Annals of the New York Academy of Sciences 935*: 50–61.

Meaney, M.J. (2010) Epigenetics and the biological definition of gene × environment interactions. *Child Development 81*: 41–79.

Mitchell, S.A. (2000) *Relationality: From Attachment to Intersubjectivity*. Hillsdale, NJ: The Analytic Press.

Moodley, R. (2005) 'Diversity matrix revisited: criss-crossing multiple identities in clinical practice'. Keynote paper at Multicultural and Counseling symposium. Ithaca, NY: Cornell University.

Paul, S. and Charura, D. (2015). *An Introduction to the Therapeutic Relationship in Counselling and Psychotherapy*. Los Angeles: SAGE.

Piaget, J. (1971) Developmental stages and developmental processes. In: Green, D.R., Ford, M.P. and Flamer, G.B. (eds) *Measurement and Piaget*. New York: McGraw-Hill, pp. 172–188.

Pickover, S. (2002) Breaking the cycle: a clinical example of disrupting an insecure attachment system. *Journal of Mental Health Counseling 24*: 358–367.

Rogers, C. R. (1939) *Clinical Treatment of the Problem Child*. Boston, MA: Houghton Mifflin.

Rogers, C. R. (1959). A theory of therapy, personality, and interpersonal relationships as developed in the client-centered framework. In S. Koch (Ed.), *Psychology: A study of a science* Vol. 3: *Formulations of the Person and the Social Context*. New York: McGraw-Hill, pp. 184–256.

Roy-Chowdhury, S. (2010) Is there a place for individual subjectivity within a social constructionist epistemology? *Journal of Family Therapy 32*(4): 342.

Sasaki, J.Y. and Kim, H.S. (2017) Nature, nurture, and their interplay: a review of cultural neuroscience. *Journal of Cross-Cultural Psychology 48*(1): 4–22.

Schore, A.N. (1994) *Affect Regulation and the Origin of the Self*. Hillsdale, NJ: Lawrence Erlbaum Associates Inc.

Shuttleworth, J. (1989) Psychoanalytic theory and infant development. In: Miller, L., Rustin, M., and Rustin, M. (eds) *Closely Observed Infants*. London: Duckworth, pp. 22–51.

Siegel, D.J. (1999) *Developing Mind: Toward a Neurobiology of Interpersonal Experience*. New York: W.W. Norton.

Siegel, D.J. (2010) *The Mindful Therapist*. New York: W.W. Norton.

Sumontha, J., Farr, R.H. and Patterson, C.J. (2017) Children's gender development: associations with parental sexual orientation, division of labor, and gender ideology. *Psychology of Sexual Orientation and Gender Diversity 4*(4): 438–450.

Thelen, E. and Smith. L.V. (1994) *A Dynamics Systems Approach to the Development of Cognition and Action*. Cambridge, MA: Bradford Books.

Tudge, J., Mokrova, I., Hatfield, B. and Karnik, R. (2009) Uses and misuses of Bronfenbrenner's bioecological theory of human development. *Journal of Family Theory & Review, 1*, 198–210.

Vygotsky, L. (1966) Play and its role in the mental development of the child. *Voprosi Psikhologii* 6, originally published 1933, translated by Catherine Mullholland. Available at: www. marxists.org/archive/vygotsky/works/1933/play.htm (accessed 1 December 2017).

Winnicott, D. (1953) Transitional objects and transitional phenomena. *International Journal of Psychoanalysis 34*: 89–97.

Winnicott, D.W. (1960) The theory of the parent–infant relationship. *International Journal of Psychoanalysis.*, 41:585–595.

Winnicott, D.W. (1967) Mirror-role of the mother and family in child development. In: Lomas, P. (ed.) *The Predicament of the Family: A Psycho-Analytical Symposium*. London: Hogarth, pp. 26–33.

Winnicott, D.W. (1971) Playing and Reality. New York: Basic Books.

# 2

# CHILD AND YOUNG PERSON-CENTRED APPROACH

## GRAHAM BRIGHT

**This chapter will discuss:**

- **The origins and key tenets of the person-centred approach (PCA)**
- **Rogers' core conditions**
- **Person-centred practice with children and young people**

## INTRODUCTION

### History and background

The person-centred approach (PCA) to therapy is grounded in Carl Rogers' formative work with children and young people; it seems right, therefore, as a means of introduction to this chapter, to recover some of that history here. Carl Rogers (1902–1987) was born near Chicago. His family moved to live and work on a farm when he was in high school. Rogers was by all accounts a studious but shy boy who did not have many friends outside the family circle. Growing up, he had a keen interest in science, and his formative years were significantly influenced by his family's Christian beliefs. Rogers studied agriculture at college for 2 years before briefly exploring a vocation to Christian ministry. During this period he attended the International World Student Federation Conference in Beijing, which he described as 'a most important experience for me' (Kirschenbaum and Henderson, 1989: 9). Here Rogers observed a good deal of disagreement and even animosity amongst delegates, which led him to conclude that pluralistic divergence was phenomenologically inevitable. As a result, he began to question some of the more affixed doctrine that he had grown up with (Barrett-Lennard, 2013). The result – to his parents' despair – was that the newly married Rogers chose to attend a highly liberal seminary, where he was exposed to heuristic forms of inquiry that enabled Rogers and his fellow students to reach their own very personal conclusions regarding matters of faith and experience.

These student-led seminars helped Rogers to clarify his own beliefs; as a result, he felt it incongruous to continue pursuit of the ministry to which he could no longer profess. It was at this time that Rogers felt drawn to the field of child guidance, an arena that at that time was saturated by Freudian thinking. He was appointed to a team of three psychologists working with the Society for the Prevention of Cruelty to Children in Rochester, New York. Rogers recounted his time at Rochester in the psychoanalytical diagnosis and treatment of young people as being a period of deep learning, yet one that left him re-evaluating the prescriptive nature of psychoanalytical diagnostic formation and treatment. One particular incident with a mother of a challenging young boy proved to be seminal. Rogers recalled trying (without success) to offer psychoanalytical interpretation regarding the underlying nature of the family's symptomatic behaviours; later, however, the mother began to detail her own distress regarding her marriage. Rogers cited this incident as:

> one of a number which helped me to experience the fact – only fully realized later – that it is the *client* who knows what hurts, what directions to go, what problems are crucial, what experiences have been deeply buried. It began to occur to me that unless I had a need to demonstrate my own cleverness and learning, I would do better to rely upon the client for the direction of movement in the process. (Kirschenbaum and Henderson, 1989: 13; emphasis in original)

Rogers' first book, *The Clinical Treatment of the Problem Child*, was published in 1939 and viewed as a welcome contribution to an emergent field. In it kernels of what we have come to understand today as the PCA can be seen. Relational qualities between practitioner and 'patient' are described and accentuated, most notably that of non-judgemental acceptance. Here too we see the emergence of Rogers' ideas on the 'actualising tendency'. Barrett-Lennard (2013: 35) notes that 'by the time his first book was completed, what was to become non-directive client-centred therapy was germinating strongly in the thought and practice of its founder'.

## Theoretical underpinning

Over the ensuing years, Rogers refined his theory, arguing that the quality of relationship between therapist and client was central to facilitative growth and change. In Rogers' view it is unnecessary to engage in therapeutic formulation drawn from the client's past; rather, he emphasised the import of empathically experiencing *with* the client the subjective, transcendent essence of their here-and-now reality as it is fluidly experienced. In this way, Rogers' work related to Husserl and Heidegger's ideas of phenomenological construction (Cooper et al., 2013) and posited a distinct shift from directive forms of therapy, which draw upon therapist interpretation and expertise towards non-directive, facilitative work in which the client – motivated by their actualising tendency – instinctively 'understands' at different levels of their being what is needed for their own healing and growth (Rogers, 1959). Here the therapist seeks to enter and understand the Other's subjective reality as they experience it, and to offer particular conditions that enable the fluidity of the Other's experience of being and becoming as determined by their congruent response to what is happening within their field of reality (or environment) to be realised. What Rogers emphasised, therefore, is a 'way of being' with another which enables that Other to intrinsically nurture their own organismic processes without recourse to technicised therapeutic interventions that draw upon more prescribed theoretical formulations (Merry, 2008). The PCA has oft been criticised for a lack of theoretical rigour and therapeutic wizardry associated with other psychotherapeutic approaches, yet proponents would argue that it is theoretically rich and necessitates advanced levels of practitioner discipline, integration and growth – it requires, perhaps more than any other approach, that therapists bring and use their whole being to assist the client on their therapeutic odyssey (Mearns and Thorne, 2013).

Rogers' work itself was based on certain theoretical underpinnings that he described throughout his career as particular hypotheses. This ongoing experiential work led Rogers to develop and iterate his own theory of the person. Central to his postulation was that each human being has an 'actualising tendency', which Gillon (2007: 27) describes as:

> an inherent, biological tendency towards growth and development. This tendency is located at the level of the organism as a whole and is seen as the single, basic motivational force driving each human being toward the fulfilment of their unique potential.

The Rogerian vision of the person is positive and hopeful. It views with optimism the possibilities of human potential observing the self as changing and dynamic, and as responsive to different stimuli within its environment. This fluidity, however, is underpinned by particular characteristics that might be viewed as relatively consistent at given moments of time and more generally across the lifecourse (Merry, 2008). For the infant, there is no experiential division between what they perceive as internal and external to the self (Cooper et al., 2013). As they grow, babies become aware through reflective interactions with others of their separateness, resulting in experiential differentiation. Infants begin to recognise the 'I' or 'me' or 'self' as being separate from others, from which a concept of the self begins to emerge (Gillon, 2007). The self requires two principal needs to be met in order to develop higher actualised outcomes. We can, according to Merry (2008), consider these as needing positive regard from self (internal regard) and others (external regard). External regard tends to manifest itself as we grow and develop through our need of acceptance, praise and recognition from those close to us, including parents, other caregivers and those whom we admire in some way. At the same time, each individual needs to develop trust in their own intrinsic organismic processes in order that a diversity of needs are met in nourishing the potential of the actualising tendency, which Gillon (2007: 28) describes as 'an on-going, biologically-driven valuing process which allows each of us to assess experiences that are enhancing to, or maintaining for, our organismic needs and potentialities'. Such is our need, however, for others' approval that over time we adapt our intuitive feelings and behaviours and conform to meet others' expectations to the detriment of our organismic needs and processes. We become subtly, and sometimes not so subtly, subjected to and imprisoned by particular messages that become imbibed deep within us: messages of conditionality – 'I will accept you if you conceal this or "change" that … I will love you if … I like this about you, but not that … If you want my approval, then don't do the other…'. The result, as Mearns and Thorne note, is that people:

> struggle to keep their heads above water by trying to do and be those things which they know will elicit approval while scrupulously avoiding or suppressing those thoughts, feelings and activities that they sense will bring adverse judgement … They are the victims of *conditions of worth* which others have imposed on them, but so great is their need for positive approval that they accept this straitjacket rather than risk rejection by trespassing against the conditions set for their acceptability (2013: 9; emphasis in original).

Such is the assault on the person's core and the onslaught against their very being that their humanity is threatened; no longer able to trust their own inner voice, they resort to consulting external loci of evaluation and living by others' ideas, values and practices. Yet, however fragile, the actualising tendency retains the potential of hope and healing.

## Self and self-concept

For Rogers (1959), the self was the totality of human experience as it is subjectively under-stood by each individual from their own unique phenomenological worldview. An individual builds their self-concept as a result of their interactions with their world and with others in that world; the extent to which the self-concept is constructive is determined by the positive regard the individual receives from others when engaging in behaviours that are aligned with their organismic core. The individual who introjects others' wishes and values into their self-concept in order to maintain their love and affection risks such osmoses being at odds with his own organismic valuing process. The child who draws conditionality into himself increas-ingly locates his loci of evaluation externally, feeling decreasingly able to trust his own inner voice (Prever, 2010), thereby generating a corrosive effect on the self-concept. The result is an individual who feels progressively detached from his own organismic reality and who increas-ingly internalises a negative self-concept that tends to perpetuate and reinforce 'negative' behaviour and emotional-belief patterns (Mearns and Thorne, 2013). The experiential disorientation that results in the dissonant incongruence between a self-concept which has been infiltrated by a drip-feed of conditionality and the individual's resilient capacity to remain wired to their organismic potential is tangible. It is the work of the person-centred therapist to permit and enable the client to reconcile himself to that potential.

Nowhere, perhaps, are these processes more acutely noticeable than in the formative experiences of the young. They are dependent on others for their care, less able to filter out negative personal messages concerning them individually from significant adults and peers, and they are often tyrannised as groups by insidious attacks from politicians, the media and society at large. Such messages are subtle, yet strong and clear.

## THE CORE CONDITIONS

In 1957 Rogers published a seminal paper which famously declared that there are six 'necessary and sufficient' conditions required for therapeutic change:

1. Two persons are in psychological contact.
2. The first, whom we shall term the client, is in a state of *incongruence*, being vulnerable or anxious.
3. The second person, whom we shall term the therapist, is *congruent* or *integrated* in the relationship.
4. The therapist experiences *unconditional positive regard* for the client.
5. The therapist experiences an *empathic understanding* of the client's internal frame of reference and endeavours to communicate this experience to the client.
6. The communication to the client of the therapist's empathic understanding and unconditional positive regard is to a minimal degree achieved.

Conditions 3, 4 and 5 later became known as the 'core conditions' and are viewed by many therapists across modalities as the *foundation* for therapeutic work. The PCA hypothesises, however, that it is *solely* these qualities within the therapeutic relationship that matter in catalysing the client's inner resources. By inference, how the therapist embodies the core conditions is of deepest concern; rather than being something that is 'switched on' when entering the therapy room, such embodiment becomes a way of life. This demands that the therapist takes seriously her commitment to personal development, attunement and attending to self in supervision in order that she can fully 'be' with the client.

Whilst for the sake of discussion it is necessary to consider the core conditions separately, the nature of their seamless, triune integration cannot be ignored (see Fig. 2.1). Empathy, for example, cannot be understood or 'practised' on its own without reference to its dynamic interrelationship with congruence and unconditional positive regard (UPR). Together, they offer a potent way of being with oneself and with others.

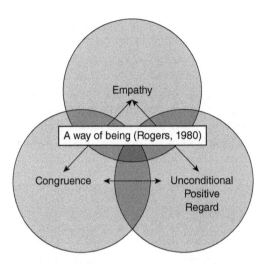

**Figure 2.1**    A way of being (Rogers, 1980)

## Congruence

The task of person-centred therapy is to nurture congruence in the client, to permit them to reconnect with the congruent experiencing of their organismic self and to re-enable trust in their internal locus of evaluation. Therapy seeks to minimise the distorted gap between the client's idealised self-concept and their real self. Here, the therapist's congruence becomes a counterpoint to the client's incongruence, a mirror held up to the client that indicates not only its possibility but its desirability also. Congruence builds trust in the therapeutic relationship (Mearns and Thorne, 2013); it expresses something of the wholeness of the person, the consistency or genuineness that exists between outward expression and inward experiencing – a gestalt, if you will. Congruence is therefore concerned with being oneself in the moment and accurately and appropriately representing the significance of that to and for the benefit of the client. The therapist who is able to be in touch with herself at some deep level, and to be accepting of that self, has a greater capacity to be attuned to the Other's process. There is no pretence; the therapist is a person willing to accompany the client on their journey, not an expert in the client's life. This message, when 'conveyed' through the therapist's way of being, moves the client from a reliance on external loci to rebuilding trust in their own inner experiential voice. Congruence therefore requires the therapist to nurture high levels of reflexive self-awareness through personal development and supervision. Mearns and Thorne (2013: 115ff.) contend that, whilst the therapist must remain intuitively aware of what is happening within her, the expression of congruent awareness to the client must be based upon what is appropriate, relevant and persistent. This is not to deny what is within the therapist's stream of consciousness, thereby unleashing incongruence; rather, the therapist is obliged to decide judiciously what might be important to explore in her own personal development or supervision and what should be shared with the client as a means of fostering benefit and realness in the therapeutic relationship.

Children and young people require their relationship with their counsellor to be trustworthy, in order that they can feel safe to explore the things they need to; secure, in order that they can go to those often difficult, painful and challenging places with the surety that they will be accompanied by someone real who can anchor their own quest for reality. Congruence fosters trust. Young clients are adept at recognising those playing a therapeutic role that is at odds with the rest of their character (Geldard et al., 2016); such insincerity dissipates therapeutic value and further undermines the client's capacity for self-trust. Congruence is therefore central to therapeutic work with children and young people.

## Unconditional positive regard

Unconditional positive regard (UPR) is founded in a deep-seated regard for others' fundamental humanity. Rogers frequently referred to UPR as 'prizing' the client. UPR is the persistent attitude of *actively* accepting and valuing the totality of each client's unique being and becoming, which, although it may be challenged, is not swerved by the client's attitude or behaviour. UPR therefore goes beyond the conditional nature of 'liking' to embrace a more essential attitude that deeply and warmly accepts the client for who he is (Mearns and Thorne, 2013). Setting the client free of conditionality is central to the process of person-centred therapy. Indeed, for Bozarth (2013: 183), UPR is the 'curative variable' in the therapy. The counsellor therefore must nurture acceptance of the client's process wherever that may take them. For the therapist, embodying UPR as part of her way of being is a challenge. She needs to be congruently aware of her true feelings regarding her clients; where persistent attitudinal conditionality exists, she must examine this with the support of her clinical supervisor.

As I noted earlier in this chapter, young people in particular are one of the most judged groups in western societies. Developmentally they are locating through experience their own values, beliefs, ideas and practices through which they construct both their sense of self and their place in the world (Corsaro, 2015). At times, however, children and young people's values and behaviours can appear to be at odds with normative adult conventions; the result is that many experience conditionality in a range of domains. In order for therapy to be an effective counterballast that enables the dissolution of conditionality and its symptoms, those working with young clients must foster and effectively convey UPR if they are to be successful in enabling their clients' therapeutic progress (Geldard et al., 2016).

## Empathy

One of the key facets of the person-centred therapeutic relationship is empathy. The counsellor's ability to lay down (without disconnecting from) her own phenomenological reality and to enter the unique perceptual world of her client, to move around in that world and to feel at home in the ebb and flow of the client's lived experiencing of it is arguably one of the most potent therapeutic capacities (Prever, 2010; Freire, 2013; Smyth, 2013). Empathic expression has often been caricatured as the therapist repeating the essence of what the client has just said. Whilst empathic understanding must be conveyed in order to be of value to the client and to meet the requirements of Rogers' sixth condition, it is so much more. It is perceiving with accuracy the subtlety of the client's feelings and meanings in the totality of their emotional, spiritual, psychological and physical being. It is conveying that understanding with tentative sensitivity to the client in a way that enables them to absorb that their experiences and meanings have been deeply understood and accepted by another, thereby releasing the client to do the same on their journey towards a congruent integration of their totality. Empathy strengthens the therapeutic alliance and enables that which is on the edge of awareness to be made known. Empathy enables the conscientisation of therapeutic material: sometimes this is as a result of 'apparently sudden light bulb moments of realisation, and sometimes through the slow burning of unconscious materials and meanings which gradually slot into place in a way that gives crystallised panoramic understanding' (Bright and Harrison, 2013: 42). Empathic understanding speaks with lucidity over the confused din of incongruence. Whilst conditions of worth lead to detachment and isolation from the self and others, empathy's gift is to enable clarity in the client's configured selves (Mearns and Thorne, 2013) and to offer connection to another who both deeply understands and accepts the client in their being and becoming. Empathy re-humanises the client; for Rogers (1986: 129, as cited by Freire, 2013: 167), it 'releases [and] confirms, it even brings the most frightened client into the human race'.

The challenge to the therapist of continually suspending her own perceptual reality in order to live within each client's internal frame of reference 'as if' it were her own is unmistakable. Such a 'task' requires time, energy, discipline, intuition, deep listening, compassion, highly developed awareness and a willingness to take risks. It requires a continual attunement to each client's 'experiences in the here-and-now' (ibid.: 168) in which the therapist must learn to flow with the client's narrative, meaning and emotions whilst remaining attentive to the changing landscape of the client's inner world.

## ROGERS' SEVEN STAGES OF PROCESS

Rogers (1961: 125ff), as summarised by Casemore (2006: 11–12 in Table 2.1), offered his view of how clients tend to process through therapy. Not all clients enter therapy at stage one and leave at stage seven; hence the seven stages of process should be regarded as a direction of

Table 2.1   Rogers' seven stages of process

| Stage | Description |
|-------|-------------|
| 1 | The client is very defensive, and extremely resistant to change |
| 2 | The client becomes slightly less rigid, and will talk about external events or other people |
| 3 | The client talks about him/herself, but as an object, and avoids discussion of present events |
| 4 | The client begins to talk about deep feelings and develops a relationship with the counsellor |
| 5 | The client can express present emotions, and is beginning to rely more on his/her own decision-making abilities and increasingly accepts more responsibility for his/her actions |
| 6 | The client shows rapid growth towards congruence, and begins to develop unconditional positive regard for others. This stage signals the end of the need for formal therapy |
| 7 | The client is a fully functioning, self-actualising individual who is empathic and shows unconditional positive regard for others. This individual can relate their previous therapy to present-day real-life situations |

travel in therapy rather than a matter of rigid linearity. However, it can be used as a reference point to consider where a client might be and might be heading in the therapeutic process; where appropriate, it might even be used with clients to discuss how they feel therapy is progressing and how they might like it to proceed.

## EXPRESSING PERSON-CENTREDNESS

The chapter to this point has sought to emphasise person-centred counselling's distinctiveness as a therapeutic way of being. However, to be effective, not only must the essential nature of the therapeutic relationship be experienced, but the embodied qualities of the therapist must also be expressed if therapeutic change is to occur (Rogers, 1957). Such ideas are, however, elusive. Person-centred therapists need to 'practise' a way of being that is congruent to them without recourse to mechanistic forms of response that might be perceived as 'wooden' and ultimately counterintuitive. Person-centred practice is fundamentally about being able to capture the essence of the client's experience as it is lived in the moment; to congruently and unconditionally accept the client in their individual process of being and becoming. Deep listening to narrative and meaning is required in order that the therapist can 'lock into' the client's internal frame of reference; however, this understanding must also be shared with the client to facilitate their process. Perhaps the key *skill* associated with this way of being is reflection. Reid and Westergaard (2011: 48) describe reflection as 'the counsellor "holding a mirror" to their client by ensuring that responses are appropriate and that they reflect accurately the words and feelings that the young person is expressing'. Thus, the counsellor reveals their understanding of the essence of the client's lived experience. Person-centred therapists who are able to synchronise their being with the client's experience are not, however, limited to words. For some, empathic understanding is 'received' through mental pictures or felt bodily sensations that, when congruently and sensitively conveyed, can facilitate powerful therapeutic movement.

## WORKING IN A PERSON-CENTRED WAY WITH CHILDREN AND YOUNG PEOPLE

Accompanying the client on *their* particular journey of growth and change is, perhaps, most accentuated in person-centred practice with children and young people, who owing to the maturational nature of lifecourse experiences are *very* much in the process of developmental change. Geldard et al. (2016) contend that therapists of all hues are most effective in practice if they are able to get in touch empathically with their own inner child or adolescent. This, they argue, enables the therapist to understand the child or young person's phenomenological experience more vividly.

Person-centred practice seeks to put the client at the centre of practice. Such an assertion means that those working with children and young people must appreciate the particular needs of these age groups, to become attuned to the appropriateness of language and expression. It has often been said that 'play is the language of the child' and, whilst more significant coverage of this claim is offered in Chapter 7, it seems right to offer some discussion here. Döring (2008: 41) argues that 'Play is spontaneous, self-initiated learning; it enables a child to acquire new abilities, problem-solving strategies and skills for coping with emotional conflicts'. Person-centred practice provides space for being and exploring; for children and young people these processes take on a variety of expressions. Behr et al. (2013) note the distinct processes in practice with children, contending that whilst adults are able to verbalise and reflect on their experiences, children symbolise their inner world via creative media like play, art, puppetry, stories, sandplay, dressing up and music (the term 'play' will be used hereafter as shorthand for all these creative media). Perhaps it is Rogers' student and colleague Virginia Axline (1989 [1969]: 69–70) who is best known for developing eight key principles for person-centred play therapy, positing that person-centred play therapists must become attuned to the child's process; offering empathic reflection of the child's symbolisation, rather than psychodynamically founded interpretation of the child's play (see Box 2.1). The language of play privileges and beckons the therapist to enter the child's world; it must therefore be honoured. Play must be treated with the same dignity that is afforded to adult clients' verbalisations. Children will only trust the counsellor and advance in the therapeutic process, when they are joined in play, and experience the core conditions through the therapeutic interactions that they initiate. The therapist needs, therefore, to follow the child's lead, to be moulded by what the child does. So, when a child sits on the floor, perhaps the counsellor should do the same. Such practice also begins to mitigate inherent power differentials that can exist between client and counsellor; it emphasises the value the counsellor has for the child and fosters equality in the relationship (Smyth, 2013).

## Box 2.1

James is busy lying on the floor, drawing a picture. The therapist lies next to him, supporting his chin in his hands.

Therapist:   'It looks like you are drawing a playground with a swing, a roundabout and a climbing frame?'

James:   'Uh-huh.'

Therapist:   'The playground looks as if it's in a park?'

James:   'Yes.'

Therapist:   'There's a boy playing in the park?'

James:   'That's me.'

Therapist:   'You've drawn a bench?'

James:   No reply (silently concentrating)

Therapist:   'It looks as if you are sitting on the bench on your own?'

James: (smiling reflectively)   'Yes, I like to be alone. I like the peace.'

Therapist:   'Peace?'

James:   'Yeah, I never get it at home – Mum and Dad are always arguing and then I have to share a room with two of my brothers …'

Adolescence is a time of profound emotional, social, physical, sexual, psychological, familial and educational change (Coleman, 2010). During this period, the process of being and becoming is perhaps highlighted more than any other. Person-centred work affords young people the space to be, to individuate, to clarify perspectives, to gain new insight and to manage relational boundaries between self and others (Bright, 2013). Working with young people during this period of their lives can be both challenging and richly rewarding as together counsellor and client observe the person who begins to emerge from the chrysalis. During this phase, young people often change their communication preferences, becoming increasingly likely to talk rather than use creative media. Adolescent communication is affected by a range of factors including culture, environment, age-related development and even time of day. Many young people feel a distrust of adults, who they perceive don't understand them (Hawkins, 2008); counsellors working with adolescents therefore must learn to empathically enter each client's phenomenological and linguistic reality and to convey their understanding of the client's internal frame of reference by paralleling the young person's communication processes (Geldard et al., 2016). Such practice fosters relational security between client and therapist and builds the young person's sense of interconnectedness (Smyth, 2013).

## SHORT-TERM WORK

As we have noted, the PCA is concerned with placing the client at the heart of practice. It expresses empowerment, democracy and the promotion of client autonomy as foundational principles. Merry (2008: 12) contends that the PCA above all others affirms an 'enduring commitment to encounter clients in a direct, person-to-person manner without providing a set of rules … that control the process'. Indeed, Smyth (2013: 163) argues that time-limited work in person-centred practice is 'anathema'. Externally imposed time constraints potentially limit the client's capacity to engage fully in the therapeutic process, and may result in 'rushing' the client towards a premature ending, thereby undermining hard-won therapeutic gains. The PCA holds that the decision to end therapy should be the client's in *conjunction* with the therapist. Externally imposed time restrictions can place counsellors under significant pressure to direct clients towards conclusions before they are ready, resulting in practice that may be unethical. The PCA therefore finds itself increasingly at odds with the assimilated wisdom of other approaches and funders' preferences for time-limited work. Pragmatically, Mearns and Thorne (2013) suggest that counselling agencies might seek to negotiate an average of, say, six sessions per client; doing so, they argue, allows practitioners to manage caseloads more effectively whilst maintaining the integrity of the approach. In practice, 'surplus' sessions from one client can then be allocated to others.

## Case Study: Sarah

Sixteen-year-old 'Sarah' was referred to me for counselling by 'Des', her Connexions Adviser. She had found school educationally disengaging and socially difficult. Sarah was also coming to terms with the recent break-up of her parents' relationship. Living with her dad, she had hardly left the house since leaving school 3 months previously. Sarah didn't want to engage with friends, and despite her love of drama felt unable be part of any group activity.

I saw Sarah for six sessions. During the first two, she was unable to look at me and spoke very little. I was aware, however, of a very damaging self-concept. As the sessions progressed, I began to question what help I (as a trainee counsellor) could be to a client who would barely speak and offered very little eye contact. I wondered whether I should integrate other approaches into my work with this client. In truth, I found the experience of working with Sarah quite disarming. In exploring this with my supervisor, I became aware of *my need* to rescue my client, of *my need* for my client to 'improve' in order to validate *me*. I was encouraged to trust the client's process, to be with her as she was, to listen empathically to her in her speaking and in her silence. I had come to realise that my expectations of Sarah's processes were counter-therapeutic, and were compounding the conditions of worth that she had experienced. To my amazement, Sarah continued to come willingly each week, slowly saying more about her experiencing and owning more of her own story. Sarah allowed me to listen beyond words, to experience empathy in the silence.

Weeks later Des called me to say that Sarah was a 'different person'. She was volunteering at a local youth project, involved in a drama group and enrolling on a training course. Des asked Sarah what had made the difference. 'Counselling', she replied. 'Graham just allowed me to be there.'

I learnt to trust the client's process!

## RESEARCH

The person-centred world appears engaged in some considerable debate concerning its involvement in particular forms of evidenced-based research, which some argue are counter-intuitive to its humanistic-phenomenological axiology. Others, meanwhile, contend that Rogers himself was an empiricist who engaged in rigorous forms of research that were concerned with both process and outcomes in therapy. Whilst there have been recent moves to produce efficacy studies via randomised controlled trials and meta-analyses on wider population studies, little has yet been specifically developed regarding the efficacy of the PCA with children and young people. This picture, however, is slowly changing, thanks to the path-breaking work of Professor Mick Cooper and colleagues, who are generating interesting evidence bases regarding the efficacy of humanistically based therapies in secondary schools (see Cooper et al., 2013; McArthur et al., 2013).

## Key Learning

- The PCA approach is rooted in the work of Carl Rogers and the central argument is that the quality of the relationship between client and therapist is central to the facilitation of growth and change.
- Rogers' vision of the person is optimistic and has a positive and hopeful view of human potential.
- In order to move towards higher actualisation, the self needs two principle needs to be met. These are positive regard from self (internal regard) and from others (external regard).
- We need to trust our own intrinsic organismic processes in order to meet a diversity of needs that will nourish the potential of the actualising tendency.
- We may become victims of 'conditions of worth' imposed by others, which results in an external locus of evaluation.

*(Continued)*

(Continued)

- The actualising tendency always retains the potential for hope and healing.
- Rogers identified six 'necessary and sufficient' conditions for therapeutic change. Three of these conditions, located in the therapist, are known as the 'core conditions'.
- Person-centred therapists need to find a congruent 'way of being' that allows them to capture the client's moment-by-moment lived experience in a congruent and unconditionally accepting way, and share this understanding and acceptance with the client.
- Person-centred therapists need to trust the client's process.
- When working with children and young people therapists must appreciate the particular needs of these age groups, to become attuned to the appropriateness of language and expression and be trustworthy so the child or young person feels safe.

## Summary

This chapter has:

- outlined the central ideas of the person-centred approach;
- considered the Rogerian postulation that particular qualities expressed within the counselling relationship are the singular requirement for therapeutic change and growth;
- explored the challenge of these relational qualities as a 'way of being' for the counsellor in accompanying the client in their journey of being and becoming;
- offered application of these principles to therapeutic practice with children and young people with particular reference to Axline's ideas on creativity and play as symbolisation of the child's inner world.

## Discussion Questions

1. Rogers contended that the six conditions that he outlined in his 1957 paper were 'necessary and sufficient' for therapeutic change. What is your view of his assertion?
2. How effective are you in offering the core conditions to clients? What might your clients say? What might be different?
3. The PCA is concerned with therapist's embodiment of a way of being. What are the particular challenges of this idea within your own personal development and professional practice?
4. Rogers (1961) proposed his seven stages of process. Map the process of a client you have been working with. What might be learnt here?

There are no specific answers to the questions – you are asked to reflect and use your own experiences.

## Develop Your Skills

Theory suggests that psychological distress occurs when we adapt our being and behaviour to meet others' demands, values and expectations. This generates disconnects between our organismic or core self and our self-concept. This, as I have argued, is particularly pertinent in work with children and young people.

Answer the following for yourself, then discuss appropriately with others (a peer, personal therapist or supervisor perhaps).

1. What conditions of worth or introjected values can you identify as having influenced your own way of being?
2. Thematically, what conditions of worth might you identify as salient for clients with whom you have worked? Where do these originate?

The PCA is a 'way of being' with self and others.

Explore with another:

3. How this challenges you, personally and professionally.
4. How accessible is your own inner child/adolescent?

## Further Reading

Cooper, M., O'Hara, M., Schmid, P.F and Bohart, A.C. (eds) (2013) *The Handbook of Person-Centred Psychotherapy and Counselling*. Basingstoke: Palgrave Macmillan.

This excellent compendium on the PCA examines theoretical concepts, underpinning values and contemporary debates and practices.

Mearns, D. and Thorne, B. with McLeod, J. (2013) *Person-Centred Counselling in Action*, 4th edn. London: SAGE.

This classic text, now in its fourth edition, from these doyens of the approach is known as 'the Bible'.

Merry, T. (2008) *Learning and Being in Person-Centred Counselling*, 2nd edn. Ross-on-Wye: PCCS Books.

A warm, accessible introduction to the PCA.

*(Continued)*

(Continued)

Prever, M. (2010) *Counselling and Supporting Children and Young People: A Person-Centred Approach*. London: SAGE.

Mark Prever's book is a much-needed addition to the literature. It examines the PCA with clarity and offers excellent application to practising counsellors and other professionals working with children and young people.

Smyth, D. (2013) *Person-Centred Therapy with Children and Young People*. London: SAGE.

David Smyth's book is written with rigour and warmth. This is a text that draws wisdom from the wells of practice.

### Online Resources

BACP website: www.bacp.co.uk, especially the BACP Children and Young People Division and the Competences for Working with Children and Young People

Counselling MindEd: https://www.minded.org.uk, especially Modules CM 07: Relational Skills, and CM 08: Therapeutic Skills

# REFERENCES

Axline, V.M. (1989) *Play Therapy*. Edinburgh: Longman.

Barrett-Lennard, G.T. (2013) Origins and evolution of the person-centred innovation in Carl Rogers' lifetime. In: Cooper, M., O'Hara, M., Schmid, P.F. and Bohart, A.C. (eds) *The Handbook of Person-Centred Psychotherapy and Counselling*. Basingstoke: Palgrave Macmillan, pp. 32–45.

Behr, M., Nuding, D. and McGinnis, S. (2013) Person-centred psychotherapy and counselling with children and young people. In: Cooper, M., O'Hara, M., Schmid, P.F. and Bohart, A.C. (eds) *The Handbook of Person-Centred Psychotherapy and Counselling*. Basingstoke: Palgrave Macmillan, pp. 266–281

Bozarth, J.D. (2013) Unconditional positive regard. In: Cooper, M., O'Hara, M., Schmid, P.F. and Bohart, A.C. (eds) *The Handbook of Person-Centred Psychotherapy and Counselling*. Basingstoke: Palgrave Macmillan, pp. 180–192.

Bright, G. (2013) *Risk, School Counselling and the Development of Resilience: Re-imagining the Empirical*. Twelfth Annual European Affective Education Network Conference, York, York St John University, 3 July 2013.

Bright, G. and Harrison. G. (2013) Switching on your curiosity: developing research ideas. In: Bright, G. and Harrison, G. (eds) *Understanding Research in Counselling*. London: Learning Matters, pp. 41–54.

Casemore, R. (2006) *Person-Centred Counselling in a Nutshell*. London: SAGE.

Coleman, J.C. (2010) *The Nature of Adolescence*, 4th edn. London: Routledge.

Cooper, M., Pybis, J., Hill, A., Jones, S. and Cromarty, K. (2013) Therapeutic outcomes in the Welsh Government's school-based counselling strategy: an evaluation. *Counselling and Psychotherapy Research 13*(2): 86–97.

Corsaro, W.A. (2015) *The Sociology of Childhood*, 4th edn. London: SAGE.

Döring, E. (2008) What happens in child-centred play therapy. In: Behr, M. and Cornelius-Whilte, J.H.D. (eds) *Facilitating Young People's Development: International Perspectives on Person-Centred Theory and Practice*. Ross-on-Wye: PCCS Books, pp. 40–51.

Freire, E.S. (2013) Empathy. In: Cooper, M., O'Hara, M., Schmid, P.F. and Bohart, A.C. (eds) *The Handbook of Person-Centred Psychotherapy and Counselling*. Basingstoke: Palgrave Macmillan. pp. 165–179.

Geldard, K, Geldard, D. and Yin Foo, R. (2016) *Counselling Adolescents: The Proactive Approach for Young People*, 4th edn. London: SAGE.

Gillon, E. (2007) *Person-Centred Counselling Psychology: An Introduction*. London: SAGE.

Hawkins, S. (2008) Working at relational depth with adolescents in school: a person-centred psychologist's perspective. In: Keys, S. and Walshaw, T. (eds) *Person-Centred Work with Children and Young People: UK Practitioner Perspectives*. Ross-on-Wye: PCCS Books, pp. 47–57.

Kirschenbaum, H. and Henderson, V.L. (eds) (1989) *The Carl Rogers Reader*. New York: Houghton Mifflin.

Mearns, D. and Thorne, B. with McLeod, J. (2013) *Person-Centred Counselling in Action*, 4th edn. London: SAGE.

McArthur, K., Cooper, M. and Berdondini, L. (2013) School-based humanistic counselling for psychological distress in young people: pilot randomized controlled trial. *Psychotherapy Research 23*(3): 355–365.

Merry, T. (2008) *Learning and Being in Person-Centred Counselling*, 2nd edn. Ross-on-Wye: PCCS Books.

Prever, M. (2010) *Counselling and Supporting Children and Young People: A Person-Centred Approach*. London: SAGE.

Reid, H. and Westergaard, J. (2011) *Effective Counselling with Young People*. London: Learning Matters.

Rogers, C.R. (1939) *The Clinical Treatment of the Problem Child*. Boston, MA: Houghton Mifflin.

Rogers, C.R. (1957) The necessary and sufficient conditions of therapeutic personality change. *Journal of Consulting Psychology 21*: 95–103.

Rogers, C.R. (1959) A theory of therapy, personality and interpersonal relationships as developed in the client-centered framework. In: Koch, S. (ed.) *Psychology: A Study of a Science*. Vol. 3: *Formulations of the Person and the Social Context*. New York: McGraw-Hill.

Rogers, C.R. (1961). *On Becoming a Person: A Therapist's View of Psychotherapy*. London: Constable.

Rogers, C.R. (1980) *A Way of Being*. Boston, MA: Houghton Mifflin.
Rogers, C.R. (1986) Rogers, Kohut and Erickson. *Person-Centred Review 1*: 125–140.
Smyth, D. (2013) *Person-Centred Therapy with Children and Young People*. London: SAGE

# 3

# PSYCHODYNAMIC APPROACHES TO COUNSELLING CHILDREN AND YOUNG PEOPLE

## SUE KEGERREIS AND NICK MIDGLEY

**This chapter will discuss:**

- A brief history of psychodynamic theory and practice
- Core beliefs that underpin the psychodynamic approach
- Key elements in psychodynamic practice

  - Observation
  - Putting feelings into words
  - Using play
  - Understanding and working with transference
  - Understanding and working with counter-transference
  - The importance of self-awareness and reflection

- Using psychodynamic approaches with children of all ages and abilities
- Working with diversity
- Short-term work
- Inter-agency working
- Findings from research

## INTRODUCTION

We will start with a description of a case:

Paolo[1] (8) was referred to the school counsellor because he was increasingly having trouble in class. He hit other children, was constantly distracted and lacked the concentration to learn effectively. He was not unintelligent but was underachieving. Psychological testing revealed a mild but significant degree of attention deficit disorder but no hyperactivity. Paolo's parents were caring and concerned. They saw the problem mainly in terms of him not applying himself, although they were aware also of him preferring to be in a world of his own. He resisted attempts to be taken out on family outings and he always wanted to play games on his phone or computer. He had always seemed different but they had not seen him as having problems until the demands of school began to bite.

In the assessment meetings, the counsellor watched whilst Paolo played rather formless games with the cars and other toys. Some had a narrative of sorts, with themes of one animal gobbling up another or shifting alliances of animals attacking each other, but the relationships portrayed were perfunctory or unclear, and the play meandered without much focus. The counsellor felt increasingly at sea, beginning to think that she had lost her expertise in understanding children or maybe never had any. Although she was an experienced counsellor who had worked with many hard-to-reach children, she felt unable to make a link with Paolo, who related to her in an affable but impersonal way.

What does a vignette like this tell us about psychodynamic counselling or therapy? And why would it help the counsellor – and more importantly, Paolo – if she is able to think psychodynamically about these encounters? In this chapter we will set out some of the key ideas behind psychodynamic counselling and psychotherapy,[2] and show how this way of thinking and working can be of value.

## BACKGROUND AND HISTORY OF PSYCHODYNAMIC WORK

Psychodynamic psychotherapy with children and young people has its origins in the work of Sigmund Freud, who first suggested that our behaviour is governed by unconscious processes, and that the core of our personality itself can often be traced back to key aspects of early

---

[1]For reasons of confidentiality all cases are fictionalised and disguised amalgamations of several actual cases.

[2]In this chapter 'counselling' and 'therapy' will be used interchangeably, although the authors are aware that these terms have different histories and are often linked to different trainings and professional groups.

childhood experience. He also argued that mental and emotional difficulties can be addressed through a therapeutic relationship that assumes that behaviour has meaning, and that exploring and coming to some understanding of one's 'internal world' is a key element of emotional well-being.

Following Freud, Hermine Hug-Hellmuth (1921), Melanie Klein (1932) and Anna Freud (1927) developed specific techniques of 'child analysis' and demonstrated the possibilities of direct work with children. Although there were strong disagreements between these early analysts, they were all agreed that children's emotional and behavioural difficulties could be understood by paying attention to the 'internal world' of the child, and that establishing therapeutic settings in which this internal world could be explored safely was key to therapeutic change. They also all agreed that play is central to the way in which children communicated about their internal worlds.

Later, Winnicott (1965) drew on his experience as a paediatrician to recognise the role of the parent–child relationship in supporting healthy emotional development, and Anna Freud highlighted how children's difficulties were sometimes based on 'deficits' in their early experience, whether due to trauma and neglect or to genetic or biological causes – or a combination. Bion (1962) introduced the important concept of 'containment', emphasising that a child's development depends on the capacity of the adults to receive and metabolise the child's powerful emotional experiences, and return them to the child in a way that could be properly processed.

Contemporary psychodynamic therapists have built on these ideas but also recognise the need to integrate findings from other disciplines. Developmental psychology, attachment theory and neuroscience all enrich both clinical and research work (e.g. Green, 2003; Alvarez, 2012; Horne and Lanyado, 2012). Systemic thinking is also incorporated, in particular the understanding that a child's problems cannot be understood outside the systems in which they are living, and that working with that system is of equal importance to working with the child's internal world.

## CORE BELIEFS WHICH UNDERPIN THE PSYCHODYNAMIC APPROACH

As indicated above, the central idea is that a child's difficulties in behaviour, emotions and responses make some kind of emotional sense. Their roots lie in the internal world of the child that has been built up from their earliest experiences and relationships. In the face of experiences that are hurtful, frightening or which engender intolerable internal conflict, a child will develop defences to make the emotional pain less overwhelming, and to keep out of awareness whatever is more than can be coped with. This clearly relates to how difficult their beginnings have been but not in a simple sense. Some children are more resilient than others and make surprisingly good progress in relatively impoverished or damaging circumstances, whilst others are more sensitive and vulnerable.

When a psychodynamic practitioner is working individually with a child, the focus will be on what is going on inside the child. What will be explored is the 'cast of characters' that has been internalised, the 'ways of being with others' (Stern, 1985), which powerfully influence how they behave and respond. The real relationships and circumstances in children's lives are of course crucial influences on how they feel about themselves and others, and family or parental work is often indicated to help address ongoing difficulties in home relationships, but in the room the emphasis will be on the child's internal world and the emotional world they bring into being with the counsellor.

It is central to psychodynamic thinking that change is painful and difficult, that defences have developed for a reason and that part of a counsellor's role is to create a space sufficiently safe for tentative moves towards more benign relationships to be encouraged. What holds a child in particular patterns of relating is in part the risk of greater vulnerability they would need to manage, and the pain they would need to face, if they were to lower their defences and experience the world more as it actually is, rather than through the lenses established from earlier experiences. The counsellor's work is to help clarify the unconscious mechanisms that get in the way of the child establishing a better relationship with themselves and with potentially helpful others, to help them make more sense of their own feelings and reactions and thus to enable the child to resume their developmental journey.

## KEY ELEMENTS IN PSYCHODYNAMIC PRACTICE

From this underlying set of ideas follows the key elements of psychodynamic practice. First the practitioner has to be able to observe extremely carefully how the child acts, reacts, responds and relates, both in the way the child speaks, plays and behaves, but also, crucially, in the way they are apparently experiencing the therapist. This emotionally sensitive and informed observation will reveal information about the internal world of the child. The therapist will be alert to clues as to what anxieties the child is most affected by, what defences they are using to keep vulnerability at manageable levels, what sorts of experiences appear to have been indigestible and what internal conflicts are causing the child's development to have stalled or become disrupted.

The emphasis on observation should not be understood to mean that the counsellor just sits back and watches. The counsellor will offer a thoughtful, attentive presence, perhaps putting into words what the child is doing, or commenting on what their play is conveying. However, it does mean that the counsellor will most likely let the child lead the session, and will usually avoid setting agendas or dictating activities. She might join in play with the child, but would take care to remain reflective and alert to the emotional dynamics, seeking guidance from the child as to what part she is supposed to play, and all the time keeping one foot outside the game, reflecting and maybe commenting on what is being brought into focus through the play. As the main aim is to find out what is going on in the child's mind and emotional life, it is essential that the child's own preoccupations are allowed to emerge rather than the practitioner impose a shape on the sessions.

Alongside the observation, therefore, the counsellor looks for ways of putting into words the child's experience. Giving children an emotional vocabulary is often of vital therapeutic value, partly because this offers acceptance and validation of often shaming or painful emotions the child may have, but also because the very act of naming a feeling makes it accessible to thinking, giving it a shape and substance that can render it less overwhelming and more available to be processed. Feeling understood is in itself a powerful therapeutic experience. So the counsellor observes, maybe making some comments about or putting into words what the child is revealing but may not be consciously able to think about.

This brings us to another central idea in psychodynamic thinking – the transference. The way the child responds to us in the counselling room is often a direct communication about how they have internalised their earlier experiences with others. We get information from them as the relationship develops as to how they see us, what issues they have with us – feeling badly treated, being wary, wanting to be the sole focus of our attention, being afraid of disapproval, expecting us to be punitive, idealising us, seeing us as useless and so on – which are good indications of the perceptions they are prone to have of others in their lives and clues as to how they have experienced aspects of their first and most important relationships.

Alongside this the counsellor will be paying attention to her own emotional state, reactions and responses, using these to provide another level of information about the child – what is called the counter-transference. The child may be relating to the counsellor in such a way that she is made to feel something the child themselves (consciously or unconsciously) struggles with, such as fear, despair, frustration, vulnerability, feeling stupid or misunderstood. The therapist in this situation is being asked to register and bear feelings which the child themselves may not be able to manage. Or, in a variation on this theme, the therapist may find herself responding as if she is a figure from the child's inner world, perhaps feeling rejecting, detached, mindless, punitive or placatory. This carries vital information about the child's inner cast of characters but also helps us understand how a child might engender unhelpful responses in those they meet.

So the psychodynamic therapist is constantly using this binocular vision, monitoring both the child's way of relating and her own emotional state. First she has to manage the impact of these, then she has to work out whether, when and how to put some of this into words for the child. If she manages to remain curious and thoughtful whilst registering and digesting the impact of the child – without getting caught up in the urge to respond in kind or retaliate – she is offering them 'containment' (Bion, 1962). This can be therapeutic in itself and is of great value in both clinical and non-clinical settings.

Out of these considerations it becomes clear that there are some personal attributes that are essential for someone working psychodynamically. The therapist needs to have a high level of self-awareness and self-knowledge, as she is using herself as the central tool of the therapy. She needs to be curious about her own feelings, so she can use her responses as a sensitive barometer for the dynamics in the room, without resorting to reaction or blocking off the impact of the child on her. She needs to be endlessly interested as to what might lie behind a child behaving or relating as they do, and above all be prepared to manage receiving the child's negative as well as positive feelings.

## USING PSYCHODYNAMIC APPROACHES ACROSS THE AGE AND ABILITY RANGE

One of the beauties of the psychodynamic approach is that it can be adapted to work with a wide range of children, both in age and in intellectual capacity. As well as in consulting rooms, psychodynamic work can take place in classrooms, children's homes or in hospitals, with individuals or with groups (see Lanyado and Horne, 2009; Kegerreis, 2010; Schmidt Neven, 2010). Since the focus is on emotional communication and interpersonal dynamics and with so much of the work being done through art, play and the therapist's processing of the relationship dynamics, children with limited verbal ability can be helped as well as those who want to talk and/or who can understand at a sophisticated level.

With younger children, art and play will most likely be the way the child communicates, with much of the processing done within the practitioner's mind, and any verbal interpretation will be geared sensitively to the child's level of linguistic ability and understanding. With older children and adolescents, more will be done in words, and interpretations may be more elaborate, making more explicit the patterns observed and their links with those from the family or from the past.

Whatever the age of the client, however, what brings about change is often less the explicit working out of a narrative link between past and present but more the way in which, during the therapy, the old and now out-of-date relationships are re-created but this time worked through differently, with the therapist reflecting on, having insight into and curiosity about their meaning, rather than just responding or retaliating. In Anna Freud's words, the therapist is both a 'transference object', and a 'new object', offering the child a different kind of experience, and thereby promoting the child's own capacity to accept and welcome new experiences.

## THE PSYCHODYNAMIC APPROACH AND DIVERSITY

Whilst the psychodynamic approach emphasises the role of the internal world, it also offers a powerful set of tools for exploring the way in which external social and cultural differences impact upon the child. By focusing closely on the way in which the world is subjectively experienced, the psychodynamic approach encourages genuine curiosity about how culture both shapes and is shaped for each individual, and how the wider social landscape is experienced.

In the past, psychodynamic practitioners were liable to overstress the individual and the internal, but more recently there has been much greater appreciation of both the obvious and more subtle ways in which such forces as racism and the social unconscious influence our relationships both with ourselves and with others.

It has already been emphasised that it is powerful for young people to have a counsellor who can clear-sightedly process the anxieties and negative feelings they may be experiencing within the therapy, and this would include their experience and understanding of any perceived differences. The counsellor needs to be alert to the child's experience and perception of her and the therapeutic setting, with openness to how much the differences between them will be shaping how she and the work might appear. The counsellor can explore how pre-judgements and expectations of pre-judgement in others affect the child, appreciating the anger and hurt they can cause but also looking into how this child particularly resonates with and responds to such pressures and their possible internalisation of or reactions to racism and cultural expectations. She needs to be attentive to her own cultural assumptions and attuned to how different from the child's her own background may be and how this has shaped her attitudes. The emphasis on the *sense* the child is making of their individual and social world means that psychodynamic work can be used to explore whatever conflicts and vulnerabilities are getting in the child's way, as well as assisting the child in processing the meaning of their own cultural journey.

Psychodynamic thinking is also immensely useful in the exploration of children's experiences of their own sexual and gender identities. It is steeped in the understanding of the complexities of individual sexual development and behaviour, and provides the counsellor with a flexible approach, whether in exploring identifications and defences against intimacy and vulnerability or in helping the child establish more clearly their own sense of who they are.

## USING THE PSYCHODYNAMIC APPROACH IN SHORT-TERM WORK

If one thinks of the essence of psychodynamic therapy being the reconfiguring of a child's inner world, removing unhelpful defences and developing more benign inner relationships, then it is true that this work can take a long time, as it involves major restructuring of the child's way of relating to the world, in the context of a safe-enough space.

However, therapists are increasingly developing more short-term approaches to psychodynamic therapy (e.g. Cregeen et al., 2017). Particularly with older children and adolescents, it is possible to help a client swiftly by helping them see what internal conflicts lie hidden in their presenting problems. For example, Sam, 15, was consciously desperate to do well in his GCSEs, particularly to impress his father who had left 2 years earlier – and to be in a position to follow in his footsteps. But he found himself endlessly procrastinating and avoiding his revision. In counselling it was quickly possible for his deep hurt and anger with his father to come to the surface, giving him insight into the unconscious sabotage that was going on. Once this was conscious he found it much easier to make himself work, on his own behalf rather than in an attempt to resolve his emotional difficulties with his father. Longer-term work might have led to deeper levels of meaning and other kinds of changes, but short-term work enabled Sam to deal with the specific problem he was facing – his problems preparing for his exams – and also awakened in him a curiosity about the links between his behaviour and his deeper thoughts and feelings about the people around him.

Uncovering patterns, making links that are as yet unacknowledged and recognising ambivalent feelings are ways in which brief psychodynamic work can be effective. Sometimes it is enough for a child or adolescent just to have their feelings recognised, named and validated as, for whatever reason, how they are experiencing things is difficult for their carers to acknowledge. This can be immensely healing in its own right.

## INTER-AGENCY WORKING

Psychodynamic thinking has been used to great effect in the understanding of organisational and network dynamics. The understanding of how projective processes and other defensive responses to anxiety can engender and exacerbate interpersonal difficulties has been applied to how colleagues and agencies relate to one another, with particular alertness to how unhelpful dynamics and enactments can occur (Obholzer and Roberts 1992). A psychodynamic practitioner can be very well placed to understand why and how well-meaning professionals might not find it easy to work well together.

For example, the care staff at Bella's (aged 5) residential home felt powerfully dismissed and undervalued by her social worker and also wary of potential adoptive parents. They were taking the brunt of aggressive but desperately needy behaviour from Bella, and felt unsupported by their own managers. Instead of all elements of the network working together on the child's behalf there was great tension between them. In many ways the staff members were re-enacting dynamics that had their origin in Bella's own fraught family background. She was expressing the damage that had been done by abusive and neglectful parents but this fed into the sense of neglect and abuse felt by the staff. The difficulty in processing her pain and the complexity of her needs led each professional to take up a place in a reworking of abuser/rescuer/helpless victim dynamic (Kegerreis, 1987), which made it difficult to collaborate effectively. The psychodynamic counsellor working with Bella gained sufficient insight into her experiences and functioning to be able to disentangle this and help each person in the network to understand more fully what was unconsciously affecting their capacity to cooperate, leading to much more effective teamwork and the eventual successful transition from the home.

Psychodynamic practitioners have long functioned well within multidisciplinary Child and Adolescent Mental Health Services (CAMHS) teams, and collaboration with other professionals is integral to their thinking. The focus on the internal world of the child is most effective if the parents are also getting support from another professional in helping the child to change and in addressing their part in the relationship.

---

## Returning to Paolo

After the discomfort of her initial feelings of being de-skilled when meeting Paolo, his counsellor was able to draw on her psychodynamic thinking, and to process her counter-transference in a number of ways. First, she realised that her lack of connection with Paolo was not just her own failure, but was similar to how the staff at school and, to some extent, his parents felt. Second, she realised that her experience of nothing making much sense and the links between things being obscure and arbitrary was an indication of how this child experienced his world.

When with Paolo she put these experiences and thoughts into words. He let her know how much difficulty he had in getting properly in touch with, let alone making sense of, his feelings. His recourse to repetitive games was in part a retreat from what baffled and perplexed him in the real world of other people. He sought distraction and excitement in a fantasy world that offered escape from his sense of disconnection and disarray. Given his difficulty in staying in touch with reality it was not surprising that applying himself to learning was a challenge.

One important strand in the work with Paolo consisted of helping him grasp and identify his own feelings. Another consisted of the counsellor first registering, then processing and bearing, then being able to feed back to him the experience – clearly one he had himself struggled with – of not being emotionally connected to. His parents were kind, but for a range of reasons had not been consistently able to reach out and try to understand this little boy. Paolo responded strongly to the therapist's interest in his emotional life and week by week built better links both inside himself and between him and others. His play became more coherent, with clear narratives and consistent relationships. He calmed down, as he no longer needed to distract himself so much from his own confusion. As he became more at ease inside his own mind, he began to be able to learn. He was also increasingly able to mentalise, that is, to be curious about his own mind and that of others, which meant that his capacity to relate to other children improved (Midgley and Vrouva, 2012). Regular meetings with his parents also helped them to see the importance of looking beyond Paolo's behaviour, and seeing him as a child with his own mind and his own feelings. The counsellor helped the parents recognise their own resistances to doing this, which led to them acknowledging their own need to address issues in the marital relationship, and they chose to attend couples counselling.

## RESEARCH INCLUDING EVIDENCE-BASED PRACTICE AND PRACTICE-BASED EVIDENCE

Paolo was helped in his counselling, but one successful case is not an evidence base. For many years psychoanalytic and psychodynamic therapies have been considered to lack credible evidence of effectiveness. However, this situation has begun to change over recent years, particularly in relation to adult work. Shedler's landmark paper on 'The efficacy of psychodynamic therapy' (2010) showed that these therapies are at least as effective as other forms of treatment long-regarded as 'evidence-based', and that patients who receive such treatment not only appear to maintain their therapeutic gains after treatment ends, but in many instances continue to improve after treatment ends.

Regarding child work, there has been a rich clinical literature, and a strong tradition of qualitative, practice-based research (see Midgley et al., 2009), but the evidence base is still a work in progress. A number of systematic reviews have now been published (e.g. Palmer et al., 2013), as well as a meta-analysis of short-term psychodynamic therapies for young people (Abbass et al., 2012). A recent systematic review (Midgley et al., 2017) gives as complete a picture as possible of the existing evidence base for individual psychodynamic psychotherapy for children aged between 3 and 18.

Key conclusions from this review included the following:

- Although few in number, studies indicate that psychodynamic treatment can be effective for a range of childhood disorders.
- Psychodynamic treatment of children and adolescents appears to be equally effective overall to comparison treatments, with some studies suggesting it is more, some less and some equally effective.
- It may have a different pattern of effect to other treatments, for example it might not be as swift but it might be more sustained, with a possible 'sleeper effect' of improvement continuing after therapy ends.
- Younger children appear to benefit more than older ones, but studies suggest that older children and adolescents can also benefit from psychodynamic therapy.
- Children with emotional or internalising disorders respond better than those with disruptive/externalising disorders, with an especially strong evidence base emerging for the treatment of children and young people with depression.

The largest ever study to take place, the IMPACT study (Goodyer et al., 2017), compared a short-term psychodynamic psychotherapy (STPP) to cognitive-behavioural therapy and to a brief psychosocial intervention, in the treatment of adolescents with moderate to severe depression. Young people in all three arms of the study showed significantly reduced symptoms, and these were sustained 1 year after the end of treatment. Indeed, 85% of adolescents receiving STPP no longer met diagnostic criteria for depression 1 year after the end of treatment. Importantly, all three treatments were equally cost-effective.

## Summary

The psychodynamic approach has three main distinctive features:

1. Emphasis on the power of unconscious dynamics at work in all of us.
2. The central importance of early experiences in shaping how we perceive, experience, behave and relate.
3. The use of the therapy relationship itself in bringing about change.

The therapist uses her observational skills to gain insight into the inner world of the child. The child may play, use art materials and/or talk, and from this and the evolving relationship with her, the therapist elucidates what conflicts, anxieties and defences are at work, and how these are interfering with the child making the most of their opportunities and relationships. She processes this and feeds back to the child where appropriate, whilst appreciating that the receiving and understanding of the child's feelings and providing the child with opportunities for emotional expression and exploration may be powerfully therapeutic in themselves.

With roots in psychoanalysis, psychodynamic work with children has been modified and extended to meet the challenges of the 21st century. Responding to theoretical refinements, clinical experience, different client groups and new knowledge about child development, it now offers a flexible yet powerful tool to help a wide range of children. Psychodynamic therapies with children and young people are also being increasingly 'manualised' (e.g. Cregeen et al., 2017), in a way that makes it clearer for others to see what this form of therapy involves, and for the approach to be scientifically evaluated.

Furthermore, because it also offers so much understanding of the impact of troubled children and families on those who work with them, and the complexity of professional interactions around challenging cases, it can be used effectively in non-clinical as well as clinical settings and to help staff as well as children and families (Kegerreis, 2011; Nicholson et al., 2011).

## Discussion Questions

1. How does the psychodynamic approach enable children to change, and to gain greater control over their behaviour?
2. Does psychodynamic thinking suggest that children with abusive pasts are bound to get into abusive relationships later in life?
3. What are the distinctive ways in which a psychodynamic practitioner would behave with and talk to a child?
4. Why would a psychodynamic practitioner pay a lot of attention to how they were feeling in their interactions with clients?
5. What toys or play materials would you provide for a child of 7? 11?

## Develop Your Skills

1. Observation:

   o  Watch someone you are not interacting with for 10 minutes and later write down in as much detail as you can exactly what you saw, heard and experienced.
   o  Discuss with a partner what you can infer from what you observed about the person.

2. Listening:

   o  With a partner, take it in turns to tell a story from your own life. The listener can practise different elements of good listening in each workshop opportunity.
   o  Listen with a view to being able to *remember the facts* and then retell to see if this was accurate, with attention paid to what might have been misremembered as well as remembered.
   o  Listen with attention *only* to the feelings being expressed – discuss.
   o  Listen with attention *only* to the listener's own sensations and responses – discuss.

3. Explore transference:

   o  Write down your feelings about three figures who have had authority over you.
   o  Are there any similarities? Key differences?

What earlier relationships might be affecting your experiences of these people?

## Further Reading

Blake, P. (2011) *Child and Adolescent Psychotherapy*. London: Karnac.

French, L. and Klein, R. (2012) *Therapeutic Practice in Schools*. London: Routledge.

Kegerreis, S. (2010) *Psychodynamic Counselling with Children and Young People: An Introduction*. London: Palgrave.

Lanyado, M. and Horne, A. (eds) (2009) *The Handbook of Child and Adolescent Psychotherapy. Psychoanalytic Approaches*, 2nd edn. London: Routledge.

### Online Resources

Self-awareness in the Therapeutic Relationship https://www.minded.org.uk/Component/Details/447322

Communicating Empathy https://www.minded.org.uk/Component/Details/447316

The Evidence for Counselling Children and Young People https://www.minded.org.uk/Component/Details/447223

## REFERENCES

Abbass, A., Town, J. and Driessen, E. (2012) Intensive short-term dynamic psychotherapy: A systematic review and meta-analysis of outcome research. *Harvard Review of Psychiatry* 20(2): 97–108.

Alvarez, A. (2012) *The Thinking Heart: Three Levels of Psychoanalytic Work in Psychotherapy with Children and Adolescents.* London: Routledge.

Bion, W. (1962) A theory of thinking. *International Journal of Psychoanalysis* 43: 328–332.

Cregeen, S., Hughes, C., Midgley, N., Rhode, M., Rustin, M. (ed. Catty, J.). (2017) *Short-Term Psychoanalytic Psychotherapy for Adolescents with Depression: A Treatment Manual.* London: Karnac.

Freud, A. (1927) Four lectures on child analysis (originally titled 'Introduction to the technique of child analysis'). In: *The Writings of Anna Freud*, Vol. 1. New York: International Universities Press, pp. 3–50.

Goodyer, I., Reynolds, S., Barrett, B., Byford, S., Dubicka, B., Hill, J., Holland, F., Kelvin, R., Midgley, N., Roberts, C., Senior, R., Target, M., Widmer, B., Wilkinson, P. and Fonagy, P., (2017) Cognitive behavioural therapy and short-term psychoanalytical psychotherapy versus a brief psychosocial intervention in adolescents with unipolar major depressive disorder (IMPACT): A multicentre, pragmatic, observer-blind, randomised controlled superiority trial. *The Lancet Psychiatry* 4(2): 109–119.

Green, V. (ed.) (2003) *Emotional Development in Psychoanalysis, Attachment Theory and Neuroscience.* London: Routledge.

Horne, A. and Lanyado, M. (eds) (2012) *Winnicott's Children: Independent Psychoanalytic Approaches with Children and Adolescents.* Hove: Routledge.

Hug-Hellmuth, H. (1921) On the technique of child-analysis. *International Journal of Psycho-Analysis* 2: 287–305.

Kegerreis, S. (1987) Saying no to psychotherapy – consultation and assessment in a case of child sexual abuse. *Journal of Child Psychotherapy* 13: 2.

Kegerreis, S. (2010) *Psychodynamic Counselling with Children and Young People: An Introduction.* London: Palgrave.

Kegerreis, S. (2011) Taking psychodynamic thinking 'home' to the workplace – how can courses manage better the impact on student and employing agency? *Psychodynamic Practice* 17(1): 23–39.

Klein, M. (1932) *The Psycho-Analysis of Children*. London: Hogarth Press.

Lanyado, M. and Horne, A. (eds) (2009) *The Handbook of Child and Adolescent Psychotherapy. Psychoanalytic Approaches*, 2nd edn. London: Routledge.

Midgley, N. and Vrouva, I. (eds) (2012) *Minding the Child: Mentalization-Based Interventions with Children, Young People and Their Families*. London: Routledge.

Midgley, N., Anderson, J., Grainger, E., Nesic-Vuckovic, T. and Urwin, C. (eds) (2009) *Child Psychotherapy and Research: New Approaches, Emerging Findings*. London: Routledge.

Midgley, N., O'Keeffe, S., French, L. and Kennedy, E., (2017) Psychodynamic psychotherapy for children and adolescents: an updated narrative review of the evidence base. *Journal of Child Psychotherapy 43* (3): 307–329, DOI: 10.1080/0075417X.2017.1323945

Nicholson, C., Irwin, M. and Dwivedi, K.N., (2011) *Children and Adolescents in Trauma: Creative Therapeutic Approaches*. London: Jessica Kingsley.

Obholzer, A. and Roberts, V.R., (1992) *The Unconscious at Work*. London: Routledge.

Palmer, R., Nascimento, L.N. and Fonagy, P., (2013) The state of the evidence base for psychodynamic psychotherapy for children and adolescents. *Child and Adolescent Psychiatric Clinics of North America 22*(2): 149–214.

Schmidt Neven, R. (2010) *Core Principles of Assessment and Therapeutic Communication with Children, Parents and Families: Towards the Promotion of Child and Family Wellbeing*. London: Routledge.

Shedler, J. (2010) The efficacy of psychodynamic psychotherapy. *American Psychologist 65*(2): 98–109.

Stern, D. (1985) *The Interpersonal World of the Infant*. New York: Basic Books.

Winnicott, D. (1965) *Maturational Processes and the Facilitating Environment*. London: Hogarth Press Ltd.

# 4

# COGNITIVE-BEHAVIOURAL THERAPY

## PAUL STALLARD

**This chapter will discuss:**

- **The development of cognitive-behavioural therapy (CBT) and the underlying theoretical model**
- **The therapeutic process of CBT and phases of treatment**
- **How CBT is adapted for use with children and young people**

## INTRODUCTION: HISTORICAL DEVELOPMENT

CBT was heavily influenced by the pioneering work of Albert Ellis (1994) and Aaron Beck (1963; 1964) and their models of rational emotional therapy and cognitive therapy. These models built upon the success of behaviour therapy by attending to the meanings and interpretations individuals make about events. Initially CBT was developed for adults and it was not until the 1990s that descriptions of the way CBT could be used with children began to emerge (Kendall, 1991). Many early studies applied CBT programmes developed for use with adults to older adolescents and how these were adapted for children received comparatively little attention. However the new millennium heralded the arrival of a number of publications that described how CBT can be adapted for use with children (see the Further Reading section).

The first randomised controlled trials evaluating the effectiveness of CBT with adolescents were published in 1990 with the following 20 years seeing an explosion of empirical studies that have established CBT as the most extensively researched of all the child psychotherapies (Graham, 2005). Early research compared CBT to waitlist control groups and found large treatment effects. The next wave of trials compared CBT with other active interventions and unsurprisingly treatment effect sizes were smaller but nonetheless positive. When CBT was compared with medication, CBT was not found to be superior, although the results confirmed that CBT offers an effective psychological intervention (Goodyer et al., 2007; Treatment for Adolescents with Depression Study (TADS) Team, 2009; Brent et al., 2008; Walkup et al., 2008). Similarly, CBT was not superior to a brief psychosocial intervention or a short-term psychoanalytical therapy group, with all interventions producing comparable effects (Goodyer et al., 2017). In terms of prevention, CBT programmes provided in schools for the treatment of anxiety or depression have demonstrated very positive results (Neil and Christensen, 2009; Calear and Christensen, 2010; Stockings et al., 2015; Werner-Seidler et al., 2017). This extensive research has resulted in CBT being recommended by expert groups such as the UK National Institute for Health and Clinical Excellence and the American Academy of Child and Adolescent Psychiatry for the treatment of children with emotional disorders including depression, obsessive compulsive disorder (OCD), post-traumatic stress disorder (PTSD) and anxiety. This growing evidence base has also prompted the development of national training programmes in CBT and the extension of the UK Improving Access to Psychological Therapies Programme to children and young people (Shafran et al., 2014).

## THEORETICAL MODEL

CBT is concerned with the relationships between cognitive, emotional and behavioural processes. Behavioural theory is based on the premise that maladaptive behaviours are learnt and draws upon the principles of classical and operant conditioning. Classical conditioning focuses upon the role of antecedent conditions in which neutral stimuli or situations (e.g. a shop) become associated with an involuntary response (e.g. anxiety). Interventions involve techniques such as learning relaxation skills to counter anxiety; the development of a hierarchy of situations that elicit anxiety; graded exposure and systematic desensitisation whereby anxiety is controlled whilst feared situations are faced and mastered.

Operant conditioning focuses upon the role of consequences in maintaining maladaptive behaviours. It assumes that behaviours that are rewarded (positively reinforced) or are followed by the removal of an aversive consequence (negative reinforcement) are more likely to be repeated. For example, a child who is anxious about leaving the house to go to school may be allowed to stay at home (i.e. staying at home is positively reinforced). If their anxiety is reduced by avoiding school, then school non-attendance is negatively reinforced (i.e. avoidance reduces anxiety). In both cases the consequences will result in the child being less likely to leave the house and go to school. Interventions involve contingency management whereby adaptive behaviours are reinforced.

Whilst behaviour therapy is effective, it fails to consider the personal meanings and interpretations that are made about the events that occur. Cognitive therapy emerged to address this issue and is based on the premise that mental health problems arise when dysfunctional and biased meanings and interpretations are made. The cognitive model proposed by Beck et al. (1979) suggests different levels of cognitions with the deepest being schemas, which are strong, global, fixed ways of thinking that underpin the meanings and interpretations that are made. Schemas can be functional and adaptive but some are overly rigid, negative and dysfunctional. They are assumed to develop during childhood as a result of significant and/or repeated experiences. Poor attachment, maltreatment or overly critical and demanding parents may, for example, lead a child to develop a cognitive schema that they are 'unlovable' or a 'failure'.

Schemas are activated by events reminiscent of those that produced the schema. Once activated attention, memory and interpretation processing biases filter and select information that supports the schema. Attention biases result in attention being focused upon information that confirms the schema whilst neutral or contradictory information is overlooked. Memory biases result in the recall of information that is consistent with the schema whilst interpretation biases serve to minimise any inconsistent information.

The most accessible cognitions are automatic thoughts or 'self-talk', which represent the involuntary stream of thoughts that run through the mind providing a continuous commentary about events. These are functionally related to schemas with dysfunctional schemas producing negative automatic thoughts. Negative automatic thoughts tend to be biased and self-critical and generate unpleasant emotional states, for example, anxiety, anger, unhappiness and maladaptive behaviours such as social withdrawal or avoidance. The unpleasant feelings and maladaptive behaviours associated with these dysfunctional cognitions and processing biases serve to reinforce and maintain them as the individual becomes trapped in a self-perpetuating negative cycle as highlighted in Fig. 4.1.

In addition to the different levels of cognitions, CBT is concerned with the specific content of dominant cognitions, which varies according to the particular psychological problem. Depression, for example, tends to be related to cognitions concerning loss, deprivation and failure; anxiety to cognitions of personal threat, vulnerability and inability to cope; OCD to cognitions of personal responsibility for harm; PTSD to current threat and panic with catastrophic interpretations of physiological symptoms.

The aim of CBT is to identify, test and reappraise dysfunctional and unhelpful cognitions. Testing involves challenging selective attention biases by attending to overlooked information; challenging memory biases by recalling contradictory experiences; and challenging interpretation biases by exploring alternative explanations. Two key methods of achieving this are Socratic dialogues and behavioural experiments.

Socratic dialogues help to discover new information that questions or contradicts the meanings or interpretations that are made. Attending to new or overlooked information challenges internal, stable and global beliefs (e.g. I am stupid; no-one likes me) and helps to develop functional cognitions by establishing limits (e.g. maths is hard but I am good at art; none of the people I know have the same interests as me).

Behavioural experiments provide an objective way of testing assumptions and beliefs. A belief 'no-one likes me' could be tested by recording how many times a young person receives a text, email, Facebook hit or phone call in a week. A prediction is made at the start of the experiment about what will happen (e.g. no-one will contact me), which is compared with the outcome. Through this process limits are placed around global schemas, which helps to promote more balanced and functional cognitions.

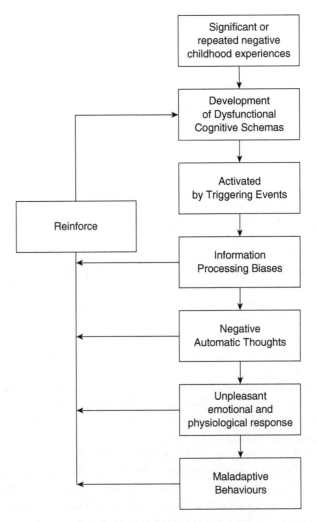

**Figure 4.1**  The development of dysfunctional cognitions and their impact on emotions and behaviour

## THERAPEUTIC PROCESS

CBT occurs within the context of a strong therapeutic relationship. The relationship needs to be open, honest and non-judgemental, and is conveyed through a genuine, warm and respectful rapport. The process is one of collaborative empiricism in which the therapist and child actively work together to test the child's beliefs and interpretations. Stallard (2005) has defined the key elements of this process with children using the acronym PRECISE.

- P: Highlights the need to develop a therapeutic partnership based upon collaborative empiricism and emphasises the central role of the child and their parents/carers in securing change.
- R: Draws the therapist's attention to developmental considerations and the need to ensure that the intervention is consistent with the child's cognitive, linguistic, memory and perspective-taking abilities.
- E: Highlights the need to develop and maintain an empathic relationship that conveys warmth, genuine concern and respect.
- C: Identifies the need to be appropriately creative in conveying the concepts of CBT in ways that match the child's developmental understanding and interests.
- I: Highlights investigation and the need to adopt a curious, open and inquisitive stance in which thoughts are subject to objective evaluation through Socratic dialogues and behavioural experiments.
- S: Encourages the development of self-efficacy and learning through reflection and assimilation of new information.
- E: Highlights the importance of engagement and enjoyment and the need to ensure that the child's interests and motivation can be maintained.

## PHASES OF CBT

CBT typically involves the four phases of psycho-education and relationship-building, skills development, consolidation and relapse prevention.

## Psycho-education and relationship-building

During this initial phase the primary focus is upon engagement, developing the therapeutic partnership, and socialising the child and their family into the cognitive model. Information is provided about the cognitive model (the link between events, thoughts, feelings and behaviours) and an overview of what therapy will involve. The idea of learning together (collaborative empiricism) and the active role of the child in testing ideas and undertaking experiments is emphasised. A shared understanding of the child's problem within a CBT framework (a cognitive formulation) is jointly developed and treatment goals are identified.

The therapist has a fairly active role during this stage as she provides information and develops the therapeutic alliance. This is a key task since typically children are referred because of concerns from others and may have no ownership of the referred problem or little motivation to change. Engaging and motivating the child is a prerequisite to the subsequent stages of CBT. The therapist therefore presents as open, understanding, positive and hopeful as she elicits commitment from the child to 'give it a try'.

## Skills development

The second phase focuses upon the development of skills to counter dysfunctional cognitions and processing, unpleasant emotional states and maladaptive behaviours. The particular skills and domains covered in the intervention will be informed by the formulation. In the cognitive domain cognitive enhancement will help the child assess the accuracy and usefulness of their cognitions and to develop more helpful balanced cognitions. Different types of cognitions (helpful and unhelpful thoughts), processing biases (thinking traps) and common dysfunctional cognitions will be identified through thought monitoring. Behavioural experiments and Socratic dialogues will be used to systematically test these unhelpful cognitions and processes to identify new or overlooked information. This process results in limits being placed around dysfunctional global beliefs and negative thoughts, and provides alternative interpretations that are more balanced and functional.

Emotional skills may be enhanced to promote better understanding, awareness and management of unpleasant emotions. Emotional monitoring can help to identify links between emotions, events and thoughts, and those situations that are associated with particularly strong, unpleasant or prolonged emotional states. Emotional management may be developed through relaxation training, positive imagery or activity rescheduling to reduce the intensity or frequency of unpleasant emotions.

In terms of behaviour, the intervention may involve developing more adaptive behaviours in which problem-solving, social and personal effectiveness skills such as assertion and negotiation are enhanced. This may involve techniques such as role-play, observational exercises, graded exposure, behavioural activation or response prevention. Finally, the child is encouraged to notice and reinforce positive attempts to change.

During the skills development phase the therapist adopts an open and curious approach to encourage the child to experiment and discover skills and strategies that are particularly helpful for them.

## Consolidation

The third stage is consolidation where the new skills are practised and integrated into the child's everyday repertoire. By this stage the child has a good understanding of the key elements of the cognitive model, their key cognitions and thinking traps. Regular practice through out-of-session assignments is a particularly important aspect of CBT at this stage. Through these assignments the child is encouraged to systematically face and cope with increasingly difficult situations and problems as they use their new skills to regain control of their life.

The therapist becomes more reflective as the child is increasingly encouraged to take a lead role in analysing difficult situations and finding solutions. The therapist reminds the child of the core elements of the CBT model and the skills they have acquired and encourages them to apply this framework and skills.

## Relapse prevention

The final stage is relapse prevention, where the child is encouraged to reflect on those aspects of the intervention that have been most helpful, prepare for possible relapse and to develop a contingency plan in case problems re-emerge. Their own specific thinking traps are highlighted, and the skills and techniques that have helped to challenge dysfunctional internal, stable and global cognitions identified. The child is prepared for relapse and a plan developed to deal with short-term problems and triggers for seeking further help identified. During the final phase the therapist is a facilitator who encourages the child to process their learning and apply it to future situations and events.

## ADAPTING CBT FOR CHILDREN AND ADOLESCENTS

CBT was originally developed for work with adults. It relies heavily on verbal and memory skills and involves advanced meta-cognitive skills that require individuals to be both aware of their cognitions and able to reflect upon them. Through this process the individual is helped to find overlooked information and new meanings, which leads to the development of alternative more functional cognitions.

Childhood and adolescence are characterised by significant and rapid development of cognitive, linguistic and memory skills. It is generally recognised that children from 7 years of age can engage in CBT, although the content and process will need to be adapted to reflect their developmental level. Younger children, for example, may have problems with some cognitive tasks such as identifying and appraising cognitions. This does not necessarily imply that they cannot engage in CBT, but indicates that some preparatory psycho-educational work may be required to help them identify and find ways to communicate their cognitions. This may involve use of worksheets, where the child is given a picture with a single thought bubble (e.g. footballer preparing to take a penalty) and asked to identify what the person may be thinking. Extra thought bubbles can be added to introduce the child to the notion of alternative thinking, that is, there may be different thoughts about the same situation (e.g. a picture of someone receiving a present with two or three thought bubbles).

Whilst younger children can typically generate some cognitions, they may not necessarily be able to understand general or overarching cognitive patterns, their cognitive processes or generalise dysfunctional patterns from one situation to another. The therapist may need to be more focused and use the cognitive framework to increase their understanding of specific events or difficulties.

Young children may also find the process of cognitive appraisal difficult, although they can be helped to engage with this if provided with a clear framework. They could be encouraged to become detectives and to actively seek 'evidence' for and against their way of thinking. Once the evidence has been collected the child can be encouraged to 'weigh it up' and to decide how well it fits the evidence. Sayings such as 'catch it, check it, change it' can be helpful. This reminds the child to 'catch' their common dysfunctional thoughts and to 'check' them to see if they make them feel good and help them to face challenges. If not, the final step is to 'change' them into more functional and activating thoughts that make them feel good.

Metaphors can be a helpful way of relating abstract concepts to familiar everyday situations. A washing machine can be used to explain the way some thoughts tumble around and around in our heads. 'Computer spam', 'thought invaders' or the metaphor of a CD playing in one's head can be used to explain automatic thoughts and how they just pop up without being requested and are difficult to ignore. These can be developed into coping strategies. For example, children could be encouraged to develop a computer firewall, shoot down their invading thoughts or to turn the volume down on the CD so they can stop listening to their negative thoughts. The metaphor of an anger volcano can help children understand the cognitive and emotional build-up that occurs before they lose their temper. Once the stages have been mapped, strategies can be developed to stop the volcano from blowing. Finally a metaphor of traffic lights can be used to discuss dysfunctional and functional thoughts and how they affect our behaviour. Red thoughts (dysfunctional thoughts) stop us from doing things, whilst green thoughts (functional) are empowering and activating.

Adolescents have more developed cognitive abilities and often enjoy the debate of the Socratic dialogue. Most are able to identify, test and challenge their cognitions, and many are able to engage in more complex cognitive work in which common themes and processes are identified. It is not however uncommon to find that adolescents hold very strong beliefs and are unable to see alternative explanations. This can result in the therapist becoming increasingly active in generating alternative views, which are simply dismissed by the adolescent as the Socratic dialogue becomes lost. It is therefore important that the therapist remains open, non-judgemental and curious, and maintains an objective focus to help the adolescent reflect upon and question their beliefs.

## Non-verbal methods

CBT with children also requires greater use of non-verbal methods. Drawings can be helpful and provide a useful way of externalising problems and separating them from the child. For example, children with OCD can be encouraged to draw and give a name to their OCD, which they can then learn to boss back. Games such as emotional charades can be used to act out different emotions to help children identify facial expressions associated with different emotions. Brightly coloured worksheets provide engaging ways to help children map physiological changes associated with different emotions onto outline body shapes. The development of a feelings scrapbook can be a fun way for young children to establish a library of pictures expressing different emotions.

Puppets can provide an engaging way to help young children talk about their worrying thoughts and feelings. Problem situations can be acted out and children encouraged to suggest what the puppets might be thinking in order to identify potentially important cognitions. They can also be used to develop skills by encouraging children to coach their puppet through a difficult situation.

With adolescents a greater use of technology can be helpful. Video or YouTube clips can provide a visual introduction to many of the key areas of CBT, and can be used to introduce, highlight or facilitate discussions. Computer logs can be used as methods of self-monitoring and email as a way of reminding young people about out-of-session assignments and for providing feedback. The internet provides a rich source of information, which individuals can be encouraged to use to seek evidence that might challenge their beliefs, for example, fears about contamination or transmission of disease. Pie charts provide useful visual ways of challenging and reappraising beliefs about responsibility or blame. Similarly, quizzes can help young people identify different types of thinking traps.

Finally, visual diagrams depicting a problem formulation or the link between events thoughts, feelings and behaviours can provide helpful ways of reinforcing the cognitive model. Printed material can supplement the session and provides a fuller and more accurate record of discussions and key points. Similarly, visual rating scales help to quantify belief in thoughts or strength of feelings and provide a useful way of demonstrating change over time.

## DIVERSITY

CBT needs to consider and address the diverse needs of children and young people arising from their race, ethnicity, faith or culture. In many respects diversity is embedded within the CBT model, with the focus on understanding the unique beliefs, values and cognitions of the individual, which, in turn, determine their perception of events. Similarly, the therapist and client seek to establish an equal partnership in the therapeutic relationship. This provides an opportunity for the therapist to actively ask and learn from the client about important diversity issues in order to consider how standard CBT ideas and methods needs to be adapted. For example, standard CBT worksheets involving thought bubbles may not be understood or computer-supported interventions may not be feasible (Levinson, 2012). The premise of CBT that problems arise due to the way the child thinks may be in conflict with some cultures where the cause of mental illness is viewed as external to the young person and not within their direct control to change. In terms of the therapeutic process, the underpinning principle of collaborative empiricism may be alien to those expecting to receive direct advice. Greater involvement of the family in the intervention may be required, thereby challenging many traditional protocols that focus primarily on working with the child. The content of metaphors needs to be considered to ensure that they are relevant and understandable. Culturally sensitive examples or relevant role models need to be carefully identified to emphasise ideas or concepts. Finally, CBT needs to be modified to meet any specific learning or developmental needs. A study by Visagie et al. (2015), for example, describes how tactile materials were used as an alternative to visual materials for visually impaired children.

## Case Study

Sarah (13) was referred by her GP with severe anxiety. She had a long history of anxiety but this was increasingly interfering with everyday life to the extent that she was now reluctant to go out and was experiencing panic attacks.

### Psycho-education and Relationship-building

The first assessment session was with Sarah and her mother. Sarah presented as bright, articulate, readily engaged with the meeting and appeared very motivated to control her anxiety.

The second session completed the assessment with information from standardised anxiety measures complementing the clinical interview. This confirmed that Sarah had a generalised anxiety problem that was resulting in panic attacks in public. At the end of the session Sarah agreed to complete a mood diary and to record any times she became anxious

The diary was reviewed in session three and identified three anxious situations. All occurred when Sarah was invited out (to the cinema, to sleep at a friend's, shopping) and resulted in her being unable to go. This information was used to map a formulation that highlighted the connection between her thoughts ('I won't be able to cope') and her emotions (anxiety) and behaviour (avoid leaving home). Finally the process of CBT was discussed and how the therapist would help Sarah to discover ways to manage her anxious feelings. Sarah agreed to complete another diary describing the bodily signals she noticed when she became anxious.

### Skills Development

The fourth session focused upon emotional recognition. The physiological anxiety reaction was explained and the signals that Sarah recorded in her diary were discussed (racing heart, difficulty breathing, hot and sweating). Sarah was then asked to record any thoughts she noticed when she became anxious and what she did.

Session five focused upon the development of anxiety management skills. A number of anxiety management skills were identified and potentially useful ideas practised. In particular, controlled breathing, listening to music and visualising a relaxation place were identified as potentially useful. Sarah agreed to practise these methods at home each day and agreed to record her thoughts when she became anxious.

The diary was reviewed in session six. Controlled breathing was helpful when Sarah began to feel anxious, whilst listening to music and visualisation helped her to prepare for potentially worrying situations. There was one situation when Sarah was invited shopping but was unable to control her anxiety. She recorded her thoughts ('I will become anxious and won't be able to cope'; 'I always panic when I go shopping'; 'I will make a fool of myself'). This led to an exploration of processing biases and how Sarah had fallen into the 'fortune teller' thinking trap where she was predicting failure. Sarah agreed to keep the diary for another week.

In session seven Sarah reported that she had gone to the school dance. She had become anxious before she went ('I look awful in this dress') but successfully managed this with her visualisation. However, whilst at the dance she was constantly looking for signs that she did not look nice. The 'negative glasses' thinking trap was discussed and a Socratic dialogue used to help Sarah find information that she had overlooked (e.g. comments from her best friends; postings on Facebook). This provided a direct challenge to Sarah's thoughts and helped her to recognise that others thought 'she looked nice'. This event also challenged Sarah's belief that she was not safe and unable to cope when she was out. The session ended with Sarah agreeing to develop a list of activities that she would like to do.

## Consolidation

In session eight Sarah was encouraged to use her skills to cope with challenging situations. The activity that Sarah felt would be the easiest to manage was to go with her best friend to the local coffee shop. Sarah was asked what she thought would happen (have a panic attack) and she rated her belief that she wouldn't be able to cope (80/100). A behavioural experiment was agreed to test her belief. Helpful skills were rehearsed. Relaxing visualisation before she went and controlled breathing if she felt anxious whilst out. Functional cognitions were practised ('I have done this before so I can only give it a go and see what happens') and a way of countering her thinking trap (negative glasses) by focusing upon what she was achieving rather than what she felt she could do better was rehearsed.

Session nine revealed that Sarah had successfully been to the coffee shop with her friend. She did not become unduly anxious and rated the belief that she wasn't able to cope as 40/100. Over the next three sessions further experiments were agreed upon culminating in Sarah going out one Saturday shopping with her friends.

## Relapse Prevention

The final sessions were monthly and encouraged Sarah to reflect on what she had discovered and the skills she found useful. Possible setbacks were discussed and a written coping plan developed. She continued to face and cope with increasingly difficult situations, and 6 weeks after the final appointment she sent a postcard from London where Sarah had gone shopping with her friends.

## Key Learning

- CBT is a theoretically informed intervention.
- It has a strong evidence base and is effective as an intervention for psychological problems and to inform emotional health prevention programmes.
- The process of CBT is based on a strong therapeutic partnership that promotes self-discovery through collaborative empiricism.
- CBT needs to be adapted to the specific needs of the child.
- Children may respond better to non-verbal methods and simpler cognitive techniques.
- Adolescents have better developed cognitive, linguistic and reasoning skills and can engage in more abstract Socratic dialogues.

## Summary

Although developed from work with adults CBT can be used with children from 7 years of age if it is carefully adapted to the developmental level of the child. With younger children CBT may need to be simpler, made concrete through the use of familiar everyday metaphors and involve less verbal and more visual techniques. Adolescents will have more developed cognitive and verbal skills and may be able to engage in more sophisticated and abstract verbal discussions.

CBT provides an evidence-based approach to the treatment of emotional problems in children and adolescents:

- It is based on the premise that psychological problems arise from dysfunctional and unhelpful cognitions that are maintained by attention and memory biases, emotional responses and maladaptive behaviours.
- Through the process of collaborative empiricism dysfunctional cognitions are subject to objective evaluation through techniques such as Socratic dialogues and behavioural experiments.
- These result in the discovery of new or overlooked information and alternative meanings about events, which leads to the development of more functional and balanced cognitions.
- Coping is enhanced through the development of emotional literacy and management skills and performance through behavioural and problem-solving skills. Enhanced coping and performance results in greater reinforcement of positive and adaptive behaviours.

## Discussion Questions

1. How would you explain CBT to a 9- or 10-year-old child with an anxiety disorder?
2. You would like to find out more about the negative thoughts a 14-year-old boy is having and think that a thought diary would be helpful. How would you go about doing this?
3. Design an experiment to test a belief that 'I never get my school work right'.
4. Think about some Socratic questions you could use with adolescents.

Turn to p.443 for possible answers.

## Develop Your Skills

1. How might you incorporate more non-verbal techniques into your practice?
2. When you ask a child or young person 'What were you thinking?' they reply 'Nothing' or 'I don't know'. Does this mean that they are not able to engage in CBT?
3. What tends to be the content of negative automatic thoughts associated with anxiety and depression?
4. What are the key characteristics of functional and dysfunctional thoughts?

Turn to p.444 for possible answers.

## Further Reading

### Adapting CBT

Friedberg, R.D. and McClure, J.M. (2015) *Clinical Practice of Cognitive Therapy with Children and Adolescents: The Nuts and Bolts*. New York: Guilford Press.

Stallard, P. (2002) *Think Good – Feel Good: A Cognitive Behaviour Therapy Workbook for Children and Young People*. Chichester: John Wiley.

### Online Resources

British Association of Behavioural and Cognitive Psychotherapy website. This is the lead organisation for CBT in the UK. www.babcp.com/Public/What-is-CBT.aspx

MindEd website for information about CBT and how it is used to treat different problems. https://www.minded.org.uk

## REFERENCES

Beck, A.T. (1963) Thinking and depression. 1. Idiosyncratic content and cognitive distortions. *Archives of General Psychiatry 9*: 324–333.

Beck, A.T. (1964) Thinking and depression. 2. Theory and therapy. *Archives of General Psychiatry 10*: 561–571.

Beck, A.T., Rush, A.J., Shaw, B.F. and Emery, G. (1979) *Cognitive Therapy for Depression*. New York: Guilford Press.

Brent, D., Emslie, G., Clarke, G., et al. (2008) Switching to another SSRI or to venlafaxine with or without cognitive behaviour therapy for adolescents with SSRI-resistant depression. The TORDIA randomised controlled trial. *Journal of the American Medical Association 299*(8): 901–913.

Calear, A.L. and Christensen, H. (2010) Systematic review of school-based prevention and early intervention programs for depression. *Journal of Adolescence 33*(3): 429–438.

Ellis, A. (1994) *Reason and Emotion in Psychotherapy: Comprehensive Method of Treating Human Disturbances*, revised and updated. New York: Citadel Press.

Goodyer, I., Dubicka, B., Wilkinson, P. et al. (2007) Selective serotonin reuptake inhibitors (SSRIs) and routine specialist care with and without cognitive behaviour therapy in adolescents with major depression: randomised controlled trial. *British Medical Journal 335*(7611), p. 142.

Goodyer, I.M., Reynolds, S., Barrett, B. et al. (2017) Cognitive behavioural therapy and short-term psychoanalytical psychotherapy versus a brief psychosocial intervention in adolescents with unipolar major depressive disorder (IMPACT): a multicentre, pragmatic, observer-blind, randomised controlled superiority trial. *The Lancet Psychiatry 4*(2): 109–119.

Graham, P. (2005) Jack Tizard Lecture: cognitive behavior therapies for children: passing fashion or here to stay? *Child and Adolescent Mental Health 10*(2): 57–62.

Kendall, P.C. (1991) *Child and Adolescent Therapy: Cognitive-Behavioral Procedures*. New York: Guilford Press.

Levinson, M. (2012) Working with 'diversity' in CBT. In W. Dryden and R. Branch (eds), *The CBT Handbook*. Los Angeles, CA: Sage, pp 162-178.

Neil, A.L. and Christensen, H. (2009) Efficacy and effectiveness of school based prevention and early intervention programmes for anxiety. *Clinical Psychology Review 29*: 208–215.

Shafran, R., Fonagy, P., Pugh, K. and Myles, P. (2014) Transformation of mental health services for children and young people in England. *Dissemination and Implementation of Evidence-Based Practices in Child and Adolescent Mental Health*: (158). New York, NY: Oxford University Press.

Stallard, P. (2005). *A Clinician's Guide to Think Good Feel Good: The Use of CBT with Children and Young People*. Chichester: John Wiley.

Stockings, E.A., Degenhardt, L., Dobbins, T., Lee, Y.Y., Erskine, H.E., Whiteford, H.A. and Patton, G. (2015) Preventing depression and anxiety in young people: a review of the joint efficacy of universal, selective and indicated prevention. *Psychological Medicine 46*(1): 11–26.

Treatment for Adolescents with Depression Study (TADS) Team (2009) The treatment for adolescents with depression study (TADS): outcomes over 1 year of naturalistic follow-up. *American Journal of Psychiatry 166*: 1141–1149.

Visagie, L., Loxton, H. and Silverman, W.K. (2015) Research protocol: Development, implementation and evaluation of a cognitive behavioural therapy-based intervention programme for the management of anxiety symptoms in South African children with visual impairments: original research. *African Journal of Disability 4*(1): 1–10.

Walkup, J.T., Albano, A.M., Piacentini, J. et al. (2008) Cognitive behavioral therapy, sertraline, or a combination in childhood anxiety. *New England Journal of Medicine 359*: 2753–2766.

Werner-Seidler, A., Perry, Y., Calear, A.L., Newby, J. M. and Christensen, H. (2017) School-based depression and anxiety prevention programs for young people: a systematic review and meta-analysis. *Clinical Psychology Review 51*: 30–47.

# 5

# GESTALT

## BELINDA HARRIS

**This chapter will discuss:**

- Key gestalt concepts and relational processes that inform a gestalt understanding of human development
- The development of gestalt theory, and significant influences on its formulation and evolution
- Key features of and relational processes involved in gestalt practice, illustrated by thickly disguised case vignettes
- The research evidence for gestalt practice with children and young people
- Gestalt as a brief therapy

## INTRODUCTION

As a humanistic teacher and counsellor working with adolescents in schools in challenging circumstances, I was drawn to gestalt because of familiarity with its underlying philosophical approach, including a focus on the whole person (holism), on awareness of immediate, present-centred experience (existential-humanism), and on the way the individual perceives and engages with reality (phenomenology). Gestalt's particular appeal, however, lay in the emphasis placed on the young person in their situation (field theory).

## Field theory and the evolution of self

The concept of field has two meanings here: the first focuses on the way the person organises their inner experience (*perceptual field*) to make meaning of their situation; the second (derived from Lewin's (1935) field theory) recognises that the person and their world are inseparable and interdependent parts of a dynamic whole, or *gestalt*. Gestalt recognises human development as a lifelong, co-creative and intersubjective process, embedded within a cultural context (i.e. here-and-now cultural norms, values and behaviours, and also power relations between own group and others in society). The self-experience of the infant and the self-experience of the parent therefore co-evolve within a dynamically unfolding relational and cultural field. It is the present-moment experience (sensory, physical, emotional and cognitive) *between* adult and child that enables the child to differentiate between the '*I*' and the '*not I*', and the adult to develop their felt sense as a parent (e.g. competent or incompetent) in relation to the child.

This energetic meeting at the '*contact boundary*' (Perls, Hefferline and Goodman, 1951) leads to an iterative, vibrant integration of experience: a perspective that is consistent with Stern's infant observation research (1985), and with recent findings in affective neuroscience (Lee, 2007). The gestalt therapist's focus, therefore, is on the young client within their social and cultural situation, and may involve working with members of the child's relational field to enhance their capacity to effectively support the child. Such work may involve parents, caregivers and other professionals (e.g. teachers, social worker, welfare officer) as relevant, in order to create a community of support around the young client.

## The relational field

The relational field has two elements:

1. The *ground* of the relationship, which includes, for example, the child's unique characteristics (e.g. health, temperament, etc.) and the parents' culturally informed mental model of parenting, their values and support systems.
2. The *figure* – the dominant need informing the relational contact (e.g. the child is tired and needs to be carried).

These elements combine in the embodied, present-centred experience of child and adult at the contact boundary, as each makes a '*creative adjustment*' (Perls, Hefferline and Goodman, 1951) to the other. If the need is met and assimilated, the gestalt is closed and a state of balance is restored (i.e. the child is rested and re-energised; the parent feels competent). McConville (2007) argues that two ground conditions are particularly important in supporting child development: namely, the extent and ways in which power is exercised to influence the child's choices and behaviours; and the way the boundaries of the relationship are organised and transformed over time to meet the child's emergent developmental needs.

When the use of power and boundaries is sufficiently attuned to the actual needs and capabilities of the child *and* the here-and-now situation, then the child's organismic self-regulation process (Perls, 1948: 576) is activated and their evolving sense of self is supported. For example, when a toddler moves towards danger (e.g. an electrical socket), the parent acts decisively but gently to divert their attention elsewhere. Such contact alters the ground of the child–adult relationship and the toddler learns to trust the relational field to meet their need for safe, self–environment exploration.

Conversely, if the toddler's needs for safety and containment are ignored or responded to with rigidity, harshness or contempt, then the flow of their experiencing is interrupted. Where inflexible responses, neglect or abuse persist, the creative adjustment needed to manage and make meaning of the situation is likely to result in a fixed gestalt, or rigid way of being at the contact boundary when similar situations occur. This is evident, for example, when a distraught, sobbing boy is scornfully told to 'stop being a sissy and act like a man'. If repeated over time, the child's *creative adjustments* might include learning not to approach another for support when he is distressed, learning to stop himself from crying and, eventually, becoming unaware of his need to cry when he is hurting. In this way *creative adjustments* may lead to a *fixed gestalt* to safeguard a sense of belonging and acceptability within a particular (family, community, societal) culture, and equally be indicative of an unfinished situation.

## Unfinished situations

Perls (1969 [1947]) identified a physiological–biological 'cycle of interdependency of organism and environment' (1969 [1947]: 45), which Goodman (Perls, Hefferline and Goodman, 1951) subsequently categorised as fore-contact, contact, final contact and post-contact. If followed sequentially, these stages of contact between the child and others in their environment enable them to create a meaningful whole (gestalt) from their experience. The sense of completion and closure of the gestalting process is experienced intuitively as 'right', and is accompanied by a sense of calm, satisfaction, peace or fulfilment. However, if progression through the cycle is thwarted in some way, and the gestalt remains incomplete, then unfinished business results.

The therapeutic relationship provides a here-and-now situation in which closure (Perls, 1975 [1959]) can be experienced viscerally and emotionally. For example, a child whose parents are overprotective may need support to define and express their own needs and wants. The parents may also need help with unfinished situations (e.g. traumatic experience in childhood) to manage their hyperanxiety about safety and reduce the power they exert over the child's choices within the relational field.

## The relational field of childhood

In early childhood the child's primary need is for 'embedding' (McConville, 1995), a sense of connection where they feel safe and protected enough to explore the environment, to express themselves physically and emotionally, and to trust in others for stimulation, comfort and support. During the embedding phase the child needs a 'porous relational boundary' (McConville, 2007: 9) where significant adults are intensely involved with the child's physical growth and well-being. Adults use their power to soothe and support the child's affective experiencing, as well as to firmly and decisively inhibit behaviours that could do harm, and refuse to accede to the child's excessive or inappropriate wants. In other words, the child experiences support whilst also learning to manage their emotions (fear, sadness, anger, joy) and tolerate disappointment.

## The relational field of adolescence

In contrast, the adolescent is focused on the process of 'disembedding' (McConville, 1995) from the family and other adult systems of support. This involves a major reorganisation of the field, based on differentiation of self from others and integration of the evolving self into new *Gestalten* or wholes. The adolescent is actively involved in stretching and redefining their power and boundaries, and needs significant adults (and their therapist) to support a 'safe emergency' (Perls et al., 1951) of the adult self, *and* of their worlds, whether family, social or educational. 'Safe emergency', a term coined by Perls et al. (1951), highlights the importance of *just enough* support to risk experimenting with new behaviours, in service of 'becoming' whole.

McConville (2007) emphasises the key role of negotiation in this process, so that adult and adolescent meet at the contact boundary as separate individuals. Here they discuss what actions are reasonable and acceptable according to the adolescent's immediate wishes, and in the context of the environmental situation. Handled well, such negotiations are characterised by and nourish mutual respect and a flexible, rather than rigid, responsiveness. The adolescent is held accountable for their behaviours and there is a positive shift in the ground of the child–adult relationship, whereby the adolescent disembeds from the family without losing their sense of belonging, and the family slowly adjusts to and appreciates the emerging adult without a loss of connection to their child or sibling.

## The shame–support dynamic

The reader may have noticed the frequent use of the word 'support', and gestalt therapists are curious about the quality and quantity of support in the person–environment field. Where, for example, the demands of the environment and the needs of the child conflict, then the creative adjustment required of the child and/or the environment to accommodate the other may be costly. For example, for children and young people with complex trauma, the behaviours required of them in school settings constitute a big ask, and without sufficient support the student is likely to fail in some way and experience further punishment, rejection and humiliation.

From a gestalt perspective such situations manifest as shame, which is '*a major regulator of the boundary between self and other*. It is a field variable, a ground condition that is the opposite of *support*' (Lee, 1996: 10; emphasis in original). Shame is an excruciating sense of self-disgust and isolation, in which the individual's yearnings for connection are unmet. This creates a 'shame bind' (Kaufman, 1989), whereby the individual withdraws from the environment rather than reaching out. This is often as true of parents, who feel judged and blamed for their child's misdemeanours, and therefore avoid contact with the school. The shame bind not only inhibits the awareness and expression of vital, positive energy, but also creates strong neural pathways for experiencing self-disgust and rejection in early childhood (Philippson, 2004).

In this situation the therapeutic process involves novel experiences that foster the development of new neural pathways. A gestalt therapist develops an in-depth appreciation of shame dynamics and uses the relational field within and beyond the therapy room to support the young client's connection with self and others. Such long-term work requires a therapist who has enough self-support to lean into the shame – experiencing the client's resistance to being accepted and to stay present at the contact boundary. Despite being repeatedly mistrusted, verbally attacked and rejected, the therapist remains solidly present until there is 'at least a thread of a relationship' (Oaklander, 2006: 20), when the therapeutic work can begin.

## HISTORY AND BACKGROUND OF THE GESTALT APPROACH

The early 20th century saw major developments in science and technology and a rise in radical socialist movements, challenging the prevailing order. New movements in the arts also challenged bourgeois values and norms, as evidenced by Expressionist paintings depicting the subjective feelings and fantasies of the artist. The founders of gestalt therapy embraced the creativity, spontaneity and intuition of Expressionism alongside the existential focus on 'being' (what is) and 'potential being', which is experienced through the exercise of choice with self-responsibility.

Fritz Perls is considered the father of gestalt therapy, yet his two co-founders, Laura Perls (dancer and philosopher) and Paul Goodman (radical thinker, activist and writer), were significant contributors to its evolution. The Perls were trained as Freudian analysts and critiqued Freud for refusing to evolve his theory further in the light of new influences and information. In contrast, the founders eschewed dogmatism in favour of 'the experimental, insecure, but creative, pioneering attitude' (Perls, 1948: 586). The Perls broke their ties with psychoanalysis (Perls, 1969 [1947]) and, having escaped German fascism, settled in New York in 1946, joining with Goodman to develop their theory of gestalt practice. For this, they drew on direct experiences of working with key professionals over previous decades.

Of particular relevance for this chapter are the influences of Martin Buber, Laura Perls' teacher; the neuropsychologist Kurt Goldstein, in whose clinic for soldiers with traumatic brain injuries Perls worked (Goldstein identified the concept and process of self-actualisation two decades before Abraham Maslow popularised it); Jacob Moreno, who emphasised the client 'showing' and experiencing rather than talking 'about'; and Wilhelm Reich, whose breath- and body-oriented approach illuminated the processes of working holistically.

Violet Oaklander is responsible for developing a comprehensive account of gestalt therapeutic process with children. Originally trained as a teacher, in the 1960s she found her niche with emotionally disturbed children. In childhood Oaklander experienced long-term hospitalisation and major surgical interventions. As a parent she was further traumatised when one of her children was diagnosed with terminal lupus. Whilst he was dying in hospital, she attended a 1 week gestalt group experience, which she described as life changing (Elsbree, 2009). She attributed this impact to the quality of the relationship with the group therapist, Jim Simkin:

> He got me working on my grief, on my anger, on my avoidance … my denial of what was happening … everything, but at the same time he was always with me. Talk about an 'I–Thou' relationship, he was with me … He really got me working. When I say it changed my life, I mean it somehow transformed me. (Elsbree, 2009: 205)

Oaklander then trained as a gestalt therapist and began to present and write up her work. *Windows to Our Children* (1978/2007) was adapted from her doctoral thesis, and has been translated into 13 languages. Her experience with Simkin and other gestalt trainers, including Laura Perls, whom she described as a 'loving presence', informed her understanding of therapeutic process, which is characterised by contact, awareness and dialogue on the bedrock of a safe, trustworthy, engaged relationship.

Whilst Oaklander still dominates the field, other gestalt therapists continue to evolve the theory and practice of gestalt (e.g. Harris, 2011), to acknowledge and incorporate the neuroscientific evidence that affirms gestalt's original emphasis on the embodied (e.g. Tervo, 2007) and relational fields (e.g. Lee and Harris, 2011) with reference to a range of presenting issues (e.g. eating disorders, sexuality, grief, trauma, learning disabilities) and age groups (e.g. Blom, 2006). In the next section I will illuminate the theory–practice relationship with reference to case vignettes from practice.

## TRANSLATING THEORY INTO PRACTICE

### The person of the therapist

Perls (1970: 15) recognised that talking *about* issues inhibits awareness and that it is sensory, embodied experiencing within the therapeutic relationship that opens the door to change. Using their awareness as a searchlight, the gestalt therapist endeavours to tune into the field, noticing their own experiencing (e.g. sensation, physicality, feelings, fantasies) and moment-by-moment changes in the client's contact (e.g. skin tone, eye contact, posture, breathing, emotional expression), to be fully present to *what is*.

---

## Case Study: Meera

Meera is 8 years of age, and I notice my throat and chest tighten as she looks vacantly round the room, before choosing to sit on a beanbag. Her breathing is shallow and her chest looks collapsed, as if defeated. I sense that she needs me close, so I softly offer her the choice 'Do you want me to join you or sit over here?' She shrugs her shoulders, and yet moves over to create space, so I sit down alongside her. We are quiet and there is a sense of calm between us. After a few minutes like this, she turns to look up at me and quietly says 'Jodie, my dog, died'. I notice my throat and chest relaxing, and tears welling up behind my eyes. She swallows hard and her chest tightens, so I gently offer, 'It's okay to cry when someone you love dies', and she bursts into tears.

---

This deliberate use of the embodied self is predicated on self-awareness, and gestalt training is an intensive experiential process supported by ongoing in-depth personal therapy. The trainee becomes acutely aware of their own *fixed gestalten* and any unresolved issues, which may impair their capacity to respond to the client's situation. They also deepen awareness of their contact processes, their embodied presence and how these impact on others. Therapy requires humility and awareness that within the co-emerging field anything can happen. There is no room for complacency or grandiosity.

Creativity lies at the heart of gestalt practice and the therapist must be imaginative and comfortable playing in an uninhibited way with children and young people at all developmental levels. Within the creative play the therapist is a willing participant in the client's efforts to define themselves, express their emotions, and gain some sense of their potency and efficacy.

Oaklander (2006) describes vividly participating in games where she was bossed about, handcuffed or tied up by young clients who needed an embodied experience of feeling powerful and in control. I have certainly played the cowering pupil of a shaming, angry 11-year-old teacher, in the service of completing an unfinished situation. In this process clear limits and boundaries are vital, as is modelling 'No' appropriately.

Rigorous attention to self-care, self-support and use of supervision are essential when the therapist is committed to supporting the young client within their field. Working with children and adolescents requires stamina and emotional resilience.

## THE NATURE OF THE RELATIONSHIP

For many young people, the therapist is just another adult who will let them down. Therefore, being met at the contact boundary in a new way enables the client to resensitise their awareness of the *now*, and of the totality of their experiencing, for example, their likes and dislikes, their similarity to and difference from the therapist. Such awareness helps the young person to define themselves and develop self-support, and is built on solid ground.

## Establishing the ground of the relationship

Oaklander (2006: 27) compares therapy with children to a dance – 'Sometimes I lead and sometimes the child leads'. There is movement between directivity and non-directivity according to the demands of the situation. In the early stages of the relationship the focus is on safety and trust-building through the dialogic 'I–Thou' relationship (Buber, 1959 [1937]). Here the therapist's authenticity and equanimity meet the child where they are, as an equal and separate individual.

Through their embodied presence and ability to honour and respect the client's resistance, contact style, rhythm and pace, they lay foundations for the work. They are not interested in creating dependency or being a surrogate parent, but commit to being a caring, supportive presence, holding an attitude of '*creative indifference*' (Friedlander, 1918), or neutrality. This attitude supports 'responding' (Parlett, 2000), whereby the client develops response-ability and responsibility for their choices through a gradual expansion of experiences they can assimilate.

---

### Case Study: Syed

Syed, aged 12, was referred for therapy by his teacher because of his constant distracting of others and inability to sit still. Initially I copied his running and darting around the room, and voiced my experience out loud, for example, 'I'm enjoying this pace'; 'I'm hot and stopping for a moment'. Each week the amount of time we spent in this cat and mouse game gradually decreased and he slowed down, becoming interested in exploring other games we could play together.

I was the first adult to accept and join Syed in his restlessness. It was the experience of being met and responded to where he was, and my willingness to be open about my embodied experiencing that enabled him to expand his repertoire of behaviours, and to disclose his experiences as a child refugee whose family had literally been 'on the run' for several months.

---

## Developing the client's sense of self

Once the relationship is established, we work together to develop the child's 'embodying' ability (Parlett, 2000), including awareness of their senses, their breathing, the way they use their body, and express their thoughts and feelings. In all this the therapist is a playmate or friendly companion who is genuinely interested in and welcoming of the whole child, however they present.

Having fun is part of childhood and helps to build the relational field. If a child is anxious and their breathing is shallow, I may suggest that we blow bubbles or play tin whistles to see how much noise we can make. I may offer pieces of fabric doused with aromatherapy oils, to support choosing between two scents, or tasting two different fruits. I may ask adolescents to bring their favourite music CD, or use fashion magazines to create a collage of their ideal personal wardrobe. Guided imagery and meditation techniques serve as strategies to calm and settle themselves in times of stress. Such work also supports self-definition, and Oaklander (2006) gives numerous examples of helping clients to use 'I' statements, as they clarify who they are and who they are not.

Opportunities for play and 'experiencing mastery' (2006: 28) are also important for clients who have had insufficient support and grown up too quickly. Even adolescents can become absorbed in tidying the doll's house, building lego scenes or writing a poem. Through such activities they gain a sense of satisfaction in their achievement and consolidate their evolving capacity for self-support.

## Expanding the client's sense of self

Once the sense of self is sufficiently robust, the experience of imaginative play enables the therapist to support the client's imaginal world. Using whichever creative materials they are drawn to, the client is encouraged to create a scene, and these scenes are often representations of their situation. Listening intently, the therapist invites the client to describe what they have created, and to 'be' one or more of the characters, for example, 'I am the fat controller and I decide where the naughty engines go'. The therapist encourages the client to say more, and asks questions, for example, 'Which engine is the naughtiest?'; 'What do they do that is naughty?' These projections offer the therapist a sense of the client's world and the client experiences being heard, accepted and responded to in their fantasy world. They also practise 'experimenting' (Parlett, 2000), where they begin to risk novel ways of being, acting and thinking.

## Completing the gestalt

The fantasy is a kind of a bridge into aspects of the self that they don't even know are parts of the self. The child begins to relate to those parts and gets to the point where they can own them. It's like they're looking into a window of the self. (Oaklander, in Mortola, 2011: 346)

Oaklander does this by inviting the client to dialogue with the characters in their picture or sand-play, for example, 'How could you help the fat controller?'; 'What would you like to tell him?' She emphasises, however, that such work is founded on the therapist's relationship with and support for the child, which enables them to engage in the fantasy, relate to different aspects of self and own them. Such work strengthens 'self-recognising' (Parlett, 2000), or knowing one's own truth, and young clients may use the relationship with the therapist to develop and embody new competences, such as exerting power and control over others in the service of completing *gestalten*.

This stage also supports 'inter-relating' (Parlett, 2000): the ability to relate to others according to the needs of the situation. The process of gestalt completion may happen within one session or take many sessions. The therapist needs to stay alert to the client's resistance surfacing at any stage, as expressed through a change in energy, or suddenly diverting attention elsewhere. Such resistance is honoured and respected, so clients learn to trust their natural cycle of contact and withdrawal. The therapist has faith that that they will return to complete the gestalt when they are ready.

## BRIEF THERAPY

Houston (2003) provides a powerful rationale for the relevance and value of brief gestalt therapy with adults. She offers the reader a useful framework for supporting the client through their contact cycle towards completion of their need, and case studies that illuminate how individual and group gestalt practice may enhance clients' abilities to impact and respond to their environment. Here I focus on three aforementioned aspects of gestalt practice that support the relevance and value of gestalt for brief work with children and young people.

First, gestalt emphasises process, or what is happening in the here-and-now between therapist and client, whereby the client's dominant need organises their perceptual field. The therapist stays open to the totality of the experience of the young person's impact on her and uses this awareness to inform her way of being with the client in the present moment. Second, the therapist is willing to enter their client's world as an attuned playmate or companion and meet them exactly where they are. This experience of support helps to interrupt any shame processes, and affects the client's self-experiencing at the contact boundary, potentially opening them up to new possibilities. Third, the therapist is committed to supporting the client's potential for creative experimentation so they may try out novel experiences (e.g. being the centre of loving attention, expressing anger) as a means to complete their dominant need or unfinished situation. Such work may take place within one session, or over a number of sessions, depending on how successfully the ground of the relationship is established.

Oaklander's reports of her work with young clients demonstrate that brief work can be effective for many children and young people, and in some cases may be as much as they can assimilate at a given stage in their own developmental process. In the final section I offer a brief account of contemporary research evidence for a gestalt approach to working with children and young people.

## THE RESEARCH EVIDENCE

Greenberg (2008) argues that process–outcome research studies have proved a valuable way of generating evidence-based data on gestalt therapy with adults over many years. Recently, gestalt practitioners working in the NHS found a practice-based research network (PBRN) approach to collecting methodical, rigorous, clinically based, mostly quantitative data to be more workable in a context where minimum funding and voluntary effort is required. Their 3-year study found gestalt psychotherapists to be as effective as therapists trained in other modalities working in the NHS and in primary care (Stevens et al., 2011). Although an equivalent study of gestalt therapy with young people in the NHS is feasible, one is yet to be conducted.

Barber and Brownell (2008: 37) argue that 'Gestalt therapists are practitioners who work with direct perception to discover how a person is sensing, thinking, feeling and imaginatively projecting information to constellate the world … they are well on the way to conducting qualitative inquiry'. Trustworthiness is a key criterion when assessing the reliability and validity of qualitative research and Oaklander's collected works are a prime example of such trustworthiness in action. Her subsequent papers in *Windows to Our Children* (1988) and her final book, *Hidden Treasure* (2006), added to the practice-based evidence in the original volume, and more recently set out the theoretical framework she created and developed over 60 years of practitioner research.

### Case Study: Eze

Eze was 15 years old when she was referred for counselling as an alternative to exclusion from school. Her tutor reported that Eze had arrived aged 14 with a glowing report of her academic and social skills. However, neither had been evident since then and her attitude to authority, behaviour and academic work had caused concern, despite teachers' best efforts to engage her and hold her to account. Her parents had apparently been uncooperative.

Initially Eze seemed hesitant, sneaking a glance at me before plonking herself down on the chair closest to the door. I sensed her resistance, 'I guess you don't want to be here with me. I understand … you didn't choose to come. So we both need some time to check each other out.' She looked askance at me, so I continued, explaining that I would meet her parents separately and explain our contract together, including issues of confidentiality. When asked if she had any questions she sat up and informed me that speaking to her parents would be a 'waste of time'. I thanked her for her honesty and asked 'How are you feeling now you've told me that?' 'Fine' came the prompt reply. 'Are you willing to try something with me?' I inquired. 'You can stop whenever you want.' She looked nonplussed but nodded. 'Okay, let's take in some short, shallow breaths, like this. How was that?' 'Easy.' 'Good, shall we try another way now?' Eze nodded, so we took some longer, deeper inhalations and exhalations. I noticed her face soften and her upper body relax as we did this, and we ended the session with an agreement to 'do more stuff like that' the next week.

On meeting Eze's parents, they insisted I get her 'back on track'. When I inquired whether anything had happened that would account for the changes in her behaviour, they were quiet and looked away. Her mother abruptly stood up and proclaimed, 'It's just puberty, it's normal!' before walking out.

Eze and I continued to work together on sensory activities to deepen awareness of herself and her preferences. One day she expressed some muted anger towards her parents and I invited her to choose some objects to represent her parents and place them in the sand tray. She became totally absorbed creating a scene with four figures, a lion cub lying in the sand with a lion on each side and another cub hidden from view behind a mud wall. She poured sand over the lying cub until it was completely covered. I suggested she 'be' one of the figures in the scene and speak 'as if' she were them. She looked embarrassed, so I encouraged her to focus on the breathing and grounding techniques we had practised. Tuning into her growing capacity for self-support, she was able to speak as the buried cub: 'I want to live. Help me.' As the cub behind the wall she said, 'I am so lonely. I wish I had died, not you.' I was touched by the agony in her voice and took a moment before asking her what this scene meant for her. Tearfully, she told me her twin sister had died of a congenital disease 18 months earlier. She had neither been allowed to visit her bedside towards the end, nor to attend the funeral. Since then, it had been taboo to speak of her sister at home, as 'it would kill her mother'. Within 6 months of their bereavement her parents had sold the family home and moved to a new suburb.

In this case study, it is possible to see how the work developed over time, by acknowledging and leaning into Eze's resistance, by clarifying boundaries and providing opportunities for her to self-soothe and ground herself. Once trust had been established Eze used the sandplay to illustrate the unfinished situation underlying her presenting behaviour. Once this was clear, Eze and I co-created a way to complete the gestalt with support from her classmates, and to engage her parents in taking Eze's truth seriously.

## Key Learning

- There are multiple realities involved in any given situation. Consider the young person's presenting issue as an expression of something happening in their situation.
- Recognising and working with shame dynamics is essential when developing a therapeutic alliance with young clients.
- The therapeutic relationship provides a safe space in which any unfinished situations can be creatively completed.

*(Continued)*

(Continued)

- Gestalt practice is experiential and experimental. The therapist provides neither solutions nor interpretations. Instead, she supports the client's creative expression of their thoughts, feelings and fantasies.
- The Gestalt therapist is willing to be an active playmate or co-actor in a young person's drama. She has worked in depth on her own unfinished situations and can use herself fully in service of the child's needs.

## Summary

- Gestalt works with the totality of the child's relational field, and recognises the dynamic interplay of field variables. These are experienced at the *contact boundary* between adult and child. Here, both co-evolve in response to one another and the demands of the situation.
- It is assumed that everyone is doing the best they can with the resources they have in the moment. This involves making *creative adjustments* to the situation in order to achieve a satisfactory ending, or *complete gestalt*.
- Shame and belonging are key field variables affecting experience at the contact boundary. Two ways of being at the contact boundary are of particular importance for child development: the way power is exercised and the way boundaries are organised to meet the child's emergent needs.
- The therapist is a fully *embodied, energetically available presence* and meets the child where they are, offering an 'I–Thou' experience at the contact boundary. It is recognised that no therapeutic work will occur until the relationship is established.
- Gestalt therapy may be *directive or non-directive* depending on the demands of the situation and the present moment. The therapist partners with the child and *co-creates* what happens with as much support as possible and as little support as possible, to activate the client's organismic self-regulatory process.
- Gestalt is a *creative* therapy and uses multisensory media to support the client's experiencing of self at the contact boundary, and hence self-definition. From this ground the client can explore other aspects of self that have been neglected, become fixed or disowned in some way.
- Clients are creatively supported to understand and own their feelings, offered opportunities to unblock emotions that interfere with their capacity to function healthily, and to learn how to express difficult feelings safely.

## Discussion Questions

1. There is a field between you the reader and the text. How are you experiencing this field here and now? What did you bring to the field by way of (a) your previous experience of gestalt, and (b) your own assumptions and beliefs working with children and young people? How did both of these affect your reading? How, if at all, has your thinking been supported and/or challenged or changed as a result of reading the chapter?
2. What are the implications of a person–environment (field theory) perspective for therapists working with children and young people? How might this influence the therapist's way of being with the client? With their caregivers? With other professionals involved?
3. When engaging with the young person's relational–cultural field, what relational and professional ethics are involved? How might you use your own power in service of the young person and the situation? What are the risks?
4. How does the notion of 'creative adjustment' affect your perception of a child/young person's presenting issue? How might this perspective influence your responses to a client's presenting issue and related behaviours?
5. How do the concepts of embedding and disembedding work for you when thinking about the child's and adolescent's relationship with significant others? How might the way you exercise your power and hold boundaries change over time as a young person moves through the school years?

## Develop Your Skills

1. Listen to your body as well as your mind. Practise being fully in contact with your embodied self. Now practise being in contact with another person without losing the connection with your embodied self. Keep shuttling and back and forth until this comes with ease.
2. Develop your ability to explore the ground of the young client's presenting figure, including any cultural and power dynamics, and the creative adjustments made to manage the situation. This work takes time and may involve listening to multiple realities and understandings of the same situation. Build respectful alliances with everyone involved.
3. Assume nothing. Practise being curious and asking open questions to deepen not only your own but also your client's/a parent's/another professional's awareness of a situation. Remember you are not the expert on a situation.

*(Continued)*

(Continued)

4.  Learn to recognise, accept and befriend your own shame and how this affects your way of being with others, for example, peers, family, authority figures. This will help you reach and make contact with a shame-bound young person.
5.  Ask for feedback on your helping style: learn to differentiate between enough support and too much support – learn to feel the boundary between mobilising and stifling your client's autonomy.
6.  Develop a degree of comfort and confidence in your own creative expression – try art, media, drama, play and games to communicate your own feelings, thoughts and fantasies.
7.  Learn how to communicate and negotiate safe boundaries depending on the child and environment. Within that framework, learn how to relinquish control and play a part in the young person's spontaneous creative process (unfinished situation), whilst remaining vigilant and able to resume control if necessary to maintain safe boundaries.
8.  Practise inviting clients to 'do something', and practise letting go if the invitation is resisted or refused. Never take their response personally.

## Further Reading

DeMille, R. (1997) *Put Your Mother on the Ceiling: Children's Imagination Games*. Cambridge, MA: The Gestalt Press.

Kanner, C. and Lee, R.G. (2005) The relational ethic in the treatment of adolescents. *Gestalt Review* 9(1): 72–90.

Lampert, R. (2003) *A Child's Eye View: Gestalt Therapy with Children, Adolescents and Their Families*. Cambridge, MA: The Gestalt Press.

Oaklander, V. (1979) A gestalt therapy approach with children through the use of art and creative expression. In: Marcus, E.H. (ed.) *Gestalt Therapy and Beyond*. Cupertino, CA: Meta Publications, pp 235–247.

Oaklander, V. (1992) Gestalt work with children: Working with anger and introjects. In: Nevis, E.C. (ed.) *Gestalt Therapy: Perspectives and Applications*. New York: Gardner Press, pp 263–287.

Oaklander, V. (1999) Group play therapy from a gestalt therapy perspective. In: Sweeney, D.S. (ed.) *Group Play Therapy: Theory and Practice*. New York: Charles C. Thomas, pp 162–175.

### Online Resources

BACP website: www.bacp.co.uk, especially the BACP Children and Young People Division and the Competences for Working with Children and Young People

Counselling MindEd: https://www.minded.org.uk
   Hard-to-Reach Families
   Designing Home/Community Interventions
   Providing Care in the Right Way
   Collaborative Working
   Cultural Competence
   Therapeutic Skills
   Using Supervision

## REFERENCES

Barber, P. and Brownell, P. (2008) Qualitative research. In: Brownell, P. (ed.) *Handbook for Theory, Research, and Practice in Gestalt Therapy*. Newcastle: Cambridge Scholars Publishing, pp. 37–63.

Blom, R. (2006) *The Handbook of Gestalt Play Therapy*. London: Jessica Kingsley.

Buber, M. (1959 [1937]) *I and Thou*. Edinburgh: T&T Clark.

Elsbree, C. (2009) Interview with Violet Oaklander. *International Gestalt Journal 32*(2): 183–213.

Friedlander, S. (1918) *Schöpferische Indifferenz*. Munich: Georg Müller.

Greenberg, L.S. (2008) Quantitative research. In: Brownell, P. (ed.) *Handbook for Theory, Research, and Practice in Gestalt Therapy*. Newcastle: Cambridge Scholars Publishing, pp. 64–89.

Harris, N. (2011) Something in the air: conditions that promote contact when meeting young people who have stories of early trauma and loss. *British Gestalt Journal 20*(1): 21–28.

Houston, G. (2003) *Brief Gestalt Therapy*. London: SAGE.

Kaufman, J. (1989) *The Psychology of Shame*. London: Routledge.

Lee, R.G. (1996) Shame and the gestalt model. In: Lee, R.G. and Wheeler, G. (eds) *The Voice of Shame: Silence and Connection in Psychotherapy*. Cambridge, MA: The Gestalt Press, pp. 3–22.

Lee, R.G. (2007) Shame and belonging in childhood: the interaction between relationship and neurobiological development in the early years of life. *British Gestalt Journal, 16*(2): 38–45

Lee, R.G. and Harris, N. (2011) *Relational Child, Relational Brain*. New York: Routledge, Taylor & Francis.

Lewin, K. (1935) *A Dynamic Theory of Personality*. New York: McGraw-Hill.

McConville, M. (1995) *Adolescence: Psychotherapy and The Emergent Self*. San Francisco, Jossey-Bass

McConville, M. (2007) Relational modes and the evolving field of parent–child contact. *British Gestalt Journal 16*(2): 5–12.

Mortola, P. (2011) You, me, and the parts of myself I'm still getting to know: an interview with Violet Oaklander. In: Lee, R.G. and Harris, N. (eds) *Relational Child, Relational Brain*. New York: Routledge, Taylor & Francis, pp. 339–348.

Oaklander, V. (2006) *Hidden Treasure*. London: Karnac

Oaklander, V. (1978/2007) *Windows to Our Children*. Gouldsboro, MA: Gestalt Journal Press

Parlett, M. (2000) Creative adjustment and the global field. *British Gestalt Journal 9*(1): 15–27.

Perls, F.S. (1948) Theory and technique of personality integration. *American Journal of Psychotherapy 2*(4): 565–586.

Perls, F.S. (1969 [1947]) *Ego, Hunger and Aggression*. New York: Vintage Books.

Perls, F.S. (1975 [1959]) Resolution. Paper presented at Mendocino State Hospital, California. In: Stevens, J.O. *Gestalt Is…* Moab, UT: Real People Press, pp. 69–74.

Perls, F.S. (1970) Four lectures. In: Fagan, J. and Shepherd, I.L. (eds) *Gestalt Therapy Now*. New York: Harper & Row, pp. 14–38

Perls, F., Hefferline, R. and Goodman, P. (1951) *Gestalt Therapy: Excitement and Growth in the Human Personality*. New York: Delta.

Philippson, P. (2004) The experience of shame. Reprinted in Philippson, P. *Gestalt Therapy: Roots and Branches – Collected Papers*. London: Karnac Books, pp. 167–177.

Stern, D. (1985) *The Interpersonal World of the Infant*. New York: Basic Books.

Stevens, C., Stringfellow, J., Wakelin, K. and Waring, J. (2011) The UK Gestalt Psychotherapy CORE Research Project: the findings. *British Gestalt Journal 20*(2), 22–27.

Tervo, D. (2007) Zig zag flop and roll: creating an embodied field for healing and awareness when working with children. *British Gestalt Journal 16*(2), 28–37.

# 6

# BECOMING AN INTEGRATIVE PRACTITIONER

## NIKI COOPER AND KELLI SWAIN-COWPER

**This chapter will discuss:**

- Common features of integrative practice
- The challenges and benefits of becoming an integrative practitioner
- An integrative practice-based model that uses a developmental perspective to integrate aspects of attachment, psychodynamic, person-centred, play therapy and systemic thinking
- A case history to illustrate core principles of theoretical synthesis

## INTRODUCTION

The world of child counselling and psychotherapy has a tradition of warring schools of thought or 'schoolism', which took root in the earliest days of its development. 'Schoolism' is perhaps an understandable strategy to manage the uncomfortable muddle that is the human psyche and we are still a long way from having all the answers about best practice with children or adults. However, the contemporary sense of competition for increasingly limited resources perpetuates these rivalrous stances, despite limiting the creative possibilities in evolving our understanding and practice. The role of a counsellor, especially for children and young people (CYP), is to strive, with humility, to develop and broaden our creative human qualities so that we can more accurately attune to the needs of a diverse range of others. Our commitment must be to keep the dialogue alive and practice-led. It is hoped that what will emerge is an understanding of how the different schools of counselling are essentially, as Castonguay (2006) said, 'trying to make sense of the same beast'. As such, the differences can offer helpful perspectives that give fuller dimension to our understanding of ourselves as therapists, as well as our CYP clients. We will show that recent developments in the field of infant development and neuroscience go some way in helping us to integrate these different perspectives.

## HISTORY AND BACKGROUND

Practitioners have been continually integrating new concepts into existing frameworks throughout the history of psychotherapeutic work. It is, however, the legacy of 'schoolism' that many innovative clinicians and theorists have been eager to be associated with or set directly against existing historical positions. It is a recent development that clinicians have openly acknowledged finding a variety of theories from different historical lines relevant to practice and have coined the term 'integrative' practice.

What do we really mean by 'integrative' practice and how does this differ from what some might describe as 'eclectic' or 'pluralistic' practice? Eclecticism is where different tools and techniques from different schools are used without any particular regard to their philosophical underpinnings (Hollanders, 1999). A pluralistic model suggests that each client needs different interventions at different stages of their therapeutic journey (Cooper and McLeod, 2007). Integration is where diverse theoretical concepts and techniques have been synthesised together to form a new coherent theoretical position (Hollanders, 1999). Arguably, 'integrative' practice itself could be viewed as the formation of yet another 'school' of thought. The difference may be that 'integrative' practice directly pays homage to each of the historical evolutions from which it borrows.

Some research suggests that although just 42% of experienced counsellors declare themselves to be eclectic or integrative, as many as 98% make use of techniques from different theoretical orientations (Cook et al., 2010). A recent national scoping report of counselling in primary schools (Thompson, 2013) estimates that 61% of the child practitioners would call themselves integrative and that play-oriented, art and psycho-educational techniques are used by at least half of all responding individuals and organisational providers. This research implies that the reality of the work with children requires elements of theoretical and technical integration. However, it is hard to know what exactly these integrative therapists 'really do in practice'. Identifying core principles that define how theories can be woven together to connect and co-create a therapeutic relationship is the topic of this chapter.

The process of synthesising different frameworks into a coherent position presents a number of challenges to both the individual and training programmes. There are an infinite number of possible combinations of theory and the specific manner in which they are interwoven will, necessarily, be affected by the personality of the tutors, the supervisors, the practitioner and the cultural context. In support, McLeod (2004) argues that good counselling – and, by inference, training – must be authentically grounded in our own experience and values rather than a wholesale adoption of a set of skills and techniques. Being familiar with the assumptions that we bring to the work can enable us to ensure that our practice is not limited or confined by our own social or cultural constraints, yet assist us in finding an authentic presence in the work. Together, these are perhaps some of the influences that come together to define what Stern et al. (1998) refer to as the 'therapist's personal signature'.

There are a number of examples of therapists who have created integrative models for work with children. Dowling and Osborne (2003) combine the systemic family theory and traditional psychoanalytic thinking and apply them to a child in the context of home and school.

Geldard and Geldard's SPICC model (2013) generally supports the idea of a:

- person-centred approach for the therapeutic relationship;
- psychodynamic thinking for processing and surviving the complexities of the relationship;
- systemic thinking for looking at the social and cultural context of the child to locate obstacles to change and conflicts in cultural norms;
- cognitive-behavioural approaches to change behaviour and/or thinking.

These approaches see the components working together in different ways. The creative challenge for an integrative practitioner is to find and identify the underlying philosophy that will make for a 'coherent' theoretical position that is helpful in practice.

Hollanders (1999) identifies what may be another challenge to becoming an integrative practitioner, suggesting that integration is an ever-evolving process rather than a fixed position. Perhaps the challenge of becoming an integrative practitioner is ultimately a benefit in working with the 'untameable nature of clinical reality' (Castonguay, 2006). It is the integrative practitioner who has developed a capacity to manage the inevitable ambiguities, uncertainty and not knowing who can remain open to the creative potential, the ruptures and repairs, and the possibility of meeting the child in a collaboratively defined intersubjective moment.

## THEORETICAL UNDERPINNING: THEORY INTO PRACTICE

### Identifying practice-led core principles

The integrative model we are presenting views each therapeutic journey as a unique series of co-created moments. However, we have identified core factors that facilitate growth and resilience in CYP and bring about therapeutic change (Lee et al., 2009). These consist of:

- building a therapeutic relationship;
- the ongoing development of self-awareness in the counsellor and the CYP;
- engaging with children, young people and adults through the medium of play or playfulness in its broad sense.

Use of these core factors in our integrative practice has yielded positive outcomes, with 77% of primary aged children who started with severe difficulties improving according to teachers, and 82% improving according to parents in 2015/16 following their therapeutic intervention (Place2Be, 2017).

The identification of these core factors that affect change is not, however, a 'coherent theoretical position', as earlier defined. Yet it becomes clear that any relevant model for working with children and young people must address these core principles.

## A practice-led integrative model

The practice-led model of integration presented here begins with the general concept that CYP are oriented towards growth, development and forming relationships, and that the nature of these relationships will affect the development of the self. We believe that, from birth, humans are driven to form secure bonds with others and that the capacity to make and build helpful relationships is the cornerstone for sound mental health. Play, in its widest definition, is an integral language to facilitating this process of development. And finally, it is through these relationships and experiences that children develop and evolve a sense of themselves that influences their way of functioning in society.

## Transcultural challenges

An evaluation of this general theory will reveal that the underlying 'philosophical assumptions' place an emphasis on a relational-based self-understanding and identity, the importance of play, the social context of mental health, the primacy of early carer relationships and an implicit valuing of a child's experiences. Many assumptions that underpin counselling trainings, both in the content and structure, have a Euro-American cultural standpoint. For example, some cultures may place a greater emphasis on the 'we' rather than the 'I', more importance on the community or intergenerational aspects of carer relationships over the mother (Music, 2011), or privilege religious or spiritual philosophy over social context in the understanding of mental health. Music (2011) poignantly exemplifies the subtleties and power of such differences when he cites a study where mothers of two different cultures are shown videos of each other's caretaking styles, resulting in each group's cringing bewilderment at the other. Given the vastness of cultural differences, we cannot hope to achieve a fully global perspective, but perhaps, as McLeod (2004) argues, being explicit about our beliefs and values, aware of a tendency towards ethnocentricity and acknowledging the cultural limitations of our assumptions, we can remain more flexible and open to a dialogue that will aspire to greater inclusivity, open acknowledgement of difference and increased accessibility.

## Relationship, self-awareness and play: Using a developmental perspective to weave together an integrative approach

We believe that the therapist must engage their mind and their body, their whole self in the therapeutic relationship with the child. The role that we play in promoting the emotional health of the client requires a repertoire as diverse, complex and layered as that of a primary carer to an infant, translated to the boundaries and framework of the therapeutic relationship. Person-centred presence, regard and empathy for the other with the offering of relational contact and a psychodynamic understanding of the conscious and unconscious forces within therapeutic transference relationship can all help us to translate this stance in an appropriate way. This thinking is supported by recent developments in infant mental health research and neuroscience as purported by many including Daniel Stern et al. (1998), Allan Schore (2011) and Graham Music (2015). This research offers us more nuanced understanding of the role of the primary carer in co-regulating using mind and body – to make meaning and offer reciprocal moments of pleasurable connection. In turn, this leads to healthy brain development and a coherent and resilient sense of self. This understanding of the carer–infant dance can guide how we engage with clients, how we think of what we do and the way we conceptualise the ideas of what is a helpful response: head to head, heart to heart, stomach to stomach (Music, 2015).

The work of Bowlby (2005), Winnicott (1965) and Stern (1985) places importance on the capacity of the mother to emotionally attune to the infant's communications in order to help the baby manage and make sense of the chaotic array of stimulation from within and without that they are as yet unable to do themselves. Stern (1985) helps us to understand these sensory and pre-verbal aspects of communication that often happen intuitively in the good-enough carer–infant relationship. He views the good-enough mother's repertoire as offering vitality, experiences of being with another and a co-regulating other. The dance between a mother and baby is responsive to the baby's innate senses of self, which Stern referred to as the emergent self, the core self and the core self with an other. These selves are described as a newborn baby's sense of its own integrity as sensing, experiencing, continually existing beings with some awareness of and readiness to experience and engage with an other. He sees these domains of self as co-existing and forming the basis for relationship, or what he referred to as core-relatedness. It is also the foundation upon which other domains of self, for example, the intersubjective, verbal and narrative self, will later be layered (Fig. 6.1). It is important to note that these layers of self continue into adulthood and form the foundation of the whole self. As such, our pre-verbal, sensory adult selves continue to need attention and connection. Stern sees these selves as existing together like strings on a violin and views our interactions and activities as activating or attending to different selves at different times. He views it as possible to have them all vibrating in harmony, or simply one or two at a time.

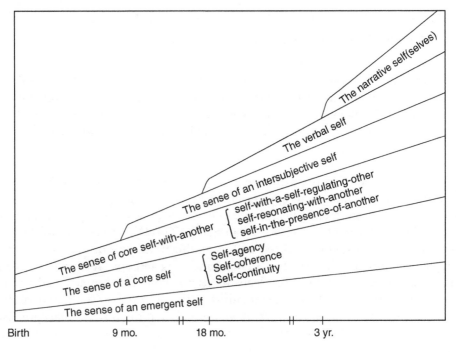

**Figure 6.1**   The interpersonal world of the infant (Stern, 1985: xxv)

The model we have presented is but one way of integrating different therapeutic understandings, theories, experiences, research and philosophies into a working model of practice, and we include it here as an illustration of integration. We continue with an illustration of how our model is applied in practice.

## Case Study: Abdi

### Background and Referral

Abdi is 10 years old. He is Somali and arrived in Britain when he was 5 years old. He lives with his mother and two older sisters. Abdi has attended a multicultural urban primary school, staffed by predominantly white British-born females, where there is a well-established Somali community. Four years had passed and the family were very recently granted leave to remain in Britain. Abdi has been referred to the school counsellor by the inclusion manager because he is often sent out of class, does not appear to have close friendships and his attainment is below expectation.

## Assessment

### *Mother*

The counsellor, John, met with Abdi's mum for an assessment and learnt the family's story. Mother described the family in Somalia, her husband and two daughters, as being secure, settled and thriving. She recounted being excited about her pregnancy with Abdi, her third child, when a sudden outbreak of war ravaged a nearby village and changed everything. Her husband had quickly organised for her and the girls to flee to a Kenyan refugee camp. He had planned to send for them when the trouble had passed, but she had never heard from him again. She confided that she had suspected he had been killed, but that as she was not sure she didn't ever talk about it to the children. The uncertainty around her husband's where-abouts and the rudimentary facilities in the refugee camp had made her depressed and unsettled in the time following Abdi's birth to their move to London. Abdi had always been very difficult and demanding and she felt he had missed out on having a man about to dis-cipline him. Things were still difficult for the family as they had only recently been given leave to stay in the UK, but she was feeling more settled and optimistic now. She explained that his two sisters were doing well at school and had good friends. She had friends and family in the area and was volunteering for a local Somali family project. She wanted Abdi to settle down at school so that he could learn and behave more respectfully at home. She worried that he might get into serious trouble when he moved to secondary school.

### *Abdi*

In the assessment session Abdi moved constantly and flitted excitedly from one activity to the next, leaving a trail of toys and mess behind him. He spoke English well, but used short, fragmented sentences. He did not make much eye contact or appear to want to talk about his life. When the counsellor gently spoke of the concerns of his teacher and mother, Abdi looked fleetingly out of the window and continued to move around. Abdi seemingly ignored the counsellor, then said that he was good at football, but that he was always treated unfairly. He said he liked coming to the lunchtime self-referral sessions because he liked playing and drawing. He was delighted to be offered more time in the playroom.

## Formulation

The counsellor thought that the dislocation, trauma and hardship of securing basic needs would have likely affected Abdi's mother's sense of self, which in turn would impact on her capacity to provide emotional attunement, playful and co-regulating experiences with her baby – perhaps, at times, leaving Abdi with a sense of overwhelming anxiety and a feeling of 'falling to pieces' (Winnicott, 1965). In light of Bowlby's (2005) attachment theory, a fundamental sense of trust and security would have been at stake in these early experiences. Abdi's domains of self and first experiences of being with and being co-regulated by an other, the very foundations for intersubjective experiences, may have thus been affected (Stern, 1985).

Taking a systemic perspective, the counsellor was also aware of how isolated Abdi was becoming by being 'sent out' of his class and football games, becoming the 'excluded' one. Culturally, his family had been uncertain of their 'right to belong' in Britain for the past 4 years. Whilst his mother and sisters were achieving and thriving, Abdi held a place within the family system of being undisciplined and reckless with his educational and social opportunities, which were deemed by his mother as very important. Abdi's mother's belief was that her son was missing a 'man to discipline him', whilst what the school was offering was counselling. There existed the potential for culturally conflicting messages between the predominantly white British female school staff and Abdi's Somali, Muslim, first-generation immigrant home culture. His presentation as the 'one who does not belong' made sense in the context of his worlds.

Abdi did have resiliencies to build on. He had made use of the self-referral lunchtime service and enjoyed the play and artwork that he had done in the room. He had used this service repeatedly, demonstrating that his internal expectations of relationships did allow for the identification of some helpful relationships and a willingness to seek them out. The counsellor decided that he would continue to work with Abdi's mum and teacher to ensure that their perspectives were honoured and that there was consistency in the adults' approach to him. He offered Abdi one-to-one weekly counselling and hoped that having his story heard would create a secure enough base from which Abdi could begin to experience the world in a less uncertain way. This would, in turn, make him less anxious in the learning setting, and more able to concentrate and maintain helpful relationships with his peers and other adults.

## Beginning the relationship

The playroom was equipped with a range of play and art materials, including a sand tray, an array of small world figures, paints, modelling material, coloured pens and pencils, and puppets. John spent the first session with Abdi drawing up a contract on paper for their work together that named the basic boundaries of safety for them both, the times and days of their sessions, and depicted the limited confidentiality that he could offer. Abdi chose to draw pictures to represent the contract but finished as quickly as he could, saying that he wanted to come for counselling so he could be captain of the football team and so he could miss numeracy. They agreed to use the time together to think about how he could get better at football and what he would need to do to become captain.

John, inspired by person-centred play therapy, offered warmth, a positive regard and empathy to Abdi. He viewed Abdi's process of development as driven by an actualising tendency and felt that if he offered the right conditions to Abdi, he could fulfil his potential.

He allowed the child to lead the play and choose what he wanted to do in the room. However, whilst a therapeutic alliance had been tentatively formed in so far as a shared goal had been agreed, forging a helpful relationship with Abdi was challenging.

John sat alongside Abdi whilst he moved from one activity to another. Abdi would use fragmented sentences to describe some goodies or baddies, but this seemed more inwardly directed. John observed Abdi carefully and noticed that they rarely made eye contact. John felt invisible, bored and found it difficult to stay focused on Abdi's play. Abdi enacted one battle after another. At the end of each story everyone died and no-one came to the rescue. John reflected aloud on the stories, offering some emotional and narrative reflection on the battles. He got no response and the battles continued on in the same manner. This persisted for a number of weeks.

## Supervision

In supervision John and the supervisor considered Abdi's apparent rejection of John's verbal reflections and John's sense of being bored, invisible and useless. The supervisor encouraged John to reflect on his bodily response to Abdi. As John reflected on this, his supervisor noticed John sinking into his seat and his shoulders slumping as he let out a big sigh and dropped his eyes to the floor, his facial expression becoming blank and flat. They discussed the possibility that John's sense of not mattering and being invisible was a projection from Abdi describing his own internal experience.

By attending to John's bodily response to Abdi, they were able to enhance their understanding of the transference, a client's internal relationship models unconsciously communicated within the therapeutic relationship. They considered John's withdrawal and disconnection, experienced both emotionally and physically, as a counter-transference response. Abdi's transference was towards a preoccupied and disconnected parent. By thinking about it together, John could integrate his thinking with his physical and emotional experience and respond to the boredom and inattentiveness in a helpful way rather than acting in the counter-transference. John realised that despite the warmth and good intention that he thought he was offering, Abdi's internalised expectations of relationships, expressed in his verbal and non-verbal communications, were pressuring John to repeat these earlier caregiver experiences. This realisation allowed John to stay alive and empathic to Abdi's vulnerability being expressed in the endless battles.

They concluded that Abdi's lack of response to verbal interventions appeared to show that Abdi was not ready for an intersubjective moment that was expressed verbally and narratively. In referring back to Stern's (1985) layered domains of self, they viewed John's rejected attempts to narrate the play in order to attune to Abdi as 'plucking the wrong string'. They felt that Abdi's non-verbal selves, particularly the core self with another, would need to be attuned to before any experiences of intersubjective meeting could happen.

## Deepening the relationship

In the following sessions John felt a deepened sense of empathy for Abdi and observed him more closely and spoke less. He empathically attuned to Abdi's taut body language and breathing and, when Abdi vigorously threw a tiger down into the sand, John spontaneously reflected the 'whatness' of the moment throwing both hands outwards with a loud sigh. Abdi looked at him wide-eyed and nodded. In that moment Abdi recognised John's expression as an accurate reflection of his own, rather than John's, emotional state. He picked up two more figures and did the same. John again responded and this continued for the rest of the session, with Abdi exploring slight variations on the narrative each time. Occasionally John ventured a cross-modal sound reflection, offering a 'hmph' or 'grrr' when it matched his movements, gently bridging the domain from Abdi's non-verbal selves to a verbal self, thereby helping Abdi to regulate his anxiety. Abdi was fully present and they experienced a 'moment of meeting' (Stern et al., 1998), a sense that an inner experience had been shared and the intersubjective field had expanded. This represented a significant step forward in their relationship. John had attuned to Abdi's pre-verbal layers of self. Like a mother in the early infant dance, he used his body, his expression, his deeply felt empathy to offer Abdi a chance for his core selves to be in the presence of, resonating with and co-regulated by another. At the next session the battle of the goodies and baddies continued – only this time an ambulance arrived to tend to the wounded. The work with Abdi was slow and painstaking. John continued to deepen the relationship and strengthen the alliance by focusing on Abdi's pre-verbal domains of self and by being consistent and holding the boundaries of the contract.

By the end of the first term Abdi had invited John to join in with his storytelling, and was using a wide variety of media to tell his stories. He would spend more time on one activity before moving onto the next. He enjoyed painting different characters and asking John to give voices and actions to them. At times, John stayed in the metaphor and expressed the experience of a character in dramatic voice or encouraged joint reflection on a situation by talking about the story from a bird's eye view. Thus began the co-creation of a more coherent narrative self through metaphorical storytelling. Abdi's use of John to fill in the narrative corresponds to the role a parent takes in co-creating a coherent narrative for a toddler. John was also aware of Abdi's still fragile sense of pre-verbal self and continued to be mindful of when this needed attention.

## Ending

As the work was coming to an end, John and Abdi were firmly venturing into Abdi's sense of verbal and narrative self. There were occasions when Abdi talked about home, Kenya or his classmates, and they wondered together about Abdi's thoughts and feelings. Abdi might still need additional support at some point in his future. John was aware that the absence of Abdi's father had only been touched upon when it had been present in the transference relationship. John felt that Abdi might one day need to make greater sense of the loss of his father and incorporate it into his narrative understanding of himself. However, John felt confident that Abdi was taking with him a different kind of 'good-enough' experience of a helping relationship and would be more likely to seek out this kind of help when he needed it.

## Behavioural change

John met with Abdi's teacher and thought about Abdi's difficulties in experiencing others as helpful in regulating his experiences. She began understand his behaviour as anxious and over-stimulated, rather than naughty. Eventually, she found that he was more receptive to her helpful interventions. She found a non-verbal co-regulating 'deep breath' or a light touch on a shoulder could be received helpfully, and slowly he became more able to engage with lessons. By the end of the year, Abdi had managed three matches in the football team without being sent off, appeared pleased with himself, and able to survive the moments of tension and excitement.

Practice-led models require us to truly engage with the children and young people who we work with and, when we do, we believe an integrative approach is inevitable. Abdi benefited from an integrative approach that made use of a developmental perspective. A brief therapy approach relies on narrative and coherent cognitive functioning, and so would not have been appropriate for Abdi because he needed time to support the foundations of his pre-verbal self. Play, music, drama, art and movement are essential tools in work with CYP because they offer a language to pre-verbal aspects of self. John's use of this integrative framework allowed him to empathically connect Abdi in both non-verbal and verbal ways in order to help him make sense of himself and his experiences.

## Key Learning

- As counsellors with CYP, it is important to attend to the whole self: mind and body, verbal and non-verbal.
- Awareness of our cultural identity and the cultural assumptions in our counselling philosophy may help us identify difference. Consequently, we can be more open to each individual's experience and our impact as practitioners.
- Integrative practice requires a coherent theoretical framework to guide our understanding, yet enough flexibility to adjust uniquely to new situations and a diverse range of CYP.
- New developments in infant mental health research and neuroscience assist us in integrating psychodynamic, developmental and humanistic perspectives on working with CYP.
- Supervision can be enhanced by reflection on the emotional and physical states of the counsellor and client to provide insight into the transference/counter-transferential relationship.

## Summary

This chapter has argued that:

- Integrative models require a sound, coherent theoretical basis within the practitioner, but are flexible and responsive to each co-created therapeutic relationship.
- The integrative practitioner's capacity to connect with children is enhanced by attending, attuning to and communicating with the verbal *and* sensory non-verbal layers of self.
- Maintaining coherence, authenticity and flexibility to co-create unique therapeutic relationships requires the integrative practitioner to have a commitment to ongoing training and self-development.
- Continuing to articulate what we do and why means that good practice can be shared and the dialogue can continue.

## Discussion Questions

1. From a systemic perspective, what might a more extensive, supporting intervention by the counsellor look like?
2. What might a follow-up intervention look like for Abdi?
3. What race, culture and age did you picture John to be?

Turn to p.444 for possible answers.

## Develop Your Skills

### Activity 1: Practice Being with Another, Focusing on the Non-Verbal 'Domains of Self'

When we have a conversation with a friend, our focus is on connecting and communicating with the other through our 'narrative' and 'verbal' selves. At times, many new child counsellors are less aware of and sensitive to both their own and others' non-verbal ways of being and communicating.

Sit with a willing other and try, without using words, to connect and attune to them. Experiment with your body positions:

- Sit side by side.
- Sit facing each other.
- One of you sit on a chair, the other on the floor.

Move closer and then further apart, monitor your physical and emotional responses to the different positions and distances, reflect together on the 'dance' between you and discuss what made you feel connected and understood, and what was uncomfortable.

- Did your perceptions differ?
- How aware were you of your partner's felt experience?

### Activity 2: Supervision Activity for Abdi

Daniel Stern's child development model suggests that both verbal and pre-verbal aspects of self need to be attended to in order for a child to thrive emotionally. This activity helps to articulate how Abdi's layers of self are being addressed.

- Choose one small world figure to represent Abdi's verbal layers of self and another to represent Abdi's pre-verbal layers of self. Think about which object or figure you choose for each and where they are placed in relation to each other.
- How might these figures relate to each other, what might they say to or need from each other? Would another constellation of figures be more helpful to Abdi's well-being? What would need to change?

## Further Reading

Alvarez, A. (2012) *The Thinking Heart: Three Levels of Psychoanalytic Therapy with Disturbed Children*. London: Routledge.

Recommended to begin to conceptualise different levels of intervening in the therapeutic work with children, which we believe bridges very well with Stern's different layers of self.

Boston Process of Change Study Group (BPCSG) (2010) *Change in Psychotherapy – A Unifying Paradigm*. New York: W.W. Norton & Company.

An influential book that details the findings of the BPCSG and translates the nuances of the carer–infant dyad into a therapeutic frame.

Geddes, H. (2005) *Attachment in the Classroom*. London: Worth Publishing.

Recommended to build an understanding of how attachment patterns in children affect their classroom behaviours and approaches to learning.

Kegerreis, S. (2010) *Psychodynamic Counselling with Children and Young People: An Introduction*. London: Palgrave.

*(Continued)*

(Continued)

A good introduction to the dynamics of the counselling relationship and understanding transference and counter-transference.

Landreth, G. (2002) *Play Therapy: The Art of the Relationship*. New York: Brunner-Routledge.

An overview of a person-centred approach to play therapy.

Lanyado, M. (2004) *The Presence of the Therapist: Treating Childhood Trauma*. Hove: Routledge.

A sensitively written book that acknowledges our 'presence' as therapists and as an individual person and how who we are affects the work in the room. This book uses descriptions of powerful case material to illustrate this.

Music, G. (2011) *Nurturing Natures*. Hove and New York: Taylor & Francis Group Psychology Press.

A compelling and accessible book that examines child development in a cultural as well as neuroscientific context.

Wilson, P. (2004) *Young Minds in our Schools: A Guide for Teachers and Others Working in Schools*. London: YoungMinds.

A guide for school staff describing how children may bring their life experiences into the school in their behaviour and interactions.

### Online Resources

BACP website: www.bacp.co.uk, especially the BACP Children and Young People Division and the Competences for Working with Children and Young People

Counselling MindEd: https://www.minded.org.uk

Counselling in Schools

Counselling in Primary Schools

Counselling in Universities and Colleges

## REFERENCES

Bowlby, J. (2005) *A Secure Base*. Abingdon: Routledge Classics.

Castonguay, L. (2006) Personal pathways in psychotherapy integration. *Journal of Psychotherapy Integration* 16(1): 36–58.

Cook, J., Biyanova, T., Elhai, J. Schnurr, P. and Cones, J. (2010) What do psychotherapists really do in practice? An internet study of over 2000 practitioners. *Psychotherapy Theory, Research, Practice and Training* 47(2): 260–267.

Cooper, M. and McCleod, J. (2007) A pluralistic framework for counselling and psychotherapy: implications for research. *Counselling and Psychotherapy Research 7*(3): 135–143.

Dowling, E. and Osborne, E. (2003) *The Family and the School: A Joint Systems Approach to Problems with Children*. London: Routledge.

Geldard, K. and Geldard, D. (2013) *Counselling Children: A Practical Introduction*, 4th edn. London: SAGE.

Hollanders, H. (1999) Eclecticism and integration in counselling: implications for training. *British Journal of Guidance and Counselling 27*(4): 483–500.

Lee, R., Tiley, C. and White, J. (2009) The Place2Be: measuring the effectiveness of a primary school-based therapeutic intervention in England and Scotland. *Counselling and Psychotherapy Research 9*(3): 151–159.

McLeod, J. (2004) *The Counsellor's Workbook: Developing a Personal Approach*. Maidenhead: Open University Press.

Music, G. (2011) *Nurturing Natures*. Hove and New York: Taylor Francis Group Psychology Press.

Music, G. (2015) Bringing up the bodies: psyche-soma, body awareness and feeling at ease. *British Journal of Psychotherapy 31*(1): 4–19.

Place2Be (2017) *Impact and evidence*. Available at: https://www.place2be.org.uk/impact-evidence (accessed 6 February 2018).

Schore, A. (2011) The right brain implicit self lies at the core of psychoanalysis. *Psychoanalytic Dialogues 21*, 75–100.

Stern, D. (1985) *The Interpersonal World of the Infant*. New York: Basic Books.

Stern, D.N., Sander, L.W., Nahum, J.P., Harrison, A.M., Lyons-Ruth, K., Morgan, A.C., Bruschweilerstern, N. and Tronick, E.Z. (1998) Non-interpretive mechanisms in psychoanalytic therapy: the 'something more' than interpretation. *International Journal of Psycho-Analysis 79*: 903–921.

Thompson, M. (2013) *School-based counselling in UK primary schools*. BACP: Lutterworth

Winnicott, D. (1965) *Maturational Processes and the Facilitating Environment*. London: Hogarth Press Ltd.

# 7

# PLAY THERAPY

## LISA GORDON CLARK

**This chapter will discuss:**

- A definition of play therapy, its historical development, theoretical underpinnings and evidence base including that from a neurobiological perspective
- A continuum of play types and of therapeutic approaches from non-directive to directive
- Clinical applications and considerations when setting up a play therapy intervention
- A case study to illustrate a fairly typical play therapy process

## INTRODUCTION: WHAT IS PLAY THERAPY?

Play therapy is an increasingly recognised, reputed and respected therapeutic approach with children and young people. In 1996 The British Association of Play Therapists adopted the following definition of play therapy:

> Play Therapy is the dynamic process between child and play therapist in which the child explores at his or her own pace and with his or her own agenda those issues, past and current, conscious and unconscious, that are affecting the child's life in the present. The child's inner resources are enabled by the therapeutic alliance to bring about growth and change. Play Therapy is child-centred, in which play is the primary medium and speech is the secondary medium.

> Play Therapy encompasses many approaches but the foundation of all approaches is child-centred. (www.bapt.info/aboutbapt.htm)

Whilst there is a spectrum of approaches in current play therapy practice, all share the understanding that play is the natural, instinctive means through which all children learn, communicate and explore their worlds and gain a sense of identity. Play is universal and vital to every child's social, emotional, cognitive, physical, creative and language development. It is generally held that conventional talking therapies are inappropriate for young children, who struggle to find the words to describe complex feelings. Rather than having to explain what is troubling them, as adult therapy and more cognitive approaches usually expect, in play therapy children use play to communicate at their own level and pace, without feeling pressurised or interrogated. The symbolic distance of play enables children to express their feelings, thoughts and beliefs surrounding difficult life experiences. These experiences are explored and made sense of through the dynamic interaction between the child and the play therapist.

Play therapy utilises metaphors inherent in children's play, art and narratives; therefore, it feels less threatening for a young person than the expectation that they explain, describe or depict factual reality. This symbolism has been termed 'aesthetic distance' and is critical for the safety of the abused child (Cattanach, 1997). Play therapy is not a quest to elicit some objective factual truth – 'what really happened'; rather, the play therapist works with the subjective meanings that the child has made of their experiences and the feelings generated – meanings and feelings that are made manifest in their play and responded to by the therapist in the same metaphorical mode. 'The therapist acknowledges that the child has had life events which might need some sorting and the play will not be to talk about these experiences but to make up stories in which the characters might have had the same things happen to them as have happened to the child' (Cattanach, 1997: 11).

The plots, themes and storylines the child creates may indeed have links to real-world experiences, but the play therapist will not interpret back to the child along the lines of: 'I see – what you really meant in that story was that the dragon is your stepfather and you are like that hedgehog', but will instead work safely and playfully with the metaphors the child has chosen. For example, 'That tiny hedgehog is so scared of that huge dragon when he roars fire! He has to curl up in a little ball to try and make sure the dragon won't see him. I wonder if he hopes that might keep him safe?', etc. The child is thus enabled to explore feelings and experiences, make sense of them and cope better thereafter, without it ever being made explicit that the story is 'really' about them and their lives. Indeed, a critical assumption for play therapy is that therapeutic change may occur without a conscious awareness of the association between the life experiences that relate to the child's difficulties and the symbolic manner in which these are expressed.

Since play therapy uses the child's natural 'language' – play – the level of sophistication of this language will reflect the child's age and developmental stage. A typical play therapy session with a 3-year-old will inevitably be rather different from that with a 13-year-old – although the teenager may very well need to regress back to missed earlier play experiences, so there may also be many similarities! Jennings (1994) proposed a continuum along which children's play may be described: the earliest type of play (both in normal childhood development and as featuring in a play therapy session) is 'embodiment play', whereby the child explores the world through their senses and in which their own physical being is central. Sensory or embodiment play allows the child literally to 'get in touch with' their physical selves, to differentiate what is 'me' and 'not me', to get a sense of what they like and dislike at the sensory level as a prerequisite to being able to understand and express their emotional feelings. Sensory play taps into primitive parts of the brain accessing pre-verbal experiences. Many children who come to play therapy have not had adequate embodiment play opportunities and the chance to indulge in regressive sensory play: running their hands through wet sand, poking holes in soft clay, exploring the 'puerile' delight of slime and fart putty can be liberating and cathartic, and provide an awareness of the bodily self perhaps hitherto suppressed or undeveloped.

The next stage on Jennings' continuum is that of projective play – when objects (the toys or play materials) and images take on metaphorical significance as the child projects meaning onto them. A simple stick can be a sword, a magic wand or a fishing rod, and symbolic potential is limited only by the child's imagination. In projective play the child makes use of objects other than their own bodies to externalise their inner worlds. This symbolic play often develops into story-making in which significant narratives are created or co-created that allow a child's inner thoughts and feelings to be safely expressed and contained, heard and healed.

Finally, in role-play, the last stage on Jennings' continuum, the child – and often the therapist too, at the child's invitation – assumes roles within dramatisations that may also be metaphorically rich. In dramatic play the child takes on roles in stories usually through improvisation, and may involve the play therapist in the scene. Dramatic role-play gives permission to do things that in everyday life would not be permissible or 'socially acceptable'.

Elements of all three play types may well feature in a typical play therapy case: the young person may feel more comfortable in one play mode but it is likely that there will be movement back and forth along the continuum as the intervention progresses.

## PLAY THERAPY: HISTORY, BACKGROUND AND CONTEXT

The use of play in therapy was pioneered in the field of child psychotherapy in the early 20th century. Anna Freud (1928) and Melanie Klein (1932) were among those who proposed a theoretical premise for the use of play. Freud used play to maximise the child's ability to form a 'therapeutic alliance' with the therapist, introducing games, toys and magic tricks to interest the child patient in the therapy and in the therapist. Klein claimed that a child's spontaneous play was a direct substitute for the free association used within adult psychoanalysis. These child psychotherapy traditions share the common central proposition that play communicates the child's unconscious experiences, desires, thoughts and emotions. However, it could be argued that such early analytical approaches used the medium of play to indicate the source of the problem, rather than viewing play as a curative or healing factor itself.

Whilst play therapy emerged from these elements of child psychotherapy, its specific theoretical foundation owes much to the work of Carl Rogers (1951), who established a new model of psychotherapy – client-centred therapy (later termed person-centred therapy), a humanistic psychology tradition born out of a protest against the diagnostic, prescriptive perspectives of his time. Rogers emphasised a relationship between therapist and client based upon genuineness, acceptance (or unconditional positive regard) and trust (see Chapter 2 for further details).

Influenced by this person-centred approach, Virginia Axline (1989; 1990) developed a new and succinct therapeutic approach for working with children – non-directive play therapy (NDPT). Like client-centred counselling, NDPT holds a central hypothesis of the individual's innate capacity for growth and self-direction and a belief in the child as the chief agent in their own therapy. Axline's eight principles, which emphasise the core importance of a warm, accepting relationship, underpin the work of most play therapists today.

American play therapists such as Moustakas (1953), Schaefer (1979) and Landreth (2012) progressed Axline's formulations and devised differing models, integrating elements of systemic family therapy, narrative therapy, solution-focused therapy and cognitive-behavioural therapy. One of the most significant developments has been an increasing emphasis on the role of the environment in the formation of children's personality and mental/emotional health and, pivotal within this, the role of attachment.

Recent advances in neuroscience have also informed the theoretical and clinical development of play therapy: the more that is understood about how early experiences shape and impact on brain structures and neural functioning, the better play therapists are able to comprehend resulting behaviour and to demonstrate the importance and efficacy of early interventions. Of particular fascination to play therapists practising today are enhanced insights into the neuropsychology of attachment and trauma such as Perry's (2001) findings that children raised in environments characterised by domestic violence, physical abuse or other persistent traumas develop an overly active midbrain/brainstem, resulting in an over-reactive stress response and predisposition to impulsiveness and aggression. Equally it has been shown that an infant who grows up surrounded by traumatic unpredictability will inevitably develop neural systems and functional capabilities which reflect that disorganisation. Such evidence confirms that therapy must do more than talk if the child is in a persistent hyperarousal state, for the child's brain may well be unresponsive to verbal interactions that rely on more sophisticated cortical functioning. In order to heal a 'damaged' brain, interventions must activate those portions of the brain that have been impacted. Furthermore, brain research (e.g. Siegel, 2012) confirms that the core therapeutic aspects that alter neuronal function and brain structure are experience and relationship – core elements emphasised in all models of play therapy. Accordingly, a child who comes from a deprived early experience will benefit from attachment-based play therapy that offers the experience of caring, attuned interaction, comparable to that of a responsive primary caregiver. This new caring experience calms the limbic area of the brain and helps to create new neural pathways that lead to building a healthy attachment relationship.

## The where, when and with whom of play therapy

Many qualified play therapists work on a freelance basis, but play therapy is now increasingly available in clinical and statutory settings in the UK, for example, within Child and Adolescent Mental Health Services (CAMHS), bereavement organisations, 'looked-after children' teams of social services departments and in the voluntary sector. There has been a growth in charitable organisations offering packages of play therapy to clusters of local authority schools as well as in the use of governmental Pupil Premium funding for 'disadvantaged' pupils, on social and emotional learning (SEL) interventions, which have been shown to have an identifiable and significant impact on attitudes to learning, social relationships in school and attainment itself (Education Endowment Foundation, 2017). Even if not school-funded it is nevertheless common for a play therapist to work with a child on school premises, predominantly within the primary school age range, but also in secondary school settings – particularly, perhaps, emotional and behavioural difficulties (EBD) schools or in specialised units within mainstream schools. Play therapists generally work with individual children, but some have experience of working with groups and with siblings.

One of play therapy's strengths is its universality: the approach can be adapted to suit different developmental levels and is appropriate for children of all ages, and those from different cultures, genders and abilities. A study by Shen (2016) of US-based school counsellors found that students of most ethnic groups, those with special needs, and of both genders tended to be more responsive to play therapy than talk therapy alone. As Thomas (2016) points out: 'The universal and cross-cultural approach of child-centred play therapy [transcends] most barriers to knowledge and understanding' (2016: 52). Preparing an intentionally welcoming and inclusive play therapy environment requires knowledge of both the needs of the individual and the various systems in which he or she is embedded. Gil and Pfeifer (2015) note that recognising, addressing, and celebrating diversity should be considered essential elements of all children's play therapy regardless of the reason for the referral.

Play therapy is an effective intervention for children with a variety of presenting problems and childhood difficulties (Bratton et al., 2005; BAPT, 2009; Bratton, 2010). These include children:

- who have been abused: physically, sexually or emotionally;
- who have experienced loss through bereavement, family breakdown or separation from culture of origin;
- who are terminally ill or disabled, or who cope with carers or siblings with disabilities or illness;
- who have witnessed violence or the abuse of substances;
- who are displaying behaviour that is regarded as a problem by those who care for them – they may be difficult to control, withdrawn or not reaching their potential;
- who externalise their difficulties with antisocial, aggressive, bullying behaviours;
- who internalise their problems – the often-overlooked victims, prone to low self-esteem, anxiety, depression or self-harm.

LeBlanc and Ritchie (2001) conducted a meta-analysis of 42 research studies of play therapy which demonstrated that it is also a viable intervention for children with various additional emotional and physical needs. Further evidence has demonstrated play therapy is effective in a number of areas, including: prevention programmes (medical); conduct disorder; oppositional/defiant disorders; social skills problems; sexual behaviour problems; attachment disorders; children in divorce; attention deficit hyperactivity disorder (ADHD); and with autistic spectrum disorders (ASDs). Whatever the presenting difficulties, it is essential to ensure that a child is currently safe enough for the therapy to commence. Although this is sometimes a grey area, as a rule of thumb play therapy should be considered a 'post-change intervention', for children who have experienced problems in their past circumstances but are now in a safer and more stable environment where they can work through their unresolved worries, fears and hurts.

## PLAY THERAPY THEORY AND APPLICATION TO PRACTICE

The format of exploration of the child's difficulties is determined by a variety of factors, including the child's needs, the therapist's theoretical perspective and their work setting. Most play therapists adhere to child-centred principles in that the child is given significant choices about how to use the time and the play materials, but there is a continuum from pure non-directive approaches to more focused techniques.

Non-directive play therapists abide by the humanistic principles prescribed by Axline (1989) and emphasise the child's ability to choose those materials that make most sense to them, and to utilise the play experience and therapeutic relationship in their own way and in their own time: the child is in control of the process and directs the agenda, focus and timing. The non-directive play therapist follows the child's lead, verbally tracking what they are doing, acknowledging non-judgementally the choices they make and voicing ongoing empathic reflections of the feelings they convey. A core aim of the non-directive play therapist is simply to 'be with' the child (Landreth, 2012) and to provide the optimum conditions that allow the child to develop their inherent potential.

Some play therapists take a more directive approach, using focused techniques with defined goals in which it is the therapist who formulates the agenda, with greater emphasis on 'doing' than 'being'. Therapist-directed interventions influenced by structured approaches such as cognitive-behavioural therapy, have specific aims such as helping bereaved children to explore grief and loss, or aggressive young people to manage their anger.

In the middle of this continuum fall play therapists who follow a more eclectic or collaborative approach, utilising both non-directive and directive methods, allowing the child and therapist equal power to direct the agenda, focus and timing of the play therapy. Cattanach (1997), for example, advocated storytelling techniques in the co-creation or 'co-construction' of a narrative of the child's experiences that evolves in the interaction between therapist and child.

Central to all play therapy approaches, however, is the relationship between therapist and child. The development of a constructive, trusting therapeutic relationship is a vital component of the play therapy process.

In any play therapy intervention, the efficacy and legacy of the work with the child client will depend greatly on liaison with parents/carers and on important inter-professional communication. A child does not exist in isolation – the family and social systems in which they live and function can compound or perpetuate their difficulties, and if significant adults in the child's life are supportive of the play therapy, the child is more likely to engage. The work has a better prognosis when there is a sense of team commitment. Most play therapists will therefore meet with key adults such as parents, teachers, social workers and learning mentors to gather a thorough understanding of the child's background and needs from their varied perspectives before commencing therapy, and will maintain this relationship via regular review meetings throughout the intervention. Whilst adherence to client confidentiality is imperative, insights can be shared and advice given that can help to shift others' perspectives too and extend the benefits. The potential impact of a play therapy intervention is greatly enhanced if there is ongoing constructive liaison with 'the team around the child' and multi-agency working is therefore regarded as best clinical practice.

## THE PLAY THERAPY APPROACH

Play therapists will commence their intervention with a careful assessment, building up a comprehensive profile of the child, their early history, family background and the nature of the difficulties as perceived by others as well as by the child themselves. In addition to building up a positive working relationship from the outset by meeting with parents/carers, the play therapist may require several referral meetings with other professionals such as school staff and social workers, and ask for access to reports and existing assessments before actually introducing herself to the child. This assessment process, which begins at referral, does not stop once the clinical work begins but is ongoing, with speculations and hypotheses remaining open to re-evaluation as the therapeutic relationship develops.

Wherever the work is located it is crucial that the room where the therapeutic work takes place is private and free of interruptions. It need not be large or have any existing equipment – peripatetic play therapists will usually bring their own play materials. Some will also bring a mat as a wipeable playing surface, which both minimises the impact of any mess and defines the therapeutic space, differentiating it from the room as it is normally used. Access to a sink is an advantage, especially when several children are seen in succession.

The selection of toys and play materials should facilitate children's expression by providing a wide range of play activities at their developmental level. These may include:

* *Toys for sensory/embodiment play:* A sand tray (and water), clay, playdough, slimes, putties, bubbles, assorted stretchy and tactile balls, etc.

- *Toys for projected/symbolic play:* A dolls' house, miniature human figures (various ages and ethnicities), hero and monster figures, toy soldiers, cars and other vehicles, animal families, miniatures of current popular film and TV characters (it is important to keep abreast of trends), etc.
- *Real-life toys for role-play:* Dressing-up clothes, realistic dolls and baby accessories, puppets, masks, pretend food, toy 'weaponry', play mobile phones, doctor's kit, etc.
- *Toys for creative expression:* Paper, paints, finger-paints, felt-tip pens, crayons, chalk, collage materials, glues, scissors and sticky tape, percussion musical instruments, etc.

These lists are not exhaustive and the range of equipment may be conditional on storage/transportation factors.

The security of a predictable, consistent time for the play therapy session aids the development of therapeutic trust. If working in a school it is also imperative that all appropriate members of school staff are apprised of the nature of the work and understand that attendance at play therapy is not conditional on good behaviour. The misconception that play therapy is a treat and that when a child has misbehaved in class they do not 'deserve' to have this 'reward' can be hugely counterproductive.

Once initial assessments have been undertaken and practical logistics organised, the play therapist will meet the child for the first time. Depending on the context of the referral, and on the young person's age and level of cognitive understanding, it may be supportive for a key adult to be present at this first meeting. It is critical that the child knows why they are there, so some discussion about the reason for play therapy needs to be addressed at an age-appropriate level. It is important to emphasise that the referral has not been made because the young person is 'in trouble' – if it is perceived as a punishment then the intervention is tarnished from the outset. Naturally the request for play therapy may be linked to a prevalence of 'unacceptable behaviour' in school or at home, but the play therapist will need to stress that the therapeutic support is to help the child with the feelings that underlie the behaviour. To reduce the negative perception that the referral is to meet an adult behaviour modification agenda, it is helpful to get a sense from the young person themselves of what they hope for from the therapeutic support.

Early sessions may well involve some limit-challenging as the child tests out the boundaries that the play therapist has outlined. Equally, many young clients are sceptical about the confidential nature of the therapy, and this is another aspect of the play therapist's credibility and trustworthiness that may be questioned and challenged. A young person whose previous relationships with adults have been characterised by negativity, abuse, inconsistency or punitive criticism may expect the same from all relationships, so establishing and consolidating therapeutic trust may take several weeks.

The expectation for child-centred play therapy is that, through the play therapist's consistent, empathic acceptance and respectful reflections, the young person will develop *self*-respect and *self*-acceptance, and that improved self-esteem and capacity for self-regulation will generalise to outside the play therapy space. Ongoing liaison with key adults in the child's life will help determine when the therapeutic goals have been met sufficiently to close the work. Endings must be carefully planned: many young people will have experienced these as traumatically abrupt in the past, so preparation for the end of play therapy must be sensitively managed. The efficacy of the play therapy intervention can be ascertained by qualitative or quantitative outcome measures, and reports provided. The requirement for brief working tends to be more budget-driven and thus more goal-oriented and the pressure to prove efficacy is increasingly acute in such contexts.

## Case Study: Elijah

Elijah was 10 years old at referral. Concerns from infancy about his speech and language development had led to a Statement of Special Educational Needs, which ensured ongoing in-class learning support. He struggled to make sense of lessons, did not cooperate with teachers and found social situations, for example, playtime, difficult to manage. His emotional well-being was connected to contexts that he found challenging to interpret: his responses could appear impulsive and unpredictable so that interactions with peers often escalated to conflict. He would sometimes express his frustration in screaming and lashing out and often labelled himself negatively: 'I'm really bad'. Elijah's mother told me he occasionally 'zoned out' when overwhelmed and that he had obsessive 'specialist interests' – then predominantly basketball. Whilst there had been no formal diagnosis, there was an unvoiced implication in these behaviour patterns that Elijah might be on the autistic spectrum and there was heightened concern about his impending transition to secondary school. Play therapy was introduced with the aim of increasing emotional stability and coping strategies, and thus decreasing inappropriate behaviour. It was envisaged that it would also improve understanding of self and others (especially around feelings and the link to behaviour), thus building empathy, and would strengthen his self-esteem.

At the introductory meeting in the presence of his mother and the special educational needs coordinator (SENCO), Elijah was initially subdued and chose to lie on the floor rather than sit on a chair – I joined him there, which immediately helped put him at ease. He listened attentively whilst I explained the reasons for play therapy. He was particularly fascinated by the sensory materials and spontaneously involved us by showing his discoveries. I drew attention to his reactions, and to those of his mother and teacher where these might differ from his own: he was able to guess that Mummy would think the slime was 'disgusting' whereas he was enthralled by it, suggestive of an unexpected potential capacity for empathy.

In the first session alone with me, Elijah asked many interested questions in an evident bid to build a relationship. He also showed a surprising facility for dramatised role-play: playdough became a delicious pizza, which he invited me to share. Whilst we carefully clarified that this was all pretend – 'Don't eat it for real!' – Elijah's ability to initiate and sustain an imaginative mime required an awareness of 'other ways of being' and an understanding of non-literal meaning, which ran counter to the suspected ASD label.

As the intervention progressed Elijah blossomed. Whilst obviously hampered by language-processing difficulties, he seemed desperately needy to engage with other people, greeting me each week with garrulous enthusiasm. He soon began drawing, and the metaphors in his prolific and skilful cartoons of basketball players in action provided rich therapeutic material. Themes of competition and rivalry, of fairness and unfairness, of triumph and failure, of pride and shame/despair were all vividly symbolised in his basketball imagery. Later the drawings broadened out to enactments of imaginative scenes – he role-played post-match interviewers, jubilant winners and despairing losers, describing their supposed emotions in powerful language. He was even able to understand the inherently contradictory concept of sarcasm, which had been the trigger of many a playground dispute in the past.

After six sessions, teachers reported that Elijah had started to behave more like his peers and that he was better at completing educational tasks. Towards the end of the second term there were no further incidents of being sent 'on referral' and he had been able to stay calm throughout his Year 6 Standard Assessment Tests (SATs).

The focus of my work shifted towards preparing Elijah for the move to secondary school – having been at the same school since nursery, this was a major transition so a specially devised statement included the provision of ongoing play therapy in the new educational context. Written reports and advance liaison with the new school facilitated this.

As the end of his primary schooling loomed, Elijah's mixed feelings of excitement and fear were expressed in metaphors of basketball players preparing to transfer to different teams for the new season: what would their new coach and team-mates be like? Would they like the huge training facilities? Elijah's basketball players conceded that their feelings might change as they familiarised themselves with the new environment. By addressing this apprehension and ambivalence within the safety of play therapy, Elijah coped with it in reality – in the event, the loss of all his primary school friends and surroundings was not as traumatic as many had anticipated.

After one term at secondary school, feedback was so positive that just five further fortnightly sessions were scheduled. At the final review the SENCO reported: 'We are pleased with his progress. Elijah is a popular member of the class and staff report he is pleasant and attempts work set. He interacts appropriately with his peers and has a good sense of humour. He is functioning well and has had no detentions.' Elijah's mother was grateful: play therapy had helped her son understand his own and others' feelings and had enhanced his self-esteem. My empathic reflections, unconditional acceptance and playful, empowering child-led approach were held to have been key mechanisms of change. Play therapy also highlighted the potential for Elijah to develop further in his social competence than early assessments had implied and thus facilitated his adjustment into secondary school life.

# Key Learning

- The symbolic distance of play, children's natural language of communication, enables them to express their feelings, thoughts and beliefs about difficult life experiences in a non-threatening way and at their own pace.

*(Continued)*

(Continued)

- Central to all play therapy approaches is an empathic, trusting and non-judgemental relationship between therapist and child.
- Types of play may be perceived along a continuum from sensory or embodiment play, through projective play to role-play, and various resources can facilitate each type.
- Play therapists view children as embedded within a system – the efficacy and legacy of the work with the child client will depend greatly on engaging constructively with parents/carers and on important inter-professional liaison.
- Clear and consistent boundaries and adherence to appropriate limits aid the development of therapeutic trust.

## Summary

- This chapter has summarised the historical development of play therapy tracing its theoretical underpinnings and evidence base.
- A continuum of play therapy approaches was described, from non-directive to therapist-directed, stressing that in all a trusting therapeutic relationship is as crucial as the play itself, as are appropriate recognition and involvement of the wider system in which the child lives.
- Some practicalities of setting up a play therapy intervention were outlined, including the environment and selection of appropriate resources.
- A detailed case study, based on real client material (anonymised to protect client identity), illustrated a fairly typical process and progress of a young person receiving play therapy in school, bridging the transition from primary to secondary education.

## Discussion Questions

1. Non-directive play therapists need to be unconditionally accepting of the young person – why do you think this is important and what obstacles might there be to you in achieving this non-judgemental attitude?
2. Whilst play therapy is relatively free of 'rules', there are certain boundaries that do need to be in place – what is the justification for this and what limits might you establish?
3. What long-term value do you think there may be in messy play and in role-play?

   Turn to p.445 for possible answers.

## Develop Your Skills

1. Think back to your own earliest play memories: what do you recall that was especially pleasurable or significant in your childhood play experiences? Consider the type of play you remember most fondly – was it messy or orderly? Creative/imaginative or structured and rule-bound? Solitary or with peers/siblings or in a team? Contemplate how this play has influenced how you behave as an adult.
2. Rediscover your 'inner child' and nurture your own playfulness: inspired by activity 1, do something playful or creative that you have not made time to enjoy for too long. It is important that play therapists are comfortable with all types of play so maybe also try something new – and relish the excuse to get messy!
3. Practise your tracking skills: watch a television programme with the sound muted and give a running commentary of the key action you see. Label the emotions you can perceive in the facial expressions and body language of the actors.
4. Go to a charity shop or car boot sale and build up your collection of small toys and play resources: other people's discarded 'junk' can be a play therapist's treasure trove!

## Further Reading

The following core texts elaborate on some of the theoretical underpinnings to play therapy outlined in the sections above and will enhance and deepen understanding of this clinical approach and the contexts in which it is practised.

Axline, V.M. (1990) *Dibs in Search of Self: Personality Development in Play Therapy*. London: Penguin Books.

Cattanach, A. (2003) *Introduction to Play Therapy*. Hove: Brunner-Routledge.

Cochran, N.H., Nordling, W.J. and Cochran, J.L. (2010) *Child-Centred Play Therapy: A Practical Guide to Developing Therapeutic Relationships with Children*. New York: John Wiley & Sons.

Crenshaw, D.A. and Stewart, A.L. (eds) (2015) *Play Therapy: A Comprehensive Guide to Theory and Practice*. New York: The Guilford Press.

McMahon, L. (2009) *The Handbook of Play Therapy and Therapeutic Play*, 2nd edn. Abingdon: Routledge.

Schaefer, C.E., O'Connor, K.J. and Braverman, L.D. (eds) (2016) *Handbook of Play Therapy*, 2nd edn. New York: John Wiley & Sons.

*(Continued)*

---

(Continued)

Van Fleet, R., Sywulak, A.E. and Sniscak, C.C. (2010) *Child Centered Play Therapy*. New York: Guilford Press.

West, J. (1996) *Child Centred Play Therapy*, 2nd edn. London: Arnold.

Wilson, K., Kendrick, P. and Ryan, V. (2001) *Play Therapy: A Non-Directive Approach for Children and Adolescents*. London: Bailliere Tindall.

### Online Resources

BACP website: www.bacp.co.uk, especially the BACP Children and Young People Division and the Competences for Working with Children and Young People

British Association of Play Therapists (BAPT) (2006) *Ethical Basis for Good Practice in Play Therapy*. Weybridge: BAPT. Available at: http://www.bapt.info/play-therapy/ethical-basis-good-practice-play-therapy/

British Association of Play Therapists (BAPT) *Play Therapy in Action*. Available at: http://www.bapt.info/play-therapy/training-dvd/ This is a 3-minute clip of play therapy and the page has links that will enable you to order the whole DVD, more than 2 hours in length

Counselling MindEd: https://www.minded.org.uk

Introducing Creative and Symbolic Methods, session reference: 412-034

The Range of Creative and Symbolic Methods, session reference: 412-035

Creative Methods in Action: Client Study, session reference: 412-036

---

# REFERENCES

Axline, V.M. (1989) *Play Therapy*, 2nd edn. Edinburgh: Churchill Livingstone. (1st edn 1947)

Axline, V.M. (1990) *Dibs in Search of Self: Personality Development in Play Therapy*. London: Penguin Books.

British Association of Play Therapists (BAPT) (2009) *Play Therapy – Its Relevance to 21st Century Needs of Children, Young People and Families*. Available at: http://www.bapt.info/resources-research/research/ (accessed 7 February 2018).

Bratton, S. (2010) Meeting the early mental health needs of children through school-based play therapy: a review of outcome research. In: Drewes, A.A. and Schaefer, C.E. (eds), *School-Based Play Therapy*. 2nd edn. Hoboken, NJ: Wiley, pp. 17–58.

Bratton, S., Ray, D., Rhine, T. and Jones, L. (2005) The efficacy of play therapy with children: a meta-analytic review of the outcome research. *Professional Psychology: Research and Practice 36*(4): 376–390.

Cattanach, A. (1997) *Children's Stories in Play Therapy*. London: Jessica Kingsley.

Education Endowment Foundation (2017) *Social and Emotional Learning*. (www.educa tionendowmentfoundation.org.uk/resources/teaching-learning-toolkit/social-and-emotional-learning).

Freud, A. (1928) *Introduction to the Technique of Child Analysis*. Clark, L.P., translator. New York: Nervous and Mental Disease Publishing.

Gil, E., and Pfeifer, L. (2015) Issues of culture and diversity in play therapy. In: O'Connor, K.J., Schaefer, C.E. and Braverman, L.D. (eds), *Handbook of Play Therapy*. Hoboken, NJ: John Wiley & Sons, Inc. pp. 599–612.

Jennings, S. (1994) *Introduction to Developmental Play Therapy*. London: Jessica Kingsley.

Klein, M. (1932) *The Psycho-Analysis of Children*. London: Hogarth Press.

Landreth, G.L. (2012) *Play Therapy: The Art of the Relationship*, 3rd edn. New York: Brunner-Routledge (1st edn, 1991).

LeBlanc, M. and Ritchie, M. (2001) A meta-analysis of play therapy outcomes. *Counselling Psychology Quarterly 12*(2): 149–163.

Moustakas, C. (1953) *Children in Play Therapy: A Key to Understanding Normal and Disturbed Emotions*. New York: McGraw-Hill.

Perry, B.D. (2001) The neuro-developmental impact of violence in childhood. In: Schetky, D. and Benedek, E. (eds) *Textbook of Child and Adolescent Forensic Psychiatry*. Washington, D.C.: American Psychiatric Press, pp. 221–238.

Rogers, C.R. (1951) *Client-Centred Therapy: Its Current Practice, Implications and Theory*. London: Constable.

Schaefer, C.E. (ed.) (1979) *The Therapeutic Use of Child's Play*. New York: Aronson.

Shen, Y.-J. (2016) A descriptive study of school counselors' play therapy experiences with the culturally diverse. *International Journal of Play Therapy 25*(2): 54–63.

Siegel, D.J. (2012) *The Developing Mind: How Relationships and the Brain Interact to Shape Who We Are*, 2nd edn. New York: Guilford Press.

Thomas, G. (2016) Bridging the cultural divide. In: Le Vay, D. and Cuschieri, E. (eds) *Challenges in the Theory and Practice of Play Therapy*. London: Routledge, pp. 52–70.

# 8

# OTHER CREATIVE APPROACHES

## BARBARA SMITH, KAYE RICHARDS, KAREN LOWE AND PETER LOWE

**This chapter will discuss:**

- A number of creative approaches used in counselling and psychotherapy, many of which have long-standing traditions and are underpinned by a wide range of theoretical perspectives
- An insight into alternative ways of engaging children and young people with the integrated use of creativity. This will draw upon the experience of the authors, who use a range of modalities (person-centred, transactional analysis and cognitive-behavioural therapy) and creative approaches (drama, sand-play, outdoor adventure, clay-work, music, etc.)
- Case study material to illustrate creative working in action, to serve as a reminder that sometimes talking alone isn't always enough

This chapter explores the practical matter of helping children and young people to open up through a variety of creative and 'alternative' methods, some of which are covered in more detail in other parts of the book.

## INTRODUCTION

Even a minor event in the life of a child is an event of that child's world and thus a world event.

*Gaston Bachelard, 1884–1962*

Being allowed into the world of a child or young person is a privilege and an adventure. Every encounter provides an opportunity for healing: every smile; every greeting; each time we laugh at a child's humour; sharing aspects of our own experience; and offering a safe space in which to explore past experiences and worries goes a little way to healing the hurts that bring them into therapy. As adults, we often focus on the 'problems' that children bring: trauma, bereavement and other transitions; the effects of bullying, depression and all manner of anxious states (Bailey and Shooter, 2009). In this chapter, as well as acknowledging children's distress, we want to also highlight the strengths that children and young people bring: resilience, power, humour, imagination, experience and creative possibilities that help them to overcome difficult life experiences or worries.

Creative work is particularly relevant when working with children and young people. Axline (1947) believed that because they express themselves through play, it is a natural therapeutic medium for children. She saw that the child would direct the play in a way that is productive in helping them to work through their struggles. Children dealing with particular issues will 'play out' what they can't 'talk out' about difficult life events (e.g. parental separation, conflict and bereavement), enabling them to resolve issues that they cannot express through words.

Malchiodi (2005) distinguishes between those therapists who have in-depth training in various creative therapies and those who integrate expressive therapies into their psychotherapy work. This chapter focuses on the latter group, in that it introduces ideas that have been successfully integrated into the authors' own practice, and in doing so is not offering a detailed examination of specific creative therapies, such as art, drama and dance therapy. Carson and Becker (2004), however, refer to 'creativity in counselling', describing the therapist's willingness to respond in a flexible and creative way, attuning to a client's creative possibilities. It is hoped this chapter explores, therefore, the broader creative potential of therapeutic practice.

## TAKING CREATIVITY INTO THERAPEUTIC PRACTICE

The value of creativity in the therapeutic process is not a new phenomenon: McNiff (1981) discusses the use of art in healing throughout the ages and Malchiodi (2005) builds on this, highlighting how artistic activity was used in ancient Egypt to help people with mental illness. She describes how the Greeks used drama and music for healing, and how Goodenough (1926) was analysing children's drawings early in the last century. In 1939 Margaret Lowenfeld developed the 'Lowenfeld World Technique' from her work with sand trays, toys and models. The children Lowenfeld worked with called her 'wonder box' of play materials 'the world' and started to create scenes and worlds in the sand box in her playroom (Lowenfeld, 1993).

The use of creative therapies is increasing its standing in the statutory mental health field. For example, in 2009 the National Institute for Health and Clinical Excellence (NICE) recommended that art therapy be considered as a supplement to standard care in patients with schizophrenia. A systematic scoping review undertaken by Harris and Pattison (2004) revealed a range of evidence-based studies supporting the use of creative therapies with children and young people: group drama therapy for children with behavioural and emotional problems in the school setting (McArdle et al., 2002), group work and role-play for improving levels of acting out, distractibility and sociability with learning-disabled children (Omizo and Omizo, 1987), humanistic play therapy effective in reducing anxiety in children whose parents have divorced (Dearden, 1998), and play therapy to reduce anxiety and build self-esteem and cognitive skills in schoolchildren (Sherr and Sterne, 1999). What follows are illustrative case study examples of how, as authors, we have used creativity in our therapeutic work with children and young people, employing a variety of media.

## WORKING IN THE SAND TRAY AND STORYTELLING

Sand tray work is a creative and popular approach, especially in working with younger children. The use of small toys and figures in sand tray work is highlighted by Geldard and Geldard (2002). They describe a goal of sand tray work as giving children an opportunity to tell their story with symbolism and metaphor, using model trees, fences, cars, soldiers, heroes, dragons and animals. This enables the child to express fears and fantasies in the small safe 'world' of the sand tray. Children use their imagination and subconscious to create a microcosm of their inner world. Below is an example of sand tray work with 'Tom'. In a discussion of metaphor and symbolism in creative work, Bonnie Meekums (MindEd) notes the importance of non-evaluative and non-interpretive approaches to this work, and this was important for Tom.

### Case Study: Tom

Tom, aged 10, was in care and had been referred because of his withdrawn behaviours, enuresis and occasional aggressive physical outbursts. He found it hard to regulate his feelings and would often seem to be 'in a world of his own' – disconnected – and finding it difficult to express himself verbally. He was significantly developmentally delayed in his speech, cognitively, and in his social and emotional skills. Before meeting Tom I had read a comprehensive referral document detailing some of his early experiences. It was heartbreaking to read. He and his siblings had been severely neglected from an early age and he had taken a great deal of responsibility for his three young brothers and little sister. He had been denied food, water and stimulation. He had also been physically and emotionally abused by his stepfather. Tom had had a number of fostering placements.

Tom was invited to explore the playroom and to choose what media he would like to use. He loved the sand tray. He chose a variety of toys, including trees and wild animals. Over the weeks as he played in the sand, his story of abuse and fear unfolded as the giraffe shouted at the monkey 'Get in there *you*', 'Don't you get out of that bed', 'Stand *there*'. Other times animals would be buried deep in the sand – 'disappeared'. These scenes were played over and over until he moved onto another theme from his difficult past.

During the early stages of our work together he had been told that he was moving to another placement. Whilst therapeutic work can be contra-indicative for a child who is not in a settled placement, this was another unexpected twist in his troubled and unsettled life. Whilst waiting for his new placement, Tom continued his sand tray work. One day he drew a line down the middle of the sand. One side was his old life and one side was his new life. In exploring his old life, he made several purposeful trips to the imaginary skip, throwing out all the 'old stuff'. In his new life he created a veritable little paradise, speaking about his hopes and expectations of his new placement.

Whilst Tom never spoke verbally about his experiences prior to coming into care, he took the opportunity, through the sand, to communicate his distressing feelings of fear and anger. Tom is now thriving in his new placement; he is dry day and night, and expressing his thoughts and feelings in more helpful ways within the nurture and care of a loving family.

## WORKING WITH ART MATERIALS

Art is commonly used across a range of psychotherapies as a vehicle for self-expression and understanding and can employ a variety of media. In a discussion of working therapeutically with clay, Geldard and Geldard (2002) emphasise its pleasant texture when 'feeling, stroking, pressing, punching, squashing and shaping'. They highlight the benefits of being able to change its shape, allowing the exploration and development of emerging themes to symbolically express held-in feelings. Emotionally blocked children are able to contact and express their feelings through working with clay. Sherwood (2010) suggests that using clay in therapy provides therapists with a powerful medium to help clients work through many core issues such as anger, grief and fear.

## Case Study: Jess

Jess, a black child, aged 5, was referred by her social worker after becoming 'looked-after' because her mother's partner had pushed her down the stairs. Other physical abuse became apparent during the investigation and, despite the man being convicted of the assault, Jess's

*(Continued)*

(Continued)

mum refused to acknowledge the danger that he posed to her daughter. Jess was placed with her maternal aunt but was distressed and confused about not living with her mum. She was an anxious little girl who sometimes had distressing 'outbursts' where she was clearly overwhelmed by her difficult feelings. Jess had no understanding of how to regulate her difficult emotions.

When Jess was invited to work with the clay, she built a fort with no doorway. She also built a jail. In exploring the jail, she was able to talk about where the bad man went, whether he might come and 'get her' and who would save her. Jess was expressing her fear of the man who abused her and letting me know about her precarious sense of safety. We were able to explore who was there to look after her (safe adults, police, social worker, the judge) and how the bad man would have to learn his lesson in jail about how to be good. As the session progressed, Jess created a door in the fort 'for the people to get in and out' (the jail stayed firmly locked). As Jess's anxieties were addressed, she was able to contemplate allowing others into her clay refuge and also to venture outside.

## Case Study: John

Many children who have experienced trauma will project their internal feelings in ways that are difficult for children and young people to understand and explain. A 'parts of self' exercise offers a visual way of helping children and young people to think about both positive and negative aspects of self (Bomber, 2007). Bomber states that once we give children a language for both negative and positive parts of themselves, we have a tool that can be used to diffuse conflicts and move children into other states and experiences. This will mean that they start to realise that they can take some control over the parts that make them who they are, especially in relation to escalating tensions. In order to make it something that young people relate to, a pizza is used to illustrate the parts. John, aged 13, was referred because he projected negative feelings towards his parents and teachers, and was on the verge of being excluded from school. Over several sessions, the pizza parts exercise gently supported John to identify his strengths and difficulties. The pizza parts process encouraged John to openly explore both his good and bad experiences. John began to recognise that he was kind, generous and had a good sense of humour. The pizza parts exercise enabled John to recognise his positive as well as his negative traits. John looked forward to reviewing his pizza parts, and talking about the positive changes and progress he was making in his life. Having the visual image of a pizza with its segmented parts appeared to be important part of this process. As a result, John was able to able to take greater ownership and responsibility for the choices he made, his anger subsided, and his relationships at home and in school dramatically improved.

# CREATIVE RISK-TAKING: OUTDOOR ADVENTURE THERAPY

There has been a long tradition of using outdoor adventure activities for the personal and social development of young people (Ogilvie, 2013). The psychological and physical demands of outdoor and adventure settings are often so different and so much more intense than those experienced in everyday life that they offer psychological, sociological and physiological benefits (McCormick et al., 2003). Research indicates a range of psychological benefits from participation in structured outdoor activities (Fiennes et al., 2015), and psychological benefits have been identified with a range of client groups, for example, addictions and post-traumatic stress disorder (Ragsdale et al., 1996), survivors of sexual abuse (Levine, 1994), eating disorders (Richards et al., 2002) and psychiatric patients (Blanchard, 1993). Psychotherapeutic approaches in the outdoors are more specifically defined as adventure therapy, wilderness therapy, adventure-based counselling and nature-based therapies, and these exist in wide international contexts (Richards et al., 2011).

The elements of novelty and challenge are key ingredients that differentiate adventure and wilderness therapy from more conventional experiential therapies. A young person's perception of the risk involved may be such that they have an additional emotional level of arousal to manage. This invites young people to step outside their comfort zone and in so doing examine the experience they have of themselves, in a new zone of disequilibrium (Gass, 1993). Gass (1993) describes this as 'edge work'. It holds the view that clients may find it difficult to achieve change in the context of their normal everyday circumstances. In such settings, much in their lives and thinking will conspire to keep things the same. If clients are facilitated to work at 'the edge', or even step over the edge of their comfort zone, then they are likely to experience, at best, new aspects of themselves and new ways of coping, or at least gain some insight into their habitual coping behaviour.

Geidd (2008) suggests that adolescence is a time of substantial neurobiological and behavioural change. The behaviours that accompany these changes include separation from family of origin, an increase in risk-taking and increased sensation seeking. 'These changes and the plasticity of the teen brain make adolescence a time of great risk and great opportunity' (Geidd, 2008: 341). Similarly, Hasset (2012: 70) suggests that 'increased risk-taking in adolescence is normative, biologically driven and inevitable'. Speaking of the adaptive role of adolescence, he states that a biological wedge is naturally driven between young people and their parents to aid transition to independence. He also states that 'you need to engage in high-risk behaviour to leave your village and find a mate' (Hasset, 2012: 72). Adventure therapy enables young people to engage in creative risk-taking, allowing the experience of authenticity and subsequent psychological change.

## Case Study: Danny

Danny, aged 14, had been diagnosed with attention deficit hyperactivity disorder (ADHD) some years ago and had had a troubled past. He was being raised by his dad, his mum having died when he was 8. Since his mum's death Danny had become difficult to manage at school and at home. He had been referred for bereavement support through his school counsellor, but did not return after the first session. He had begun to seriously self-harm by cutting his arms, was hanging around with much older boys and was drinking alcohol harmfully. He was reluctantly placed in a single occupancy residential placement with 'round-the-clock' care.

As the staff team began to win Danny's trust, he would talk to them about his mum and his past, but he continued to harm himself and put himself at considerable risk in the community. An offer was made to work on a one-to-one basis with Danny in the outdoors, and, though initially he flatly refused, he was shown the website of the venue where the work would be undertaken. This seemed to 'hook' Danny's adventurous spirit. After meeting with Danny, it was evident that there were areas that could possibly be impacted by the use of a variety of outdoor adventurous activity, including rock climbing, mountaineering and high ropes courses. The therapists agreed to offer opportunities to experience issues of 'trust', safe 'risk-taking' and 'accepting support'.

Danny arrived at the outdoor venue and was introduced to the activities for the 2 days. The first was a ropes course, where we invited Danny to engage in a childlike way, quite different from the moody adolescent façade we were used to. In the paradoxical experience of fear and excitement, Danny showed his authentic feelings of enjoyment, unable to maintain the indifferent and disconnected persona that had kept him 'safe' and others at bay for many years. As the outdoor trainer and therapist worked together to enable Danny to express his feelings more openly, he began to acknowledge his fears and uncertainty about the future. His sense of self-efficacy was compromised due to his early life experiences. Offering him opportunities to experience his capabilities was crucial in the outdoor adventure work.

Given this, the team decided to facilitate Danny on a mountainous rock climb to build a sense of competence and resilience. At first Danny was doubtful about the task in hand – he had never climbed roped on a mountain before; he felt unsure about his ability and anxiety about entering an unknown environment. This was the kind of risk Danny had never previously encountered. During the climb, a number of pivotal moments occurred. As he became more confident in the climb, Danny began to connect more openly with the therapists, sometimes offering support and even requesting support – something that Danny had previously resisted. Importantly, he began to play, making Tarzan noises as he became more relaxed and playful. Hearing Danny's laughter and Tarzan cry echoing across the mountains was a joy for the therapists. Danny had resumed his journey.

# A CREATIVE GROUP WORK APPROACH TO SCHOOL TRANSITION

Significant research has been conducted into children's concerns about the primary–secondary transition (Zeedyk et al., 2003; West et al., 2010; Rice et al., 2011). Zeedyk et al. (2003) found that bullying was a major concern for all respondents, followed by getting lost, increased workload and peer relationships. Research has shown that group work is an effective intervention to use with children, partly because they spend a significant amount of time with peers, and groups are a socialising influence (Kulic et al., 2001; Landreth and Sweeney, 2001). Group members are given the opportunity to experience themselves in relation to others and reflect on peer relationships, which is not available to a child working in individual therapy (Woolf, 2011). The sharing of difficult experiences in a safe environment with peers helps children feel relaxed and recognise that they are not alone in their distress as well as enabling them to help each other (Shen, 2002). However, group work is not suitable for all children – for example, those who have significant issues of risk, or those whose distress or behaviour cannot be contained sufficiently in a group environment (Pearce et al., 2014). Although there is a shortage of studies directly exploring children's experience of play therapy group work in relation to their concerns about the transition from primary to secondary school, there is literature available on the use of play therapy group work with other child populations (Danger and Landreth, 2005; Baggerly and Jenkins, 2009; Dayle Jones, 2002).

## Case Study: A Bag of Worries

A creative/play therapy group work was set up to offer an effective, low cost, targeted intervention that would act as support and preparation for four Year 6 children who were anxious about the transition from primary to secondary school. The group included two boys and two girls from the same class, and they were all worried and anxious about attending secondary school, and teachers and parents also felt they would struggle. The children formed group rules to reinforce safety, respect, trust and appropriate behaviour (Geldard and Geldard, 2001), and to promote group coherence before the sessions began. Musical instruments promoted relaxation (Malekoff, 2004; McMahon, 2009). Other creative media were used including arts and crafts materials, puppets, therapeutic stories and stories compiled by the children. Art materials were used for each child to create their own Huge Bag of Worries (Ironside, 2004), which was then shared with the other children in the group. Common themes across the group were fear of being bullied, getting lost, new teachers or difficult schoolwork. Once fears were identified, the children used puppets to act out their anxieties.

*(Continued)*

(Continued)

This experience appeared cathartic, empowering the children to strengthen resilience, develop coping strategies and gain mastery over their worries. The children were also encouraged to draw their concerns using a six-part story-making model (Lahad, 1992). Knowing that they were not alone with their anxieties empowered the children to draw or act out their worries alongside their peers, enabling them to access peer support.

By week 3, the children were laughing about how they never really got to know each other, although they had been in the same year group for 2 years. They reported feeling supported now and making new friends who understood their worries. As a result, the children's worries were reduced and replaced by feelings of excitement and confidence. In week 5, one child became upset because of a bullying issue outside of the group, and the other children offered solutions, including letting her play with them, speaking to the teacher and approaching the bully to explain the hurt caused. In the final week, the group chose to tie their worries to a balloon and let the balloon fly away. One child stated 'It's just like the girl in *The Huge Bag of Worries* book – we have shared our worries with each other and now we don't have them anymore. We can let them go.'

## RESEARCH ISSUES

Recently, Cooper and McLeod (2010) presented the concept of pluralistic counselling and psychotherapy. Citing Lazarus' (2005) multimodal approach, they suggest that different clients are helped by different methods. They also highlight the development of practice which incorporates the whole range of concepts and therapeutic methods. Two key principles underpin the pluralistic approach: (1) lots of things can be helpful to clients; and (2) if we want to know what is most likely to help clients, we should talk to them about it (Cooper and McLeod, 2010: 6). In understanding what is helpful to children, research needs to examine wider creative processes and practices and ascertain more clearly the potential benefit of these. This will help to better guide practitioners on the application of creative approaches for achieving long-standing psychological change.

## Key Learning

- Helped you to develop your skills in recognising the opportunities to engage young people in creative ways of communicating that they understand and enjoy.
- Increased your knowledge of how giving children and young people a broad of creative media can both enhance therapeutic possibilities and give them a wider choice in how therapy is conducted.
- Led to a greater understanding of the ways in which children and young people express their feelings in a language different to adults.

## Summary

In conclusion, counsellors can help children and young people to engage through a variety of creative and 'alternative' methods, whereby the sensory nature of creative work enables children and young people to express their feelings in a language they can take more ownership of. Employing creative media and techniques requires the therapist to be able to connect with the symbolism and imaginative essence of the child's world. And working creatively with children and young people teaches us how to reconnect with aspects of ourselves perhaps long-forgotten. It is well documented that children and young people contact the world through play and creativity – our task is to harness the therapeutic potential that these things bring and thus embrace more of a pluralistic approach to our creative practices. In the words of Picasso, 'Every child is an artist – the problem is staying an artist when you grow up'.

## Develop Your Skills

So now time to get creative yourself. The invitation is to simply take some time to do some of the creative activities highlighted. The goal is not to overthink it – just create a quiet space, gather the relevant resources and allow yourself some creative time.

1. Mould clay to music: Letting your creativity flow in response to music can have a meditative quality. Let your feelings out, or just relax and enjoy the sensory experience of moulding clay. See what textures, shapes and images emerge.
2. Go outdoors: Take a walk outside in a local green space area. As you walk, take notice of natural things that you see – take time to look, sense, touch and smell these. As you do, take note of the thoughts and feelings that these natural things stir in you. Do they provide symbols to you? Do you notice metaphors that relate to you – feelings, dilemmas, thoughts, hopes, etc.? After a short time find a suitable safe spot to sit down. Take time to reflect more on your experience of nature, jot down thoughts, images, feelings, etc. If you collected any natural things replace them after you have made some notes. Do the same walk for a number of days or weeks. Allow your journey each time to unfold and don't let rain deter you from going outside!

## Further Reading

Axline, V. (1947) *Play Therapy*. Boston, MA: Houghton Miffin.
An older but nevertheless classic text for play therapy with children that still stands strong today.

*(Continued)*

(Continued)

Emunah, R. (1994) *Acting for Real: Drama Therapy Process, Technique and Performance.* London: Brunner-Routledge.

This offers a good overview of the field, so will set the scene well.

Karkou, V. (ed.) (2010) *Art Therapies in Schools: Research and Practice.* London: Jessica Kingsley.

Focused on practice in both mainstream and special schools, and across the different art therapies (e.g. music, dance and art), it offers a good overview.

Gass, M.A., Gillis, H.L. and Russell, K.C. (2012) *Adventure Therapy: Theory, Research and Practice.* London: Routledge.

It has a North American slant, but still offers a good context, with helpful signposting to literature. Also see International Adventure Therapy Conference Proceedings over the past 20 years; excellent accounts of theory and practices with different client groups across the world.

### Online Resources

BACP website: www.bacp.co.uk

BACP Children and Young People Division – see Competences for Working with Children and Young People

Counselling MindEd resource: Overview www.bacp.co.uk/ethics/Resources/MindEd.php

Online resource: click on therapeutic skills section for the range of creative and symbolic methods. See: https://www.minded.org.uk/Catalogue/Index?HierarchyId=0_36300_36301&programmeId=36300

Institute for Outdoor Learning: www.outdoor-learning.org. The UK professional body for learning outdoors, range of signposts to information and resources working outdoors.

## REFERENCES

Axline, V. (1947) *Play Therapy.* Boston, MA: Houghton Miffin.

Baggerly, J. and Jenkins, W. (2009) The effectiveness of child-centered play therapy on developmental and diagnostic factors in children who are homeless, *International Journal of Play Therapy, 18*(1), pp. 45–55.

Bailey, S. and Shooter, M. (eds.) (2009) *The Young Mind: An Essential Guide to Mental Health for Young Adults, Parents and Teachers.* London: Bantam Press.

Blanchard, C.W. (1993) 'Effects of ropes course therapy on inter-personal behaviour and self-esteem of adolescent psychiatric patients.' PhD Dissertation, New Mexico State University, Las Cruces.

Bomber, L.M. (2007) *Inside I'm Hurting: Practical Strategies for Supporting Children with Attachment Difficulties in Schools*. London: Worth Publishers.

Carson, D., and Becker, K. (2004). 'When lightning strikes: Re-examining creativity in psychotherapy'. *Journal of Counseling and Development 82*(1): 111–115.

Cooper, M., and McLeod, J. (2010). Pluralistic Counselling and Psychotherapy. London: Sage Publications.

Danger, S. and Landreth, G. (2005) Child-centered group play therapy with children with speech difficulties. *International Journal of Play Therapy 14*(1): 81–102.

Dayle Jones, K. (2002) Group play therapy with sexually abused preschool children: group behaviors and interventions. *Journal for Specialists in Group Work 27*(4): 377–389.

Dearden, C. (1998) The children's counselling service at Family Care: an evaluation. Loughborough, Leics.: Loughborough University

Fiennes, C., Oliver, O., Dickson, K., Escobar, D., Romans, A. and Oliver. S. (2015) *The Existing Evidence-Base about the Effectiveness of Outdoor Learning*. The Belgrave Trust: Giving Evidence.

Gass, M. (1993) *Adventure Therapy: Therapeutic Applications of Adventure Programming*. Dubuque, IA: Kendall Hunt.

Geidd, J.N. (2008) The teen brain: insights from neuroimagining. *Journal of Adolescent Health 42*(4): 335–343.

Geldard, K. and Geldard, D. (2001) *Working with Children in Groups*. Basingstoke: Palgrave.

Geldard, K., and Geldard, D. (2002) *Counselling Children: A Practical Introduction* (2nd ed). London: Sage Publications.

Goodenough, F. (1926) *Measurement of Intelligence by Drawings*. New York: Harcourt, Brace and World.

Harris, B. and Pattison, S. (2004) *Research on Counselling Children and Young People: A Systematic Review*. Rugby: BACP.

Hasset, A. (2012) Unpublished PowerPoint presentation 'Adolescence, adolescent development and adolescent brain development'. Permission granted for use.

Ironside, V. (2004) *The Huge Bag of Worries*. London: Hodder Children's Books.

Kulic, K., Dagley, J. and Horne, A. (2001) Prevention groups with children and adolescents. *Journal for Specialists in Group Work 26*(3): 211–218.

Lahad, M. (1992) Story-making in assessment method for coping with stress; six part story-making and BASIC ph. In: Jennings, S. (ed.) *Dramatherapy: Theory and Practice 2*. London: Routledge, pp. 150–163.

Landreth, G. and Sweeney, D. (2001) Child-centered group play therapy. In: Landreth, G. (ed.) *Innovations in Play Therapy: Issues, Process and Special Populations*. New York: Taylor & Francis, pp. 181–202.

Levine, D. (1994). Breaking through barriers: Wilderness therapy for sexual assault survivors. *Women & Therapy, 15*, 175–184.

Lowenfeld, M. (1993). *Understanding Children's Sandplay: Lowenfeld's World Technique*. Great Britain: Antony Rowe Ltd.. (Originally published as *The World Technique*, George Allen & Unwin Ltd., 1979)

Malchiodi, C.A (ed.) (2005) *Expressive Therapies*. New York. The Guilford Press.

Malekoff, A. (2004) *Group Work with Adolescents* (2nd ed). New York: The Guilford Press.

McArdle, P., Moseley, D., Quibell, T., Johnson, R., Allen, A., Hammal, D. and LeCouteur, A. (2002) School-based indicated prevention; a randomised trial of group therapy. *Journal of Child Psychology and Psychiatry* 43(6): 705–712.

McCormick, B., Voight, A. and Ewert, A. (2003) Therapeutic outdoor programming: theoretical connections between adventure and therapy. In: Richards, K. with Smith, B. (eds) *Therapy with Adventure. Proceedings of the Second International Adventure Therapy Conference*. Augsburg: Zeil Verlag, pp. 155–174.

McMahon, L. (2009) *The Handbook of Play Therapy and Therapeutic Play*, 2nd edn. Hove: Routledge.

McNiff, S. (1981) *The Arts and Psychotherapy*. New York: Charles Thomas.

Ogilvie, K.C. (2013) *Roots and Wings. A History of Outdoor Education and Outdoor Learning in the UK*. Lyme Regis: Russell House Publishing.

Omizo, M.M. and Omizo, A.O. (1987) The effect of group counselling on classroom behaviour and self-concept among elementary school learning disabled children. *The Exceptional Child*, 34(1) 57–64.

Pearce, P., Proud, G. and Sewell, R. (2014) Group work. In: Pattison, S., Robson, M. and Beynon, A. (eds) *The Handbook of Counselling Children and Young People*. London: SAGE, pp. 212–228.

Ragsdale, K.G., Cox., R.D., Finn, P. and Eisler, R.M. (1996) Effectiveness of short term specialised inpatient treatment for war-related posttraumatic stress disorder. A role for adventure based counselling and psychodrama. *Journal of Traumatic Stress* 9(2): 269–283.

Rice, F., Frederickson, N. and Seymour, J. (2011) Assessing pupil concerns about transition to secondary school. *British Journal of Educational Psychology* 81: 244–263.

Richards, K., Peel, J., Smith, B. and Owen, V. (2002) *Adventure Therapy and Eating Disorders: A Feminist Approach to Research and Practice*. Ambleside: Brathay Hall Trust.

Richards, K., Harper, N. and Carpenter, C. (eds) (2011) Looking at the landscape of adventure therapy: making links to theory and practice. *Journal of Adventure Education and Outdoor Learning* 11(2): 83–90.

Shen, Y. (2002) Short-term group play therapy with Chinese earthquake victims: effects on anxiety, depression and adjustment. *International Journal of Play Therapy* 11(1): 43–63.

Sherr, L. and Sterne, A (1999) Evaluation of a counselling intervention in primary schools. *Clinical Psychology and Psychotherapy*, 6: 286–296.

Sherwood, P. (2010). *The Healing Art of Clay Therapy*. Melbourne: Acer Press.

West, P., Sweeting, H. and Young, R. (2010) Transition matters: pupils' experiences of the primary-secondary school transition in the west of Scotland and consequences for well-being and attainment. *Research Papers in Education* 25(1): 21–50.

Woolf, A. (2011) Everyone playing in class: a group play provision for enhancing the emotional well-being of children in school. *British Journal of Special Education* 38(4): 178–190.

Zeedyk, M., Gallagher, J., Henderson, M., Hope, G., Husband, B. and Lindsay, K. (2003) Negotiating the transition from primary to secondary school: perceptions of pupils, parents and teachers. *School Psychology International* 24(1): 67–79.

# PART 2

## COUNSELLING PRACTICES AND PROCESSES

# 9

# REFERRALS AND INDICATIONS FOR THERAPY

## ANI DE LA PRIDA AND WENDY HAY

**This chapter will discuss:**

- Policy background and current system
- The importance of diversity
- Referral and initial assessment
- Indications for therapy and presenting problems
- Influence of counselling settings on referral process
- Developing practitioner skills

## INTRODUCTION: POLICY BACKGROUND AND CURRENT SYSTEM

At present in the UK there is no single system or policy for referral, but a variety of ways in which children and young people come to counselling. Referral is further complicated by the variation in legislation, policy and commissioning, and a lack of shared understanding resulting in a concerning lack of any comprehensive structure and accessibility in mental health care provision for children and young people (Children's Commissioner for England, 2016). Until now Child and Adolescent Mental Health Services (CAMHS) provision in the UK has been organised around a four-tier system of assessment and delivery of services first outlined in an NHS Health Advisory Service review (1995).

- Tier 1 services can be delivered by GPs, health visitors, school nurses, teachers and voluntary agencies who provide treatment for conditions such as mild depression, whilst offering an assessment service for children and young people who would benefit from referral to a more specialist service.

- Tier 2 provides assessment and treatment of more severe or complex mental health needs. Counsellors and psychologists work at this level.
- Tier 3 services are providing assessment of more severe, complex and persistent mental health conditions, delivered by a multidisciplinary team, such as a psychiatrist, social worker, educational psychologist and occupational therapist.
- Tier 4 provides specialist services for children with the most serious problems, such as violent behaviour, a serious or life-threatening eating disorder, or a history of physical and/or sexual abuse.

However, the UK mental health care system is currently in the process of organisational change and transformation as outlined in *The Five Year Forward View for Mental Health* (The Mental Health Taskforce, 2016), with fundamental changes to the referral system planned, including replacing the current four-tier system with a new model.

A British Association for Counselling and Psychotherapy (BACP) scoping report points to recent figures which suggest that the numbers attending school-based counselling are similar to the numbers attending specialist CAMHS services (Cooper, 2013). The report suggests that counselling is currently available in approximately 60–85% of secondary schools in the UK, whilst there is mixed provision in primary schools (Spong et al., 2013). Cooper (2013) highlights that sources of referral to school counselling services include parents and self-referral. However, the most common referral source is school staff members, and in particular pastoral care teachers, who were reported to be involved in approximately two-thirds of referrals.

Research highlights that children and young people are more likely to be referred to a professional for behaviour than for emotional difficulties, with mental health support being provided principally by teachers (DfE, 2011). More worryingly, the DfE report states that in their study 'no primary or secondary schools reported using approaches that involved following a rigorous protocol' (2011: 10). This picture suggests children and young people may not always be referred for counselling when appropriate or needed.

Within the current system, less than 25% of children and young people with diagnosable mental health conditions access support (DoH, 2017). Restrictions on referral and threshold criteria imposed by many specialist CAMHS means that many children and young people who are referred don't meet the soaring thresholds for support (Children's Commissioner for England, 2016). For example, in 2015 of the 3000 children referred to specialist CAMHS with serious life-threatening issues (suicide, psychosis, self-harm), worryingly, 14% were not allocated any provision, and 51% were placed on a waiting list (Children's Commissioner for England, 2016). This means that only 35% of these most serious referrals were allocated prompt support. In addition, for those who are allocated support, there are often long waits, with an average wait of 32 weeks for a routine appointment (DoH, 2017).

The lack of a shared language and approach to mental health care is further complicating referrals and cross-agency working (Values-Based Child and Adolescent Mental Health System Commission, 2016). In addition, tackling stigma around mental health issues by improving how we talk about mental health is also suggested (Values-Based Child and Adolescent Mental Health System Commission, 2016). The use of the term 'emotional health', rather than 'mental health' may be more appropriate and help reduce stigma in many instances. Proposed changes from the current organisational needs-based system towards a more values-based system will hopefully promote the development of more collaborative referral forms and systems.

## REFERRAL AND ASSESSMENT

Clear referral protocol is a vital part of the counselling process, although one that may be overlooked at times. When considering the counselling process as a whole, it is perhaps difficult to determine the most significant aspect that enables change to occur for each client. Of recognised importance to the counselling process are the therapeutic conditions (Prever, 2010) and therapeutic alliance (Muran and Barber, 2010), but the referral is where we really start the work with each client. It is where a therapist can begin to develop a relationship with the unmet client, where we gain a 'picture' of the client in context and where we have an opportunity to create dialogue that can contribute towards therapeutic change.

It is difficult to separate referral and assessment, as the two are linked and often intertwined. Different theoretical orientations have different ways of assessing (or not assessing) clients, which will discernibly influence the information sought as well as the referral process. The structure of the setting and localised policies will also shape the referral process both in terms of information requested and also in terms of who is seen or referred on. Therefore, there is a huge diversity in terms of referral and assessment practices in the UK, and referral policies and forms will naturally reflect this.

Some settings prefer a written referral to be completed before seeing a client, for example, specialist CAMHS require written referrals from a GP, social worker or other professional. Drop-in centres, schools-based counselling services and community-based services may not require referral or assessment documentation, whilst counselling services may ask clients to meet with a counsellor to complete a referral or assessment form during an initial session. Assessment tools may be used, such as CYP CORE, or the CAMHS Current View Tool (CAMHS Press, 2013).

All referral processes need to be age-appropriate. Practitioners need to be aware of legal aspects when contracting to work with young people. Children under the age of 16 years may be considered Gillick competent to make their own choices according to a number of factors, including age, maturity and capacity for understanding of issues. Where they are considered not to be competent (for further discussion, see Chapter 17) someone with parental responsibility must give consent.

Ideally, information on a referral form would include the client's voice (including whether the client wants to come to counselling), the nature of the problem, how long the difficulty has been experienced and any information considered relevant to the issue. For example, in the case of bereavement the form should include details of the loss. Information about the context of the client may be useful, for example, if the child has just moved to the school or local area. The form should also contain information about any serious issues, such as child protection.

Decisions to accept referrals would be informed by modality, limits of competency and counselling service policy. Referral forms could be considered inherently flawed in that they are predominantly created for the needs of the setting rather than the client, they often contain other people's perceptions and the younger the child the less likely that they will contain the client's words or view.

Although a referral form can contain much information about a client, it is important to remember that it may contain biased opinion, for example, one teacher may see behaviour as unmanageable that others, and the client, would view as acceptable. Referral information may not be accurate, for example, informal assessments and diagnoses such as 'Jane has low self-esteem' may be inaccurate. It is important to be able to hold the information on a referral form in mind without allowing it to prejudice your view or opinion of the client before you have even met.

Relevant information may also be missing at referral, so it is important that the counsellor checks if there is 'anything else' during the initial meeting. Perceptions of those referring may be distorted by their own difficulties, and projected onto the child.

The requirements and structure of counselling settings will often create dilemmas, challenging ethical boundaries, theoretical stance and counsellor competence. For example, a counselling service policy to decline referrals for pre-trial therapy for children involved in court proceedings because of the risk and complexity of managing the counselling without prejudicing the client's evidence (for further discussion, see Chapter 17). This may not be in the client's interest, however, and could be seen as contrary to the ethical principles of autonomy and beneficence (BACP, 2013).

Theoretical and organisational stance can also give rise to dilemmas with referral. For example, specialist CAMHS services, particularly when working from systemic and integrative perspectives, have historically declined referrals for counselling for children in care on the basis that they must be in a stable environment before engaging in therapeutic work. Other service providers working from modalities such as person-centred therapy do not see this as a barrier to therapeutic work. In fact, it can be argued that the child's need is greater during periods of instability than when their environment is stable. Declining requests for therapy on this basis are contrary to the ethical principles of autonomy and beneficence (BACP, 2013), and recent legislation now states that therapy must not be refused because of short-term placements (*Promoting the health and well-being of looked-after children Statutory guidance for local authorities, clinical commissioning groups and NHS England*. DfE, 2015).

At referral it good practice to include information on:

- client's voice;
- current family status (both parents, lone parent, step-parent, carer, adopted);
- whether the child is subject to a child protection plan/order;

- whether the child is a looked-after child, and, if they are, their placement history;
- any current medications;
- behaviours or issues causing concern;
- what is the hoped for outcome of therapy;
- any recent losses, bereavements, or major changes.

## The importance of diversity

As previously discussed, upon receipt of a referral we begin loosely formulating our hypothesis of each case. At this early stage we need to consider our understanding of the child within their cultural heritage and their world. There is no such thing as 'normal' and, if we do not have awareness of this, we end up on a slippery slope, which may be lubricated with stereotyping, patronising and ignorance. All practitioners at this early stage of the therapeutic alliance have to give consideration to differences. The important aim is to be inclusive – assess each individual's needs without stereotyping or forming an opinion. When a child walks through the counselling door our perception must not be based on our perceptions of their life, image or appearance. We always need to begin by ensuring we are going to be diverse in our thoughts around the child within their own world.

## INITIAL ASSESSMENT MEETING

Initial referral meetings can often include the child and parent. This meeting gives the counsellor an opportunity to hear where the difficulties may lie, and how these are being felt and displayed by the child or young person. This is also an opportunity to ensure that both parties fully understand what counselling is, and just as importantly, what it is not. With an older young person who doesn't have an adult present, it is important to ensure that you check their understanding throughout the process. For a younger child the initial consultation session can be a transitional space for parents and child before moving to having individual sessions. Sometimes this may be a difficult session for the child. They may not want the adults to share information about them, or they may not agree with what is being said. It is important to ensure that the child has a voice at these meetings. It can also be a difficult session for the counsellor, who may experience the parent as judgemental or punitive towards the child. Managing boundaries and expectations is important, and this initial referral meeting can help build a therapeutic relationship and ensure clear understanding of the boundaries and legal responsibilities of the counselling work.

Difficulties can also arise around expectations at referral stage. Clear information and contracting can support the work by informing realistic expectations and verbalising therapeutic aims. For example, a parent who brings a child who is 'sad' to counselling may become disturbed if their child appears to become angry or unhappy through counselling. Changes that occur as part of the client's therapeutic growth process – for example, because the child is revealing previously hidden feelings such as anger – can make it seem that counselling isn't working or is even making things worse. Discussing this at referral can help support the therapeutic work. It is important, therefore, to give clear information at the outset for parents/ referrers, explaining what may occur as part of the counselling process.

At referral stage it is important to understand the circumstances and relationships surrounding the child or young person. Dilemmas can arise when the client's difficulties are being created by parents, or the family situation, perhaps unconsciously. Taking time to create a genogram with the family is usually helpful in looking at the wider context. A child may possibly disclose abuse or neglect at referral. This can be difficult in any setting, but particularly when challenging the parent could result in them ending counselling for the client. Working with a child or young person's issues when the parent is contributing to or compounding a child's difficulties is difficult and demanding for a counsellor to manage, therefore supervision is an essential support.

To help reflect on the dynamics in the child or young person's world, and help your understanding, the puzzle grid (Figure 9.1) (adapted from a systemic model) can be a useful and easy-to-use reflection tool for the counsellor (Carr, 2004).

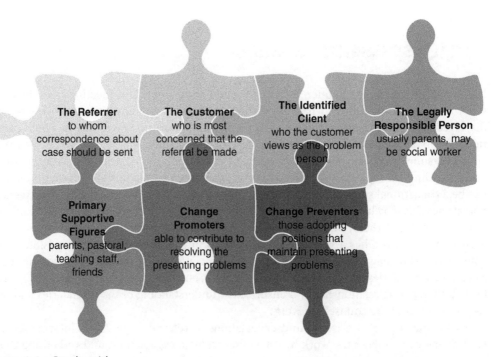

**The Referrer**
to whom correspondence about case should be sent

**The Customer**
who is most concerned that the referral be made

**The Identified Client**
who the customer views as the problem person

**The Legally Responsible Person**
usually parents, may be social worker

**Primary Supportive Figures**
parents, pastoral, teaching staff, friends

**Change Promoters**
able to contribute to resolving the presenting problems

**Change Preventers**
those adopting positions that maintain presenting problems

**Figure 9.1**   Puzzle grid

The puzzle grid tool can be used as a guide to identify key people in the child's world and can help the counsellor gain an overview of the dynamics surrounding the child or young person. In using the tool it is important to ask the following questions:

- Who has decided the child needs therapy?
- Who is referring them?
- Why are they referring this child?
- Does the child know about the referral?
- What does the child feel about the referral?

The case study below illustrates how one counsellor used the puzzle grid tool to enable a deeper understanding of the client's context, and of the therapeutic process.

---

## Case Study: Phillipa

Phillipa was an extremely shy 12-year-old girl living alone with her mother after her Dad left 9 months ago. Phillipa was refusing to go to school and was referred by her GP after seeing her at an appointment with her mother, who was described in the referral letter as 'beside herself with worry'. During the first contracting session Phillipa seemed anxious and tearful a lot of the time. Using the puzzle grid, Phillipa is 'The Identified Client' and her mum is in the role of 'Customer and Legally Responsible Person'. Counselling began and a teacher was identified as 'Primary Supportive Figure'. The counsellor recognised two of Phillipa's friends as 'Change Promoters'. Sessions progressed and the work flourished, with Phillipa improving and returning to school on a phased basis. At this point, her mum contacted the counsellor, worried that Phillipa was being bullied at school, and concerned about her getting the bus to school in the mornings. There had been a minor incident, but exploring with Phillipa it become clear that her mum's distress was the cause of Phillipa's difficulty in leaving in the mornings. Using the grid, her mum was identified as in the role of 'Change Preventer' – her anxiety following the departure of Phillipa's dad was possibly being unconsciously projected onto Phillipa. The counsellor showed empathy and compassion towards Phillipa's mum and suggested she engage in her own counselling. She went ahead with this and became able to separate her anxieties from Phillipa, and moved from being a Change Preventer to a Change Promoter for Phillipa.

---

## INDICATIONS FOR THERAPY AND PRESENTING PROBLEMS

The current transformation of mental health provision will necessitate a more holistic and less diagnostic view of referral. In relation to children the National Institute for Health and Clinical Excellence (NICE) refers to three domains:

- emotional well-being – feeling happy, confident and not anxious or depressed;
- psychological well-being – autonomy, problem-solving, managing emotions, empathy, resilience, attentive;
- social well-being – good relationships with others, not disruptive, violent or bullying.

Therefore, a child experiencing difficulty in any of these areas could be seen as being in need of emotional or mental health support. However, a key question must also be whether the child or young person wants help and support, and also what type of support they feel would help.

## COUNSELLING SETTINGS

Counsellors work in a variety of settings, and the setting in which the client is seen will impact on the referral and on the therapeutic work. Whether in private practice or within service providers such as voluntary or statutory agencies and schools, surprisingly children's rights – and consequently their rights within a therapeutic relationship – vary. The diagnostic labels used to describe children's behaviour and distress can vary between agencies (Malek, 1991: 1993), and it is not unusual, therefore, for counsellors and therapists to become confused as to the limits of their work with the child. Knowing when to refer on to specialist CAMHS, or when specialist CAMHS should refer on to counselling, is therefore not always clear.

## Schools

Counsellors in schools can find that some children perceive counselling as stigmatising or as part of the disciplinary system, although the opposite can also be true, with children finding school counselling less stigmatising than other mental health interventions (Cooper, 2013). Work may be needed to particularly draw attention to the child or young person's autonomy to choose whether they wish to engage with counselling. Provision of school counsellors is increasing (Cooper, 2004; 2006; McGinnis, 2006), and drop-in sessions within schools are becoming more common. Counselling in schools without education of school staff may lead to it becoming part of the disciplinary system, which may be stigmatising. Practitioners establishing or working within a school setting are invited to consider the guidelines and resources in the Welsh Toolkit (BACP 2011).

## Statutory agency

A significant level of therapeutic work is provided by statutory agencies, such as children's services departments, specialist CAMHS, the NHS and youth services of local authorities.

Provision is variable, although a more comprehensive and integrated provision is being developed in response to guidance and directives (Spong et al., 2013). Assessment-focused, time-limited and risk-averse policies are likely issues for counsellors in practice in statutory agencies, all of which can influence the referral process.

## Voluntary and community sector

Given current constraints affecting statutory bodies, some of the greatest opportunities for child-centred therapeutic practice are in the voluntary and community sector (Daniels and Jenkins, 2010). Clients highlighted the strengths of this provision as the non-stigmatising settings, holistic approach and initial contact at referral (Street, 2013). However, agencies may have limited administrative ability to gather data on outcomes or referrals, and agencies may be reluctant to engage with routine monitoring (Street, 2013). Agencies will have their own specific referral policies in place and practitioners need clear understanding of these to ensure they work with cases appropriate to the agency's work. For example, some agencies work only with sexual abuse, whilst others may refer on young people who are using drugs. Each individual agency will also have policies relating to confidentiality and child protection, for example information about self-harm may be sought at referral with one agency, whilst another may not require this.

## Private practice

There are many counsellors and therapists working with children and young people within their own private practice. Rather confusingly, these practitioners are not necessarily bound by the same requirements, such as referral policies or specific requirements related to their therapeutic work, as those working in statutory or voluntary agencies. For example, in terms of child protection, there is no legal requirement to report suspected child abuse to the authorities, although the therapist would be justified in doing so in the 'public interest' (Daniels and Jenkins, 2010). The increased freedoms in private practice run parallel to an increase in the responsibility and complexity carried by the practitioner. The self-referral process can leave practitioners vulnerable. For example, risk assessment may be more difficult when working in isolation. Additionally, working in your own home carries vulnerability for the counsellor that can affect the referral process. For example, a counsellor working alone at home may choose not to see clients with a history of violence, and therefore this may form part of the information sought at initial referral. All of these scenarios can make private practice a complex area to work within, particularly as payment can create an additional dynamic with parents. Boundaries and risk need to be clearly and ethically explored by the practitioner.

## Referring on to other agencies

There are various reasons for referring a child or young person on to another agency and at the core of this action is recognition that this is in the child's best interests. Onward referral should never be viewed as a sign of a practitioner's weakness, or lack of skill, but in fact quite the opposite. There are a number of possible reasons for referring a child or young person on to another agency. These may include:

- The child's presenting problems are outside the remit of the agency or counsellor.
- The counsellor knows the child or the family on a personal basis.
- It is appropriate for the child to access additional sources of support.
- The child requires more specialist intervention, or a clinical assessment for a mental health difficulty.
- The child or child's family asks for referral.

It is important when referring on to check that the parent and the client clearly understand the reason(s) and do not interpret the referral as being because they are 'too difficult', 'too complex' or 'too ill'.

Research has found that '92% of counsellors feel clear about when to refer a young person on to specialist CAMHS or other services' (Cooper, 2013: 5). The Current View Tool (Cooper, 2013) may be used to assess at referral.

## Abuse and investigations

There are difficulties with a referral for children and young people when there are issues of abuse under investigation. There are risks and fears associated with seeing clients in this situation – for example, that a counsellor may potentially damage the case by influencing a client's testimony (see Chapter 17 for further discussion). This situation in itself is not a reason to decline a referral, although many agencies may wrongly believe this to be the case.

There may be fear around the possibility of notes being requested, or of a counsellor being required to give evidence. A disproportionate fear of the risk means that services may decline referrals until after the court case rather than risk damaging the prosecution, or opening a counsellor to scrutiny. However, a client may be in great need of support at this time, and *The Cleveland Report* states: 'there is a danger that in looking to the welfare of children believed to be victims of sexual abuse the children themselves may be overlooked. The child is a person and not an object of concern' (Butler-Sloss, 1988: 245).

Children have a right to influence decisions made about them (HMSO, 1989, *The Children Act 1989*), and before declining a referral the potential impact on a client in this circumstance must also be considered in terms of the ethical framework (BACP, 2013).

Careful assessment, understanding of legal issues, and clear and open communication with referrers can help ensure good practice.

## Key Learning

- There is no single referral system in the UK.
- CAMHS provision in the UK has been organised around a four-tier system of assessment and delivery of services.
- The UK mental health care and referral system is undergoing a transformation of service and provision, which started in 2016. The new system will be based on a more holistic and collaborative system of referral and mental health care without tiers.
- Referral is influenced by counselling setting, service provider policy, modality and client's context.
- It is important to recognise that the information received at referral may be inaccurate or incomplete and the child or young person's views may not be present.

## Summary

To revise, it is important for referrers to aim to provide clear, unbiased and accurate referrals. The referral system surrounding the child or young person can be complex at times. Policies, organisational settings and theoretical stance can influence the process in ways that may not be in the client's interest. Information received at referral may be incomplete, inaccurate or biased. For the practitioner, remaining able to meet the child without a prejudiced view caused by information at referral isn't easy and can be challenging. Experience, supervision and reflection can help to develop the counsellor's capacity to manage the challenges of referral when counselling children and young people.

## Discussion Questions

1. How might a counsellor's theoretical stance influence what information is sought at referral?
2. Working as a school counsellor, when a child is referred to you for counselling how might you enable and protect the young person's autonomy to choose to engage or not with counselling?
3. Ethical practice includes knowing when to refer a potential client to more appropriate support. Discuss where you might refer to, and how you would manage the process.

## Develop Your Skills

1. Using one of your clients, apply the puzzle grid to identify the various roles surrounding the child in order to gain a deeper understanding of the client's situation. Then discuss with a peer, tutor or supervisor.
2. Reflect on what equality and diversity mean to you. Consider your views on the following statement: 'A child's background doesn't matter to me, I treat everyone the same'.
3. Design your own referral form, giving consideration to the information you would want the form to contain that would enable you to make an informed choice about accepting the client or referring on. Then discuss with a peer, tutor or supervisor.
4. Work through the Counselling MindEd module CM 2.6 on risk assessment, available at https://www.minded.org.uk.

## Further Reading

Burton, M. Pavord, E. and Williams, B. (2014) *An Introduction to Child and Adolescent Mental Health*. London: SAGE.

Guishard-Pine, J. (2016) *Supporting the Mental Health of Children in Care*. London: Jessica Kingsley.

Midgely, N., Hayes, J. and Cooper, M. (2017) *Essential Research Findings in Child and Adolescent Counselling and Psychotherapy*. London: SAGE.

Padmore, J. (2015) *The Mental Health Needs of Children and Young People: Guiding You to Key Issues and Practices in CAMHS*. Maidenhead: Open University Press.

Prever, M. (2010) *Counselling and Supporting Children and Young People: A Person-Centred Approach*. London: SAGE.

Timimi, S. (2009) *A Straight Talking Introduction to Children's Mental Health Problems*. Ross-on-Wye: PCCS Books.

Vohra, S. (2018) *Mental Health in Children and Young People: Spotting Symptoms and Seeking Help Early*. London Sheldon Press.

### Online Resources

Counselling MindEd: https://www.minded.org.uk

CM 2.1: What is Assessment in CYP Counselling?
CM 2.2: Engaging the CYP in Collaborative Assessment

CM 2.3: Areas to Consider Assessing with the CYP

(online experiential learning toolkit)

The Mental Health Taskforce (2016) *The Five Year Forward View for Mental Health.* [online]. NHS England. Available at: https://www.england.nhs.uk/wp-content/uploads/2017/03/fyfv-mh-one-year-on.pdf (accessed 2 May 2017).

(details fundamental changes to the referral system planned, including replacing the current four-tier system with a new model)

www.rcpsych.ac.uk (2017) The scandal of underfunded child and adolescent mental health services laid bare in new research from the Royal College of Psychiatrists. [online] Available at: www.rcpsych.ac.uk/mediacentre/pressreleases2016/underfundedcamhsresearch.aspx (accessed 28 March 2017)

(addresses the key issue of funding, and concern that despite increased provision for mental health services for children, funding isn't always reaching front-line services, with some clinical commissioning groups spending as little as £2 per head on mental health services for children)

# REFERENCES

BACP (2013) *The Ethical Framework for Good Practice.* Lutterworth: BACP

BACP (2011) School Based Counselling Toolkit. *BACP online.* Available at https://www.bacp.co.uk/media/2057/bacp-school-based-counselling-toolkit-welsh-english.pdf. (Accessed 30 March 2018).

Butler-Sloss, E. (1988) *Report of the Inquiry into Child Abuse in Cleveland 1987.* Cm 412. London: HMSO.

CAMHS Press (2013) *Current view tool completion guide.* [online] Available at: https://www.ucl.ac.uk/ebpu/docs/publication_files/current_view (Accessed 7 May 2017).

Carr, A. (2004) *Family Therapy: Concepts, Process and Practice.* Chichester: John Wiley & Sons.

Children's Commissioner for England (2016) *Lightning review: access to child and adolescent mental health services.* [online] London: Children's Commissioner for England. Available at: https://www.childrenscommissioner.gov.uk/wp-content/uploads/2017/06/Childrens-Commissioners-Mental-Health-Lightning-Review.pdf (Accessed 7 March 2017).

Cooper, M. (2004) *Counselling in Schools Project: Evaluation Report.* Glasgow: University of Strathclyde.

Cooper, M. (2006) *Counselling in Schools Project Phase 2: Evaluation Report.* Glasgow: University of Strathclyde.

Cooper, M. (2013) School-based counselling in UK secondary schools: a review and critical evaluation. [online] Glasgow: University of Strathclyde. Available at: https://www.bacp.co.uk/media/2054/counselling-minded-school-based-counselling-uk-secondary-schools-cooper.pdf (Accessed 7 May 2017).

Daniels, D. and Jenkins, P. (2010) *Therapy with Children: Childrens Rights, Confidentiality and the Law.* 2nd edn. London: Sage Publications.

DfE (2011) Me and My School: Findings from the National Evaluation of Targeted Mental Health in Schools 2008-2011. Research Report DFE-RR177. *Department for education.* [online] Available at https://www.gov.uk/government/publications/findings-from-the-national-evaluation-of-targeted-mental-health-in-schools-2008-to-2011 (Accessed on 17 March 2014)

Department of Health (2017). *FIVE YEAR FORWARD VIEW FOR MENTAL HEALTH: ONE YEAR ON.* [online] Redditch: NHS England. Available at: https://www.england.nhs.uk/wp-content/uploads/2017/03/fyfv-mh-one-year-on.pdf (Accessed 4 April 2017).

Department of Education (2015) *Promoting the health and well-being of looked-after children Statutory guidance for local authorities, clinical commissioning groups and NHS England.* (2015). [online] Department of Education, Department of Health. Available at: https://www.gov.uk/government/uploads/system/uploads/attachment_data/file/413368/Promoting_the_health_and_well-being_of_looked-after_children.pdf (Accessed 7 April 2017).

Her Majesty's Stationery Office (HMSO) (1989) *The Children Act 1989.* London: HMSO. Available at: www.legislation.gov.uk/ukpga/1989/41/contents (accessed 8 February 2018).

Malek, M. (1991) *Psychiatric Admissions: A Report on Young People Entering Psychiatric Residential Care.* London: Children's Society

Malek, M. (1993) *Passing The Buck: A Summary of Institutional Responses to Controlling Children with Difficult Behaviour.* London: Children's Society.

McGinnis, S. (2006) *Good Practice Guidance for Counselling in Schools,* 4th ed. Lutterworth: British Association for Counselling and Psychotherapy.

Muran, J.C. and Barber, J.P. (2010) (eds) *The Therapeutic Alliance: An Evidence-Based Guide to Practice.* New York: Guilford Press.

Prever, M. (2010) *Counselling and Supporting Children and Young People: A Person-Centred Approach.* London: SAGE.

Spong, S., Waters, R., Dowd, C. and Jackson, C. (2013) *The Relationship between Specialist Child and Adolescent Mental Health Services (CAMHS) and Community-based Counselling for Children and Young People.* Lutterworth: BACP/Counselling MindEd. Available at: https://www.bacp.co.uk/media/2052/counselling-minded-relationship-between-camhs-school-community-based-counselling-spong.pdf (accessed 8 February 2018).

Street, C. (2013) *Voluntary and Community Sector (VCS) Counselling Provision for Children, Young People and Young Adults in England.* Lutterworth: BACP/Counselling MindEd.

Values-Based Child and Adolescent Mental Health System Commission (2016). *What Really Matters in Children and Young People's Mental Health..* [online] Royal College of Psychiatrists. Available at: http://www.rcpsych.ac.uk/pdf/Values-based%20full%20report.pdf (Accessed 28 March 2017).

# 10

# PREPARATION FOR THERAPY: BEGINNINGS

## EDITH BELL AND DAVE STEWART

**This chapter will discuss:**

- The primary importance of listening to children and young people (CYP) in the preparation for therapy process and the need to include relevant stakeholder adults
- The need to tune into different ages, developmental presentations and preferences to help children and young people access and articulate their thoughts and feelings in the preparation phase
- The importance of a more 'active counsellor' stance in assisting young clients to feel more confident in expressing emotion and more at ease in the therapeutic relationship
- 'Collaborative assessment' as a development within the CYP counselling field
- Seven collaborative assessment tasks that together create a 'preparation for therapy map'
- Some of the key constructs from within child development theory that underpin safe and effective preparation for therapy are: Piaget's (1969) theory of cognitive development (including 'schema' formation), Bronfenbrenner's (1979) 'ecological systems theory', Gardener's (1983) 'multiple intelligences' and Vygotsky's (1934) ideas about the 'zone of proximal development'

## INTRODUCTION: LISTENING TO CHILDREN AND YOUNG PEOPLE – THE CRITICAL PREPARATION TASK

In his book *Equals*, child psychotherapist Adam Phillips (2003) invites us to reconsider therapy as a 'listening' – rather than 'talking' – 'cure'. Few of us would argue about the prime importance of listening in our work. Why then can it be so difficult to *really* listen to children?

Why do we sometimes find it hard to let go of 'counsellor-knows-best' when deciding how to shape work with young people? What barriers do therapists face in centralising the voice of a child/young person in therapy? In hearing the views of key adults in a child's world – often an important part of the initial listening process – how do therapists hold and contextualise the potential 'clash' of voices? What structures might helpfully scaffold the preparation process to enable a young client to define what they want from counselling? And what theories should counsellors be aware of when preparing a CYP for therapy?

## Preparation for therapy – unexplored territory within CYP counselling

For the first edition of this book a search of British Association for Counselling (BACP) journals over the 5 years prior to its publication confirmed that this was not a priority area for research, and for the second edition we must report that in research terms the situation remains largely the same. The field of practice is developing beyond the available research base and requires a flowering of research in this underconsidered field. Practice mainly draws on common factors research, and that of empirically supported therapies, much of which is from an adult perspective. For further reading on this we direct you to *The Heart and Soul of Change* (Duncan et al., 2010), or to the work of Wampold and Imel (2015).

Whilst *Therapy Today, Counselling and Psychotherapy Research* and *Counselling Children and Young People* host a good number of articles on research, theory and practice with CYP, there are only two pieces specific to the preparation therapy phase. Ruth Schmidt Neven (2010) was interviewed about her book *Core Principles of Assessment and Therapeutic Communication with Children, Parents and Families*; however, it comes from the tradition of psychoanalytic child psychotherapy, as opposed to CYP counselling. The second is a short article by Liana Lowenstein (2011) looking at creative assessment techniques, within an integrative orientation.

Overall, however, it would appear that preparation and assessment of CYP from a humanistic orientation is a neglected area within the literature. This in itself is a diversity issue. How can we be sure that CYP can engage in a way with counselling that supports Gillick assessment without understanding what prepares them for a successful outcome? Perhaps counselling preparation is unexplored because they are seen as places *outside* the core humanistic counselling map whose roots are within the 'anti-medical model'. Assessment can be seen as antithetical to counselling. It is seen as labelling, prescribing and diagnosing and is beyond counselling's horizon. Indeed some counsellors might agree with Worrall (2006) that the only task during preparation/contracting is 'to create with them [the client] a relational climate that will most effectively facilitate their self-directed exploration and development' (2006: 52). For others there is a conviction that it is even contrary to Rogers' 'core conditions':

within the person-centred domain the question of assessment is ridiculous: the assessor would have to make a judgement not only about the client but on the relational dimensions between the client and the counsellor. (Mearns, 1997: 91)

## Contemporary developments and their impact on preparation practice in CYP counselling

However, the ever-growing field of CYP counselling is pushing at historical boundaries of what is necessary within the counselling map. It is articulating more clearly what it does and how its work, of necessity, differs from adult counselling. For instance, BACP's 'CYP Competency Framework for Humanistic Counselling' (2014) has 'ability to conduct a collaborative assessment' as one of its generic therapeutic competences. To create safe and effective practice counsellors must scaffold the preparation process in developmentally attuned ways that both facilitate each CYP to draw a map of *their* territory and enable the counsellor to finetune the picture to illuminate any areas of risk or vulnerability. They must help the client create and expand a schema for therapy that makes autonomous sense for them using sensory, motor and cognitive pathways.

This means assuming a more active role in the preparation phase. Katie McArthur's (2013) research of secondary school counselling highlights that 'emotional expression' is seen by young people as the most helpful aspect of their therapy, with difficulties in talking about emotions the key hindering factor.

Young people in the study also preferred a more 'active counsellor' approach: asking questions, offering advice, providing psycho-education and self-help strategies. These counsellor-led activities are seen to reduce anxiety, overcome barriers to emotional expression and create a sense of ease in the relationship.

Similarly, research carried out by Barnardo's (Regan and Craig, 2011) with primary school children indicated that 'talking about feelings' and 'counselling activities' were the two aspects children mentioned the most in interviews.

Developmentally and preferentially attuned activities help mediate the content of these preparation phase conversations. The right activity helps a child access and express emotion. Perhaps what looks like non-engagement is really crying out for a less verbal, more 'right-brain' approach. Here we might find that visual techniques, like a series of 'feelings faces' to map responses to key areas in a client's life, can break the silence. Or use of the sand tray to 'tell a story of me and my world' will unlock the communication pathway.

For others, activity is more 'left brain' and verbal, with structured questions establishing grounds for conversation: 'In your family … who is the safest person to talk to when you've had a hard day? Who is the best at being angry? Who is the one who sorts out fights between you and your brothers?' Scaling might also help a child with a more cognitive preference:

'On a scale of 1–10, where 1 is the worst and 10 is the best, how would you score your relationship with your teacher ... the two friends you mentioned ... your new stepdad?' A client's self-perception in relation to the reason(s) they are seeking support is another area often requiring a lateral approach from counsellors. Here asking a CYP how their 'best friend ... mum ... favourite teacher' might describe them, their strengths and qualities, can help access a useful self-perspective.

By adopting this flexible, adaptable approach counsellors can scaffold their input, moving until they find the right 'fit' for each client's developmental presentation and preferences. This 'back-and-forth' movement calls for a capacity to 'learn from our mistakes and mis-attunements' in a creative listening process that ultimately helps access the CYP's voice and story.

Our experience is that none of this is at odds with counselling's commitment to the therapeutic alliance, client autonomy and self-determination. Assessment *can* be a highly collaborative activity, a rich opportunity to get to know a CYP, partnering and catching a view of their territorial map. It is about generating 'constructive understanding' (Sharry, 2004) to inform preparation for therapy and its development at each successive phase.

## MAKING A COLLABORATIVE 'PREPARATION-FOR-THERAPY MAP': SEVEN KEY TASKS

We have identified seven key tasks in making the 'preparation-for-therapy map' (see Figure 10.1).

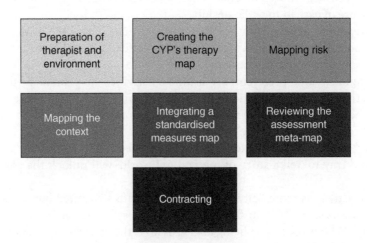

**Figure 10.1  Seven key tasks of the preparation-for-therapy map**

## First task: pre-preparation – therapist and environment

The preparation process begins before client and counsellor meet. In her article 'Therapist as host: making my guests feel welcome' (2006), Aman notes the importance of attending to the physical environment where we see clients, hypothesising that 'a calm space supports a person in getting distance from the immediacy of their experience, therefore enhancing the effectiveness of the conversations' (Aman, 2006: 8).

Leaflets, voicemail messages and websites need to have a warm, welcoming approach, and Aman gives examples of children's art work and a child-friendly introductory letter from her website. Her 'therapist as host' metaphor is useful for shaping therapists' own preparation before work with a new client:

> Treating someone as a cherished guest addresses the power differential undisputable in a therapeutic relationship by elevating the status of the person who comes to consult the therapist. (Aman, 2006: 4)

Addressing the power differential is of particular importance in CYP counselling, where elevating the status of the CYP serves against a 'therapist-knows-best' attitude. Children begin life as visual processors in the world and only acquire formal language later, so our space should be visually inviting with information conveyed through verbal and visual means. This is crucially important for younger children, those with special needs and those whose first language is not English.

## Second task: facilitating the CYP to create a personal preparation-for-therapy map

This involves accessing CYP's views on why they are coming to therapy and their perceptions of the impact that problems, issues and situations are having on their personal, family, school, friendships/relationships, hobbies and values/beliefs. In this task CYP map the strengths and resources they identify in themselves, their family, peer group, school and the wider community. This promotes a clear sense of autonomy and self-efficacy from the outset. Identifying strengths provides a bridge from problem perception to goal setting.

The map should include specific goals; usually about three is manageable for most CYP. This creates a transparent baseline for what change will 'look like'. Goals are best expressed as adding something new. 'I want to start doing X' rather than 'stop doing Y.'

Approaches and techniques include the strengths-based information gathering by Sharry (2004), the creative techniques indicated by Liana Lowenstein (1999, 2011) and structured therapeutic games such as *All About Me* (Hemming/Barnardo's). Age, developmental level, diversity and temperament/specific interests will dictate the best fit for each CYP.

## Third task: mapping risk

Issues of safety are central within CYP counselling. Historical, existing or potential risk must be part of the mapping process. When working with children under 12, this includes engaging with parents/carers in risk identification and assessment. The risk map should consider:

- parent/carer or young person with mental illness, current or historical;
- child/young person on the 'at risk' register;
- young person indicating wish or intent to harm self or others;
- history of abuse, neglect, domestic violence, other trauma;
- misuse of alcohol and/or other drugs;
- parent/family member in prison;
- newcomer/immigrant black/ethnic minority family;
- multiple bereavements;
- poor school attendance;
- poor parental involvement (for children 6–12);
- impact of learning or other disabilities;
- emotional communication difficulties;
- significant life cycle transitions in combination with any of the above.

Risk assessment informs whether counselling is a feasible support at this time in a young client's life. It contextualises other decisions too, including the counselling goals agreed – *what is realistically possible given the risks identified?* – the timeframe for reviews – *should reviews occur more often in the light of risk?* – and any risk assessment management required for safe, effective counselling to occur.

Risk assessment means asking about other services involved with the family, for example, social services and Child and Adolescent Mental Health Services (CAMHS), and explicitly contracting to liaise with these services as part of the assessment. With identification of risk there is a need to ensure that counselling is contextualised within a network of supports.

## Fourth task: mapping the context

To understand the diversity of the CYP's personal map we must contextualise it within the larger territory of family, school and community maps. This is particularly important in work with under-12s and with young people who present developmentally as 12 or under, due to learning or other disabilities.

Supporting adult carers during the preparation phase, including school staff members in school counselling, recognises the key role they play in defining or constraining the maps children live by (Szalavitz and Perry, 2010). Assessment with parents/carers can happen with adults only, or with the CYP present for all or part of the meeting(s). This covers the same ground as the CYP assessment, inviting caretakers to be part of the change process and 'change allies' with the child (Freeman et al., 1997). It may be that an interpreter is also part of this process for parents who are disabled or have English as a second language.

Encouraging caretakers to shift their map boundaries in terms of compassion, understanding, relationship or behaviour can free the child to make changes. In some instances the adults *must* make a change before change is a possibility for the child, for example, an acrimonious divorce where hostility pressurises a child to 'take sides', or where a school has a negative view of a pupil and cannot see the efforts she is making to change (see Example 1 below).

---

## Case Study 1: How a Change in Perspective for Adults Increases the Possibility of Change for a Child

Simon is 10 years old. He is identified as the school 'trouble-maker'. Early during counselling preparation Simon said he was always in conflict with his brother and peers at school. He was distressed by this as he was blamed as instigator on every occasion. As a result Simon was feeling very down on himself, though this went unrecognised behind the conflict. In the school's opinion he *was* the trouble-maker.

During pre-therapy assessment Simon identified that he wanted to change his behaviour, and how he saw himself. He wanted others to think more positively of him. The counsellor invited Simon's teacher to closely observe how often he got into trouble and what led up to it. The teacher discovered that Simon's behaviour was often a reaction to someone else's taunt. This observation saw the teacher become more compassionate towards Simon. She started to notice changes in his behaviour and encouraged him. This helped Simon to step back from situations of conflict. A new pre-therapy story about Simon was emerging, made possible through the involvement of a key adult who was willing to rethink an established story that could have hindered counselling progress.

As a young person increases in age there is less reliance on direct adult involvement because of their developmental capacity for increased autonomy and personal problem-solving. However, it is worth bearing in mind that young people may wish to continue to involve parents/carers in the work, especially where relationships are a source of distress.

---

## Case Study 2: Re-connecting Family Relationships in the Face of Suicidal Thoughts

Mark was 16 when he self-referred to the school-based counselling service in a school for pupils with mild to moderate learning disabilities. Mark initially presented with high levels of

*(Continued)*

(Continued)

emotional distress, finding it hard to verbalise his thoughts and feelings. However, he was able to indicate that things had got so bad that he had been thinking of taking his own life. Given Mark's level of distress and his difficulty in articulating it, the counsellor tentatively suggested completing the 'young person's stress profile'. Mark agreed and found it useful to communicate and clarify his distress this way.

It emerged that Mark greatly valued the relationship with his parents but felt it had been difficult lately. He began to identify this as a key contributor to his current feelings of stress and isolation. Taking Mark's lead, the counsellor indicated it would be possible to meet with his parents in a counselling session. Mark was interested in this idea. The next session was a conversation between Mark, his parents and the counsellor. During the session the counsellor facilitated a discussion about how much the whole family valued the close relationship they had and the things they did together to maintain it. Mark also got to hear directly from his parents what it was they particularly valued about him and their hopes for his future.

At the following session Mark completed the stress profile again to find significantly reduced scores. Mark saw the conversation with his parents as pivotal to his change in outlook. Given Mark's age, it would have been easy to overlook the relevance of parental involvement in the counselling assessment.

## Fifth task: integrating the map of standardised measures

Standardised measures are not incompatible with relational counselling practice. Using them does not require counsellors to resolve a clash between the 'art' and 'science' of preparation/assessment. Rather, it's about how to interconnect the analytical perspective of a measure with the more intersubjective, relational knowledge of a therapeutic conversation. Interconnection enriches potential for a fuller understanding of all the assessment material for the counsellor and CYP. The counsellor's task is to hold together the different – sometimes clashing – emerging perspectives, whilst centralising the voice of the CYP.

Several standardised measures have gained prominence within UK CYP counselling, namely the Strengths and Difficulties Questionnaire (SDQ) (Goodman, 2001) (available at www.sdqinfo.com) and the Young Person's Clinical Outcomes in Routine Evaluation (YP-COre) (Twigg et al., 2009).

The use of session-by-session measures has emerged over the past 5 years. Collecting outcome information at each session is a great way of gathering 'practice-based evidence'. Session-by-session measures improve effectiveness, reduce drop-out and prevent deterioration (Duncan and Sparks, 2010) without asking counsellors to make any other changes to how they work. In addition to the popular ten-item YP-Core, there is also a suite of measures called the Outcome Rating Scale (ORS) (Duncan et al, 2006), which tracks distress/well-being and the therapeutic alliance session-by-session. The ORS is validated for use with young people 12 and up; there is a version for children aged 6–11 called the Child Outcome Rating Scale (CORS) (Duncan et al., 2003), and one for children under 6 called the Young Child Outcome Rating Scale (YCORS). Quick to complete and useful as a clinical as well as an outcome tool, these measures have been widely used in school-based counselling services in Northern Ireland since 2008. They are available at www.heartandsoulofchange.com, and more information can be found in Stewart (2012).

Scoring the measure and sharing the result with the client, including an outline of its meaning in relation to the clinical cut-off, provides a final reference point in the collaborative preparation process. It further informs its outcome and decisions about counselling suitability.

## Sixth task: reviewing the 'assessment meta-map'

The endpoint of the preparation listening process will be the creation of a larger 'assessment meta-map'. Therapist and client, including key adults with younger children, need to review the meta-map together and agree on the suitability of counselling.

## Seventh task: contracting

If a period of counselling is agreed, a contract should be drawn up with the young client covering the following areas:

1. *Who will be involved?* Agreeing the level and extent of systemic involvement (if any).
2. *Where and when will the counselling happen?*
3. *What will happen in sessions?* Outlining the range of approaches and activities the counsellor can offer and ascertaining any immediate client preferences (e.g. sand tray work; psycho-education; therapeutic assessment game).
4. *Why might counselling be useful?* Establishing focus/purpose/goals; this includes talking with younger children (4–12 years) about why key adults feel it would be useful and checking this against their views.
5. *What about confidentiality?* Establishing confidentiality and its limits.
6. *What about counselling records?* Outlining the policy on record-keeping and gaining consent from the young person (or parent/carer if not 'Gillick competent').
7. *What about complaints?* Outlining the complaints policy and agreeing whether a nominated 'trusted adult' is required to represent the child's views.

## THEORETICAL UNDERPINNING

It is a pleasure to listen attentively to children because listening opens windows onto the child's world. As therapists, as we accept their invitation to explore their world, we quickly understand our dependency on them as our guides. The CYP's understanding of their world differs from the adult experience in a myriad of ways. I am reminded of the CYP who was exploring the experience of loss of a much loved adult with a parent. The parent had explained euphemistically that the adult had 'gone to be with Jesus'. The CYP thought for a moment, and then helpfully clarified, 'So they're in Bethlehem then'. A charming anecdote, or a sharp reminder of the literal way children understand the world.

Listening to the client involves not only what clients say but also being attuned to their age and stage of development. In laying the theoretical foundations for sensitive and autonomous therapy we believe that focusing on developmental theories will provide clear signposting and guidance. We advocate a framework for integration of counselling theory and child-centred practice as the basis for preparing CYP clients for therapy. We also believe that, given the CYP's embedding within their family system, it is essential to take the widest possible view of who and what needs to be prepared if CYP are to gain all they can from their experience of therapy. A diagram of the specifics of such individualised tasks might look something like the one in Figure 10.2.

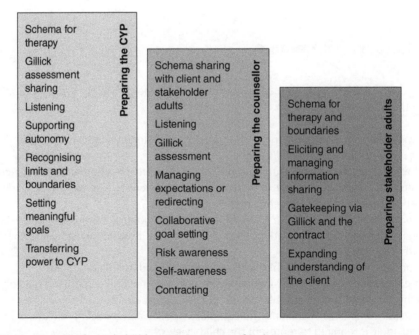

**Figure 10.2**   Key tasks for stakeholders in preparation for therapy.

To assist us in laying a theoretical basis for the work, we propose briefly to explore Piagetian theory, Bronfenbrenner's ecological systems theory, schema theory and the application of Vygotsky's theories to the process of preparation for therapy.

## Age and stage

Piaget asserted that childhood is not just *quantitatively* but *qualitatively* different from adulthood, as shown in the example above. Adults selectively mis-attend to this sometimes. As the counsellor enters into the process of preparing themselves for working therapeutically they must actively engage with the age-appropriate aspects of the CYP's voice. The counsellor must be listening so actively as to hear variations in the range of development between CYP within ages, stages and particular needs. The counsellor must understand the normative issues that development itself generates, whilst also being aware that every child is part of a particular complex familial, cultural and societal system. An applied understanding of diversity is essential to this approach and the counsellor must constantly challenge their own narrative and cultural understanding of the client and their world.

---

### Case Study 3: Listening to the Developmental Voice

Samira, aged 9, self-referred to a school counsellor after her mother had slipped into a diabetic coma in the early hours of the morning. Her mum had managed to call the emergency services when she felt unwell. The police had to break into the house and Samira was worried about her mother dying in the future. She had talked to her mum about this but her mum said she was 'being silly'. Mum felt Samira should be over it by now and didn't need counselling. Samira's view of illness and death differed markedly from her mum's. At 9, Samira was on the cusp of developing a more mature concept of death and dying. She had begun to recognise that death is permanent and irreversible, felt fiercely protective of her mum and did not want to distress her. Her mum had talked to her about diabetes as a manageable illness but Samira was unable to understand this because she had not yet developed a scientific view of illness as a process. Preparation for therapy involved acknowledging Samira's fears and concerns, whilst helping her mum to understand the need for a safe place for Samira to ask potentially upsetting questions, and explore different ways of understanding how human beings with illness survive with an intact sense of self. The developmentally aware counsellor in this case was actively engaged with understanding development and its effect on the client and was able to share it with the parent and young person.

## Individual variation

CYP are not a homogeneous group, despite the fact that we often talk about them as if they are. Individual children and young people differ markedly from each other in culture, temperament, experience, understanding and capacity to process many elements that represent the beginning of the therapeutic experience. CYP practitioners employ many different skills and tools and we should be respectful of other model-specific ways of working. Counsellors can also benefit from a more global understanding of how CYP engage with taking information from their environment. Gardener's theory of multiple intelligences alerts us to the fact that 'the brain has evolved over millions of years to be responsive to different kinds of content in the world. Language content, musical content, spatial content, numerical content' (Gardener, 1983). Learning styles theory encourages us to engage with the CYP styles of encountering the world, so preparation for therapy should include auditory, visual, read/write and kinaesthetic ways of introducing the therapeutic process. CYP counsellors value the client, their right to autonomy, and to safe, sensitive and appropriate access to therapy that makes human sense to the client (Donaldson, 1978). In order to ensure this, we must always take the CYP as our guide for the start of the therapeutic process, committing to setting aside our adult assumptions, frameworks and language. General history-taking and specific measures like YP-CORE or SDQ can support this.

## Context is everything

Ecological systems theory illustrates the complex systems in which the CYP lives. This helps us conceptualise the interacting and reciprocal effects of these systems on the client (and counsellor) whilst allowing for change due to the impact of time (Figure 10.3). Whilst Bronfenbrenner (1986: 2005) does not offer a counselling theory, he reminds us of the who, what and how of preparation as we engage in the pre-therapeutic process.

Whilst children are regarded as autonomous beings from the counsellor's perspective, and within the BACP ethical framework, not everyone within the child's social system may understand or accept this. The counsellor may have a differing view of autonomy from parents, social workers, teachers or other adults who have an interest in the therapeutic process. The CYP may have an unexplored understanding of their autonomy. The counsellor may need to prepare the CYP or stakeholder adults for this. Views of autonomy and control may differ between the multidisciplinary team in a school or CAMHS. Theoretical orientation also places demands on how counsellors prepare CYP for therapy work. The counsellor should move beyond this normative preparation by engaging with the legal and ethical framework within the CYP's system. In doing so the counsellor must hold the CYP's needs and rights as paramount. In practice this is rather like engaging in a multiplayer video game in which the counsellor is central because it involves the counsellor in mediating CYP intrapersonal issues

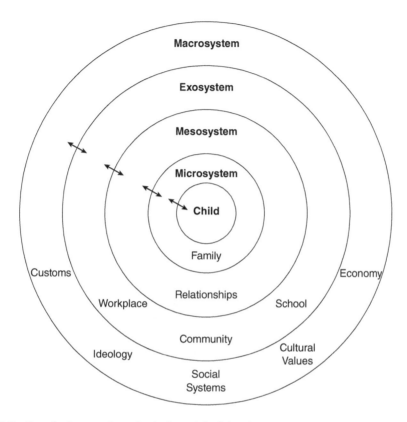

**Figure 10.3**   Bronfenbrenner's ecological model of development

like competence, capacity and consent, systemic interpersonal issues such as risk, safeguarding and confidentiality, and societal issues such as legal requirements regarding disclosures, role limits and boundaries. For example, CYP can often disclose safeguarding issues at an initial meeting. When dealing with complexity, a clear, simple plan is often best. Therefore, many of these issues can be dealt with at the outset of the preparation for therapy phase by clear communication with the CYP, their carers and any other interested parties, for example, social services.

## Developing a schema for therapy

CYP, carers and other interested adults often have no idea of what counselling is. Just as we have no schema for astrophysics (unless somebody helps us acquire one!) so CYP, carers and

## Case Study 4: Holding the Client Central

Cody is a 15-year-old boy who has cancer. He and his parents know that his disease is terminal. He has been offered a place on a drug trial that may extend his life by a few months. His parents want him to agree to the trial and have asked him to spend time considering this in counselling. Cody is clear that he has made the decision to decline the drug trial. He wants to spend his time in counselling discussing how to tell his parents and plan for the last months of his life.

Cody's case is just one example of many where competing expectations, hopes, needs, desires and interests can benefit from open, thoughtful and honest preparation for therapy. Preparation for therapy involves the counsellor in the process of actively engaging with competing interests whilst advocating for the client. It requires counsellors to use age-appropriate, high-level skills to establish excellent psychological contact with the client. Once this has been established, respectful, collaborative assessment of the CYP's developmental ability and potential, reasoned professional judgements about their ability to understand and consent to counselling, and honest communication can be entered into. Only by doing so can we ensure that young people have opted to attend counselling freely (not because their mum, dad or social worker felt it would be good), understand the consequences of counselling and speak openly owning the therapeutic space as theirs. Through a process like this Cody was able to own the counselling space and his parents were helped by him to let go. Preparation for therapy for the parents was an essential adjunct to this process.

interested adults need the counsellor to help them develop a schema for therapy. It is the role of the counsellor to provide a window into the world of therapy. This builds engagement and provides a narrative for the process. Clear information leaflets, using visual images and simple words and website statements need to be offered. Care must be taken to understand the translation pitfalls when using an interpreter too. For example, an interpreter translated 'confidentiality' to a child as a 'professional secret' and this had to be explored and challenged at depth until full understanding was attained. Pre-therapy conversations need to be had with CYP and adults that emphasise that the CYP, and not the parent/carer, is the client. Clear, picture-based, verbal, age-appropriate descriptions of what counselling is (and is not) need to be provided for CYP and stakeholders (Arnold, 2010). Expectations on all sides need to be elicited and explored. In Cody's case this was essential. Interested adults need to be freed up from the 'counsellor as fixer' paradigm because CYP are not 'broken'. They are themselves, and we respect them as such. Counsellors need to establish clear confidentiality, safeguarding and risk boundaries to the preparation for therapy schema so that young people are not shocked or disappointed when, during or after assessment, a counsellor must report a disclosure or take action because a CYP is at risk of significant harm. A positive view of standardised and session-by-session measures should be built from the outset. We are strongly of the opinion that measures are there to aid the client in their understanding of self, change and development. However, in order for the client to be positive the counsellor must have honestly explored and engaged with their barriers and biases to the use of such resources. It is fascinating to see even very young clients use skills they have learnt to develop positive personal evaluation skills that build their confidence in school, with friends or at home.

## Preparing for good outcomes – the zone of proximal development (ZPD)

This leads us to the final girder in our theoretical underpinning of preparation for therapy. Vygotsky (1934) postulated that the work of development can be described as the acquisition of cultural tools. As counsellors we might describe the process as a gateway to more useful ways of being for the client. He postulated that understanding and meanings are acquired through interactions between adults and children, and that this begins 'first as an interpersonal process before it appears in the child as an intrapersonal process' (Vygotsky, 1988, cited in Lee and Das Gupta, 1995: 13). He also introduced the concept of the ZPD (Vygotsky, 1934). This means that children can get a certain way on their own initiative but the presence of a respectful, listening and engaged adult increases the child's developmental reach. The difference between where they are and where they can get to is the ZPD. This is the counselling space.

# Key Learning

- The process of preparing children to engage successfully with counselling and therapy involves the management of sensitive, ethical and careful interactions with both the CYP and the system in which they live.
- Careful preparation of client, parents and other adults will support the CYP's autonomy from the outset of the process.
- Systemic influences that are actively engaged with and managed will have a positive impact on the CYP's experience o f counselling and therapy for the young client, and ultimately for their family.
- Key developmental issues have an impact on the process of engaging with CYP.
- If these developmental issues are well understood and respected by counsellors and therapists, clients will experience more satisfactory outcomes.
- In applying some research and key considerations from the outset of therapy that keep the CYP central, a model for preparation for therapy might begin to emerge.

## Summary

- A 'collaborative assessment' is essential for safe and effective preparation for therapy with children and young people.
- There are seven key collaborative assessment tasks that make up a 'preparation-for-therapy' map:

  - pre-preparation (therapist and therapy environment);
  - facilitating a personal preparation-for-therapy map with a child/young person;
  - mapping risk;
  - mapping the context;
  - integrating outcome measures;
  - reviewing the assessment 'meta-map';
  - contracting.

- Counsellors should have a working knowledge of developmental theory if they are to provide safe and effective therapy.
- Counsellors need to draw on this knowledge in order to tune into the age and stage of each client's developmental presentation.
- CYP are not a homogeneous group and the counselling approach should reflect awareness of 'multiple intelligences' and cater for a range of 'learning styles' – visual, auditory, read/write and kinaesthetic – to help scaffold a schema for therapy.
- In the presence of a respectful, engaged and attuned therapist the counselling space can become a ZPD for CYP, where they can extend their developmental reach and make positive life changes.

## Discussion Questions

The purest form of listening is to listen without memory or desire. (Wilfrid Bion, 1897–1979)

1. How might the counsellor's experience of their own childhood or their experience of parenthood have an impact on their understanding of how to prepare children, young people and parents for the experience of therapy? How might culture intrude on this?
2. The process of counsellor reflection is vital to preparing ourselves for undertaking therapeutic work with any client group. It is particularly important in working with CYP because

the counsellor may find themselves 'staring into the mirror of (their) own grief' (Formica, 2009). As a consideration of the potential for parallel processes in the room, what memories or desires might I need to deal with?

3. What knowledge, skills, attitudes and values do I have in assessing the capacity, competence and ability of CYP to give consent to counselling? What knowledge and skills do I need to acquire? What personal, cultural and professional attitudes and values do I need to reflect on and process, to assist myself, children, parents and other concerned adults in the process of understanding the autonomy of CYP?

## Develop Your Skills

### Activity 1 – Hearing Your Own Voice

Record yourself explaining the process of counselling to a child, adolescent, parent. Play it back and reflect on what you have learnt from listening. Think about diversity as you do this.

### Activity 2 – Preparing the Setting

You are a counsellor in a school setting. A teacher comes to you and asks for advice. A client's parent has made it explicit that they want to withhold consent for their 14-year-old to attend counselling. The young person is clear in their own mind that they do wish to attend. What processes would you as a counsellor have to undergo to prepare yourself to work with this situation? What might you as a therapist be able to say to the teacher, the young person, the parent, that might add clarity to the pre-therapy process?

### Activity 3 – Preparing the Client

Consider the following clients:

- an 8-year-old, who is described by a parent as being very anxious;
- a 14-year-old newcomer who has fled ethnic violence;
- a 10-year-old who has been exposed to domestic abuse at home;
- a 15-year-old wanting to explore issues around gender identity and sexuality.

What preparation might you need to set in place that is specific to these clients as you consider working with them?

## Further Reading

CYP counsellors require a developmental meta-rationale for how they begin, engage in and work with their clients. Learning about development as a precursor to preparing for therapeutic work is both a joy and a challenge. For CPD reading about child development and child centred assessment we recommend:

Bion, W. (1967) Second Thoughts. London: Karnac Books.

Daniels, H. (ed.) (2005) An Introduction to Vygotsky. Abingdon: Routledge.

Duncan, B., Miller, S., Wampold, E. and Hubble, M. (eds) (2010) *The Heart and Soul of Change: Delivering What Works in Therapy*, 2nd edn. Washington, DC: APA.

Hubble, M. (eds) (2010) *The Heart and Soul of Change: Delivering What Works in Therapy*, 2nd edn. Washington, DC: APA.

Lowenstein, L. (1999) *Creative Interventions for Troubled Children and Youth*. Toronto: Champion Press.

Music, G. (2011) *Nurturing Natures: Attachment and Children's Emotional, Socio-Cultural and Brain Development*. Hove: Psychology Press.

Santrock, J. (2010) *Child Development: An Introduction*. New York: McGraw-Hill.

Sharry, J. (2004) *Counselling Children, Adolescents and Families*. London: SAGE.

Vygotsky, L. (1935) Mind in Society: The Development of Higher Psychological Processes. Cole, M., John-Steiner, V., Scribner, S. and Souberman, E. (eds) (1978) Cambridge, MA: Harvard University Press.

Wampold, B.E. (2015) How important are the common factors in psychotherapy? An update. *World Psychiatry 14*: 270–277. doi:10.1002/wps.20238

### Online Resources

BACP website: www.bacp.co.uk, especially the BACP Children and Young People Division and the Competences for Working with Children and Young People

Counselling MindEd: https://www.minded.org.uk, especially modules CM 0103: Presenting Issues and CM 06: Using Measures

## REFERENCES

Aman, J. (2006) 'Therapist as host: making my guests feel welcome'. *The International Journal of Narrative Therapy and Community Work* 3: 3–10.

Arnold, C. (2010) *Understanding Schemas and Emotions in Early Childhood*. London: SAGE.

BACP (2014) *CYP Competency Framework for Humanistic Counselling*. Lutterworth: BACP. Available at: https://www.bacp.co.uk/media/1954/bacp-competences-working-with-children-young-people-counsellors-guide.pdf

Bronfenbrenner, U. (1979). *The Ecology of Human Development: Experiments by Nature and Design.* Cambridge, Massachusetts: Harvard University Press.

Bronfenbrenner, U. (1986) Ecology of the family as a context for human development. *Research Perspectives Developmental Psychology 22*(6): 723–742.

Bronfenbrenner, U. (2005) *Making Human Beings Human.* London: SAGE.

Donaldson, M. (1978) *Children's Minds.* London: Fontana.

Duncan, B. and Sparks, J. (2010). *Heroic clients, heroic agencies: partners for change*, 2nd edn. Jensen Beach, FL: Author.

Duncan, B., Miller, S. and Sparks, J. (2003). *Child Outcome Rating Scale.* Jensen Beach, FL: Author.

Duncan, B., Miller, S., Wampold, E. and Hubble, M. (eds) (2010) *The Heart and Soul of Change: Delivering What Works in Therapy*, 2nd edn. Washington, DC: APA.

Formica, M.J. (2009) *Enlightened living, mindfulness practice in everyday life.* Available at: www.psychologytoday.com/blog/enlightened-living/200901/the-me-in-you-parallel-process-in-psychotherapy (accessed 8 February 2018).

Freeman, H., Epston, D. and Lobovits, D. (1997) *Playful Solutions to Serious Problems.* New York: W.W. Norton & Company.

Gardener, H. (1983) *Frames of Mind: The Theory of Multiple Intelligences.* New York: Basic Books.

Goodman R. (2001) 'Psychometric properties of the strengths and difficulties questionnaire'. *Journal of the American Academy of Child and Adolescent Psychiatry 40*(11): 1337–1345.

Lee, V. and Das Gupta, P. (1995) *Children's Cognitive and Language Development.* Milton Keynes: Open University Press.

Lowenstein, L. (1999) *Creative Interventions for Troubled Children and Youth.* Toronto: Champion Press.

Lowenstein, L. (2011) 'Assessing creatively'. *Counselling Children and Young People Journal.* BACP. https://www.bacp.co.uk/bacp-journals/bacp-children-young-people-and-families-journal/september-2011/

Mearns, M. (1997). Person-centred Counselling Training. London: Sage.

McArthur, K. (2013) *Change processes in school-based humanistic counselling: a qualitative interview study.* Paper presented at the 19th BACP Research Conference, Birmingham.

Phillips, A. (2003) *Equals.* New York: Basic Books

Piaget, J. and Inhelder, B. (1969 [1936]) *The Psychology of the Child* (Reprint, 2000). New York: Basic Books

Regan, H. and Craig, E. (2011) 'A thematic analysis of schools' and children's experiences of the Barnardo's primary school counselling service 'Time 4 Me' unpublished paper, Barnardo's N. Ireland.

Schmidt Neven, R. (2010) *Core Principles of Assessment and Therapeutic Communication with Children, Parents and Families: Towards the Promotion of Child and Family Wellbeing.* London: Routledge.

Sharry, J. (2004) *Counselling Children, Adolescents and Families.* London: SAGE.

Stewart, D. (2012) 'Giving the client a voice: client-directed, outcome-informed work with children and young people'. *Children and Young People's Counselling* 3.

Szalavitz, M. and Perry, B.D. (2010) *Born for Love: Why Empathy is Essential and Endangered.* New York: Harper.

Twigg, E., Barkham, M., Bewick, B., Mulhern, B., Connell, J. and Cooper, M. (2009) The young person's CORE: development of a brief outcome measure for young people. *Counselling and Psychotherapy Research* 9(3): 160–168.

Vygotsky, L. (1934) *Thought and Language.* [Translation] Revised and edited by Kozulin, A. (1986). Cambridge, MA: MIT Press.

Wampold, B.E. and Imel, Z.E. (2015) *The Great Psychotherapy Debate: The Evidence for What Makes Psychotherapy Work.* 2nd edn. New York: Routledge.

Worrall, M. (2006) 'Contracting within person-centred counselling and psychotherapy'. In C. Sills (ed). *Contracts in Counselling and Psychotherapy*, 2nd edn. London: Sage.

# 11

# THE THERAPEUTIC ALLIANCE IN COUNSELLING PROCESS

## SUE PATTISON AND SANDRA BELL, WITH ACKNOWLEDGEMENT TO MARK PREVER

This chapter will discuss:

- The concept of therapeutic alliance
- Building a therapeutic relationship
- The therapeutic process
- Stages of counselling

## INTRODUCTION

This chapter explores the concept of the 'therapeutic alliance', so critical in counselling, but especially so in work with children and young people. When a counsellor goes to meet a new young client, it is often the issue that concerns them most. Will it be possible to build a relationship with this young person? Will it be possible to establish a climate of trust and respect? Many counsellors express concern about their ability to establish a therapeutic relationship, which ensures that therapy can take place. The relationship we build with clients impacts on the counselling process and the client's process and progress.

## THERAPEUTIC ALLIANCE

The therapeutic alliance may also be referred to as the 'working alliance' but, put simply, the therapeutic alliance indicates the degree to which the child or young client trusts and believes in the counsellor and whether they 'like' them or not. It refers to the collaborative aspect of the relationship between a young client and their counsellor. Forming such an alliance is especially important when working with children and young people, who may come for counselling having already experienced a range of 'interventions', where a therapeutic outcome has been second to behavioural or attitudinal change.

The importance of the relationship in therapy and counselling with children and young people did not begin with Carl Rogers, although his substantial work remains a very important component and the essence of any discussion about the relationship between client and counsellor. In his seminal article published in 1957, Carl Rogers set out his understanding of the relationship in therapy as well as its centrality. The 'conditions of therapeutic change' influenced all his subsequent works and the development of what later became known as 'person-centred therapy'. Rogers argued that therapy is less about what the therapist does to a client and more about the quality of that relationship and the therapeutic conditions, which he felt were essential in any therapeutic work. These were defined as empathy, unconditional positive regard and congruence; that is, being yourself, non-judgemental and real with a client. It is worth noting that empathy is an important component of the therapeutic alliance across all models of counselling theory and practice (Feller and Cottone, 2003). Rogers also emphasised the need for what he termed 'psychological contact', by which he meant that both client and therapist need to be aware of the presence of each other for a relationship to occur. It is hard to see how a therapeutic alliance can be formed with a young client where such contact does not exist.

The concept of the therapeutic alliance has its roots in psychoanalytic theory with its emphasis on the transference relationship between therapist and client where the work is based around the client's previous experiences of relationships such as with parents or significant others. A comprehensive and detailed history of the concept of the therapeutic alliance can be found in Horvath and Luborsky (1993). This analysis stretches as far back to the work of Freud, where, according to the authors, he refers to the analyst maintaining 'serious interest' in and 'sympathetic understanding' of the client to allow for the client to attach themselves positively to the analyst. Greenson (1967) has also added to the discussion around the concept of the working alliance in psychoanalytic theory (see also Kanzer, 1981). Focused discussion of the concept begins with the work of Bordin (1979), who suggested that the working alliance in therapy comprised three elements: *tasks*, *goals* and *bonds*. These were later developed by Dryden (1989), who included a new component, 'views', which he felt should be included in any expanded discussion of the therapeutic alliance. Bordin believed that the therapeutic alliance was an essential component in counselling and was possibly the most important factor in bringing about change in the client.

Goals are the outcomes which the client and counsellor have agreed to work towards together. In other words, a mutual understanding of what might be causing the client's problems or unhappiness. Such an agreement is more likely to lead to a successful outcome for the client. Tasks are the things that the counsellor does to help the client achieve their goals. These may be problematic where there has been a lack of contracting with the young client or where there are misunderstandings around the way the work will proceed.

Dryden (1989) sees the client's attitude to the counsellor as important. This might include things like trust in the counsellor and feelings of safety in the relationship. He also refers to the client's faith in the counsellor to bring about change in their lives. He notes that clients will often bring with them to the counselling room 'pre-formed tendencies', which have the potential to impact markedly on the counselling process. His reference to 'client reluctance' may be relevant to work with children and young people who may have developed pre-conceived ideas about adults in their livesand whether they can invest trust in them.

Dryden is clear that the establishment of a therapeutic alliance is most likely to occur where the views held by both client and counsellor are convergent, and where they are not, they need to be explored as part of the counselling work. Views held by both client and counsellor around issues such as the nature of the client's problems, how these are best addressed and how this will happen also require exploration leading to common understanding.

In drawing on the work and extending it to children and adolescents, Campbell and Simmonds (2011) found that empathy and trust were highly valued by young people, whilst an additional parental support dimension was identified as of particular importance, especially where the counsellor was able to show understanding, reassurance and support. It is not surprising to find that research has shown a strong correlation between the establishment of an effective working alliance and 'success' in therapy. An excellent and detailed analysis of the arguments around this can be found in Muran and Barber (2010). Equally, it follows that where there are obstacles to the establishment of an effective working alliance, client progress will be limited – if, indeed, the child or young person continues to regularly attend sessions. Most research into the therapeutic alliance has related to work with adults, but this is changing, and some useful papers can be found in the Further Reading section below.

What can hinder the therapeutic alliance? Ackerman and Hilsenroth (2001) looked at the personal attributes of the therapist that might interfere with the therapeutic alliance. These included: rigidity; uncertainty; being critical, distant, tense and distracted. They also noted that the therapeutic techniques of the counsellor were an important factor and a negative influence on the working alliance where sessions were overstructured, where there was inappropriate self-disclosure, an overuse of transference interpretation and an unhelpful use of silence. In recent years there has been increasing academic discussion around the concept of 'ruptures' or a 'weakening' in the therapeutic alliance and their repair. Interested readers might want to look at Eubanks et al. (2010) and Safran and Muran (2000). We know when a therapeutic alliance has been established with a young client: we have a sense that our young client is engaged with the process, and we seem to understand each other. The client is open and appears to trust us. We have a feeling that progress is being made. We feel a sense of rapport and that we are doing what we are meant to be doing. Conversely, where there is a lack of understanding and communication between counsellor and young client, it is likely that a working alliance has not been established. Where the client becomes frustrated with the counsellor, expressing anger or anxiety or, indeed, a lack of interest, it might be suggested that the working alliance is in difficulty.

Returning to the influence of Carl Rogers, there exists a consensus that regardless of counselling orientation, it is hard to see how without the 'core conditions', a therapeutic relationship can be established. It doesn't matter how much training a person has done or what counselling qualifications have been achieved, it is difficult to see how these professional developments alone are sufficient for the building of a therapeutic working relationship. This is possibly even more marked when working with children and young people who may already have suspicions about professionals and who desire a helping relationship that is characterised by warmth, acceptance, trust, realness and an empathic ability to feel what they are feeling.

My (Sue) experience of working with children and young people indicates to me that a therapeutic alliance is more likely when the counsellor is able to address issues of power and authority, suspend the ego, and bring some equality and mutual respect into the relationship. Other important dimensions to the relationship are that it should be characterised by warmth, friendliness, honesty, openness, a lack of judgement, real empathy, showing energy and interest in the child or young person and their story. Children and adolescents need to feel that their counsellor is a real person and not somebody in a role.

Bryant-Jefferies (2004: 6–7) draws our attention to the work of Everall and Paulson (2002), which focused specifically on the needs of adolescents. Based on a series of semi-structured interviews, three themes were explored in relation to the therapeutic alliance: therapeutic environment, uniqueness of the therapeutic relationship and therapists' characteristics. They observed that a therapeutic alliance was characterised by acceptance, supportiveness, trustworthiness and the appropriateness of the therapeutic tasks and goals. Bryant-Jefferies notes how it is important for the young client to see the therapeutic relationship as special, and indeed the counsellor as their 'special friend', and the relationship experienced by the young person as being different to those normally experienced with an adult. In this sense, there is the expectation that the counsellor will adapt their working style to suit the age of their client.

At the relational level, it is important that the counsellor can help the client to find a sense of meaning and hope, allow the child to talk about what is important to them and not show frustration or impatience when the young person has lost hope, is sad or despairing. The literature reveals an acceptance that the therapeutic alliance or its equivalent is an essential part of any therapeutic work, regardless of orientation or modality. Muran and Barber (2010) refer to Wolfe and Goldfried's (1998) description of it as 'the quintessential integrative variable' and most quoted 'common factor' in psychotherapy as discussed by Wampold (2001). However, they also refer to a growing number of writers who have challenged this assumption or see the matter as being of greater complexity than first understood. Some of these points are explored in the literature listed in the Further Reading section.

## COUNSELLING PROCESS AND STAGES

Counselling with children and young people is undoubtedly for many a rewarding and yet challenging area of work. I (Sandra) often find myself remembering my own early childhood and the anguishes I encountered, recollecting times when life absolutely seemed so unfair, of getting blamed for something I didn't do and of having to take my younger sister out with me wherever I went. I have worked as a counsellor in schools for over 11 years and in this time, I have seen a significant increase in terms of 'self-referrals' from young people. One can only suggest that this is a positive move and inclines towards counselling for young people becoming less stigmatising and more of a 'norm'. However, I know this is more likely to do with the ethos of the school as well as the school's budget. A recent study of school-based counselling suggests having access to emotional well-being expertise in a school context plays a crucial role in improving the mental health of young people in the UK. Furthermore, Cooper (2013) and Street (2013) suggest a frequent reason for referral to school counselling is for 'family relationship' problems and that young people most frequently present at school counselling with concerns around family difficulties. This they say equates to approximately a third of all young people with issues around 'anger' being the second most common reason for referral especially for boys.

In this part of the chapter we will look at the therapeutic process of counselling with young people and identify specific stages with the help of an anonymised case study. Although there can be marked differences in the counselling process within the contrasting fields, each one typically emphasises the importance of nurturing the therapeutic relationship in order to make effective change or bring new awareness to light. In the course of my work as a school counselling service manager, I too am seeing an increase in the number of referrals for young people struggling to deal with issues around significant relationships in their lives. Though managing this process can often be a difficult time for many adolescents it can be more challenging when there is added anxiety and stress. When this happens, it can have a significant impact upon other important relationships in the lives of young people. As a consequence, typically it is often the relationship with parents or carers which seems to be affected the most (Cooper, 2013; Street, 2013).

It cannot be overemphasised how important it is to establish a strong therapeutic alliance with young people to begin to really understand what might be troubling them. Subsequently, the stages of progression (or regression) of this process will be determined by many factors, not least the counsellor's ability to connect with the young person, or what Geldard and Geldard (2010) term as the counsellor's ability to 'join' with the child or young person. In the well documented series of books by Geldard and Geldard relating to counselling with children and young people, they refer to the term a 'Proactive Approach' for counselling adolescents. More than that, they suggest that when young people are progressing satisfactorily along their developmental path from childhood to adulthood, they generally feel okay about themselves and usually do not need counselling help (Geldard and

Geldard, 2010). However, this, they imply can be interrupted for a number of reasons and for some young people being able to tap into their own inbuilt resources is enough to get them through a difficult period. For other young people this may be different, and they might instead reach out for support from either close friends or relatives, or confide in a favourite teacher they can trust. However, Geldard and Geldard (2010) propose that when a young person's problems become more serious or start to increase they may be unable to cope and need the help of a counselling professional, which is when the Proactive Approach to counselling could be considered. The Proactive Approach consists of five key points that counsellors need to consider:

1. Being responsive to the adolescent's developmental needs.
2. Believing the adolescent.
3. Joining an adolescent style of communication.
4. Being proactive.
5. Respecting the adolescent's disclosure processes.

Geldard and Geldard also draw attention to the need for counsellors to be more flexible and spontaneous when working with young people and that the process itself is less likely to be clear cut. They put forward the idea that young people are often struggling with changing constructs and are sometimes unable to see the bigger picture of the world in which they are living (Geldard and Geldard, 2010). What's more they support the idea that a young person's process of discovery is about striving to make sense and connect with separate parts of themselves. Their work promotes the idea that when counsellors are faced with young people in sessions who are constantly changing from one subject to another, counsellors could facilitate this exploration by using the Proactive Approach. They suggest that this approach allows for and also requires the counsellor to be 'spontaneous, creative, flexible and opportunistic', whilst at the same time remaining focused on the counselling relationship and process (Geldard and Geldard, 2010)

It is also important to recognise that each young person is unique, with a unique set of circumstances that brought them to counselling in the first place. For this reason, the way in which they progress or regress through the stages of counselling will vary. It can on occasion feel like a game of Snakes and Ladders for both the counsellor and the young person. There are some young people who appear to be progressing well through the changing stages of the relationship, starting to climb a ladder with a clearer picture beginning to emerge, only to find that during the week, life has thrown them a 'double six' and down the snake they go, right back to where they started from. For this reason, not only do we need to be mindful that this can happen; we should in some ways expect it too, as this is often the nature of adolescents presenting difficulties – up one minute and down the next. As a result, we need to pay attention to both the personal and interpersonal relationships of our young clients on a session-by-session basis and be ready to work in the 'here-and-now' with however a young person presents.

In the same way, Tudor (2008) says the therapist needs to:

Attune to the pace of the particular young person's process on a moment-to-moment basis, if this is felt to be too slow by the young person, they are likely to lose interest and disengage. If this is felt to be moving too quickly, the young person may well feel overwhelmed, and could potentially draw negative self-conclusions, for example, 'this is going over my head. I must be really stupid'. Tudor (2008: 46)

Humanistic therapies stress the need for counsellors to be able to engage with the young person's perspective by having an ability to 'stay close to the young person's language, emotional state and developmental capacities' (BACP, 2015: 40). In doing so, they suggest counsellors have the ability to help a young person express themselves verbally by 'scaffolding' communication. This means having the ability to be creative and adaptive. As well as this they suggest counsellors should be able to encourage a young person to express themselves by thinking aloud for them, for example, 'I wonder if…'. Or by offering an opinion 'Do you think that …' (BACP, 2015: 41). These are important recommendations, not only because they can facilitate the growth of the therapeutic relationship, but also because they can help determine the process and stages of the therapy. Similarly, the same document refers to counsellors having the capacity to maintain the alliance and being able to recognise when the alliance might threaten the progress of therapy, and states:

A counsellor should have the ability to give and ask for feedback about what is happening in the here-and-now interaction, in a manner which invites exploration with the client. (BACP, 2015: 47)

We will now consider the following case study and the different stages of therapy. In addition we will reflect on the importance of developing, sustaining and pacing the therapy by carefully attuning and matching our young adolescents in therapy.

## Case Study: Nabil

Nabil is a 14-year-old boy and lives at home with his mum and stepdad and one older sister, Leila, who is 18. Leila is at university studying law. Nabil is a high achiever expecting to gain mostly As in his final exams. He has a close group of friends and he is well liked by both peers and teaching staff. His parents would like him to follow his sister to university to study for a career in law too. Nabil feels under immense pressure to follow the same career path and is worried about upsetting his parents, but feels as if he is losing his own identity. All of this was beginning to have an adverse effect on Nabil's relationships in school as well as at home. He was also becoming extremely anxious and easily upset.

*(Continued)*

(Continued)

Nabil was very close to his maternal grandfather, who recently passed away. The counselling referral emphasised Nabil did not wish his parents to know he was in counselling and said he wouldn't talk to anyone if they had to be told. Nabil was anxious about being in session and this was observed and sensitively acknowledged by the counsellor. He emphasised on no account did he want his parents to know that he was coming for counselling, stating 'I would never come back if they knew'. The therapist began the relationship-building initially by explaining the confidentiality and limits of this and then proceeded based on the Gillick guidelines, reaching an acceptable agreement with Nabil. The counsellor helped him explore his thoughts around his belief that his mum never listened to him as he spoke about the unfairness of not been understood. Nabil explained how he desperately wanted things to be different at home and was becoming convinced that his mum really disliked him and favoured Leila. He spoke about his mum always seeming irritated when he was around and felt she just wanted him out of the way. The counsellor was able to facilitate the active relationship-building by accurately summarising Nabil's comments and reflecting both content and feelings back to him around wanting things to be different at home with his mum. The middle stages of counselling were focused on helping Nabil to gain further insight and understanding of his problems. One approach was the use of the 'I'm wondering if …' question:

Therapist:  'I'm wondering if not being listened to by Mum is what's really making you unhappy?'

Nabil:  'Yes, exactly, it's like I may as well not be here. It's do this, no, do that, and she knows I've got homework to do as well, but she always wants me to do what she wants straight away, like my feelings don't matter!'

Therapist:  'That sounds quite difficult and maybe a bit confusing at times? When you are asked to do different things … And it sounds like your homework is really important too?'

Nabil:  'Yeah, I just get so angry … and if I try to explain why I can't do the jobs she wants me to do because I've got homework, she just grounds me!'

Paralleling the adolescent communication by agreeing with Nabil's point of view around feeling unheard helped to validate his feelings and maintain the trusting relationship that had begun to develop.

Therapist:  'Mmm, so it sounds like you would really like Mum to understand that doing your homework is a priority for you, but that if you try and explain this, you might get grounded?'

Nabil: 'Exactly, that's what's so frustrating. It's like I don't count anymore.'

Therapist: 'You don't count anymore? Was there a time when you felt you did count, Nabil?'

Nabil: 'Yeah, before my grandad died … (Nabil became upset at this point) 'I could tell Grandad anything, he was the only person who understood how I felt, and he could always make Mum understand.'

Therapist: 'It sounds like Grandad was very important to you and really understood you? And that maybe he could put things across in a way that made Mum understand? You must really miss him?'

Nabil: 'Yes … I do, that's just it … He could always make her listen … but I can't.'

This was active relationship-building by helping to understand the difficulty Nabil was encountering with the use of open-ended questions and accurate reflective feedback. Likewise, the use of exception-oriented questions, such as asking Nabil if there was a time when he felt he did count, enabled the counselling relationship to further progress.

In the concluding stages of counselling Nabil began to recognise and acknowledge that although he was grieving for the loss of his grandad, his mum was probably still grieving too. Nabil was keen to mention how he thought coming to the counselling sessions was making a difference to his mood and the way he was beginning to feel about himself. He also confessed the way in which he answered his mum at times probably angered her a lot and was likely the cause for the awful arguments at home.

Therapist: 'You know in our last session, Nabil, you said that counselling was beginning to help you? I'm wondering if you can tell me in what way it's helping.'

Nabil: 'Yeah it's mainly that I've got someone else that I can talk too about my feelings, without bottling it all up. I get listened to again.'

Therapist: 'And being listened to is really important for you?'

Nabil: 'Yes, it just makes me less angry. It's like I can think clearer.'

Therapist: 'Do you think anything's changed since you've been able to think clearer?'

Nabil: 'Yeah loads, you know when you asked if I thought could Mum still be grieving too? Well, I'd never thought of it in that way, I just thought she hated me. So last night when she asked me to tidy my room, I just took a deep breath (pause) and I answered her in a calmer voice.'

Therapist: 'And then …?'

*(Continued)*

(Continued)

Nabil:      'She said I could finish my homework first, and then tidy my room. I couldn't believe it! Then asked me if I fancied a pizza take out later!'

Therapist:  'So talking in a calmer voice gets you a pizza takeout?!'

The counsellor made use of the humour in this situation to maintain the positive relationship. With reference to specific competences for working with young people, the British Association for Counselling and Psychotherapy (BACP) outlines the importance of counsellors having an ability to respond to humour and play as it can help young people to normalise feelings and lessen anxiety (BACP, 2015: 36). Similarly, Geldard and Geldard (2010) advocate for counsellors being able to use appropriate humour to effect change in a young person, but emphasise the importance of paying careful attention to when this is applied. Preparation for the end of therapy was considered and both Nabil and his therapist agreed that a 'countdown' method would be beneficial. Nabil was reminded of how many sessions were left before the final one, which allowed for Nabil and his counsellor to review what, if anything, had changed or had particularly worked well, and to look at what could be improved on. Nabil liked the idea of having time to prepare for the end of therapy and came up with the following metaphor:

It'll be a bit like when I practise my rock climbing, I don't just get to the top and then jump off, I've got to work my way down slowly.

The counsellor acknowledged Nabil's use of such a symbolic metaphor and said 'Sounds like you really understand the process of how we might prepare to end our sessions together?'

Nabil:      'Yeah, I have I suppose and that's what this has been like for me. It's been my rock.'

## DIVERSITY

We realise that the content of this chapter is based on western therapeutic approaches, developed and published in the English language. However, we are also aware of the varied range of ethnicities and languages within the contexts in which counselling takes place. Within my own family there are at least five different languages spoken and a range of nationalities and ethnicities. One of the challenges faced by counselling services is to provide access to a diverse range of young clients, including those with mental or physical impairment. This means that facilitating the therapeutic relationship, accessing the counselling process, and a range of creative techniques and strategies needs to be made inclusive (see Chapter 19). The therapeutic relationship is built on mutual respect and unconditional warmth and acceptance, which cross boundaries of language, ethnicity and mental or physical impairment.

## Key Learning

- In this chapter you have explored the concept of therapeutic alliance and what it means in theory.
- You have looked at applying theory to practice in building a therapeutic relationship through case study material.
- You have widened your knowledge and understanding of the therapeutic process.
- You have had the opportunity to learn more about the stages of counselling.

## Summary

This chapter has shown that:

- The therapeutic alliance is critical to any work with a child or young person. Without this qualitative aspect of the therapeutic relationship, counselling with a young client becomes something else. Whilst different models of counselling place a different emphasis on the importance of this relationship, most see it as an essential component and prerequisite for therapy.
- As counselling moves through several phases, the therapeutic alliance has to be maintained and nurtured to ensure that client and counsellor remain in contact with each other and with some shared understanding of the work and the way an outcome can be achieved, whatever form that takes.
- Whilst many organisations working with children and young people are required to submit detailed statistics on the work of the service as a whole, individual reviews with clients provide the kind of feedback and mutual exploration required for the work to grow and develop.

## Develop Your Skills

1. Think of examples from your own practice where you have felt a rapport and common sense of purpose with a young client. Can you build on this to develop your relationship skills with other young clients?
2. If you have personally been in the role of client, reflect upon your experiences of the therapeutic relationship, or otherwise. This will help you to develop your skills and build deeper therapeutic relationships.
3. If you reflect on your learning from working with a diverse range of young clients, you can use your knowledge and understanding of cross-cultural dimensions to help establish more effective therapeutic alliances.

## Discussion Questions

1. Are there differences in the nature of the therapeutic alliance when working with children and young people and with adults?
2. In your work with young clients, how would you know if a strong therapeutic working alliance had been established?
3. How might a counsellor working with a child or young person build trust?
4. BACP have set out core competences for work with young people (11–18).

Under generic competences:

- ○ Choose two that you consider could be the most challenging for you to carry out.
- ○ Consider why it would be important to make use of measures (including monitoring outcomes).

Under basic competences for humanistic counselling with young people:

- ○ Consider how you would maintain an authentic relationship with a young person.
- ○ How might you establish and agree therapeutic focus/goals with a young person?
- ○ How might you conclude the counselling relationship?

## Further Reading

Clarkson, P. (2003) *The Therapeutic Relationship*. London: Whurr Publishers.

Cooper, M. (2009) The young person's CORE: development of a brief outcome measure for young people. *Counselling and Psychotherapy Research 9*(3): 160–168.

Feltham, C. and Horton, I. (2000) *The SAGE Handbook of Counselling and Psychotherapy*. London: SAGE.

Levy, S. (2000) *The Therapeutic Alliance*. Madison, CT: Psychosocial Press.

Mearns, D. and Thorne, B. (2013) *Person-Centred Counselling in Action*, 4th edn. London: SAGE, chapter 8.

Nelson-Jones, R. (2002) *Essential Counselling and Therapy Skills: The Skilled Client Model*. London: SAGE, chapter 12.

---

**Online Resources**

BACP website: www.bacp.co.uk, especially the BACP Children and Young People Division and the Competences for Working with Children and Young People

Counselling MindEd website: https://www.minded.org.uk, especially MN 12.01: Empowerment, Activation, and Tackling Passivity and Stigma; CM: Establishing a Therapeutic Alliance; CM 2.2: Engaging the CYP in Collaborative Assessment; CM 2.4: Establishing a Therapeutic Goal/Focus with CYP; and CM: Using Process Measures in Counselling

---

# REFERENCES

Ackerman, S.J. and Hilsenroth, M.J. (2001) A review of therapists' characteristics and techniques negatively impacting the therapeutic alliance. *Psychotherapy: Theory, Research, Practice, Training* 38(2): 171–185.

BACP (2015) *Competences for Working with Young People (11–18 years)*. Lutterworth: BACP.

Bordin, E.S. (1979) The generalizability of the psychoanalytic concept of the working alliance. *Psychotherapy: Theory Research and Practice* 16: 252–260.

Bryant-Jefferies, R. (2004) *Counselling Young People: Person-Centred Dialogues*. Oxford: Radcliffe Medical Press Ltd.

Campbell, A.F. and Simmonds, J.G. (2011) Therapists' perspectives on the therapeutic alliance with children and adolescents. *Counselling Psychology Quarterly* 24(3): 195–209.

Cooper, M. (2013) *School-based counselling in UK secondary schools: a review and critical evaluation*. Available at: www.iapt.nhs.uk/silo/files/school-based-counselling-review.pdf (accessed 18 July 2013).

Dryden, W. (1989) The therapeutic alliance as an integrating framework. In: Dryden, W. (ed.) *Key Issues for Counselling in Action*. London: SAGE, pp. 1–17.

Eubanks, C., Muran, J.C. and Safran, J.D. (2010) Alliance ruptures and resolution. In: Muran, J.C. and Barber, J.P. (eds) *The Therapeutic Alliance: An Evidence-Based Guide to Practice*. New York: Guilford Press, pp. 74–93.

Everall, R. and Paulson, B. (2002) The therapeutic alliance: adolescent perspectives. *Counselling and Psychotherapy Research* 2(2): 78–87.

Feller, C.P. and Cottone, R.R. (2003) The importance of empathy in the therapeutic alliance. *Journal of Humanistic Counselling, Education and Development* 42(1): 53–61.

Geldard, K. and Geldard, D. (2010) *Counselling Adolescents: The Proactive Approach for Young People*, 3rd edn. London: SAGE.

Greenson, R. (1967) *The Techniques and Practice of Psychoanalysis*, Vol. 1. New York: International Universities Press.

Horvath, A.O. and Luborsky, L. (1993) The role of the therapeutic alliance in psychotherapy. *Journal of Consulting and Clinical Psychology 61*(4): 561–573.

Kanzer, M. (1981) Freud's 'analytical pact': the structured therapeutic alliance. *Journal of American Psychoanalytic Association 29*(1): 69–87.

Muran, J.C. and Barber, J.P. (eds) (2010) *The Therapeutic Alliance: An Evidence-Based Guide to Practice.* New York: Guilford Press.

Rogers, C.R. (1957) The necessary and sufficient conditions for therapeutic change. *Journal of Consulting Psychology 21*: 95–103.

Safran, J.D. and Muran, J.C. (2000) *Negotiating the Therapeutic Alliance: A Relational Treatment Guide.* New York: Guilford Press.

Street, C. (2013) *Voluntary and Community Sector (VCS) Counselling Provision for Children, Young People and Young Adults in England.* Lutterworth: BACP/Counselling/MindEd.

Tudor, K. (2008) *Brief Person-Centred Therapies.* London: SAGE.

Wampold, B.E. (2001) *The Great Psychotherapy Debate: Models, Methods and Findings.* Mahwah, NJ: Lawrence Erlbaum Associates.

Wolfe, B.E. and Goldfried, M.R. (1998) Research on psychotherapy integration: recommendations and conclusions from an NIMH workshop. *Journal of Consulting and Clinical Psychology 56*: 448–451.

# 12

# THERAPEUTIC SKILLS

## CLAIRE HARRISON-BREED, WITH ACKNOWLEDGEMENTS TO SALLY INGRAM AND MAGGIE ROBSON

**This chapter will discuss:**

- Generic therapeutic skills we use when working with children and young people rather than describing the skills used in a specific modality
- A brief review of the research into the types of counselling and psychotherapy interventions that appear to work the best
- A definition of therapeutic skills
- An outline of the British Association for Counselling (BACP) (2014) Competences for Working with Children and Young People
- The argument that active listening is a generic therapeutic skill relevant across modalities
- Identification of the differences between working with children, young people and adults
- A discussion of the issue of working briefly

## INTRODUCTION

This chapter focuses on the therapeutic skills we use when working with children and young people. These skills are related to our knowledge, best practice research evidence and our beliefs about what we feel is effective. These beliefs often rest upon our theoretical orientation. So, the first question we may need to ask is 'what works best?' This is addressed in Chapter 16 of this handbook, 'Evaluating Counselling'. However, probably the most comprehensive overview of research into the efficacy of working with children and young people is to be found in the BACP scoping review on research on counselling and psycho-therapy with children and young people by McLaughlin et al. (2013). The study examined evidence from meta-analyses, systematic reviews from controlled trials, cohort studies, case studies, observational and exploratory studies, and 'methodological papers that raise issues for future research in this field' and so gives an exceptional overview of research in this area.

The review builds on the previous scoping review by Harris and Pattison (2004) and asks the same question: Is counselling and psychotherapy effective for children and young people? Three sub-questions are also explored:

1. Which types of counselling and psychotherapy interventions work?
2. For which presenting problems?
3. For whom?

In terms of techniques, cognitive-behavioural therapy (CBT), psychodynamic, play therapy, humanistic therapies and interpersonal psychotherapy were all found to be beneficial. It is, however, worth noting that depending on the presenting issues, specific approaches may be more beneficial; for example, trauma-informed practice and protocols recognise the importance of client-centred directive work, due to the trauma avoidance and dissociation that survivors of trauma may experience (Struik, 2014).

Bratton et al. (2005) conducted a meta-analysis into the efficacy of play therapy. They found that the results were more positive for humanistic approaches and that inclusion of parents in play therapy was associated with a positive outcome. Part 1 of this handbook explores the therapeutic techniques of these different theoretical approaches, whilst this chapter considers the knowledge and skills that underpin all therapeutic encounters with children and young people, regardless of orientation. It focuses, in part, on the therapeutic relationship and the skills utilised to offer this. Rather than repeat the content of other chapters, the reader is advised to read the relevant chapters to support understanding of this chapter. Chapter 1 is relevant to the discussion of child development and attachment. Chapters 2–8 outline different theoretical approaches. In addition, the reader is also advised to read Chapters 17 and 18 when considering law and policy and ethics, and Chapter 16 when curious about evaluation.

Lambert and Barley (2001) identified four factors that influence the outcome of therapy: These were:

> extra therapeutic factors, expectancy effects, specific therapy techniques, and common factors. Common factors such as empathy, warmth, and the therapeutic relationship have been shown to correlate more highly with client outcome than specialized treatment interventions. (Lambert and Barley, 2001: 357)

And they suggest that:

> decades of research indicate that the provision of therapy is an interpersonal process in which a main curative component is the nature of the therapeutic relationship. (Lambert and Barley, 2001: 357)

They argue that we need to tailor our relationship to our individual clients, in this case children and young people, and improve our ability to relate to them.

## WHAT ARE THERAPEUTIC SKILLS?

Therapy is a process of relationship-building and trust acquisition between the therapist and the client. To facilitate this relationship counsellors need highly developed therapeutic skills. Therapeutic skills are verbal and non-verbal ways of engaging with clients in order to establish an emotional environment where a therapeutic alliance can be created, maintained and safely terminated. This relationship is vital if we are to assist clients in exploring how their life experiences have informed their way of being and, if they choose, find new meanings and ways of relating to self, others and life.

Corey (2001) reminds us that irrespective of one's core therapeutic model, effective counselling skills should be a carefully balanced blend of attention to our client's emotions, thoughts and actions. In this way, we can enable our clients to reflect upon their belief systems, experience the emotional depths of their internal and external struggles and use these to aid new ways of being.

Rather than detail specific therapeutic skills, BACP has developed a set of competences for therapists who work with young people. These are available on its website (www.bacp.co.uk). These competencies have been developed as humanistic competencies but the core and generic competencies, in our view, detail the general therapeutic skills and knowledge relevant to all practitioners working both with children and young people regardless of theoretical orientation. Some of the issues identified in these core competencies are explored in detail within this handbook, reflecting the importance of these areas when working therapeutically with children and young people.

Competencies identified by BACP (2014) include knowledge of child and family development and transitions, and knowledge and understanding of mental health issues. Knowledge of legal, professional and ethical frameworks is considered essential, including an ability to work with issues of confidentiality, consent and capacity. BACP (2014) suggests that therapists need to be able to work across and within agencies and respond to child protection issues. In addition, therapists need to be able to engage and work with young people of a variety of ages, developmental levels and backgrounds, as well as parents and careers in a culturally competent manner. They also need to have knowledge of psychopharmacology as it relates to young people. The generic competencies relate to knowledge of specific models of intervention and practice, an ability to work with emotions, endings and service transitions, an ability to work with groups and measurement instruments and to be able to use supervision effectively. The ability to conduct a collaborative assessment and a risk assessment is paramount. Crucially, BACP (2014) suggests the therapist needs to be able to foster and maintain a relationship that builds a therapeutic alliance and understands the client's 'worldview'. In our experience most proficient therapists, irrespective of their modality, work to achieve this trusting relationship necessary for human change. Four broad areas of the therapist's intent within this relationship are described below.

## Attention-giving

This is where we actively demonstrate to clients through verbal responses, facial expressions, eye contact and body posture that we are in a supportive, respectful, accepting and authentic relationship with them. This builds respect and trust in the therapist–client relationship.

## Observing

This is where we observe the client's verbal and physical expressions to enable us to more fully understand our client's experience, their relationship with the therapy process, their life experiences and us. We believe that noticing these leads to greater relational depth (Mearns and Cooper, 2005). This relational depth allows the client to feel safe enough to try out new ways of being, which can be a prelude to trying these outside the counselling relationship.

## Listening

This is where we are *actively listening* (Rogers and Farson, 1987) to the content and emotional experience of a client's story, whilst listening out for indicators of how the client defines their experience. At the same time, we are continuously communicating back to the client that we have heard and understood their phenomenological perspective. Active listening and affirming what we have heard imbues in the client a sense of being understood and accepted.

## Responding

This is where we are responding to a client's core communication. This involves reflecting the content and feeling of the client's expressions whilst offering summaries, or questions that can lead to further expression or exploration of how the client wishes to move forward from current or historical experiences. This also gives the client the opportunity to modify the internal view of their external experience, as they hear it reflected back to them. As we discuss later in the chapter, the way we respond will need to be developmentally appropriate and may use other mediums of communication such as play.

Although specific orientations, for example CBT, will have specific skill sets, the four broad areas described above are often seen as the basis for therapeutic work with children and young people. Taken together, these four areas can be described as demonstrating the skill of active listening. Rogers and Farson (1987: 1) argue that:

> People who have been listened to in this new and special way become more emotionally mature, more open to their experiences, less defensive, more democratic, and less authoritarian.

The fundamental premise is that these therapeutic skills span all client groups irrespective of age, gender, sexuality, cultural background and life experiences. What is key is how we adapt attention-giving, observing, listening and responding to meet the unique needs of the client before us. This is true for all client groups but never more so than for those of us working with children and young people. For younger children, we may adapt our active listening by communicating through play, whereas older young people may be more able to tolerate a more adult type of counselling experience.

Rogers and Farson (1987) describe the skills required for active listening. They argue we need to really understand what the speaker is saying from their perspective and communicate that we have done this. When we listen, we have to listen for 'total meaning' – both the content of the communication and the feeling and/or attitude underneath this. We need to 'respond to feelings'. The feelings can be much more important than the content. Finally, we must 'note all cues'. This means attending to non-verbal as well as verbal communication and being aware of how something is communicated, hesitantly or confidently, for example. Again, we will adapt our skills to the age and developmental level of our client and communicate through appropriate mediums. For work with children, play is often the preferred way of working and this is described in Chapter 7, 'Play Therapy'. Within the play we may say, 'Teddy is crying, I wonder how he is feeling right now'. We can also differentiate feelings from thoughts so could respond, 'Oh teddy is crying, I wonder what he is thinking right now'. Young people and adults can also find play therapy very powerful but may feel it's babyish, so age-appropriate ways of working need to be employed. It is not uncommon for children who have missed out on particular play stages to want to go back and experience this at a later date. Younger adolescents may find it difficult to tolerate the focused attention of the therapist so a third focus, often creative work, can be offered.

Using age-appropriate mediums will make the communication of active listening more accessible. It is acceptable to be creative and not be fearful of inviting the client to consider working in this way. Chapter 8, 'Other Creative Approaches', offers some ideas, and it may also be useful to offer life simulation computer games as a powerful vehicle for the client to express their world. Clients may choose to use mobile phone texting to share some of the toughest experiences they are not able to verbalise. This may require a service phone specifically for this purpose and some pretty fast texting skills on the counsellor's part.

Another important part of active listening is the therapist's skill in attuning to what the child or young person's body is communicating. Noticing breathing or shifts in body posture enables the therapist to track changes in emotional state that the child may be experiencing. Being curious about what the body is telling us enables the therapist to work with the unconscious processes (Rothschild, 2017). For example, 'I notice that you fold your arms every time that you mention your dad. If your folded arms could speak, what would they say right now?'

In addition to offering active listening skills, which can be viewed as one of the underpinning skills of all interpersonal encounters, there is also a need for the specialist skills that fit with different modalities and relationship needs of the client. Therapeutic skills when working with children and young people will be used to orperationalise the philosophy of the particular modality. Person-centred counsellors will focus on offering a relationship characterised by the core conditions (Rogers, 1951). Cognitive-behavioural therapists will be looking to develop the therapeutic alliance to help the client make connections between thought, emotions and behaviour. The psychoanalytic therapist will be aiming to develop a relationship in which transference can occur and where unconscious material can be made available to the conscious mind (Corey, 2001).

## What are the differences between working therapeutically with adults, children and young people?

Although there are similarities between all types of therapeutic work, there are some important differences. These include:

- Differing stages of development – emotional, moral, physical and cognitive. See Chapter 1 of this handbook, 'Child Development and Attachment'.
- Ethical and power issues: see Chapter 17 ('Law and Policy') and Chapter 18 ('Ethics') of this handbook, and Daniels and Jenkins (2010).
- The role of the family, school and community in the therapeutic process.

Therefore, as has been suggested in the BACP (2014) Competences for Working with Children and Young People, a knowledge of child and family development is essential, as well as a knowledge of legal frameworks and an ability to work with issues to do with confidentiality and capacity.

Therapeutic skills that enable us to work with adults are not necessarily suitable for work with children and young people. In addition, those suitable for young people (adolescents) are not always suitable for working with children (primary school-aged children and younger). Those commissioning therapy for children and young people share this understanding (Pattison et al., 2007). We need to appreciate what separates children from young people and young people from adults, and how having a therapeutically differentiated strategy can be the crucial element in providing safe yet effective therapeutic outcomes. What should inform this strategy is an understanding of the developmental stages young people go through, discussed in Chapter 1.

Counsellors need to be aware of the significant impact these developmental stages have on childhood understanding and communication, and must be willing to adapt their way of work to accommodate these variants. Specific skills for working with children and young people need to be developed. Part 1 of this handbook, particularly Chapters 2–8, describes the theoretical base and skills needed for a number of modalities for working in this field.

The key stages of development include social, physical, emotional and cognitive functioning. These stages are rarely synchronised with each other and we would argue that the chances of them being disharmonious is greater in young people who have suffered early life trauma. Developmental trauma teaches the child that the world is an unsafe place and that people cannot be trusted so will let you down or hurt you. The body enters a state of high arousal as the child stays on guard in an attempt to protect themselves (Van Der Kolk, 2015). This flow of adrenalin and cortisol creates symptoms in the child causing restlessness and lack of concentration. All of these processes interrupt the young person's capacity to be spontaneous and absorbed in difficult to concentrate on tasks that build development such as education, play and fun. This means that many of our clients may present as being under- or overdeveloped physically, emotionally and/or psychologically in relation to their expected stage of development. Client presentations of development will often not parallel each other: a client could be physically overdeveloped and emotionally underdeveloped. The case study is an example of this, the issues it may cause and the skills a therapist may employ to manage this.

Culture may also affect the development of children and young people and how we view their development. The age at which a child becomes a young person or an adult varies from culture to culture and so we need to move away from adopting one static theory of child and adolescent development and select one that can form a 'baseline starting point from which to modify and improve upon so that they maintain their relevance in a rapidly changing multicultural society' (Walker, 2005). He maintains:

> We also need to reflect upon our own perceptions and beliefs concerning child development and avoid rigid understandings. We need to ensure that we come from an open, curious and culturally pliable position. (Walker, 2005: 15)

Another difference when working with children and young people is that of boundary keeping, especially confidentiality. Children and young people are, in general, much less autonomous than adults and have several groups of people interested in, concerned for and responsible for their welfare (parents, relatives, carers, teachers, social workers, school meal assistants, for example). In our experience, to stick to the normal adult limits of confidentiality can risk alienating the people responsible for the care of the child or young person and may ultimately put them at risk. The carer may feel that the child or young person is sharing 'secrets' that they feel threatened by, or that you have an intimate connection with your client that could jeopardise the relationship they have. In order to keep this boundary sensitively, we need to develop communication skills that will allow us tell the carers enough to keep them involved but not enough to violate the child or young person's privacy. Generalities such as 'Things seem to be going well' or 'How are you feeling about the therapy?' may suffice, but thought needs to go into what it is and isn't okay to say. Supervision can help with these decisions and, if possible, the client should also be involved. Sometimes the client wants you to act as a spokesperson for them to their carers, so a careful discussion of what is to be shared is vital. The therapist needs to be aware of the processes outside of the therapy room and the team around the child. It is important that we do not pathologise the child as 'the problem' that needs 'fixing' through therapy, but consider the wider system that the child is embedded in. It may be that family work is needed to address wider issues and create a firm base before individual work with the child can take place.

The mechanics of therapy may also be different when working with children and young people. Adults usually refer themselves for therapy but children and young people may be referred by others, usually carers or teachers. If this is the case, both the client and referrer need to understand what therapy is and the client needs to want to engage. It may be appropriate to offer a home visit to explain the purpose and procedure of therapy to both the client and the carer. In the case of a teacher referral, a programme of education and information would ideally have been undertaken within the school.

In our experience, in private rather than school settings, we feel it may be better if a carer could accompany a younger child and wait outside the therapy room, as the child may want to leave early. Also, having the carer involved in the practicalities of therapy can help the therapist maintain a positive relationship with them.

For more complex issues that involve the whole family, systemic family therapy may be required as a starting point before moving onto individual work. Systemic therapy is an evidence-based approach that recognises that from a very early age children entertain complex triadic relationships, with a range of emotional dimensions in the process. The nature of the child–parent interaction and the developmental stage of the child are explored, and the therapist works to understand the interrelated elements of the family relationships (marital sub-system; parental and co-parental sub-system; sibling's sub-system; extended family sub-system) all of which significantly influence each other. This process is similar to thinking in terms of a goldfish in an aquarium. If we only care about the fish, and overlook the overall health of the aquarium, it is usually not going to end well for the fish. Systemic family therapy works to develop and strengthen family relationships and work through any difficulties that the family may be experiencing, creating a solid place for individual work to occur.

As with adult clients, it is important to work and plan for the ending of therapy right from the beginning, and, if possible, to include the client in planning the final session. It is also helpful, in our view, to try and finish therapy at a time that would resonate with a normal end, for example, the end of the school term.

## Relationship of personal qualities or attributes to therapeutic skills

It has been suggested that the therapist needs special qualities or attributes when working with children and young people (West, 1996; Geldard, 2013). These qualities or attributes are conveyed using therapeutic skills. They, and the associated skills, will depend, to a certain extent, on the therapist's theoretical orientation. West's (1996) description, although quite dated, is one that would be familiar to child-centred play therapists. She suggests personal qualities should include the ability to:

- relate to, through and with feelings;
- understand and come to terms with what has happened in their own childhood, adolescence and adulthood, including child-rearing and parenting issues;
- work within a child-centred framework;
- communicate with children;
- play;
- work alongside troubled children without being damaged by the children's pain;
- act as an advocate for the children they have in play therapy. (West, 1996: 150)

Geldard (2013), working from a more CBT stance, suggest four attributes for therapists:

1. congruence;
2. in touch with own inner child;
3. accepting;
4. emotionally detached. (Geldard, 2013: 21)

The final one, 'emotionally detached', may be shocking for some therapists, but they do qualify this by saying that this 'does not mean that the counsellor needs to be limp, lifeless and remote. On the contrary, the child does need to feel comfortable with the counsellor' (2013: 23).

Whatever personal qualities or attributes we develop to further our work will be communicated using therapeutic skills. Each modality will dictate what we are trying to convey to our clients and how we use our skills to do that. The use of active listening skills can express empathy and attention-giving, which are qualities commonly valued by all approaches.

## Working briefly

Working briefly with children and young people will not necessarily change the skill set employed by the therapist but can put pressure on the therapist to 'solve' the problem rather than concentrating on building a strong relationship with the client. As has been suggested earlier, clients, particularly younger children, can find it helpful to end therapy where a break in their routine would occur naturally, for example, at the end of a school term. Brief or time-limited therapy may not allow this to happen.

---

## Case Study: Andrew

This case study demonstrates work with a client whose physical development had overtaken his cognitive and emotional development and the skills the therapist used to help her client explore the meaning of his experiences.

Andrew was 14 years old when he was referred to Liz, the school counsellor. He'd been at his new school only 5 months after his mother had moved to the area seeking a fresh start after the end of another violent relationship. Andrew had two younger female siblings who had different fathers. Andrew was not in contact with his father, but his sisters' fathers kept in sporadic contact. Their life had been nomadic since Andrew was about 2 years old.

Prior to the referral, at least three teachers had reported that Andrew's behaviour was becoming more disruptive in class and one teacher had asked that Andrew be excluded permanently from his class, after Andrew had 'faced him off in front of other pupils'.

Other staff and pupils reported that they found it hard to warm to Andrew and that he had done little to integrate himself into his new school community. Andrew's year head accompanied him to his first counselling session to 'make sure he bothered to turn up'.

The first thing that struck Liz about Andrew was his physical presence. Andrew was incredibly tall and broad for his age and could easily have passed for a baby-faced adult man. Andrew's posture, attitude and general manner seemed to demonstrate nonchalance bordering on arrogance. Liz opened the early stages of her work with Andrew by congruently reflecting the path by which he had arrived at counselling. Liz explained it felt their coming together had been coerced. She disclosed her own dissatisfaction about this, and explained that one of the fundamental tenets of counselling was that it had to be a voluntary process that both parties wished to freely engage in.

Andrew said he had no problem attending counselling, but he did not know why others thought he would benefit from it. Referring to his teachers, he stated that the only thing that would be gained by counselling was that others would be pleased because he would be 'out of the way as usual'. Despite his physical stature, Liz noticed that when Andrew said this, he seemed small and diminutive; his posture was hunched and almost foetal like. Liz reflected to Andrew that he didn't seem pleased by the idea that people wanted him out of the way and asked if his teachers were the only people who seemed to enjoy his absence.

Andrew then gave an outline of his life, explaining that it was only men who wanted him out of the way – male teachers, his mum's boyfriends and male peers. Most of Andrew's early years had been deeply fractured; he could report no consistent male role model, just a series of men who drifted in and rather violently out of his family's life. Despite his apparent physical maturity, it was clear that Andrew carried a rather young and naive sense of blame for the patterns in his mother's relationships. 'They get sick of me you see'; 'They don't mind my little sisters, it is only my dad who doesn't keep in touch'.

Liz invited Andrew to explore how he felt about 'being out of the way' and he explained that sometimes it was for the better. For many years there had been multiple violent incidents that he had heard and observed. These culminated in his mother being so badly beaten that she had a punctured lung and was unconscious. Andrew was deeply disturbed by this incident, explaining he regularly 'saw' it when he closed his eyes and he 'daydreamed' about it. With the help of supervision Liz began to realise that Andrew was describing early signs of post-traumatic stress and that his daydreaming appeared to be an indicator of intrusive daytime imagery. Liz's supervisor encouraged her to give Andrew more space to explore his daydreams.

Andrew explained daydreaming was why he had been excluded from class. He was seen as uncooperative and had been described as blatantly ignoring classroom instructions. In fact, what Andrew said was happening was that he was 'zoning out' in thinking about what had happened to his mum. Liz worked with Andrew's dissociation, looking at ways to stabilise him through grounding techniques and increase his capacity to stay in the here-and-now. Throughout the work Liz also supported Andrew to process his memories of what happened to his mother.

In his own language, prompted by accurate reflections from his therapist, Andrew began to articulate the internal conflict he experienced between physically appearing as an adult whilst internally feeling young and fearful. 'I'm built like a brick shithouse; I should be able to protect my mom. I'm big enough but I'm a pussy.'

Andrew's stature was a real hindrance to him as he was regularly perceived as being an adult. This led others to place unrealistic expectations upon him in terms of his behaviour, attitude and emotional resilience. Andrew had internalised many of these expectations, especially when it came to protecting his mother. His inability to live up to these internalised standards ultimately led Andrew to feel a great sense of shame and physical and emotional impotence. Andrew's arrogance, nonchalance and burgeoning aggression seemed to be his way of covering what he felt sure others could see in him.

Liz recognised initially she had also been a little blinded by Andrew's stature and that she had the challenge of building a relationship with a vulnerable young man whose sense of self was incredibly fragile. The work began to focus on what attributes Andrew wanted people to see. Andrew said he wanted people to see his sporting and artistic skill, although he wrestled with the latter as this was 'a wussie's game'. The remainder of Liz and Andrew's work focused on attending to the common question that is present for many adolescent clients: 'Who will I be?'

Over the following weeks Liz and Andrew returned to Andrew's image of who he might be and explored which elements of this could be facilitated through change within his life

*(Continued)*

(Continued)

and which elements needed to be accepted as currently unachievable. During one particularly difficult session, Andrew became distressed when he realised that he could never have protected his mum from domestic abuse as for many years he'd been physically unable to because of his youth and small stature. His recent physical development had left him with a feeling that he should have done something to protect his family. This led Andrew to look at the limits and scope of his own personal responsibility. Andrew found this frustrating but was willing to accept on a cognitive level that he had not had the capacity to protect his family and, because of this, he could not be responsible. Throughout the counselling encounter Liz used active listening to try and enter Andrew's world and congruently worked with the dissonance between his developmental levels.

## Key Learning

The key learning to be taken from this chapter is in:

- The consolidation of the generic therapeutic skills we use when working with children and young people.
- Knowledge of research into the types of counselling and psychotherapy interventions that appear to work the best.
- Defining therapeutic skills and how they are used with children and young people.
- Knowledge of the BACP (2014) Competences for Working with Children and Young People.
- Identification of the differences between working with children, young people and adults.

## Summary

In this chapter we have:

- Argued that we need different therapeutic skills and knowledge when working with children and young people.
- Detailed the competencies required and highlighted the importance of the skill of active listening.
- Considered the impact of the developmental stage of the client on the therapy.

- Explored the differences in working therapeutically with children, young people and adults.
- Provided a case study to demonstrate the dissonance that can occur between different elements of development and how the therapist uses her therapeutic skills to attend to the whole client experience.

## Discussion Questions

1. Can you think of a child or young person whose physical, emotional, cognitive or behaviour development is not synchronised? Does this cause issues?
2. Are there any special attributes or qualities that you feel a therapist working with children and young people should have? If so, what are they and why?
3. Why might it be important to communicate to the carers of the child or young person something of what is happening in your therapy sessions?
4. What is the role of the family and school when working with children and young people?
5. What do you think are the most important skills for a therapist when working with children and young people?

## Develop Your Skills

1. Think about your school days and about your teachers. Think of one good teacher and one bad teacher. What were the qualities/behaviours/attributes that made them good teachers? What were the qualities/behaviours/attributes that made them bad teachers? Can you list them? Think about your 'good' list. Does it connect in any way to the suggestions made by Rogers and Farson (1987) about how to listen actively?
2. Write a list for yourself of the different skills required to work with children and young people. If you do not already have these skills, where could you learn them? Do a search for training providers.
3. West (1996) suggests that in order to work with children and young people we need to 'understand and come to terms with what has happened in [our]/their own childhood, adolescence and adulthood, including child-rearing and parenting issues'. How could you do this?
4. West (1996) also suggests that we 'work alongside troubled children without being damaged by the children's pain'. What sort of strategies can we put in place for ourselves to help us manage this?

## Further Reading

Baruch, G. (2001) *Community-Based Psychotherapy with Young People: Evidence and Innovation in Practice*. Philadelphia, PA: Taylor & Francis.

Bowman, R.P. and Bowman, S.C. (1998) *Individual Counselling Activities for Children*. Chapin, SC: Youth Light.

Harris, B. and Pattison, S. (2004) *Research on Counselling Children and Young People: A Systematic Scoping Review*. Rugby: BACP.

Lines, D. (2002) *Brief Counselling in Schools: Working with Young People from 11 to 18*. Thousand Oaks, CA: SAGE.

Luxmoore, N. (2000) *Listening to Young People in School, Youth Work and Counselling*. Philadelphia, PA: Taylor & Francis Group.

McLaughlin, C., Holliday, C., Clarke, B. and Llie, S. (2013) *Research on Counselling and Psychotherapy with Children and Young People: A Systematic Scoping Review of Evidence for its Effectiveness from 2003–2011*. Rugby: BACP.

Mapes, K. (2000) *Stop! Think! Choose! Building Emotional Intelligence in Young People*. Tucson, AZ: Zephyr Press.

Ponterotto, J., Casas, M.J., Suzuki, L.A. and Alexander, C.M. (2001) *Handbook of Multicultural Counselling*, 2nd edn. Thousand Oaks, CA: SAGE.

Schaefer, C. (ed.) (2003) *Foundations of Play Therapy*. Hoboken, NJ: John Wiley & Sons.

Simpson, A.R. (2001) *Raising Teens: A Synthesis of Research and a Foundation for Action*. Boston, MA: Center for Health Communication, Harvard School of Public Health.

## Online Resources

BACP website: www.bacp.co.uk, especially the BACP Children and Young People Division and the Competences for Working with Children and Young People

Counselling MindEd: https://www.minded.org.uk, especially Modules CMD 02: Participation and Empowerment; CMD 03: Legal and Professional Issues; CMD 04: Cultural Competence; CMD 05: Initiating Counselling; CMD 07: Relational Skills; CMD 08: Therapeutic Skills; and CMD 10: Concluding Counselling

Children and Young People's Improving Access to Psychological Therapies (CYP IAPT): www.cypiapt.org

# REFERENCES

Bratton, S.C., Ray, D., Rhine, T. and Jones, L. (2005) The efficacy of play therapy with children: a meta-analytic review of treatment outcomes. *Professional Psychology: Research and Practice 36*(4): 376–390.

Corey, G. (2001) *Theory and practice of counseling and psychotherapy* (6th edn). Belmont, CA: Brooks/Cole Thompson Learning

Geldard, K. (2013) *Counselling Children: A Practical Introduction* (4th edn). London: Sage.

Griffiths, G. (2013) *Helpful and Unhelpful Factors in School Based Counselling: Client's Perspective. Counselling MindEd Scoping Report*. Available at: https://www.bacp.co.uk/media/2049/counsel ling-minded-helpful-unhelpful-factors-school-based-counselling-griffiths.pdf.

Daniels, D. and Jenkins, P. (2010) *Therapy with Children: Children's Rights, Confidentiality and the Law* (2nd edn). London: SAGE.

Harris, B. and Pattison, S. (2004) *Research on Counselling Children and Young People: A Systematic Scoping Review*. Rugby: BACP.

Lambert, M.J. and Barley, D.E. (2001) Research summary on the therapeutic relationship and psychotherapy outcome. *Psychotherapy: Theory, Research, Practice, Training, 38*(4): 357–368.

McLaughlin, C., Holliday, C., Clarke, B. and Llie, S. (2013) *Research on Counselling and Psychotherapy with Children and Young People: A Systematic Scoping Review of Evidence for its Effectiveness from 2003–2011*. Rugby: BACP.

Mearns, D. and Cooper, M. (2005) *Working at Relational Depth in Counselling and Psychotherapy*. London: SAGE.

Pattison, S., Robson, M. and Beynon, A. (2007) *Handbook of Counselling Children and Young People*. London: SAGE.

Rogers, C.R. (1951) *Client-Centred Therapy: Its Current Practice, Implications and Theory*. London: Constable.

Rogers, C.R. and Farson, R. (1987) Active Listening. In: Newman, R.G., Danzinger, M.A, and Cohen, M. (eds) *Communicating in Business Today*. Washington D.C: Heath & Company, pp. 28–30.

Rothschild, B (2017) *The Body Remembers Volume 2: Revolutionising Trauma Treatment*. New York: W.W. Norton & Company.

Struik, A. (2014) *Treating Chronically Traumatized Children: Don't Let Sleeping Dogs Lie*. London: Routledge.

Van Der Kolk, B. (2015) *The Body Keeps the Score: Brain, Mind, and Body in the Healing of Trauma*. New York: Penguin.

Walker, S. (2005) *Culturally Competent Therapy: Working with Children and Young People*. London: Palgrave Macmillan.

West, W., (1996) Using human inquiry groups in counselling research. *British Journal of Guidance and Counselling, 24*(3) 347–355.

# 13

# SUPERVISION

## PENNY LEAKE, ANN BEYNON AND JENNY BIANCARDI

**This chapter will discuss:**

- Background to supervision of work with children and young people
- Theoretical underpinning to supervising counsellors working with children and young people
- Supervisees' feelings
- Issues of power
- Communication and symbolism
- Action methods in supervision

## INTRODUCTION

Supervision of work with children and adolescents is different from that of work with adults.

There have been many definitions of the triple function that supervision serves in work with adults, and we have chosen Houston's (1990) description of 'policeman, plumber and poet' to look at in the context of child and adolescent work. Houston's use of metaphor in her definition seems appropriate when we think about work with children, their communication being so rooted in symbolism. This creativity, so frequent in the therapy itself, can get forgotten as a tool in the supervisory process.

## BACKGROUND

In the 1960s and 1970s, the 'birthing period' of counselling for children and young people in education, approaches to counselling practice learnt much from the developing fields of child psychiatry and social work, not least in terms of the integrated models of management supervision in delivering effective practice.

During these early years supervision or tutorial sessions had become an integral part of generic counselling training programmes and finally became recognised as a requirement for professional accreditation by the British Association for Counselling and Psychotherapy (BACP) and other professional bodies. A number of training courses were developed in the 1980s and 1990s based on a variety of theoretical models.

In the past 20 years significant developments in understanding the nature and complexity of child development, most currently in the field of neuroscience, have underlined the need for further specialist training.

In recent years many counsellors have initiated peer mentoring services in their schools, working in partnership with other members of staff.

Provision for integrated supervision for both mentors and staff is crucial to sustained service development. Cowie and Wallace (2000: 78) go as far as to say:

> If there is really not enough time to supervise peer supporters regularly, perhaps it is not the best time to set up a peer support service.

Thus, with an infrastructure of consistent and creative management and supervision, the value of these outreach services alongside a counselling provision can actively influence an ethos of mutual awareness and openness in a school community.

## THEORETICAL UNDERPINNING

### The relationship

Houston's 'policeman' metaphor reminds us that the ultimate function of supervision is to benefit and protect the child client, even though the practitioner is likely to experience it as a benefit to themselves. In their extensive writing on supervision of adult work, Inskipp and Proctor (1993) conclude that it is not possible to have an exact parallel of Rogers' core conditions in the supervisory relationship, because the need for rigour is not compatible with a completely non-judgemental attitude. A clinical supervisor, just like a line manager, has a vicarious liability for the standard of work. The version of the core conditions that Proctor and Inskipp describe is one of empathy, respect and genuineness.

The kinds of duties that the 'policeman' may have to fulfil are best discussed between the supervisor and the practitioner at the outset and set out in a written contract in order to avoid any later discomforts.

A crucial difference from supervision of adult work is the need to keep in mind the legal framework that surrounds practice with children. Sometimes the practitioner can lose sight of this in the midst of the therapeutic relationship. Legal issues (such as safeguarding, parental responsibility or the child's competence to make decisions) can lead to difficult dilemmas for the practitioner around confidentiality. It is good to have reference in the supervision contract to what kind of issue can stay within supervision and what may need to go outside. If the practitioner works for an agency there will be times when agency policy must be followed quickly and the line manager consulted rather than the clinical supervisor. See the 'Discussion Questions' section for further examples of contract contents.

The level of experience of the supervisee is likely to affect how frequently the 'policeman' function comes to the fore.

This can also affect the character of the 'plumber' aspect, by which Houston means looking at the nuts and bolts of the day-to-day work, the discussion of individual sessions, the progression of the series, the need for additional training, etc. If the supervisee is on a qualification course, or if she feels the need for some minute attention to a session, this may take the form of looking at a video recording together. The supervisor might give straightforward advice in a case like this. Supervisors of work with children and adolescents need to have experience in the field themselves. Sometimes drawing on this to make practical suggestions may be helpful, but too much may interfere with the collegial exploration that is likely to be the most successful.

This 'plumber' work may well be done cognitively, but there will be times when the supervisee brings feelings of stuckness which she finds elusive and difficult to describe. This is an ideal opportunity for the supervisor to invite the supervisee to use creative ways of exploring, such as by using psychodrama, stones, art, play therapy figures, etc. In so doing, the supervisee's unconscious emotions about the work are likely to come to the fore, and parallel processes may emerge. This is where the third function of supervision, the 'poet' work, is crucial.

The 'poet' in the supervisor listens out for themes and patterns, but above all listens to the music under the words, which gives clues on any unconscious feelings about the child and the child's system.

However, our feelings when working with children can go beyond counter-transference, as we are working with an actual unhappy child in real time, and this may bring out natural protective instincts that can lead to rescuing and unhelpful mothering behaviours. The practitioner needs to stay with the child's pain, and this is difficult to do. She needs to be able to bring these feelings to supervision in order to lessen them, both for her own sake and for that of the child.

When working with adolescents, more negative feelings may be triggered if hostility and attachment difficulties are being directed towards the counsellor. Practitioners may find working with suicidal ideation, self-harm and disordered eating particularly anxiety-provoking.

Other people in the child's system may cause the practitioner to feel professionally isolated, angry or inadequate. It is the feelings of inadequacy and other vulnerabilities that cause practitioners to want external clinical supervision rather than any that may be contracted within their agency. This is the effect of the power issues inherent in any supervisory relationship, irrespective of how good the agency's supervisor (or, indeed, line manager) may be. If choice is not possible, because of tight accountability needs in the agency, a clear three-way specimen contract from a potential clinical supervisor may help here.

Sometimes, however, a carefully boundaried in-house supervision programme can be useful – such as when both co-facilitators of a group can be supervised together.

## Systemic thinking

A fundamental difference of this work is that children, in particular, and young people, to a large extent, do not have personal autonomy. They are part of a system that includes parents, foster carers, culture, school and possibly other agencies. If a parent is hostile to the idea of therapy for a younger child, they have the power to forbid it, sabotage it, withhold it as a punishment or turn it into a scapegoating process. A Gillick competent young person may be able to have counselling in a school setting without their parents' knowledge, but here the system of the school could itself cause tensions. The supervisee can find that many people besides the child are taking up her headspace. She may need the supervisor's help to sort out which of these extra players need to be centre stage and which can be in the wings.

She may also need a safe place to vent frustrations about parts of the system, and a containing supervisor can help with any accompanying issues of splitting and activation of Karpman's (1968) Drama Triangle. The supervisor may be able to spot if the agency is mirroring the issues of the client group they work with, if practitioners are mirroring family dynamics or if a parallel process is emerging in the supervisory relationship.

Anything that can be done to get the system on board is likely to make the therapy more effective. This is especially important when working with a young client from an eastern culture, where 'collectivism' carries more weight than individualism. Initial work to bring the family on side, especially the father, may be essential with young Muslim clients (see Khan, 2017).

Sometimes family therapy is needed rather than individual, and this may become clear through discussion in supervision. Sometimes the supervisor has to support the therapist in facing the fact that her work can only be damage limitation, and that a good therapeutic relationship now may enable the child to seek therapy again when an autonomous adult.

Information-sharing within the system is always tricky, especially with looked-after children. If a practitioner was originally trained in adult counselling, the principle of tight confidentiality may still be rooted in them, and the supervisor can help with the discomfort that information-sharing brings.

In the event of an ethical dilemma, it is good to look together at the ethics of the practitioner's professional body in supervision. BACP's 2016 'Ethical Framework for the Counselling Professions' (EFCP) contains sections on work with children and on supervision. For more depth, there is a suite of detailed Good Practice in Action (GPiA) resources, including decision-making tools, on the BACP website (www.bacp.co.uk). Also the wide variety of MindEd resources, particularly tailored for work with children and young people, can be helpful.

## Developmental issues

Both practitioner and supervisor need to have a good understanding of child development, especially emotional development. A framework such as that of Erikson (1965) can be helpful, combined with an understanding of how trauma and disability can skew these stages, and how the 'we' consciousness of eastern cultures may set up conflicts within such a model.

A young person who is considered Gillick competent can reasonably expect that their issues will be kept confidential, with the usual exceptions of harm to self or others. However, degrees of harm may cause grey areas that need to be explored in supervision. The thought of the law, parental anger, cultural opposition and possible court appearance can make the practitioner feel precarious. Consultation with the Coram Children's Legal Centre may be helpful. On the other hand, a therapist trained in adult work may need reminding that promises of confidentiality to a young child can have resonance of 'our special secret', which can cause confusion rather than healing.

Practitioner and supervisor may wish to discuss how far Rogers' concept of 'the wisdom of the client' can apply to this client group. Children may well have perfect wisdom over the pacing of their sessions and the methods of communication they will use. There will, however, be some decisions, depending on age and understanding, that they cannot make and, sometimes, should not be asked to make. Supervision may be a good time to think about whether a child's presence at the adults' feedback meeting is likely to be helpful or harmful.

The supervisee, too, has stages of development, and the supervisory relationship may need to adapt accordingly to advancements and to any regressions caused by professional or personal insecurity.

## Attachment issues

Attachment patterns are likely to be acted out in the therapy room, and may cause a variety of discomforts for the practitioner.

The early stages of the work may echo the child's attachment experience – anxiety, hostility and avoidance or the wish to please that can come with ambivalent attachment. It can be difficult to judge when the child has been securely attached to the practitioner long enough to be able to move on. The subjects of dependency and endings are likely to be brought to supervision, and the supervisee's own feelings may well need to be disentangled from the needs of the child. The supervisor can help the practitioner to feel that the child is getting a good, predictable ending rather than the many unpredictable ones they have had in the past.

The attachment issues of adolescents are additionally complex because of their need to begin attaching to peers and push away parent figures. Moving from individual to group work is therefore ideal here. If the practitioner is facilitating a group, there are many people, issues and powerful feelings that will be present in the supervision room, and the use of creative methods can help to make this feel more clear and manageable.

## The supervisee's feelings

It is difficult for a counsellor to stay with the pain of adults, but staying with the pain of children is especially hard. There is a great temptation to minimise, distract and rescue.

Supervisees can bring complex and overwhelming feelings to supervision. Issues of counter-transference may be at work, but so too may real-time sympathy or despair – for example, for a vulnerable young child, sexually exploited teenager, female genital mutilation survivor or unaccompanied young refugee. A child can silently call to the supervisee's inner child, or evoke feelings about children in her family, or lack of them. Through projective identification, the therapist may get an unbearable feeling of what it is like to be this child. If those feelings are those of guilt and inadequacy, the supervisor may be able to point out the process that is happening, and so normalise what the therapist may be feeling about her competence, disentangling what is hers and what is the child's.

The supervisor, too, may experience strong feelings, and generally these can be brought into the room so that an exploration of parallel processes can help with the clarification. Both counsellor and supervisor may sometimes feel bewildered by the rapid changes in the world in which young people live – for example, gender fluidity and the increasing number of children addicted to watching pornography.

Counsellors and therapists constantly have to swallow down children's pain, and this needs to be assuaged in supervision and in other replenishing activities. If it is not, it can become toxic to the practitioner, or lead to defences which protect the therapist but can give a subtle message to the child that there are some no-go areas in therapy.

We know from neuroscience that a practitioner can be simultaneously flooded with the same unhealthy cortisol as is the child they are listening to. Equally, the child can pick up the opioids generated by calmness and containment. The supervisee needs a containing supervisor to increase her own opioids and diminish cortisol. So, too, the supervisor has to hear pain and contain splitting, and he needs to keep up his own regular supervision for identical reasons.

The supervisor's overview of many cases can help him to remember that children heal more quickly than adults given the right circumstances, and this can help to keep the therapist's optimism alive. Sometimes, however, the supervisor may sense that the supervisee's usual resilience is being chipped away, and the subject of time out and/or burn-out may have to be raised, with the help of a diagnostic questionnaire if necessary. Sometimes there are so many personal issues impacting on the work that it becomes clear that the supervisee needs to look for personal therapy rather than let clinical supervision become a kind of counselling.

## Legal Issues

It is the practitioner's responsibility to be familiar with all issues of safeguarding children, Gillick competence, parental responsibility (PR), the basics of current Children Acts, the latest assessment framework, and his or her own agency's procedures. The supervisor also needs knowledge on these matters, for example, the need for their own Disclosure and Barring Service (DBS) clearance if supervising on premises where children may be present.

Even with damage limitation in mind, the necessary acting on disclosures of abuse can be distressing for both child and practitioner. There will also be a need for the therapist to seek legal advice on how soon play therapy or counselling can be resumed after legal proceedings have begun. With both children and adolescents there is a greater danger of the practitioner being accused of 'coaching' the child in their evidence than there is in equivalent adult work. The supervisor can model the careful record-keeping that is always necessary in child therapy, and there can be discussion on the complexities of this, together with signposting to relevant BACP guidance and professional literature. Any court appearance is likely to be stressful for the practitioner, who will need support from both supervisor and line manager.

Both practitioner and supervisor need to keep up to date with developments in the law in a changing society, for example, the law on 'sexting' and on gender reassignment under the age of 18.

## Power Issues

A clause in the contract about regular review should help with the power issues inherent in all supervisory relationships, especially long-term ones.

Karpman's Drama Triangle of victim, rescuer and persecutor can be activated especially easily in therapy with children because children have little power and we frequently see them as victims, even without any other barriers to their inclusion in society. It would be easy for this dynamic to be mirrored in the supervision process, and supervisors need to be on their guard against acting on such feelings, especially that of wanting to rescue. That is not to say that supervisees do not need to hear their good work regularly praised to keep up their enjoyment of what they do. A containing adult-to-adult atmosphere will make Drama Triangle dynamics less likely.

The power/powerlessness issues of difference and diversity are important here. Amongst the many conscious and unconscious triads that feature in supervision, there can be a sub-system of two and an odd one out. Already the practitioner and supervisor are adult, unlike the client. If in addition the supervisee and supervisor are, for example, white and the child is black, it is possible for unconscious filtering and collusion to occur. Equally, there could be times when child and therapist are in a sub-system that is causing boundary difficulties, and the objectivity of a supervisor from a different grouping might be helpful. The supervisor, like the therapist, needs to be vigilant as to whether he is working within his competence, or whether some parts of the work might need to be supervised elsewhere, for example work with children with significant learning disabilities or sexually harmful behaviour.

## COMMUNICATION AND SYMBOLISM

Practitioners may find that older children communicate like adults do, using words and perhaps art. It is important to remember, however, that Muslim values could prevent a young person from depicting faces. Adolescents may also be disconcertingly silent. Their preferred style of communication may be online, even if it is the problems of cyberspace that have brought them to counselling in the first place. BACP's MindEd portal is helpful for online therapy (www.bacp.co.uk).

For younger children, their natural medium for communication is symbolic play, and the play therapist and supervisor are likely to spend much time discussing hypotheses about what has happened in the session. If this is done mutually, without the supervisor doing all the interpretation, it can be fascinating and rewarding for both, even if the material is sad. Sometimes the therapist will bring feelings of frustration and isolation because of constantly having to explain to others that the child is not 'just playing'.

The supervisor and therapist together can look for the signs that the urgent symbolic play is diminishing, and ordinary playfulness is increasing – a sign that the work is nearing its end.

Ideally the supervisor will offer creative methods in supervision so that the unconscious and the right brain are as active for the therapist as they are for the child.

## ACTION METHODS IN SUPERVISION

### Overview

Without video, the supervisor needs a high degree of trust and self-awareness from the counsellor to give him the information he needs to provide safe and supportive supervision. The supervisor normally only has the counsellor's conscious perception and conscious insight into what is happening. By moving into action, the counsellor's feelings towards the child become visible and unconscious insights are brought to light, helping the counsellor, supervisor and child.

The working in action methods described here use chairs to represent the child, different aspects of the counsellor and others as necessary. Moving into a chair (and what it represents) enables the counsellor to have a deeper understanding of what that person – or aspect of a person – feels.

Briefly, the benefits of using action methods are: to free the counsellor from her own material; to bring material that is just out of their conscious awareness into awareness; to increase empathy towards the child; and to enable the counsellor to share with the supervisor difficult or unacceptable feelings she may have, so avoiding these being acted out in the session with the child.

In all these methods, the supervisor needs to be active and physically supportive by standing beside (or if doubling – described later – behind) the counsellor. The supervisor behaves as if the chair were occupied and looks at it, rather than the counsellor. After using any of these techniques, the counsellor and supervisor review what has been learnt.

The four methods described below are used as the need arises.

### Role reversal

This rapidly increases empathy for the child.

The supervisor has the counsellor sit in a separate chair to her own – or on a cushion – in role as the child, asking her to take the posture and show the behaviour the child may express. If the counsellor's name is Susan, the supervisor might address the chair and ask: 'What does Susan need to know about you that she doesn't understand?', or 'What do you think Susan feels about you?', or 'What do you most want Susan to know about what your life is like?'

Whilst in the role of the child, the counsellor frequently experiences much deeper empathy and understanding of how the child feels. Because it is often so painful and difficult to be truly aware of the distress the child feels whilst you are in role as the counsellor, the counsellor protects herself. But at a subliminal level, we are picking up the feelings, and this can be accessed using these methods.

The supervisor then puts the counsellor back into the counsellor's chair, giving her a chance to verbalise anything she understood or felt to the now-empty child's chair. This is not a rehearsal for their next session, but a chance to explore and deepen their understanding.

Role reversal is not advised if the counsellor is already over-identified with the child.

## Multi-chair method

This method is useful for discovering and freeing the counsellor from transferential feelings, where she is attributing material and feelings from her own past, to the child.

This method starts with an empty chair for the child, with the counsellor sitting facing the child's chair. The supervisor encourages the counsellor to describe her feelings towards the child. It is often useful if the counsellor is asked what her gut feeling is when she looks in her diary and sees the child's name. Is it heart-sink, or a feeling of pleasure? The supervisor is trying to find the essence of the counsellor's feelings towards the child.

The supervisor then puts a chair between the counsellor and the hypothetical child's chair and encourages the counsellor to think about any other relationship from the past where she had similar feelings. This might include parts of herself as possible candidates for the different parts of self and the relationship with each part. So, this middle chair now holds the memory of a past relationship.

Once the counsellor has recognised the connection (e.g. 'Yes, she reminds me of my sister who was always getting attention'), the supervisor asks for three ways in which the relationship just described is different from the counsellor's relationship with the child. Differences might include how responsible she feels, age, place, gender or power balance.

This is supervision – not therapy – so keep this brief. The supervisor now names the differences. For example, 'So, in that relationship you were a child; they had the power, you were a relative'. The supervisor then moves the empty chair to a distance, or out of sight.

Moving the middle chair reveals the child's chair, now free of any transference. The difference this makes to the counsellor's feelings towards the child is often significant.

## The unreasonable chair

This is often a popular chair. In this chair, the counsellor is encouraged to express all the feelings she cannot normally express, or feels she should not have about the child or herself.

The counsellor is given a chair for her professional self, and next to it a second chair, which is the unreasonable chair. The counsellor then moves between these chairs as needed. Usually the counsellor starts in the professional chair and starts to express her feelings towards the empty (child's) chair opposite her. When she needs to express difficult or unacceptable feelings she does that from the unreasonable chair.

For example, 'You do the same thing every session. It is so boring.' Or 'You are so angry all the time'. Or 'You make me feel helpless/useless/stuck/exhausted/overwhelmed …'

One of the difficult things about working with children, particularly using play therapy, is that the child will treat the counsellor in the same way that they have been treated. Whilst this is useful information, we are human, and have all been children, so this experience can trigger the counsellor's own feelings of being left out, being bullied, being treated unfairly or being ignored.

Expressing these uncomfortable feelings and thoughts is often a relief, and – as in many other situations in life where feelings have been suppressed or denied – more positive and acceptable feelings then often surface.

It is important to end this method with the counsellor back in the professional chair, where she expresses what she has experienced.

## Doubling

'Doubling' can be an effective strategy and is used to help the counsellor to gain clarity in relation to feelings and difficulties experienced when working with specific clients. The supervisor can offer insights into any feelings or difficulties the counsellor is experiencing. Alternatively, the supervisor might model a possible response.

In doubling, the supervisor stands behind the chair of the counsellor, and speaks as the counsellor in the first person to an empty chair in which the imagined child is sitting. So, for example: 'I feel so helpless when you shout all the time. I want to help, but I feel pushed away.' Any statements the supervisor makes are then checked with the counsellor: 'Is any of that right?'

These interventions are often empathic or congruent. They are given as suggestions only: it is always important that the supervisor gets the counsellor to find her own words for what she needs to say.

The supervisor can also put in positive support when doubling as the counsellor. For example, directing to the child the statement: 'I'm trying so hard to be helpful, but you are really exhausting', lets the counsellor know the supervisor is on her side, freeing her to find new ways to be.

## Concluding comments about action work

Gaining practice with colleagues, or attending appropriate training, will give you confidence and fluidity in these methods.

# Case Study

Pippa had worked for 3 years in a Child and Adolescent Mental Health Services (CAMHS) outreach team. She had been trained in adult counselling, but had had regular in-house training in therapeutic work with children and adolescents.

When Pippa was allocated a new case, even the referral details made her feel overwhelmed. Adam was 9, a looked-after child, with slight learning difficulties, from a white working class background, living with his grandparents. By the time he was 6, he had been physically, emotionally and sexually abused, and had seen his mother die of a cerebral haemorrhage in front of him as she was cooking the tea. For 3 years he had been quiet and no-one had thought he needed therapy, but now he was being oppositional and destructive at home, and his grandmother (Nana) was not sure that she could continue to look after him like this.

Pippa took her feelings of being overwhelmed to supervision even before her first session. She had never known a child suffer so much, and even his system, which included complex reconstitutions, was more than she could grasp. Jane, her supervisor, suggested using Russian dolls to clarify this, and this externalising and miniaturising helped Pippa to feel less submerged.

Before the first session, Pippa had put out excessive amounts of paint, because Nana had said Adam liked art. She realised later in supervision that this was her 'rescuer' at work. Adam had squirted paint wildly, staining the carpet, and made much mess with sand and water. He had also banged loudly on the walls. Pippa found herself worrying about what other people would say, and was powerfully reminded of when her own toddler made a mess in someone else's house. She had coped with boundary-testing before, but realised there was rightly no mention of mess or noise in the ground rules that she had outlined earlier. Nana looked worried by his excited presentation when she came to collect him. She wanted to talk to Pippa in front of him, but Pippa gently put her off. Pippa went home worrying that she might have done more harm than good in letting him be so wild.

She had lots of unease to share at her next supervision. Jane made the practical suggestion that Pippa might change the therapy day to one when no-one was using the room next door. This was simple but effective 'plumber' work. Jane also contained Pippa's feelings in a calm and respectful way. They reflected together on what mess might mean to Adam, and Jane suggested slightly re-stating the ground rules to 'no damage that can't be put right'.

As Pippa stayed with the process more confidently, Adam's mess began to focus itself into a game of a naughty, messy baby. He sucked on a baby's bottle, and wrenched Pippa's heart by crawling round saying someone had taken his bottle away and he couldn't find it.

However, Nana had been worried by Adam's telling her he was drinking from a baby's bottle, and she had shared her fears of regression with a liaison teacher, who rang Pippa and said, 'He needs to be made to talk', and had advised immediate referral to someone else. After a moment of indignation, Pippa went into self-doubt, and suddenly felt inexperienced. Jane was able to help her to see that the established good relationship meant she was the right person to do the work, but that she had taken insufficient account of systemic issues.

*(Continued)*

(Continued)

Pippa quickly arranged a programme of regular feedback meetings, which Adam had no objection to, some just with Nana and some with the professional system as well. Nana was also signposted to counselling for her own grief and anxiety. Once the system was fully supportive, the therapy was enhanced by changes made in the outside world.

Pippa had to contain Adam's splitting of his vulnerability and his anger in many dizzying role reversing dramas, which she took for her own containment to supervision. Just as she was beginning to gain more confidence, she heard from Nana that Adam had shown some distressing sexualised behaviour at a family party. Pippa's experience was with victim issues, not with sexually harmful behaviour. She needed all Jane's 'policeman, plumber, poet' functions, together with line management involvement. Pippa's growing attachment to Adam tempted her to minimise what had happened, but Jane was clear that the behaviour had to be addressed at once and mainly cognitively, both supportive and challenging, neither underreacting nor overreacting. She pointed towards an age-appropriate assessment tool, which included other members of the system, to see if this was an 'amber light' or a 'red light' situation. Because everyone concluded it was the former, it was felt Pippa could do the work herself with Jane's supervision and some further reading.

Adam showed no more sexually inappropriate behaviour. He resumed his symbolic play, integrating his earlier splitting by acting as a kickboxing baby. He invited Pippa to be 'the Mam'. Over the weeks, he directed Pippa in dramas in which the mother was angry with the messy baby, and their mutual anger and rejection escalated to the point where the mother died – died cooking the tea. Pippa knew the theory of children's magical thinking about their own responsibility, but she had never felt it in her stomach until that day. She needed to discharge her pain in supervision, and also to talk about the way forward, whether it was right to stay indefinitely with this bleak pain or intervene to move it on. Jane pointed her in the direction of literature which suggested that repeated post-traumatic play does need to be interrupted.

Fortified by this, Pippa was able next time to make the dying mother say words of reconciliation and reassurance that he was not to blame. After that, Adam's play showed themes of forgiveness, hope and growing self-esteem. Ordinary interactive games began to appear.

Pippa's shared journey made her reluctant to let him go, even though she knew the work was done and that he was behaving well and starting to transfer his attachment to his grandmother. Jane reminded her that it is the therapist's job to make herself unnecessary. Pippa took comfort from this and made it her mantra. She was able to do a good ending, and she and Jane looked back together with satisfaction on what had eventually been achieved from such a daunting beginning.

## RESEARCH

Recent evaluations of school counselling, such as the Counselling in Schools Project in Scotland 2004 and the Welsh School-based Counselling Strategy 2011, provide encouraging detailed evidence of the effectiveness of counselling in schools but, and maybe appropriately for their focus, with little or no reference to the place of the supervisory relationship in the service delivery. Similarly in *Research on Counselling Children and Young People: a Systematic Scoping Review* (Harris and Pattison, 2004), the function of and training requirements for supervision are absent.

However, the BACP's Supervisors' Workshop devised for circulation by Inskipp and Proctor (1993) evidenced a growing recognition of the integral importance of supervision in counselling practice.

The recent BACP Children and Young People Practice Research Network (CYP PRN), which now provides support to practitioners to undertake research projects, is a welcome base into the future.

The BACP's Ethical Framework, redeveloped in 2018, recognises the qualitative and creative nature of the supervisory relationship whilst introducing the value of shared reviewing of the supervisees' practice. This strengthening of the framework for therapeutic practice has equally enhanced the reference potential for research projects.

The ETHOS study is a current example of the use of this potential. From April 2016 to April 2019 the ETHOS Project, a randomised controlled trial led by Professor Cooper at Roehampton University with researchers from other universities and organisations, aims to evaluate the effectiveness and cost-effectiveness of school-based humanistic counselling 'to positively impact the provision of mental health support for young people'. Supervision has a well-blended part to play in this project both for the counsellors' practice and the purpose of the research. The supervisor is expected to be 'an active member of the research counselling team: participating in the research orientation and training'.

With the inclusion of supervision in this and ongoing research, counselling practice commissioners will hopefully grow to understand the need for supervision in their budget proposals – a serious professional concern in these straitened times.

## Key Learning

The supervisor needs:

- To understand the importance of the counsellor working with the child's system, especially in some ethnic communities.
- To be ready to contain the counsellor's emotions, and to seek his own supervision for this.
- To be up to date on the law regarding children.
- To be prepared to mirror the creativity of children within supervision.

## Summary

The supervisor of work with children and young people fulfils the same functions of 'policeman, plumber and poet' as with adult work, but has to bear in mind the ways in which these client groups are different. The power/powerlessness issues of society, and hence of any therapeutic or supervisory relationship, are likely to be accentuated in this field. It is also even more difficult for the practitioner to stay with the pain of children than it is to stay with that of adults. The supervisee is likely to bring powerful and complex feelings to supervision, which can often best be explored creatively. Children's healing can be faster than that of adults however, and seeing this brings great reward to both practitioner and supervisor.

## Discussion Questions

1. As a supervisor how much do I need to be needed?
2. Do I feel uncomfortable setting limits?
3. What are the key elements of a supervision contract with a supervisee working with children and young people?

   Turn to p.446 for possible answers.

## Develop Your Skills

1. For supervisor: Think of one of your supervisee's clients and construct her family system as you understand it at this moment, using objects or drawing a map with the child in the central position. Use this in your supervision, or peer consultation, to clarify your own reactions and ownership of issues.
2. For supervisor and supervisee – evaluation exercise: Design and use a questionnaire to focus on the purpose, model and outcomes of your work in supervision for an agreed period, perhaps 6 months or a year.
3. Practise, in a safe context, one of the skills described in the action methods section in this chapter.

## Further Reading

British Association for Counselling and Psychotherapy (BACP) (2016) *Ethical Framework for the Counselling Professions*. Rugby: BACP

Bond, T. and Sandhu, A. (2005) *Therapists in Court: Providing Evidence and Supporting Witnesses*. London: Lutterworth/SAGE/BACP.

Henderson, P. (2009) *Different Wisdom Reflections on Supervision Practice*. London: Karnac Books.

Khan, M. (2017) Working with young Muslim clients. BACP Children and Young People, March. Available at: https://www.bacp.co.uk/bacp-journals/bacp-children-and-young-people-journal/march-2017 (accessed 12 February 2018).

Landreth, G.L. (2002) *Play Therapy: the Art of the Relationship*. New York: Brunner-Routledge.

### Online Resources

BACP Counselling MindEd e-portal – https://www.bacp.co.uk/events-and-resources/ethics-and-standards/competences-and-curricula/counselling-minded/

School-based counselling in UK primary schools

BACP PRN – www.bacp.co.uk/schools

BACP Research – www.bacp.co.uk/research/networks

Coram Children's Legal Centre – www.coram.org.uk/legalcentre

Ethos Project – www.roehampton.ac.uk/researchcentres/ethos

Gillick competency – www.nspcc.org.uk/gillick-competency-fraser-guidelines

## REFERENCES

Cowie, H. and Wallace, P. (2000) *Peer Support in Action*. London: SAGE.

Erikson, E.H. (1965) *Childhood and Society*. London: Hogarth Press.

Harris, B. and Pattison, S. (2004) *Research on Counselling Children and Young People: A Systematic Scoping Review*. Rugby: BACP.

Houston, G. (1990) *The Red Book of Supervision and Counselling*. London: Rochester Foundation.

Inskipp, F. and Proctor, B. (1993) *Making the Most of Supervision.* Cardiff: Cascade Publications.

Karpman, S. (1968) Fairy tales and script drama analysis. *Transactional Analysis Bulletin,* 7(26): 39–43.

Khan, M. (2017) *Working with young Muslim clients. BACP Children and Young People,* March. Available at: https://www.bacp.co.uk/bacp-journals/bacp-children-and-young-people-journal/march-2017 (accessed 12 February 2018).

# 14

# GROUP WORK

## PETER PEARCE, GWEN PROUD AND ROS SEWELL

**This chapter will discuss:**

- Some of the key applications of group work with children and young people
- Some of the benefits and advantages of this work
- Considerations necessary for setting up group work
- Identification of many of the attributes required of a group facilitator as well as behaviours that are not facilitative
- Details of some of the theoretical ideas about group work and group dynamics
- The history and background for group work
- Current research on group work

## INTRODUCTION

Children's health services today place high value on the provision of a range of interventions to improve accessibility in supporting the mental health of the individual. Group work may be a worthwhile option to consider: the literature on the subject shows an increase in its use and effectiveness to help young people cope with shared problems such as living in families where social problems or illness exist.

In a climate of limited resources, particularly one that can be dominated by concerns about results and statistics, as within a UK school environment, therapeutic group work can be seen as cost-effective and time efficient. In an *International Scoping Review of School*

*Counselling*, Harris (2013) found that school counselling was well established in 62 countries and that the majority of those counsellors had experience of group work as well as individual counselling. It can be attractive to stakeholders to know that 12 people are being seen in a group. Groups might also be seen as a way to address particular issues, for example, bullying or anger management. So there may be considerable pressure for group work to be offered. The key benefit of therapeutic group work is that it results in interaction and social contact, which does not occur in the individual client and therapist model. In this way therapeutic groups can offer participants the potential to develop their understanding of themselves and others by being in relation to other group members. The social, interpersonal context for issues is played out live through embodied experiencing. Groups can also become rich feedback environments where any participant can be facilitative, not only the therapists, and this can support increased self-awareness and awareness of what others see. It can be very validating and potentially developmental for a participant who, because of previous experiences, may feel they have nothing to offer others to begin to experience that they can be facilitative and that they might receive something valuable for themselves in return.

In a group new responses and ways of being can be tried out in relative safety. Participants have the opportunity to be more than the person they have come to be known as, providing the opportunity for harsh introjects and conditions of worth to be dissolved and offering important preparation for using newly learnt behaviours in other areas of their lives.

The facilitative conditions can begin to be 'held' and communicated by the group, as participants begin to challenge and keep each other on track. Participants may also be triggered by others' material into a range of emotional responses, giving the opportunity for vicarious learning and, particularly with young people, for building on emotional literacy. The effect of working in this way therefore can have a profound impact on personal awareness and development. All of this makes group work a suitable choice for effective work with children and young people in a variety of contexts such as schools and children's services, particularly when the problems are recurring, isolating and stigmatising.

Therapeutic group work involves the bringing together of a carefully selected group of individuals to meet regularly with a therapist. The purpose of such work may include assisting each individual in emotional growth and personal problem-solving to identify and increase the use of strengths and to increase well-being.

Generally, therapeutic group work will be adopted for children and young people whose problems relate to social and/or relational difficulties. It is about helping people within a social setting to grow and develop their social skills, personal resources and their relationships with other people. In the school setting, therapeutic group work can have a variety of applications including prevention (e.g. peer pressure), problem-focused (e.g. parental separation) and information-focused (e.g. study skills), with the decision to offer group work often influenced by time constraints.

Much of the literature points to the supportiveness of groups made up from children sharing similar experiences. Three implications arising out of this common experience are: it makes it safe to be social; they know you are not the only one; and coping strategies can be shared, thus building on resilience.

Small group work, facilitated by a mental health professional with knowledge and experience of how to use the group process to promote the individual, can be a useful intervention to attend to self-esteem and social difficulties. Within the group context the group process is viewed as an integral agent for change in individuals. Although beneficial outcomes can be achieved from educational and guidance group interventions, a counselling/therapy approach, which addresses internal difficulties in an environment of support and group cohesiveness and enables freedom of self-expression, has the potential for greater intrapersonal gains relating to self-esteem and locus of control.

The culture of group work is somewhat informal, every member sitting in a circle, though there will usually be inbuilt safe working practices, including mutually consented boundaries and meeting in the same room, that provide privacy, appropriate space for movement, light and resources.

Carl Rogers describes the group as an organism with an inherent actualising tendency, which means that, given a reasonably healthy psychological climate (i.e. characterised by the presence of Rogers' six conditions), the group will move towards health. Facilitation of group work ensures a climate that is psychologically safe for the participants through being authentic, offering empathic understanding and acceptance of each individual, and the group itself. Culturally competent group work requires a capacity in the practitioner to value diversity and maintain an active interest in how individual young people and their families experience specific beliefs, practices and lifestyles, whilst considering how these might impact on their ability to access and experience group work. It also requires a capacity for cultural self-awareness in the practitioner and a willingness to adapt practice skills to fit the cultural context.

Therapeutic group work can offer participants the opportunity to become more aware of their own beliefs, values and potential prejudices and more sensitive and accepting of others, acting as a sort of sensitivity training. During therapeutic group work, participants may also begin to see that they are not alone in experiencing difficulty in life and can find it comforting to hear that others have similar difficulties, or have already worked through an issue that is problematic for another group member. Yalom and Leszcz (2005) describe this therapeutic factor as 'universality'. Other therapeutic factors of group work identified by Yalom (Yalom and Leszcz, 2005) are outlined in Table 14.1 on the next page.

Yalom's therapeutic factors are consensually accepted and remain widely debated and researched.

## Therapeutic group work as an economic intervention

A considerable benefit of the group modality is that professionals can work with a larger group of young people at one time. This possibility offers a degree of relief in child-based health care systems, which are often bound by restrictions on time and resources. A particular benefit is the opportunity to alleviate pressure on waiting lists, allowing clients to be seen sooner and helping prevent difficulties increasing or a decline in coping that may occur during a long waiting period.

Table 14.1   Therapeutic factors of group work (Yalom and Leszcz, 2005)

| Therapeutic factor | Definition |
| --- | --- |
| Altruism | Participants gain a boost to self-concept through extending help to other group participants |
| Instillation of hope | Members recognise that other participants' success can be helpful and they develop optimism for their own improvement |
| Imparting information | Education or advice provided by the therapist or group participants |
| Family re-enactment opportunity | To re-enact critical family dynamics with the group; the corrective recapitualisation of the participant's primary family experience |
| Development of socialising techniques | The group provides participants with an environment that fosters adaptive and effective communication |
| Imitative behaviour | Participants expand their personal knowledge and skills through the observation of group participants' self-exploration, working through and personal development |
| Cohesiveness | Feelings of trust, belonging and togetherness experienced by the group participants |
| Existential factors | Participants accept responsibility for life decisions |
| Catharsis | Participants' release of strong feelings about past or present experiences |
| Interpersonal learning input | Participants gain personal insight about their interpersonal impact through feedback provided from other participants |
| Interpersonal learning output | Participants provide an environment that allows them to interact in a more adaptive manner |
| Self-understanding | Participants gain insight into psychological motivation, underlying behaviour and emotional reactions |

## Selecting participants for group work

It is important to consider the basis on which individuals are brought together to work in a group. Candidates for therapeutic group work should be offered a group that is best suited for their identified needs. This is different from forming a group based on a diagnosis or label. Consideration of the rights of children and young people, including full and appropriate consent, needs to be an integral part of the recruiting process.

In order for a therapeutic group to function effectively care needs to be taken in group selection. Points to consider could include that need is compatible with the goals of the group, that the group is mixed (i.e. not a group of young people all of whom have behavioural difficulties – which might be in danger of entrenching existing self-images and becoming the 'naughty boys' group), motivation to participate and capacity to perform given group tasks. It is also useful to have a balance between those who speak easily in a group and those who find it more difficult.

The size of groups can range from between 5 to 12 participants, but eight participants would generally be considered as the optimal size. Whilst therapeutic groups will normally have one or two group facilitators, it is worth considering the benefits of having two facilitators. Greater opportunity for observing and noting the group dynamics is afforded, there is improved access to adult support when needed for certain tasks, less chance of disruption should a facilitator be unable to be present for any reason and less chance of leaving a group unattended in a situation that might require a facilitator to seek help.

It is recommended that prospective group work participants meet in advance with group facilitators to determine suitability. This provides the opportunity for the group facilitators to explain the purpose and format of group work and answer any questions that will help in deciding whether to participate.

## Attributes of a group facilitator

We have found that to be effective group facilitators with young people we have had to be:

- flexible, willing to start where the participants can;
- willing to really hear the young people and honour each person's unique contribution and frame of reference;
- willing to allow conflict in the room and support others to be okay with this too;
- unafraid of the process and non-defensive;
- able to stay in relation;
- attentive to the process and sensitively observant;
- open to welcome different parts of participants and open to people changing;
- 'in the moment';
- equipped with a sense of humour;
- willing participants in the group ourselves and consider self-disclosing when it feels appropriate;
- good advocates for the group outside of the group setting and represent it positively to others;
- mindful of child protection issues and safety in the group;
- consistent in maintaining a quietly positive invitation to participants that signals hope and welcomes potential;
- warm, accepting and able to set clear boundaries.

We have found that these attributes, which might all be part of one-to-one work or other group work too, need to be developed further in this setting, which can then feel more intense and issues amplified.

Corey (2013) identifies some behaviours which he sees as non-facilitative. These include: giving frequent interventions, pushing or manipulating the group towards their own unspoken goal, judging the success of a group by the dramatics (how many people cried), acting as an expert with superior knowledge and withholding of self, using 'we' statements and implying there is no free choice – 'now we will do an exercise', etc.

## Life cycle of the group dynamic in group work

Though theories exist about group work dynamics and life cycle, there is no definitive model of group stage development. It is generally considered that the group process is fairly predictable and that therapeutic groups change and evolve over time. Within that process the therapist can determine the development of the individual and the group as a whole, as well as providing opportunity to evaluate and formulate specific interventions. Information coming out of recent studies indicates that paying attention to group dynamics is crucial to the maintenance and success of group work, highlighting the importance of a welcoming and supportive atmosphere, with equity and comfort also being important factors.

Harbin and Murphy (2000) draw attention to the influence on dynamics of groups made up of young people of different ages pointing out how it can have a detrimental impact on behaviour and concentration levels within the group.

Tuckman (1965) has been highly influential in providing insight into the possible factors involved in group dynamics. Rogers advocated that group facilitators become participants and that they have influence but not control. He placed emphasis on trusting the group process for therapeutic potentiality with reliance on the wisdom of the group for recognising and dealing with unhealthy elements.

Studies of group development are generally consistent with the Tuckman model, which considers the developmental stages (from conception to the end) to be the most significant dynamic. Tuckman identified five stages through which groups progress. The first stage is 'forming' and involves a number of group participants experiencing levels of uncertainty and anxiety, whilst others will experience feelings of positive anticipation or even excitement. Expectations about what might happen in the group will vary from member to member. Participants will be appraising how trustworthy or safe the group feels for them and will generally be looking to the facilitator for guidance. The second stage, 'storming', involves the formation of a group identity and is more challenging in character than the forming stage because of increased active participation and the emergence of personalities ranging from dominant to withdrawn. This is the time when the boundaries and skills of the facilitator will be tested, and the importance of tolerance and patience, and being able to demonstrate firmness, fairness and support, will be imperative for the future triumph of the group. Tuckman's third stage, 'norming', involves participants having a sense of belonging, giving up their own interests to the interests of the group, and establishing group 'norms' that enable a sufficient sense of trust and safety. The resulting shift in the power dynamics means that participants will begin to feel comfortable enough to work together on given tasks with less reliance on the facilitator and will in effect be 'performing'. The final 'adjourning/mourning' stage of the group process is concerned with the phase that includes ending the group work when the work is completed and the group breaks up. This will present varying levels of emotional challenge for participants depending upon their experience of change and former endings in their lives. Great consideration and care needs to be given to participants during this phase. Preparing participants for the end of the group work may include an acknowledgement and celebration of work accomplished and completed, facilitating the expression of feelings about ending and engaging in some kind of evaluation process.

The perspective of the group dynamic of Slavin differs from that of Tuckman with its emphasis on the importance of individual behaviours of group participants and the effect they have on the group dynamic. Individual participants begin to adopt roles that influence the direction of learning and group process which will be significantly impacted, for example, by the absence of a particular group member.

Lewin was responsible for coining the term 'group dynamics' with a focus on group behaviour and suggested that the individual exists in a psychological field of forces. He noticed the impact of the group on the individual and consequent change in behaviour followed by the individual then impacting on the group, which he defined as 'group pressure'.

## HISTORY AND BACKGROUND

The therapeutic power inherent in groups was recognised in the early 1900s by Boston physician Joseph Pratt working with impoverished sufferers of tuberculosis. Pratt initiated group intervention for his patients for efficiency purposes and learnt from observations that healing qualities emerged from the group process involving mutual concern and learning. The efficacy of the work demonstrated by Pratt sparked an interest in group work as a therapeutic intervention in the field of psychology based on the dual belief that many individual problems are social in origin and that people sharing a common problem can be helpful to each other. The formation of Alcoholics Anonymous is a notable example. The ensuing widespread practice of group therapy and the growing body of literature commending the benefits of group work resulted in firmly establishing its practice across populations and settings.

The developmental roots of therapeutic group work with children and young people are founded in the social and theoretical changes relating to psychology. A noteworthy example is that of S.R. Slavson and his role in the establishment of the American Group Psychotherapy Association. Slavson became interested in social group work within his New York neighbourhood in 1911. His educational convictions, viewed as progressive, determined the nature of the group work. In 1934 he introduced a child guidance clinic for small groups of socially alienated girls. Structured activities using arts and crafts materials allowed complete freedom of self-expression devoid of any didactic or judgemental elements in the belief that self-expression and creativity are key to human happiness and constructive social adjustment.

From the 1950s great strides were made towards the development of group therapy with increasing focus extending to other areas including education and child guidance. A humanistic approach was brought to group psychotherapy by Dreikers, Adler and Rogers, and significant contributions by Corsini, Rosenberg and Berne, amongst others, helped to illuminate the role of group dynamics and environment in successful therapeutic outcomes.

## Theoretical underpinning

A person-centred or child-centred theoretical orientation provides an appropriate context for group therapy and is in line with contemporary guidance and policy for psychological interventions with children and young people (e.g. the UN Charter on Children's Rights). Therapeutic group work with children and young people is rooted in the humanistic tradition of psychology and Carl Rogers' theory of person-centred practice, which centres on the individual's potential to be self-directive within a facilitative environment. A doctoral student of Rogers, Virginia Axline (1947), outlined important child-centred principles for providing an effective framework for group therapy practice. They include: that the therapist develops a warm, friendly relationship with the child; the child is accepted exactly as they are; that only those limitations that are necessary to anchor the therapy to the world of reality are established; that the child is made aware of their responsibility in the relationship; that a deep respect is maintained for the child's ability to solve their own problems if given an opportunity to do so; that the responsibility to make choices and to institute change is the child's.

## MODELS OF GROUP CONTRACTING AND MAINTENANCE

As in all therapeutic work it is imperative to establish clear boundaries. At the outset of group work the boundaries can be incorporated into a contract, which involves participants of the group, including the facilitators, working together to produce a statement setting out the general responsibilities and expectations for the course of the group work. As the group develops, it is possible that the contract may need to be reviewed and revised to reflect altering conditions and expectations. Revisions happen as a result of increased meaning and significance of the contract for participants brought about from experiential learning and group process. Some group contracting models require participants to sign the contract, agreeing to abide by its conditions. A copy of the group contract is generally available for reference at every session.

The content of the group contract should reflect that it is designed to provide a safe and cohesive environment for participants including the valuing of one another. It may include agreements about conflict resolution, attendance expectations, terms of withdrawal from the group, confidentiality, physical contact limits, the right to 'pass' on an activity, and how feedback, evaluation and information are handled and shared.

Regular attendance and punctuality increase value for participants and contribute to creating a climate of cohesiveness and purpose. Participants may need to be helped to appreciate that their participation makes an important contribution to the group process and is therefore helpful not only personally but also to the other group participants. Leaving a group is an important process because of the feelings involved. The terms might usefully encourage discussion of any concerns a member may have initially within the group so that efforts can be made to find a satisfactory resolution.

An atmosphere of trust is essential for group participants to feel safe enough to share material and disclose their feelings and problems. Participants should be asked not to discuss anything outside the group, using the principle of 'what is said in the group stays in the group'. It is the group facilitator's job to help each member understand that it is their responsibility to protect the names and identities of fellow group participants. At the same time, because sharing themes of the group work and their personal material with significant others can be an important element of personal growth for participants, the facilitator should not discourage it as long as it does not contravene confidentiality boundaries. An element of safety can be provided by including the right to 'pass' on any activity that may cause a member of the group to feel uncomfortable and this helps to establish trust that may enable fuller participation as confidence grows.

Contracting will also need to make clear the limitations of what can remain private and that the group facilitators have an obligation under child safeguarding requirements to share with relevant parties any disclosures that indicate serious risk of harm.

Generally group contracts will specify that there should be no uninvited physical contact. This is important because young people will have different personal histories and interpretations of what touch means. Exceptions include drama and dance groups, where touch will form a natural and normative part of the group work.

Group function and maintenance are supported by careful selection of activity and instruction. Preference should be given to collaborative and fun activities that promote mutual support and interdependence rather than independence (Gitterman, 2006). Giving specific instructions about how long an activity should take and explicit prompts, such as 'take turns' or 'ask your group mates', enables effective functioning and the comfort of knowing how to proceed.

## CONTEXT OF THE GROUP

Therapeutic group work acknowledges that personal well-being depends to some extent on how the individual constructs the self in social terms and the strong relationship between emotion and social interaction. This approach takes a holistic view of the complex range of human need, conceiving human problems in context.

## Methods of outcome evaluation

Evaluating the outcomes of group therapy can be useful to determine whether the intervention is suitable to a child's needs and is achieving the goals that were identified at assessment. An evaluation can provide important information on the effectiveness of the content of group work as well as ideas for improvements. Essential characteristics of outcomes evaluation include the use of reflective practice, clinical supervision, gathering feedback from participants about their experience of the intervention, and overall authoritative monitoring and assessment.

Evaluation may involve measuring numerous outcomes such as behaviour changes, attainment of skills, group process, goal attainment and participant satisfaction. It may take the form of both quantitative and qualitative assessment measures and, in work with children and young people, may also involve taking into account assessments obtained from significant others such as parents and teachers. Debate surrounds this practice because of the potential for bias and personal interest influencing assessment.

## AN EXAMPLE OF THERAPEUTIC GROUP WORK

The group was a closed group of 12 students and we met together for one and a half terms. All the students were aged 14–15 years old and had been selected by their year head for a variety of reasons. The presenting issues from the school's perspective were mainly behavioural issues that affected the school, for example, 'challenging behaviour', 'withdrawn', 'violent', 'rude to staff', 'aggressive' and 'silly in class'. With only this information about the students the group was formed, so our beginning point with this group was knowing their behavioural history at school but very little about them as people. What unfolded in the group were the group members' individual stories. These were moving and helped us to make sense of their behavioural issues.

One of the challenges in this setting is to collect and assemble a group in the designated room. These particular students were drawn from a pool of students who were seen as 'problem students' – those whom the staff found 'difficult to work with'. It was our task to try to move the students through the school in a group. Moving around the school together caused problems for other classes, as the group members were often shouting, disruptive and knocking on classroom doors en route. This can present problems for counsellors working within a school environment as the role of group facilitator may become compromised by enforcing discipline, and of course the rules of the environment need to be respected if any group is to go ahead. The tension between these attitudes is always present for a school counsellor, and working with groups seems to highlight this issue.

Our experience with this particular group was that once we had arrived at the room it was always difficult to begin. We would invite an opening circle. We found that by asking each member of the circle to share the best and the worst part of their week this helped to invite them to a reflective place. This process was a struggle to achieve. During the opening circle, we modelled trying to listen respectfully whilst openly acknowledging the difficulties of speaking over each other and striving to manage this without being critical or telling the participants off. We were seeking to invite a different experience of mutual respect for each other in the group, helping to create a safe space where all the participants could share openly.

## Case Study

C:       'The best bit of my week was …'

D:       'The best bit of his week was shagging his girlfriend.'

(All the group participants laughing and commenting 'whooo, yeah', etc.)

D:       'Yeah – he thinks he's fit, innit?'

(All the group participants laughing and commenting 'whooo, yeah', etc.)

C:       'Shu' up.'

D:       'No, you shu' up!'

(The whole group just began taking sides and shouting 'shu'up' at each other)
We waited for a break in the shouting.

Peter:   (to C, said with warmth) 'It didn't feel like you really got a chance to speak, C, do you want to carry on?'

The therapist's response here was just enough to create some space and allow the group to continue, and we were able to complete the opening round. L was the first person to speak after the opening round. She told the group that she had noticed how dark it was this morning on her way to school and said how she hated it and it made her feel a bit 'rotten'.

J:       'What d'you mean rotten?'

L:       'Well … a bit sad I think.'

*(Continued)*

(Continued)

Ros:   'You feel a bit sad?'

L:     'Yeah sad, because it was in the winter when I had to go and live with my nan and she lives so far away from the school that I had to leave early when it was dark … *[silence]* and I think the dark reminds me of that time.'

F:     'Why were you living with your nan?'

L:     'It was when my mum died.'

(There was absolute silence whilst the whole group watched and listened attentively and a palpable feeling of warmth and empathy entered the room)

C:     'I didn't know your mum had died.'

(Various group members said 'nor did I', 'how sad', 'that's awful')

C:     'I don't know how to say this … I just feel so sad for you … and I want to say … I'm here for you.'

L:     (Sat quietly for a while – then cried – L got up and moved towards C and they hugged each other and the whole group cried together)

This example demonstrates the capacity that group members have for listening to each other and for reaching out with empathy. The group moved from all shouting at each other in the early part of the session to being able to be empathic without the need for 'facilitation'.

## RESEARCH

Therapeutic group work is a well-established and widespread approach and has a good evidence base for its potential benefits. A systematic scoping review for the British Association for Counselling and Psychotherapy (BACP) (Harris and Pattison, 2004) reviews a number of controlled trials and meta-analyses that include group therapy interventions for children and young people. Group play therapy (Bratton et al., 2005; Danger and Landreth, 2005), group cognitive-behavioural therapy (CBT) (Kaufman et al., 2005; Carpentier et al., 2006), school-based group psychotherapy (Layne et al., 2008), and group humanistic and interpersonal therapies (Shechtman and Pastor, 2005; Rosselló et al., 2008) all show some evidence of effectiveness. Baskin et al. (2010), examining data from 107 studies, found that treatment groups that were predominantly male or female did better than mixed gender groups, and suggest that the flexibility of schools to offer multifaceted interventions seem to demonstrate an advantage of the school setting over mental health clinic settings. In a randomised controlled trial by Stice et al. (2010), adolescents with mild to moderate depression were randomised to one of the following: supportive group therapy vs. CBT group therapy vs. CBT bibliotherapy vs. controls. In this study those who received supportive therapy showed comparable benefits to those in CBT. These benefits were sustained at 2-year follow-ups and were much better than the control group.

The BACP scoping review also identifies that future research needs to be rigorous and transparent to capture the complexity of routine practice with this client group. The authors recommend a wider range of research methodologies, attention to the transfer of research findings into clinical settings, consideration of the relationship between age and treatment outcome specifically adapting interventions to the different developmental stages of adolescence and pre-adolescence, and research into the long-term impact of interventions with children and young people. They also note the relative absence of research relating to certain issues, particularly self-harm and eating disorders.

In a research review of school-based counselling in UK secondary schools, Cooper (2013) highlights that, both for young people themselves and other stakeholders, there tends to be a preference for school-based counselling services that offer a wider array of interventions beyond the one-to-one counselling setting. It further identifies that there is evidence to suggest that mental health and well-being interventions are more helpful when a 'whole-school' approach is adopted, targeting interventions at the wider school context and the groups within it, rather than just the individual young person's problems and needs.

Cooper identifies how the extent to which counsellors can expand their services will depend on the resources available but also identifies that there may also be issues of training, and of how the school-based counsellor role is conceptualised.

## Key Learning

This chapter has provided you with knowledge and information to help develop a greater understanding of group work with children and young people. The knowledge base includes:

- Identifying the key benefits of group work and when to offer this modality.
- How to understand young people's issues in the wider context of home and family and the wider world.
- How to apply theory to the practice of setting up and facilitating groups.
- The place of evaluation of outcomes.

## Summary

- The key benefit of therapeutic group work is that it results in interaction and social contact, which do not occur in the individual client and therapist model.
- The group context offers a method of intervention that acknowledges individual problems in relation to the wider social world.
- Therapeutic group work is a suitable intervention in a variety of contexts such as education and family work for problem-solving, social skills building and addressing socially constructed problems.
- An understanding of issues for children and young people and related mental health problems is necessary for implementing effective support.
- Awareness of the emotional and social aspects of child development is important for understanding how social situations impact on child well-being.
- Therapeutic group work acknowledges the relevance of group process as a helping technique in personal development.
- There are a variety of methods for measuring the outcomes of interventions. The choice of method may be governed by available resources.
- Preliminary discussion and preparation are key factors in conducting successful group work.
- The environment in which therapeutic group work takes place needs to be supportive, with a therapist whose approach is sensitive and respectful.
- Feedback from group work participants and other interested parties is a necessary part of the evaluation process and provides a cross-reference against group work aims and objectives.
- Therapeutic group work has a proven record of significant benefit and is becoming a common choice for therapeutic use. If introduced at a grassroots level, such as within schools, it can provide a great opportunity to address specific social and emotional needs preventatively to support healthy development as part of a school well-being service.

## Discussion Questions

1. What kinds of characteristics are common to group work development across different theories?
2. When might therapeutic group work not be suitable?
3. What might be some of the advantages of the therapeutic group?
4. What are some of the ethical considerations of group work?

# Develop Your Skills

You can use the following scenarios to look at how you would respond, skills you would need and how you will develop these through continuing professional development or practice. You can also reread the chapter to identify useful skills.

Scenarios – how would you respond?

1. The head has asked you to organise a group to address an escalation in bullying that has been identified within the school.
2. A year head has given you a list of boys who really need to 'work on their anger' and asks you to sort it out.
3. A group of girls, including one of your current clients, asks if they can all come together to talk in a group.
4. A teacher who you know really values your work asks you to help her with her class tomorrow after registration as she needs to address their disruptive behaviour.

# Further Reading

Bratton, S.C., Ray, D., Rhine, T. and Jones, L. (2005) The efficacy of play therapy with children: a meta-analytic review of treatment outcomes. *Professional Psychology: Research and Practice* 36(4): 376–390.

Carpentier, M.Y., Silovsky, J.F. and Chaffin, M. (2006) Randomized trial of treatment for children with sexual behaviour problems: 10-year follow-up. *Journal of Consulting and Clinical Psychology* 74(3): 482–488.

Cooper, M. (2013) *School-Based Counselling in UK Secondary Schools: A Review and Critical Evaluation*. Glasgow: University of Strathclyde.

Danger, S. and Landreth, G. (2005) Child-centred group play therapy with children with speech difficulties. *International Journal of Play Therapy* 14(1): 81–102.

Gitterman, A. (2006) Building mutual support in groups. *Social Work with Groups* 28(3–4): 91–106.

Kaufman, N.K., Rohde, P., Seeley, J.R. et al. (2005) Potential mediators of cognitive-behavioral therapy for adolescents with co-morbid major depression and conduct disorder. *Journal of Consulting and Clinical Psychology* 73(1): 38–46.

*(Continued)*

(Continued)

Layne, C.M., Saltzman, W.R., Poppleton, L. et al. (2008) Effectiveness of a school-based group psychotherapy program for war exposed adolescents: a randomized controlled trial. *Journal of the American Academy of Child and Adolescent Psychiatry 47*(9): 1048–1062.

McLaughlin, C., Holliday, C., Clarke, B. and Llie, S. (2013) *Research on Counselling and Psychotherapy with Children and Young People: A Systematic Scoping Review of Evidence for Its Effectiveness from 2003–2011*. Lutterworth: BACP.

Rosselló, J., Bernal, G. and Rivera-Medina, C. (2008) Individual and group CBT and IPT for Puerto Rican adolescents with depressive symptoms. *Cultural Diversity and Ethnic Minority Psychology 14*(3): 234–245.

Shechtman, Z. and Pastor, R. (2005) Cognitive-behavioural and humanistic group treatment for children with learning disabilities: a comparison of outcomes and process. *Journal of Counseling Psychology 52*(3): 322–336.

Stice, E., Rohde, P., Gau, J.M. and Wade, E. (2010) Efficacy trial of a brief cognitive-behavioral depression prevention program for high-risk adolescents: effects at 1- and 2-year follow-up. *Journal of Consulting and Clinical Psychology 78*: 856–867.

Westergaard, J. (2009) *Effective Group Work with Young People*. Milton Keynes: Open University Press.

Yalom, I.D. and Leszcz, M. (2005) *The Theory and Practice of Group Psychotherapy*, 5th edn. New York: Basic Books.

### Online Resources

BACP website: www.bacp.co.uk, especially the BACP Children and Young People Division and the Competences for Working with Children and Young People

Counselling MindEd: https://www.minded.org.uk, especially the modules on the Counselling Context, CMD 0104–0108, and CMD 0110

## REFERENCES

Axline, V. (1947) *Play Therapy*. Boston, MA: Houghton Miffin.

Baskin, T.W., Slaten, C.D., Sorenson, C., Glover-Russell, J. and Merson, D.N. (2010) Does youth psychotherapy improve academically related outcomes? A meta-analysis. *Journal of Counseling Psychology, 57*(3): 290–296.

Bratton, S.C., Ray, D., Rhine, T. and Jones, L. (2005) The efficacy of play therapy with children: a meta-analytic review of treatment outcomes. *Professional Psychology: Research and Practice 36*(4): 376–390.

Carpentier, M.Y., Silovsky, J.F. and Chaffin, M. (2006) Randomized trial of treatment for children with sexual behaviour problems: 10-year follow-up. *Journal of Consulting and Clinical Psychology 74*(3): 482–488.

Cooper, M. (2013) *School-Based Counselling in UK Secondary Schools: A Review and Critical Evaluation.* Glasgow: University of Strathclyde.

Corey, G. (2013) *Theory and Practice of Counselling and Psychotherapy.* India: Cengage.

Danger, S. and Landreth, G. (2005) Child-centred group play therapy with children with speech difficulties. *International Journal of Play Therapy 14*(1): 81–102.

Gitterman, A. (2006) Building mutual support in groups. *Social Work With Groups 28*(3–4): 91–106.

Harbin, F. and Murphy, M. (eds.) (2000) *Substance Misuse and Child Care.* Lyme Regis: RHP

Harris, B. (2013) *School-based Counselling Internationally: A Scoping Review.* Lutterworth: BACP.

Harris, B and Pattison, S. (2004) *Research on Counselling Children and Young People: A Systematic Scoping Review.* Rugby: British Association for Counselling and Psychotherapy

Harrison, A. (2009) Setting up the doll house: a developmental perspective on termination. *Psychoanalytic Inquiry 29*: 174–187.

Kaufman, N.K., Rohde, P., Seeley, J.R. et al. (2005) Potential mediators of cognitive-behavioral therapy for adolescents with co-morbid major depression and conduct disorder. *Journal of Consulting and Clinical Psychology 73*(1): 38–46.

Layne, C.M., Saltzman, W.R., Poppleton, L. et al. (2008) Effectiveness of a school-based group psychotherapy program for war exposed adolescents: a randomized controlled trial. *Journal of the American Academy of Child and Adolescent Psychiatry 47*(9): 1048–1062.

Rosselló, J., Bernal, G. and Rivera-Medina, C. (2008) Individual and group CBT and IPT for Puerto Rican adolescents with depressive symptoms. *Cultural Diversity and Ethnic Minority Psychology 14*(3): 234–245.

Shechtman, Z. and Pastor, R. (2005) Cognitive-behavioural and humanistic group treatment for children with learning disabilities: a comparison of outcomes and process. *Journal of Counseling Psychology 52*(3): 322–336.

Stice, E., Rohde, P., Gau, J.M. and Wade, E. (2010) Efficacy trial of a brief cognitive-behavioral depression prevention program for high-risk adolescents: effects at 1- and 2-year follow-up. *Journal of Consulting and Clinical Psychology 78*: 856–867.

Tuckman, B.W. (1965) Developmental sequence in small groups. *Psychological Bulletin 63*: 384–399.

Yalom, I.D. and Leszcz, M. (2005) *The Theory and Practice of Group Psychotherapy*, 5th edn. New York: Basic Books.

# 15
# ENDINGS
## DEE C. RAY

**This chapter will discuss:**

- A review of outcome goals to guide the ending process in order to improve intentionality when approaching the ending of the counselling relationship
- Unique themes encountered by therapists in ending therapy with children, including developmental and attachment considerations
- Types of endings encountered in most counselling relationships and how to manage endings when they come too soon
- Affective elements that impact a therapist's decision-making and approach to ending and children's affective and behavioural responses to ending counselling
- Skills, scripts, and activities to facilitate the process of ending

## INTRODUCTION

The purpose of this chapter is to explore the closing phase of the counselling relationship specific to the developmental level of children and review attitudes, obstacles and skills related to effective approaches to ending. As a therapist for over 20 years, I have experienced ending a great number of therapeutic relationships with children. In my early career I worked with young adolescents in a residential setting where endings varied from abrupt runaways to very satisfying completion of therapeutic relationships. In later years, as a school counsellor, my endings were often softened by the reassurance that I would see the children throughout the school day, even if I no longer engaged in counselling with them. And in recent years, I have worked at a university-based counselling centre where I teach, supervise and facilitate the counselling of children in an agency setting and a school outreach programme. Currently, my role entails ending counselling relationships on a weekly basis. As I supervise the ending of counselling relationships facilitated by my supervisees and students and as I experience my own endings with children, I recognise and honour the emotional process involved in this final stage of the counsellor–child relationship.

Endings start at the beginning. The therapist's job is to facilitate expression and functionality so that each child can move towards optimal development. The ending of therapy must be part of the therapist's vision at initial contact with a child. The therapist visualises the child at a point in time when obstacles to growth are removed and the child progresses to a state of interdependent and healthy functioning. The therapist sees the end as the real beginning for the child. Ironically, the goal of therapy is to end therapy.

Ending is typically viewed as the resolution of the counselling process. However, closing therapy may possibly be an active part of the counselling process that allows children to create meaning (Harrison, 2009) or experience new ways of coping with loss (Many, 2009). Within the process of ending, the therapist and child collaborate to make sense of the counselling relationship and develop new directions for growth. Ending is the catalyst for the child's movement into the world minus the extra emotional and behavioural supports provided by the therapist.

Although the closing phase is critical to all endings of counselling with children, the level of emphasis or time spent on ending is affected by several factors. First, endings in more relationally oriented treatment relationships necessitate more emphasis by the therapist on the ending and loss of a meaningful relationship (Joyce et al., 2007). Brief and skill-oriented therapies may require less reflection by both therapist and child. Additionally, younger children may require less verbalisation and reflection on the counselling process usually addressed in endings. Extensive talk and requests by the therapist to verbally address the closing of therapy may be confusing and disconcerting to young children due to their limited ability to grasp timelines. Finally, premature ending initiated by a parent or managed care entity may influence a therapist's presentation and processing of ending with a child. Timing, emphasis and approaches to endings are addressed throughout this chapter.

## Goals of endings

Because ending is a phase within the therapeutic process, there are goals to guide this phase just as there are goals for other stages of treatment. Joyce et al. (2007) identified three outcomes related to successful endings in adult therapy that can be applied to working with children, including the consolidation of therapy, resolution of relationship and preparedness for progress. In the following segment, I will define each of these goals and present a child case study that exemplifies each of the desired outcomes in endings. Because most literature regarding endings is contextualised in adult therapy, application to the developmental needs of a child is often challenging. The sample case study portrays the application of the theoretical process of therapy to children.

One notable goal of the ending process in therapy is consolidation of the therapy process and gains made in treatment. The focus on recognising the progress made during treatment when ending therapeutic relationships is one of the top commonalities among therapists across counselling approaches (Norcross et al., 2017). When described within the context of adult therapy, this phase requires a review of the therapeutic relationship since the beginning of therapy and self-assessment by the client regarding changes in functioning. Although a verbal review of therapy would be a meaningless task for a young child, this outcome can be addressed through skilful therapist introduction of ending and facilitating the child's natural response.

Second, during the ending phase, the therapist seeks to resolve issues within the therapeutic relationship. In most cases, children develop intimate relationships with their therapists. During the ending phase, the child will experience a sense of loss and will respond to that loss. The success of this outcome is related to the child's view of the therapist and view of self outside of the relationship with the therapist.

Finally, the third goal of endings is related to the child's preparedness for continuing progress and functioning following counselling (Joyce et al., 2007). For this outcome, the child internalises the counselling process and the therapist's role in that process. In other words, the child reveals self-reliance and confidence in abilities to work through future challenges.

## Case Study: Seth

### Consolidation of Therapy

Seth was a 7-year-old client whom I saw over 8 months for selective mutism. I introduced ending in the following way, 'Seth, do you remember when you first came here and you never talked at school?' Seth nodded. I continued, 'And now you figured out how to feel good about talking at both home and school? Also, you used to never talk to me but now you talk to me a lot?' Seth nodded. He said, 'Now I talk all the time'. I responded, 'Yep, you sure do. Now that you're feeling good about yourself and you can figure out ways to feel good about talking, I think that it's time for us to stop seeing each other. We'll have four more playtimes together.' Seth nodded and then responded, 'I also used to act like a dog but I don't do that anymore. I talk instead of bark.' The brief verbalisation by reviewing Seth's progress served to consolidate Seth's view of the changes he made. Seth further acknowledged his growth by identifying a previous coping skill that kept him from connecting to others (barking) that he replaced with a more functional skill (talking).

### Resolution of Relationship

In the session following the announcement of ending to Seth, I gave a 5-minute warning for the end of the session. He threatened to cut my neck with a rubber knife if I stood up from my chair to leave. After threatening me a few times, I responded, 'You don't want me to leave, but our time is up for today'. He said, 'I guess you can go'. In our second to final session, Seth painted a picture of a woman handing a bouquet of flowers to a child. He did not describe the picture but he presented it to me by saying, 'This is for you'. Both the threats and painting were new behaviours for Seth in which he had not engaged until ending was presented. These behaviours appeared to be his attempt to let me go and acknowledge what he had been given in our relationship.

### Preparedness for Progress

In Seth's final sessions, he initiated a new type of play with a toy he had not used prior to the endings phase. Seth picked up a turtle and placed it in the sand box. Seth drowned the turtle in the sand and then brought the turtle back to the surface over and over again. He verbalised, 'This turtle just keeps coming back to life'. The continued resurgence of the turtle seemed to imply that Seth knew he was resilient and could thrive when things get tough. He acknowledged his readiness to face the challenges before him.

## CONSIDERATIONS FOR CHILD ENDINGS

## Development

A child's understanding of ending is directly related to age and developmental stage. Child therapists are charged with having extensive and substantial knowledge regarding the maturational stages of children and how development may affect ending of therapeutic relationships (Ray, 2016). In the pre-operational stage of cognitive development (ages 2–6; Piaget, 1965 [1932]), a young child has difficulty grasping the permanence of loss and timelines set for an impending loss. Giving a young child 5 weeks' notice for ending of therapy may be understood as a lengthy time period. If not reminded, the child is surprised by the quick end of therapy and has difficulty managing the processing of ending. Yet, a child in concrete cognitive operations (ages 6–12) may assume that if the counselling relationship is ended, then logically she will never be able to see her counsellor again, leading to significant grief. A therapist may need to reassure the child that the relationship can be continued at a later point or the child can contact the therapist after ending.

Due to egocentricity states of children, children may feel that therapy is ending due to something they have done wrong or that they have been bad in some way. Helping children understand the reasons for ending therapy, and reminding them as needed throughout the closing process, is one way to address a child's tendency to interpret events negatively (Moore et al., 2008). Also, young children may often misunderstand the permanency of ending or they may come to understand permanency only after weeks of not seeing the therapist. They may gleefully run out of the therapist's office with no goodbye after the last session. In these cases, the therapist may send a note following the final session or suggest the parent facilitate a note from the child to the therapist if the child needs to send a last goodbye.

Another factor related to endings and development is acknowledgement of the child's need to revisit issues related to treatment as they reach new developmental stages. Even if children have progressed well through therapy, meeting all treatment goals, it is likely that they will revisit old issues with each new developmental phase. In a case where a 6-year-old child has been sexually abused and the child has worked through fear and pain related to the abuse, it is likely that the same child will revisit issues related to cognitive understanding of those events when they reach a concrete level of operations, attempting to make cognitive sense of the situation. And again, when the same child reaches puberty, there may be a need for extra support as the child attempts to understand the self as a sexual being. Therapists help parents understand that many issues related to child challenges are not simply resolved in one period of time. There is a need to encourage parents to seek therapy when they see their children struggling at subsequent developmental stages. In the ending phase of child treatment, the therapist emphasises the fluidity of development and the likelihood of the need for additional therapy.

## Attachment

Endings are addressed sporadically and incompletely in the literature, and endings in child therapy are even less addressed. However, one element that is emphasised in the few manuscripts addressing endings is the relationship between ending, attachment and loss. Joyce et al. (2007) claimed that a history of serious loss during critical developmental periods increases the importance of endings for adult therapy, whilst Marmarosh (2017) emphasised the relationship between attachment and loss that is triggered during therapeutic endings. In humanistically and psychodynamically inclined therapies, the therapist works with diligence to facilitate a relationship with a child that emphasises trust, acceptance, genuineness and warmth. If a child is able to perceive these therapist attitudes, an attachment bond is formed and valued. Ending is a direct threat to this bond and may cause feelings of grief, loss, abandonment, anger or rejection (Moore et al., 2008).

Due to the fact that children presented to therapy typically have multiple risk factors, often related to significant histories of loss and abandonment, the issue of attachment is a key feature of treatment and endings (Many, 2009). Children seek the stability of a therapeutic relationship and are often positively responsive to such a relationship. When such a relationship is established and treatment goals are met, a conflict ensues regarding how therapy can end whilst the child maintains relational gains. Additionally, the child does not just lose the therapeutic relationship but also loses the stability of therapy itself, such as the therapy room, materials, rituals, and people related to therapy, such as administrative staff (Zilberstein, 2008). The loss is relationally intense and structurally broad.

Historically, the ending phase signified a definitive end to therapy. Therapists were seen as crossing over professional boundaries with clients if they maintained contact following the completion of therapy. In recent literature, it is suggested that a therapist should consider ending as transitional, not resolved (Zilberstein, 2008). Suggestions related to addressing attachment issues within the ending phase offer the therapist various opportunities for contact with the child. A therapist may taper sessions from once a week to once every 2 weeks to once a month as a move towards ending. Therapists may provide follow-up sessions at various intervals to check in with the child, such as once every 6 months or year. Providing children with transitional objects such as pictures and crafts during the ending phase is suggested. Additionally, a therapist may want to provide the child with a way to contact the therapist following the closing of therapy through notes or phone calls. With opportunity for subsequent contact, the therapist allows the child to transition from the therapeutic relationship on a timeline that fits the child's needs.

Both Many (2009) and Zilberstein (2008) suggest that a gradual and transitional approach to ending offers a child with attachment difficulties an experience outside of her reference, an opportunity for non-traumatic loss. Whilst preparing the child for loss, the therapist will also want to prepare the parent for the child's loss. Collaborating with parents regarding time and structure of closing offers parents an opportunity to face their own losses and prepare to support their children. The parent's acceptance of the end of therapy helps them to model acceptance for the child. In a developmentally sensitive approach to attachment and loss, Gil and Crenshaw (2016) further suggested the potential benefits of an 'open-door' (2016: 27) policy towards ending therapy in which the child and parents seek further counselling at later times and various intervals.

The process and structure of endings has not been explored in the research. The field of psychotherapy lacks knowledge on clients' responses to endings or its effects on counselling outcome. Although some counsellors believe that endings should be final with no contact between therapist and clients, others believe that tapering of sessions or continued contact after ending is the most effective way to close the counselling process. Yet, there is no research to substantiate either practice.

## Cultural sensitivity

Some therapists have suggested that timing and pace of therapy may be influenced by cultural differences among clients and warn against approaching the ending of therapy according to uniform standards and approaches (Wilcoxon et al., 2008). Standard length and types of treatment may be insensitive to values within some cultural communities. In addition, the decision of a third party or the therapist to end therapy may discount cultural norms of clients in which familial and community decisions are held as most valuable. In order to provide culturally sensitive services, Gil and Crenshaw (2016) recommend that the child and the family be involved in decision-making regarding when and how therapy will end. Therapists may be called upon to advocate for cultural sensitivity to clients in systems in which client decision-making is disregarded.

## TYPES OF ENDINGS

### Natural endings

In the ideal therapy world, therapy is completed when a child, parent and therapist agree that treatment goals have been met, emotional needs have been addressed, and the child is ready to operate independently from the therapist. This leads to a natural ending. Most child therapists experience natural endings in a minority of cases. Rarely do therapists, parents and children come to the same conclusion at the same time. Natural endings may be initiated by any of the three parties involved in therapy. Therapists are probably the most likely to initiate a natural ending by highlighting therapeutic progress with the parent and child. Children will often initiate ending through verbal or behavioural signs such as 'I want to go to football practice instead of coming here', or being bored in session. Parents are often hesitant to end therapy if progress has been made due to fears of regression. They tend to address the topic of ending hesitantly: 'I think he's doing better but I'm just not sure if this is the right time to end'.

### Premature endings

#### Client/parent-initiated

Premature ending initiated by the client, more typically initiated by the parent in child therapy, is also referred to as dropping out of therapy. The drop-out rate is cited with a substantial range depending on individual studies but, on average, appears to be hovering at approximately 50% (Venable and Thompson, 1998). Often, therapy ends abruptly at the will of the parent without therapist or child consent. The abrupt ending to therapy is disconcerting for a child and may result in the child's interpretation that they did something wrong or that the therapist no longer wants to see them (Ray, 2011). Child therapists first address endings in

---

### Example Note

Dear Michael, I am writing this note to tell you that I cherished our time together for the last few weeks. I enjoyed talking with you and getting to know you. I hope that you enjoy your karate lessons. Please take care of yourself and remember how special you are. Thank you for sharing time with me. Suzanne

initial parent consultations, explaining the need for a planned approach to ending therapy. When parents decide that ending is in order before the therapist or child agrees, the therapist makes a concerted effort to contact the parent to plead the case for one last session with the child. If parents do not concede to bring the child in for a last session, the therapist may decide to send a note as one method of ending.

Research has focused on variables related to premature endings with children, emphasising characteristics of clients that lead clients to end therapy early. Kazdin and Mazurick (1994) found children at one site were more likely to prematurely end therapy at early stages (six or fewer sessions) if children had higher impairment in conduct, academic and social behaviours, parents were younger, children came from a single-parent home, parents identified with a minority group or parents reported higher levels of stress. Children were more likely to prematurely end therapy at later stages (7–14 sessions) if mothers were younger, children had a history of antisocial problems, children had lower intellect scores, children were in a household with a non-biological parent or children had poor adaptive functioning reported at school. Venable and Thompson (1998) found that caregivers who were highly self-critical or held personal guilt for the predicament of the child were more likely to initiate premature endings. It appears that reasons for ending prematurely are cross-cultural, as found by McCabe (2002), who reported that Mexican-American children were more likely to drop out of therapy if parents had a lower level of education, perceived barriers to treatment initially, believed that increased discipline addressed emotional problems, or experienced lack of client–therapist ethnic match.

Children who dropped out of play therapy at one site were more likely to be from single-parent homes, have younger mothers or have mothers with lower levels of education (Campbell et al., 2000). And parents at another site who had very high or very low expectations for therapy were more likely to complete therapy, whilst parents with moderate expectations were most likely to end the sessions prematurely (Nock and Kazdin, 2001). Overall, children with higher levels of behavioural problems were more likely to end therapy prematurely (Tsai and Ray, 2011). This extensive research on premature endings offers explanations for why child clients drop out from therapy early but it offers no insight into best practices for the process of endings. Because endings are a significant stage of therapy, there is a need for researchers to focus on variables related to process and structure of the final stage of therapy.

## Therapist-initiated

When therapists initiate premature endings, typically referred to as forced endings, a client is informed by the therapist that counselling will be ended even if treatment goals have not been met. Forced endings are usually triggered by professional and personal changes in the therapist's life such as moves, new professional opportunities or changes in family situations. Although forced endings are to be expected, they are particularly difficult to address in child therapy. It is often hard for a child to understand that he will be losing his therapist because she is having a baby or moving with a new partner. Forced endings are more likely to be met with feelings of rejection by the child and feelings of guilt by the therapist.

Pearson (1998) and Bostic et al. (1996) suggested several implications for counselling related to forced endings. Forced endings require the therapist to conduct a thorough review of each child's case and consider the child's response to an unexpected ending. If a therapist is open in sharing why he is leaving and where he is going, such openness helps to soothe the child's personalisation of the ending. Genuineness on the part of the therapist by sharing emotions about leaving helps a child feel valued. Additionally, a therapist should expect a child to respond in a variety of ways from apathy, to anger, to sadness. The therapist is open to the child's response and need for expression of the loss. Wittenberg (1999) emphasised the therapist's emotions of guilt, followed by defensiveness, which sometimes interfere with the therapist's ability to hold the child's emotions. Therapists will often experience intense feelings related to difficult endings and benefit from additional supervision (Bamford and Akhurst, 2014). Additionally, allowing children to have subsequent contact through notes and letters can be helpful to the separation process. In the case of child therapy, Moore et al. (2008) cautioned against accepting children with attachment disruptions in therapy if the therapist knows that treatment will end early due to forced ending situations.

## Managed care

Often, ending of therapy is decided by a third party who is uninvolved in the process yet a decision-maker about length of therapy. In these cases, the therapist is typically aware of the limited time for therapy at the beginning of the relationship. Although children may be developmentally limited in their understanding of time, facilitating therapy under management of an outside entity requires that children are fully informed of therapy time limits from the beginning of the relationship. If only eight sessions are allowed, the therapist should emphasise in the first session that 'we will meet together eight times'. Clarity helps children understand the concreteness of the limitations. Just as in adult therapy, children will make a choice consciously or unconsciously regarding how they will use their time in therapy and the limitations of the therapeutic relationship.

## AVOIDING ENDINGS

Child therapy is particularly susceptible to a therapist's or child's desire to prolong therapy and avoid the ending of the relationship. Because children are in a constant state of development, therapists might aspire to be involved in each developmental stage or issue to ensure the child is progressing well. There is a tendency for some therapists to prolong therapy until the child's situation is 'perfect' – waiting for the parents to establish complete stability or the school to offer a perfect learning environment. Moore et al. (2008) warned that prolonging therapy may be motivated by a therapist's personal issues and may inadvertently undermine the independent functioning of the child and parent. Boyer and Hoffman (1993) found that counsellors were more anxious regarding endings if they had a personal history of loss or if they perceived the client would be sensitive to loss. Knowing that almost all children are sensitive to loss, especially children with attachment issues, may inspire therapists to continue therapy beyond necessity. In supervision of new therapists, I often find that they must be prompted to end therapy when it appears that treatment goals have been met. Often therapists feel that they provide the only predictable stability in the child's life and hesitate to end the relationship. Such feelings prompt discussion about the therapist's role in the child's life and counter-transference issues. With supervision or consulting support, therapists work through their hesitancies and intervene for the benefit of the child.

A child's hesitancy or reaction to ending therapy is complicated. As a normal reaction to ending, a child might regress in behaviour and emotions, reverting back to negative coping skills used in the beginning of the relationship. Often, the therapist can be reassured that this is a natural response to ending the relationship and the child will return quickly to the new behaviours acquired during therapy. Yet, children often seem to organically know what is in their best interests when provided with a stable and emotionally supportive environment. Hence, when it appears that a child does not want to end therapy, the therapist needs to ask if she should take the child's lead and extend the relationship. A close attunement between therapist and child, along with the therapist's trust in the child, typically result in the most effective therapeutic judgement. If consideration of all factors does not clarify the therapist's direction, a therapist may want to offer ending as a break for a few weeks instead of ending therapy permanently. Interrupting therapy for 1 or 2 months may provide clarity regarding the child's readiness for ending.

## APPROACHES TO ENDINGS

### Timing

There is no clear timeline suggested for the ending phase of child counselling. Some have suggested two to three sessions (Moore et al., 2008), yet others encourage 4–6 months (Wittenberg, 1999). Adult therapy guidelines tend to indicate that the longer a therapy relationship has been established, the more time is needed for termination. Yet, developmental considerations of children indicate that drawn out periods of endings may actually induce anxiety. Knowledge and attunement with the child, as well as a collaborative relationship with parents, help inform the therapist in decision-making about ending timelines. However, a minimum of three to five sessions is encouraged for most children. Additionally, the view of endings as a transitional period for children may also influence a therapist's approach to timing. For example, an endings phase of frequent weekly sessions may be shorter if the therapist plans to taper to monthly sessions.

## Preparing parents

Parents are often hesitant to end therapy, especially if they have established a trusting and stable relationship with the therapist just as their child has. In these cases, the therapist has become part of the family system and it is difficult for the parents to visualise themselves without the support of the therapist. The therapist presents the subject of ending to the parent before the subject is approached with the child. The therapist may need to provide several sessions of support to the parent in preparation of ending. During this time, the parent is advised to not inform the child of impending ending until the parent is confident about the ending of therapy.

In some cases, the ending phase will consist of reminding the parent of the skills they acquired over the time of therapy and continuing to bring up the inevitability of ending. Meetings with the parent may become more frequent to provide emotional support for ending. Once the parent agrees to ending, the therapist will introduce ending to the child. Therapists are very encouraging during this phase of therapy, reminding parents of their growth that correlated with the child's development. The therapist will discuss options for returning if the parent feels that the child is in need of therapy following closure of therapy.

## Preparing the child

The therapist needs to offer a developmentally appropriate explanation for ending therapy. Although some children may be unable to process extensively, they may be able to connect behaviours with new situations, indicating that they have integrated a newly revised sense of self. Child therapists are often surprised, sometimes disappointed, by a child's reaction to endings. A child may respond with a simple 'Okay' and it is never spoken of again. At the last session, the child may simply wave goodbye to the therapist without any demonstrable sadness or upset. Although this may be hurtful to the therapist's feelings or bruising to the ego, this type of ending is developmentally appropriate. In addition, a simple ending to the relationship indicates that the child was ready to end and progress to the next stages of self-actualisation without dependence on the therapist.

## Activities and gifts

Child therapists will often ask if they should give the child something or do something different in session to mark endings. If the therapist decides to do something to mark the ending of therapy, it is purely for the therapist, not for the client. Creating crafts, exchanging gifts and hosting parties are common rituals indicating the end of the therapeutic relationship. Generally, large gifts are discouraged but sharing small gifts is often understood as a cultural custom. The most essential element to activities that address endings is a focus on the ending of the therapeutic relationship. An ending activity should represent the value of both people within the relationship and a celebration of what each has contributed to the relationship. This celebration may include shared drawings, photographs or notes.

Children may want to give something to the therapist to mark an ending. In these cases, if the child asks first, 'What do you want me to give you for our last time?', I will respond, 'Anything that you make is something I will like'. If a child wants to celebrate the ending of the relationship with a symbolic token, I truly want to participate in that celebration. I attempt to avoid any encouragement for the child to buy a gift but if a child arrives at our last session with a gift (of small monetary value), I will usually accept such a gift as a way of honouring the child's intention. Whether the child acknowledges ending or not, I commemorate our relationship by taking a few minutes to review the child's file by reading through all the documents in a personal way before filing my final treatment summary.

## Key Learning

- Ending therapy is a phase within the process of therapy and should be anticipated by the therapist at initial contact with the child.
- Ending therapy involves review of therapeutic gains, address of the therapeutic relationship and preparation for the future.
- The developmental level of children necessitates responsiveness on the part of the therapist, specifically responding to the child's limitations regarding verbalisation, understanding permanence, and previous experience with loss and relationship.
- Therapeutic endings can be initiated by the child, therapist, family or external circumstances. Each scenario requires a sensitive response from the therapist.
- Therapists work to prepare children and parents for ending therapy through consideration of timing and groundwork.

## Summary

Ending counselling with children is a significant undertaking within the therapeutic relationship. Endings involve the consideration of specific outcomes such as the need for integration of changes adopted by the child during counselling, synthesis of the counsellor–child relationship and acceptance that closing of therapy is the beginning, not the end. Some key points to remember from this chapter include:

- Due to developmental and attachment factors, counselling endings with children require a high level of personal awareness by the therapist, as well as ability to respond affectively and effectively to children's reactions to the endings phase. Emphasis and timing of endings are influenced by the significance of the therapeutic relationship and the counsellor's attunement to child needs.
- Endings involve goals that address the affirmation of the counselling process, resolution of the relationship between counsellor and child and preparation for the child's progress following counselling.
- Types of endings include natural endings, which take place when therapeutic goals are met and a child is ready for ending, and premature endings, which may be required when a parent withdraws a child from counselling or a counsellor ends therapy prior to a natural ending. A counsellor seeks to prepare a client according to the experienced type of ending.
- In contrast to historical approaches to endings, new ways of conceptualising the ending of counselling involve possible ongoing contact between therapist and child to address issues of loss and independence.
- Activities or shared gifts may be ways to help a child and counsellor commemorate their shared relationship and offer a symbolic gesture of care to one another when ending a therapeutic relationship.
- The ending of the counselling relationship can be the catalyst for effective relationships over the lifetime of a child. Hence, a counsellor is most therapeutic when acknowledging the ending of counselling as an essential part of the therapeutic relationship.

## Discussion Questions

1. What are the implications of working with children who have significant attachment problems regarding endings? How might a past history of attachment disruptions negatively affect the ending process?
2. How do endings of counselling with children differ from endings with adults? How would a therapist approach endings differently with children?

3. How can a therapist react in an effective way to premature endings in the three identi-fied situations: parent-initiated endings, managed care endings and therapist-initiated endings?
4. What is your history of personal loss? How might this affect your approach to endings?
5. What is your reaction to conceptualising endings as a transition, not an ending? What effect, if any, will this conceptualisation have on your approach to endings?

Turn to p.446 for possible answers.

## Develop Your Skills

1. Imagine you have been seeing a child for 6 months in therapy. The child had a significant history of loss and abandonment and has made great gains in therapy. Write an ending note to the child.
2. With a partner, practise presenting the ending phase to the same child.
3. With a partner, practise presenting the ending phase to a parent of a child you have seen for 3 months.
4. Imagine you have seen a child for 6 weeks in therapy and the parent meets with you to tell you that she is dissatisfied with therapy and will not be bringing her child back. With a partner, practise what you would say to that parent.
5. Create a shared ending activity and role-play the activity with a partner.

### Possible Group Activities

- As a group, create a variety of scenarios with children of different ages and presenting issues in which the therapist initiates termination within session. Play out or write a script for the therapist and brainstorm how the children may reply.
- Within a small group, discuss how previous personal losses may affect your experiences of endings in therapy.
- Brainstorm a list of possible feelings and thoughts that a child may experience when ending is initiated.
- Create a variety of shared activities that can be done with a child during ending sessions.
- Develop a list of self-care activities for a therapist who experiences a challenging ending to a counselling relationship.
- Have each person in the group write an ending note to a child. Exchange notes with each other and discuss the different ways group members expressed themselves. Discuss details of notes, such as vocabulary level, how the note might be interpreted by a child or when the note should be sent.

## Further Reading

Gil, E. and Crenshaw, D. (2016) *Termination Challenges in Child Psychotherapy*. New York: Guilford Press.

Joyce, A., Piper, W., Ogrodniczuk, J. and Klein, R. (2007) *Termination in Psychotherapy: A Psychodynamic Model of Processes and Outcomes*. Washington, DC: APA.

Landreth, G.L. (2012) *Play Therapy: The Art of the Relationship*, 3rd edn. New York: Routledge.

Marmarosh, C. (2017) Fostering engagement during termination: applying attachment theory and research. *Psychotherapy 54*: 4–9.

Norcross, J., Zimmerman, B., Greenberg, R. and Swift, J. (2017) Do all therapists do that when saying goodbye? A study of commonalities in termination behaviors. *Psychotherapy 54*: 66–75.

Novick, J. and Novick, K. (2006) *Good Goodbyes: Knowing How to End in Psychotherapy and Psychoanalysis*. Lanham, MD: Jason Aronson.

O'Donohue, W. and Cucciare, M. (eds) (2008) *Terminating Psychotherapy: A Clinician's Guide*. New York: Routledge.

Ray, D. (2011) *Advanced Play Therapy: Essential Conditions, Knowledge, and Skills for Child Practice*. New York: Routledge.

Ray, D. (ed.) (2016) *A Therapist's Guide to Child Development: The Extraordinarily Normal Years*. New York: Routledge.

Wilson, K., Kendrick, P. and Ryan, V. (2001) *Play Therapy: A Non-Directive Approach for Children and Adolescents*. London: Bailliere Tindall.

### Online Resources

BACP website: www.bacp.co.uk, especially the BACP Children and Young People Division and the Competences for Working with Children and Young People

Counselling MindEd: https://www.minded.org.uk, especially Module CMD 10: Concluding Counselling

# REFERENCES

Bamford, J. and Akhurst, J. (2014) She's not going to leave me – counsellors' feelings on ending therapy with children. *British Journal of Guidance and Counselling 42*: 459–471.

Bostic, J., Shadid, L. and Blotcky, M. (1996) Our time is up: forced terminations during psychotherapy training. *American Journal of Psychotherapy 50*: 347–359.

Boyer, S. and Hoffman, M. (1993) Counsellor affective reactions to termination: impact of counsellor loss history and perceived client sensitivity to loss. *Journal of Counselling Psychology 40*: 271–277.

Campbell, V., Baker, D. and Bratton, S. (2000) Why do children drop-out from play therapy? *Clinical Child Psychology and Psychiatry 5*: 133–138.

Gil, E. and Crenshaw, D. (2016) *Termination Challenges in Child Psychotherapy*. New York: Guilford Press.

Harrison, A. (2009) Setting up the doll house: a developmental perspective on termination. *Psychoanalytic Inquiry 29*: 174–187.

Joyce, A., Piper, W., Ogrodniczuk, J. and Klein, R. (2007) *Termination in Psychotherapy: A Psychodynamic Model of Processes and Outcomes*. Washington, DC: APA.

Kazdin, A. and Mazurick, L. (1994) Dropping out of child psychotherapy: distinguishing early and late dropouts over the course of treatment. *Journal of Consulting and Clinical Psychology 62*: 1069–1074.

Many, M. (2009) Termination as a therapeutic intervention when treating children who have experienced multiple losses. *Infant Mental Health Journal 30*: 23–39.

Marmarosh, C. (2017) Fostering engagement during termination: applying attachment theory and research. *Psychotherapy 54*: 4–9.

McCabe, K. (2002) Factors that predict premature termination among Mexican-American children in outpatient psychotherapy. *Journal of Child and Family Studies 11*: 347–359.

Moore, B., Bursch, B. and Walshaw, P. (2008) Termination of psychotherapy with children. In: O'Donohue, W. and Cucciare, M. (eds) *Terminating Psychotherapy: A Clinician's Guide*. New York: Routledge, pp. 251–267.

Nock, M. and Kazdin, A. (2001) Parent expectancies for child therapy: assessment and relation to participation in treatment. *Journal of Child and Family Studies 10*: 155–180.

Norcross, J., Zimmerman, B., Greenberg, R. and Swift, J. (2017) Do all therapists do that when saying goodbye? A study of commonalities in termination behaviors. *Psychotherapy 54*: 66–75.

Pearson, Q. (1998) Terminating before counseling has ended: counseling implications and strategies for counselor relocation. *Journal of Mental Health Counseling 20*: 55–63.

Piaget, J. (1965 [1932]) *The Moral Judgment of the Child*. New York: Free Press.

Ray, D. (2011) *Advanced Play Therapy: Essential Conditions, Knowledge and Skills for Child Practice*. New York: Routledge.

Ray, D. (ed.) (2016) *A Therapist's Guide to Child Development: The Extraordinarily Normal Years*. New York: Routledge.

Tsai, M. and Ray, D. (2011) Children in therapy: learning from evaluation of university-based community counseling clinical services. *Children and Youth Services Review 33*(6): 901–909.

Venable, W. and Thompson, B. (1998) Caretaker psychological factors predicting premature termination of children's counseling. *Journal of Counselling and Development 76*: 286–293.

Wilcoxon, S.A., Magnuson, S. and Norem, K. (2008) Institutional values of managed mental health care: efficiency or oppression? *Journal of Multicultural Counseling and Development 36*: 143–154.

Wittenberg, I. (1999) Ending therapy. *Journal of Child Psychotherapy 25*: 339–356.

Zilberstein, K. (2008) Au revoir: an attachment and loss perspective on termination. *Clinical Social Work Journal 36*: 301–311.

# 16

# EVALUATING COUNSELLING

## KATIE MCARTHUR AND MICK COOPER

**This chapter will discuss:**

- **The experience of evaluation for clients and therapists**
- **The impact of evaluation on therapeutic outcomes**
- **The interrelationship between research and practice**
- **Evidence-based practice and practice-based evidence**
- **Outcome and process feedback**
- **Qualitative and quantitative evaluation methods**

## INTRODUCTION

Across UK child and adult services, there are many counsellors – particularly those of a more relational orientation – who are disinclined to participate in formal outcome evaluation (Daniel and McLeod, 2006). Internationally, there is also little evidence that counsellors working with children and young people are formally evaluating their work. This reluctance has been noted by the Department of Health's Improving Access to Psychological Therapies (IAPT) programme (Wheeler and Elliott, 2008). In spite of this, evaluation of therapeutic outcomes is often necessary for counselling services to secure and retain funding, and may be seen by stakeholders as essential.

## THE EXPERIENCE OF EVALUATION FOR CLIENTS AND THERAPISTS

In addition, research suggests that the evaluation process may be a positive experience for both clients and therapists. Recent studies in the context of school-based counselling, for instance, have shown that young people report positive responses to completing psychometric measures at regular intervals before, during and after counselling (Hanley et al., 2011). Indeed, an interview study of young people allocated to the waiting list condition of a randomised controlled trial of school-based counselling (Daniunaite et al., 2012) found that some participants were able to make substantial progress from participation in the research project alone – without an active counselling intervention.

From the practitioners' perspective too, a Northern Irish study showed that the process of participating in a large-scale school counselling evaluation garnered considerable benefits for practice and professional development, although the experience was described as challenging (Tracey et al., 2009).

## THE IMPACT OF EVALUATION ON THERAPEUTIC OUTCOMES

There is also some evidence that evaluation improves therapeutic outcomes. In the field of adult psychotherapy, Lambert and Shimokawa (2011) published a meta-analysis of studies investigating the effects of providing systematic feedback to clients. Their results showed that clients who are given systematic feedback on progress were 3.5 times more likely to experience reliable positive change, and had less than half the chance of deteriorating, when compared with clients who received no formal feedback.

The potentially therapeutic effects of research also appear to extend to young people in counselling. For example, Saunders and Rey (2011) found that screening and assessment procedures contributed to improvement for 12–25-year-olds with alcohol problems. A recent evaluation study (Cooper et al., 2014) on school-based counselling for young people obtained a substantially larger effect size for counselling (1.26; see Box 16.1) than the mean weighted effect size (0.81) calculated in a comprehensive meta-analysis of UK audit and evaluation studies (Cooper, 2009). The key difference between this and previous evaluation studies was that counsellors administered weekly session-by-session outcome measures. This suggests that completing measures at every session, as opposed to only at the beginning and end of the entire counselling period, may improve outcomes for young people in school-based counselling. In fact, the results of another study of school-based counselling using systematic feedback with children as young as 7 suggest that feedback may as much as double the impact on reducing psychological distress (Cooper et al., 2012).

However, Davidson et al. (2015) recently conducted a systematic review that questioned the generalisability of findings that feedback improves outcomes. They point out that many of the studies in this area take place in university counselling clinics with mainly Caucasian, female, young adults. They argue, therefore, that these results cannot be generalised to other ethnic groups, male clients, older adults or children and young people. They also highlight that, in client populations with more severe psychiatric problems, studies show a reduced effect overall and suggest that feedback to therapists may only improve outcomes for those who are not improving in therapy. This indicates that session-by-session feedback may only be helpful in cases where therapy is not progressing well. More research is required to establish the impact of feedback on outcomes for black and minority ethnic (BME) clients, male clients and those of different age groups including children and young people.

## THE INTERRELATIONSHIP BETWEEN RESEARCH AND PRACTICE

Research activity among counselling practitioners is now widely encouraged, and counsellors in training are expected to develop interest in research evidence and understanding of methods with a view to actively participating and securing the future of counselling as a profession (Wheeler and Elliott, 2008). Outcomes of counselling with children and young people, in particular, have seen a flourish of research interest, and the British Association for Counselling and Psychotherapy (BACP) launched a practice-research network specifically dedicated to this area: Children and Young People Practice Research Network (CYP PRN). Its aims and objectives include promoting the interrelationship of research and practice and creating a sustainable network of practitioner-researchers to engage in ethical practice-based research. In addition, a practitioner- and student-oriented review of research findings in this field is now available: *Essential Research Findings in Child and Adolescent Counselling and Psychotherapy* (eds Midgley, Hayes and Cooper, 2017, SAGE).

Wheeler and Elliott (2008) outline three key questions for the evaluation of practice: (1) Do clients change substantially over the course of counselling? (2) Is counselling substantially responsible for these changes? (3) What specific aspects of counselling contribute to client change? Adequately answering these questions, and the many further questions that they inspire, requires that they are addressed from a range of different perspectives, using a range of different tools.

## EVIDENCE-BASED PRACTICE AND PRACTICE-BASED EVIDENCE

Although the counselling and psychotherapy field requires rigorously controlled research designed to meet the demand for *evidence-based practice*, this must be balanced with the real-world perspective provided by *practice-based evidence*. Evidence-based practice is a philosophical approach used in medicine and gaining ground in counselling and psychotherapy, whereby empirical research is systematically reviewed to develop practice guidelines on which clinical decisions are based. Research studies are selected and interpreted according to specific methodological criteria governing what constitutes 'evidence'. Research is considered on a spectrum of rigorousness, typically leading to qualitative data (which may be considered anecdotal) being disregarded in favour of quantitative studies conducted according to strict methodological criteria.

Practice-based evidence is one way of informing evidence-based practice, rather than an opposing concept. It is the exercise of drawing evidence from practice settings in order to take this into account along with data from controlled experimental studies to form the basis for clinical decision-making. In other words, rigorous research is conducted in routine clinical practice, and this evidence feeds into decisions about clinical practice.

In established counselling services for children and young people, outcome measures can easily be incorporated into everyday practice, resulting in the potential to generate a large body of evaluation data, which can be a powerful aid to the interpretation and application of evidence.

## OUTCOME AND PROCESS FEEDBACK

Outcome feedback is the process of monitoring change in individuals, with the aim of using this information systematically to improve practice. In counselling, it is complicated by the fact that practitioner-researchers from different theoretical approaches may have different aims and different concepts of 'improvement' for clients. For instance, cognitive-behavioural therapy aims to address specific problems, such as obsessive compulsive behaviour, and measures its outcomes accordingly. Conversely, person-centred counselling focuses on the client's intrinsic needs and wants and may be more appropriately tested by measuring overall well-being. Typically, outcome measures used to evaluate counselling interventions focus on constructs such as psychological distress, or difficulties. Some have a more 'positive' focus, attempting to measure well-being or achievement of personal goals.

### Box 16.1   Effect Sizes

Even when different outcome measures are used in evaluation studies, direct comparisons can be made between them by calculating standardised 'effect sizes', which is a way of reporting the amount of change observed. The most common effect size in the counselling and psychotherapy literature is Cohen's d, which is the amount of difference between two groups on some variable (e.g. pre- and post-counselling scores on the Clinical Outcomes in Routine Evaluation – Outcome Measure (CORE-OM)), divided by their 'standard deviation' (a measure of the amount of variability across scores).

Cohen (1988) proposed that in the social sciences, standardised effect sizes can be understood in the following way:

Small effect ≥0.2
Medium effect ≥0.5
Large effect ≥0.8

In addition to the specific outcome measure used, decisions regarding when and how to administer these measures influence the results of outcome studies, and must be carefully considered. Traditionally, measures are taken before counselling begins, and immediately after it ends. This approach allows practitioner-researchers to assess the amount of change that has occurred in a given domain (according to the specific outcome measure used) during the counselling period. However, a key recommendation for practice research networks like CYP PRN is for members to routinely collect data from all clients on a session-by-session basis rather than only at the beginning and end of counselling. One reason for this recommendation is that weekly monitoring allows practitioner-researchers to collect more robust evaluation data than pre–post measurements alone. The majority of practice-based evidence is limited by the problem of missing data, and this is true of school-based counselling studies too (see Cooper, 2009). Crucially, when measurements are taken at the beginning and end of counselling only, the endpoint data collected come exclusively from clients who participated in a planned ending with the counsellor. Cooper (2009) found that in school-based counselling studies, the mean response rate was less than 65%, suggesting that a large proportion of young clients are not represented by these studies due to dropping out of counselling before completing endpoint questionnaires. This means that calculated effect sizes cannot accurately reflect the whole population of young people in school-based counselling. This is a particularly pressing problem given that those who complete counselling tend to have better outcomes. Using weekly outcome monitoring ensures that data are available for all clients, producing more reliable evidence. Therefore, studies that use weekly session-by-session monitoring overcome one of the major limitations of practice-based research and have a greater chance of influencing clinical guidelines.

Some of the most frequently used tools for evaluating counselling with children and young people are detailed in Table 16.1.

As noted, clients in general tend to respond positively to outcome measures, and some may have additional benefits. For instance, the opportunity to collaborate on goals with a counsellor, which is part of completing the Goal-Based Outcome Record, has been shown to improve outcomes for clients (Tryon and Winograd, 2011).

As well as outcome measures, questionnaires are available to investigate the therapeutic process and clients' experiences in counselling. One of the most commonly used tools here is the Child Session Rating Scale (CSRS), which invites children and young people to rate the

**Table 16.1** Most frequently used tools for evaluating counselling with children and young people

| Name | Acronym | Key publication | Age range | Prevalence | Strengths | Limitations |
|---|---|---|---|---|---|---|
| Young Person's CORE (Clinical Outcomes in Routine Evaluation) Outcome Measure | YP-CORE | Twigg, E., Cooper, M., Evans, C., Freire, E., Mellor-Clark, J., McInnes, B. and Barkham, M. (2016) Acceptability, reliability, referential distributions and sensitivity to change in the Young Person's Clinical Outcomes in Routine Evaluation (YP-CORE) outcome measure: replication and refinement. *Child and Adolescent Mental Health* 21(2): 115–123. doi: 10.1111/camh.12128 | 11–16 years | Most widely used in UK school-based counselling | Sensitive to change Appropriate for brief interventions Concise User-friendly; simple, easy scoring system Suitable for weekly use | Not suitable for use with children <11 years |
| Strengths and Difficulties Questionnaire | SDQ | Goodman, R. (2001) Psychometric properties of the strengths and difficulties questionnaire. *Journal of the American Academy of Child and Adolescent Psychiatry* 40(11): 1337–1345. | Self-report version: 11–16 years Parent- and teacher-rated versions: 3–4 years and 4–16 years | Most widely used in specialist CAMHS (Child and Adolescent Mental Health Services) | Four distress-related sub-scales allow comprehensive view of difficulties; one sub-scale dedicated to pro-social behaviour Excellent evidence of reliability and validity Translated into a range of languages | Not suitable for brief interventions Not suitable for weekly use Relies on adult caregivers' perceptions for children <11 years |
| (Young) Child Outcome Rating Scale; from Partners for Change Outcome Management System (PCOMS) | CORS/YCORS | Duncan, B.L., Sparks, J.A., Miller, S.D., Bohanske, R. and Claud, D.A. (2006) Giving youth a voice: a preliminary study of the reliability and validity of a brief outcome measure for children, adolescents, and caretakers. *Journal of Brief Therapy* 5(2): 66–82 | CORS: 6–11 years YCORS: children <6 years | Used internationally, with growing popularity in UK | Focuses on child's own perception of well-being Concise User-friendly Appropriate for brief interventions Designed for session-by-session use | Psychometric validity yet to be well-established |

| Name | Acronym | Key publication | Age range | Prevalence | Strengths | Limitations |
|---|---|---|---|---|---|---|
| Goal-Based Outcome Record | G-BOR | Law, D. (2011) Goals and goal-based outcomes (GBOs): some useful information. Internal CORC publication. Available at: www.corc.uk.net | 11–16 years Can be completed by parent/ caregiver for children <11 years | Growing use in specialist CAMHS in UK | Measures what child or young person wants to achieve Incorporates collaboration with counsellor on therapeutic goals Concise Appropriate for brief interventions Suitable for weekly use | Relies on adult caregivers' perceptions for children <11 years |
| Revised Children's Anxiety and Depression Scale | RCADS | Ebesutani, C., Chorpita, B.F., Higa-McMillan, C.K., Nakamura, B.J., Regan, J., & Lynch, R.E. (2011). A Psychometric Analysis of the Revised Child Anxiety and Depression Scales—Parent Version in a School Sample. *Journal of Abnormal Child Psychology*, 39(2), 173–185. http://doi.org/10.1007/s10802-010-9460-8 The Research Network on Youth Mental Health. *Journal of Abnormal Child Psychology* 38(2): 249–260. | 6–18 years, (both self-report and parent/ caregiver report versions) | Increasingly widespread use in specialist CAMHS | Evaluates changes in anxiety symptoms across range of sub-scales Includes assessment of depression symptoms Can be completed by both child/young person and adult caregiver | Limited to specific disorders (based on DSM-IV diagnostic criteria for range of anxiety disorders) |
| Health of the Nation Outcome Scales for Children and Adolescents | HoNOSCA | Gowers, S.G., Harrington, R.C., Whitton, A., Beevor, A., Lelliott, P., Jezzard, R. and Wing, J. (1999) Health of the Nation Outcome Scales for Children and Adolescents (HoNOSCA). Glossary for HoNOSCA score sheet. *British Journal of Psychiatry 174*: 428–431. | 3–18 years | Estimated use of <10% among CAMHS in UK | Sensitive to change Good validity, reliability and feasibility 15 scales allow comprehensive view of difficulties | Primarily relies solely on clinician's report, though self-rated and parent-rated versions are available Designed to be used only by clinicians who know the child or young person well |

extent to which they felt listened to in the therapeutic work, and the degree to which the work met their personal needs and preferences. In addition, satisfaction questionnaires such as the Experience of Service Questionnaire (developed for children and young people by Bury NHS Trust) can give valuable insight into clients' views of counselling. This measure asks young people to rate their experience of a service on 12 items related to satisfaction, such as 'I feel that the people who saw me listened to me'. Both of these measures are available to download from the Child and Adolescent Mental Health Services Outcome Research Consortium (CORC) at https://www.corc.uk.net/outcome-experience-measures/.

## QUALITATIVE AND QUANTITATIVE EVALUATION METHODS

Whilst outcome studies focus on quantitative data taken from psychometric measures, qualitative data can also have a role in evaluation. Conducting semi-structured interviews is a potential way of collecting clients' views about the outcomes of therapy, and can provide a more in-depth perspective than psychometric measures. Whilst outcome measures give valuable information about effectiveness and appear to have benefits for young people in their own right, combining this kind of data with qualitative records from children and young people can enrich and support findings, providing crucial depth and context to our understanding of the counselling process. This form of interviewing generally involves using a pre-set series of open-ended questions and prompts, and allowing the respondent to take the conversation in new directions as they come up. Robert Elliott (1999) designed an interview schedule entitled the Client Change Interview, which asks clients whether and how they feel they have changed since beginning counselling, to what they attribute the change and how much it has impacted on their lives, as well as covering the client's overall experience of counselling. This has recently been adapted for use with young people in school-based counselling (Lynass et al., 2012).

Once semi-structured interviews have been conducted and transcribed, they can be analysed in various ways. Thematic analysis is a commonly employed method, and involves searching text for emerging themes and categories of responses. Using this approach, Lynass et al. (2012) found that young people in school-based counselling tended to experience positive changes in emotional, interpersonal and behavioural domains. When asked about the helpful aspects of counselling, young people mentioned talking and 'getting things out', as well as specific counsellor qualities.

A different approach to qualitative data is discourse analysis, which investigates a text on the level of underlying meanings as opposed to face value. A recent example of this method is Prior's (2012) investigation of how young people manage stigma in relation to accessing a school counselling service. He described how young clients demonstrated critical views of help-seeking, which they had internalised, before going through a process of reformulating those critical views, so that they came to see their own behaviour (seeking counselling) as a sign of strength and self-empowerment.

Randomised controlled trials (RCTs) are the most politically powerful method of evaluation in health research, since clinical guidelines groups (such as NICE, the National Institute for Health and Clinical Excellence, and SIGN, the Scottish Intercollegiate Guidelines

Network) primarily draw on RCTs to develop guidelines for evidence-based practice. The basic principle is that quantitative measures are taken from a sample of participants (the larger the sample, the more powerful the trial), who are then randomly allocated to two or more conditions: the treatment under investigation, and a control (or controls), which either involves not receiving the treatment, or receiving a comparative treatment. Then measures taken from both groups at the end of the trial period are compared to assess differences, which are assumed to be solely caused by the treatment(s) under investigation, since random allocation is assumed to control for individual differences. One recent RCT (McArthur et al., 2013) compared Young Person's Clinical Outcomes in Routine Evaluation (YP-CORE) scores from young people who attended school-based counselling with those of young people who were on a waiting list, and found that those in counselling showed significantly more improvement in psychological distress. More recently, the Economic and Social Sciences Research Council has funded a fully powered RCT of school-based humanistic counselling, the ETHOS study (www.roehampton.ac.uk/ETHOS), which will evaluate the effectiveness and cost-effectiveness of this therapy in over 300 young people (aged 13–16 years old). The results of this study are due in approximately 2019 and may have significant implications for policy decisions regarding youth counselling in coming years.

## Key Learning

- Outcome evaluation is a means by which counsellors can reflect on the effectiveness of their work: both generically and with individual clients.
- Process evaluation and feedback gives counsellors an opportunity to consider means by which they might improve their work with children and young people.
- Research evidence is a means by which the counselling community can demonstrate the value of its work, and identify important areas for development.

## Summary

- Measuring outcomes of counselling is increasingly necessary to secure funding.
- Outcome research appears to have considerable benefits for clients and counsellors.
- Weekly outcome monitoring has further benefits for creating a robust evidence base.
- A wide range of measures are available for children and young people.
- Evaluation methods available to counselling practitioner-researchers are both qualitative and quantitative.
- Counsellors interested in becoming more involved in research can benefit from practice-research networks.

## Discussion Questions

1. How and why might research in various forms contribute to therapeutic change for children and young people?
2. How easy is it to incorporate an evaluation project into an existing service? What might be the impact of this for a service?
3. What might be the barriers to introducing evaluation to a service, and how might they be overcome?

Turn to p.447 for possible answers.

## Develop Your Skills

1. Join the BACP CYP Practice Research Network (PRN): www.bacp.co.uk/schools.
2. Work through the three Counselling MindEd e-learning modules on Using Measures (CMD 06, freely available through www.minded.org.uk).
3. Download some examples of measures from www.corc.uk.net/outcome-experience-measures/. What do you think of them? How do you feel about completing them? Do you prefer some to others, and if so why? If possible, role-play how you might use these measures whilst counselling a child or young person. What impact do you think they might have?
4. Download the Goal-Based Outcome Record from https://www.corc.uk.net/outcome-experience-measures/practitioner. Imagine you are a client beginning therapy, being asked what things you would like to achieve by the end. What kind of goals would you set yourself? How does it feel to compose and rate these life goals?
5. Try to design a research project to investigate any aspect of counselling children and young people. This could be a project to evaluate an entire service, or focus more specifically on your own practice. What would you want to find out? How would you go about it? What ethical issues might it raise?

## Further Reading

McLeod, J. (2014) *Doing Research in Counselling and Psychotherapy*, 3rd edn. London: SAGE.

Sanders, P. and Wilkins, P. (2010) *First Steps in Practitioner Research: A Guide to Understanding and Doing Research for Helping Practitioners*. Ross-on-Wye: PCCS Books.

For counselling practitioners or trainees who are new to research, and interested in getting involved, these introductory texts are ideal. They explain the basic principles in an accessible manner, covering quantitative and qualitative methods, and include practical advice on ethical considerations, getting started and ways of presenting research to others.

Fraser, S., Lewis, V., Ding, S., Kellett, M. and Robinson, C. (eds) (2004) *Doing Research with Children and Young People*. London: SAGE.

This text provides information and advice on the specific issues relating to research with children and young people.

McLaughlin, C., Holliday, C., Clarke, B. and Ilie, S. (2013) *Research on Counselling and Psychotherapy with Children and Young People: A Systematic Scoping Review of the Evidence for its Effectiveness from 2003–2011*. Rugby: BACP.

This report provides an excellent grounding in counselling research conducted with children and young people, which is essential to planning future research projects and addressing gaps in knowledge.

Deighton, J., Croudace, T., Fonagy, P., Brown, J., Patalay, P., and Wolpert, M. (2014). Measuring mental health and wellbeing outcomes for children and adolescents to inform practice and policy: a review of child self-report measures. *Child and Adolescent Psychiatry and Mental Health, 8*, 14. doi: 10.1186/1753-2000-8-14

An overview of outcome measures, including those discussed in this chapter and many others, is given in this report. The CORC website (www.corc.uk.net) is an excellent resource for practitioner-researchers interested in work with children and young people.

Hill, A., Cooper, M., Pybis, J. et al. (2011) *Evaluation of the Welsh School-Based Counselling Strategy*. Cardiff: Welsh Government Social Research.

This is a landmark piece of research evaluating the Welsh Assembly Government's School-Based Counselling Strategy, employed since 2008. The study incorporates outcome measurement, interviews and surveys with key stakeholders such as counsellors and link teachers. The findings showed reduction in psychological distress associated with counselling, with greater improvements than in previous studies of UK school-based counselling services.

Cooper, M. (2011) Meeting the demand for evidence-based practice. *Therapy Today 22*(4): 10–16.

McArthur, K. (2011) RCTs: a personal experience. *Therapy Today 22*(7): 24–25.

Rogers, A., Maidman, J. and House, R. (2011) The bad faith of 'evidence-based practice': beyond counsels of despair. *Therapy Today 22*(6): 26–29.

These three articles published recently in *Therapy Today* give an introduction to the debate surrounding evidence-based practice and the use of RCTs in relational counselling.

*(Continued)*

(Continued)

**Online Resources**

Counselling MindEd: https://www.minded.org.uk, especially Module CMD 06: Using Measures

Children and Young People's Improving Access to Psychological Therapies Programme (CYP IAPT): https://www.england.nhs.uk/mental-health/cyp/iapt/

Griffiths, G. (2013) Helpful and Unhelpful Factors in School Based Counselling: Client's Perspective. Counselling MindEd Scoping Report. Available at: https://www.bacp.co.uk/events-and-resources/ethics-and-standards/competences-and-curricula/counselling-minded/

# REFERENCES

Cohen, J. (1988) *Statistical Power Analysis for the Behavioral Sciences*, 2nd edn. Hillsdale, NJ: Lawrence Erlbaum.

Cooper, M. (2009) Counselling in UK secondary schools: a comprehensive review of audit and evaluation studies. *Counselling and Psychotherapy Research* 9(3): 137–150.

Cooper, M., Stewart, D., Sparks, J.A. and Bunting, L. (2012) School-based counseling using systematic feedback: a cohort study evaluating outcomes and predictors of change. *Psychotherapy Research.* 23(4): 474–488. DOI:10.1080/10503307.2012.735777.

Cooper, M., McGinnis, S. and Carrick, L. (2014) School-based humanistic counselling for psychological distress in young people: a practice research network to address the attrition problem. *Counselling and Psychotherapy Research.* 14(3): 201–211. DOI: 10.1080/14733145.2014.929415.

Daniel, T. and McLeod, J. (2006) Weighing up the evidence: a qualitative analysis of how person-centred counsellors evaluate the effectiveness of their practice. *Counselling and Psychotherapy Research* 6(4): 244–249.

Daniunaite, A., Ali, Z.A. and Cooper, M. (2012) Psychological change in distressed young people who do not receive counselling: does improvement happen anyway? *British Journal of Guidance and Counselling* 40(5): 515–525.

Davidson, K., Perry, A. and Bell, L. (2015) Would continuous feedback of patient's clinical outcomes to practitioners improve NHS psychological therapy services? Critical analysis and assessment of quality of existing studies. *Psychology and Psychotherapy: Theory, Research and Practice* 88: 21–37.

Elliott, R. (1999) Client Change Interview protocol. *Network for Research on Experiential Psychotherapies.* Available at: http://experiential-researchers.org/instruments/elliott/changei.html.

Hanley, T., Sefi, A. and Lennie, C. (2011) Practice-based evidence in school-based counselling. *Counselling and Psychotherapy Research 11*(4): 300–309.

Lambert, M.J. and Shimokawa, K. (2011) Collecting client feedback. *Psychotherapy 48*(1): 72–79.

Lynass, R., Pykhtina, O. and Cooper, M. (2012) A thematic analysis of young people's experience of counselling in five secondary schools in the UK. *Counselling and Psychotherapy Research 12*(1): 53–62.

McArthur, K., Cooper, M. and Berdondini, L. (2013) School-based humanistic counseling for psychological distress in young people: pilot randomized controlled trial. *Psychotherapy Research 23*(3): 355–365.

Midgley, N., Hayes, J. and Cooper, M. (2017) (eds) *Essential Research Findings in Child and Adolescent Counselling and Psychotherapy*. London: SAGE.

Prior, S. (2012) Overcoming stigma: how young people position themselves as counselling service users. *Sociology of Health and Illness 34*(5): 697–713.

Saunders, J.B. and Rey, J.M. (2011) *Young People and Alcohol: Impact, Policy, Prevention, Treatment*. Oxford: Blackwell.

Tracey, A., McElearney, A., Adamson, G. and Shevlin, M. (2009) Practitioners' views and experiences of participating in a school counselling evaluation study. *Counselling and Psychotherapy Research 9*(3): 193–203.

Tryon, G.S. and Winograd, G. (2011) Goal consensus and collaboration. In: Norcross, J.C. (ed.), *Psychotherapy Relationships that Work: Evidence-based Responsiveness*, 2nd edn. New York: Oxford University Press, pp. 153–167.

Wheeler, S. and Elliott, R. (2008) What do counsellors and psychotherapists need to know about research? *Counselling and Psychotherapy Research 8*(2): 133–135.

# PART 3
## PRACTICE ISSUES

# 17

# LAW AND POLICY

## PETER JENKINS

**This chapter will discuss:**

- **An outline of the main sources of the law relating to children and young people**
- **Information on some of the key areas likely to cause anxiety, both to novice and more experienced therapists, their supervisors and managers**
- **Policy and law relating to children and young people, for example, school-based counselling, mental health services and pre-trial therapy**
- **Key aspects of the law, such as the rights of children and parents, confidentiality, safeguarding, diversity, information-sharing, contracting, record-keeping and appearing in court**

## INTRODUCTION

This chapter starts by acknowledging the very real concerns held by many therapists about the impact of law and policy on their therapeutic work with children and young people. It is designed to be read in tandem with Chapter 18 on 'Ethics'.

## What is 'the Law'?

The term 'law', in this context, refers to all legal systems applying in the UK, with particular reference to England and Wales. Reference will also be made to the law applying to Scotland and Northern Ireland, where relevant. The law includes statute, that is, Acts of Parliament, or devolved legislation, such as via the Welsh Government, common law and case law (for a more detailed discussion of these terms, see Jenkins, 2007). 'Policy' refers to the statutory and voluntary provision of counselling services, including relevant mental health services. This is based on legal requirements, codes of practice, government reports and established 'custom and practice', in relation to counselling services.[1]

The law can seem complex and intimidating at first sight. This chapter takes an explicitly *rights-based approach*, as a way of making sense of the (sometimes conflicting) legal pressures weighing upon the individual counsellor. This model is presented in more detail in Chapter 18 on 'Ethics'. A rights-based approach considers the entitlement of children and young people to specific responses by counsellors, social workers, parents, etc., regarding young people's rights to welfare, participation and autonomy. A right is defined as 'a claim to treatment which an individual can make, by reason of law, code of practice or otherwise' (Jenkins, 2013a: 5). A child, in legal terms, is defined as a person under the age of 18, as per section 105, Children Act 1989. Whilst not a legal definition as such, it can also be useful to bear in mind the distinction between *children*, of roughly primary school age, that is, 6–11 years, and *young people* of secondary school age, that is, 11–18 years, respectively.

These broad age bands may carry differing levels of legal entitlement to autonomy, in terms of decision-making by younger people. Young people under the age of 16 of 'sufficient understanding' have a right to confidential medical treatment, *without* parental knowledge or consent, under the *Gillick* case (1986), or via the Age of Legal Capacity Act 1991 in Scotland. This right can logically be extended to include access to confidential counselling.

This model can be useful in helping therapists to distinguish between rights that are driven more by *adult perceptions*, for example, protecting a child from harm, and those that are more about the *empowerment of young people*, for example, promoting autonomy. However, a rights-based approach to the law and policy may have its weaknesses. It may appear to overemphasise the position of individuals, such as an entitlement to confidentiality, at the expense of wider social considerations, for example, the value of having mandatory reporting systems for abuse. However, the advantage of this model is that it permits a useful

---

## Reflection

Take some time out to think about your own experience of and attitude towards the law. What do you already know about the law with regard to working as a counsellor with children and young people? In what areas are you less confident with your existing knowledge? How could you develop your knowledge in this area – for example, by starting a resource file of relevant articles for future reference?

---

[1] At this point, you can refer to Counselling MindEd (free online training material) (www.minded.org.uk): Jenkins, P. (2018) *Applying the Law*. MindEd.

point of cross-over with ethics, as a decision-making aid, as the concept of rights embraces *both* formal legal entitlements *and* the corresponding ethical obligations for counsellors.

## Ethical dimensions of legal practice in counselling young people

The British Association for Counselling and Psychotherapy (BACP) Ethical Framework clearly recognises the specific features of working with children and young people, in terms of capacity and consent:

Careful consideration will be given to working with children and young people that:

a.  takes account of their capacity to give informed consent, considering whether it is appropriate to seek the consent of others who have parental responsibility for the young person, and their best interests
b.  demonstrates knowledge and skills about ways of working that are appropriate to the young person's maturity and understanding. (BACP, 2018: 21)[2]

Legally informed therapeutic work with children and young people thus has an *ethical* dimension, just as ethical practice also has a *legal* aspect to it. The key BACP statements regarding the law include:

(14) (f) keeping up to date with the law, regulations and any other requirements, including guidance from this Association, relevant to our work. (2018: 8)

(42) We will give conscientious consideration to the law and how we fulfil any legal requirements concerning our work (2018: 26)

The BACP Ethical Framework (2018) has a specific requirement regarding the law in relation to working safely with children and young people, namely that the practioner:

c.  demonstrates a sound knowledge of the law relevant to working with children and young people and their human rights" (2018: 21).

Practitioners clearly need, as with any client group, to be fully aware of the law, understand it and be accordingly accountable for their own professional practice.

The BACP Core Curriculum for counselling training for work with children and young people further sets out the requirement for knowledge of capacity, informed consent, parental/carer

---

[2]At this point, you can refer to: Counselling MindEd (free online training material) (www.minded.org. uk): Jenkins, P. (2014) *Confidentiality, Consent and Capacity and Ethical Frameworks*. MindEd.

responsibilities, contractual obligations and a wide range of relevant legislation, covering mental health, education, data protection, disclosure of information, discrimination and safeguarding (2016: 15). The curriculum also carefully distinguishes between different jurisdictions, such as Wales, Scotland, Northern Ireland and England. Whilst this is a useful starting point, the curriculum seems to focus largely on legislation, that is, Acts of Parliament, rather than on influential case law, and has little to say on the key emerging topic of children's *privacy rights*. BACP has produced a range of resource and reference materials on the law relating to children and young people (www.bacp.co.uk/ethical_framework/documents/GPiA002.pdf).

## Research on law and policy for counselling children

The limited research base on counsellors and the law tends to be drawn primarily from practice-based evidence. Brown identified critical ethical dilemmas for generic counsellors (n: 20), which broadly relate to issues of risk of harm/child protection issues, information-sharing and record-keeping (2006: 101). Confidentiality emerges, unsurprisingly, as a key, but still problematic, issue in counselling young people in particular. Confidentiality is highly valued by young people working with voluntary agencies (LeSurf and Lynch, 1999; n: 42), and in schools (Cooper, 2009). It is seen by young people as being particularly important in relation to the provision of counselling and treatment on sexual health issues (Carlisle et al., 2006; n: 18). This expectation appears to have carried some weight in the judge's decision in the *Axon* case in 2006.

## POLICY AND LAW RELATING TO COUNSELLING CHILDREN AND YOUNG PEOPLE

The term 'policy' with regard to counselling for children and young people has two main dimensions in this context. One refers to a range of sources of official guidance to therapists, and the other to the actual provision of counselling services. It may be tempting to see the law and policy as being completely 'black and white', with no room for professional discretion over decision-making, but this is far from being entirely the case. It is also important to understand that law and policy may be 'out of synch' with each other. It may be the case that children and young people are entitled to certain rights according to the *law*, but these are not afforded in practice by counselling providers, due to the operation of a particular *policy*. One example of this would be where young people under 16 in England and Wales are afforded autonomy rights via the law, in terms of the *Gillick* case, but providers actually insist on evidence of parental consent, due to their own agency or school policy. This would be an example of young people's autonomy rights being overridden by reference to paternalistic rights (see Chapter 18 for the corresponding framework of children's rights).

## Law relating to counselling children and young people

The law, as suggested above, refers to all systems of law in the UK. The law varies between different parts of the UK, so that child care law for England and Wales is determined by the Children Acts of 1989 and 2004, in Northern Ireland by the Children (NI) Order 1995 SI 1995/755 (NI 2), and in Scotland by the Children (Scotland) Act 1995. Common legal principles may apply in each legal context, but, equally, there may be significant differences. This discussion will cover mainly the law relating to England and Wales, on the basis that much will also be common to the other jurisdictions in the UK. However, therapists will need to check the detail of the law applying to their own practice, as the law is subject to constant updating and change.

The term 'law' includes statutes, that is, Acts of Parliament, such as the Children Act 1989. Statute law has an added significance for therapists, in that some therapists, such as psychologists, are subject to statutory regulation, via formal bodies such as the Health and Care Professions Council. In addition, some forms of counselling provision are provided on a statutory basis, that is, school counselling in Wales. This may help to protect its resource base and impose a greater degree of public scrutiny of appropriate professional standards.

The term 'common law' refers to law that is decided by judges on a custom and practice basis over centuries, such as the law relating to confidentiality. Case law refers to key legal decisions, such as the *Gaskin* and *Gillick* cases. In the first case, Graham Gaskin, a young man formerly in care of Liverpool Social Services, sought to gain access to his own social work file. He partially won his case at the European Court of Human Rights at Strasbourg, opening the door for client access to social work, education and medical files, a decade before the Data Protection Act 1998 came into force (*Gaskin v. UK* (1988) [1990]; Jenkins, 2007: 140). In the second case, that is, *Gillick*, it was decided by the House of Lords that a young person under 16 could receive confidential medical treatment without parental knowledge or consent, if judged to have 'sufficient understanding' by a health practitioner. This decision was confirmed in the subsequent *Axon* case in 2006.

Another reference point is provided by the United Nations Convention on the Rights of the Child (UNCRC) (1989). This is increasingly emerging as a key reference point, for example, in influencing childcare legislation by the Welsh Assembly, and also decisions in the courts in England and Wales. It has provided a strong case, as an international treaty ratified by the UK in 1991, for the rights of children under 18 to provision, protection and participation. However, whilst this is an extremely useful step forward, the UNCRC has, unfortunately, done nothing to develop the rights of young people to exercise higher level rights to *autonomy*, in sharp contrast with the *Gillick* and *Axon* cases.

It is also important for counsellors to recognise that the law is constantly changing, often through the efforts of young people themselves to protect or extend their own rights to autonomy. At the time of writing (2018), one young person of 14 had launched a legal challenge against Facebook, in order to remove a naked photo from social media, as a clear breach of her rights to privacy and to data protection principles. She successfully achieved an out-of-court confidential settlement with the company (McDonald, 2018).

## SOURCES OF LAW RELATING TO COUNSELLING PRACTICE

In terms of the full range of statements on law and policy, there are statutory codes of practice, which derive from specific Acts of Parliament. For example, the Code of Practice for the Mental Health Act (MHA) 1983 sets out authoritative guidance for practitioners working with adults and young people under 18, within the mental health services in England and Wales (DoH, 2015). The Health and Care Professionals Council (HCPC) Code, Standards of Conduct, Performance and Ethics (2016) set out a clear duty for its registrants, in relation to protecting children from harm. Arguably, statutory codes such as the HCPC (for HCPC registrants only) and MHA 1983 (for mental health practitioners) would carry significant weight in a court of law, in determining a judge's perception of the appropriate professional responses made by a therapist (DoH, 2015).

In terms of sources of guidance, this would include statutory guidance, government circulars and statutory instruments. For counsellors, the key examples here would include the relevant guidance on child protection and safeguarding, such as *Working Together* (DfE, 2015), and its equivalent versions for Wales and Scotland. A second example would include practice guidance on the provision of pre-trial therapy, which is discussed in the section on 'Pre-Trial Therapy' (CPS et al., 2001). Other levels of this range of sources regarding legal perspectives on good professional practice could also include influential reports, such as Lord Laming's report on failures of child protection in the Victoria Climbie Inquiry (Laming, 2003) and, not least, professional codes of ethics by therapist organisations (BACP, 2018), setting out ethical principles, values and minimum standards of therapist competence.

Table 17.1    Sources of law and their application to counselling practice with children and young people

| Sources of law | Examples potentially applying to counselling practice |
| --- | --- |
| Statute, i.e. Act of Parliament | Children Act 1989; Data Protection Act 1998; Equality Act 2010; School Standards and Organisation (Wales) Act 2013 |
| Common law | Law relating to confidence/confidentiality |
| Case law | *Gaskin* case (1990); *Gillick* [1986]; *Axon* [2006]; *Campbell* [2003] |
| International treaty | United Nations Convention on the Rights of the Child 1989 |
| Statutory codes of practice | Health and Care Professions Council Code (2016); Mental Health Act Code (2015) |
| Statutory guidance | Working Together (2015) (England) and equivalent guidance on child protection for Wales and Scotland; Practice Guidance on pre-trial therapy for children (2001, 2002); Information Sharing (2015) |
| Government reports | Laming Report on Victoria Climbie Inquiry (2003) |
| Professional codes of ethics | BACP Ethical Framework (2018) |

# POLICY AND PROVISION OF COUNSELLING SERVICES

This section covers a number of key areas of counselling provision for children and young people, for example:

- school-based counselling;
- working across organisations and in multidisciplinary teams;
- counselling as part of mental health services;
- pre-trial therapy (i.e. counselling for a child witness prior to a criminal trial).

## School-based counselling

Historically, counselling has mainly tended to be provided on a voluntary, non-statutory basis within the UK, by a wide range of providers. This has included provision by voluntary or third-sector agencies (Street, 2013) and by private and independent therapists. Counselling has been long established within the further and higher education sectors as an element of pastoral care, for students moving from adolescence into young adulthood. School counselling within secondary schools saw a decline from a peak of influence in the 1960s, but has since undergone a resurgence, with an estimated 80% of secondary schools in England now providing counselling for pupils, and 100% in Wales (Hanley et al., 2012). Secondary school counselling is now a statutory requirement in Wales, under s 92, School Standards and Organisation (Wales) Act 2013. Increasing numbers of primary schools also provide counselling for children (Thompson, 2013: 4).

Table 17.2   School-based counselling: Comparison of current and potential future patterns of counselling practice (adapted from Jenkins and Polat, 2006: 11)

| | *Potential* future pattern | |
| --- | --- | --- |
| **Current pattern** | | |
| **Model of confidentiality** | Child-centred orientation<br>Exclusive model of confidentiality<br>Limited sharing of client information | Family-centred orientation<br>Inclusive model of confidentiality<br>Routine sharing of client information |
| **Professional orientation** | Role-based professional boundaries<br>Individual focus of therapy | Task-based professional boundaries<br>Systemic and community focus of therapy |
| **Relationship to other professions** | Status as individual practitioner<br>Loose integration with other support services | Member of multidisciplinary team<br>High levels of integration with other support services |

## Working across organisations and in multidisciplinary teams

The rapid expansion of school-based counselling has made this provision available to a growing number of young clients, in a non-stigmatising and accessible format (Cooper, 2013). However, it has also brought with it some major challenges to the counselling profession, particularly those of integrating therapy within schools, as highly complex, bureaucratic organisations, with their own distinct ethos and culture. Thus, the BACP *Curriculum for Working with Young People (11–18 Years)* includes the requirement to 'work effectively within and across agencies, particularly with regard to confidentiality and consent' (2016: 33). It could be argued, perhaps controversially, that the traditional model of child-focused counselling has been strongly challenged by the safeguarding agenda (see section on Safeguarding and Child Protection). This has led to pressures for the adoption of a more multidisciplinary, team-based approach, with different expectations about confidentiality and information-sharing. Counsellors need to be increasingly skilled at adapting to and working within organisations such as schools, or programmes, such as Improving Access to Psychological Therapies (IAPT), each with its own very distinct ethos and culture. Classically, trying to provide therapeutic services within such organisations and programmes can entail strong challenges to the normal, established boundaries and elements of counselling practice, such as privacy, confidentiality, record-keeping and supervision (Jenkins, 2017: 85–87).

In addition, counsellors are increasingly involved in working within multidisciplinary teams. A school counsellor, for example, is likely to need to liaise on a day-to-day basis with a wide range of other, largely education-based professionals. At best, counsellors therefore need to be 'organisationally savvy'; at minimum, counsellors need to have a good working knowledge of what other non-therapists do and develop respect and good working relationships with other members of such teams, in the interests of the service and of the client (see Figure 17.1).

## Counselling as part of mental health services

Counselling can also be provided as part of mental health services. The Mental Health Act 1983 Code of Practice for England shows strong signs of influence by the *Gillick* case. It confirms the rights of young people under 16 to confidentiality, if of sufficient understanding (DoH, 2015: 169, 172). Provision of mental health services for children and young people is determined within England and Wales by the National Service Framework, setting out relevant standards (DfES/DoH, 2004). This has identified problem areas, such as the relative lack of provision for 16–17-year-olds, the perceived gap between adolescent and adult services, and the inappropriate placement of some adolescents on adult psychiatric wards. Other weaknesses include problems transferring between adolescent and adult services, and the lack of provision for self-referral by young people, in order to access mental health services. Mental

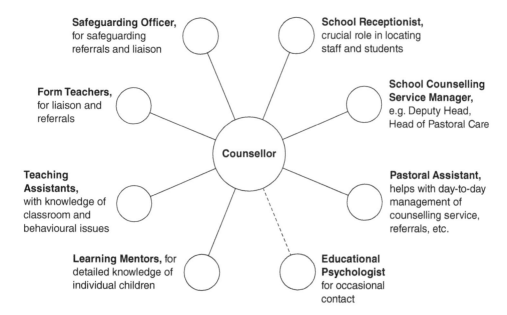

**Figure 17.1**    School counsellor working as part of a multi-disciplinary team (Jenkins, 2017: 84)

health provision for children and young people in England and Wales has been the subject of a recent UK government consultative Green Paper (DHSC/DfE, 2017).

Counselling provision within mental health services within England is provided via Child and Adolescent Mental Health Services (CAMHS). This operates on a four-tiered level of service:

Tier 1: Primary level of service, such as initial assessment and referral by GPs.
Tier 2: More specialised provision, by child psychologists and some school counsellors.
Tier 3: Specialist provision via multidisciplinary teams, such as CAMHS.
Tier 4: Highly specialist outpatient and inpatient services for severe mental health problems, such as eating disorders.

Mental health services provide medication and psychological therapy. Both are governed by reference to National Institute for Health and Clinical Excellence (NICE) guidance, for example, regarding the use of antidepressants for under-18s. It also applies in relation to evidence-based therapies, such as cognitive-behavioural therapy (CBT), for a wide range of presenting problems, such as anxiety, depression and self-harm.

Access to CAMHS is governed by referral gateways, such as via GPs, school counsellors and social workers. Increasingly, CAMHS services are mapped onto the tiered system used by the Young People – Improving Access to Psychological Therapies Programme (CYP IAPT) (Spong et al., 2013). This was initially aimed primarily at adults and has now been extended to include children and young people (see Table 17.3). Counselling services within CYP IAPT are closely evaluated via a battery of outcome measures. CYP IAPT services for children and young people may provide a wider range of types of therapy than its adult equivalent. However, CBT may hold a key position in terms of recommended treatment, given its privileged, evidence-based status within NICE guidelines (for a summary of NICE guidance for children and adults, see Jenkins, 2017: 89–90).

**Table 17.3** Stepped care model for the CYP IAPT service (Bala et al., 2011: 24)

| Stage/step | Services | Interventions available |
|---|---|---|
| Step 5 | CAMHS psychiatrist | Specialist services (Tier 4 CAMHS) |
| | Inpatient CAMHS services | |
| Step 4 | Core CAMHS team | Secondary care services (Tier 3 CAMHS) |
| Step 3: High intensity interventions | Core CAMHS team | Systemic, narrative and solution-focused therapies |
| | CAMHS outreach team (children in need/looked-after children) | CBT |
| | | Face-to-face counselling |
| | Primary care children and young persons worker team | Family counselling |
| | | Bereavement counselling |
| | Bereavement service | Play therapy |
| | | Psychology |
| | | Specialist parenting groups |
| | | Psycho-educational and psychotherapeutic groups |
| | | Signposting/assessment/step up/step down |
| Step 2: Low intensity interventions | Streetwise | Guided self-help based on CBT |
| | Action for Children | Parenting groups |
| | Targeted Adolescent Mental Health Services Team | Behavioural activation |
| | | Structured physical activity |
| | Psychological well-being practitioners 16–19 | Computerised cognitive-behavioural therapy (CCBT) |
| | | Bibliotherapy |
| | | Psycho-educational workshops and groups |
| | | Signposting/assessment/step up/step down |
| Step 1: Primary care | GP | Watchful waiting |
| | Children's health services | Advice and information |
| | Education | Local parenting groups |
| | Social care services | |

The model opposite is based on the work of Bury NHS Primary Care Trust. It is included simply as an illustration of CYP IAPT provision for children and young people, rather than claiming to be either representative, or prescriptive. The CYP IAPT model in general may well be significant for the future of counselling provision for children, in adopting a systemic, tiered approach, using a wide range of therapeutic interventions, for targeted treatment and therapy for assessed psychological difficulties, which are then subject to comprehensive outcome measurement.

## Pre-Trial Therapy

Where a child or young person is potentially a witness in a criminal trial, for example, as the victim of alleged abuse, therapy is governed by practice guidance issued by the Crown Prosecution Service (CPS) and other agencies (CPS et al., 2001). This sets out very clear and specific parameters for the provision of counselling. Any pre-trial counselling must be provided in close liaison with the CPS and avoid rehearsing evidence, or revisiting the original alleged abuse. This is in order to pre-empt future claims by the defence solicitors that the child's evidence has been 'contaminated' by the therapy, or that the child has been 'coached' by the therapist. The counsellor is required to keep careful records of therapy, which are accessible to the CPS. Any fresh disclosures of abuse, or material changes to the child's evidence, must be reported to the CPS. The guidance lists certain types of therapy, including hypnotherapy, psychodrama and group therapy, amongst others, which are identified as presenting particular problems for the child later giving evidence in court. Anecdotal evidence suggests that some children are still being actively discouraged by the authorities from attending counselling before the criminal trial, despite this advice running directly counter to the ethos of this guidance. Pre-trial therapy for child witnesses and victims of abuse has received relatively little research attention, despite its prominence as a complex and significant issue for many practitioners and clients. Plotnikoff and Woolfson (2009) (n: 182) found continuing delays in child abuse cases going to court, and high levels of anxiety amongst young witnesses.

## KEY ASPECTS OF THE LAW RELATING TO COUNSELLING CHILDREN

There are a number of key aspects of the law relating to counselling children and young people. These include:

- rights of children and parents;
- confidentiality and privacy;

- safeguarding and child protection;
- respecting diversity;
- information-sharing with other professionals;
- contracts and contracting;
- record-keeping and data protection;
- appearing in court.

## Rights of Children and Parents

Children and young people under the age of 18 in the UK have extensive rights to the provision of counselling, to participation in decisions and to autonomy (for a detailed outline of this framework, see Jenkins, 2013a; for its application to counselling, see Jenkins, 2013b, and Daniels and Jenkins, 2010). The rights of parents were substantially recast by the Children Act 1989, to assume the much narrower form of 'parental responsibility'. This legal power is not limited to biological parents, but can be legally acquired by other significant figures in a child's life, such as a grandparent. The notion of 'parental rights' has been radically reframed and slimmed down, to now include essentially, parental *duties* to provide for, educate and protect children (see Daniels and Jenkins, 2010: 18). Counsellors should therefore be wary of accepting at face value any claim to 'parental rights' as affording a parent the authority to intervene into the counselling space where the client is a child or young person.

## Confidentiality and Privacy

Young people aged 16 to 17 years have the same entitlement to confidentiality as would an adult, under Section 8, Family Law Reform Act 1969. Under the age of 16, young people in England and Wales, with 'sufficient understanding', are deemed capable of consenting to medical treatment by a health practitioner, following the *Gillick* case. Confidentiality is an essential pre-condition for exercising such consent, according to the *Axon* case in 2006. This confirmed that '*Gillick* remains good law' (*Axon* (2006) at 24). Following the principles set out in *Gillick*, it follows that parental consent is, therefore, *not* a legal requirement for counselling a young person under 16 with 'sufficient understanding'.

   Children of any age also have the right to respect for their private and family life, under Article 8 of the Human Rights Act 1998. In 2003, Naomi Campbell won a key legal case and was awarded damages for breach of privacy, when the *Daily Mirror* published photos of her leaving a meeting of Narcotics Anonymous. Following the *Campbell* case (2004), it could be argued that this right of *privacy* extends to the very fact of actually *attending* counselling. This may be true even for those primary school age children, who may be considered as too young to qualify for confidentiality under the *Gillick* criteria (Daniels and Jenkins, 2010: 135).

## Safeguarding and Child Protection

There is now an extensive safeguarding and child protection agenda in place, designed to protect children under 18 from abuse. Child abuse is defined as 'significant harm', under Section 47 of the Children Act 1989 for England and Wales. Children and young people within these jurisdictions are protected via the Children Acts of 1989 and 2004, the safeguarding provisions of the Education Act 2002, and the vetting provisions of the Safeguarding Vulnerable Groups Act 2006 and Protection of Freedoms Act 2012. These are then set out in detail, at an operational level, by statutory guidance, such as *Working Together* (DfE, 2015) and the equivalent guidance applying variously to Scotland, Wales and Northern Ireland.

There is, however, a widening gap between the formal *law* on this issue and the *policy* of many agencies, with regard to the *reporting* of alleged abuse. It is quite clear that 'there is no mandatory reporting law in England and Wales', according to Hoyano and Keenan (2007: 444). However, many agencies operate on the basis of an obligatory abuse reporting *policy*, which is imposed as a term of the counsellor's contract of employment. This can clearly be justified by appeals to the concept of social justice and by being demonstrably 'in the public interest'. Nevertheless, it can also raise acute ethical and professional dilemmas for counsellors working with mid- to late-age-range teenagers. Such clients may be making highly conflicted disclosures of abuse, but might not be perceived by the counsellor as being at *immediate* risk of exposure to current or continuing significant harm.

This issue of mandatory reporting of child abuse has been the subject of several research reports relevant to current debates about safeguarding. Goldman and Padayachi (2005) found a tendency for school counsellors in Australia (n: 122) to *underreport* their suspicions of child sexual abuse, possibly due to their lack of confidence in accurately identifying symptoms of abuse. Bryant and Baldwin (2010) found a similar reticence regarding reporting abuse amongst school counsellors in the US (n: 193), which has a similar system of mandatory reporting. These research findings would suggest that counsellors' abuse reporting practice relies on more than a simple legal requirement to do so, and is, in part, mediated by professionals' own perceptions and practices. The issue of introducing mandatory reporting of child abuse was the subject of a major consultation exercise by the Independent Inquiry into Child Sexual Abuse (Jenkins, 2016).[3] However, the consultation indicated overwhelming opposition to the introduction of mandatory reporting by most professionals, so the government has decided not to introduce this radical legislative change into English law.

---

[3]At this point, you can refer to: Counselling MindEd (free online training material) (www.minded.org. uk): Jenkins, P. (2018) *Safeguarding Young People and Vulnerable Young Adults*. MindEd.

## Respecting diversity

Respect for client diversity is an ethical obligation under the BACP Ethical Framework (2018). It is also a legal requirement to avoid discrimination against clients with 'protected characteristics', under the terms of the Equality Act 2010. 'Protected characteristics' include the following:

1. age;
2. disability;
3. gender reassignment;
4. marriage and civil partnerships;
5. maternity and pregnancy;
6. race;
7. religion or belief;
8. sex;
9. sexual orientation.

School counsellors will already be familiar with the duty of schools and education authorities to make 'reasonable adjustments' for pupils with disability, for example, by providing additional support, specialist software or laptops. More generic counsellors working with young people are aware of the steep rise in enquiries and self-referrals around issues of sexual orientation and transgender issues, for example (NSPCC, 2016: 8). With regard to diversity, the BACP Ethical Framework clearly states: '(23) We will take the law concerning equality, diversity and inclusion into careful consideration and strive for a higher standard than the legal minimum' (2018: 20). Counsellors therefore need to know the law regarding equality and diversity, to be attuned to the wide variety of their clients' experiences and to be proactive in raising these issues appropriately within their own counselling agencies.

## Information-sharing with other professionals

In legal terms, information-sharing with other professionals can be justified by obtaining the consent of the child or young person. It can also be carried out *without* consent, if it can be justified as being 'in the public interest', that is, in preventing significant harm to the child or young person concerned (HMG, 2015). On information-sharing practice within safeguarding, Bunting et al. (2010) provide an extensive literature review. Brown's research (2006) has identified some of the role strain experienced by counsellors between, on the one hand, respecting client confidentiality and, on the other, becoming involved in information-sharing with other professionals. Cromarty and Richards (2009) found less evidence of this difficulty amongst school counsellors (n: 16). However, they identified a preference amongst counsellors for sharing information with trusted individuals, rather than in a group setting, where there was less control over its subsequent use. Rees et al. (n: 24) found similar concerns about retaining control over information amongst young people, in making disclosures of abuse to social workers. 'For young people, the relationship with social work practitioners was central to disclosure and protection' (2010: 52).

## Contracts and contracting

In England and Wales, young people under 18 (under 16 in Scotland) are not usually deemed capable of entering into a legally binding contract, with certain rare exceptions (Mitchels and Bond, 2010: 64). Where counselling is being directly paid for, then the contract would often be between the counsellor and the parent concerned. The terms of the contract need to specify the limits to confidentiality applying to the therapeutic work and any restrictions on the nature of the counsellor's reporting back to the parent(s) of the process and content of therapy. In other contexts, it may be that the counsellor is carrying out their work under contract to an *agency*, such as children's services. Again, the specific terms of the contract may include provisions for returning completed case files to the agency purchasing the service, and an obligation to report any disclosures of abuse made during therapy.

Mitchels and Bond (2010: 65–66) discuss the capacity of children and young people to make 'therapeutic contracts', according to their age, understanding and legal jurisdiction. Where these are not properly legally binding contracts, these might be more accurately described as 'consent agreements', or even as 'working charters'. This is precisely to avoid any potential confusion over their legal status. Such an agreement can set out clearly practical arrangements for therapeutic work, any limitations to confidentiality, data protection requirements and provision for client complaint, in the event of dissatisfaction.

## Record-keeping and data protection

Record-keeping in counselling children and young people is covered by the somewhat complex guidance derived from data protection law, based on the General Data Protection Regulation and the forthcoming Data Protection Act 2018 (ICO, 2016). The law essentially parallels provision for record-keeping for adult clients, but with certain increased rights for younger clients (see Jenkins, 2018). Data protection requirements cover all processing of personal data, that is, client recording, in electronic/computerised, including audio, video and digital recording, and manual/handwritten formats. Records must be accurate, relevant, not excessive for their purpose and kept no longer than necessary.

Record-keeping in therapeutic work with children may be governed by agency policies, regarding their content and time limits, but these clearly need to be consistent with data protection law. Generally, as with adult clients, compliance with data protection requirements has seen a marked shift away from the keeping of therapist- and process-focused recording, towards much briefer, primarily factual, records. Records of therapy with pre-trial child witnesses need to follow this approach and are, in principle, accessible to the CPS (CPS et al., 2001). Children and young people have rights as data subjects to access their own files, to have the privacy implications of record-keeping outlined in appropriate language, and do not require parental consent for recording which is for counselling or preventive purposes (ICO, 2016) The rights of children and young people can be directly challenged, however, when parents seek to access health, education and counselling records, independently of the child, as may happen in contested cases concerning divorce, or medical treatment.[4]

## Appearing in court

All counselling records are potentially accessible to the courts via a court order. Counsellors do not possess legal privilege in the UK, with the limited exception of marital relationship counsellors (Jenkins, 2007: 105). Equally, a counsellor may be called upon to write a report for the court, as either a professional witness, or as an expert witness. The tasks of report writing, or appearing as an expert witness, for the court require substantial professional experience and, ideally, specialist training. Where therapists are asked to provide court reports, these are often related to the assessment of attachment, parenting, child development, trauma or child abuse. This may be in the context of proceedings connected with divorce, separation, parental contact, domestic violence, adoption or child care proceedings.

Counsellors called to court can obtain expert legal advice from their employer, if applicable, and from their professional indemnity insurance society, or the Psychologists Protection Society (PPS). Counsellors employed by large organisations may have an advantage over colleagues in private practice, in having easier access to the legal resources of the relevant employing local education authority or NHS Trust. Legal information and professional advice may also be obtained from professional associations, such as BACP, the United Kingdom Council for Psychotherapy (UKCP), the British Association for Behavioural and Cognitive Psychotherapies (BABCP) or the British Psychological Society (BPS), as appropriate. Counsellors providing pre-trial therapy for child witnesses in alleged abuse cases need to be particularly mindful of the practice guidance governing therapy in these circumstances and to follow it closely (CPS et al., 2001). Advice for counsellors on appearing in court is aptly summarised as 'Dress up, stand up, speak up and shut up!' More generic suggestions for giving evidence in court are outlined in Jenkins (2007: 52–73).

---

[4]At this point, you can refer to: Counselling MindEd (free online training material) (www.minded.org. uk): Jenkins, P. (2018) *Record-Keeping, Data Protection and Access to Records*. MindEd.

# Case Study: Parveen

Parveen worked as a counsellor in a secondary school run by the local authority, and developed a particularly close therapeutic alliance with Simon, aged 12 years, who came from a fairly chaotic family background. There was some evidence of poor parenting by his mother, a single parent with multiple domestic and housing problems. Parveen met with Simon on a regular basis, with no missed sessions. She was actively supported in this work by the head teacher, who saw the counselling as enabling Simon to engage as well as he could with his studies, as an 'oasis' in an otherwise stormy life. Simon's social worker was also highly appreciative of this therapeutic work, but respectful towards the ongoing therapy as a 'private space', whilst also trying to support his mother with her daily struggles.

The situation changed drastically when Simon's case was taken over by a new social worker, with a very different attitude towards the counselling. The new social worker instructed Parveen to attend a 'team around the child' meeting, where she would be expected to update the professionals attending on the fine detail of what Simon was discussing in therapy. Parveen was concerned at this, as Simon was not prepared for the detail of the counselling session to be shared in this way. The social worker's view was that the school counsellor was now part of a multidisciplinary team, and that Parveen was duty-bound to share all relevant information about Simon, as a 'child in need', under the Working Together guidelines. Parveen's referring to the BACP Ethical Framework was dismissed as being 'just a code of ethics', even though the head teacher supported Parveen in her defence of client confidentiality. Parveen was informed in no uncertain terms by the social worker that, if she failed to attend the meeting and share all relevant information, Simon would be referred to CAMHS, with the result that the school counselling would cease forthwith.

# Key Learning

- Law and policy may be perceived by practitioners as being highly complex, but they provide a framework for working therapeutically with children and young people in the UK.
- Sources of guidance on the law include statute, case law, codes of practice, statutory codes of practice, official reports and professional codes of ethics.
- Policy overlaps with this legal framework, in setting out the requirements for counselling provision, for example, within mental health services, CYP IAPT and NICE guidelines.
- Much counselling provision, for example, in schools or in voluntary organisations, currently sits outside these statutory frameworks, but is heavily influenced in practice by statutory provision, such as in CAMHS, or by the safeguarding and child protection agendas.
- Counsellors are increasingly required to adapt to working across organisations and within multidisciplinary teams.
- A rights-based model offers a way of grasping the rights of young people, and protecting the 'confidential space' in which counsellors do their valuable work.

## Summary

This chapter has set out the main sources of the law relating to children and young people, including:

- Information on some of the key areas that can cause anxiety to students, counsellors just starting out and more experienced therapists, their supervisors and managers.
- Policy and law relating to children and young people and their context, for example, safeguarding in the family, school-based counselling, mental health services and pre-trial therapy.
- Key aspects of the law, such as the rights of children and parents, caregivers and the wider family, confidentiality, safeguarding, diversity, information-sharing, contracting, record-keeping and appearing in court.

## Discussion Questions

1. What are the rights of the child in the situation discussed above?
2. What is the legal situation for the counsellor in this situation?
3. What are the options available to the counsellor in this situation?

   Turn to p.448 for possible answers.

## Develop Your Skills

1. Check online for the latest version of *Working Together* (DfE, 2015) or its equivalent and read the sections on:

   o information-sharing;
   o a child in need;
   o safeguarding.
2. Check the safeguarding policy of your own counselling agency, and how it might apply in this situation.
3. Construct a possible solution that might offer a way forward in this complex situation and discuss it with your tutor, supervisor or line manager.

## For Trainers – Group Activity

Divide the group into two equal sub-groups and organise a debate for and against on the topic of either:

○ Children's rights – have they gone too far?
○ Should we have mandatory reporting of child abuse?

# Further Reading

Daniels, D. and Jenkins, P. (2010) *Therapy with Children: Children's Rights, Confidentiality and the Law*, 2nd edn. London: SAGE.

Jenkins, P. (2007) Therapy with children and young people. In: *Counselling, Psychotherapy and the Law*, 2nd edn. London: SAGE, pp. 151–176.

Jenkins, P. (2011) *A Confidential Space: Ethical Considerations When Counselling Children and Young People*. DVD: University of Wales. Available at: http://hss.newport.ac.uk or https://sites. google.com/site/counsellingdvds/a-confidential-space (accessed 14 February 2018).

Jenkins, P. (2013) *Children's Rights and Counselling*. Brighton: Pavilion.

## Online Resources

Temenos online archive of interviews (free registration and online access for counselling students):

Peter Jenkins (2015) *Working with Children and Young People: An Ethical and Legal Minefield?* https://www.onlinevents.co.uk/category/portfolio

## Legal Cases

*Axon, R. (on the application of) v. Secretary of State for Health and Anor* (2006) EWHC 37 (Admin).

*Campbell v. MGN Ltd* (2004) UKHL 22.

*Gaskin v. UK ECHR 2/1988/146/200* (1990) 1 FLR 167.

*Gillick v. West Norfolk AHA* (1985) 3 All ER 402; (1986) AC 112.

## REFERENCES

Bala, P., Pratt, K. and Maguire, C. (2011) The needs of children and young people: developing a new service. *Healthcare Counselling and Psychotherapy Journal* April: 20–24.

British Association for Counselling and Psychotherapy (BACP) Professional Standards (2016) *Young People (11–18 Years) Training Curriculum: An Evidence-Informed Curriculum Framework for Young People*. Lutterworth: BACP.

British Association for Counselling and Psychotherapy (BACP) (2018) *Ethical Framework for Good Practice in Counselling and Psychotherapy*. Lutterworth: BACP.

Brown, A. (2006) 'In my agency it's very clear – but I can't tell you what it is': work settings and ethical challenges. *Counselling and Psychotherapy Research* 6(2): 100–107.

Bryant, J. and Baldwin, P. (2010) School counsellors' perceptions of mandatory reporter training and mandatory reporting experiences. *Child Abuse Review* 19: 172–186.

Bunting, L., Rosenblatt, B. and Wallace, I. (2010) Information-sharing and reporting systems in the UK and Ireland. Professional barriers to reporting child maltreatment concerns. *Child Abuse Review* 19: 187–202.

Carlisle, J., Shickle, D., Cork, M. and McDonagh, A. (2006) Concerns over confidentiality may deter adolescents from consulting their doctors: a qualitative exploration. *Journal of Medical Ethics* 32: 133–137.

Cooper, M. (2009) Counselling in UK secondary schools: a comprehensive review of audit and evaluation studies. *Counselling and Psychotherapy Research* 9(3): 137–150.

Cooper, M. (2013) *School-Based Counselling in UK Secondary Schools: A Review and Critical Evaluation*. Lutterworth: BACP/Counselling MindEd.

Cromarty, K. and Richards, K. (2009) How do secondary school counsellors work with other professionals? *Counselling and Psychotherapy Research* 9(3): 182–186.

Crown Prosecution Service (CPS), Home Office and Department of Health (2001) *Provision of Therapy for Child Witnesses Prior to a Criminal Trial*. Bolton: CPS.

Daniels, D. and Jenkins, P. (2010) *Therapy with Children: Children's Rights, Confidentiality and the Law*, 2nd edn. London: SAGE.

Department for Education (DfE) (2015) *Working Together to Safeguard Children: A Guide to Inter-Agency Working to Safeguard and Promote the Welfare of Children*. London: Stationery Office.

Department for Education and Skills/Department of Health (DfES/DoH) (2004) *Child and Adolescent Mental Health Services (CAMHS) Standard: National Service Framework for Children, Young People and Maternity Services*. London: DfES/DoH.

Department of Health (DoH) (2015) *Mental Health Act 1983 Code of Practice*. London: DoH.

Department of Health and Social Care (DHSC) / Department for Education (DfE) (2017) *Transforming Children and Young People's Mental Health Provision: A Green Paper*. DHSC/DfE: London.

Goldman, J. and Padayachi, U. (2005) Child sexual abuse reporting behaviour by school counselors and their need for further education. *Health Education Journal* 64(4): 302–322.

Hanley, T., Jenkins, P., Barlow, A., Humphrey, N. and Wigelsworth, M. (2012) *A Scoping Review of the Access to Secondary School Counselling*. BACP Internal Document. Lutterworth: BACP.

Health and Care Professions Council (HCPC) (2016) *Standards of Conduct, Performance and Ethics*. London: HCPC.

Her Majesty's Government (HMG) (2015) *Information Sharing: Advice for Practitioners Providing Safeguarding Services to Children, Young People, Parents and Carers*. London: HMG.

Hoyano, L. and Keenan, C. (2007) *Child Abuse: Law and Policy across Boundaries*. Oxford: Oxford University Press.

Information Commissioner's Office (ICO) (2016) *Overview of the General Data Protection Regulation*. Wilmslow: ICO.

Jenkins, P. (2007) *Counselling, Psychotherapy and the Law*, 2nd edn. London: SAGE.

Jenkins, P. (2013a) *Exploring Children's Rights: A Participative Exercise to Introduce the Issues Around Children's Rights in England and Wales*, 2nd edn. Brighton: Pavilion.

Jenkins, P. (2013b) *Children's Rights and Counselling: A Participative Exercise to Introduce the Issues around Children's Rights in England and Wales and Their Access to Counselling*. Brighton: Pavilion.

Jenkins, P. (2016) Telling secrets to protect children? *Children and Young People* December: 40–43.

Jenkins, P. (2017) *Professional Practice in Counselling and Psychotherapy: Ethics and the Law*. London: SAGE.

Jenkins, P. (2018) An upgrade for data privacy? *Counselling at Work*, 95: 22–27. https://bacp-live-fe.azurewebsites.net/bacp-journals/counselling-at-work/january-2018/

Jenkins, P. and Polat, F. (2006) The Children Act 2004 and implications for counselling in schools in England and Wales. *Pastoral Care in Education* 24(2): 7–14.

Laming, Lord (2003) *The Victoria Climbie Inquiry: Report of an Inquiry by Lord Laming*. Cm 5730. London: Stationery Office.

LeSurf, A. and Lynch, G. (1999) Exploring young people's perceptions relevant to counselling: a qualitative study. *British Journal of Guidance and Counselling* 27(2): 231–243.

McDonald, H. (2018) Facebook warned of rise in 'revenge porn' lawsuits. *Guardian,* 13th January.

Mitchels, B. and Bond, T. (2010) *Essential Law for Counsellors and Psychotherapists*. London: BACP/SAGE.

National Society for the Prevention of Cruelty to Children (NSPCC) (2016) *It turned out someone did care: Childline Annual Review 2015/16*. London: NSPCC.

Plotnikoff, J. and Woolfson, R. (2009) *Measuring Up? Evaluating Implementation of Government Commitments to Young Witnesses in Criminal Proceedings: Executive Summary.* London: NSPCC.

Rees, G., Gorin, S., Jobe, A., Stein, M., Medforth, R. and Goswami, H. (2010) *Safeguarding Young People: Responding to Young People Aged 11 to 17 Who Are Maltreated.* London: Children's Society.

Spong, S., Waters, R., Dowd, C. and Jackson, C. (2013) *The Relationship Between Specialist Child and Adolescent Mental Health Services (CAMHS) and School- and Community-Based Counselling for Children and Young People.* Lutterworth: BACP/Counselling MindEd.

Street, C. (2013) *Voluntary and Community Sector (VCS) Counselling Provision for Children, Young People and Young Adults in England.* Lutterworth: BACP: Counselling/MindEd.

Thompson, W. (2013) *School-based Counselling in UK Primary Schools.* Lutterworth: BACP: Counselling/MindEd.

# 18
# ETHICS
## PETER JENKINS

**This chapter will discuss:**

- An exploration of some of the different approaches to ethics within counselling and psychotherapy, and the particular issues of concern with regard to counselling younger and more vulnerable clients
- The value of adopting a rights-based approach to addressing ethical dilemmas in therapy with children and young people, and an exploration of a number of key areas of concern to therapists, including contracting, and undertaking research with children
- A discussion of recent research evidence on how practitioners actually work in practice with some of the key issues confronting them in their day-to-day practice with children and young people

This chapter is designed to be read in conjunction with Chapter 17, 'Law and Policy', in this volume.

## INTRODUCTION

Counsellors often tend to see the subject of ethics as a topic that is dry and academic, or as being worthy, but slightly dull, or even as an 'add-on' to the more *central* task of actually working in therapy with children and young people. This is a real misreading of the importance and value of ethics, which is defined as 'a generic term for understanding and examining the moral life' (Beauchamp and Childress, 2008: 1). Ethics is concerned with addressing, and attempting to find answers to, key therapeutic dilemmas such as:

- a child's parents *insisting* on knowing what is said in the therapy session;
- an agency requiring *all* underage sexual activity to be reported as a risk factor;
- defining the *age* at which a child becomes self-determining and acquires a right to greater autonomy.

## ETHICAL PRACTICE AND CODES OF ETHICS

The counselling profession attempts to support, monitor and reinforce ethical practice amongst its members, by providing codes of ethics, or ethical frameworks, for decision-making, and by implementing complaints procedures, in order to offer redress to aggrieved parties. Codes of ethics are, in turn, not set in stone, but change over time. They are influenced by changing professional perceptions, broadening experience, key cases or complaints, and by the changing legal and policy context. Codes attempt to embody the current professional wisdom of the time, but they cannot realistically seek to answer every issue confronting a counsellor or supervisor. Instead, codes offer a *framework* for responding to both everyday and more complex and unusual challenges to therapeutic practice.

Professional approaches to ethics also vary between professional associations and change over time. A key moment in the development of the counselling and psychotherapy profession was marked by the decisive shift by the British Association for Counselling and Psychotherapy (BACP), from the former *Code of Ethics* (BAC, 1998), to the *Ethical Framework for the Counselling Professions* (BACP, 2018). It is often not fully appreciated that codes or frameworks speak with different tones or authority, in setting out, for example, what counsellors *may* do (or may *not* do), and what they *must* do. These tones, or requirements, can be described as including the following:

- *Advisory*: Psychologists '*should* practice within the boundaries of their competence' (BPS, 2009: 16).
- *Prescriptive*: 'We will respect our clients' privacy and dignity' (BACP, 2018: 20).
- *Mandatory*: 'You must keep full, clear and accurate records ...' (HCPC, 2016: 10).[1]

The BACP Ethical Framework contains a variety of different authoritative tones, but marks a distinct shift away from the earlier binding set of prescriptions. It recognises that counsellors need a more flexible set of ethical guides, where there are competing claims for action, and there is not necessarily one single, right answer to a pressing ethical dilemma.

---

[1] At this point, you can refer to: Counselling MindEd (free online training material) (www.minded.org.uk): Jenkins, P. (2018) *Using the BACP Ethical Framework*. MindEd.

Within philosophy, there is a wide range of different approaches to the study of ethics. These different approaches include the following:

- *Deontological*, that is, *rule-following*, prescriptive: 'You *must not* break client confidentiality'.
- *Teleological*, that is, based on achieving a positive *outcome*: 'You *may* decide to break confidentiality, *in order* to avert client suicide'.
- *Rights-based*, that is, based on an active appreciation of the *rights* of all parties involved, for example, 'You need to *balance* the child's right to privacy, *versus* their right to protection from harm'.

The approach taken in this chapter follows an explicitly *rights-based model*, whilst acknowledging the valuable contribution of both rule-following and outcomes-based approaches. It also needs to be borne in mind that the practical application of ethics in

## Reflection: Exploring the origins and sources of your own personal sense of ethics

Look at the following list of possible influences on your own ethical stance. Take a moment to reflect on the sources of your own ethics as a therapist. What are the main influences on you regarding your own ethical stance? What aspects have had the least influence and why?
    These influences could include your:

- personal values;
- family upbringing;
- religious faith or worldview;
- understanding of the law;
- agency policy (if relevant);
- philosophical stance;
- prior professional role or training (e.g. as a nurse, social worker, etc.);
- professional code of conduct;
- experience of working with dilemmas or difficult moral issues in your own personal or professional life. (Jenkins 2017: 132)

### Possible Group Activity

1. Work on exploring the sources of your own ethical stance, as in the exercise above for 10 minutes.
2. Work in pairs, sharing your experiences for another 10–15 minutes each.
3. Plenary session: Report back your main findings from your individual and joint work to the group and its facilitator for further group discussion and flipcharting of main themes.

counselling does not solely revolve around the ethical stance adopted by the counsellor. It is increasingly clear that children and young people also bring their own expectations and a strong sense of ethics and fairness to therapy, which can become a key factor in the unfolding of the therapeutic work (Jenkins, 2010).

## ETHICAL APPROACHES TO WORK WITH CHILDREN AND YOUNG PEOPLE

Discussion of ethical approaches to work with children tends to have a distinct nature, marking it apart from more generic discussions about ethics in counselling with adult clients. This is so for a number of reasons. The terms 'children' and 'young people' cover a wide range of age groups and situations: the 'child' in question may be aged 17 (using the term 'child' in a strictly legal sense); or the 'young person' may be aged 12 or 13. The terms children and young person/young people are used here to denote persons of roughly primary school age, that is, 6–11 years, or secondary school age, that is, 11–18 years, respectively. This follows a broad distinction, between *children*, who are assumed not to be mature enough to make decisions for their own care, and *young people*, who may have developed sufficient maturity to do so. However, this broad distinction is no more than a very rough guide, as there will emerge situations where these categories are not particularly useful in guiding ethical decision-making by the counsellor.

Counselling work with children and young people is also considered to be a distinct field in terms of ethics, because of the child or young person's developmental, physical and emotional vulnerability. The long-term adverse effects of child abuse, trauma, bullying and emotional abuse are by now well-established. Children and young people may also be more subject to manipulation by powerful and respected adult authority figures, perhaps lacking an adult's wider experience of relationships, on which to judge a counsellor's influence. By definition, children and young people are also heavily dependent upon adults for their everyday care, protection and control, whether in a family, hospital, residential care home or in a custodial setting. It is also probably much more likely that counselling will involve potential contact by the counsellor with *adult third parties*, who take an active interest in the process and outcomes of therapy, whether as parents, foster parents, social workers, teachers or judges, than would normally be the case with an adult client. This vulnerability to harm, and corresponding dependence upon adult caretakers, is recognised by specific provision for children and young people under the law, which then becomes a further crucial element, in terms of ethical decision-making by counsellors.[2]

---

[2]At this point, you can refer to Counselling MindEd (free online training material) (www.minded.org.uk): Jenkins, P. and Williams, A. (2018) *Key Differences in Counselling Adults and Children*. MindEd. See also: Jenkins, P. (2011) *A Confidential Space: Ethical Considerations When Counselling Children and Young People* for a brief outline of the impact of the Gillick case on child-centred counselling.

There is limited counselling-based research on how counsellors work with ethical dilemmas in their practice, mostly drawn from practice-based evidence, such as work by Brown (n: 20), in exploring the uncertainties experienced by counsellors in confronting issues that relate to young people, such as child protection (2006: 102). Research on the nature of the therapeutic alliance in working with young people has emphasised the key role of the therapeutic alliance and, within this, confidentiality as a central component of the therapeutic environment (Everall and Paulson, 2002). This latter small-scale survey (n: 18), carried out in Canada, found that many young clients did not grasp that the *context* of therapy radically influenced the limits of confidentiality, hence underlining the need for careful initial contracting to set out the limits of confidentiality. This finding is echoed by LeSurf and Lynch, in their research with young clients of a counselling agency (n: 42). They found with young people that 'their desire for confidentiality related not so much to concerns for privacy, but to a wish to retain control over the material which they disclosed' (1999: 237). A study by Finkenauer et al. (2002) (n: 227) found that the provision of client confidentiality, in essence the keeping of secrets from parents and authoritative adults, had an additional and unexpected *developmental* value, in promoting a stronger sense of autonomy amongst young people.

## BACP Ethical Framework

The BACP Ethical Framework (2018) will be taken as the main reference point for discussion, whilst acknowledging that there are other, equally valid, ethical codes available for practitioners belonging to other professional associations. The Ethical Framework refers to values, ethical principles and (often overlooked) the *personal qualities* of therapists, as components of informed ethical decision-making. These separate elements amount to a kind of 'scaffolding', which supports and empowers counsellors, in making often difficult decisions. The Framework makes the key point:

> Careful consideration will be given to working with children and young people that:
>
> a. takes account of their capacity to give informed consent, considering whether it is appropriate to seek the consent of others who have parental responsibility for the young person, and their best interests
> b. demonstrates knowledge and skills about ways of working that are appropriate to the young person's maturity and understanding. (BACP, 2018: 21).

In addition, the BACP Training Curriculum, for working with children and young people, identifies a number of key areas for special attention in relation to professional and ethical work (BACP, 2016: 21):

- applying key ethical principles;
- knowledge of potential ethical conflicts;

- understanding how to deal with ethical conflicts via supervision;
- understanding own limits of competence;
- identifying and minimising the potential for harm;
- collaborating with other professionals;
- gaining consent in appropriate ways;
- evaluating risk to ensure safeguarding;
- maintaining confidentiality;
- storing, managing and sharing information;
- having an in-depth knowledge of record-keeping;
- knowledge of appropriate communication with service users, other professionals and services;
- understanding how to advocate for service users.

The areas that are identified as especially sensitive, or even problematic, could easily occupy a special ethical framework, simply for work with children and young people. The complexity of devising a set of ethics for work with children and young people is further recognised in discussion of the possible constraints to a key ethical principle – that of autonomy. The Ethical Framework sets out key principles, including respect for autonomy, that is, respect for the client's right to be self-governing' (2018: 11). However, this quality of autonomy may be radically compromised by the immaturity of a child, or young person, in the role of client. For example, a 10-year-old client may be exposed to, or encouraged to drink, alcohol in their home by older peers, or by parents. The child's autonomy in choosing to experiment in this way may be in conflict with their lack of maturity in making such a decision, which then places them at risk of harm.

# A RIGHTS-BASED APPROACH TO THERAPY WITH CHILDREN AND YOUNG PEOPLE

The field of ethics in therapy with children and young people is often seen as being hugely complex and risky, not least for practitioners. The advantage of a rights-based approach is that it offers a way of categorising a wide range of conflicting material, of identifying key underlying ethical principles in decision-making and of linking ethical choices with the often closely related legal framework underpinning such decisions. This framework is developed in more detail elsewhere (Daniels and Jenkins, 2010; Jenkins, 2011, 2013a, 2013b).

Within this model, a right is defined as 'a claim to treatment which an individual can make, by reason of law, code of practice or otherwise' (Jenkins, 2013a: 5). Thus, a child may have a right to *privacy*, regarding accessing therapy, which is both an *ethical* imperative for the counsellor and agency, and also, arguably, a *legal* right under the Human Rights Act 1998. In some cases, a child may require the proper support of an adult, in order to claim such a right, whether in the role of advocate, solicitor or social worker.

Briefly, the model suggests four types of rights for children and young people with regard to counselling:

Level 1: Children have *no rights* to counselling.
Level 2: Children have rights to *welfare and protection*, decided by adults.
Level 3: Children have a right to *participate in decisions* made about them.
Level 4: Children have rights *independent of their parents*.

## Level 1: Children have no rights to counselling

This category relates to children effectively being denied access to counselling, or having their access severely and unjustifiably constrained. Examples would include a requirement for parental consent to access counselling provided in secondary schools; proposals for the mandatory reporting of underage sexual activity by counsellors in sexual health clinics; constraints and limitations on the discussion of sexuality in state schools; age limitations on referrals to counselling services in primary care; and refusal of self-referrals by young people to mental health services.

## Level 2: Children have rights to welfare and protection, decided by adults

Within this category, children and young people have rights to the provision of counselling, for example, for gay and lesbian young people in care, and for children with a disability, under Guidance and Regulations for the Children Act 1989; for children and young people in schools in Wales; for children who have broken the law, under the UN Convention; and to access pre-trial therapy, when awaiting court action as a witness in the case of alleged abuse. In addition, children and young people have a right to be protected from significant harm, including physical and sexual abuse, under the Children Act 1989.

## Level 3: Children have a right to participate in decisions made about them

Under the Children Act 1989, children in care, or those appearing in civil court, have rights to be consulted about decisions being made about them, depending on their age and level of understanding. This right is extended to *all* children by Article 12 of the UN Convention, ratified by the UK government in 1991. This right would include an entitlement to be actively consulted in the contracting process within therapy, for example, regarding the proposed limits to confidentiality; it should also include young people being consulted about school policies on parental permission for accessing counselling, and on proposed closures of youth counselling services by local authorities.

## Level 4: Children have rights independent of their parents

Children and young people also hold substantial rights in relation to counselling, which are independent of parents or adult caretakers. Young people aged 16 to 17 have rights to consent and confidentiality equivalent to adults. Young people under 16 have rights to counselling confidentiality and to consent to medical treatment, if of 'sufficient understanding', in the view of the relevant medical practitioner, and, arguably, of the counsellor. Some of these rights are non-age-dependent, in that the child has rights to confidentiality of personal data, and to privacy, regardless of age.

In ethical terms, these sets of rights correspond to key ethical principles. Level 1 concerns the *denial of rights* to children and young people, presumably on the basis of age, thereby contradicting the ethical principle of justice. Level 2 rights relate to *classic welfare rights*, including the ethical principles of beneficence, or welfare, and non-maleficence, namely the avoidance of harm to the client. Level 3 rights directly express the broader social value of the child's *participation in decision-making*, which can be linked to the ethical principle of fidelity, or trust. Finally, Level 4 rights are primarily concerned with *autonomy*, and promoting the developing capacity of the child, or young person, for greater independence and acknowledging, in the words of the UN Convention, the 'evolving capacities of the child' (UNICEF, 1989: 5).

In practice, the rights of the child or young person might well be in direct conflict with each other. A child may be entitled to confidentiality (Level 4), but also require immediate protection from harm (Level 2). The age of the child and an assessment of the degree of perceived risk are crucial here. Conversely, a young person may be entitled to privacy in attending a sexual health clinic (Level 4); a parent may claim, however, to be entitled to be informed of this, given their (assumed) rights as a parent (Level 1). The model offers an initial way of recognising complementary, competing and sometimes *conflicting* rights of all the various parties, who are frequently involved in accessing counselling services for children and young people.

Clearly, a rights-based approach to ethics has its own weaknesses. Critiques might point to the implicit emphasis on the value of *autonomy*, as betraying either gender-informed assumptions about desirable developmental norms, or a narrow, cultural bias towards western expectations for family life. However, a rights-based approach does also offer a way of understanding a major anomaly within the field of counselling provision for children and young people. This is the pronounced influence of *context and institutional setting* on professional and ethical approaches to therapy with children and young people.

Practitioner approaches, for example, to confidentiality, can vary enormously between school, medical centre, voluntary agency and private practice, in a confusing range of apparently inconsistent policies. Given that the rights of children and young people are heavily determined by institutional context, a rights-based approach can clarify why the same young person can be offered confidentiality for contraceptive treatment in a general practitioner setting, but be effectively denied confidentiality in a secondary school, via a policy-based requirement for prior parental permission to access counselling (Jenkins, 2013a, 2013b).

## CURRENT ISSUES WITHIN *RULE-BASED* AND *OUTCOME* APPROACHES TO ETHICS

There are a number of crucial ethical principles contained in the BACP Ethical Framework, drawn from a wider tradition of discussion on ethics. These principles include *beneficence*, that is, promoting welfare, and *non-maleficence*, that is, avoiding harm. Given some of the factors referred to previously, such as the vulnerability of children and young people, their developmental immaturity and their dependence on adult caretakers, ethical discussion about work with this client group often seeks to emphasise the need to promote welfare and avoid harm, at the expense of limiting autonomy. A consequent shift towards a rule-following approach seems to be explicit in BACP-endorsed literature on safeguarding, with the strong recommendation that 'All therapists should comply with child protection law' (Mitchels and Bond, 2010: 38). This statement appears to present safeguarding law and practice in education as the template for good practice for *all* work with children and young people, rather than considering how best practice needs to take account of differing opportunities and constraints for promoting adolescent autonomy, as, for example, can be found in the third, or voluntary, sector.

## ETHICAL CHALLENGES TO MAINTAINING COUNSELLING CONFIDENTIALITY

No conscientious counsellor would want to place, or leave, a child or young person at evident risk of harm. However, the reality is that many young clients are already engaged in risky behaviour, or have a history of being abused, *before* coming into therapy. Adopting an ethically informed stance of always reporting such risk or harm, against the client's expressed wishes, runs the risk of breaking the therapeutic alliance, and even of the client later retracting, or minimising, their original disclosures. Daniels and Jenkins present a sustained argument for providing 'confidential spaces' in working with children and young people, and suggest possible factors to consider, in deciding whether to initiate a report to the authorities (2010: 99). This stance receives support from a perhaps surprising quarter. The National Society for the Prevention of Cruelty to Children (NSPCC) presented evidence to the Laming Review (2009), which argued for a 'mixed economy' of services for children, offering differing levels of confidentiality, in order to provide a range of choices and appropriate support for children and young people (2008: 32).[3]

Confidential counselling can offer a safe space for young clients to disclose very private material, often relating to risk of harm or experience of abuse. Research by Rees et al. (n: 24) emphasises the key *relational dimension* to such disclosures, that is, 'a consistent relationship with a professional they felt they could trust' (2010: 52). This finding is paralleled by Ungar et al. (2009) researching patterns of disclosure of abuse by young people in Canada (n: 1621). They describe such disclosure as 'an interactive process', a 'co-construction'. Disclosure of abuse depended heavily on the young person's perception of the *quality* of their relationship with a trusted adult.

Brown (2006) found that school counsellors (n: 30) were often challenged by dilemmas around confidentiality, with competing demands for information from head or class teachers, and parents. Jenkins and Palmer (2012) found, in a relatively small-scale survey (n: 6), that counsellors worked to protect client confidentiality as far as possible, with the exception of overt child protection incidents, in order to manage high levels of risk for young clients, without breaking the therapeutic frame. In a relatively rare piece of research, on the perceived benefits of supervision for school guidance counsellors in Australia, McMahon and Patton (n: 51) reported on the value of supervision as ongoing support, in 'reducing the professional isolation' of counsellors facing ethical and professional dilemmas (2000: 344).

## KEY ISSUES AND CONCERNS IN ETHICAL PRACTICE WITH CHILDREN AND YOUNG PEOPLE

It is, perhaps, evident from the foregoing discussion, that there are no easy answers, in exploring ethical practice in therapy with children and young people. This discussion will now focus on key areas presenting a major challenge to therapists:

1. ethical issues in contracting;
2. working with diversity;
3. ethics in counselling research with children and young people.

---

[3]At this point, you can refer to Counselling MindEd (free online training material) (www.minded.org. uk): Jenkins, P. (2014) *Confidentiality, Consent and Capacity and Ethical Frameworks*. MindEd.

# Ethical issues in contracting

The process of contracting with the child or young person is important, for clarifying mutual expectations in therapy. This needs to be done in age-appropriate language, geared to the child or young person's level of understanding and verbal ability. For a younger child, starting play therapy will require a very different type of explanation from that needed for an older teenager entering into therapeutic work with a mutually agreed focus. The younger the child, the more likely it is that parents, or adult caretakers, will be party to the therapeutic contract. In law, children and young people cannot enter into a contract, with certain very specific exceptions, so any contract for payment will need to be made with parents, or those with parental or other formal responsibility for the child. The contract then essentially requires all three parties, that is, the child, therapist and those paying for the therapy, to agree the form, focus and duration of the therapy, with discussion obviously taking account of the child's level of understanding. Child psychoanalysts have pointed out that contractual therapy is usually initiated by the parents, as the child may have limited understanding of their own distress, or that their behaviours are becoming problematic for others, or, indeed, of what therapy itself entails. As Anna Freud expressed it, with regard to therapy for younger children: 'The situation lacks everything which seems indispensable in the case of the adult: insight into illness, voluntary decision, and the wish to be cured' (Freud, 1974 [1927]: 6).

Contracting, from a rights-based approach, is consistent with honouring the child's right to participate in decisions, within the limits of their understanding. From an ethical point of view, the counsellor needs to work within the limits of her own professional competence, to refer to more a specialist service if necessary, not prolong the therapy beyond the point at which it appears to be of value to the client and to clarify limits to confidentiality regarding any disclosures of abuse, or parental access to detailed information on the therapy itself.

With older children, it is important to spell out the limits to confidentiality very clearly within the contracting process, as young people may not fully appreciate the contextual constraints on reporting disclosures. Research suggests that retaining some element of *control* over disclosures is very important to this older age group, in terms of maintaining their trust in the therapeutic alliance (Rees et al., 2010).

# Working with diversity

Therapists are increasingly required to embrace diversity as a core part of their therapeutic work, in turn reflecting the increasingly diverse nature of society. Counselling may be provided for children and young people who are refugees, or asylum seekers, carers for others or who are 'looked-after children' in the care system, or with mental health problems, or from black and minority ethnic (BME) backgrounds. Young clients may have been disadvantaged by social class, insecure housing, having special educational needs or low educational achievement, or a lack of parental support, for example, through a parent being in prison, or an ex-offender. They may identify as being lesbian, gay, bisexual, transgendered, queer or questioning (LGBTQ+) or be subject to bullying, harassment or discrimination. Counsellors are thus required to incorporate working with diversity into their daily practice.

In terms of ethics, working with client diversity has two main sources within the BACP Ethical Framework. The first flows from a commitment to clients, that is, a requirement to show our respect, by 'valuing each client as a unique person' (BACP, 2018: 7). Second, there is the ethical principle of justice, namely that of providing 'the fair and impartial treatment of all clients and the provision of adequate services' (BACP, 2018: 11).

Any of the distinct and overlapping aspects of diversity outlined above could be the focus of detailed exploration, but we will look briefly at one emerging area, which has received relatively little attention in the past. The counselling agency, Childline, has recorded a significant increase in counselling sessions on the topic of sexuality, gender identity and transgenderism, or gender dysphoria, to use a more diagnostic language (NSPCC, 2016: 8). Young callers have described feeling 'trapped' in the wrong body, and may be left feeling overwhelmed and confused about their gender. One anonymous young person was described as saying:

> I'm feeling really down at the moment. I want to come out as transgender but I'm not sure how to talk about it with my family. The only person I have told other than Childline is some trans people who I met online. (NSPCC, 2016: 22)

Counsellors thus need to adapt to the rapidly changing world encountered by young people, often negotiated online, as with this caller, and to promote an effective, ethically informed, therapeutic response to their needs.

## Ethics in counselling research with children and young people

Counselling research activity with children is driven by the need to promote the well-being of children. However, research with children is also heavily influenced by the need to avoid causing harm to them, on account of their age and vulnerability, both physical and emotional. The major safeguard employed, to promote the rights of children within research and to protect them from harm, is via applying the concept of *informed consent*. Children, and their parents or caretakers, need to be able to give valid consent, on the basis of being provided with sufficient information, so as to make a reasoned choice as to whether or not to participate in any research activity.

Following the Inquiries at Alder Hey Hospital in Liverpool and at Bristol Royal Infirmary, more stringent conditions have been introduced, to protect the rights of parents and children taking part in both medical and social research. Department of Health guidance defines informed consent as being 'at the heart of ethical research' (DoH, 2005: 7). This concept is also emphasised by relevant professional codes of ethics (BACP, 2018). The *age* of the child taking part in research is seen as a key factor. The BPS code on Human Research Ethics requires that children and young people under 16 need to have consent from their parents, in order to participate (BPS, 2014: 32), unless this is in a school or institutional setting, and where there is judged to be no significant risk (2014: 17).

Research ethics committees have been heavily criticised for introducing bureaucratic procedures into the research process. These procedures can also be notoriously risk-averse, regarding research with children. The effect has been, arguably, to limit counselling research with some marginalised groups of children and young people, seen to be 'high-risk' in research terms, such as LGTBQ+ (McDermott, 2010), or young women with eating disorders (Halse and Honey, 2005). From a *rights-based perspective*, research committees may thus be in danger of adopting a paternalist or protectionist approach, but at the cost of denying the potential for *autonomy* of young research subjects. This risk-averse stance is therefore likely to further limit and constrain research into key sensitive areas, such as young people experiencing transgender issues.

Seen from a narrowly legal perspective, research codes may also be in danger of making a number of errors with regard to children taking part in counselling research. First, the law requires only the lower standard of *consent* for research participation (other than clinical trials), rather than the higher, ethically driven standard of *informed consent* (Masson, 2004: 50). Second, children under 16 in England and Wales can consent on their own to taking part in research, on the basis of their demonstrating 'sufficient understanding', following the *Gillick* decision. This view is also clearly stated in the Mental Health Act Code of Practice (DoH, 2015: 176).

Best practice in counselling research ethics continues to rest on the process of obtaining informed consent from children, and, in the case of younger children, also from their parents or caretakers. The process of obtaining informed consent from a younger research participant is illustrated below. Here, the researcher was looking at adoption support services, and initially explained the research to the child's parent, leaving an information pack for the 8-year-old daughter. In a later phone call made by the researcher with the permission of the girl's parents, the girl asked the following questions about the research itself (DoH, 2005: 12):

- How long do you want to talk to me?
- Will you tell anyone what I say?
- Will you write down what I say?
- Will anyone reading the book know me?
- Will you all come to speak to me?
- What if I'm not sure? Can I change my mind?

In essence, this girl is covering, in her own way, the essential features of confidentiality and informed consent.

## Case Study: Richmond Moves to Reassure Critics over Catholic 'Counselling' Body in Schools

The London Borough of Richmond upon Thames has tried to reassure critics about its decision to award an £89,000 contract to the Catholic Children's Society to offer counselling and support to children in the borough's schools. It comes after Baroness Jenny Tonge – an ex-MP for Richmond Park – said: 'It is unfair and irrational for the council to impose Catholic thinking on the entire population of young people in this borough, the vast majority of whom are not Catholic or may have no religion at all'.

But Richmond Council insisted that staff from the Catholic Children's Society were committed 'first and foremost' to their professional standards and 'not by standards of the Catholic Church'. The Society, which is accredited by the British Association for Counselling and Psychotherapy, said in a statement that its counsellors respect other beliefs and would not try to convert or pass judgement on children.

It said: 'Issues raised in counselling are therefore explored in a way which respects the autonomy of the individual receiving counselling. On matters pertaining to sexual health, such as contraception and teenage pregnancy, we ensure that young people are referred to medical health services where the appropriate professional advice and guidance can be given. In particular, young people who come to our counsellors because they are unsure about their sexuality and may be frightened and confused are treated with sensitivity. On the matter of homophobic bullying in schools, we work with students to use the appropriate policies and procedures within schools to address this.'

The Society was required to sign the Council's equalities policy before it won the contract in February (20 May 2011; abridged. Reprinted with the kind permission of the National Secular Society. Available at: www.secularism.org.uk/richmond-moves-to-reassure-criti.html, accessed 12 November 2012).

## Key Learning

- Ethics is concerned with addressing, and attempting to find answers to, key therapeutic dilemmas.
- Professional codes of ethics, such as the BACP Ethical Framework (2018) offer a *framework*, to support counsellors in responding to both everyday and more complex and unusual challenges to therapeutic practice.
- Approaches to ethics can include rule-following, outcomes-based and the explicitly rights-based model underpinning the arguments put forward in this chapter.
- This chapter follows a very broad distinction, made between *children*, that is, 6–11 years, who are assumed not to be mature enough to make decisions for their own

care, and *young people*, that is, 11–18 years, who may have developed sufficient maturity to do so.

- Counselling work with children and young people is often considered to be a distinct field in terms of ethics, because of the child or young person's developmental, physical and emotional vulnerability, requiring correspondingly higher levels of ethical awareness and therapeutic competence from practitioners.

## Summary

This chapter has explored and discussed:

- Different approaches to ethics within counselling and psychotherapy, and issues of concern to practitioners with regard to counselling younger and more vulnerable clients.
- The value of adopting a rights-based approach to addressing ethical dilemmas in therapy with children and young people, and an exploration of several key areas of concern to therapists, including contracting, and undertaking research with children.
- Recent research evidence on how practitioners work in practice with some of the key issues confronting them in their day-to-day therapy with children and young people.

## Discussion Questions

1. What are the rights of children and young people in the situation discussed above?
2. How can the rights of children and young people be maintained and protected in this situation?
3. How might the rights of children (i.e. aged 6–11 years) be different from those of young people (i.e. aged 11–18 years) when accessing counselling from this agency?

Turn to p.448 for possible answers.

## Develop Your Skills

1. Read the case study opposite:
   - Should counselling services be awarded to faith-based organisations?
   - What ethical issues might this faith-based counselling provision raise for children and young people accessing this service?

*(Continued)*

(Continued)

    ○ How might the professional and ethical standards of a faith-based counselling service be monitored, in order to ensure compliance with equal opportunities principles?

2. Look at the ethical principles contained in the BACP Ethical Framework (2018).

    ○ Which of these principles are potentially *consistent* with faith-based provision of a counselling service for children and young people?

    ○ Which principles might potentially *conflict* with faith-based counselling provision for children and young people?

    ○ How might any such ethical conflicts be addressed and resolved?

3. Review the material in this chapter on approaches to ethics, that is,

    ○ rule-following;

    ○ outcomes-based;

    ○ rights-based.

4. How might each of these ethical approaches be applied to this situation? Where would the significant differences, if any, be found between these approaches?

## Background Material on Activities and Case Study

- In 2009, the Catholic Children's Society withdrew from the process of approving same-sex adopters, on the grounds that this was incompatible with the teachings of the Church. This requirement was brought into law by the Equality Act (Sexual Orientation) Regulations of 2007.
- The decision by Richmond Council to award a contract for the provision of counselling services to the Catholic Children's Society was criticised by gay, secular and humanist organisations, as being likely to lead to potential bias against, or exclusion from, helping services, of young people, given the religious beliefs of the provider.
- The Catholic Children's Society is accredited by the BACP, and must comply with its Ethical Framework (2018). It is also subject to the complaints and disciplinary procedures of the BACP.
- The Catholic Children's Society has agreed to comply with the Council's equalities policy, as a necessary part of the process of being awarded the contract. The Catholic Children's Society has also stated that it will respect the autonomy of children and young people, make appropriate referrals to medical and sexual health centres, and respond sympathetically to young people experiencing homophobic bullying in schools and elsewhere.

## Using Different Models of Ethics with the Case Study

*Rule-following approach*: The counselling provision could be monitored by the Council and by the BACP, or by an independent body, to ensure compliance with the existing equalities policy and with key ethical principles, such as autonomy and justice, drawn from the BACP Ethical Framework.

*Outcomes approach*: The provision could be monitored and evaluated by the Council, BACP or by an independent body, to ensure a continuing rate of referrals to gay counselling organisations, and to sexual health clinics. Rates of access (or non-access) by young people from a range of religious backgrounds, race, ethnicity and sexual orientation could be audited, to identify the effects of faith-based provision.

*Rights-based approach*: The ongoing practice of the agency could be monitored and evaluated, to identify the extent to which attitudes and professional counselling practice reflected particular models of rights, for example, potential denial of rights to gay and lesbian young people; welfare rights of provision and protection from harm; rights to participation in decision-making; and rights to autonomy consistent with the *Gillick* decision.

# Further Reading

British Association for Counselling and Psychotherapy (BACP) (2018) *Ethical Framework for the Counselling Professions*. Lutterworth: BACP.

Daniels, D. and Jenkins, P. (2010) *Therapy with Children: Children's Rights, Confidentiality and the Law*, 2nd edn. London: SAGE.

Jenkins, P. (2013a) *Exploring Children's Rights: A Participative Exercise to Introduce the Issues around Children's Rights in England and Wales*, 2nd edn. Brighton: Pavilion.

Jenkins, P. (2013b) *Children's Rights and Counselling*. Brighton: Pavilion.

Jenkins, P. (2017) *Professional Practice in Counselling and Psychotherapy: Ethics and the Law*. London: SAGE.

United Nations Children's Fund (UNICEF) (1989) *The United Nations Convention on the Rights of the Child 1989*. London: UNICEF.

## Online Resources

Counselling MindEd (free online training material) https://www,minded.org.uk, especially Module CMD 03: Legal and Professional Issues.

Jenkins, P. (2014) *Confidentiality, Consent and Capacity and Ethical Frameworks*. MindEd.

Jenkins, P. (2018) *Using the BACP Ethical Framework*. MindEd.

*(Continued)*

(Continued)

Jenkins, P and Williams, A. (2018) *Key Differences in Counselling Adults and Children*. MindEd.

Temenos online archive of interviews (free registration and online access for counselling students): Peter Jenkins (2015) *Working with Children and Young People: An Ethical and Legal Minefield?* https://www.onlinevents.co.uk/category/portfolio

# REFERENCES

Beauchamp, T. and Childress, J. (2008) *Principles of Biomedical Ethics*, 6th edn. Oxford: Oxford University Press.

British Association for Counselling (BAC) (1998) *Code of Ethics and Practice for Counsellors*. Rugby: BAC

British Association for Counselling and Psychotherapy (BACP) Professional Standards (2016) *Young People (11–18 Years) Training Curriculum: An Evidence-Informed Curriculum Framework for Young People*. Lutterworth: BACP.

British Association for Counselling and Psychotherapy (BACP) (2018) *Ethical Framework for the Counselling Professions*. Lutterworth: BACP.

British Psychology Society (BPS) (2009) *Code of Ethics and Conduct*. Leicester: BPS.

British Psychology Society (BPS) (2014) *Human Research Ethics*. Leicester: BPS.

Brown, A. (2006) 'In my agency it's very clear – but I can't tell you what it is': work settings and ethical challenges. *Counselling and Psychotherapy Research 6*(2): 100–107.

Daniels, D. and Jenkins, P. (2010) *Therapy with Children: Children's Rights, Confidentiality and the Law*, 2nd edn. London: SAGE.

Department of Health (DoH) (2005) *Research Governance Framework for Health and Social Care*, 2nd edn. London: DoH.

Department of Health (DoH) (2015) *Mental Health Act 1983 Code of Practice*. London: DoH.

Everall, R. and Paulson, B. (2002) The therapeutic alliance: adolescent perspectives. *Counselling and Psychotherapy Research 2*(2): 78–87.

Finkenauer, C., Engels, R. and Meus, W. (2002) Keeping secrets from parents: advantages and disadvantages of secrecy in adolescence. *Journal of Youth and Adolescence 31*(2): 123–136.

Freud, A. (1974 [1927]) *Introduction to Psychoanalysis*. London: Hogarth.

Halse, C. and Honey, A. (2005) Unraveling ethics: illuminating the moral dilemmas of research ethics. *Signs: Journal of Women in Culture and Society 30*(4): 2141–2162.

Health and Care Professions Council (HCPC) (2016) *Standards of Conduct, Performance and Ethics*. London: HCPC.

Jenkins, P. (2010) Having confidence in therapeutic work with children and young people: constraints and challenges to confidentiality. *British Journal of Guidance and Counselling 38*(3): 263–274.

Jenkins, P. (2011) *A Confidential Space: Ethical Considerations When Counselling Children and Young People*. DVD. Counselling DVDs, in association with University of Wales: Newport.

Jenkins, P. (2013a) *Exploring Children's Rights: A Participative Exercise to Introduce the Issues around Children's Rights in England and Wales*, 2nd edn. Brighton: Pavilion.

Jenkins, P. (2013b) *Children's and Young Person's Rights to Counselling: A Participative Exercise to Introduce the Issues around Children's Rights in England and Wales and Their Access to Counselling*. Brighton: Pavilion.

Jenkins, P. (2017) *Professional Practice in Counselling and Psychotherapy: Ethics and the Law*. London: SAGE.

Jenkins, P. and Palmer, J. (2012) 'At risk of harm?' An exploratory study of school counsellors in the UK, their perceptions of confidentiality, information-sharing and risk management. *British Journal of Guidance and Counselling* 40(5): 545–559.

Laming, Lord (2009) *The Protection of Children in England: A Progress Report*. HC 330. London: Stationery Office.

LeSurf, A. and Lynch, G. (1999) Exploring young people's perceptions relevant to counselling: a qualitative study. *British Journal of Guidance and Counselling* 27(2): 231–243.

Masson, J. (2004) The legal context. In: Fraser, S., Ding, S., Kellett, M. and Robinson, C. (eds) *Doing Research with Children and Young People*. London: SAGE/Open University, pp. 43–58.

McDermott, E. (2010) *Researching and Monitoring Adolescent Sexual Orientation*. London: Equalities and Human Rights Commission.

McMahon, M. and Patton, W. (2000) Conversations on clinical supervision: benefits perceived by school counsellors. *British Journal of Guidance and Counselling* 28(3): 339–351.

Mitchels, B. and Bond, T. (2010) *Essential Law for Counsellors and Psychotherapists*. London: BACP/SAGE.

National Society for the Prevention of Cruelty to Children (NSPCC) (2008) *Evidence to Lord Laming's Review of Child Protection*. London: NSPCC.

National Society for the Prevention of Cruelty to Children (NSPCC) (2016) *It turned out someone did care: Childline Annual Review 2015/16*. London: NSPCC.

Rees, G., Gorin, S., Jobe, A., Stein, M., Medforth, R. and Goswami, H. (2010) *Safeguarding Young People: Responding to Young People Aged 11 to 17 Who Are Maltreated*. London: Children's Society.

Ungar, M., Barter, K., McConnell, S., Tutty, L. and Fairholm, J. (2009) Patterns of abuse disclosure among youth. *Qualitative Social Work* 8: 341–356.

United Nations Children's Fund (UNICEF) (1989) *The United Nations Convention on the Rights of the Child 1989* London: UNICEF.

# 19

# INCLUSION: WORKING WITH DIFFERENCE

## DIVINE CHARURA, TOM MCANDREW AND SUE PATTISON

This chapter will discuss:

- The importance of transcultural working with children and young people
- Neurological development and damage due to traumatic experiences related to diversity such as disability, discrimination or asylum and its causes
- Communicating with deaf young people
- Communication with children and young people who have learning disabilities

## INTRODUCTION

Over the past couple of decades, the importance of the diversity of children and its impact on bio-psycho-social development has continued to be recognised as an important factor to consider when working with children. It is generally now accepted that poverty, violence, chaos/neglect at home, pollution, malnutrition and abuse are all factors that have an impact on both neurological development and emotional processing (Hayasaki, 2016; Immordino-Yang, 2017). With this understanding it is clear that working with children and young people in therapeutic settings is work that is highly important and work that has many dimensions of influence. Children and young people are a heterogeneous group with diversity in language, culture, family histories, social classes and experiences of life events. For those who come for counselling or are in contact with diverse therapeutic/care services, their experiences may include abuse, neglect, adoption, bereavement, and other multiple levels of loss and trauma. Such diversity of experiences and backgrounds has led to the development of specialist transcultural and diversity practice. It is not possible to cover the full range of diversity and related counselling practices in this chapter. However, this chapter can be viewed as a taster, something to stimulate further thinking on the overt and covert aspects of diversity. The authors have knowledge and experience in the fields of counselling, psychotherapy, education and working in practice with the diverse range of young clients referred to in the text. Divine and Sue are researchers, psychotherapists and educationalists, whilst Tom is a qualified and experienced teacher of the deaf. Each of us has developed a range of skills and techniques to aid communication and we have learnt from each other through collaborating on the writing of this chapter. At the heart of our work we share fundamental values, those of acceptance, empowerment, the rights of the child, inclusion and a love of humanity.

## THE IMPORTANCE OF TRANSCULTURAL WORKING WITH CHILDREN AND YOUNG PEOPLE

Transcultural and intercultural therapy was pioneered in response to dissatisfaction of therapists trying to apply Eurocentric models of training and practice in their work with non-European migrants and their families (Kareem and Littlewood, 1992; Lago, 2011). Differences in cultural, racial, ethnic class and diversity of family practices are important aspects to consider when thinking about the wider impact of these factors on individual children. It is also important to consider the socio-political and economic influences on the therapeutic relationship.

Within the past two decades many parts of the world, including within the UK, have become increasingly multicultural. This has influenced further development of transcultural counselling and multicultural practice within therapy (Lago, 2011). As such, this way of working has permeated not only in working with adults in therapy but also in working with children and young people whose wider experiences are reflected in therapy, and they show how they are increasingly influenced and affected by not only personal but also wider societal and cultural issues. Several factors are central to transcultural counselling, including the importance of the awareness and development of skills in meeting the needs of children and young people from diverse backgrounds in the therapeutic relationship, and counsellor self-reflection in responding to dynamics and interventions specific to working with diversity and within transcultural settings. Griffin (2008) highlighted the importance of inclusion, equality and diversity in working with children. All these factors inform practitioners' thinking when assessing children, and will influence decision-making as well as the therapeutic process when issues of race, culture, disability, ethnicity discrimination and education are taken into account. The role of therapy with children and young people is to provide a safe and ethical way to explore their experiences, unpack their problem story and its cultural underpinnings, explore their concept of self as a result of the experience and also to make visible information or perspectives that are neglected through the problem story filter (Beaudoin, 2004, 2005).

Therapists have noted that clinical practice and research indicate just how important it is for the therapist to both respect and acknowledge diversity and difference in the therapeutic setting (Lago, 2006; Griffin, 2008; Charura and Paul 2015). That is, the capacity of therapists to recognise and value unconditionally the (diverse) clients and their circumstances. Smith and Widdowson (2003) highlighted the importance of child-centred practice. They identified the disadvantages and experiences faced by black, disabled or working class children. They presented a framework to work from and stated that children who are different will be acutely aware of their difference and hence will need affirmation for that difference. Children and young people from minority ethnic groups have specific identity needs relating to knowledge about their cultural roots/identity and hence it is important to respond to this as to ignore it may disadvantage them in later life in their understanding and acceptance or comfort of self (Smith and Widdowson, 2003). Furthermore, Charura (2012) highlighted the importance of therapists and professionals carefully considering the hypersensitivity and the skills necessary in working with children and young people. When working with difference, transcultural counselling is an example of working with diversity in children that embraces the child's diversity/difference. It uses the recognition that within the therapeutic relationship the child can be helped to integrate their experience and accept their identity and cultural roots (Charura, 2012).

## COUNSELLING CHILDREN IMPACTED BY ABUSE OR TRAUMA RELATED TO THEIR DIFFERENCE

Unsurprisingly, the children and young people who access therapy or services are often referred because they have experienced abuse or trauma related to their difference, which has had a negative impact on their lives. At times they may want to deal with existential experiences such as bereavement, abandonment, loss, disability, discrimination, migration or other experiences affecting them. They may also want to work through other aspects of themselves such as sexuality, body image or psychological distress, for example, depression, anxiety, psychosis, eating disorders, obsessive compulsive problems and so on. In thinking about this it is also important to therefore understand that children and young people may have their own ways of understanding their experience that are different to how therapists or professionals may see it. Therefore, it is essential that we continue as therapists to become aware of the growing range of modalities to support children and the research evidence of their effectiveness.

As with any therapeutic approach, such new approaches need to be viewed with caution and the first intention should be 'to do no harm'. There is a large body of literature and research pointing out the dangers of retraumatising children by involving them in a retelling of their story, including traumatic experiences (White and Epston, 1990; Durrant and White, 1992; Adam-Westcott and Isenbart, 1995; White, 2004). Many of these articles are drawn from family therapy theory (narrative therapy), which engages people in a process that distances them from their experience of problems in ways that can allow them to re-examine, reflect and deconstruct problems' influence over their lives (Freedman and Combs, 1996; Beaudoin, 2005).

Scott and Stradling (2006) provide information on another approach to working with children and young people experiencing post-traumatic stress. They suggest four goals that counsellors can work towards:

1. Developing a strong therapeutic alliance/relationship of safety with the child/young person.
2. Obtaining a clear description of the trauma or experience the child or young person is presenting.
3. Focusing on working with problematic behaviours (we assert here the importance of not labelling the child as problematic or difficult).
4. Helping the young client to understand the connections between thoughts and feelings.

As with all interventions that value anti-discriminatory practice, this way of working should also at all times consider the differences in children and young people and the influences of culture/experiences on the articulation of emotions and feelings, along with the child's willingness to engage with the therapeutic process.

Therapeutic interventions for children who have had difficult and traumatic experiences can be invaluable, and it is important that counsellors can offer supportive and therapeutic interventions that are reparatory and can respond to the needs of a diverse young population. Engaging children and young people in therapy or services is specialist work, which needs to be carried out with expertise, caution and care in order to avoid further damage or retraumatisation, leaving both the young person and therapist stuck. Professional organisations such as the British Association for Counselling and Psychotherapy (BACP), the United Kingdom Council for Psychotherapy (UKCP), the British Psychological Society (BPS) and the Academy of Play and Child Psychotherapy (APAC) provide good practice guidance for working with children and young people and ethical frameworks that can help counsellors to make decisions about their practice based on judgements made in relation to potential harm weighed against the benefits of individual therapies. The issues discussed in this chapter therefore raise important points for therapeutic arenas in the offering of therapeutic modalities that employ a true valuing of diversity in helping children and young people.

## Case Study: Ishtar

Ishtar is a young Syrian girl, aged 15 years. She came to the UK from Syria as an unaccompanied minor over 3 years ago following serious political violence aimed against her, which included rape and torture. Ishtar also witnessed most of her family members being killed.

*(Continued)*

(Continued)

She was referred by a health professional in the UK to an organisation that works with refugees and asylum seekers following serious concerns of depression, obsessive compulsive behaviours, which included numerous rituals such as counting and continued handwashing, as well as an episode of self-harm. This episode followed reports of being bullied in school and being called names because she is a foreigner/refugee.

Initially in therapy, despite being supported to communicate by a translator, Ishtar was unwilling to talk about her experiences. However, as the weeks went on Ishtar referred to her life prior to coming to the UK and in particular her childhood experiences. She was forced to be a war rebel's sex slave, and described nearly being killed on two occasions as well as witnessing the murder of her parents and young sister. In counselling, she often described how she felt that she was no longer the person she thought she would be. She stated that she had discussions with two adult women from her country she met at the Mosque she now goes to and told them about her family and her situation. She was informed by them that all her life experiences were influenced by transgenerational misfortune. She shared some of her cultural metaphors with the counsellor, including the misfortune that was often spoken about in her family when she was much younger. In working creatively with the therapist she would often draw pictures of decapitated bodies. Ishtar told her therapist that a child psychiatrist/psychologist who had worked with her in the past had suggested that any connotations of misfortune were not scientifically founded and that her rituals were a result of irrational thoughts. Ishtar shared with the therapist how she believed that her rituals would stop the war in Syria and protect other family members and young cousins whom she had been separated from. She also believed that her parents were constantly watching her and protecting her and that she could talk to them.

Issues raised in this case study include working with trauma, depression, rape, multiple levels of loss and bereavement, religion, beliefs on death and life, and also working with a young person who presents with multiple experiences/manifestation of psychological distress. It also raises questions and issues regarding the type of support that can be provided for such a young person, including the need for a translator. Thus, the case presented demonstrates the level of complexity that therapists can often find themselves working with. It is worth considering how you would work with Ishtar.

## NEUROLOGICAL DEVELOPMENT AND DAMAGE DUE TO TRAUMATIC EXPERIENCES RELATED TO DIVERSITY

Developmental processes are discussed more fully in Chapter 1. However, a brief look at neurological development here is intended to refresh the reader's memory and make the material more accessible when applied to aspects of diversity. The importance of love and attachments within primary relationships and their impact on children's mental and physical well-being is well documented (Joseph, 1999; Gerhardt, 2015). Joseph (1999) highlighted the relationship between children's experiences and neurological development at different age stages.

Van der Kolk (1994, 2005) describes the neurological impact of trauma in childhood and how the child's detachment is expressed in their body, by a 'shutting down' of sensation, the body protecting itself from trauma, for example, rape, torture and natural disasters, as experienced by some children and young people from war-torn countries who may access our counselling services as refugees. This 'shutting down' affects how the child or young person feels, learns and moves in the world as they are developing their vital physical skills. This highlights the neurological impact of trauma on children's behaviour and self-concept. This can continue to be evident in early adulthood manifesting as disruptive behaviour, inability to connect emotionally and personality complexities if therapeutic change does not occur. Cook et al. (2010) identify a wide range of areas in which deficits arise after early relational trauma: cognition, self-concept, affect regulation, attachment, biology, behavioural control and dissociation. Goldfinch (2009) concurs with this and further states that when children experience trauma early in life, when their nervous system is immature, then the development of their concept of self and of others is disturbed. She further argues that young children are more vulnerable to trauma because they are more dependent on their environment and less able to self-regulate than adults. Charura and Paul, alongside other authors (2015), offer a collection of perspectives on love and therapy in which they argue about the importance of love as a curative and reparative ingredient of therapy. They concur that therapists in their work should at all times work ethically and embrace non-discriminatory practice regardless of their modality of practice. In line with these we cite here numerous researchers have also contributed compelling arguments on the most current and innovative neurobiological, cognitive, clinical and legal research on trauma, stress memory development and diversity (Cicchetti et al., 2008; Rinne-Albers et al., 2013).

## COMMUNICATING WITH DEAF CHILDREN AND YOUNG PEOPLE

Although there are many types of disability that can affect communication in the counselling context, hearing impairment can fundamentally affect how a child or young person communicates and the quality and type of communication possible. Communicating with young deaf people can be challenging and, in order to be effective and make counselling accessible, a range of skills, some knowledge and experience is very useful. In this section we look at some of the areas you will need to consider. Over 40% of deaf people have additional special needs, such as autism, Down's syndrome or other congenital disorders, and they may have physical disabilities or may be deaf-blind. This section refers specifically to young deaf clients without additional complex needs.

## Terminology

The term 'deaf' is often used to refer to people with a hearing loss. However, 'Deaf' with a capital 'D' refers to people who identify themselves as being part of the sign language-using Deaf Community. In the UK, the Deaf Community communicates in British Sign Language (BSL). There is a spectrum of hearing loss across the frequency range and it is rarely uniform: hearing loss can be mild, moderate, severe or profound. People with mild to moderate hearing losses may refer to themselves as hearing impaired or hard of hearing. The latter term is more widely acceptable internationally, although both are used in the UK. For counselling purposes, it is important to be aware of these basic differences in terminology to minimise the risk of offence.

## Cultural and educational backgrounds

Over 90% of deaf children in the USA are born to hearing parents (Mitchell and Karchmer, 2004) and for most of these hearing parents it comes as a shock to have a deaf child, especially if there has been no history of deafness in the family. They often go through a grieving process and may have difficulties accepting their child's deafness. Hearing parents of deaf children rarely have sign language skills at the time of diagnosis and, although some parents may take on board learning about deafness, baby signing and BSL, others may choose not to learn BSL – they may not have the necessary motivation to learn this language or indeed be advised not to learn it by some, otherwise well-meaning professionals.

Many deaf children of hearing parents (DCHP) take an oral pathway in education and are fully integrated into mainstream schools or go to mainstream schools with a hearing impaired (HI) unit attached. Consequently, these children have not grown up as members of the Deaf Community and may not have developed the sign language skills that enable communication with this community. They do not necessarily share the same cultural values and could feel they belong more to the wider hearing community, an issue around diversity that counsellors may need to be aware of.

Of the 10% of deaf children of deaf parents (DCDP), many are members of the Deaf Community from birth since they more are likely to grow up with BSL as a preferred/first language and have contact with Deaf Clubs and organisations associated with the Deaf Community from an early age, which helps to nurture a distinctive Deaf culture. Deaf parents are more likely to opt for a sign-based educational pathway (e.g. Total Communication or Sign Bilingual Education) for their deaf children. However, it needs to be emphasised that some DCDP take oral pathways in education and some DCHP take sign-based educational pathways, which means that forms of communication cannot be assumed by the counsellor. The pathway taken depends on the level of hearing loss, aids used (e.g. hearing aids or cochlear implants) and the availability/type of specialised deaf education institutions near to where they live and, of course, parental choice.

Deaf children, especially teenagers and young adults, could be very confused as to whether they belong to the Deaf Community or not. A deaf child whose preferred language is spoken English and who has more of an affinity with the wider hearing society may join the Deaf Community through later association with its members. It is also important to realise there are different sign languages for each country and there are regional variations within countries too. Deaf people from ethnic minorities in the UK will also have been exposed to their parents' native language (whether through speech sounds or writing) as well as another sign language. Deaf and young people who have sought refuge in the UK with or without their families may be more vulnerable regarding lack of communication than others due to their exposure to trauma, loss and unavailability of sign language translators from their linguistic or cultural background. In addition to these difficulties, some young people may have been deafened through the violence of armed conflicts without any opportunity for treatment or education in forms of communication. Their experience can be extremely traumatic and enduring. For the counsellor, the context or setting they work in is likely to determine the resources available and whether the communication needs of the deaf child or young person can be met. For example, in a school for the deaf, the counsellor may sign, or there will be a support worker with signing skills. On the other hand, in a mainstream school, there may not be the communication resources available to support counselling a deaf young person.

## Methods of communication

There are various ways of communicating with young deaf people. BSL and other sign languages have already been mentioned as well as speech for mild to moderately deaf people (or deaf people with cochlear implants). However, there are also other sign systems that can aid communication with young deaf people. Although the examples presented here cannot be detailed in a chapter, there is much information available through a range of websites. Examples of other sign systems include: Sign Supported English (SSE), Manually Coded English (MCE), Seeing Exact English (SEE), Signed English (SE), Cued Speech, Paget–Gorman, Makaton and Finger-spelling (Swanwick et al., 2016). These systems are mainly used in deaf education to help support and encourage speech, written grammar, spelling (Finger-spelling) or to communicate on a basic level with deaf people with complex needs (Makaton). It must be emphasised that they are not languages; they are methods of communication used by professionals and deaf people in specific contexts.

This section does not describe the full variety of communication systems in detail. However, if a young client does express a wish for one of the above systems to be used, then the counsellor may consider learning more about this particular method or contacting a competent user to act as a form of interpreter. Another aid to communication is lip-speaking. A trained lip-speaker can use facial expression and clearer lip patterns to make the speaker more easily understood. This is an option that also needs to be taken into consideration by the counsellor.

## Long-term preparation for counselling deaf children and young people

Going on a Deaf Awareness course is a fundamental starting point for counsellors who want to work with young deaf clients. The next step would be to start learning BSL, ideally progressing to a highly competent level but at least to a basic level so that introductions and basic conversations can be held. This would reassure the young Deaf client that their counsellor is aware of their language and culture and should have the effect of putting them at ease and promoting the development of a stronger therapeutic relationship.

Eventually being a fluent signer of BSL will enable a counsellor to directly communicate effectively to young members of the Deaf Community without recourse to booking an interpreter. Two-way rather than three-way communication will lead to more effective counselling and safeguard against confidentiality issues (interpreters, by the very nature of their job, will be privy to very personal information about the deaf client). However, counsellors cannot assume that young deaf clients value confidentiality in the same way that hearing clients do; by the very nature of the world in which a deaf young person operates, familiarity may foster greater trust and confidence. If a BSL/English interpreter is required, BSL users usually have a preferred interpreter who may be a family member or someone they use on a regular basis in contexts other than counselling. The young deaf person may feel more comfortable with an interpreter they are familiar with. Many parents and guardians of deaf young people will book an interpreter themselves, but it is wise to check just in case the family expects the counsellor to organise this service. Also, it is prudent to have the contact details of one or two BSL/English interpreter agencies in case the client's usual interpreter is not available. The issue of funding for interpretation services should be addressed by all counsellors prior to beginning a therapeutic intervention. The initial assessment stage of counselling may need to be longer to make sure that the needs of the young client are met in the most effective and appropriate way.

There may be other difficulties around the provision of communication support for young deaf clients, for example, family members who take on the role of interpreters for their children may not be ideal during counselling sessions because their signing skills may not necessarily be of a high enough level. In addition, the child's trust or confidence in their family members, especially when discussing sensitive personal feelings, cannot be guaranteed. Most competent BSL/English interpreters will be members of the Association of Sign Language Interpreters (ASLI) and work to a Code of Practice that includes confidentiality in relation to the content of their interpretation.

To offer inclusion in counselling services, Childline launched a deaf counselling service in 2017, giving deaf children the option to chat in sign language directly to a counsellor or via an interpreter, to use online chat or email. Considering that deaf and disabled children are three times more likely to be abused or neglected than non-deaf and disabled children and are also less likely to receive the protection and support they need when they have been abused, this provides a welcome and essential service. In addition, deaf children and young people are 60% more likely to suffer mental health problems than other children (Public Health England, 2016).

## Deaf Awareness

The following guidance cannot replace a course on Deaf Awareness but it can help counsellors with the basics. Regardless of the client's level of hearing loss, it is good practice always to face the client whilst talking/communicating, to speak clearly and evenly rather than exaggerating facial expressions. The background environment is also important, with the counsellor being more visible when sitting in front of a plain background, rather than, for example, highly patterned wallpaper or pictures. It is more difficult for a young deaf client to lip-read the counsellor or interpret signs, if using BSL, with an irregular background.

It is useful for counsellors to have an awareness of the range of technology to help deaf young people maximise the use of their residual hearing (remember, most deaf people are not profoundly deaf). For many, a particular model of behind-the-ear (BTE) digital hearing aid or one of the other types of hearing aid will be worn. More and more deaf young people have cochlear implants and the recent trend is for young people to have cochlear implants for both ears. However, these are simply aids to using residual hearing – not cures for deafness.

When using a BSL/English interpreter, it is good practice for the counsellor always to address the client, not the interpreter. It is useful to be aware that there will be a short time delay between the words you have spoken and the interpreter's signed translation. BSL interpreters work to a strict Code of Practice and, if there is only one translator, the counsellor should make sure they give the interpreter short breaks every 15 minutes since it is a very intense and tiring activity. If you want to get your client's attention, tap them on the shoulder or give a hand signal that is appropriate and clearly visible (mainly for severe to profoundly deaf clients; for mild to moderately deaf clients this may not be required). This may go against some counsellors' practice of not touching clients. However, to provide an appropriate service to young deaf clients, flexibility rather than rigidity is essential.

## COUNSELLING YOUNG CLIENTS WHO HAVE INTELLECTUAL DISABILITIES

If we could offer one piece of advice or guidance to counsellors wanting to be more inclusive of children and young people who have intellectual disabilities, we would say: 'be proactive'. The concept of being proactive was addressed by Viktor Frankl in his book *Man's Search for Meaning* (1992) and has at its heart a process of taking responsibility, not looking to others or outside circumstances, but having the courage, perseverance, awareness of the existence of choices, regardless of the situation or context. Martin (2001) refers to Frankl's work in his assertion that 'the active choice is to play the game; the proactive choice is to change the rules of the game, especially when the rules of engagement are unfair'. The rules of 'the game' are inherently unfair for children and young people who have an intellectual disability, present during childhood, or acquired following disease or accident, impacting on developmental processes and manifesting in a variety of ways including the presence of a significantly reduced ability to understand new or complex information, to learn new skills (impaired intelligence, usually an IQ below 70; WHO, 2003), with reduced ability to cope independently leading to impaired social functioning (DSM-5, APA, 2013; ICD-11, WHO, 2018). The major argument for specifically including young people with learning disabilities in counselling is related to human rights. Human rights policies that provide the impetus for inclusive counselling are the Disability Rights Commission Act (1999); Human Rights Act (1998); United Nations Declaration of the Rights of Disabled People (1975); United Nations Convention on the Rights of the Child (UNICEF, 1989); United Nations Standard Rules on the Equalization of Opportunities for Persons with Disabilities (1993); and the National Advisory Committee on Creative and Cultural Education (1999).

Research carried out by Pattison (2010) indicates that counsellors who are proactive in raising awareness of the service to young people, their parents or carers, and within organisations working with young people (reaching out), and who provide inclusive initial assessments, found that the level of inclusivity in their practices and processes increased and they saw more young people with learning disabilities in their counselling rooms. Similarly, a proactive use of advocacy through the young person's teacher, support worker, parent or peers improved inclusivity. Moreover, an integrated partnership approach, including building relationships with parents/carers, school staff, statutory health and social care professionals, and/or voluntary agencies and charitable trusts, raised inclusiveness in counselling. To support these processes counsellors may require specialist training in learning disability issues. In Pattison's (2010) study, linked to counsellors' expressed need for specialist training was the need for experienced supervision. In the school context counsellors' requirement for supervisors experienced in working with children and young people, along with knowledge and experience of the school context, is well documented (WAG, 2008). However, no mention is made of the value of knowledge and awareness of learning disability issues. This highlights the poor visibility of this client group in mainstream policy documents.

The most inclusive counsellors are clear about what works for them and they proactively include young people with learning disabilities in both their practices and processes. By far the most effective factor is building relationships: with the client, with members of staff who have enabling roles in schools, health and social care services, and with parents/carers. In terms of specific client work, the engagement and process of counselling is enabled through proactive relationship-building and communication. Pattison (2010) found that by trying out various imaginative and creative approaches and the use of simplified language, most importantly at the initial assessment stage, counsellors discovered ways of communicating that worked. The barriers to inclusion were largely located in systems, for example, resources, time, money and training. In order to overcome these barriers, a proactive approach to the operationalisation of equal opportunities policies is recommended, and this brings us back to the quote at the beginning of this section by Martin (2001) with reference to Frankl's (1946) work. The overt rules of the game appear inclusive, supported by policies and legislation. However, the hidden organisational, social and political discourses, or covert 'rules of the game', may differ and relate more to resource management and educational, health and social care agendas that are adopted by organisations in response to central policies, for example, meritocratic goals and league table achievements in schools and a hierarchy of resource distribution in the NHS and social care services. These dual discourses and agendas may extend into the counselling service, impacting on practices and processes in ways that can exclude some young people from counselling when they may benefit from the service, for example, referral for behavioural programmes when the young person's behaviour is an external expression of their emotional distress. Martin (2001) proposes that Viktor Frankl's proactive stance builds upon foreknowledge (intelligence) and creativity to anticipate and see situations as opportunities and to influence systems constructively for the good of the client.

## Key Learning

- In this chapter you have learnt about the importance of transcultural working with children and young people and can reflect on how this can be applied to your own practice.
- You have explored how counselling children can be impacted by abuse or trauma related to their difference.
- You have read about neurological development and the damage that can be caused to children and young people due to traumatic experiences related to diversity.
- You have had the opportunity to learn more about communicating with deaf children and young people, and ways to develop more inclusive practices and processes.
- The services provided for counselling young clients who have intellectual disabilities rely on the development of inclusive practices by counsellors. You have explored how counselling can be made more inclusive and can apply this to your own practice context.

## Summary

As identified in the introduction to this chapter, working with children and young people in therapeutic settings is specialist work. We identified that children and young people are not a homogeneous group and display diversity in language, culture, family histories, social class and life experiences. The reasons for therapy are also diverse, and young

*(Continued)*

(Continued)

people's experiences may include abuse, adoption, death of loved ones, and other psychological distress or multiple levels of loss and trauma. It has not been possible to cover the full range of diversity and related counselling practices. Therefore, this chapter has focused on:

- transcultural working with children and young people;
- neurological development and damage due to traumatic experiences related to diversity such as disability, discrimination or asylum and its causes;
- communicating with deaf young people;
- communicating with young people who have intellectual disabilities.

## Discussion Questions

1. What challenging issues can you identify in the case study – Ishtar?
2. What therapeutic approach would you take in supporting Ishtar?
3. How could you prepare for future work with deaf children and young people?

Turn to p.449 for possible answers.

## Develop Your Skills

1. Contact your local Deaf Club – the college of further education in your area will be able to provide contact details. You may be able to visit and get to know some useful contacts, building up a network to draw upon when you need a BSL translator or advice and guidance on deaf issues.
2. Look at the antidiscrimination policies in your counselling setting and assess accessibility for children and young people of difference.
3. Familiarise yourself with current language that young people use to describe their socio-political issues as well as emerging evidence-based practice.
4. Get to know the local community where you are based for your counselling work, and get a feel for issues around diversity that impact generally on that community.

## Further Reading

Charura, D. and Paul, S. (2015) *Love and Therapy: In Relationship*. London: Karnac Books.

Cicchetti, D., Goodman, G.S. and Howe, M.L. (2008) *Stress, Trauma, and Children's Memory Development: Neurobiological, Cognitive, Clinical, and Legal Perspectives*. Oxford: Oxford University Press.

Griffin, S. (2008) *Inclusion, Equality and Diversity in Working with Children*. Oxford: Heinemann.

Glickman, N.S. (2013) *Culturally Affirmative Psychotherapy with Deaf Persons*. New York: Routledge.

Hayasaki, E. (2016) How poverty changes the brain: new research reveals the connection between stress, poverty and brain development in children. *Newsweek 8*. Available at: www.newsweek.com/2016/09/02/how-poverty-affects-brains-493239.html [Accessed 25 March 2018]

Immordino-Yang, M. (2017) Embodied brains, social minds, cultural meaning: integrating neuroscientific and educational research on social-affective development. *American Educational Research Journal 54*(1): 344–367

Lago, C. (ed.) (2011) *The Handbook of Transcultural Counselling and Psychotherapy*. Maidenhead: Open University Press/McGraw-Hill.

Paul, S. and Charura, D. (2014) *An Introduction to the Therapeutic Relationship in Counselling and Psychotherapy*. London: SAGE.

Rinne-Albers, M.W., van der Wee, N.A., Lamers-Winkelman, F. and Vermeiren, R.M. (2013) Neuroimaging in children, adolescents and young adults with psychological trauma. *European Child and Adolescent Psychiatry 22*(12): 745–755.

Zand, D.H. and Pierce, K.J. (eds) (2011) *Resilience in Deaf Children: Adaptation through Emerging Adulthood*. New York: Springer.

### Online Resources

BACP website: www.bacp.co.uk, especially the BACP Children and Young People Division and the Competences for Working with Children and Young People

Counselling MindEd: https://www.minded.org.uk MN8 Cultural Competence and Equalities Issues for CYP and Families, MN 8.01, MN 8.02, CM

http://limpingchicken.com/2017/05/17/deaf-news-childline-launches-deaf-counselling-service-bsl

## REFERENCES

Adam-Westcott, J. and Isenbart, I. (1995) A journey of change through connections. In: Freedman, S. (ed.) *The Reflecting Teams in Action: Collaborative Practices in Family Therapy*. New York: Guilford Press, pp. 331–352

American Psychiatric Association (2013) *Diagnostic and Statistical Manual of Mental Disorders* (5th edn.). Washington, DC: APA.

Beaudoin, M.N. (2004) Problem with frogs, clients and therapist: a cultural discourse analysis. *Journal of Systemic Therapies* 23(3): 51–64.

Beaudoin, M.N. (2005) Agency and choice in the face of trauma: a narrative therapy map. *Journal of Systemic Therapies* 24(4): 32–50.

Charura, D. (2012) What's a disrupted and traumatic childhood got to do with it? *Exploring therapeutic ways of working following childhood disruption with asylum seekers' concept of self and identity in adulthood*. Paper presented at the Annual Conference of the UK Oral History Society – Displaced Childhoods: Oral History and Traumatic Experiences. Solent University, Southampton, UK.

Charura, D. and Paul, S. (2015) *Love and Therapy: In Relationship*. London: Karnac Books.

Cicchetti, D., Goodman, G.S. and Howe, M.L. (2008) *Stress, Trauma, and Children's Memory Development: Neurobiological, Cognitive, Clinical, and Legal Perspectives*. Oxford: Oxford University Press.

Cook, J., Biyanova, T., Elhai, J., Schnurr, P. and Cones, J. (2010) What do psychotherapists really do in practice? An internet study of over 2000 practitioners. *Psychotherapy Theory, Research, Practice and Training* 47(2): 260–267.

Counselling MindEd Scoping Report. Available at: https://www.bacp.co.uk/media/2048/counselling-minded-elearning-for-counsellors-working-with-children-young-people-rodgers.pdf [Accessed 23 March 2018]

Durrant, M. and White, C. (1992) *Ideas for Therapy with Sexual Abuse*. Adelaide: Dulwich Centre Publications.

Frankl, V.E. (2006 [1946]) *Man's Search for Meaning*. Boston, MA: Beacon Press.

Freedman, J. and Combs, G. (1996) *Narrative Therapy*. New York: Norton.

Gerhardt, S. (2015) *Why Love Matters: How Affection Shapes a Baby's Brain*, 2nd edn. London: Routledge.

Goldfinch, M. (2009) 'Putting Humpty Together Again': working with parents to help children who have experienced early trauma. *The Australian and New Zealand Journal of Family Therapy* 30(4): 284–299.

Griffin, S. (2008) *Inclusion, Equality and Diversity in Working with Children*. Oxford: Heinemann.

Hayasaki, E. (2016) How poverty changes the brain: new research reveals the connection between stress, poverty and brain development in children. *Newsweek 8*. Available at: www.newsweek.com/2016/09/02/how-poverty-affects-brains-493239.html [Accessed 25 March 2018]

Immordino-Yang, M. (2017) Embodied brains, social minds, cultural meaning: integrating neuroscientific and educational research on social-affective development. *American Educational Research Journal* 54(1): 344–367.

Joseph, R. (1999) *Neuropsychiatry, Neuropsychology, Clinical Neuroscience*, 3rd edn. Philadelphia, PA: Lippincott Williams & Wilkins.

Kareem, J. and Littlewood, R. (eds) (1992) *Intercultural Therapy*. Oxford: Blackwell.

Lago, C. (2006) *Race, Culture and Counselling: The Ongoing Challenge*. Maidenhead: Open University Press/McGraw-Hill.

Lago, C. (ed.) (2011) *The Handbook of Transcultural Counselling and Psychotherapy*. Maidenhead: Open University Press/McGraw-Hill.

Martin (2001) *Harnessing the Power of Intelligence, Counter-Intelligence and Hitch-Hiking on Surprise Events*. Toronto: Executive Organizational Press.

Mitchell, R.E. and Karchmer, M.A. (2004). Chasing the mythical ten percent: parental hearing status of deaf and hard of hearing students in the United States . *Sign Language Studies* 4(2): 138–163.

Pattison, S. (2010) Reaching out: a proactive process to include young people with learning disabilities in counselling in secondary schools in the UK. *British Journal of Guidance and Counselling* 38(3): 301–311.

Public Health England (2016). *The mental health of children and young people in England*. London: PHE

Rinne-Albers, M.W., van der Wee, N.A., Lamers-Winkelman, F. and Vermeiren, R.M. (2013) Neuroimaging in children, adolescents and young adults with psychological trauma. *European Child and Adolescent Psychiatry* 22(12): 745–755.

Scott, M.J. and Stradling, S.G. (2006) *Counselling for Post-Traumatic Stress Disorder*, 3rd edn. London: SAGE.

Smith B. and Widdowson M. (2003) 'Child-Centred Counselling', in C. Lago and B. Smith (eds), *Anti-Discriminatory Practice in Counselling and Psychotherapy*. London: Sage.

Swanwick, R., Wright, S. and Salter J. (2016). Investigating deaf children's plural and diverse use of sign and spoken languages in a super diverse context. *Applied Linguistics Review*. 7(2): 117–147.

United Nations Children's Fund (UNICEF) (1989) *The United Nations Convention on the Rights of the Child 1989*. London: UNICEF. Available at: www.unicef.org/crc.

Van der Kolk, B. (1994) The body keeps the score: memory and the evolving psychobiology of post-traumatic stress. *Harvard Psychiatric Review* 1(5): 253–265.

Welsh Assembly Government (WAG) (2008) *A National Strategy for a School-Based Counselling Service in Wales*. Cardiff: DELLS/WAG.

White, M. (2004) Value, resonance, and definitional ceremony. *International Journal of Narrative and Community Work 1*. Adelaide: Dulwich Centre Publications.

White, M. and Epston, D. (1990) *Narrative Means to Therapeutic End*. New York: Norton.

World Health Organization (WHO) (2001) *The World Health Report*. Geneva: World Health Organization.

World Health Organization (WHO) (2018) https://icd.who.int/dev11/l-m/en [Accessed 25 March 2018]

# 20

# BEREAVEMENT

## MAGGIE ROBSON

This chapter will discuss:

- Loss and bereavement
- Whether therapeutic interventions can help children and young people who have experienced significant loss
- The differences when working with children and young people
- The theoretical underpinning of the experience of grief and its relationship to attachment and developmental stages
- Issues of diversity

## INTRODUCTION: DEFINITIONS AND THE LOSS EXPERIENCE

Bereavement and loss are terms that are often used interchangeably but which have slightly different meanings. Bereavement is commonly used to mean mourning after the loss by death of a significant person in our life. Loss may be described as any loss experience that causes an individual to re-evaluate their worldview, as well as their past, present and future, as a result of that experience. Loss can thus encompass bereavement and can include the results of other experiences such as divorce, abuse, death of a pet and moving house. This re-evaluation means that we can no longer take for granted assumptions about our world; our assumptive world changes (Parkes, 1993). For example, if a young girl's mother dies, she can no longer assume that her mum will greet her at the door on her return from school. She can no longer assume she can share the ups and downs of her day with her. A small boy can no longer assume that his older brother will be there to protect him in the playground or to play football. However, we need to have assumptions in our internal world in order to function as psychologically healthy people. The process of bereavement, therefore, is about adapting to these losses in our internal world and restoring a degree of denial that life is transient and fragile.

Loss is strongly connected to change as most change involves some loss and loss always involves change. Parkes (1993) argues that bereavement may be viewed as a process of adaptation to change (a psychosocial transition) whilst also acknowledging the role of attachment in shaping our responses to loss. The significance of the loss experience may not necessarily be confined to physical loss but can be symbolic in nature, depending on the meaning the individual attributes to the experience, for example, lost childhood due to abuse.

Grief is the result of experiencing both bereavement and loss and is the process we go through when mourning. In bereavement, we may be consumed by images and thoughts of the dead person, feel overwhelmed by sadness and also experience more unexpected emotions such as guilt that we have survived or that we did not prevent the death, anger at the dead person for dying and leaving us, relief that the dead person is no longer in pain or even relief that the dead person is no longer able to harm us. In other losses we may experience a similar complex and possibly ambivalent mix of thoughts and feelings, which may have an effect upon our behaviour.

The emotions we experience when we are bereft can be overwhelming – we can feel that we will never be able to function 'normally' again or be the same as we were before the experience. Although most theories of loss and bereavement (Bowlby, 1980; Worden, 1991; Stroebe and Schut, 1999) tend to talk about adjusting to the loss and disengaging from the deceased in order to reinvest our emotional energy in others, Silverman and Klass argue that the process of mourning is about maintaining the relationship with the deceased, albeit in a different form:

> rather than emphasising letting go, the emphasis should be on negotiating and renegotiating the meaning of the loss over time. Whilst the death is permanent and unchanging, the process is not. (1996: 18)

If our loss is significant, it may be that part of us always remains grieving (Hunt, 2004). This does not mean that we cannot still lead satisfying and fulfilling lives but that our grieving self will always be with us, sometimes very much in the background of our lives, but sometimes in the forefront, and can feel as raw as when first experienced. This rawness, however, may be present less and less as time passes. The effects of loss can be imagined as being like ripples in a pond after a stone has been thrown in, with the biggest waves nearest the stone, getting smaller and gentler as they get further away. However, big waves can come and take us by surprise! The effects of loss can also be physical – we can feel as if our heart is breaking and, in fact, the experience of grief can be linked to depression, somatic symptoms and interpersonal problems (Goodman and Brown, 2008).

# IS THERAPEUTIC INTERVENTION HELPFUL WHEN CHILDREN AND YOUNG PEOPLE EXPERIENCE LOSS?

All human beings are driven to try and make sense of their experiences even though, in the case of significant loss, there may seem to be no sense to it, and the grieving process is a way of making this sense. Counselling can help us to do this but may not always be the most appropriate response for children and young people.

Bereavement and loss can be viewed as a 'natural' part of our experiencing. There is, therefore, a debate about whether counselling is appropriate for people who have experienced loss as loss is a normal and natural part of our life, not something pathological or unusual (Bonanno and Lilienfeld, 2008). Parkes (1998: 18) suggests that there is:

> no evidence that all bereaved people will benefit from counselling and research has shown no benefits to arise from the routine referral to counselling for no other reason than that they have suffered a bereavement.

However, just because these may be universal experiences, it doesn't make them less painful or individual. Grief is a process that is both unique to the loss we experience and to us as people.

Counselling, both for children and young people and for adults, can be helpful if normal social support is either not available or if it is limited in some way, and/or if the grief is complicated or the effects last for a long time. Adams (2012: 3) argues that:

> Grief is not an illness or a condition, it is normal, as are extreme responses to it. It is when these responses continue into the long term that there may be cause for concern. A young person will not get over their grief, but with timely and appropriate support, they will hopefully learn to live with it. If it is preventing them from engaging with normal life, do not hesitate to seek help. Most young people will not need professional help but some will need a bit of extra support. Others will require a more in-depth approach with bereavement counselling, or therapy.

Children and young people may have a very supportive social network but often the most intimate supporters (family and friends) are also devastated by the same loss and so are unavailable. Sometimes the young people are afraid to utilise the family support for fear of upsetting the people around them, and sometimes the people who could be of most support feel as though they haven't the knowledge or expertise to help. Adults may find it easier to deny the idea that the child might be grieving. Perhaps, because we all share a knowledge of the impact and pain of loss on ourselves, we can find it difficult to witness this in children and young people and are tempted to downplay the effect that it may be having on them. 'She's too young to understand what's happening' is not an uncommon response to a bereaved child. It can sometimes feel overwhelming for us to witness the pain of a young person and can feel more comfortable if we minimise, in our minds, the pain we are seeing.

Additionally, it is important to acknowledge that children and young people do understand death differently and grieve differently to adults, and this is sometimes misinterpreted as them being unaffected by the loss. Although they may experience the same range of feelings as an adult and process the loss in a similar way, they may lack the conceptual skills to talk about it and their distress may become apparent through their behaviour (Turner, 2006: 13–15). In my experience, therapeutic help can be of benefit when this occurs.

In situations where carers lack the confidence to work with the child or young person, perhaps the most helpful thing a professional therapist can do is to support the family/friends to support the young person. This can be done through information giving and talking through what may be helpful.

Counselling may also be helpful if the grief is complicated by unsureness about how we felt about the deceased. Although we are often taught not to speak ill of the dead, some of the significant losses we experience are of people with whom we had an ambivalent relationship and perhaps even hated. This can lead to a complicated grief response. The type of loss can also trigger more difficult grief responses; for example, sudden, unexpected loss, loss by suicide, murder, and loss where the body is unrecoverable or not found. Children and young people may also need to mourn a loss at different stages of their lives. For example, a young girl whose mother died when she was 6 may mourn the loss again when she goes to secondary school, gets married, has her first baby and at other significant points in her life. Also, we may not recognise the full impact of the loss at the time but may come to recognise it gradually or at a later date. For example, a child who has been adopted and has no details of their birth family's medical history may grieve anew when a doctor asks if some condition 'runs in the family'.

## HISTORY AND BACKGROUND

In its present form, counselling has only been available in the UK since the 1950s, although helping with psychological distress has historically been a part of the function of all societies (McLeod, 2013). Bereavement counselling similarly has a short history. Perhaps the best known charity offering bereavement counselling in the UK is CRUSE, founded in 1959. Its initial remit was to help bereaved adults, although it now offers a website for bereaved young people. Initially, bereavement support services rarely extended their work to children and young people, but recently these services have been developed (Rolls and Payne, 2003). Some local therapeutic services are available and schools who offer access to counselling often find bereavement and loss to be common issues brought to therapy. Cooper (2013) reports that bereavement issues make up about 10% of the concerns that young people attending counselling in schools present.

There is little research into the efficacy of therapeutic interventions with children and young people who have been bereaved (Wilkinson et al., 2007). The lack of research using randomised control trials (RCTs) is perhaps understandable given the ethical issues raised in denying some of the population support during bereavement, but qualitative research is sparse too. Wilkinson et al. (2007: 405) attempted an RCT trial but had to abandon it due to lack of participation, however, they did conduct a study of parents' perceptions of a family bereavement support service in seven UK hospices. They concluded that 'support interventions for bereaved children can have a positive impact on post-bereavement adjustment'. It is an interesting study but has quite a limited scope and more research needs to be developed to examine more fully the efficacy of bereavement work with children and young people, and also needs to include the views of the children.

## THEORY THAT TRIES TO EXPLAIN RESPONSES TO LOSS IN CHILDREN AND YOUNG PEOPLE

Why do we grieve? We grieve because we have lost something or someone with whom we had formed an attachment. Parkes suggests 'that it is the nature and quality of the attachment that determines the intensity of the grief, rather than the magnitude of the psychosocial transition that results' (1993: 246). In other words, it is the importance we attach to the loss rather than the disruption in our lives that affects the depth of our grief. This seems to be true whether the attachment experienced is positive or negative, or, in Bowlby's (1969, 1973, 1980) terms, secure or insecure. This concept is explained in detail in Chapter 1, 'Child Development and Attachment'.

The idea that early relationships are important in healthy development permeates all development theory, and it is interesting to note that attachment theory implies a causal relationship between loss and our responses, and is seen, as Fraley and Shaver report, to determine our grief responses:

> whether an individual exhibits a healthy or problematic pattern of grief following separation depends on the way his or her attachment system has become organised over the course of development. (1999: 740)

Bowlby (1969, 1973, 1980) conceptualises grief as separation anxiety (caused by separation from an important attachment figure), so the way we manage grief is dependent upon our attachment style and whether the 'internal working models' we hold in mind are positive or negative. Broadly, secure individuals are believed to be able to recognise their losses and deal with them and to seek support. Anxious-ambivalent individuals are thought to focus on their distressing thoughts and feelings more in order to maintain contact with the person or thing they have lost. They may have difficulty 'moving on'. Avoidant individuals are thought to be more likely to minimise their grief and to 'move on' quickly (Cassidy and Shaver, 1999).

There do seem to be some commonalities within models of the grieving process, as seen below, but the intensity, duration and experience is a very individual one. Most models of the process suggest that it is either phased (moving through various phases of grief, e.g. Bowlby, 1980; Parkes, 1986), tasked (having to complete a variety of tasks to successfully negotiate the process, e.g. Worden, 1991) or an oscillation between grieving and coping, as in the Dual Process Model (DPM) (Stroebe and Schut, 1999).

Bowlby's phase model is derived from his attachment theory and has similarities to the phase model proposed by Parkes (1986), where the following phases are identified: numbness (denial and shock), pining (yearning and protest), disorganisation and despair, reorganisation (recovery).

Stroebe and Schut's (1999) DPM describes our grieving process as an oscillation between focusing on the emotions surrounding our loss and avoiding the loss. We engage in restorative behaviour as well as experiencing the meaning of our loss. Stokes et al. (1999) suggest this model is useful in helping us understand the behaviour of children and young people in managing their grief. They suggest, for example, that if the child or young person senses the adult is distressed when talking about the dead person, they may attempt to distract the adult or avoid talking about the dead person themselves. This can be a helpful strategy but can also be misconstrued by the surrounding family and friends as an indication that the child or young person is not affected by the loss.

## HOW CHILDREN AND YOUNG PEOPLE MAY GRIEVE

Although all of these models may help our understanding of the process of bereavement and loss children may experience, we need to remember that grief is unique. Children and young people understand death differently at different developmental stages and are likely to deal with it in a different way to adults (Slaughter, 2005; Himebauch et al., 2008).

Four concepts are commonly used in the literature (e.g. Willis, 2002) to judge whether children and young people understand death or not. These are:

1. Do children understand that death is irreversible?
2. Do they understand it is final?
3. Do they understand it is inevitable, that all living things die?
4. Do they understand causality, that there is a physical cause to death – the body stops working?

There are huge differences of opinion about the age at which a child can understand these concepts, with some authors believing that children as young as 6 months can understand and others believing understanding only emerges in adolescence (Willis, 2002: 222). Broadly, however, understandings that children and young people have relate to the developmental stages they have reached, which are, in turn, related to the development of cognitive understanding. As suggested in Chapter 1, Piaget (1965 [1932]) argued that children's thinking is structurally different from that of adults and suggested a theory of cognitive development based on the way that children and young people at different ages function. These ideas can be used to understand children's developing concept of death and dying (Himebauch et al., 2008).

## Box 20.1   The development of the concept of death in children and young people related to developmental stage

### Sensory Motor Stage: 0–2 years approximately

Normally, there appears to be little cognitive understanding of death or loss but the child does respond to separation and is often very in tune with parents' emotions. However, Raphael (1984) suggests that we may be unconsciously aware of our losses:

> David, a young man of 22 who saw a dead woman being taken from the site of an accident on a stretcher. Her arm was hanging over the edge and her breast was partially exposed. This awakened a vivid and previously repressed, memory of his attempts to suckle the breast of his dead mother when he was 10 months old. (p. 79)

### Pre-operational Stage of Development: 2–7 years approximately

Up to around 5 years, a child is usually able to use words about death relatively appropriately but really it seems to be 'pretend' and there is little concept of the irreversibility or finality of death. It is common to confuse death with sleeping and death may be seen as a punishment. They may feel they have caused the death although guilt is a common feeling associated with grief right through life, including adulthood. We need to be very careful with the language we use to explain death as the misunderstanding reported by Raphael (1984) demonstrates:

> Jason (2½) … He and his father used to go to a nearby airport to see planes together. When his father, to whom he was intensely attached, died, he was told he had 'gone to Heaven to be with Jesus' … he ran away on many occasions and was found … [near the airport] where he had gone to 'get in a plane to go to the sky to Daddy'. (pp. 86–87)

Between the ages of around 5–8 years, children gradually see death as possible but not for them, and usually associate death with old age. They begin to accept that death is an end and begin to realise death is not reversible. They often have a real curiosity about the idea of death.

### Concrete Operational Stage: 7–11 years approximately

Children are much more able to see death in abstract terms and can understand as much as people will tell them. They begin to realise death may include them and to understand the irreversibility of death. They are able to differentiate between living and non-living.

### Formal Operational Stage: 11–16 years approximately

The young person begins to have a more adult understanding. Because they are able to think more abstractly, they understand implications of death more fully. It is possible that some may think suicide is a means of getting back at someone, but they may also see it as reversible (as some survive) and re-occurrable (as some try more than once). Desperate young people can engage in risk-taking behaviour, which can result in death.

The descriptions of Harry Potter's experience of Dumbledore's death provide an illustration of the range of emotions an adolescent might experience – sadness, mirth, regret, curiosity, suppression of emotion, accumulation of grief and loss, isolation (Rowling, 2005: 599–600).

## Case Study: Sharon

Sharon was 9 years old and was referred because her older brother was killed in a car accident, which Sharon witnessed. She, understandably, was having difficulty processing this experience.

Her mother, because of her own distress, felt unable to offer Sharon appropriate responses to her questions about the death of her brother, and because Sharon's 'supporters' were also bereft they were unable to help her to find a voice for her feelings of loss.

Sharon and I met for ten sessions of play therapy where the purpose was to use the child's natural medium of communication, 'play', to make some sense of her experience. Rather than interpret the meaning of the play, I look for themes and the themes in her play were predominantly about making order out of chaos and about nurturing. She rarely talked directly about her experiences or acknowledged her feelings.

The major theme of Sharon's play was nurture. She played most of the time with the doll's house, which 'Mammy' or 'Daddy' kept clean and where they looked after the children. In session two, a new theme occurred through her stories, that of sudden happenings, then things returning to normal, but nothing ever being the same again.

Sharon's play became much more expressive in the seventh session and she spoke for the first time of the things that had happened to her. She again played with the doll's house and the theme of creating order out of chaos was apparent.

Session eight seemed to mark a change in Sharon's behaviour. She was much more assertive and more playful. The themes included being in control and, although terrible things happened in her stories, they had a happy ending and seemed less chaotic. This continued in session nine.

In session ten, themes of order and normality were very apparent and the session seemed very peaceful. Her play was still very ordered but seemed less stressed. The children in the doll's house did not seem to need quite so much looking after and could be very independent.

The final session was a very tranquil session and old themes and play were revisited. The chaos seemed to have receded and some sort of order established in her life. Perhaps the therapeutic play space had allowed her to make some sense of her experience.

## ISSUES OF DIVERSITY

It has been argued throughout this chapter that the response to loss and bereavement is very individual and is dependent upon the meaning that loss has for the child or young person. Cultural differences may dictate how that response is manifested but many of the emotions will be common to all cultures. Parkes et al. (2015) support this view:

> … all societies see death as a transition for the person who dies. How people prepare themselves for this transition and survivors feel and behave after a death has occurred varies a great deal but even here there are common themes. (p. 5)

The same argument holds for children and young people with a learning difficulty. Their understanding of, and response to, the loss will be shaped by their developmental level and the meaning the loss has for them (Read, 2014).

---

## Key Learning

- The process of grieving involves adapting to changes in our internal world and restoring a degree of denial.
- Therapeutic interventions are not always helpful or needed when children and young people have experienced a loss.
- There is little research as to the efficacy of bereavement counselling with children and young people and more is needed. Chapter 16 explores the efficacy of counselling in general with young people and concludes it can be helpful.
- There are several theories to explain children and young people's response to loss.
- Children and young people have differing understandings of death dependent upon their stage of development.
- Each child or young person's response to loss is unique and will be shaped by their culture, developmental stage and social setting as well as by the meaning the loss has for them.

---

## Summary

How a counsellor works therapeutically with children and young people who have been bereaved will depend upon their theoretical orientation (see Chapters 2–8 in this handbook). However, in this chapter I have suggested:

- The meaning associated with the loss is what is central in understanding the loss and to working with grieving children and young people.
- Reactions to loss are individual and range from feelings of sadness to serious physical, emotional, behavioural and cognitive reactions.
- Responses are dependent both on the meaning of the loss and the development stage of the child or young person.

### In addition:

- To understand how children and young people perceive loss and grieve, it is important for us to appreciate how working with this issue with this population may affect us. It is often very difficult to witness pain in others, especially if we see the others as vulnerable children. This may make us reluctant to 'hear' the children, so we need to make sure we are well supported.
- How we work therapeutically with our young clients will depend upon our training, orientation, work setting and experience, but we all need to be aware of the possible effects on us. Working with loss can make us aware of our own mortality and the mortality of those we care about, and we can become supersensitive to risk, which can be paralysing.
- We need good supervision and good self-care in order to keep ourselves open to our clients and safe.

## Discussion Questions

Some of these activities, as with all personal development work, may be upsetting, so make sure you are well supported if you choose to do them.

1. Think about a loss you have experienced; write down an account of your process?
2. How well do the descriptions of how death is conceptualised at different developmental stages in Box 20.1 fit with your experience of children and young people? Where is it the same, where different? Why might that be?
3. Why is it important to keep parents and carers 'on board'?
4. What strategies would you use to do this whilst still maintaining confidentiality?
5. When do you think it would not be appropriate to offer a therapeutic intervention to a bereaved child or young person?
6. You are working with children and young people who are bereft. What support do you have? How will you look after yourself so you can be open to listen to your clients?

## Develop Your Skills

Again, some of these activities, as with all personal development work, may be upsetting so make sure you are well supported if you choose to do them.

Theory suggests that our response to loss is associated with our attachment style. When working therapeutically with loss, our own attachment style as a therapist can impact upon our work so these first two activities are designed to help us explore our own styles.

1.  Answer the following questions by yourself then discuss with a partner:

    a.  Who do you like to spend most time with? Why?
    b.  Who do you miss most during separations? Why?
    c.  Who do you feel you can always count on? Why?
    d.  Who do you turn to for comfort when you're feeling down? Why?

2.  Is there any particular type of loss you think you would find hard to work with; death by suicide, murder, road accident, cancer for example? With a partner, discuss why you think this may be difficult.
3.  Sit quietly by yourself. Let an image of death and/or dying come into your head. Does it have a size, a shape, colour, texture, smell? Does it change or remain the same? Is there anything else about it? When you feel you know your image, then draw, sculpt, make a collage or write about it. Share with a partner.
4.  You are working with children and young people who are bereft. What support do you have? How will you look after yourself so you can be open to listen to your clients?

## Further Reading

Gerhardt, S. (2004) *Why Love Matters: How Affection Shapes a Baby's Brain*. London: Routledge.

She argues much of our brain and connections develop after birth, ready to be shaped and learnt from the environment we are born into.

Gersie, A. (1991) *Story Making in Bereavement: Dragons Fight in the Meadow*. London: Jessica Kingsley.

This is a lovely book which introduces stories connected to death that can be used therapeutically or just enjoyed.

Golding, K. (2008) *Nurturing Attachments: Supporting Children Who are Fostered or Adopted*. London: Jessica Kingsley.

This book contains good descriptions of attachment types.

Mallon, B. (2011) *Working with Bereaved Children and Young People*. London: SAGE.

This is a comprehensive book that combines theory with practice and the latest research. Each chapter ends with a reflective exercise that adds interest.

### All About Me

This is a game (currently £45) developed by Barnardo's that is designed for use in therapy to help children and young people talk about difficult feelings.

Pennells, M. and Smith, S. (1999) *The Forgotten Mourners: Guidelines to Working with Bereaved Children*, 2nd edn. London: Jessica Kingsley.

Although quite an old resource, this book offers very practical and straightforward advice about working with bereaved children and young people.

### Online Resources

BACP website: www.bacp.co.uk, especially the BACP Children and Young People Division and the Competences for Working with Children and Young People

Counselling MindEd: https://www.minded.org.uk, Although there are no specific modules on working with bereavement and loss with children and young people, there are a number of useful general modules regarding working with this client group

# REFERENCES

Adams, J. (2012) Understanding grieving teenagers. Information Sheet. *Child Bereavement UK*. Available at: https://childbereavementuk.org/for-families/support-for-bereaved-children/

Bonanno, G.A. and Lilienfeld, S.O. (2008) Let's be realistic: when grief counseling is effective and when it's not. *Professional Psychology: Research and Practice* 39(3): 377–378.

Bowlby, J. (1969) *Attachment and Loss: Attachment*. Vol. 1. New York: Basic Books.

Bowlby, J. (1973) *Attachment and Loss: Separation – Anxiety and Anger*. Vol. 2. London: Hogarth Press.

Bowlby, J. (1980) *Attachment and Loss: Loss – Sadness and Depression*. Vol. 3. London: Hogarth Press.

Cassidy, J. and Shaver, P.R. (eds) (1999) *Handbook of Attachment: Theory, Research, and Clinical Applications*. New York: Guilford Press.

Cooper, M. (2013) *School-Based Counselling in UK Secondary Schools: A Review and Critical Evaluation*. Available at: https://pure.strath.ac.uk/portal/en/publications/schoolbased-counselling-in-uk-secondary-schools(4aa2cbb1-3b83-4a24-936f-f4d6beb7f3da).html

Fraley, R.C. and Shaver, P.R. (1999) Loss and bereavement: attachment theory and recent controversies concerning 'grief work' and the nature of detachment. In: Cassidy, J. and Shaver, P.R. (eds) *Handbook of Attachment: Theory, Research, and Clinical Applications*. New York: Guilford Press, pp. 735–759.

Goodman, R.F. and Brown, E.J. (2008) Service and science in times of crisis: developing, planning, and implementing a clinical research program for children traumatically bereaved after 9/11. *Death Studies 32*(2): 154–180.

Himebauch, A., Arnold, R.M. and May, C. (2008) Grief in children and developmental concepts of death. *Journal of Palliative Medicine 11*(2): 242–243.

Hunt, K. (2004) 'An exploration of the experience of loss and its relationship to counselling practice'. PhD dissertation, University of Durham, UK.

McLeod, J. (2013) *An Introduction to Counselling*, 5th edn. Maidenhead: Open University Press.

Parkes, C.M. (1986) *Bereavement: Studies of Grief in Adult Life*, 2nd edn. London: Penguin.

Parkes, C.M. (1993) Bereavement as a psychosocial transition: processes of adaptation to change. In: Dickenson, D. and Johnson, M. (eds) *Death, Dying and Bereavement*. London: SAGE.

Parkes, C.M. (1998) Editorial comments. *Bereavement Care 17*(2): 18.

Parkes, C.M., Laungani, P. and Young, B. (2015) *Death and Bereavement across Cultures*, 2nd edn. Hove: Routledge.

Piaget, J. (1965 [1932]) *The Moral Judgment of the Child*, 2nd edn. New York: Free Press.

Raphael, B. (1984) *Anatomy of Bereavement: A Handbook for the Caring Professions*. London: Hutchinson.

Read, S. (ed.) (2014) *Supporting People with Intellectual Disabilities Experiencing Loss and Bereavement*. London: Jessica Kingsley

Rolls, L. and Payne, S. (2003) Childhood bereavement services: a survey of UK provision. *Palliative Medicine 17*: 423–432.

Rowling, J.K. (2005) *Harry Potter and the Half Blood Prince*. London: Bloomsbury.

Silverman, P. and Klass, D. (1996) Continuing bonds. In: Klass, D., Silverman, P.R. and Nickman, S.L. (eds) *Continuing Bonds. New Understandings of Grief*. Philadelphia, PA: Taylor & Francis.

Slaughter, V. (2005) Young children's understanding of death. *Australian Psychologist 40*(3): 179–186.

Stokes, J., Pennington, J., Monroe, B., Papadatou, D. and Relf, M. (1999) Developing services for bereaved children: a discussion of the theoretical and practical issues involved. *Mortality 4*(3): 291–307.

Stroebe, M.S. and Schut, H. (1999) The dual process model of coping with bereavement: rationale and description. *Death Studies 23*: 197–224.

Turner, M. (2006) *Talking with Young People about Death and Dying*, 2nd edn. London: Jessica Kingsley.

Wilkinson, S., Croy, P., King, M. and Barnes, J. (2007) Are we getting it right? Parents' perceptions of hospice child bereavement support services. *Palliative Medicine 21*(5): 401–407.

Willis, C. (2002) The grieving process in children: strategies for understanding, educating, and reconciling children's perceptions of death. *Early Childhood Education Journal 29*(4): 221–226.

Worden, J. (1991) *Grief Counselling and Grief Therapy: A Handbook for the Mental Health Practitioner*, 2nd edn. New York: Springer.

# 21

# DEPRESSION AND ANXIETY: COMMON CHALLENGES FOR CHILDREN AND YOUNG PEOPLE

## JENNIFER BAGGERLY

**This chapter will discuss:**

- Depression and anxiety in children and young people
- Risk factors
- Multidisciplinary treatment interventions
- Counsellor's practice

## INTRODUCTION

Depression and anxiety are so prevalent that they are often considered the common cold of mental health. In fact, the World Health Organization (WHO, 2017) estimates that more than 300 million people worldwide have depression and even more have anxiety. Unfortunately, rates of anxiety and depression increased by nearly 50%, from 416 million to 615 million between 1990 and 2013 (WHO, 2016).

In the USA, one in five children either currently or at some point in their life has had a serious mental health disorder (Merikangas et al., 2010). In the USA, 2.1% children who are 3–17 years old have depression and 3.0% have anxiety (CDC, 2013). However, rates are even higher among adolescents. A survey of 10,123 USA adolescents ages 12 through 18 years old found that 14.3% had been diagnosed with a mood disorder (i.e. major depressive disorder, dysthymia, bipolar I or II) and 31.9% had been diagnosed with an anxiety disorder (i.e. agoraphobia, generalised anxiety disorder (GAD), social phobia, specific phobia, panic disorder or separation anxiety disorder) (Merikangas et al., 2010). When considering age of onset, it was found that 50% of those with anxiety disorders started having symptoms by age 6, whilst 50% of those with mood disorders started having symptoms by age 13 (Merikangas et al., 2010).

Despite this prevalence, approximately 64% of adolescents with depression and/or anxiety will not receive professional mental health services due to lack of awareness, resources or stigma (Merikangas et al., 2011). Left untreated, depression and anxiety can contribute to academic failure, social isolation, substance abuse and criminal activity among adolescents (Merikangas et al., 2011). Therefore, it is imperative for human services professionals and educators to recognise and understand the treatment of depression and anxiety in children and adolescents.

## DEPRESSION: WHAT IS IT?

Most children experience sadness numerous times throughout their childhood. Perhaps they broke a toy, lost a pet, fought with their friend, received a low grade in school, moved away or learnt their parents were divorcing. Yet, depression is far more serious than situational sadness. Depression entails persistent sadness, loss of pleasure and/or fatigue that occurs for at least 2 weeks and has multiple associated symptoms. According to the International Statistical Classification of Diseases and Related Health Problems (ICD-10) (WHO, 1992), the diagnostic criteria for depression are as follows.

- Key symptoms – at least one experienced most days for at least 2 weeks:
  - persistent sadness or low mood; and/or
  - loss of interest or pleasure;
  - fatigue or low energy.

- Associated symptoms – defines degree of depression:
  - disturbed sleep;
  - poor concentration or indecisiveness;
  - low self-confidence;
  - poor or increased appetite;
  - suicidal thoughts or acts;
  - agitation or slowing of movements;
  - guilt or self-blame.

- Not depressed (fewer than four associated symptoms).
- Mild depression (four symptoms).
- Moderate depression (five to six symptoms).
- Severe depression (seven or more symptoms).

In addition to these symptoms, the American Psychiatric Association's (2013) *Diagnostic and Statistical Manual of Mental Disorders, Fifth Edition* (DSM-5) adds (1) the symptoms must be a change from his or her baseline presentation; (2) must cause significant impairments in school, social settings and/or family; and (3) are not better accounted for by a grief reaction, substance abuse or medical illness.

Prominent psychologist Aaron T. Beck (1979) described depression as consisting of three cognitive distortions (i.e. errors in thinking), in which a person views: (1) self as negative; (2) the world as pessimistic; and (3) the future as hopeless. These thinking errors were also found to occur in children and adolescents with depression (Braet et al., 2015). Children may hold maladaptive schemas or patterns of beliefs such as 'I am stupid', 'There is nothing in the world that makes me happy' and 'My future is ruined'. It is these maladaptive schemas that result in feelings of depression and self-defeating behaviours (e.g. aggression towards peers, isolating self in room, sleeping all day). Depression in children and adolescents can be dangerous, if left untreated, due to the risk of suicide.

## ANXIETY: WHAT IS IT?

Fear is a common experience of children since they are more vulnerable than adults due to their limited physical size, cognitive development and lack of experience. Fear is an emotional response to real or perceived imminent threat (APA, 2013). Children are often afraid of the dark, monsters or inclement weather. In contrast, worry and anxiety are anticipation of future threat. Worry is also common in children throughout their development. Perhaps they are worried about getting in trouble at home, going to school for the first time, taking a test, having no-one to sit with at lunch, body changes from puberty or finding a date for a school dance. Yet, anxiety is far beyond typical childhood worry and fear. Anxiety is excessive fear and worry in the absence of real threat that results in physical and behavioural symptoms out of proportion to what is considered typical in a given environment (APA, 2013).

According to ICD-10 (WHO, 1992), the diagnostic criteria for anxiety disorder are as follows:

- Anxious feelings, dread or fear without actual threat.
- Physical symptoms such as restlessness, tension, tachycardia (racing heartbeat) and dyspnoea (laboured or difficult breathing) when there is not a clearly identifiable stimulus.
- Other symptoms include irritability, anxious expectations, pangs of conscience, anxiety attacks or phobias.
- Experience is persistent and disabling to typical functioning.

The DSM-5 (APA, 2013) specifically defines GAD as having the following symptoms that are clearly excessive for at least 6 months, making it difficult to carry out day-to-day activities (going to school, getting along with others, participating in hobbies):

- The presence of excessive anxiety and worry about a variety of topics, events or activities that is disproportionate to an identifiable threat.
- Worry is experienced as very challenging to control.
- The child has one of the following symptoms.
  - edginess or restlessness;
  - tiring easily, more fatigued than usual;
  - impaired concentration or mind going blank;
  - irritability;
  - increased muscle aches or soreness;
  - difficulty sleeping (trouble falling asleep or staying asleep, restlessness at night);
  - sweating, nausea or diarrhoea.

In order to meet the criteria for a GAD, these symptoms of anxiety cannot be due to a medical condition, medications, alcohol or recreational drugs, and cannot be better explained by a different mental disorder. Children and teens with GAD often worry excessively about their performance at school or in sports and catastrophes such as earthquakes or war (NIMH, 2016a).

Other anxiety-related diagnoses include separation anxiety disorder (fear of being away from a close family member), selective mutism, panic disorder (i.e. sudden onset of intense fear with pounding heart, shortness of breath), specific phobic disorder (i.e. excessive fear of something particular like dogs or trucks), agoraphobia (i.e. excessive fear of crowded spaces or enclosed public places) and social anxiety disorder (i.e. high anxiety in social or performance situations, feeling extremely self-conscious and fearing others will judge them). It is important to note that both obsessive compulsive disorder and post-traumatic stress disorder are no longer listed in the DSM-5 chapter on anxiety disorders but rather have their own chapter.

## RISK FACTORS FOR DEPRESSION AND ANXIETY

Depression and anxiety often occur together. The causes of depression and anxiety are thought to be a combination of genetics, psychodynamic make-up and environment interacting together (NIMH, 2016a, 2016b). A recent study of twins found that depression and anxiety are explained by 44% genetic heritable characteristics, 25% shared environment and 31% non-shared environments (Ask et al., 2016). Genetics can influence the activity of neurotransmitters, causing chemical imbalances in serotonin and norepinephrine that are implicated in depression and anxiety (Little et al., 2015). Genetics also influence the functioning of the two structures within the limbic system, the amygdala and the hippocampus, which help modulate emotions and memories, respectively (Little et al., 2015).

The psychodynamic make-up that contributes to depression and anxiety is identified by Erk (2008: 83–84) as 'the quality of their attachment relationships, how they were reinforced or punished, their social learning situations, their cognitive skills, how they interpreted their inter- and intrapersonal feeling states, and how life events shaped their lives at developmentally crucial periods'. Environmental factors that contribute to anxiety and depression may be poverty, divorce, death of family members, abuse, neglect, substance abuse, racial oppression, community violence or disasters (Erk, 2008).

Common risk factors for depression and anxiety include:

- family history of depression or anxiety;
- parent psychopathology;
- stress or trauma;
- female gender;
- sexual minority status (gay, lesbian, bisexual, transgender);
- chronic medical illness;
- neighbourhood and social instability;
- immunosuppressive medications (e.g. corticosteroids, interferon);
- substance use/abuse;
- poor performance in school.

For anxiety, additional risk factors include shyness in childhood and elevated afternoon cortisol levels in the saliva (NIMH, 2016a).

Rates of anxiety and depression are common across racial and ethnic groups (Merikangas et al., 2011). However, anxiety is higher among non-Hispanic black adolescents compared to non-Hispanic white adolescents. Depression is higher among Hispanic adolescents compared to non-Hispanic whites. Despite the higher rate of depression and anxiety, Hispanic and non-Hispanic black adolescents are less likely to receive treatment (Merikangas et al., 2011).

Parental characteristics correlated with anxiety are parents who are divorced or separated (Merikangas, 2011). In contrast, lower rates of depression are correlated with children of parents who were never married. Parental aggression or lower levels of positive parenting can impact serotonin transporter gene, resulting in increased depression and anxiety in adolescents (Little et al., 2015).

It is important to examine particular risks of depression due to the associated risk of suicide. In a 2-year longitudinal study of 324 adolescents, risk factors for depression that leads to suicidal ideation were found to be negative adjectives to describe self (in females), rumination in response to negative affect (i.e. repeated focus on negative emotions) and negative inferential style (i.e. assume negative results for self and future) (Burke et al., 2016). Protective factors against suicidal ideation were distraction and problem-solving skills (Burke et al., 2016). These research findings imply that treatment should focus on cognitive processes for adolescents.

## MULTIDISCIPLINARY TREATMENT APPROACHES

Depression and anxiety are not something that children and adolescents simply 'outgrow'. Rather, they may need a comprehensive, multidisciplinary treatment approach, including counselling. This allows parents and professionals to contribute expertise based on their role for the common good of a child or adolescent. Whilst psychologists may focus on psychological assessment and treatment planning, counsellors can provide individual counselling, perhaps in the school environment, group work and family counselling to promote choices and changes. Social workers tend to link children and adolescents to resources and work on systemic improvements. Medical doctors such as psychiatrists evaluate physical health and prescribe medications. Teachers adapt curriculum and facilitate positive social interactions. Parents provide in-depth information about their child and coordinate services. Community leaders develop needed services such as recreational activities, sports, youth groups and laws that protect children and adolescents.

Counsellors can assess children and young people for depression and anxiety, within the school context or in a community or medical setting. Common assessments for depression and anxiety in children and adolescents include the Child Behavior Checklist versions of Parent Report, Teacher Report and Youth Self-Report (Achenbach, 2017); the Children's Depression Inventory (Kovacs, 1980); the Revised Children's Manifest Anxiety Scale (Reynolds and Richmond, 1978); and the Revised Child Anxiety and Depression Scale (Chorpita et al., 2005). This range of tools may be used within a multidisciplinary approach.

Typical multidisciplinary treatment approaches begin with psycho-education for the child and parents, as well as a lifestyle assessment and recommendations for changes in diet and exercise (NIMH, 2016a, 2016b). The counsellor can provide talking therapy approaches or therapeutic play, depending on the age of the child. Counselling may be provided within a package of care including psychiatric care and medication. A meta-analysis research study, which statistically analyses numerous other studies, found that adolescents in a treatment group with both psychotherapy and medication improved in their global functioning better than those in a group with just medication (Calati et al., 2011).

## SPECIFIC COUNSELLING STRATEGIES

### Play therapy

Children below the age of 11 typically do not have the cognitive ability to understand abstract reasoning that requires theoretical and hypothetical thought. According to Piaget (1952), children aged 2–7 function in the pre-operational level of cognitive development whilst children aged 7–11 function in the concrete operational level. This cognitive limitation makes 'talk therapy' difficult and uninteresting to children. Play therapy addresses this problem by providing a therapeutic relationship between a trained play therapist and children that allows the children to use their natural medium of communication, play, to express their feelings, thoughts and experiences in order to resolve psychological difficulties (Landreth, 2012). The play therapist creates a safe playroom with selected toys and provides therapeutic responses such as tracking play behaviour, reflecting feelings, returning responsibility, building self-esteem, facilitating understanding and setting therapeutic limits whilst the child plays (Landreth, 2012).

Research shows that play therapy is helpful in reducing children's anxiety and depression. In Stulmaker and Ray's (2015) study of 53 children with borderline or clinical levels of anxiety, children receiving Child Centered Play Therapy (CCPT) demonstrated statistically significant decreases in worry and overall anxiety when compared to the active control group. Reyes and Asbrant (2005) found significant reductions in anxiety and depression after 9 months of play therapy in children who disclosed sexual abuse. Baggerly (2004) found a significant decrease in anxiety and negative mood after CCPT for children residing in a homeless shelter. A meta-analysis that examined the combined overall treatment effects of 93 play therapy studies found a statistically significant overall effect size of 0.80, indicating a large treatment effect for play therapy (Bratton et al., 2005). The US Substance Abuse and Mental Health Services Administration National Registry of Evidence-based Programs and Practices listed CCPT as a promising practice in the treatment of anxiety.

## Cognitive-behavioural therapy

Cognitive-behavioural therapy (CBT) is a psychotherapy that teaches children and adolescents different ways of thinking, behaving and reacting through cognitive, emotional and behavioural strategies (Beck, 1979; Friedberg and McClure, 2015). CBT is considered the treatment of choice in resolving anxiety and depression in children and adolescents due to the plethora of research studies proving its effectiveness (NIMH, 2016a, 2016b).

Cognitive strategies begin with the counsellor teaching children and adolescents about the cognitive triangle, in which their thoughts, rather than an event, influence their feelings and behaviour (Beck, 1979; Sburlati et al., 2011). For example, if a girl's friend does not say 'Hello' to her in the school cafeteria, the girl who thinks 'She must hate me now' will feel sad and avoid her friend. In contrast, a girl in the same situation who thinks 'That is strange; I wonder if she is preoccupied' will feel curious and will approach her friend. The next cognitive strategy is to explain thinking errors, sometimes called cognitive distortions, as follows (Beck, 1979; Friedberg and McClure, 2015):

- All-or-nothing thinking: an either/or belief with no middle ground such as 'Either I am perfect or I am a failure'.
- Magnifying the negative: only looking at or for negative parts and ignoring the positive such as 'My mother yelled at me this morning so I will not notice anything nice that she does for me the rest of the week'.
- Overgeneralisation: making a general conclusion based on one single piece of evidence such as 'That girl was rude to me so all girls in the entire school will be rude to me'.

- Catastrophising: expecting disaster to occur from one small thing such as 'It rained this morning so my home is going to be flooded and all my clothes will be ruined'.
- Shoulds: demanding that self, or others should or must behave in a certain way and if they do not, there should be punishment such as 'My brother should play with me when I want and if he does not then he should be punished'; also demanding that a situation or event should meet expectations and if it does not then there will be hell to pay, such as 'My computer should work faster and if it doesn't then I'll slam it down'.
- Mindreading: assuming what another person is thinking without evidence such as 'My teacher thinks I'm stupid because I forgot my homework'.
- Personalisation: believing that others' actions are because of something wrong with you and comparing self to others such as 'My friend forgot to give me a birthday card so I must not be as good as her other friends'.
- Trashcan labelling: negative judgement of self or others that results in a negative label such as 'I'm a loser' and 'My teacher is a witch'.

Once these thinking errors are identified in children and adolescents, then counsellors help them examine evidence to see if the thought is really true and if the conclusion is accurate. For example, the counsellor may ask 'Just because you made a bad grade on your math test, does that really mean you will never make a good grade?' or 'There are hundreds of girls in your school, how do you know that every single one of them is rude – have you spoken with all of them?' When evidence has been examined, the counsellor helps create a more reasonable, balanced thought. For example, 'Although I am disappointed in my math grade, it does not mean that I'll always make a horrible grade because I can get help' or 'Some girls may be rude but certainly not all 100 are rude so I can be friendly to find a few who are nice'. Thought stopping and thought replacing can be taught by telling children to clap their hands and say 'Stop' when they have thinking errors and then replacing them with a balanced thought.

Emotional regulation strategies often begin with mindfulness or paying attention to what is going on right here, right now inside and outside of self without judgement but with kindness and curiosity (Burdick, 2014). One mindfulness activity is to ask children to describe the colour, shape, details, texture, feel, smell and sound of an object without giving an opinion if it is good or bad or pretty or ugly. This activity helps children to slow down their mind, focus on the here-and-now, think objectively and maintain calmness. Deep breathing, which also helps regulate emotion, is taught by inhaling slowly through the nose to the count of four with stomach expanding and exhaling through pursed lips to the count of eight with stomach going in. This is repeated three to four times and then regular breathing is resumed. Identifying levels of emotions from low to high such as annoyed, angry, irate or disappointed, sad, hopeless can help children lower the intensity of their emotions. Creating gratitude is achieved by asking children to remember a positive or happy time, imagine that they are sending a thankful feeling to self or others and dismissing thoughts that distract them from the thankfulness (Burdick, 2014). Progressive muscle relaxation helps decrease emotions of anxiety that are stored in the body (Sburlati et al., 2011). It is accomplished by asking children to tighten fists for 10 seconds and then relax them for 10 seconds, followed by doing the same for biceps, triceps, eyebrows, eyelids, mouth, shoulders, shoulder blades, stomach, back, bottom, thighs, calf muscles and toes (Burdick, 2014). Other emotional regulation skills are singing or humming lullabies, biting down on a chopstick sideways in the mouth so that the child is smiling, playing a game and talking to a friend about their favourite things.

Behavioural regulation strategies often begin with activity scheduling in which pleasurable activities such as exercising, walking, sports, watching a comedy on television or going somewhere new are scheduled for each day (Friedberg and McClure, 2015). Graded task assignments help children learn to break down big tasks such as cleaning their room or doing a school project into small steps with a set amount of time for each step. Positive reinforcement increases a desired behaviour by providing a desired reward (e.g. time on mobile phone, going to a movie, praise from a parent). For anxiety, gradual exposure to the feared stimuli (e.g. going to school, speaking in public, being near dogs) is paired with the relaxation of deep breathing and imaging a calm place (Friedberg and McClure, 2015).

## Case Study: Depression

Debbie is a 15-year-old girl who was referred to counselling for missing numerous days of school. Her parents report that for the last 6 months she has stayed in her room playing video games most of the time, does not engage with friends other than her 17-year-old boyfriend Charlie, eats sweets and chips constantly resulting in significant weight gain, refuses to help around the house and constantly complains about everything. The counsellor reflects the parents' feelings by saying 'You are very worried about Debbie. You care for her so much that you want a better life for her.'

When meeting Debbie, the counsellor observes that she walks slow, speaks slow, does not make eye contact and is not well groomed. Debbie states that she does not need counselling because 'it is stupid' and says she would rather die than come to counselling. She states she does not care about going to school or a future job as she will probably get pregnant and be a stay-at-home mother. The counsellor reflects her feelings and summarises by saying 'You are angry about being here. It seems to you that nothing will help you feel less down about now and the future.' The counsellor can see that Debbie is depressed.

To engage Debbie in the counselling process, the counsellor says 'Since you are here anyway, we might as well have some fun' and asks Debbie to take out her mobile phone and play her favourite song. Together, they examine the song lyrics, make up dance moves and poses for each key lyric, and decide which lyrics are life-giving (i.e. make life pleasurable and meaningful). The counsellor builds on this by explaining how thoughts can influence behaviour and feelings. They review thinking errors and find that Debbie often has all-or-nothing thinking (i.e. 'Life sucks'), catastrophising (i.e. 'I'll probably get pregnant like my best friend did and will be stuck in poverty the rest of my life') and magnifying the negative (i.e. 'Schoolwork is too hard and my mother always yells at me for not doing my homework'). The counsellor teaches Debbie to examine the evidence for each thinking error and helps her to develop balanced thoughts (e.g. 'Although I am not currently enjoying life, I can find some pleasurable things to enjoy'; 'I always have choices and can choose to be proactive to prevent pregnancy and lifetime poverty'; and 'Although homework is difficult, I can learn to tolerate it, ask my teachers for help and tell my mom my plans for getting homework done').

Over the next ten sessions, the counsellor worked with Debbie and helped her to develop some strategies, such as thought stopping, mindfulness strategies, deep breathing, charting feelings in relation to thoughts, creating gratitude, activity scheduling, graded task assignments and positive reinforcements. She made slow but steady progress in returning to school, making three new friends and identifying two career options.

## Case Study: Anxiety

Adam is a 7-year-old boy who was referred to counselling for excessive whining, crying and clinging when his mother would try to leave him at school, church or any activity. His mother reported the behaviour began when his father moved out of town after their divorce last year. She said Adam does not eat breakfast due to an upset stomach, has lost weight and does not sleep well. The counsellor identified issues with separation and anxiety.

Although Adam was initially reluctant to enter the counselling room, he eventually began playing with the toys. He set up the army men in two rows facing each other and then knocked each of them down while he made a groaning noise. The counsellor worked with therapeutic play, and tracked play behaviour and reflected feelings by saying 'Each one falls down and gets hurt. Each army man is in pain and may be scared.' Then, Adam grouped the farm animals together in families and slammed a dinosaur through them separating the families. He moved the baby animals and said 'Dad, where are you? Mom, where are you? Help me!' The play therapist reflected and facilitated understanding by saying 'The little ones are scared and confused. They need protection from danger and need help calming down. Sometimes children need that too.'

Adam attended ten sessions of counselling and worked with play. At the end of the play time, the play therapist met with Adam and his mother together to help them develop mindfulness strategies, deep breathing, progressive muscle relaxation, emotional rating via a daily feelings thermometer (i.e. colouring in how anxious he was on a thermometer scale of 1–10), thought stopping, activity scheduling and positive reinforcement when he enters school successfully.

## Key Learning

- Knowledge and understanding of depression and anxiety in children and young people.
- Risk factors.
- Counselling and multidisciplinary treatment interventions.
- Counsellor's practice and useful approaches.

## Summary

Depression and anxiety are common but debilitating mental health disorders in children and adolescents. Depression is more than situational sadness and anxiety is more than typical childhood fears. Both impair the functioning of children and hinder their healthy development. The causes of depression and anxiety are genetics, psychodynamic characteristics and environment. Play therapy or therapeutic play is a promising practice that helps resolve symptoms of depression and anxiety in children below age 11. CBT is considered the treatment of choice for treating depression and anxiety in older children and adolescents. Cognitive, emotional and behavioural strategies can be implemented with children and adolescents to help them be free from depression and anxiety.

## Discussion Questions

1. What is the difference between typical 'blues' (i.e. sadness) and depression in children? Describe the difference in beliefs and behaviour for each. If you had a video of an adolescent who just had the blues and a video of an adolescent who was depressed, what difference would you see?
2. What is the difference between typical worry and anxiety in children? Describe the difference in beliefs and behaviour for each. If you had a video of an adolescent who just worried and a video of an adolescent who had anxiety, what difference would you see?
3. Think of a person you know or a famous person or a TV/movie character who has depression or anxiety. Describe how the depression or anxiety has impacted him or her. What were some of the risk factors that contributed to depression or anxiety?
4. When considering a multidisciplinary approach, which role would you enjoy the most? Why?

## Develop Your Skills

1. *Reflect feelings*: When you see a child who is upset, a good starting place is to reflect their feelings by stating the feelings you see in them. Practise saying this sentence out loud in a way that both matches the feeling you just stated and expresses concern (i.e. slowly, softly, eye contact, wait and listen). 'You look _____' (state the feeling you see such as sad, down, depressed, worried, uptight, anxious).
2. *Amplify*: In order to help the child say more and gain awareness, practise saying these sentences out loud in a way that expresses concern (i.e. slowly, softly, eye contact, wait and listen). 'I'm sorry to see you feeling so bad. What's been going on? How long have you felt like this? What was happening when you first started feeling like this? What changes have you noticed in yourself and your life since this began?'
3. *Express concern*: Practise saying these sentences out loud in a way that expresses concern (i.e. slowly, softly, eye contact, wait and listen). 'I am really sorry to hear about your difficulty. You are a good person and deserve to feel happy and calm. I care about you and hope that you will start to feel better soon. Please let me know what I can do to help you.'

## Further Reading

Burdick, D. (2014) *Mindfulness Skills for Kids and Teens*. Eau Claire, WI: PESI Publishing.

Friedberg, R.D. and McClure, J.M. (2015) *Clinical Practice of Cognitive Therapy with Children and Adolescents: The Nuts and Bolts*. New York: Guilford Press.

Landreth, G. (2012) *Play Therapy: The Art of the Relationship*. New York: Routledge.

### Online Resources

Anxiety disorders, https://www.nimh.nih.gov/health/topics/anxiety-disorders/index.shtml

Association for Behavioral and Cognitive Therapies, www.abct.org/Home

Association for Play Therapy, www.a4pt.org

Child and Adolescent Mental Health, www.who.int/mental_health/maternal-child/child_adolescent/en

Depression, https://www.nimh.nih.gov/health/topics/depression/index.shtml

Depression, www.who.int/mediacentre/factsheets/fs369/en

Suicide Prevention Lifeline, https://suicidepreventionlifeline.org

# REFERENCES

Achenbach, T. (2017) *Achenbach System of Empirically Based Assessment.* Burlington, VT. Available at: www.aseba.org/schoolage.html (accessed 21 February 2018).

American Psychiatric Association (APA) (2013) *Diagnostic and Statistical Manual of Mental Disorders,* 5th edn. Washington, DC: American Psychiatric Association.

Ask, H., Waaktaar, T., Seglem, K.B. and Torgersen, S. (2016) Common etiological sources of anxiety, depression, and somatic complaints in adolescents: a multiple rater twin study. *Journal of Abnormal Child Psychology* 44(1): 101–114. DOI: 10.1007/s10802-015-9977-y.

Baggerly, J. (2004) The effects of child-centered group play therapy on self-concept, depression, and anxiety of children who are homeless. *International Journal of Play Therapy* 13(2): 31–51.

Beck, A.T. (1979) *Cognitive Therapy of Depression.* New York: Guilford Press.

Braet, C., Wante, L., Van Beveren, M. and Theuwis, L. (2015) Is the cognitive triad a clear marker of depressive symptoms in youngsters? *European Child and Adolescent Psychiatry* 24(10): 1261–1268. DOI: 10.1007/s00787-015-0674-8.

Bratton, S., Ray, D., Rhine, T. and Jones, L. (2005) The efficacy of play therapy with children: a meta-analytic review of treatment outcomes. *Professional Psychology: Research and Practice* 36(4): 367–390. DOI: 10.1037/0735-7028.36.4.376.

Burdick, D. (2014) *Mindfulness Skills for Kids and Teens.* Eau Claire, WI: PESI Publishing.

Burke, T.A., Connolly, S.L., Hamilton, J.L., Stange, J.P., Abramson, L.Y. and Alloy, L. B. (2016) Cognitive risk and protective factors for suicidal ideation: a two year longitudinal study in adolescence. *Journal of Abnormal Child Psychology* 44(6): 1145–1160. DOI: 10.1007/s10802-015-0104-x.

Centers for Disease Control and Prevention (CDC) (2013) *Mental health surveillance among children – United States, 2005–2011. MMWR* 62: 1–35. Available at: https://www.cdc.gov/childrensmentalhealth/features/kf-childrens-mental-health-report.html (accessed 21 February 2017).

Calati, R.P., Favero, F.I. and Riboni, E. (2011) Is cognitive behavioural therapy an effective complement to antidepressants in adolescents? A meta-analysis. *Acta Neuropsychiatrica* 23: 23–271.

Chorpita, B.F., Moffitt, C.E. and Gray, J. (2005) Psychometric properties of the Revised Child Anxiety and Depression Scale in a clinical sample. *Behaviour Research and Therapy* 43: 309–322.

Erk, R.R. (2008) Understanding the development of psychopathology in children and adolescents. In: Erk, R.R. (ed.) *Counseling Treatment for Children and Adolescents with DSM-IV-TR Disorders.* Upper Saddle River, NJ: Merrill Prentice Hall, pp. 39–91.

Friedberg, R.D. and McClure, J.M. (2015) *Clinical Practice of Cognitive Therapy with Children and Adolescents: The Nuts and Bolts.* New York: Guilford Press.

Kovacs, M. (1980) Rating scales to assess depression in preschool children. *Acta Paedopsychiatrica 46*: 305–315.

Landreth, G. (2012) *Play Therapy: The Art of the Relationship.* New York: Routledge.

Little, K., Olsson, C.A., Youssef, G.J. et al. (2015) Linking the serotonin transporter gene, family environments, hippocampal volume and depression onset: a prospective imaging gene × environment analysis. *Journal of Abnormal Psychology 124*(4): 834–849. DOI: 10.1037/abn0000101.

Merikangas, K.R., He, J., Burstein, M., Swanson, S.A., Avenevoli, S., Cui, L., Benjet, D., Georgiades, K. and Swendsen, J. (2010) Lifetime prevalence of mental disorders in US adolescents: results from the national comorbidity study–adolescent supplement (NSC-AP). *Journal of American Academy of Child and Adolescent Psychiatry 49*(10): 980–989. DOI: 10.1016/j.jaac.2010.05.017. Available at: https://www.ncbi.nlm.nih.gov/pmc/articles/PMC2946114.

Merikangas, K.R., He, J., Burstein, M., Swendsen, J., Avenevoli, S., Case, B., Georgiades, K., Heaton, L., Swanson, S. and Olfson, M. (2011) Service utilization for lifetime mental disorders in U.S. adolescents: results of the National Comorbidity Survey – Adolescent Supplement (NCS-A). *Journal of American Academy of Child and Adolescent Psychiatry 50*(1): 32–45. DOI: 10.1016/j.jaac.2010.10.006. Available at: https://www.ncbi.nlm.nih.gov/pubmed/21156268.

National Institute for Mental Health (NIMH) (2016a) *Anxiety Disorders.* Rockville, MD: Author. Available at: https://www.nimh.nih.gov/health/topics/anxiety-disorders/index.shtml (accessed 21 February 2016).

National Institute for Mental Health (NIMH) (2016b) *Depression.* Rockville, MD: Author. Available at: https://www.nimh.nih.gov/health/topics/depression/index.shtml (accessed 21 February 2016).

Piaget, J. (1952) *The Origin of Intelligence in Children.* New York: International University Press, Inc.

Reyes, C.J. and Asbrand, J.P. (2005) A longitudinal study assessing trauma symptoms in sexually abused children engaged in play therapy. *International Journal of Play Therapy 14*(2): 25–47.

Reynolds, C.R. and Richmond, B.O. (1978) What I think and feel: a revised measure of children's manifest anxiety. *Journal of Abnormal Child Psychology 6*: 271–280.

Sburlati, E.S., Schniering, C.A., Lyneham, H.J. and Rapee, R.M. (2011) A model of therapist competencies for the empirically supported cognitive behavioral treatment of child and adolescent anxiety and depressive disorders. *Clinical Child and Family Psychology Review 14*(1): 89–109. DOI: 10.1007/s10567-011-0083-6.

Stulmaker, H.L. and Ray, D.C. (2015) Child-centered play therapy with young children who are anxious: a controlled trial. *Children and Youth Services Review 57*: 127–133. DOI: 10.1016/j.childyouth.2015.08.005

World Health Organization (WHO) (1992) *The ICD-10 Classification of Mental and Behavioural Disorders: Clinical Descriptions and Diagnostic Guidelines*. Geneva: World Health Organization.

World Health Organization (WHO) (2016) *Investing in treatment for depression and anxiety leads to fourfold return*. Available at: www.who.int/mediacentre/news/releases/2016/depression-anxiety-treatment/en (accessed 21 February 2018).

World Health Organization (WHO) (2017) Depression. Fact sheet. Available at: www.who.int/mediacentre/factsheets/fs369/en (accessed 21 February 2018).

# 22

# SELF-HARM AND SUICIDE

## SUM YU PANSY YUE AND DENNIS OUGRIN

**This chapter will discuss:**

- **Definition of self-harm**
- **Self-harm prevalence in adolescents**
- **Self-harm as a risk factor for future suicide**
- **Basic risk assessment and red flags**
- **Therapeutic interventions for adolescent self-harm**
- **Common therapeutic challenges**
- **Adolescent self-harm and suicide prevention**

## INTRODUCTION

## What is self-harm?

'Self-harm' can be defined as self-injury or self-poisoning, irrespective of the intent of the action. It is sometimes referred to as 'deliberate self-harm' (DSH). As such, this encompasses a wide spectrum of behaviour that can be categorised into self-harm with suicidal intent (suicide attempts), self-harm without suicidal intent (non-suicidal self-injury, NSSI) and self-harm with undetermined intent. In this chapter, the term 'self-harm' will be used as per the broad definition given above.

## Prevalence of self-harm in adolescents

Self-harm and suicide are common in adolescence. Both are more common in females than males. Suicide is the second most common cause of death in young people aged 15–29 years old internationally, with 804,000 suicides worldwide in 2012 alone according to statistics from the World Health Organization (WHO). A systematic review of international self-harm literature (52 studies) found that the mean lifetime prevalence in adolescents was 18% for NSSI and 16.1% for DSH, with no significant difference in mean prevalence between the two (Muehlenkamp et al., 2012). These paradoxical findings where DSH has lower mean lifetime prevalence than NSSI highlight the variation in methodology and definitions used in prevalence studies, and hence the difficulty in comparing self-harm prevalence rates between studies and across countries.

## Self-harm, a strong risk factor for future suicide

NSSI and suicide attempts often co-exist. The exact relationship between the two remains controversial, as some researchers believe that NSSI activity is a protective, coping mechanism to regulate negative emotions, whereas others postulate that NSSI may actually be a precipitating factor on a spectrum of behaviour that escalates up to suicidal ideation and suicide attempts (Grandclerc et al., 2016). Nevertheless, it is clear that some of the risk factors for NSSI and suicide overlap; these include psychiatric co-morbidities such as depression and borderline personality disorder (BPD), as well as a personal history of sexual or physical abuse. NSSI itself is also an independent risk factor for future suicidal behaviour. In fact, a long history of NSSI behaviour, the use of varied methods for NSSI and the absence of physical pain during NSSI have all been associated with an increased risk of suicide attempts.

# RISK ASSESSMENT

Given the prevalence of adolescent self-harm and suicidal behaviour, being able to conduct a comprehensive risk assessment for those who present with such behaviour is a useful skill for any health professional. Here, we will identify and explore some of the key aspects of a basic risk assessment, including red flag symptoms and the use of common risk assessment tools.

## Basic risk assessment

A risk assessment can be defined as a:

> detailed clinical assessment that includes the evaluation of a wide range of biological, social and psychological factors that are relevant to the individual and, in the judgment of the healthcare professional conducting the assessment, relevant to future risks, including suicide and self-harm. (NICE, 2011)

The range of risk factors to consider in a risk assessment can be divided into risk factors related to the index self-harm event, proximal risk factors and distal risk factors (Ougrin et al., 2012).

## The index event

It is important to fully explore the index self-harm episode, with particular attention paid to the method chosen, the motivation behind the episode (e.g. to relieve the emotional pain, to escape from thoughts or to die) and the presence of any suicidal intent. In exploring the method of self-harm, access to the chosen method and other more lethal methods such as firearms or sharp objects must be considered. The lethality of the method should be evaluated, both objectively (the actual degree of danger to life of the method used) and subjectively (the degree of danger to life as perceived by the adolescent). The objective lethality may correlate poorly with the suicidal intent of the adolescent or child, so lethality should not be used as a surrogate marker of suicidal intent.

With regard to suicidal intent, several factors should be elicited. One factor is the degree of planning and preparation made for the episode. When did they first think of hurting themselves? How long did they spend thinking or planning before the actual episode of self-harm? Did they do any research on the method selected? Did they choose a significant date, time or place? Was any alcohol or drugs used prior to self-harm? Did they give their possessions away? Did they leave a suicide note? Another is whether any attempts were made to prevent their discovery. Were they alone or did they ensure they were alone for the episode? Did they, for example, lock the door of their bedroom? Did they resist help when offered? A third factor is whether the youth discussed their intentions to self-harm with others or made anyone aware of the episode prior to it happening. It is often useful to ask the individual to reflect on their self-harm episode. What do they think of the episode now? Any regrets? Do they want to self-harm again? Do they still want to die? If they have changed their mind since, what has changed? Many adolescents may also be ambivalent as to whether they live or die.

## Proximal and distal risk factors

Proximal risk factors can be defined as recent stressful life events, recent changes in physical or mental state and substance abuse (Ougrin et al., 2012). They can precipitate an episode of self-harm. Stressful life events can include bereavement, arguments or break-ups of family or romantic relationships, school-related factors (e.g. exams, bullying, self-harm or suicide in friends), recent diagnosis of physical or mental health problems, increasing suicidal thinking (in frequency and severity), as well as abuse (physical or sexual, or triggers from past episodes of abuse). Like lethality, the subjective and objective amount of stress triggered by a life event may differ significantly depending on the individual.

Distal risk factors are those that are long-standing. These include socio-demographic (females are more likely to self-harm but males are more likely to succeed in completing suicides), psychiatric (co-morbid diagnoses including anxiety, mood disorders, eating disorders, psychotic disorders) and psychological risk factors (personality traits such as impulsivity, neuroticism, perfectionism).

## Red flags

In addition to exploring the aforementioned risk factors, one should look out for red flag symptoms that may indicate a higher risk of future self-harm or suicide. These include:

- current suicidal ideation;
- detailed planning behind self-harm episode;
- suicide note or giving away possessions prior to event;
- attempts to prevent being found or resisting help (for suicide attempts);
- previous history of suicide attempts;
- family history of suicides;
- feeling hopeless;
- isolated or lack of social support (from family, friends, school);
- psychiatric co-morbidities (anxiety, depression, psychosis);
- significant changes in mood, behaviour or personality.

## Common risk assessment tools

To support clinicians in risk assessing young people who present with self-harm, a variety of tools have been developed. They are often in the form of a questionnaire or checklist to be completed either by the patient (e.g. Suicidal Behaviour Questionnaire SBQ, University of Washington) or the clinician (e.g. Galatean Risk Screening Tool Child-Adolescent Version,

GRIST). They generally generate a crude indication of risk of a specific outcome (e.g. the Behavioural Research and Therapy Clinics Imminent Suicide Risk and Treatment Actions Note generates an indication of the imminent risk of suicide).

Whilst risk assessment tools can be helpful, current National Institute for Health and Clinical Excellence (NICE) guidelines recommend that risk assessment tools and scales are not to be used in isolation to predict future self-harm or suicide, to determine whether the patient should be offered treatment or whether they are suitable for discharge (NICE, 2011).

## Summary of risk assessment

A thorough risk assessment of a young person presenting with self-harm is a key part in determining the subsequent, most appropriate management for the individual patient. A detailed history, including that of the index self-harm episode and other related risk factors (both proximal and distal), is indispensable. Risk assessment tools can be used to help structure and supplement risk assessments but cannot in isolation replace a clinical assessment of the patient.

## THERAPEUTIC INTERVENTIONS FOR ADOLESCENT SELF-HARM

Whilst no pharmacological intervention has yet been found to be effective at treating adolescent self-harm, there is a wide range of non-pharmacological, psychosocial interventions available for adolescent self-harm management. They include individual-based, group-based and family-based interventions.

## Individual-based interventions

Individual-based interventions include interpersonal psychotherapy (IPT) and cognitive-behavioural therapy (CBT). IPT is an established intervention for depression in adolescents but currently lacks evidence of its efficacy on self-harm or suicidal behaviour in adolescents. It is a time-limited intervention of 12–16 weeks, where the individual attends weekly therapy sessions with an IPT therapist who links the individual's diagnosis with their interpersonal problems. The sessions will then focus on learning skills and thus solving interpersonal problems, providing symptomatic improvement. IPT may be a potential suicide prevention intervention, as it has been shown in one randomised controlled trial (RCT) to reduce depression, suicidal ideation, anxiety and hopelessness in depressed adolescents with suicidal risk compared to treatment as usual (TAU).

Like IPT, CBT has been used to treat depression in adolescents with clinically significant benefits. However, as CBT itself is not specifically aimed at self-harm management, it remains unclear as to whether CBT is effective in improving self-harm-related outcomes. Relatively large RCTs, including the TADS study, the ADAPT trial and the TORDIA study, have been conducted on adolescent cohorts with depression. Overall, the evidence from these trials has been mixed, with the TADS study, for example, showing reduced suicidal events and suicidal ideation with CBT, but the ADAPT trial finding no significant difference in clinical outcomes when CBT was added to routine care with selective serotonin-reuptake inhibitor (SSRI) treatment (Ougrin and Yue, 2016).

CBT has also been adapted into different related interventions, such as computerised CBT (cCBT), mindfulness-based cognitive therapy (MBCT) and manual-assisted cognitive therapy (MACT). MACT has in particular been shown in a few trials to be feasible and effective in reducing self-harm behaviour, but this has not yet been explored in purely adolescent cohorts aged 18 years old or below. In addition, a CBT-based intervention called an adjunctive cognitive-behavioural family-based alcohol, DSH and HIV prevention programme (ASH-P) has been developed. It involves small adolescent and parent group workshops (two workshops over 2 weeks lasting 12 hours in total plus one 2-hour booster session 2 weeks post-workshops). In its pilot RCT of adolescents ($n = 81$ adolescents and a parent) who were receiving community mental health treatment at the time of recruitment, it found that ASH-P was associated with lower odds of DSH at 12-month follow-up relative to an assessment-only control (Esposito-Smythers et al., 2016). This suggests that CBT-based family approaches have some promising potential in reducing self-harm, but only a small percentage of participants had self-harm at baseline and there has been no independent replication of the study yet.

## Individual and family-based interventions

Mentalisation-Based Therapy for Adolescents (MBT-A) is an adolescent version of MBT, a therapy originally developed for BPD. It aims to enhance the individual's ability or capacity to mentalise, the process in which we explicitly and implicitly interpret our own actions and that of others, thereby improving affect regulation and impulse control. MBT-A, a 12-month, manualised, psychodynamic intervention, comprises weekly individual therapy sessions and monthly family therapy sessions. Only one RCT has been conducted of MBT-A ($n = 8$, 85% female), but MBT-A was found to be more effective than TAU in reducing self-harm and depression (Ougrin et al., 2015).

Another intervention combining both individual-based and family-based elements is the modified Dialectical Behaviour Therapy for adolescents (DBT-A). DBT-A is an intensive intervention lasting up to 12 weeks, comprising weekly individual therapy sessions, weekly skills training group sessions with family members included and a 'Walking the Middle Path' skills module aiming to improve often problematic relationships between adolescents and their family members. Despite the intensive nature of the programme, RCTs have found it to be a feasible and acceptable intervention for adolescents who self-harm. In addition, DBT-A has been shown to have some long-term efficacy. In an RCT of outpatient adolescents who engage in self-harm ($n = 77$, 88.3% female), it was effective in reducing self-harm frequency relative to enhanced usual care (19 weeks of usual care plus at least one therapy session weekly), even at 52 weeks of follow-up (Mehlum et al., 2016). However, independent replication of the promising findings is needed, with larger sample sizes. Future research should also aim to explore the potential of DBT-A interventions in adolescent inpatient cohorts as well.

## Group-based intervention

An example of a group-based intervention is Developmental Group Psychotherapy (DGP). DGP, unlike other interventions such as CBT, was specifically designed for adolescents who self-harm. It involves three phases, with the first being the initial assessment phase, the second being six 'acute' group sessions and the third being weekly 'long-term' group therapy sessions. There is no explicit time limit for the latter 'long-term' phase.

The pilot study for DGP ($n = 63$) conducted in Manchester, 2001 was in fact the first to show that a psychological intervention could successfully reduce adolescent self-harm (Ougrin and Yue, 2016). Following the pilot study, larger replication studies were conducted in Australia ($n = 72$) and in northwest England ($n = 366$). However, both replication studies failed to replicate the promising findings of the pilot study (Ougrin et al., 2015). Reasons for this may include that the adolescents in the replication studies generally had more severe levels and longer histories of self-harm at baseline than in the pilot study. Of the latter replication study participants, 86% also had significant ongoing therapy with Child and Adolescent Mental Health Services (CAMHS) during the follow-up period, which may have contributed to the overall improvement seen across the whole cohort. Notably, DGP did not offer any significant improvement in self-harm outcomes compared to routine outpatient care and was also shown to be less cost-effective than routine care only. Nevertheless, follow-up of this large and well-characterised cohort may be of benefit in the future.

## Summary of interventions

In spite of the paucity of evidence available, there is promising evidence that overall, non-pharmacological interventions may be effective in managing adolescent self-harm. However, there is an urgent need for independent replication of the trials that have been conducted, preferably with larger sample sizes and longer follow-up periods, to validate and support the implementation of the aforementioned therapeutic interventions.

# COMMON THERAPEUTIC CHALLENGES THAT MAY ARISE

## Poor engagement with therapy

Although a wide range of therapeutic interventions are available for the management of adolescent self-harm, they all rely on the individual to engage or be compliant with the intervention to be of benefit. Poor engagement and compliance with therapy are common challenges in the management of adolescent self-harm. It is particularly common in outpatient settings, where up to 77% of adolescents disengage from treatment and approximately half of the patients attend four or fewer follow-up appointments (Ougrin and Latif, 2011).

Since poor engagement with therapy has been associated with poor psychosocial outcomes in adolescents who present with self-harm, developing ways to improve engagement is key to the successful implementation of any type of therapeutic intervention to help adolescents reach their treatment goals. Whilst research suggests that specific outpatient psychotherapy is not any better than TAU for engaging adolescents in outpatient therapy (Ougrin and Latif, 2011), several factors other than the therapeutic intervention itself are likely to affect engagement as well and can be targeted in the future. This may include home-based or school-based interventions, or changing the way the initial assessment of the adolescent patient is conducted. One example of the latter is therapeutic assessment, a manualised combination of a psychosocial assessment and a 30-minute therapeutic intervention, which has shown some promise in improving engagement relative to standard psychosocial assessment alone (Ougrin et al., 2013).

## Barriers to seeking help

Many young people who self-harm do not seek help at all. One study found that for adolescents who engaged in self-harm, only 27% sought some form of help (Doyle et al., 2015). The help sought ranged from that of a friend (39%), a family member (21%), a psychologist or psychiatrist (8%), or a hospital (11.8% for previous self-harm episode, 6.9% for the latest self-harm episode). Among the reasons provided by those who did not seek help, a third were of the opinion that they did not require help, and approximately 20% did not want anyone to know about their self-harm (Doyle et al., 2015). Other reasons included the feeling that no-one would be able to help or the reluctance to 'waste other people's time'. The secretive nature of self-harm and the feeling that 'no-one would be able to help' may in part be due to the attitude of the professionals that young people come in contact with, and how they may adversely contribute to the stigma attached to self-harm. Research has shown that professionals who commonly come into contact with adolescents who self-harm (accident and emergency department (A&E), CAMHS and secondary school professionals) may lack the knowledge and training they feel they require to effectively support adolescents who self-harm (Timson et al., 2012).

Removing or minimising these existing barriers to adolescents seeking help is essential, as a thorough professional assessment and therapeutic intervention are known to reduce the likelihood of self-harm repetition. An example of a modifiable factor is the stigmatising attitude and lack of knowledge of health care and school professionals towards adolescents who present with self-harm. One possible intervention to minimise this may be to implement training at an early stage, aimed at students of health care professions. Similar interventions may be implemented to support teachers and parents of adolescents who self-harm, as they are often amongst the first to be aware of the behaviour. School-based and public health interventions may also make adolescents more knowledgeable about how best to support each other, as informal sources of help are the most likely source of help sought out by adolescents. More details on the help-seeking behaviour of adolescents can be found in the Further Reading section.

## ADOLESCENT SELF-HARM AND SUICIDE PREVENTION

Community-based and public health strategies play an important role in adolescent suicide prevention. The successful implementation of such strategies often requires the collaboration of multiple agencies, from schools to local governments.

One large community study of almost 3000 students aged 15–16 years old in the UK investigated their views on possible interventions or strategies to prevent adolescent self-harm (Fortune et al., 2008). The study found that the main sources of support identified by adolescents were their families and friends, over formal organisations (well-known national telephone counselling services and GPs). However, the adolescent cohort also identified key areas beyond their circle of friends and family that could, in their view, be improved with community-based strategies to prevent self-harm. These areas included school-based interventions, particularly with regard to the need for more effective anti-bullying interventions, having access to a school counsellor and additional support related to examinations and school assessments. Another area identified was public education, with the aim of improving adolescent awareness of what sources of help are available, the dangers of self-harm, and the negative consequences of suicide on families and friends. A small number of adolescents in the study also mentioned the role of the media, and how the media may be both beneficial (by advertising different sources of help available for struggling adolescents) and harmful (depictions of adolescent suicide as a way of getting attention) for adolescent self-harm prevention or intervention.

Given the range of strategies that can be implemented via multiple agencies, the field of adolescent self-harm and suicide prevention is a large, multifaceted one. Through dedicated suicide prevention national charities such as Prevention of Young Suicide (PAPYRUS) in the UK and the American Foundation For Suicide Prevention (AFSP) in the US, numerous campaigns exist to improve internet safety (e.g. limiting access to pro-suicide websites), encourage sensitive media reporting of suicides, improve access to high-quality and timely support services, and to educate schools, workplaces and communities about the importance of mental health.

School-based interventions have also been trialled with some success. For example, the Youth Aware of Mental Health Programme (YAM), a manualised universal school-based intervention involving a 3-hour role-play session complete with workshops, a booklet and educational posters displayed in the classrooms, was shown in a large, multicentre RCT (Saving and Empowering Young Lives in Europe, SEYLE study) to significantly reduce the number of suicide attempts (odds ratios (OR) 0.45, 95% CI 0.24–0.85, $p = 0.014$) and severe suicidal ideation (OR 0.5, 95% CI 0.27–0.92, $p = 0.025$) in adolescents at 12 months follow-up, relative to the control group where only the educational posters were put up in the classrooms (Wasserman et al., 2015). Given that the YAM is of short duration, consisting of only 5 hours in 4 weeks, the SEYLE study provides promising evidence that universal, school-based interventions may be logistically possible and effective in preventing adolescent suicide. Other school-based interventions in the US, such as the classroom-based 'Signs of Suicide' (SOS) and 'Good Behaviour Game' interventions, have also had some success at reducing the risk of suicide attempts and suicidal ideation in trials (Wasserman et al., 2015).

As research into adolescent self-harm and suicide prevention progresses, it is important for researchers to work closely with the government, schools and health care professionals (in primary and emergency care) to facilitate robust, large, multicentre trials of interventions in high-risk cohort populations. Trials with longer follow-up periods are also required to investigate whether any benefits achieved in the short term remain sustained over time. Future research may target and modify risk factors for suicide early, from childhood with family-based and school-based interventions to adolescence with peer-based and community-based interventions (Wyman, 2014). This developmental, upstream approach offers a pragmatic view to guide researchers in the field of adolescent self-harm prevention and may stimulate helpful knowledge breakthroughs in the future.

## Case Study: 'Lily'

'Lily' was 11 years old when she was referred by her GP for further assessment, after an overdose of five paracetamol tablets at school. This was her first episode of self-harm and it was preceded by a 4-week history of low mood, tearfulness, low self-esteem and occasional thoughts of suicide. Her schoolwork had recently deteriorated. It became apparent that her symptoms and deterioration in schoolwork coincided with the recent deterioration in her relationship with her father. Having moved to the UK at the age of 5, she has had no contact with her mother since, who had separated with her father prior to the move. However, she has close friends at school. She also denied any ongoing suicidal thoughts or plans.

From the initial assessment, it appeared that Lily had a moderate depressive episode. Her immediate risk of self-harm or suicide was deemed to be low and she was discharged with a community follow-up appointment a week later.

## Key Learning

- Self-harm is a broad term describing a spectrum of behaviour, including self-injury or self-poisoning irrespective of suicidal intent.
- Some researchers consider NSSI and suicide attempts separately; others disagree that suicidal intent is a reliable differentiator between the two behaviours.
- The relationship between self-harm and suicide is complex. NSSI has been shown to be an independent risk factor for future suicide attempts.
- A comprehensive risk assessment should consider risk factors related to the index event itself, as well as more distal, long-standing risk factors such as the presence of any psychiatric comorbidity.
- Risk assessment tools are helpful but should not be used in isolation to determine the risk of self-harm or suicide in a young person.
- No pharmacological agent has been shown to reduce adolescent self-harm.
- Psychosocial interventions, especially DBT, CBT and MBT may be effective in managing adolescent self-harm.
- Adolescent suicide prevention is an evolving, multidisciplinary field requiring teamwork from a range of organisations.

## Summary

Adolescent self-harm and suicide are major public health issues. Being able to conduct a thorough risk assessment for any young person who presents with an episode of self-harm is therefore a key skill that health care professionals should develop. Although no pharmacological intervention has been shown to reduce adolescent self-harm, there is some promising preliminary evidence that some psychosocial interventions, such as DBT-A, may be of benefit. However, there is a need for additional research exploring the mechanisms behind how the psychosocial interventions reduce adolescent self-harm, and a need for independent replication of trials to further explore the efficacy of such interventions.

A number of challenges remain, including the development of effective, universal public health strategies that can modify risk factors early and thus prevent adolescent suicide worldwide. Public education for adolescents themselves, their families and for front-line health care professionals is needed to break down the barriers that prevent adolescents from seeking help, as well as to improve the quality of support they receive when they do.

## Discussion Questions

Based on the case study of 'Lily' presented in this chapter, consider the following questions. Imagine you are the one performing the initial assessment of Lily after she is referred to you by her GP.

1. What key information or details would you like to know about Lily and her overdose? How would you phrase your questions sensitively to elicit the information?
2. Would you consider using a risk assessment tool to assist in your risk assessment of Lily? Why or why not? If you choose to, which tool would you use?
3. What advice would you give her father after the initial assessment for Lily's safety whilst she waits for her community follow-up appointment a week later?
4. If you were worried about Lily's immediate safety, how would you manage her case differently? What services would you consider referring her to?

## Develop Your Skills

CBT formulation is a useful skill to develop. It aims to make sense of the predisposing factors, causes and maintaining factors of the individual's psychological and behavioural problems. Formulation often takes the form of a diagram linking thoughts, feelings, bodily responses and behaviour.

Consider the case of 'Lily' and the following additional details. Her parents separated when she was very young. Growing up, there were two brief periods of time when her father travelled to the UK without her, leaving her to stay with other relatives in India. Eventually she did move to the UK to live with her father and continue primary school. Since arriving in the UK, she has had to switch primary school once due to fights and arguments at school. Some of these arguments, according to Lily, were triggered when others tried to 'control' her, by asking her to do things a certain way. Lily tells you that when she feels 'controlled', she feels angry and low in mood. Recently, she has also started to feel tired all the time, and she is struggling to sleep and concentrate at school. Her schoolwork has, as a result, deteriorated in quality.

She talks about upcoming exams at school and how she thinks she will fail them because she will fail to remember everything that the teachers have talked about in class. She states that her family will be better off without her as she is and will always be a failure. When asked to list some things she is good at, Lily struggles to do so initially, but eventually admits that she is quite good at dancing and singing. However, she no longer participates in these extra-curricular activities.

When asked about her relationship with her father, she says that her father hates her, does not understand her thoughts and feelings, and is not at all interested in her life. Although Lily says she has good friends who support her, including one who has been her friend ever since she arrived in the UK, her father tells you that he feels quite differently, stating that Lily has few friends and her friendships appear to be very unstable.

Now try to put Lily's story together in a diagram, linking her predisposing factors, core beliefs, thoughts, feelings, bodily responses and behaviours together. Discuss and compare your diagram with that of a partner. Then, assuming that Lily receives some CBT, what do you think her re-formulation would look like?

## Further Reading

Bridge, J.A., Horowitz, L.M., Fontanella, C.A., Grupp-Phelan, J. and Campo, J.V. (2014) Prioritizing research to reduce youth suicide and suicidal behavior. *American Journal of Preventive Medicine 47*(3): S229–S234.

Dudley, M., Goldney, R. and Hadzi-Pavlovic, D. (2010) Are adolescents dying by suicide taking SSRI antidepressants? A review of observational studies. *Australasian Psychiatry: Bulletin of Royal Australian and New Zealand College of Psychiatrists 18*(3): 242–245.

Hawton, K., Witt, K.G., Taylor Salisbury, T.L., Arensman, E., Gunnell, D., Townsend, E., van Heeringen, K. and Hazell, P. (2015) Interventions for self-harm in children and adolescents. *Cochrane Database Systematic Reviews* 12: CD012013.

Law, G.U., Rostill-Brookes, H. and Goodman, D. (2009) Public stigma in health and non-healthcare students: attributions, emotions and willingness to help with adolescent self-harm. *International Journal of Nursing Studies 46*(1): 107–118.

McLean, J., Maxwell, M., Platt, S., Harris, F. and Jepson, R. (2008) *Risk and Protective Factors for Suicide and Suicidal Behaviour: a Literature Review*. Edinburgh: Scottish Government Social Research.

Oldershaw, A., Richards, C., Simic, M. and Schmidt, U. (2008) Parents' perspectives on adolescent self-harm: qualitative study. *British Journal of Psychiatry 193*(2): 140–144.

Rowe, S.L., French, R.S., Henderson, C., Ougrin, D., Slade, M. and Moran, P. (2014) Help-seeking behaviour and adolescent self-harm: a systematic review. *Australian and New Zealand Journal of Psychiatry 48*(12): 1083–1095.

### Online Resources

Counselling MindEd, Self-Harm and Risky Behaviour: https://www.minded.org.uk/course/view.php?id=89

Young Minds: www.youngminds.org.uk

The National Self-Harm Network: www.nshn.co.uk

# REFERENCES

Doyle, L., Treacy, M.P. and Sheridan, A. (2015) Self-harm in young people: prevalence, associated factors, and help-seeking in school-going adolescents. *International Journal of Mental Health Nursing* 24(6): 485–494.

Esposito-Smythers, C., Hadley, W., Curby, T.W. and Brown, L.K. (2016) Randomized pilot trial of a cognitive-behavioral alcohol, self-harm, and HIV prevention program for teens in mental health treatment. *Behaviour Research and Therapy* 89: 49–56.

Fortune, S., Sinclair, J. and Hawton, K. (2008) Adolescents' views on preventing self-harm. *Social Psychiatry and Psychiatric Epidemiology* 43(2): 96–104.

Grandclerc, S., De Labrouhe, D., Spodenkiewicz, M., Lachal, J. and Moro, M.-R. (2016) Relations between nonsuicidal self-injury and suicidal behavior in adolescence: a systematic review. *PLoS One* 11(4): e0153760.

Mehlum, L., Ramberg, M., Tørmoen, A.J., Haga, E., Diep, L.M., Stanley, B.H., Miller, A.L., Sund, A.M. and Grøholt, B. (2016) Dialectical behavior therapy compared with enhanced usual care for adolescents with repeated suicidal and self-harming behavior: outcomes over a one-year follow-up. *Journal of the American Academy of Child and Adolescent Psychiatry* 55(4): 295–300.

Muehlenkamp, J.J., Claes, L., Havertape, L. and Plener, P.L. (2012) International prevalence of adolescent non-suicidal self-injury and deliberate self-harm. *Child and Adolescent Psychiatry and Mental Health* 6: 10.

National Institute for Health and Clinical Excellence (NICE) (2011) Self-harm in over 8s: long-term management. *NICE guideline* (CG133). London: NICE.

Ougrin, D. and Latif, S. (2011) Specific psychological treatment versus treatment as usual in adolescents with self-harm systematic review and meta-analysis. *Crisis* 32(2): 74–80.

Ougrin, D. and Yue, S.Y.P. (2016) *Self-Harm in Young People*. Hong Kong: iConcept Press Limited.

Ougrin, D., Tranah, T., Leigh, E., Taylor, L. and Asarnow, J.R. (2012) Practitioner review: self-harm in adolescents. *Journal of Child Psychology and Psychiatry and Allied Disciplines* 53(4): 337–350.

Ougrin, D., Boege, I., Stahl, D., Banarsee, R. and Taylor, E. (2013) Randomised controlled trial of therapeutic assessment versus usual assessment in adolescents with self-harm: 2-year follow-up. *Archives of Disease in Childhood* 98(10): 772–776.

Ougrin, D., Tranah, T., Stahl, D., Moran, P. and Asarnow, J.R. (2015) Therapeutic interventions for suicide attempts and self-harm in adolescents: systematic review and meta-analysis. *Journal of the American Academy of Child and Adolescent Psychiatry* 54(2): 97–107.

Timson, D., Priest, H. and Clark-Carter, D. (2012) Adolescents who self-harm: professional staff knowledge, attitudes and training needs. *Journal of Adolescence* 35(5): 1307–1314.

Wasserman, D., Hoven, C.W., Wasserman, C. (2015) School-based suicide prevention programmes: the SEYLE cluster-randomised, controlled trial. *The Lancet 385*(9977): 1536–1544.

Wyman, P.A. (2014) Developmental approach to prevent adolescent suicides: research pathways to effective upstream preventive interventions. *American Journal of Preventive Medicine 47*(3): S251–S256.

# 23

# SEXUAL, PHYSICAL AND EMOTIONAL ABUSE

## BEVERLY TURNER-DALY

This chapter is dedicated to Sinead Staveley, a much-missed colleague and friend whose humanity, integrity and absolute commitment to children and families will never be forgotten. 'Onwards…'

**This chapter will discuss:**

- **Definitions of abuse**
- **General principles of working therapeutically with children who have been abused**
- **Evidence-based practice**
- **The impact of abuse and therapeutic responses explored within a case study drawing on the author's clinical experience**

## INTRODUCTION

Reading this chapter will provide opportunities for you to reflect (privately and with others) on some of the complex practical and ethical issues specific to counselling and providing therapeutic support to children and young people affected by abuse. You may decide to read it in one sitting or work slowly through it, taking time to explore fully the explicit and implicit learning opportunities within. The chapter summarises what is known about the impact of abuse, outlines key principles for working with children and young people who have been abused, and describes therapeutic responses that might be offered.

The case study is fictitious but inspired by the stories of many children with whom the author has had direct or indirect contact over a 30-year period. It has been designed to bring to life the impact of child abuse and neglect, and therefore has potential to cause distress. It goes without saying that this chapter comes with a sensitivity warning and it is recommended that readers have access to appropriate support both to explore the material and any impact it has on them personally.

## DEFINITIONS OF ABUSE

Physical abuse, sexual abuse, emotional abuse and neglect are terms used to categorise the plethora of experiences that cause or are likely to cause 'significant harm' to children and young people. As our knowledge and understanding expands, so too do definitions. Mirroring a growing awareness of the extent of abuse outside the family as well as within it, we now recognise child sexual exploitation, female genital mutilation and bullying (including cyber bullying) as forms of abuse that may give rise to the need for therapeutic intervention. The government publication *Working Together to Safeguard Children* (DfE, 2015) contains an overview of official definitions of abuse, is regularly updated and available online at www.gov.uk.

## GENERAL PRINCIPLES FOR WORKING THERAPEUTICALLY WITH CHILDREN AFFECTED BY ABUSE

Children who have been abused experience a wide range of emotional and behavioural difficulties that sometimes result in them being referred for counselling or therapy (Allnock and Hynes, 2012). The effects of abuse are different for each child but in some instances, they can be enduring, impacting significantly on mental health, relationships and well-being (Pritchard, 2013).

Working with children who have been abused can be daunting, and it would help therapists enormously to have access to evidence about which approaches are most effective in which circumstances. Although there is an extensive research base relating to the long-term effects of abuse on children (Cashmore and Shackel, 2013) and evidence-informed clinical excellence guidelines exist relating to specific psychiatric disorders (NICE, 2005), the comparative value of the wide range of treatment interventions is still being explored (Myers, 2011). Until more research becomes available, it would be unwise to rule out 'unproven' interventions and more helpful, perhaps, to think in terms of key therapeutic principles that give rise to a range of possibilities. Key principles are outlined below and expanded upon further in the case study that follows.

## GETTING THE TIMING RIGHT

The 'child protection' system, with its emphasis on gathering information and preventing further abuse, can at times be disempowering to children. When statutory interventions begin, children may be overwhelmed by the impact of professional involvement in their lives and fear the consequences. This may shed light on why so many children report abuse only to retract later.

Abuse can give rise to conflicting and ambivalent feelings. Professionals sometimes assume that thoughts and feelings relating to abuse will be uppermost in a child's mind when in fact home life, school, hobbies and friendships matters more. Before embarking on therapy, the therapist should be satisfied that the child is living in a safe, secure environment where their physical and emotional needs are being met (Doyle, 2012) and, where possible, access to appropriate education is in place. Supportive carers/significant adults make strong allies and can have a significant impact on outcomes of therapeutic work; therefore, the timing of intervention needs to be compatible with all aspects of a child's life.

Child abuse can make caring adults feel incredibly responsible, sometimes 'duty-bound' to do something to compensate for the harm caused by others. Pushing for a child to receive therapy can be part of this process. Sometimes, when considering the suitability of counselling or therapy for a child who has been abused, it is important to step back, reflect on our feelings and examine carefully whose needs we are trying to meet. Counsellors and therapists may sometimes need to have uncomfortable conversations with colleagues in order to ensure that the principle of appropriate timing is followed. On occasion, the best intervention a professional can make is to recognise that therapy can go on hold in the short term whilst focus is placed on supporting the child to re-adjust to post-abuse life, centred around their wishes and feelings.

## MANAGING THE LEGAL PROCESS

The timing of therapy is further complicated by the various legal processes associated with safeguarding children. In addition to being clients in need of therapeutic services, many children who have been abused are simultaneously witnesses to a crime, required to give evidence in legal proceedings against the perpetrators of the abuse. In these situations, the therapeutic needs of individual children may be viewed by some professionals as secondary to the task of securing a conviction, thus protecting other children from harm. Counsellors who work in the field of child abuse need to be familiar with the legal and policy context of their work so that, in these instances, they are best placed to contribute to decision-making with regard to the timing and nature of therapeutic interventions. To consolidate your understanding of the legal and ethical context of safeguarding children, it is recommended you read this chapter in conjunction with Chapters 17 and 18.

## EMPOWERMENT

A universal aspect of child abuse, irrespective of type and nature, is that of disempowerment. Child abuse generally involves an abuse of power through coercion or manipulation leaving the abused feeling unable to resist or protect themselves. In terms of knowledge, experience and autonomy, children lack power in relation to adults. Disabled children are additionally vulnerable and more at risk of abuse than non-disabled children. When providing therapeutic support, it is essential we are mindful of how the 'Social Graces' such as gender, race, age, ability, social class, sexuality (Burnham, 2011) may contribute to vulnerability and make it harder to seek or receive help. Counsellors and therapists are most effective when they understand how disadvantage, discrimination and oppression may be impacting on their client and work in ways that are sensitive to diversity and place empowerment at the centre of all interventions.

Devastating though it may be, we must remember that abuse is an experience, one aspect of a child's life. Therapists and other professionals must avoid contributing to any process through which abuse becomes part of a child's identity. Children who have been abused may find the labels 'victim' or 'abused child' hugely stigmatising (Bass and Davis, 2008). It is not unusual for professionals to frame their understanding of abuse in terms of 'victims' and 'perpetrators', which is not entirely helpful. In addition to the negative connotations associated with both, this can be oversimplistic, for example, when we seek to understand abuse perpetrated by one child on another. 'Cyberbullying' and the phenomenon currently referred to as 'sexting' are without doubt harmful, whether the child is themselves bullied, they bully others or witness bullying. To think in terms of victims and perpetrators (given the age of some of the children involved in these behaviours) may restrict our understanding and limit our ability to respond appropriately to all children.

There have been occasions when the professional world has been slow to understand and respond appropriately to child abuse because of judgemental assumptions about what a 'victim' looks like and how they behave. Inquiries into cases of child sexual exploitation in recent years suggest that children and young people who do not fit a stereotype of 'victim' are not afforded sufficient protection or responded to supportively.

Abuse can be seriously damaging to a child's self-esteem and sense of identity (Sanford, 1991), therefore, counsellors, therapists and other professionals need to think of each child as a person first: a unique individual who is so much more than their 'presenting problem'. Professionals can make an important therapeutic intervention simply by being careful not to label, and by challenging those who do. By seeing beyond the abuse and emphasising that the child is so much more than their abusive experience, counsellors can begin the process of helping children to move forward. Language is vitally important in this regard. We might deliberately choose to talk about 'a child who has been abused' rather than an 'abused child' or 'victim of abuse'. We might challenge assumptions that all children who have been abused need therapy or that all children who have been abused are in some way damaged. It is not uncommon for children who have experienced abuse to feel angry, hurt, betrayed, ashamed, guilty, frightened, sad, unlovable, unworthy and culpable, and to behave in ways that reflect this. To be effective helpers, we must be aware of this but not forget to be optimistic; to balance the negatives with what we know about courage, resilience and survival. Labels are rarely helpful to anyone. In the case of child abuse, labels may reinforce the negative experiences and act as barriers to recovery and we should avoid them.

## EVIDENCE-BASED PRACTICE

At the time of writing, a discourse of evidence-based practice is widespread, underpinned by government expectation that clinical intervention should be informed by appropriate theory and research, especially in relation to efficacy. This is more complex than it may seem. One position is that it is possible through research to demonstrate the effectiveness of some forms of therapeutic intervention in the same way one might measure the effectiveness of a drug. An alternative perspective is to question the reliability of the science behind such research and suggest that, in a challenging economic climate, there is an inherent bias in favour of short-term, comparatively cheap methods. Counsellors need to be aware of current theory and research and become critical consumers of knowledge: exploring origins, considering ethical issues and measuring published findings against their own practice wisdom and experience. The effects of child abuse and choices of therapeutic intervention are inextricably linked; however, in our quest for evidence-informed practice, we must be aware of the risks of overgeneralising.

Humans are infinitely complex: the unique 'product' of what they bring into the world and what is experienced from then on in. How each child or young person is affected by abuse is unique. Factors considered relevant include: nature and duration of the abuse, relationship to abuser, age, gender, physical and emotional maturity, culture, ethnicity and race (Myers, 2011). There is much debate about core concepts such as attachment theory, vulnerability and resilience, although it has long been asserted that the quality of relationships with non-abusing significant adults is highly significant in outcomes for children (Wyatt and Powell, 1988). Given the complex interplay of a huge number of variables, counsellors need to be cautious in their use of theory and research, and true to the principle of treating each client as unique.

Whether they work with children, adults or both, counsellors require knowledge of the short- and long-term effects of abuse, and the range of therapeutic responses and interventions that may be appropriate in different circumstances. In the case of sexual abuse, it is also useful for therapists to have some understanding of what is known as the 'grooming' process – strategies used by perpetrators of abuse to intimidate, disempower and silence their victims (Finkelhor, 1984). Therapists also need to keep up to date with developments in 'child sexual exploitation' and what is known about the needs of children who harm other children.

In situations where there is uncertainty about how best to intervene, the following suggestions may be helpful. Where trauma is clearly apparent and 'symptom' reduction a priority (as in cases of post-traumatic stress) a cognitive-behavioural approach may be indicated (Deblinger et al., 2006). Where isolation and self-esteem are primary concerns, therapy within a group setting might be more effective than individual counselling (Doyle, 2012). Where trust is an issue and the client is ambivalent about being referred, it may be that progress will best be achieved through a slow, careful process such as person-centred counselling or play therapy (Doyle, 2012). Therapeutic objectives are numerous and multifaceted, ranging from working through feelings (such as anger, loss, guilt and shame) to directly focusing on reducing behaviours that may be harmful. Improving self-image and self-esteem may also be valid goals as may repairing and strengthening relationships with significant others.

In reality, it is often left to each therapist to assess and provide what they believe to be appropriate which, inevitably, is influenced heavily by each therapist's training and theoretical orientation. What a child is offered will depend to a large extent on where they live, to whom they are referred, and how knowledgeable and experienced the therapist is. Methods of intervention are likely to be influenced as much by cost and availability as suitability and efficacy, and it is not uncommon these days for therapists to be allowed only a small number of sessions in which to work with each child.

The case study below is intended to give a flavour of the various ways in which children who have been abused might be assisted. At the end is a series of questions and answers to promote reflection and consolidate learning.

## Case Study: Tina

When Tina was born, her mother experienced post-natal depression and was unable to bond with her. For the first 8 months of her life Tina received little warmth and affection and spent many hours strapped in a buggy with a soother in her mouth. Her parents' relationship involved frequent episodes of domestic violence and, on one occasion, Tina was caught in the crossfire sustaining a blow to the head that went unreported. When Tina was 2, her father moved away and ceased all contact with the family leaving Tina's mother angry and bitter. Tina bore a close resemblance to her father, which grew more noticeable with each passing year. Tina's mother often shouted at and insulted her, telling her she was 'an ugly pig, just like him!'

By the age of 11, Tina had two younger half-brothers, aged 5 and 7, whose father had left shortly after the youngest was born and had no contact with them. Tina spent most evenings and weekends looking after the boys and doing domestic chores. Her mother worked in the offices of a local taxi company and was often out during the evenings, leaving Tina to feed and supervise the boys and put them to bed. Tina loved her brothers and went to great lengths to make sure the family's domestic situation did not come to the attention of school or the local authority. Social workers had followed up anonymous referrals on two occasions but Tina and her mother had presented a united front and convinced them these referrals were malicious and without grounds. Tina stayed 'below the radar' at school, maintaining acceptable levels of attendance and avoiding attention. Tina had no friends to speak of and the only affection she received was from the boys. Tina was afraid that she and her brothers would be taken 'into care' if details of their family life were ever to be discovered.

When Tina was 13, her mother began a relationship with Dave, a man she met at work. Dave moved in with the family and life changed dramatically. Tina had never known her mother to be so happy, and the shouting and criticism that had hitherto been a constant

*(Continued)*

(Continued)

feature of her life, virtually stopped. Dave was kind to Tina and used his tips to buy her presents that he jokingly told her to keep quiet about. No-one had ever made Tina feel special before and, inevitably, she came to like and trust Dave a great deal. Tina did not know that these were the beginnings of an elaborate grooming process that would eventually lead to sexual abuse.

At the age of 15, Tina was admitted to hospital having taken an overdose of painkillers with cider. Hospital records showed that she had been admitted 3 months earlier with a broken arm that was said to have been caused by falling downstairs. During a series of interviews with a psychiatrist, Tina disclosed sexual abuse and, later, in the presence of a social worker, made a formal statement to the police alleging rape by Dave over an 18-month period. Professionals learnt that she had tried unsuccessfully to draw attention to the abuse a few months earlier by throwing herself down the stairs at home. Medical examination revealed numerous scars to Tina's arms and legs that had been self-imposed. Dave had used many strategies to silence Tina, convincing her that she was to blame and that no-one would believe her if she told. On discharging her, the psychiatrist concluded that Tina's was not a serious attempt to take her own life but rather a classic 'cry for help'. The report stated that Tina had not expressed any emotions at all during her time in hospital and seemed to have 'no sense of self-worth whatsoever'.

## Therapeutic Responses

The aftermath of the disclosure and ensuing child protection investigation was traumatic for Tina. Tina's mother did not believe her and refused to have any further contact with her. Tina was placed with foster carers who lived many miles away. She was able to speak to her brothers by telephone but opportunities for direct contact were few. Initially, Dave denied the allegations, but when faced with forensic evidence, admitted the abuse but claimed Tina had 'led him on'. He was subsequently sentenced to a term of imprisonment, something Tina felt incredibly guilty about.

A multi-agency plan was put in place to address Tina's needs. Included in the plan was a recommendation she be offered 'post-abuse counselling'. Tina found talking about the abuse very difficult and was reluctant to see a therapist but not assertive enough to refuse. During the first year following disclosure, two attempts at establishing therapeutic relationships failed, with counsellors concluding it was the wrong time.

Tina's care team prioritised her home and school life, eventually finding a foster carer, Ann, who was willing and able to commit to Tina long term. This enabled Tina to start afresh in a new school and to experience nurture and care for the first time in her life. She lost weight, joined the school running club and began to form friendships. Ann understood that Tina had difficulties expressing her emotions and was sensitive enough not to push this. She was respectful of Tina's privacy and personal space, and noticed over time that Tina became more relaxed in her presence and more able to hold short conversations. Some members of the care team remained concerned that Tina had never talked about what Dave had done to her and felt that some of the distorted thinking and self-blame that had been evident in her sessions with the psychiatrist needed to be addressed. Encouraged by Ann, Tina agreed to give counselling another go.

Tina's counsellor, Louise, was trained in person-centred counselling and play therapy. She was creative in her methods and her counselling room was bright, cheery and had artwork and poetry on display. Louise understood the importance of establishing clear boundaries and took a lot of time explaining to Tina what counselling involved, how she worked and what to expect. She involved Tina in negotiating a working agreement and made use of every opportunity that arose to empower Tina, knowing that feelings of powerlessness are common in children who have been abused. Although Louise did not know the details of Tina's early life, she was experienced enough to know that Tina's poor self-esteem and difficulties expressing emotion might pre-date the sexual abuse and that she should not allow assumptions to creep into her work. Although she was curious to know more about Tina's early years and her relationship with her mother, Louise trod carefully, letting Tina lead the way. Louise had to be strong and assertive regarding this matter. Some members of the care team did not think she could work properly with Tina without understanding what was now on record as a 'chronic history of physical, sexual and emotional abuse'. Others were concerned that the work lacked focus and that clearer objectives needed to be set in order to justify the funding. Louise trusted her instincts, refusing to allow others to set the therapeutic agenda. She relied on supervision to help her remain focused on her therapeutic process with Tina.

Over a series of 12 sessions taking place in two blocks of six with a review midway, Louise and Tina worked together, supported by Ann, who encouraged attendance but never asked to be told the details. Louise had warned Ann that there might be times when Tina would seem upset by the sessions or even that the sessions might seem to be making her worse. Louise prepared Ann carefully in order to reduce the risk of her undermining the process. She also did this with members of the care team, making clear that with the exception of information suggesting ongoing risk of harm, no detailed feedback would be provided on the content of the sessions. She explained that affording confidentiality gave the counselling a better chance of success.

Louise understood that direct conversation was hard for Tina so made use of various mediums to facilitate communication. A significant breakthrough occurred when Tina was making a pebble sculpt and Louise offered her a box of buttons to supplement the stones. Tina was drawn to a particular button, which she held and stared at. Tears began to pour down her face – the first show of emotion Louise had witnessed. Remaining calm and staying with the process, Louise used congruence to acknowledge what was happening and Tina began to talk in detail about her brothers and her sorrow at being separated from them. She also revealed snippets of the neglect, physical and emotional abuse that had characterised her early life.

*(Continued)*

(Continued)

In subsequent sessions, Tina drew pictures of herself and her brothers, representing herself as fat and ugly. She was able to tell Louise that her mother had referred to her as 'the Pig' and that she had been teased at school and on social media for being overweight and smelly. At times, Louise had to work very hard to contain her own feelings and remain focused. She longed for Tina to realise that she was in fact a very beautiful young woman and was staggered that Tina believed herself to be ugly and unlovable. She was a mother herself and could not imagine how Tina's mother could treat her own daughter in this way. She felt utter fury towards this woman whom she would never meet. At times, she fought strong urges to express this anger. Louise knew that Tina might have deep-rooted and ambivalent feelings towards her mother and that an ill-judged comment could jeopardise their working relationship. There were times during her work with Tina that Louise had a strong urge to reach out and physically comfort her.

At the start of one session, Tina asked Louise if they could play a word game she had on her mobile phone. This was slightly unconventional but Louise decided to agree and see where it went. Louise quickly realised that Tina had introduced this game so that she could talk about difficult things without needing to make eye contact. At the end of the session, she saved the game on the screen and brought it back unchanged to the next session. On the third occasion, Tina typed the word 'slut', almost inviting Louise to comment. Louise felt that a door had been opened and, taking care not to make any assumptions or judgements, she gently enabled Tina to begin talking about the sexual abuse and the impact it had had on her.

What emerged was the story of a needy, vulnerable little girl who had been desperate for affection and easy to manipulate. Dave had told Tina that she was the 'daughter he never had' and that he was going to protect and care for her the way a father should. When he had begun to sexually abuse her, he had told Tina that most fathers did this and that it was 'his job to introduce her gently to being a woman'. Tina had no friends at school and no-one to check this out with. Her mother had been less hostile towards her since Dave's arrival and Tina was terrified that confiding in her would spoil everything. By the time touching turned into rape, Tina had been made to feel that she had cooperated with the abuse, indeed had encouraged it. Dave always gave her sweets and money and made her feel that these were in payment for sex. She had thrown herself downstairs misguidedly, believing that in hospital the abuse would be discovered. Tina's overdose had been an expression of her powerlessness and self-loathing, as had several months of self-mutilation. Louise was aware that many children who have been sexually abused feel great shame about their bodies having responded (to the abuse) and to it being physically pleasurable. She took great care not to say anything about how the abuse must have felt or to make any judgements about how Tina felt about Dave.

Working with Tina's newfound openness, Louise was able to help her think about what had happened to her and begin reducing the level of self-blame that had been instilled. Louise also realised that Tina might now be able to make use of a therapeutic group where more direct approaches to challenging distorted thinking could be used.

### Group Work

Tina agreed to attend a therapeutic group for girls who had been sexually abused and made further progress as a result. Group leaders did not share any of the content of the sessions outside the group, although the weekly agenda and activities they used were passed on to other professionals and carers. Within this group, Tina was enabled to participate in activities that focused on body image and self-esteem, and was helped to realise that she was not alone in this experience and that sexual abuse is never the child's fault. She was enabled to share some of the ambivalent feelings she had towards her abuser and non-protecting parent and to hear that this was not uncommon. Tina had hoped that if she were examined, doctors would discover she was being abused; this was because she believed that signs of sexual abuse were noticeable. Many children think they are forever damaged by abuse and have heard many myths about never being able to have children, going on to become abusers and so on. Attending the group enabled some of the myths that reinforced Tina's low self-esteem to be dispelled. It also allowed taboo subjects and some of the most embarrassing, humiliating aspects of abuse to be explored in a safe and sensitive way.

## Is This Area of Work For Me?

Tina's story demonstrates that, despite the challenges, this is an extremely worthwhile and rewarding area in which to work, having potential to make a huge difference to a child's well-being both in the short and long term. Although it is rarely obvious at the outset what method of intervention is most likely to be successful, and sometimes it can be a struggle to establish the trust necessary to engage the client, the theory and research in this area can be fascinating and there is great potential for creativity in practice, making it well worth the effort of developing the knowledge and skills necessary to be effective. That having been said, working with children who have been abused is not for everyone. The emotional impact on the counsellor of hearing firsthand and in depth the stories of children who have been abused cannot be overestimated. This work carries with it a significant risk of compassion fatigue. At times it can be incredibly frustrating to witness the damage done to children both by abusers and the system around them, and to feel powerless to change this. Sometimes, through parallel process, therapists may even begin to experience some of the same feelings as their clients and it is not uncommon for them to take to supervision feelings such as anger, frustration, sorrow, fear, guilt and even shame, and it is essential the counsellor avails themselves of high-quality supervision from a supervisor who is experienced in this area.

## Key Learning

- There are many different ways in which counsellors and therapists can work with children who have been abused.
- All interventions should take into account appropriate timing, the impact of the legal process and the importance of empowerment.
- Counselling children and young people who have been abused can be very challenging, both in terms of the skills required and its highly emotive nature. It is an aspect of practice where transference and counter-transference can be very powerful and where the 'personal/professional interface' needs a high level of attention.

## Summary

- There is evidence to suggest that child abuse can have a lasting impact and that counselling and therapy may improve outcomes for children.
- The research base is developing rapidly but, as yet, there is insufficient evidence to evaluate the effectiveness of all forms of therapeutic intervention. Empirical studies into the efficacy of therapeutic interventions are limited due to the significant ethical and methodological challenges posed; nevertheless, research in this field is progressing and it has been suggested that we are moving towards a clearer understanding of the respective merits of different forms of intervention (Myers, 2011).
- This area of work can be very demanding, and counsellors should remain alert to issues of parallel process, transference and counter-transference and compassion fatigue, ensuring they have access to an appropriately trained and experienced supervisor.

## Discussion Questions

1. Do you think any of Tina's experiences are likely to affect her permanently?
2. How might intervention need to be different if there were only funding for six sessions?
3. Are there any circumstances in which therapeutic intervention should be withheld?
4. What is the ideal physical environment in which to do therapeutic work with children and young people who have been abused?
5. What level of confidentiality should be offered within the counselling relationship?

Turn to p.450 for possible answers.

## Develop Your Skills

1. Complete MindEd Module 8 (see the Online Resources section) and, on completion, discuss with your supervisor or line manager/employer. This might result in you deciding to make contact with your Local Safeguarding Children Board (LSCB) and find out what relevant training is available to you. Attending events such as 'Child Protection Awareness Workshops' will give you an opportunity to think about child abuse within a multidisciplinary forum and help you to understand how counselling fits within the wider context of safeguarding children.
2. Reflect on your theoretical orientation and preferred method of intervention, and consider the extent to which it lends itself to working with children or young people who have been abused. Does your way of working take into account the needs of all clients and is it empowering?
3. How do we know when the conditions are right for counselling and therapy to begin? What factors need to be considered? Whose opinions should be sought and how?
4. There are many myths about how children who have been abused feel about their abusers and how they behave. It can be helpful to explore this in groups with colleagues by listing possible feelings and behaviours and exploring how professionals can respond in ways that are open and non-judgemental.
5. What do you know about the process referred to as grooming? Are only victims groomed? What about family members and whole communities? What strategies are used? Is grooming always done face to face by someone who knows the child/young person? What about grooming via the internet? What about cases of child sexual exploitation?
6. In what circumstances, if any, should a counsellor offer physical comfort to a child? What issues does this raise? How might the age of the child or young person influence this? What difference does the gender and sexuality of client and therapist make, if any? In terms of comforting a distressed client, how is working with a child different from working with an adult?
7. If a child disclosed abuse during a session with you, would you know how to respond therapeutically whilst following your agency's safeguarding procedure? (If not, the workshops outlined in point 1 above will help.)

## Further Reading

Allnock, D. and Hynes, P. (2012) *Therapeutic Services for Sexually Abused Children and Young People: Scoping the Evidence Base*. London: NSPCC.

Daniels, D. and Jenkins, P. (2010) *Therapy with Children: Children's Rights, Confidentiality and the Law*, 2nd edn. London: SAGE.

*(Continued)*

(Continued)

Doyle, C. (2012) *Working with Abused Children*, 4th edn. Basingstoke: Palgrave Macmillan.

Geldard, K., Geldard, D. and Yin Foo, R. (2013) *Counselling Children: A Practical Introduction*, 4th edn. London: SAGE.

Gerhardt, S. (2004) *Why Love Matters: How Affection Shapes a Baby's Brain*. Hove: Brunner-Routledge.

Mudaly, N. and Goddard, C. (2009) The ethics of involving children who have been abused in child abuse research. *International Journal of Children's Rights 17*: 261–281.

**Online Resources**

NSPCC Research and Resources: https://www.nspcc.org.uk/services-and-resources/research-and-resources

# REFERENCES

Allnock, D. and Hynes, P. (2012) *Therapeutic Services for Sexually Abused Children and Young People: Scoping the Evidence Base*. London: NSPCC.

Bass, E. and Davis, L. (2008) *The Courage to Heal: A Guide for Women Survivors of Child Sexual Abuse*, 20th Anniversary Edition. New York: Harper & Row.

Burnham, J. (2011) Developments in Social GRRRAAACCEEESSS; visible-invisible and voiced-unvoiced. In: Krause, I.B. (ed.) *Culture and Reflexivity in Systemic Psychotherapy: Mutual Perspectives*. London: Karnac Books, pp. 139–160.

Cashmore, J. and Shackel, R. (2013) 'The long-term effects of child sexual abuse', *Child Family Community Australia Information Exchange (CFCA)*. Paper 11. Available at www.aifs.gov.au/cfca/pubs/papers/a143161/cfca11.pdf.

Deblinger, E., Mannarino, A.P., Cohen, J.A. and Steer, R.A. (2006) 'Follow up study of a multi-site, randomised controlled trial for children with sexual abuse PTSD: Examining predicators of treatment response', *Journal of the American Academy of Child and Adolescent Psychiatry*, 45:1474–1484

Department of Education (DfE) (2015) *Working Together to Safeguard Children*. London: HMSO.

Doyle, C. (2012) *Working with Abused Children*, 4th edn. Basingstoke: Palgrave Macmillan.

Finkelhor, D. (1984) *Child Sexual Abuse: New Theory and Research*. New York: The Free Press.

Gerhardt, S. (2004) *Why Love Matters: How Affection Shapes a Baby's Brain*. Hove: Brunner-Routledge.

Myers, J.E.B. (2011) *The APSAC Handbook on Child Maltreatment*, 3rd edn. London: SAGE.

National Institute for Health and Clinical Excellence (NICE) (2005) *Depression in Children and Young People: Identification and Management in Primary and Secondary Care: Update.* London: NICE.

Pritchard, J. (ed.) (2013) *Good Practice in Promoting Recovery and Healing for Abused Adults.* London: Jessica Kingsley.

Sanford, L.T. (1991) *Strong at the Broken Places: Overcoming the Trauma of Childhood Abuse.* London: Virago.

Wyatt, G.E. and Powell, G.J. (1988) *Lasting Effects of Child Sexual Abuse.* London: SAGE.

# 24

# EATING DISORDERS

## REBECCA KIRKBRIDE

**This chapter will discuss:**

- Eating disorders (EDs) and presentations involving disordered eating particularly as they relate to counselling children and young people
- The definition, possible causes and treatment of EDs
- Various ways of working with EDs in practice, including multi-agency working and involving family members in the therapy
- When an ED presentation might become a safeguarding or child protection issue
- The chapter will also provide a series of 'questions for discussion' throughout the text, in order to enhance the reader's engagement with the content

## INTRODUCTION: COUNSELLING CHILDREN AND YOUNG PEOPLE WITH EATING DISORDERS

EDs can be one of the most challenging presentations counsellors face in their practice. Young people experiencing psychological and emotional conflicts expressed via their relationship with food and their bodies are often in great need of help in understanding and working through these conflicts, and offering counselling is a natural response to this. However, the nature of an ED can mean that the client has no conscious desire to be relieved of their symptoms and may in fact fear recovery. One of the symptoms of an ED is phobia of gaining weight or getting fat, meaning that the client fears losing control of restricting food intake, overexercising and other ED behaviours. This can present challenges in the work for both counsellor and client, including the difficulty inherent in developing a therapeutic alliance with a young person who is, on a superficial level at least, afraid of getting better.

A further challenge arises because EDs are fundamentally psychological problems that often have a significant impact on the sufferer's physical health and well-being, both short and long term. Over time EDs can affect many aspects of the young person's physical and mental health. They also have a relatively high mortality rate amongst mental health presentations (Katzman and Steinegger, 2013). For this reason, counsellors seeing a child or young person with an ED will often work alongside other professionals who collaborate to ensure that both physiological and psychological needs are attended to.

## What is an eating disorder?

EDs in childhood and adolescence have been defined as, 'a disorder of childhood in which there is an excessive preoccupation with weight or shape, and/or food intake, and accompanied by grossly inadequate, irregular, or chaotic food intake' (Bryant-Waugh and Lask, 1995).

## Who is affected?

Whilst in the past it was believed that EDs were culture-bound, affecting only affluent white women and girls in the west, this view has now changed considerably. There are various socio-cultural theories (Nicholls, 2013) regarding the prevalence of EDs across different groups, along with an acknowledgement that EDs are found in diverse communities, as well as being prevalent across gender and class divides within these communities. Whilst most commonly found in adolescent and young adult girls, boys and young men also experience eating issues. EDs have been encountered clinically in children as young as 7 years old, but onset is more common during adolescence (Bryant-Waugh and Lask, 2013). Clinicians in the field of childhood EDs have argued that criteria used for diagnosing EDs in adults are not directly transferrable to children due to differences in the ways that children conceptualise issues as well as biological differences between the two groups (Nicholls et al., 2000). The most recent version of the *Diagnostic and Statistical Manual of Mental Disorders* (DSM-5) contained the new category of Avoidant/Restrictive Food Intake Disorder (ARFID), covering children affected by EDs but without a prevailing concern with weight or body image. The general criteria for anorexia nervosa (AN) and bulimia nervosa (BN) have also been updated to be more relevant for younger and diverse populations.

## Diagnostic criteria

The following diagnostic criteria, based on the DSM-5, are included to give a sense of ED criteria rather than as a guide for the diagnosis of individual clients, as this would be beyond the scope of most counselling practitioners.

Diagnostic criteria for AN include:

- Restriction of food intake leading to significantly low body weight (in context of what is minimally expected for age, sex, development and physical health).
- Either an intense fear of gaining weight or of becoming fat, or persistent behaviour that interferes with weight gain.
- Disturbance in the way one's body weight or shape is experienced.
- Undue influence of body shape and weight on self-evaluation.
- Persistent lack of recognition of the seriousness of the current low body weight.

Diagnostic criteria for BN according to the DSM-5 include:

- Recurrent episodes of binge eating characterised by both of the following:

  o Eating, in a discrete period (e.g. within any 2-hour period), an amount of food that is definitely larger than most people would eat during a similar period of time and under similar circumstances.
  o A sense of lack of control over eating during the episode.

- Recurrent inappropriate compensatory behaviour intended to prevent weight gain, such as self-induced vomiting, misuse of laxatives, diuretics or other medications, fasting, or excessive exercise.
- Self-evaluation is unduly influenced by body shape and weight.

Binge-eating disorder (BED) is characterised by the same bingeing behaviour as BN but without the compensatory behaviours. People with BED are often overweight or obese.

# CAUSES (AETIOLOGY) AND RISK FACTORS FOR EATING DISORDERS

In spite of a myriad of theories, it is hard to isolate any one cause in the development of EDs. As can be seen in the definition above, EDs are a collection of symptoms that arise for very different reasons in each person experiencing them. Their development is perhaps best understood as a dynamic process made up of the interaction of various influential factors. These influences may be internal, such as inherited genes or neural pathways, or external, such as attachment history or cultural pressures (Wood, 2011). In the following some of these factors are considered in brief, but readers are referred to the Further Reading section for more information.

## Biological and genetic risk factors

Evidence from studies examining the development of EDs in families has concluded that a female relative of someone with an ED is significantly more likely to develop an ED (Nicholls, 2013). Recent studies have also examined the likelihood of genetic inheritance of some of the personality or temperament traits that are understood to contribute to the development of EDs, such as perfectionism and interpersonal mistrust (Nicholls, 2013). Fonagy et al. (2004) suggest that interaction between an individual's genes and the environment they experience growing up may be significant in the development of EDs (2004: 117).

## Neurobiological factors

There are two main areas for consideration regarding neurobiological influences on EDs. One is whether underlying neurobiological abnormalities contribute to the development of an ED, whilst the other considers whether ED symptoms such as long-term low weight cause disruption in neural mechanisms and lead to further neuropsychological deficits (Frampton and Rose, 2013). Various models for neuroscientific-based concepts regarding the aetiology and maintenance of EDs have developed over the past decade and these could have implications for therapeutic interventions, particularly with regard to treatments that work with cognitive understanding, such as cognitive-behavioural therapy (CBT) (Frampton and Rose, 2013).

## Psychological factors

Alongside developments in understanding EDs from the genetic and neurobiological positions outlined above, the psychological roots of eating problems are still seen as key to understanding their development, maintenance and treatment. Psychodynamic concepts of EDs include viewing the development of AN in adolescence as an expression of an internal crisis regarding sexuality and the transition from childhood to adulthood (Hogan, 1992). This is one route to explaining the role of puberty in the development of an eating disorder. Crisp (1983) suggests that AN develops due to anxieties regarding separation, sexuality and the adult body, 'To the anorectic the body, especially the adult body, is perceived as alien and threatening rather than owned' (1983: 856). In this respect, the ED symptoms are understood as the psyche's attempt to hold on to, or return the body to the pre-pubescent state of childhood as a defence against growing up, with all that might mean for the individual.

## Environmental factors: Attachment and culture

Some theorists (Gander et al., 2015) suggest that environmental factors such as attachment history as well as wider social and cultural influences play a part in the development of EDs. As is shown in the following section on assessment, it is important to consider what factors in their history may have contributed to the client's current difficulties. There is also an argument that parenting styles, for example, authoritarian, and family systems are influential factors in ED development (Gander et al., 2015).

There are many different views regarding how societal and cultural influences contribute to the development of an ED. Hogan (1992) suggests that increasing societal demands 'for sexual expression and participation have placed profound social pressure on all adolescents ... At puberty such external stimulation and expectation give rise to overwhelming unconscious internal conflict' (1992: 112). Given that we now live in the digital age when there is considerable pressure for young people to conform to norms and to be constantly courting approval or 'likes' for their appearance, this view of internal conflicts seems relevant to understanding the relationship a young person might develop with their body today, given the current importance of social media.

## EATING DISORDERS IN PRACTICE

Similar to other clinical presentations, clients present with a wide range of eating issues. These issues range in severity from mild concerns regarding body image and weight at one end of the spectrum to a clinically diagnosable and severe ED requiring treatment as a medical emergency at the other. Each client presenting with eating and body image issues needs to be assessed according to their individual needs on a collaborative and ongoing basis.

The following case material offers a sense of the range of presentations that can occur.

## Case Study

### Michelle

Michelle is 12 and a pupil in Year 8. She is referred to the school counsellor because of concerns regarding low mood and bullying in school. Michelle is slightly overweight for her age and is teased by boys in her class. In her first session Michelle tells the counsellor she feels bad about herself and wishes she could lose weight. She says sometimes she fantasises about cutting the fat off her thighs. Michelle's mum is a single parent with chronic back pain and depression, and Michelle does a lot of the caring for her. Michelle tells the counsellor that she often eats sweets in the evening as a way of making herself feel better but then feels angry and bad.

### Lauren

Lauren is 15 and training to be a dancer. She is currently a pupil at a local secondary school but intends studying dance full-time when she finishes her GCSEs this summer. Her form teacher notices Lauren has recently lost a lot of weight and appears to be suffering from low mood in school. After discussing her concerns with the year nhead she refers Lauren to the school counsellor. When Lauren goes to her initial counselling session she tells the counsellor that there is nothing wrong and that she doesn't need help. She says her teacher doesn't understand that dancers need to be fit and healthy and that she needs to keep up with the others in her dance class if she is going to get a scholarship to dance school next year.

### Questions for Discussion

- How might a counsellor think about these two young people?
- Is a different approach required for each of them? What might be similar?

## Collaborative Assessment

Collaborative assessment, including assessment for risk, is a crucial part of the therapeutic process with EDs. A collaborative assessment needs to be carried out in order to get a good sense of what is happening with the client's eating and exercising behaviours, as well as any concurrent issues they may have, such as anxiety, depression and/or self-harm, presentations commonly found alongside EDs (Katzman and Steinegger, 2013). An active interest in the young person and their worldview needs to be established, as well as a sense of family dynamics, as these can be significant in the development maintenance and treatment of eating issues. It is important to get a sense of the young person's experiences in school or in their community, as well as at home. For example, in the case study above Michelle is experiencing bullying at school, which may exacerbate her issues with self-esteem, whilst Lauren seems to be feeling under pressure at dance school to compete and 'keep up with the others'. Counsellors need to look closely at areas such as these during assessment and begin to explore them with the young person, gradually moving towards a shared understanding of what might be at the root of the issues for each individual client. It is also important to consider cultural background as part of this assessment. This means exploring how body image and eating is viewed within the young person's community and taking steps to understand how this might affect their own thoughts and behaviour regarding this issue.

## Risk assessment

Risk assessment is a vital component of the assessment process for a child or young person presenting with eating and/or body image issues. As outlined previously, EDs can have both psychological and physiological components, and the ED-related behaviours of the young person may place them at risk of significant harm. There is a distinction between issues that can be managed in a weekly counselling session, such as those experienced by Michelle in the example above, and those requiring possible further intervention and outside support. It is important, therefore, that counsellors have some understanding of the range of EDs and problems. This can support in identifying and acting with awareness when a young person's thoughts and behaviours around food and eating may be developing into a specific ED, potentially requiring additional treatment if significant harm is to be prevented. If in any doubt regarding the severity of the presentation, counsellors should consult their supervisor and/or seek guidance from a mental health practitioner or child and adolescent psychiatrist. This should preferably be done with the knowledge and consent of the young person, although if the counsellor believes they have grounds for breaking confidentiality due to risk of significant harm they may need to proceed without permission. Counsellors working in agency settings will need to consult their particular agency policy at this point. Here we return to Lauren and her counsellor to see risk assessment in practice.

## Case Study

During the initial counselling assessment, Lauren is adamant she does not need counselling and is fine. However, Maya, the counsellor, is concerned that Laura's weight is low and that she seems unwilling or unable to think clearly about her health. When Maya asks Lauren about what she meant by wanting to 'keep up with the others', Lauren becomes distressed and says they are all better dancers and thinner than her. She reports that none of the other girls has breasts whilst hers are huge and she has a big tummy. Lauren is dressed for school in an over-sized jumper, making it hard to have an accurate sense of her weight and body shape. Her face and fingers are thin and her skin is pale. Maya asks Lauren if she would be willing to meet with her again as it seems there are some issues causing her stress at the moment and which it might help to talk about. Lauren again refuses, saying she doesn't need to speak to anyone. At this point, since Lauren is refusing further counselling, Maya feels that she has enough concerns regarding Lauren's weight loss as well as her attitude towards her body to refer Lauren to the school's designated safeguarding lead, Mrs Sopel. She tells Lauren that she can't make her come for counselling but that she is very concerned about her health and thinks it is best if this is investigated further by a medical professional. Maya says that she will be sharing her concerns initially with Mrs Sopel and then there may be further action, including contacting Lauren's parents. Maya tells her they need to get a better sense of whether she is losing too much weight to be healthy in order to make sure that she doesn't come to harm. Lauren is furious and storms out of the counselling room with tears in her eyes.

### Questions for Discussion

- Do you feel that Maya's actions were appropriate here?
- Are there any other options she could have explored?
- What are the likely or possible consequences of the action she has taken?

## Safeguarding

This case study above demonstrates how a young person's eating behaviour and mental state can mean that there is a safeguarding issue to be managed. Lauren's behaviour could be putting her at risk of significant harm and she could already be experiencing cognitive dysfunction due to malnutrition and low weight. In this situation, the usual therapeutic boundaries regarding confidentiality need to be considered carefully, with the best interests of the young person viewed as paramount in any decision-making. Here Maya decides that Lauren's best interests would not be met by allowing her to leave the counselling assessment without any further action being proposed. In this case Maya's concerns are such that it seems necessary to proceed without permission from Lauren. Maya is aware that Lauren may be developing an ED and that early intervention is significant for successful treatment. She also recognises that she is not qualified to diagnose an ED or to discount it in this case, and therefore a referral to another professional is the right course of action.

Risk assessment needs to be a continuous process throughout therapeutic work and practitioners working with a client with an ED or eating issues need to be alert to any signs that symptoms have worsened and are no longer manageable with counselling alone. When this is the case counsellors again should discuss their concerns in supervision before deciding on any action to be taken. Not all cases involve breaches of confidentiality, and often counselling can take place successfully with a young person with an ED, usually with other professionals working alongside the counsellor.

# WORKING THERAPEUTICALLY WITH CHILDREN AND YOUNG PEOPLE WITH EATING ISSUES

Whilst the physiological symptoms of an ED can be alarming and become the focus of the therapeutic work, it is important to remember that these symptoms are often a communication of underlying psychological issues that will need to be successfully worked through in therapy if the disordered eating behaviour is to be treated.

## Working with other agencies

The complexity and range of ED presentations means that treatment takes place at different levels of intervention as well as moving through various phases. How these develop will depend largely on the severity of the disorder and its course. If the client has experienced significant weight loss and/or other physiological symptoms, then some aspects of the treatment are likely to take place outside of counselling sessions. This may mean that a client has regular meetings throughout the counselling process with a GP, psychiatrist, paediatric nurse, dietician, or other professionals as necessary. Services might be accessed via the NHS, whilst other families may wish to access support for their child via private medical services. It can be helpful for food and weight management to be taken care of outside of the therapeutic space, leaving the counsellor free to concentrate on helping the client to understand, and work towards resolving any underlying psychological and emotional issues.

It is important to be aware of the potential for splitting when working with other professionals or family members, that is, seeing them as either all good or all bad. Counsellors need to bear in mind that others who are in contact with the client at different times may have different experiences and responses to them, and they should try not to react negatively or collude with the client's negative view of the behaviour of their family or other professionals.

## Information-sharing

Working with other agencies may mean that information needs to be shared regarding progress in counselling or any areas of concern regarding the client. When working alongside other professionals it is vital that communication is clear regarding the roles and responsi-bilities of everyone involved. This will help ensure that the client is not offered confusing or conflicting information. Counsellors need to ensure that any information given is easily accessible for clients and their families, whatever their cultural background.

Counsellors must ensure that they respect at all times their client's right to confidentiality where they are over 16 or considered to have the legal capacity to consent (see Chapter 17). Clients should be informed wherever possible of the nature of any information to be shared and this should only take place where consent is given. The exception to this is when confi-dentiality is broken due to concerns regarding significant harm to the young person, as shown in the earlier case example.

## APPROACHES TO TREATMENT

There are several different approaches to treatment and their application will depend on fac-tors such as the severity of the presentation as well as the context in which treatment is taking place. For example, treatment within NHS or Child and Adolescent Mental Health Services (CAMHS) services will often be based on cognitive-behavioural therapy (CBT) or family therapy interventions. According to National Institute for Health and Clinical Excellence (NICE) guidelines there is no particular treatment of choice for EDs and often a range of treatment will be required, tailored to individual needs (Lask and Bryant-Waugh, 2013).

## Individual counselling

As already discussed, EDs are often a response to underlying psychological and emotional issues. As treatment progresses and defensive behaviours around food and weight begin to change, these issues can emerge in the counselling and need to be worked through. Issues may include perfectionism, low self-esteem, a need for control, difficulties with separation and individuation, identity, etc., and these can be explored in counselling where physiological aspects of the ED are being managed elsewhere as appropriate. Bruch (1973) saw the goal of therapy as supporting the young person as they gain a sense of their own capabilities and resources. It is important that the counsellor supports the client's autonomy and does not repeat the young person's possible early experience of being overwhelmed by another. Bruch (1973) suggests this is important in order to avoid a situation where the counsellor 'represents in a painful way a repetition of the significant interaction between patient and parents, where "mother always knew how I felt", with the implication that they themselves do not know how they feel' (1973: 336). Very often, therapy with a young person with an ED involves support-ing them in finding their own separate sense of self and identity.

## The therapeutic relationship

For counselling to be effective, a solid therapeutic relationship must be established. As we saw in the earlier example of Lauren, this is sometimes difficult when a young person themselves cannot accept that there is a problem to be treated. Where the young person finds it hard to acknowledge their need for help, it is important to offer them the kind of conditions that are most likely to support the formation of a therapeutic alliance. As with all therapeutic relationships, empathy, warmth, and non-judgemental curiosity are crucial factors. In order for the alliance to be established the young person needs to feel that the counsellor understands their perspective, even if they don't agree or collude with it. This is shown in the following case study.

---

### Case Study: Kate and Tasneem

Kate is a counsellor working in private practice. She is seeing Tasneem, a 15-year-old girl with AN. As well as working with Kate, Tasneem also meets regularly with a child and adolescent psychiatrist and dietician attached to a private children's ED clinic. The following conversation takes place during Kate and Tasneem's third meeting.

T:  'This week has been terrible. Everyone's trying to make me eat more. Dr Lewis told my mum I had to start eating bread and pasta again or I would have to go to hospital. He just wants to scare me. No-one understands I can't eat bread. Eugh. It's disgusting.'

K:  'So bread is disgusting?'

T:  'Yes, and they all want me to eat it. They want me to get fat. I know they won't be happy until I'm enormous. Especially Mum. I'm 15 now for god's sake. They can't keep forcing me to eat like I'm in prison or something. Why can't they see I need to be thin and let me get on with it?'

K:  'It sounds like you'd like them to let you get on with being thin. Maybe we can think about that a bit. It sounds like being thin is important to you – what do you think it's about for you?'

T:  'I don't know. Mum says it's stupid. But, I suppose being thin makes me feel strong and like I can do all the stuff I want to. If I'm fat I worry I won't be as good at sport and things.'

K:  'So for you, being thin is about being strong and good at stuff?'

T:  'Yes, that's it. When they make me eat stuff I don't want to it feels like they don't want me to be strong. I know I need to eat and sometimes I feel like I should be eating more. Then another part of me says no, I need to exercise more and get stronger. So I go out for a run again.'

---

K:   'So sometimes you have mixed feelings about how much you are eating?'

T:   'I do. Not when I'm around Mum and Dad though. Then I just feel like eating nothing. They don't get that forcing me just makes me want to eat less.'

In this example, Kate uses open questions to try to encourage Tasneem to explore her own thoughts and feelings more. Kate is careful to avoid pushing an agenda with Tasneem about the food she eats or that wanting to be thin is wrong. She hears that being thin is important to Tasneem and invites her to explore this further. This is intended to gently encourage Tasneem to explore any feelings of ambivalence regarding eating and her body without the kind of pressure that is likely to meet with resistance.

One model that counsellors may wish to consider is that of motivational interviewing (MI), developed by Miller and Rollnick (2012) and based on the concept of the 'cycle of change'. Originally used as a therapeutic intervention for addiction, MI is based on the principle that a person's active desire for change goes through different stages and that counsellors need to use different skills and approaches depending on where their client is on the 'cycle of change'. Where this model is particularly useful for EDs is in allowing the client in the 'contemplative' or ambivalent phase of the cycle the space to explore reasons they should and shouldn't be concerned about their eating. They become responsible for this process rather than having all choice taken away from them via their ED behaviours. In the case of severe EDs where a young person is not capable of eating enough to keep them healthy, they won't have much autonomy regarding their food and activity choices. Using MI techniques in this way begins to allow the young person to regain autonomy in how they think about themselves and their behaviour within the containment of the therapeutic relationship. By making space for all of the client's thoughts and feelings to be expressed, the counsellor allows for the possibility that they will be able to find a way to change that feels self-determined rather than simply complying with their parents' or others' wishes.

## Family work

When working with a young person with an ED it may be useful for other family members to be involved in the counselling. This is because, as mentioned previously, some young people with EDs find it difficult to accept that they have an issue so the therapeutic alliance may initially need to be supported by the parents. Working alongside parents can be important because they are with their child far more than the therapist, and are responsible for managing meal times as well as monitoring behaviours and exercise levels. It can be useful if the counsellor is able to support them in managing this in a joined-up way during the counselling process.

Family interventions for EDs often begin with an initial phase of the parents taking full responsibility for feeding the young person when the severity of the illness means that they are not capable of doing this themselves. This can be difficult for parents who struggle with setting boundaries and dealing with the conflict that mealtimes can present. Most if not all parents in this situation will need help with providing the appropriate support. In some cases, depending on the context in which counselling takes place, counsellors may work with parents separately or along with the young person. It is important when working with other family members that boundaries around confidentiality are clearly stated and respected by all parties (Kirkbride, 2016). Some young people, especially older adolescents, may find it difficult to feel completely safe with a counsellor who is also seeing their parents, whilst other young people might welcome this connection and feel that they benefit from having someone they trust 'fight their corner' with their parents.

## Key Learning

- The causes of eating issues are complex and involve the interaction of various internal and environmental factors.
- It is important to carry out a collaborative assessment including assessment for risk when working therapeutically with EDs.
- Counselling young people with EDs may require multi-agency working alongside other professionals.
- Psychological counselling is a vital part of the treatment of the issues underlying EDs in young people.

## Summary

- The nature of therapeutic work with young people with EDs will depend to a great extent on the severity of the disorder and the treatment plans in place, as well as the context within which therapy takes place.
- Where other professionals are involved in supporting the young person and counselling takes place as part of a range of interventions it is important that the counsellor understands what their role is and how best to support the young person in their recovery.
- Eating disorder symptoms can be understood as communications of psychological and emotional distress. Through the use of therapeutic interventions and the establishment of a therapeutic relationship based on empathy, acceptance and genuineness, we can

attempt to help the young person understand the distress or unresolved conflicts that may underlie their issues with their bodies and with food itself. It is by demonstrating non-judgemental curiosity about what might be behind the young person's behaviours that a therapeutic relationship can be established, allowing for the safe exploration of symptoms as well as underlying thoughts and feelings. As this process continues it will hopefully become possible for the young person to let go of some of their previous fears and negative feelings about their body.

- Counsellors need to always bear in mind the risks of an ED and be ready to consider safeguarding measures where appropriate in order to prevent harm to the young person. Such consideration should always take place with the support of either line management or a clinical supervisor.
- Working with eating disorders can be challenging for counsellors and may lead counsellors to explore their own issues with food and their bodies, both past and present. Supervision is a vital source of support for practitioners working in this area.

## Discussion Questions

- What do you think might be the challenges for counsellors working with children and young people with EDs?
- Are these challenges different from those that other professionals encounter in work with this group?

## Develop Your Skills

- Using images from magazines, social media and the internet, consider how today's media reflects societal pressures on young people to conform in terms of their appearance. Look at how this varies across gender, sexuality and culture.
- Thinking about your own adolescence, consider whether such pressures have changed since then, and in what ways. How did the media affect your own relationship with your body when you were growing up?
- Finally, think about how counselling might help young people to manage any negative effect that such pressures may have on their healthy development.

## Further Resources

Gander, M., Sevecke, K. and Buchheim, A. (2015) Eating disorders in adolescence: attachment issues from a developmental perspective. *Frontiers in Psychology 6*: article 1136. Available at: www.frontiersin.org.

Lask, B.and Bryant-Waugh, R. (eds) (2013) *Eating Disorders in Childhood and Adolescence*, 4th edn. Hove: Routledge.

Lask, B. and Frampton, I. (eds) (2011) *Eating Disorders and the Brain.* Chichester: Wiley-Blackwell.

Miller, W.R. and Rollnick, S. (2012) *Motivational Interviewing: Helping People Change*, 3rd edn. New York: Guilford Press.

### Online Resources

MindEd: www.minded.org.uk

410-035 Eating Problems: Mimi Simic

414-016 Eating Disorders: Anorexia and Bulimia: Mimi Simic

401-0062 Eating Disorders in Young People: Dasha Nicholls

401-0063 Assessment of Eating Disorders: Dasha Nicholls

Beat is the UK's leading charity supporting anyone affected by EDs, anorexia, bulimia, eating disorder not otherwise specified (EDNOS) or any other difficulties with food, weight and shape: www.b-eat.co.uk

National Centre for Eating Disorders: www.eating-disorders.org.uk

## REFERENCES

Bruch, H. (1973) *Eating Disorders: Obesity, Anorexia Nervosa, and the Person Within.* New York: Basic Books.

Bryant-Waugh, R. and Lask, B. (1995) Eating disorders – an overview. *Journal of Family Therapy 17*: 13–30.

Bryant-Waugh, R. and Lask, B. (2013) Overview of eating disorders in childhood and adolescence. In: Bryant-Waugh, R. and Lask, B. (eds) *Eating Disorders in Childhood and Adolescence*, 4th edn. Hove: Routledge, pp. 33–49.

Crisp, A. (1983) Anorexia nervosa. *British Medical Journal 287*: 855–858.

Fonagy, P., Gergely, G., Jurist, E.L. and Target, M. (2004) *Affect Regulation, Mentalization, and the Development of the Self*. London: Karnac Books.

Frampton, I. and Rose, M. (2013) Eating disorders and the brain. In: Bryant-Waugh, R. and Lask, B. (eds) *Eating Disorders in Childhood and Adolescence*, 4th edn. Hove: Routledge, pp. 125–147.

Gander, M., Sevecke, K. and Buchheim, A. (2015) Eating disorders in adolescence: attachment issues from a developmental perspective. *Frontiers in Psychology 6: Article 1136*. Available at: www.frontiersin.org.

Hogan, C.C. (1992) The adolescent crisis in anorexia nervosa. In: Wilson, C.P., Hogan, C.H. and Mintz, I.L. (eds) *Psychodynamic Technique in the Treatment of the Eating Disorders* New York: Jason Aronson, pp. 111–127.

Katzman, D. and Steinegger, C. (2013) Physical assessment. In: Bryant-Waugh, R. and Lask, B. (eds) *Eating Disorders in Childhood and Adolescence*, 4th edn. Hove: Routledge, pp. 77–104.

Kirkbride, R. (2016) *Counselling Young People in Private Practice: A Practical Guide*. London: Karnac Books.

Lask, B. and Bryant-Waugh, R. (2013) Overview of management. In: Bryant-Waugh, R. and Lask, B. (eds) *Eating Disorders in Childhood and Adolescence*, 4th edn. Hove: Routledge, pp. 173–196.

Miller, W.R. and Rollnick, S. (2012) *Motivational Interviewing: Helping People to Change*. New York: The Guilford Press.

Nicholls, D. (2013) Aetiology. In: Bryant-Waugh, R. and Lask, B. (eds) *Eating Disorders in Childhood and Adolescence*, 4th edn. Hove: Routledge, pp. 50–76.

Nicholls, D., Chater, R. and Lask, B. (2000) Children into DSM don't go: a comparison of classification systems for eating disorders in childhood and early adolescence. *The International Journal of Eating Disorders 28*(3): 317–324.

Wood, D. (2011) Why clinicians should love neuroscience: the clinical relevance of contemporary knowledge. In: Lask, B. and Frampton, I. (eds) *Eating Disorders and the Brain*. Chichester: Wiley-Blackwell, pp. 1–18.

# 25

# COUNSELLING CHILDREN AND YOUNG PEOPLE WITH MENTAL ILLNESS – A RELATIONAL APPROACH

## PAUL NICHOLSON, DIVINE CHARURA AND BRIAN CHARLESWORTH

**This chapter will discuss:**

- Historical perspectives on mental illness in children and young people (CYP)
- The contemporary challenges and pressures of working with CYP clients with mental health issues
- Retaining professional identity and boundaries within an ever-growing diagnostic culture
- The significance of the therapeutic relationship in working with children and young people with mental health diagnoses

## INTRODUCTION

Over the past decade, there has been a growing recognition of the scale and impact of mental health problems among young people. This has been evident in the media, schools and a wide range of services responding to the high prevalence of psychological distress, anxiety, affective disorders, neuropsychological and behavioural disorders. Whilst one in ten children require treatment or support for a mental health problem or psychological difficulties, research suggests only one-quarter to one-third of children and young people with a diagnosable mental health condition seek help, and three-quarters of mental health issues facing adults will have begun before the age of 18 (DoH, 2015). In 2016, NHS England launched a new 5-year programme for mental health care, which has seen the funding for CYP's mental health rising to £214m in 2020/21, along with £30m allocated each year for tackling eating disorders among CYP, and £20m to £25m each year for reaching vulnerable groups. Whilst local to England, these figures suggest a perspective into the scale of the problem for CYP experiencing mental ill-health all over the world.

Within the counselling and psychotherapy field, the study of mental ill-health and pathological presentations in children continues to invite debate. Our intention is not to add to debate on the diversity of presentations or diagnoses, but rather clarify how therapists can conceptualise mental ill-health in order to work ethically with CYP clients and their embodied diversities.

The consideration of mental illness/psychological distress and their manifestations in CYP is one that has been noted within psychotherapy and literature and practice for many decades. Classical examples by forerunners in the field include that of Sigmund Freud, who presented one of the best known case studies of little Hans, a 5-year-old boy whose father sought help from Freud for his phobia of horses (Freud, 1909). Melanie Klein presented the case of Erna, who was a very disturbed 6-year-old girl who suffered from sleeplessness, obsessional symptoms and severe learning inhibition (Klein, 1924). Other Kleinian contributions include object relations, the development of the ego and clarification of the underlying causes of childhood psychosis – and how through play therapy contact could be made. This can be identified through the case study of a young boy (Dick) who was having psychotic experiences and who showed no emotion of any kind (Klein, 1930).

In 1943 the American psychiatrist Leo Kanner first described autism as a syndrome (Kanner, 1943), with Margaret Mahler following on from these early ideas offering hypotheses of key features of childhood psychosis and the aetiology of psychosis in children. She asserted the developmental process of the infants' psyche and its variants naming autism as one such variant (1968).

From the humanistic tradition, Carl Rogers noted his experience of such work with children in his first book *The Clinical Treatment of the Problem Child* (Rogers, 1939), and as the forces of psychology shifted, others like Piaget (1929) and Vygotsky (1987) offered cognitive and social development theories. Vygotsky emphasised children's social basis and interaction with their social environment by their speech experiences in their cognitive development, with Piaget arguing that children actively become socialised and solve the problems that the social environment causes. Bruner expounded on the notion of language acquisition and asserted that this begins before the child utters their first lexico-grammatical speech. He stated that it begins when mother and infant create a predictable format of interaction that can serve as a microcosm for communicating and for constituting a shared reality (Bruner, 1983: 18). Attachment theory also offers a perspective from which we as therapists can also understand psychological distress and separation anxiety. Based on the work of Ainsworth and Bowlby, anxiety may present similarly in children across the world but may manifest differently depending on the cultural norms that influence the family (Ainsworth and Bowlby, 1991). It thus remains important for all therapists working with children to be aware of these aspects of diversity.

These pioneers laid the foundations for understanding not only the psychic and cognitive make-up of children but also the aetiology of psychopathology as interwoven with the nature of primary relationships. In considering the evidence base for different therapies we noted that NICE recommends two trauma-focused therapies for adults: CBT and eye movement desensitisation and reprocessing (EMDR). However, for children, the guidelines are currently less specific, nominating only CBT as a therapy of choice. Thus, whilst it is plausible that psychological trauma or disturbances in attachment in childhood can be seen as the underlying cause for psychological disturbances, our experience of relational philosophy and practice draws us to a much wider body of evidence than uni-theoretical perspectives in considering effective explanations for an individual's condition and how to address it.

Contemporary writers and texts offer a broad diversity of therapeutic perspectives and treatment for children and young people experiencing mental ill-health. These include Daniel Stern's seminal work on the *Interpersonal World of the Infant* (1985); the interface of nature and nurture that occurs in the psychobiological interaction between the primary caregiver and the CYP, which has given rise to the understanding of the link between heredity and the psychological environment (Lehtonen, 1994: 28); the focus on 'interpersonal neurobiology' (Siegel, 1999); and some developments and perspectives which challenge that infant mental health is not just about the presence or absence of certain psychological functions, but is also the product of biological structural systems that are organising through the stages of infancy (Schore, 2000). Despite the promising emergence of these neuroscientific perspectives, the most recent literature indicates heavy criticism of neuroscience, suggesting much of its 'evidence' is purely speculative (Satel and Lilienfeld, 2013).

There have also been other perspectives: in the work of Geldard and Geldard (2008) importance is attributed to therapist flexibility and creativity in the therapy room when working with CYP. When there are so many sources of effective work available, we argue that rather than one particular perspective, an openness to a combination of perspectives may provide material for plausible formulations for psychological distress, including that of the client.

The relational approach to which we refer is a contemporary paradigm developed by a number of authors over the past 20 years, which considers *relationship* to be a common factor described across multiple practice models and represents a number of key themes found in therapeutic practice (Mitchell, 2000; DeYoung, 2003, Pelham, 2008; Charlesworth and Nicholson, 2014; Paul and Charura, 2015). Whilst the relational approach is currently considered to be a collection of practice principles and theoretical assumptions rather than a coherent and singular practice model (Pelham, 2008), it also has the potential to operate as a conceptual term that respects the phenomenological sense-making of the individual and as an integrative *lingua franca* for the assimilation of theory and relevant experiences within one's practice (Charlesworth and Nicholson, 2014).

A core theme in the paradigm is that our sense of self evolves and maintains itself through relationship and that 'our sense of reality and identity is formed *in relation to* our experience and the meaning we divine from it' (Charlesworth and Nicholson, 2014: 87). Consequently, the primacy of the therapeutic relationship is placed at the heart of the counselling process within this approach. Respecting how both the client and counsellor make sense of, and relate to their ontological experiencing is represented via the construction of meaning within the relationship, using co-created language that utilises theoretical vocabulary only when necessary to elucidate on material that requires exploration or understanding.

Contrary to the traditional psychiatric view, where diagnosis pre-dates and predicts the therapeutic treatment of children and young people, the case examples and theoretical perspectives we present herein embrace this relational stance to understanding mental ill-health and therapy with children and young people. Strong et al. (2015) highlighted that the search for a diagnosis by parents, or indeed young people themselves, is an understandable one. They stated that assurance that one's confusing or distressing experiences have a medical explanation or category can bring immense relief. For some this relief may be associated with the hope that, following diagnosis, there may be a corresponding scientific solution. This could be medication, evidence-based psychotherapy or some self-help strategies. Thus, Strong et al. (2015) suggest that this understanding enables therapists to have an awareness of why individuals or families may be pushing for a formal diagnosis even when as therapists we may, from our philosophical understanding of the aetiology of psychological distress, feel that perhaps no diagnosis is warranted.

The question that remains, however, is how do therapists work with those who have diagnoses? In their in-depth examination of psychopathology, Brites, Nunes and Hipólito (2016) propose psycho-emotional development perspectives that offer therapists ideas on how to work with diagnosis from a relational and person-centred perspective. Majumder (2014) identified ways to reinvent the therapeutic relationship for young people, in a context-specific and culturally sensitive manner. These writers argue that in clients with severe and enduring mental illness, supportive therapeutic alliance allows the therapist to gain essential information about their mental ill-health and symptoms.

This relational approach fosters an environment in which trust and treatment adherence can then ensue. This represents a shift in paradigm from one that focuses on psychiatric diagnosis as a reductionist dynamic and predictor of therapeutic treatment to one in which the therapeutic relationship is central to a way of being that is empathic, flexible, non-prejudiced, open minded and culturally sensitive when working with the narratives of young people.

## RETAINING THE ROLE OF THERAPIST

Within this contemporary era of medicalised health care, the rise in awareness of mental health issues has resulted in the familiarisation of the general public with a number of diagnostic terms for mental health conditions. Labels such as 'depression', anxiety, post-traumatic stress disorder and obsessive compulsive disorder are all terms in common parlance within popular culture. This familiarity has resulted in additional pressure for the contemporary counselling practitioner to be seen as conversant with a broad range of conditions and diagnostic language as well as being able to offer explanations and curative treatment for the young people who exhibit mental health difficulties (Carlson and Kees, 2013). However, whilst many counsellors working with young people consider themselves proficient in dealing with a range of mental health issues related to their clients, *Diagnostic and Statistical Manual of Mental Disorders* (DSM)-related diagnoses such as schizophrenia and psychotic disorders are considered amongst the main conditions practitioners felt least confident working with (Carlson and Kees, 2013).

Outside of the family, schools are often the first places where childhood mental health issues emerge, yet Westergaard (2013) highlights that counselling within such settings is often difficult. With young clients frequently inconsistent in attendance and therapeutic work often influenced by future-focused issues, the school's academic agenda is often a dominant force in proceedings. Whilst often difficult to fully grasp, the challenges of working alongside local authorities, managers, teachers and those involved in pastoral care who are obliged to address well-being issues in their non-therapeutic roles is something that can be more fully articulated through supervision.

The case study that follows outlines a range of issues at play for therapists working within the secondary school via a summary of the supervisory discussions.

---

### Case Study: Challenges for Counsellors in the School System – a Supervision Perspective

Mary is a school counsellor working in a local secondary school in the northeast of England with a population of children who have shown a widening range of mental health issues during the time spent in the organisation. She presents a range of issues to discuss in supervision, many of which are focused on the difficulties in working within a multidisciplinary environment, where consensus on treatment and the conditions themselves is rare.

Whilst client need is always foremost in Mary's mind, sharing this duty with the multiple departments directly involved in student welfare means that an organisational 'push and pull' is an ever-present theme in the supervisory work. She reports professional relationship issues as being inextricably interwoven with therapeutic practice. Working within a complex web of involved stakeholders such as the school safeguarding team, inspection documentation, parents, social services and Child and Adolescent Mental Health Services (CAMHS), raising significant questions about how Mary's practice fits within the wider organisational context. Working alongside alternative helping roles prompts regular scrutiny from colleagues not holding a 'therapeutic mindset', which in turns prompts a pressure to explain the intentionality behind interventions. 'They don't really know what I do' is the main issue she reports and illustrates her isolation, working in a non-therapeutic environment without an effective support network of like-minded practitioners. On the most basic level, the multidisciplinary working context means that there is no agreement on the fundamental question of what to call the service user (client, patient or pupil?), and this makes holding a sense of professionalism as a qualified therapist with a depth of experience a persistent challenge for her. Organisational issues take precedence despite therapeutic process being reviewed productively, with significant time given to how Mary manages interactions with other stakeholders. The impact on deciding what is considered meaningful continuing professional development (CPD) – whether to go with the need to be aware of policy-driven systems or to further develop professional practice – remains a point of continued doubt and cuts to the heart of what it means for her to practise.

The range and complexity of client presentations was varied: bullying; abuse – physical, sexual, emotional; eating disorders and poor diet; anxiety and depression; gender and sexual orientation; transsexual issues; body image; self-harm; attention deficit hyperactivity disorder (ADHD); and autism were the main issues Mary reported. When to engage new clients with difficulties quickly became a constant theme too. Despite a well-established referral route, the immediacy of distressed pupils often proved challenging for school staff and the perceived 'catch all' for all these crises is inevitably the school counsellor. Appointed sessions and holding the boundary of the 'therapeutic hour' effectively became a practitioner's fantasy as highly distressed pupils were sent to see the 'counsellor' randomly throughout the day. By employing a wealth of creative and productive interventions leading to positive and long-lasting change in many clients, Mary's professional and personal sense of self still felt nourished, but she felt that progress with certain complex cases was compromised due to the demands of other services.

The idea of symptom labelling became a contentious issue for Mary in that her practice philosophy is routed in the 'I–thou' view of responding to a client's needs (Buber, 2004) rather than the 'I–it' often linked to more symptom-driven approaches such as CBT. Because other disciplines can be nuanced in their interpretation of labels and often have widely differing *modi operandi* in approaching each stated condition, this difference in vocabulary and practice philosophy can lead to tensions in communication that at times can be a major challenge and distraction to Mary and her work.

Table 25.1    Main themes in offering psychological support within a school environment

| Working with others external and internal | Organisational push and pull | Professional issues |
|---|---|---|
| Professionals – GPs, CAMs, social workers | Accountability | Working within the espoused ethical framework |
| Information requests | Upwards – government, school governors | Attending supervision |
| Parents, guardians, foster parents | Sideways – staff and parents, clients | Seeking appropriate continuing professional development |
| Knowing who does what | | |
| Noticing perceived overlapping roles | Safeguarding – pastoral care team and wider accountability | Working within level of competency, leading to referral and signposting |

| Self-care | The therapist | Client's needs |
|---|---|---|
| Responding to the messages from inner supervisor | Use of supervision | Secure base |
| Sense of professional autonomy | What to take when? | Autonomy |
| | | Confidentiality |
| Boundary management | Crisis management contact arrangements | Crisis interventions |
| Availability – drop in, crisis, normal sessions | CPD needs | Safeguarding issues – what to share when? |
| Personal support system | Ethical issues – collaborative problem-solving | Assessment – initial and ongoing |
| Managing work load | When to engage new clients | Therapeutic timespan: brief or open-ended |
| Letting go of clients – endings | | Endings |
| Knowing when not to engage | | Onward referral |

## CONSIDERING ADAPTIVE EXPLANATIONS FOR MENTAL ILL-HEALTH

Adjusting counselling practice to accommodate diagnostic descriptions opens up a wider debate regarding the aetiology of mental illness. The accepted wisdom underpinning DSM diagnostic organisation of mental disorders has recently been questioned as an inappropriate paradigm in its current form (BPS, 2013). Research into the rise of pharmacological treatment in the last half-century suggests that a range of commercial and political factors have shaped how we understand (and, consequently, approach) the treatment of mental illness, with Mayes and Horwitz (2005) arguing that the DSM has evolved from a manual that offered broadly analytic explanations for conditions as adaptive disorders into a definitive listing of labelled diseases that may serve interests external to the client or the therapist.

With the publication of the DSM-III in 1980, the way we viewed the nature and treatment of mental illness changed fundamentally by adopting the diagnostic model from conventional medicine. With this shift in paradigm, many of the subtler explanations of mental disturbance, which included appreciation of the clients' personal experiences and ontological perspective, were now sidelined in favour of diagnostic categorisation. This shift in methodology has endured and, despite ongoing debate and requests for revision of the DSM-5 by the American Psychological Association and the British Psychological Society (Frances, 2011), it is still accepted as the foundation common practice in many areas of mental health care.

Understanding the difference between counselling a client with mental ill-health and other forms of helping that are associated with diagnoses is an important distinction for each counselling practitioner to be clear on. Confusion regarding the boundaries of the role of the therapist can lead to temptation to work outside of it, which immediately raises ethical questions related to fitness to practice, adequate training, specific supervision and appropriate competencies. Adopting relational principles in practice means that, whilst you can accept the existence of DSM-based diagnoses and the currency they have, focusing on the client who has these labels and their individual view of their experience should remain at the heart of the work. The relational approach to counselling places emphasis on the establishment of co-created meaning between client and therapist and, as such, the language created between the two parties involved is intended to accurately describe the client's experience as they experience it. This approach to assisting the client in establishing a stronger sense of understanding and relating to their experience of their mental difficulties takes primacy over external descriptors of symptomology, which are ostensibly intended for people other than the client themselves.

As an alternative to a diagnostic-focused approach to working with mental illness, this method is not without historical precedence or rationale. Regarding mental ill-health as *adaptation difficulties* offers an alternative explanation for mental illness, with each individual's symptoms a consequence of struggling to adapt to their ontological experience (Menninger, 1963; Wilson, 1993). This in turn offers a reasonable narrative for the use of counselling as a valid method to employ.


## THERAPEUTIC RELATIONSHIP WITH CHILDREN AND YOUNG PEOPLE

One of the major factors in successful therapy with any client is developing a sound therapeutic relationship (Haugh and Paul, 2008). A number of key studies have found that the primary determinant of success in therapy is the therapeutic relationship itself (Wampold, 2001; Orlinsky et al., 2004), and that that much of that success is contingent on the practitioner's individual factors, which facilitate interpersonal connection and promote relational depth (Mearns and Cooper, 2005). The individual and idiosyncratic aspects of therapeutic practice place great demands on the competency and effectiveness of the therapist, but often represent the significant moments in successful practice (Nicholson, 2017).

Sinitsky (2010) found that establishing a therapeutic relationship was particularly pertinent to counselling children and regarded holding their subjective experiences and constructed meanings as essential components of the therapy. Appreciating the child's perspective in relation to their developmental position (Sinitsky, 2010) and promoting a sense of safety are also essential factors in establishing an age-appropriate therapeutic relationship, as is a degree of adaptability when considering theoretical explanations alongside the child's interpretation of experience within the practice (Westergaard, 2013). In short, counselling CYP clients requires that you see the young person and not the diagnosis, and feel able to be creative and authentic in how you present yourself in the relationship.

The case studies that now follow demonstrate how idiosyncratic practice elements can provide the safety required for working with CYP clients and transform the therapy from a diagnosis-driven, orthodox working alliance into an authentic and meaningful therapeutic relationship.

## Case Study: Seeing the Young Person Behind the Diagnosis

Jo was a 17-year-old student of dual heritage diagnosed with depression and anxiety, who was prescribed medication to combat her symptoms. Initially, she appeared very timid and fragile, and after the preliminary contracting she recalled a long history of lifetime experiences that involved parental inconsistency, family break-up and culturally supported racial abuse whilst at school. She spoke of a very painful relationship with her father, described as a very proud and devoutly religious man, who offered her little in the way of love throughout her life but demanded absolute obedience from her in everything he asked for or implied. She described herself as 'gender neutral' and spoke of feeling so alone, yet being deeply attached to her mother and younger sister. She recalled a long history of receiving treatment for her mental health issues and had been taking medication for a number of years.

As the therapist listened, it struck him that it appeared never to have occurred to her that she was a victim in her own story – so after 20 minutes when she'd arrived at a natural pause, the therapist reflected this back to her, stating 'Jo, I've been listening to you talk about your life and I noticed that I felt really sad hearing about so many painful things you have had to deal with that you had no control over. It must have been so hard for you to cope with all that yourself.'

The effect was profound. Silently, she stared with utter disbelief. The reflection was a complete surprise to her. She had never considered herself a victim until that moment. She fought it, but then very reluctantly was overcome with emotion and broke down in tears. She sobbed for at least 10 minutes before they processed what had happened together.

The remaining sessions with the therapist, whilst productive, felt almost insignificant compared to that initial breakthrough. The one single event of hearing from an impartial observer that she looked as if she blamed herself for all she felt was, in this case, enough to change everything.

This young client had related all the events of her life by concluding that she was responsible for them all. As a consequence, she simply hated many aspects of herself – her mixed heritage, her gender, her father's behaviour – but couldn't tolerate existing with that belief either. An adaptation rationale would suggest her symptoms to be physiological responses to her ontological confusion and, with this single intervention, her understanding of the meanings she'd arrived at from the events of her existence were given the opportunity to, within the safety of an appropriate therapeutic relationship, be reviewed and revised.

## Case Study: Considering Idiosyncratic Elements of Practice in Developing Authenticity with CYP Clients

Jenny, a 15-year-old school girl, entered counselling to address what were described as 'anger issues' manifest as regular violent exchanges with other pupils in school. ADHD and borderline personality disorder were reported as possible diagnoses by practitioners previously involved in her care. She was currently in the latest of many foster placements that had failed due to her extreme presentation. Her family unit was separated, her parents and siblings unavailable and she had contact with only one older relative who lived 100 miles away.

With appropriate working conditions agreed, Jenny agreed to start therapy, but swiftly made it clear that the relationship was to be on her terms. Reluctant disclosures in the initial sessions detailed a personal history that offered insight into how she had made sense of the short life she had experienced thus far. Abused and abandoned by both parents, with her mother now deceased and all but one of her siblings inaccessible to her, the therapist could see a survivor, abused, abandoned, alone and very, very scared. The irony of being asked by school to address anger issues highlighted the disconnect between competing priorities as it seemed very clear why she was angry.

Jenny's resistance remained consistent over the next few months. Regular silences, smoke breaks and occasional insults formed an impregnable barrier to establishing any productive relationship together. Somewhat frustrated, the therapist used supervision to assess this dynamic and it ultimately became clear that what Rogers described as his first condition for

*(Continued)*

(Continued)

therapy to take place – psychological contact (1957) – hadn't been achieved. Upon returning to the work with a sense of release from the pressure to perform, the therapist immediately accessed a range of alternative resources available to engage the client, including his own experience of childhood difficulties and a more colourful use of language. Focus became less about intentional counselling but more about simple engagement with this traumatised and fiercely defensive young girl who needed to know she wasn't faced with yet another adult who would hurt her. Playful, verbal jousting became commonplace and, by meeting her at the level she was inviting, the exchanges and disclosures soon became more significant and a quality of relational depth began to emerge.

And then – it was over. Expelled from school for one incident too many, her foster placement and access to therapy were lost. And yet, 12 months later Jenny specifically asked for the same therapist to be contacted to continue the work. With trust already established, there was no need for the previous defensive posturing and work continued productively for another 20 sessions, ending with Jenny happy to move on, her behaviour and anger significantly reduced.

The work was noteworthy for the process by which the relationship became a functional, therapeutic one. Allowing opportunities for the relationship to be tested and idiosyncratic characteristics to enter into the process meant that a genuine authenticity was present between both parties. By focusing on the relationship itself, rather than professional agenda, the safety that CYP clients find so necessary for working was established, and successful therapy became possible.

## Key Learning

- The manifestations of mental illness in children and young people have been noted within psychotherapy literature for many decades.
- The aetiology of psychopathology is interwoven with the nature of primary relationships as well as consideration of diversity in the manifestation of symptoms.
- Official guidelines suggesting treatment for children with mental illness are currently less than specific.
- Whilst the search for a diagnosis is the norm within the current culture of medicalised health care, therapists must resist the pressures to work outside of their competence and offer a reasoned narrative for their practice.
- Relational explanations for mental illness as adaptation difficulties offer a valid narrative for the use of therapeutic relationship as a treatment method amongst a range of options.

## Summary

Working with CYP clients diagnosed with mental illness can prove challenging for practitioners for a broad range of reasons; however, we argue that to work effectively, you need to be confident in what it is you offer as a treatment option. The relational competencies (Paul and Charura, 2015) suggest that therapists working with CYP clients need to be competent in the following:

- Knowledge and understanding of how the particular context in which the therapist works with CYP with mental ill-health impacts on the client–therapist relationship.
- Ability to work collaboratively with the client in exploring potential barriers to challenges when considering the client's treatment and social context.
- Ability to work with difficult and complex processes.
- Ability to help clients reflect on and develop and articulate their emotions, experiences and personal meanings.
- Ability to recognise and address own prejudice in relation to working with CYP who have mental ill-health as well as their families.

## Develop Your Skills

In addition, context-specific skills must be developed in order to work effectively within multidisciplinary professional settings, such as:

- Be conversant with diagnostic language and contemporary descriptors of mental illness.
- Be aware of alternative adaptation-based interpretations of mental illness as well as culturally diverse presentations of psychological distress.
- Decide upon your own professional boundaries for working to alleviate external pressures to operate outside your role.
- Decide if establishing a therapeutic relationship to facilitate therapy is possible with the client. Ask the question – is counselling the appropriate treatment option for this client at this time?
- Establish your own effective guidelines for referral.
- Develop multidisciplinary working skills – be prepared to communicate your own practice rationale and outline its boundaries to colleagues – especially those not versed in therapeutic practice.

## Discussion Questions

1. How do you feel about working with children and young people who are diagnosed as 'mentally ill'?
2. Can you identify the professional and therapeutic pressures you associate with working with children with mental health diagnoses in your work setting?
3. Can you conceptualise and articulate your own working practice within the ever-growing diagnostic culture mental health issues are embedded within?
4. What support or additional training would you feel you need to develop further in this area?
5. In what ways could supervision help you in your work with CYP?

## Further Reading

Brites, R., Nunes, O. and Hipólito, J. (2016) Psychopathology and the person centred perspective. In: Lago, C. and Charura, D (eds) *The Person Centred Counselling and Psychotherapy Handbook: Origins, Developments and Current Applications*. Maidenhead: Open University Press, pp. 91–101.

Frances, A. (2013) *Saving Normal: An Insider's Revolt Against Out-of-Control Psychiatric Diagnosis, DSM-5, Big Pharma, and the Medicalization of Ordinary Life*. New York: William Morrow.

Geldard, K. and Geldard, D. (2008) *Counselling Children: A Practical Introduction*. Los Angeles, CA: London.

Majumder, P. (2014) Psychiatry and young people. In: Charura, D. and Paul, S. (eds) *The Therapeutic Relationship Handbook: Theory and Practice*. Maidenhead: McGraw-Hill Education/ Open University Press. pp. 207–217

Westergaard, J. (2013) Counselling young people: counsellors' perspectives on 'what works' – an exploratory study. *Counselling and Psychotherapy Research 13*(2): 98–105.

### Online Resources

MindEd – a free educational resource on children and young people's mental health for all adults: https://www.minded.org.uk

YoungMinds – a leading UK charity championing the well-being and mental health of young people: https://youngminds.org.uk

# REFERENCES

Ainsworth, M.S. and Bowlby, J. (1991) An ethological approach to personality development. *American Psychologist 46*: 333–341.

Brites, R., Nunes, O. and Hipólito, J. (2016) Psychopathology and the person centred perspective. In: Lago, C. and Charura, D. (eds) *The Person Centred Counselling and Psychotherapy Handbook: Origins, Developments and Current Applications*. Maidenhead: Open University Press, pp. 91–101.

British Psychological Society (2013) *Division of Clinical Psychology Position Statement on the Classification of Behaviour and Experience in Relation to Functional Psychiatric Diagnoses: Time for a Paradigm Shift*. British Psychological Society [online] Available at: https://https://www1.bps.org.uk/networks-and-communities/member-microsite/division-clinical-psychology (accessed 25th March 2018).

Bruner, J. (1983) *Child's Talk: Learning to Use Language*. New York: Norton.

Buber, M. (2004) *I and Thou*, 2nd edn. London: Continuum.

Carlson, L. and Kees, N. (2013) Mental health services in public schools: a preliminary study of school counselor perceptions. *Professional School Counseling* [serial online] *16*(4): 211–221.

Charlesworth, B. and Nicholson, P. (2014) Relational therapy: defining the therapeutic relationship. In: Charura, D. and Paul, S. (eds) *The Therapeutic Relationship Handbook: Theory and Practice*. Maidenhead: McGraw-Hill Education/Open University Press, pp. 87–98.

Department of Health (DoH) (2015) *Future in mind: promoting, protecting and improving our children and young people's mental health and wellbeing*. Available at: https://www.gov.uk/government/uploads/system/uploads/attachment_data/file/414024/Childrens_Mental_Health.pdf (accessed 23 February 2018).

DeYoung, P. (2003) *Relational Psychotherapy*. London: Routledge.

Frances, A. (2011) The British Psychological Society condemns DSM-5. *Psychiatric Times* 25 July. Available at: www.psychiatrictimes.com/dsm-5-0/british-psychological-society-condemns-dsm-5 (accessed 23 February 2018)

Freud, S. (1909) *Analysis of a Phobia of a Five Year Old Boy*. In: *The Pelican Freud Library* (1977), Vol. 8, Case Histories 1, pp. 169–306.

Geldard, K. and Geldard, D. (2008) *Counselling Children: A Practical Introduction*. Los Angeles, CA: London.

Haugh S. and Paul S. (2008) (eds) *The Therapeutic Relationship: Perspectives and Themes*. Ross-on-Wye: PCCS Books.

Kanner, L. (1943) Autistic disturbances of affective contact. *Nervous Child 2*: 217–250.

Klein, M. (1924) An obsessional neurosis in a six-year-old girl. In: *Psychoanalysis of Children*. London: Hogarth Press, 1975, pp. 36–7

Klein, M. (1930) The importance of symbol-formation in the development of the ego. *International Journal of Psycho-Analysis 11*: 24–39.

Lehtonen, J. (1994) From dualism to psychobiological interaction. A comment on the study of Tenari and his co-workers. *British Journal of Psychiatry* 164: 27–28.

Mahler, M.S. (1968) *On Human Symbiosis and the Vicissitudes of Individuation*, Vol. 1: *Infantile Psychosis*. New York: International Universities Press.

Majumder, P. (2014) Psychiatry and young people. In: Charura, D. and Paul, S. (eds) *The Therapeutic Relationship Handbook: Theory and Practice*. Maidenhead: McGraw-Hill Education/Open University Press, pp. 207–217.

Mayes, R. and Horwitz, A.V. (2005) DSM-III and the revolution in the classification of mental illness. *Journal of the History of the Behavioral Sciences* 41(3): 249–267.

Mearns, D. and Cooper, M. (2005) *Working at Relational Depth in Counselling and Psychotherapy*. London: Sage.

Menninger, K. (1963) *The Vital Balance*. New York: Viking Press.

Mitchell, S.A. (2000) *Relationality: From Attachment to Intersubjectivity*. Hove: Routledge.

Nicholson, P.E. (2017) Kung fu counselling. *BACP Private Practice Journal* 10–13. BACP. Summer edition.

Orlinsky, D.E., Ronnestad, M.H. and Willutski, U. (2004) Fifty years of psychotherapy process – outcome research: continuity and change. In: Lambert, M.J. (ed.) *Bergin and Garfield's Handbook of Psychotherapy and Behaviour Change*, 5th edn. New York: Wiley, pp. 307–393.

Paul, S. and Charura, D. (2015) *An Introduction to the Therapeutic Relationship in Counselling and Psychotherapy*. Los Angeles: SAGE.

Pelham, G. (2008) The relational approach. In: Haugh, S. and Paul, S. (eds) *The Therapeutic Relationship: Perspectives and Themes*. Ross-on-Wye: PCCS Books, pp. 104–116.

Piaget, J. (1929) *The Child's Conception of the World*. New York: Harcourt Brace.

Rogers, C.R. (1939) *Clinical Treatment of the Problem Child*. Boston, MA: Houghton Mifflin.

Rogers, C.R. (1957) The necessary and sufficient conditions of therapeutic personality change. *Journal of Consulting Psychology* 21: 95–103.

Satel, S. and Lilienfeld, O. (2013) *Brainwashed: The Seductive Appeal of Mindless Neuroscience*. New York: Basic Books

Schore, A.N. (2000) The self-organization of the right brain and the neurobiology of emotional development. In: Lewis, M.D. and Granic, I. (eds) *Emotion, Development, and Self-Organization*. New York: Cambridge University Press, pp. 155–185.

Siegel, D.J. (1999) *Developing Mind: Toward a Neurobiology of Interpersonal Experience*. New York: Norton.

Sinitsky, G. (2010) A trainee's experiences of counselling psychology's contribution to therapeutic work with children and adolescents. *Counselling Psychology Review* [serial online] 25(1): 52.

Stern, D. (1985) *The Interpersonal World of the Infant*. New York: Basic Books.

Strong, T., Ross, K.H. and Sesma-Vazquez, M. (2015) Counselling the (self?) diagnosed client: generative and reflective conversations. *British Journal of Guidance and Counselling* 43(5): 598–610.

Vygotsky, L.S. (1987) *The Collected Works of L. S. Vygotsky: Vol. I. Problems of General Psychology*. Rieber, R. and Carton, A. (eds), Minick, N. (trans.). New York: Plenum Press.

Wampold, B.E. (2001) *The Great Psychotherapy Debate*. Mahwah, NJ: Erlbaum.

Westergaard, J. (2013) Counselling young people: counsellors' perspectives on 'what works' – an exploratory study. *Counselling and Psychotherapy Research 13*(2): 98–105.

Wilson, M. (1993) DSM-III and the transformation of American psychiatry: A history. *American Journal of Psychiatry, 150*: 399–410.

# PART IV
## PRACTICE SETTINGS

# 26

# HEALTH AND SOCIAL CARE SERVICES

## BARBARA SMITH, SUE PATTISON AND CATHY BELL

**This chapter will discuss:**

- **Practice and policy and the development of child-focused services**
- **Working with children in care including adopted children**
- **Child and Adolescent Mental Health Services (CAMHS)**

## INTRODUCTION

The work of the professional counsellor takes place in a diverse range of practice settings and covers the main modalities and interventions, such as talking therapies in the client-centred/humanistic, cognitive-behavioural and psychodynamic approaches, and play therapy/therapeutic play, filial therapy and other creative approaches. This chapter looks specifically at the practice contexts of health care and social services where counsellors are employed to work with children and young people, either directly through the statutory organisations, NHS and local authority or sub-contracted from another service provider such as a charitable trust or agency on an employed or self-employed basis. Although the range of health and social care services is similar across the various parts of the UK, they may be organised and referred to differently in England, Northern Ireland, Wales and Scotland, and may be informed by country-specific legislation and policies. Counsellors are advised to familiarise themselves with the policies, practices and legislation most appropriate to their context. Professional counselling bodies such as the British Association for Counselling and Psychotherapy (BACP) are a good source of information or signposting.

As practitioners, we are familiar with a range of sub-contexts within the health and social care services, and we share with you our knowledge, skills and experience from our work with some of the most vulnerable children and young people. As authors we have learnt much about each others' career histories from the process of story sharing. Our joint career histories include counselling and psychotherapy, teaching, researching, writing, social work, nursing and health visiting. Our knowledge, skills and experience are brought to this chapter in a way that you, the reader, can find accessible and can engage with in ways that enable you to inform and enhance your own practice. The scope of 'health and social care services' is vast, and it is not possible to cover it all in relation to the work of counsellors.

## PRACTICE AND POLICY: THE DEVELOPMENT OF CHILD AND YOUNG PERSON-FOCUSED SERVICES

In developed countries, the notion of childhood has shifted from one of extreme vulnerability and lack of consequence to a position strengthened by human rights legislation and policy, for example, the United Nations Convention on the Rights of the Child (UNICEF, 1989). In the UK, the NHS was set up to address the needs of the post-war population and included welfare strategies to enhance the physical growth, development and health needs of mothers, babies and children (Webster, 2002). Children's developmental progress became of interest to parents and professionals, and could be measured and charted and used by UK local authorities as a yardstick for the quality of care provided by parents. Child abuse and neglect were studied and legislated for, leading to the responsibilities and powers that local authorities now have in relation to the welfare of children and young people. Alongside this, child guidance clinics attached to hospitals and in the community grew in number to provide for the needs of 'difficult' children and young people, those with behavioural problems and/ or special educational needs such as physical or learning disabilities (Sampson, 1976). The responsibility for children and young people with 'special educational needs' developed and became part of political discourses around human rights, and the concept of inclusion gained political credibility leading to the health and social care landscape of antidiscrimination, access to services for all and addressing the needs of diverse and marginalised groups (MacBeath et al., 2006).

Mention health and social care services to a counsellor working in any sector or from any modality and a variety of responses are liable to be solicited. These may range from frustrated responses such as: 'There are not enough resources, therefore, it's a postcode lottery' and 'Even though my young clients are living in extremely neglectful homes, nothing is ever done about it', to grateful comments such as: 'I'm so glad there is support out there for vulnerable young people'. The response will depend on the individual's experience, and yet when the UK NHS was set up in 1946 it was hailed as being free for all from the 'cradle to the grave' at the point of delivery. With health and social care being a devolved matter within the UK, despite shared values and similarities in legislation, policy and practice, considerable differences are continuing to develop within the systems of each of the four countries (nations) that make up the UK: Scotland, Wales, Northern Ireland and England.

As with any counselling context, it is useful for counsellors to understand what is meant by health and social care services. However, in view of the statutory nature of these services and their powers and responsibilities in respect of safeguarding children and young people, a good working knowledge of these services and how their work is impacted is essential for counsellors. For discussion on safeguarding see Chapter 17: 'Law and Policy'.

Across the countries of our world, access to health care will vary. This is largely influenced by each country's social and economic condition and the health policies in place. Some countries see health care distributed among market participants, whereas in others planning is made more centrally among governments or other coordinating bodies. The four nations of the UK can be viewed as microcosms in relation to global health and social care systems. According to the World Health Organization (WHO) a well-functioning health care system: 'Requires a robust financing mechanism with a well-trained and adequately paid workforce, reliable information on which to base decisions and policies and well-maintained facilities and logistics to deliver quality medicines and technologies' (WHO, n.d.www.who.int/topics/health_systems/en).

For the counsellor who works with children and young people this means they would be well advised to know about and have some understanding of how the health and social care services that surround that child and their family work to operate safely and ethically. In order to achieve this some health and social care authorities will purchase the services of counsellors, art therapists, play therapists, music therapists and others directly to enable a useful resource to add to an existing or developing multidisciplinary team. This approach helps to provide balance in relation to knowledge and experience. In other instances, local services may be put out to public contract, and counsellors and therapists could be employed by the local agency or charity in the voluntary or community sector that successfully applies for and is granted the tender for a specific service delivery. This is another service-building approach that can lead to shared knowledge and experience.

The modern approach to health and social care requires groups of trained professionals and para-professionals to come together as interdisciplinary teams to provide an all-round service to the child and family, known as multi-agency working (Littlechild and Smith, 2013). The cost of providing such care can be high as the number of 'problem families' in the UK rises in relation to socio-economic factors such as high unemployment and increasing demands on health care systems due to changing demographics and greater expectations.

For ease of access in deciphering the maze of health and social care services within the UK and to enable international contexts to be compared by the reader, we will look at services as they fit into the categories of primary, secondary and tertiary care. Primary care is the term for those health care services that contribute to the health and well-being of the local community. It is the first stage of any journey within health and social care, the first port of call for all who use the health care system. Such professionals could be a nurse, GP, dentist, counsellor or play therapist depending on which services a local authority or NHS Trust offers within its primary care provision. In most areas the first contact is the GP, who is the main referral agent for children and young people outside of the school context. Generally, secondary care is when a patient needs to see professionals such as cardiologists, urologists and allied health professionals, for example, counsellors, and psychologists. Secondary care is often associated with hospital care, yet a dietician, a counsellor or a psychiatrist may be seen in a local health centre, clinic or community centre. Secondary care is normally only accessed via a doctor's referral and in rare instances by a patient self-referral.

Tertiary care is specialised consultative health care and includes CAMHS. It is usually for inpatients and is reached by a referral from a primary or secondary health professional. Examples of this are cardiac surgery, advanced neonatal services, palliative care and secure or other psychiatric units. It is important for counsellors to recognise that many types of health and social care interventions take place outside of health facilities. Food safety services, needle exchange services, professionals who serve in residential and community settings, self-care, home care and assisted living treatment for substance misuse are examples of such services. The counsellor may come into contact in any counselling situation with a child or young person who has input from other professionals. In the counselling room at times it will be obvious to the counsellor that the young client has a physical disability, a communication difficulty or an illness that requires some form of health or social care support. For example, the child may be a wheelchair user or have adapted equipment to carry out everyday tasks. Some of our young clients may have a physical illness such as diabetes, asthma, epilepsy or childhood cancer. It may be useful for counsellors to be aware of any physical illness as it can have a direct impact on the counselling; for example, young people who take medication for epilepsy on a morning may be more alert in the afternoon and more able to engage with counselling. Some illnesses can cause tiredness and impact on the ability to concentrate. In our individual practices we have each had young people in the counselling room who, due to physical illness, could not have a counselling session in the afternoon as they were physically too tired. Physiotherapists, occupational therapists, specialist nurses and social workers specialising in disability could have an involvement with the young client and a team approach may (though not necessarily) be helpful. A counsellor may notice a progressive or sudden change in a young person's physical health and be required to share this information under safeguarding policies or as a specific requirement of contracts with the organisation through which they deliver counselling.

## Working with children and young people in care

There are currently about 93,000 children in care (looked-after children) in the UK (NSPCC, 2015). Looked-after children in England and Wales are those young people who are subject to 'care orders' under Section 31 of the Children Act (1989) (HMSO, 1989) or those who are voluntarily accommodated under Section 20 of the Children Act (1989).

In Scotland children will be looked after under Children (Scotland) Act (1995). Some children are looked after if they are involved with the youth justice system or subject to police protection. Some young people are looked after within foster families, whilst others are looked after by kinship carers (members of their own extended family) or in residential homes.

Of those children in care, according to the NSPCC (2015), over 60% are looked after due to abuse and neglect. It is no surprise then to learn that children in care are four times more likely to suffer mental health difficulties. The Royal College of Psychiatrists explains the way in which health risk is exacerbated due to looked-after children's previous experiences. They have significantly higher rates of emotional disorders such as anxiety and depression, attention deficit hyperactivity disorder (ADHD) and autistic spectrum conditions. More looked-after children have mental health difficulties compared to children living in private homes, and the mental health and well-being of looked-after children and young people is high on the policy agenda (Education Committee, 2016).

## Common experiences of looked-after children

When we meet any child for the first time for counselling, we are curious about what brings them into our lives. What's happened? With looked-after children we can safely assume that this child has experience of social workers, maybe police officers, judges, case conferences, not to mention what went before – the reasons why these professionals became involved in their lives. Research by Cleaver et al. (2011) found that there are particular difficulties relating to parenting capacity that impact on the health and development of children at different ages. These issues are domestic violence, drug and alcohol dependency, mental illness (the toxic trio) and learning disability. They found that it is the 'multiplicative impact' of a combination of these different problems that is more likely to be harmful and that brings children into the care system. What we have learnt about the impact of domestic violence on children and young people is that, like other abused children, they may be dealing with symptoms of post-traumatic stress disorder (PTSD) – dissociation, numbness, disturbed sleep, lack of concentration and withdrawal.

They may be experiencing flashbacks, memory problems and difficulties relating to other children (Graham-Bermann and Levendosky, 1998). Children unable to deal with these distressing feelings will often 'act out' all manner of behaviours in their attempt to survive, bringing them to the negative attention of teachers, police officers and other professionals. As a result, placement stability in care can be difficult, some children moving placements as many as three times in 1 year (Munro and Hardy, 2006). Children in care frequently suffer chronic low self-esteem and self-confidence. Fahlberg (1991) tells of the risk of problems with attachment in the early years where poor parenting through drug and alcohol use or mental illness can cause infants to see themselves as unloved and unlovable. Golding (2008) suggests an inability to regulate emotion is a consequence of a difficult infancy and early childhood, often resulting in a range of distressing emotional, psychological and behavioural problems (Golding, 2008).

In 2015, 3253 separated children claimed asylum in the UK (Gov.uk) and clearly services will need to respond through specialist provision where staff members have cultural competence, work with trauma, and understand the religious and cultural context within which a child has been raised. Not only are they dealing with grief, loss and trauma, but they can often experience ongoing alienation and stigma in the country of 'refuge'.

## Therapeutic work with children in care

Given the levels of distress of children in care it is important for counsellors, social workers, teachers and carers to have knowledge and understanding of attachment difficulties and their ensuing problems. Gerhardt (2004) writes about what neuroscience offers in understanding the internal world of the child, promising greater insight into how we can support children's emotional life in the future. In her work on the importance of affection in shaping a baby's brain, Gerhardt (2004: 49) speaks of the powerful impact of a disapproving or rejecting look, which causes 'a sudden lurch from the sympathetic arousal to parasympathetic arousal, creating the effects we experience as shame – a sudden drop in blood pressure and shallow breathing'. Some children have been raised in cold, affectionless environments and need a reparative therapeutic process to help them to heal, not just with a loving therapist, but with all adults whom they meet. For this reason, much of the therapeutic work undertaken with children in care involves foster carers and/or perhaps birth family members. As well as the different individual play therapy approaches discussed elsewhere in this book, some authors have written specifically for children traumatised in early childhood and who have attachment difficulties. According to Pinto and Woolgar (MindEd), it may be enough for a child to thrive if placed in a stable home with sensitive carers. However, they suggest that some children will need disorder-specific interventions and highlight the importance of interventions that work with carers to help them parent more effectively. Some of the therapeutic approaches used in working with looked-after children are outlined in the following sections.

## Attachment-focused parenting

Attachment-focused parenting, developed by Dan Hughes (2006), fosters a relationship between carer and child in which the child experiences a 'safe haven' and where the child feels physically, psychologically and emotionally safe. Hughes uses the acronym of PACE to describe his model – Playfulness, Acceptance, Curiosity and Empathy. The idea is to facilitate parents to engage the child expressively and playfully, giving the child the message that the relationship is stronger than any small irritations. Hughes' model suggests that an attitude of acceptance and empathy enables the adult to co-regulate the child's emotional state, enhancing the child's own capacity for emotional regulation. An attitude of curiosity and wondering enhances the child's capacity to construct meaning (Golding, 2008). This is supported by the ground-breaking work of Schore and Schore (2010), who have integrated attachment theory and neuroscience. They describe how our right brain hemisphere regulates emotion and processes our sense of self, suggesting that what we (counsellors) communicate unconsciously is essential to our clients' recovery from early childhood trauma. The PACE model, then, is based on facilitating carers to offer therapeutic environments for children in their care. Often carers have suggested that children's difficult behaviours happen suddenly 'as if a switch had been turned on' – the carer begins to recognise the onset of a child's overwhelming feelings.

## Case Study: Katy

Katy, aged 6, came for counselling with her grandmother, Joan, her kinship carer, because Katy would on occasions scream abuse and scratch and punch her grandmother 'out of the blue'. When this happened, Joan found it difficult to deal with Katy – she was hurt and angry and would threaten that Katy would have to go and live with someone else – exacerbating Katy's anguish and insecurity. Joan's own distress was getting in the way of her helping Katy to learn how to deal with her difficult emotions. It is hard to empathise with a child who is raging at you. Using an attachment-focused parenting approach Joan learns that Katy's angry displays are not about her – they are the only way Katy knows how to get through the next moment/10 minutes/hour/day. Joan needs support to stay grounded and loving when Katy is suffering in this way by learning about attachment and what is behind Katy's behaviour. Over time, Joan came to develop the PACE skills, offering Katy a containing experience (as was offered to Joan by the counsellor), and Katy's distressing episodes became less frequent and less intense. Katy is now able to deal with her feelings by asking for her needs to be met and asking for help when she is feeling upset.

## Theraplay

Another way of supporting children within their foster placements is through Theraplay, a model designed to build and enhance attachment (Booth and Jernberg, 2010). This too has a basis of playful interaction between children/young people and carers, and focuses on four essential qualities of the relationship between parent and child – structure, engagement, nurture and challenge. The notion of Theraplay was originally developed by DesLauriers and Carlson (1969) to work with children with autism. Their research focused on five severely autistic children over a 1-year period. Applying the method (now known as Theraplay), personality and socialisation qualities improved, as was evidenced by parent, clinic and therapist ratings. Emphasising the importance of an emotional connection between the child and parent/caregiver, the work differs from the work of Hughes' (2006) PACE model, in that the play is structured to attend to specific difficulties the child may be having. For example, they give specific examples of ways of working with children and young people with autistic spectrum disorder, those who have experienced complex trauma and young people who have been adopted. Such specific difficulties are met with a range of specific Theraplay activities to enhance children's functioning, but particularly to enhance the young person's attachment relationships. Counsellors may work with children, carers and others involved in the Theraplay approach, both supporting and contributing to the approach.

## Life story work

It is well documented that placement instability adversely affects the psychosocial development of children in care (Lewis et al., 2007). Furthermore, as previously mentioned, some looked-after children can have as many as three placements in the course of 1 year (Munro and Hardy, 2006). Shockingly, research by Ward and Skuse (2001) found that in a long-stay sample of 242 children and young people, 28% had three or more placements and 3% had six or more. This may be because placements are often unplanned and crisis-driven, or because of a shortage of carers and unfilled social work vacancies. When a child is moved, they not only leave their placement, but they must deal with a range of changes of school, friends or even separation from siblings. When a child has been in care for some years, particularly when they have had several placements, they can become confused about their past, and memories of different places and people become blurred. One child said 'I lived with John and Sue when I was five or it might have been when I was eight ... I think I had a dog named Boudie and I think I had a sister.'

A life story book is not only a record of places, people and events in the child's life, but an opportunity to process painful feelings about incidents and endings along the way. Whilst some people consider the life story book as an 'end product' with important information for the child, it can also be a therapeutic 'journey' in which the child makes sense of why they came into care and why they moved from one fostering or residential placement to another. If a child is not clear about why they have moved, they may experience a move as a rejection. The book is put together over a period of time covering the time from birth until the present day. It often takes the form of a scrap book with copies of their birth certificate, photographs of birth family members, and stories and photographs of foster families. Counsellors and play therapists within the local authority context, or social workers using counselling as part of their wider role may use life story work extensively to help children and young people build self-esteem and confidence, develop a sense of identity, and express and deal with difficult emotions and psychological distress.

## Therapy with adopted children

Since 2005, when the Adoption and Children Act 2002 (HMSO, 2002) was fully implemented, the law specified that only those therapists who are registered with the Office for Standards in Education, Children's Services and Skills (Ofsted) as part of an adoption support agency (ASA) can offer specific adoption services. Therefore, counsellors who work with clients for whom adoption is the main focus of therapeutic work are employed by registered adoption agencies.

Rogers (2010) highlights the work of therapists working with adopted clients. She suggests that a therapist working in the field of adoption needs 'to be able to bear the weight of all of the losses and grief of the adopted clients, adoptive parents, birth relatives and prospective adopters – and survive its enactment in the therapeutic space'. In addition, she argues, the early experience of rejection can lead the client to play out their pain in the transference relationship. Further, when intimacy is established, there may be a premature ending to the therapy: to risk intimacy might lead to further unbearable experiences of rejection and abandonment.

Adopted children have often had a turbulent history before being looked after in the care system. These early traumatic experiences of loss and separation can lead to children developing attachment disorders, behavioural difficulties and developmental problems that can disturb them long into adult life. The naive expectation that the provision of a loving home with new loving parents will lead to instant stability has long been questioned. Adopted children often believe that they are somehow fundamentally flawed. This is true for many clients from a range of backgrounds, but there is something about the experience of being adopted that gives the child hard 'evidence' that they were not wanted, not lovable enough or not good enough.

Rogers (2010) highlights the different areas of expertise required to work as an adoption therapist, including understanding issues of rejection, reunion and life story work. Themes of identity and belonging are frequently present – those often 'taken-for-granted' issues of religious background, blood relatives, cultural history, and genetic and medical history cannot be assumed for many adopted children. 'It is the not knowing that results in many adoptees having burning questions about who they are; the circumstance behind their placement, their birthparent and ultimately why they were given up' (Counselling Directory, n.d.).

Young people who have been adopted may need support in dealing with the emotional impact of tracing birth parents and the experience of reunion – both positive and negative. Birth parents may have a new family and the client has to deal with the fact that these other children were 'kept', again reinforcing long-held beliefs that it is their 'badness' that made their parent give them up. As well as intense feelings of loss and grief,

then, strong feelings of anger and shame may also be present. Approved adoption counsellors are registered with Ofsted, and are subject to regular inspections. This challenging
and rewarding work needs therapists who are resilient, knowledgeable, reliable and willing to commit to the 'long haul'.

## THE WORK OF CHILD AND ADOLESCENT MENTAL HEALTH SERVICES (CAMHS)

The information provided in the following sections on CAMHS is as accurate as is possible in
an ever-changing UK NHS environment, giving a flavour and overview of how services are
organised as providers of mental health care for children and young people. Traditionally,
CAMHS were NHS community and hospital-based mental health services for children and
young people. However, more recently a broader definition of CAMHS has emerged as community services in the voluntary sector respond to the growing number of children and young
people needing support with mental distress. The work of community CAMHS teams was
previously undertaken by the local authority child guidance clinics, until 1995 when the
*Together We Stand* document was published (NHS Health Advisory Service, 1995), offering a
coherent planning, delivery and evaluation strategy for children's mental health. The document introduced the current four-tier CAMHS framework.

Tier 1 is provided by universal services such as in-school counsellors, teachers, health
visitors and GPs, who are not necessarily specialist mental health practitioners but may have
some mental health knowledge. They offer advice and support including mental health promotion and can signpost young people to other more specialist services. Tier 2 are those
professionals working in community and primary care settings and may be counsellors, play
therapists, primary mental health workers, paediatric clinics or psychologists. They may
guide and support families, train other workers and identify young people with more severe
or complex needs. Tier 3 CAMHS provide a multidisciplinary approach usually in a community mental health clinic. The team often consists of specialists such as psychiatrists,
psychotherapists, psychologists, family therapists, mental health practitioners, play therapists
and nurse therapists. Tier 3 services support those young people with severe, complex and
persistent disorders. Typically, a Tier 3 service will take referrals from GPs, school counsellors, teachers, school nurses and social workers when young people have symptoms of mood
disorders such as depression, and anxiety disorders such as social anxiety disorder, post-
traumatic stress and phobias. Specialist CAMHS workers may also see children and young
people who need assessment for autistic spectrum disorder or ADHD (although these conditions are likely to be assessed by the community paediatric team). Tier 4 CAMHS services are
for children and young people with serious mental health problems, provided by highly specialised day units, outpatient teams or inpatient units. CAMHS may also offer 'targeted
services' for young people with learning difficulties, physical illness, behaviour difficulties or

children in care, although the scope of provision may differ in different parts of the UK and may change in response to NHS objectives. Counsellors may act as referral agents to CAMHS or be part of specialist service provision.

## Working with risk

Working with risk is relevant to all contexts of counselling children and young people (see Chapter 17: 'Law and Policy'). However, the elements of risk may be higher in children and young people who have been referred to specialist CAMHS, though this cannot be assumed. Tier 3 specialist CAMHS workers often carry a caseload of a wide range of difficulties, including young people who are persistently self-harming. This might include overdosing on medicines, using ligatures dangerously and often cutting their skin, sometimes quite deeply. Similar risky behaviours may also be seen in other counselling contexts, for example, secondary schools.

Favazza (1989: 143) suggested that 'of all disturbing patient behaviours, self-mutilation is the most difficult for clinicians to understand and treat'. A range of negative emotions are expressed by practitioners dealing with young people who self-mutilate, but particularly powerlessness, helplessness and inadequacy (Favazza, 1989; Spiers, 2001; Sanderson, 2006). In a study undertaken by Young Minds and Cello (2012), as many as one in 12 children and young people are believed to self-harm, inpatient admissions increasing by 8%. Intensive therapeutic intervention, including outreach work and telephone contact is recommended by the National Institute for Health and Clinical Excellence (NICE) for the treatment of self-harm, particularly when a young person is at risk of repetition. They also emphasise the importance of follow-up on missed appointments to lessen risk. In the Young Minds and Cello report, young people spoke of feeling unable to speak openly or ask for support and advice from professionals. Although self-harm behaviours are common in other counselling contexts when working with children and young people, the severe or more dangerous types of self-harm tend to be referred to specialist CAMHS.

According to the Royal College of Psychiatrists (2012) there are several reasons why young people harm themselves, but essentially it is a way of coping with distressing feelings building up inside. Feeling desperate with nowhere to turn may lead a child to feel helpless. This might lead to a young person cutting themselves to relieve the tension and to feel more in control. Others have reported feeling guilt and shame – self-harm being a way of punishing themselves. Some report traumatic events where they have disconnected from their bodies, the self-harm enabling them to feel alive (Royal College of Psychiatrists, 2012). It is important to distinguish self-injury from suicidal intention, and the Royal College of Psychiatrists (2010) claims that self-injury has been misperceived and confused with suicidal intent. Self-injury is often indicated when young people have a serious mental health problem, have been subject to abuse or rejection, are depressed or have an eating disorder, along with alcohol and drug problems (which indicates increased risk). Often, self-harm is triggered by arguments with family or close friends (Royal College of Psychiatrists, 2012). Whilst self-injury is often serious, it is important to know that suicide is more likely when a young person is depressed or has a serious mental illness. CAMHS practitioners assess for previous suicide attempts, and if a young person has a plan about dying in a situation where they cannot be saved. Having a relative who has killed themselves also increases risk, and if a young person is intoxicated or under the influence of drugs, they are at risk. Whitney (MindEd) highlights the potential seriousness of self-harm 'self-harm should be taken seriously; its occurrence is an identified risk factor of death by suicide as well as accidental death. The nature of the self-harm behaviour (for example, depth of cutting) does not predict underlying intent or levels of emotional distress.'

Part of the care plan for young people in this category is to ascertain the level of support within the family and to help them to find new ways of expressing their distress. Advice to parents to lock away pills or sharps is part of helping to keep young people safe until the therapeutic work can get underway and until their mood improves.

## Specialist CAMHS and cognitive-behavioural therapy

Many of the interventions recommended by NICE include an element of cognitive-behavioural therapy (CBT). For example, depression, anxiety disorders, PTSD, autism spectrum disorder and ADHD. CBT theories and interventions are addressed in Chapter 4 of this volume and therefore it is not necessary to detail the approach here. However, it is important to recognise ways in which CBT is utilised within CAMHS. School age children with a diagnosis of ADHD, for example, might be offered some CBT and/or social skills training, as well as parents being recommended parent training/education programmes (NICE, 2005). In addition, CBT has been shown to be feasible for children with ASD having a verbal IQ of at least 69 (Scottish Intercollegiate Guidelines Network, 2007). It is also recommended as a first-line treatment for moderate to severe depression in children and young people (NICE, 2005).

---

### Key Learning

- Insight into practice and policy and the development of child-focused services
- Knowledge and information on working with children in care including adopted children
- Greater working knowledge of Child and Adolescent Mental Health Services (CAMHS)

## Summary

This chapter has provided:

- An overview of health and social care services beginning with a section that looked at the development of child-focused services through practice and policy.
- Information and a case study example of counselling a looked-after child, their life experiences and appropriate therapeutic interventions such as therapeutic parenting for Katy, aged 6.
- An outline of the role of specialist CAMHS.

## Develop Your Skills

1. Read and reflect upon the attachment-focused work carried out by the counsellor working with Katy, aged 6, in the case study. What stands out about this approach?
2. How flexible do you see your practice being in terms of offering sessions to children and young people with chronic illness or chaotic lives? Reflect upon your service management and whether this would be possible.
3. What can the counsellor offer the 'looked-after' child or young person who has experience of instability and frequently changing foster placements? How might the child experience the counselling relationship?

   Turn to p.451 for possible answers.

## Discussion Questions

1. Read further around attachment theory in Chapter 1 of this book and research advances in neuroscience. What type of advances have been made over the past few years?
2. Use creative materials, narrative and photographs to look at your own life story. You may want to carry out this activity in personal therapy if you feel that it may be painful for you. How did you respond to carrying out this activity?
3. Audit your practice environment to see if it is user-friendly for children and young people who may have chronic illnesses or chaotic lives. What were the results of this audit?
4. Look at your own counselling practice and examine service policies around endings and boundaries with young clients. Are your policies in line with good practice?

## Further Reading

Gerhardt, S. (2004) *Why Love Matters: How Affection Shapes a Baby's Brain*. London: Routledge.

Golding, K (2008) *Nurturing Attachments: Supporting Children Who Are Fostered or Adopted*. London: Jessica Kingsley.

Hughes, D. (2006) *Building the Bonds of Attachment: Awakening Love in Deeply Troubled Children*, 2nd edn. New York: Jason Aronson.

Improving Access to Psychological Therapies (2012) Available at: https://www.england.nhs.uk/mental-health/adults/iapt/

### Online Resources

https://www.england.nhs.uk/mental-health/adults/iapt/

https://www.nspcc.org.uk/services-and-resources/research-and-resources/statistics/

https://www.childwelfare.gov/pubPDFs/brain_development.pdf

www.refugeecouncil.org.uk

## REFERENCES

Booth, P.B. and Jernberg, A.M. (2010) *Theraplay: Helping Parents and Children Build Better Relationships through Attachment-Based Play*. San Francisco, CA: Wiley.

Cello (2012) Available at: https://cellohealthplc.com/pdfs/talking_self_harm.pdf

Children (Scotland) Act (1995) Available at: https://www.legislation.gov.uk/ukpga/1995/36/contents (accessed 23 February 2018).

Cleaver, H., Unell, I. and Aldgage, J. (2011) *Children's Needs – Parenting Capacity: Child Abuse: Parental Mental Illness, Learning Disability, Substance Misuse and Domestic Violence*, 2nd edn. London: The Stationery Office.

Counselling Directory (n.d.) Adoption. Available at: www.counselling-directory.org.uk/adoption.html (accessed 23 February 2018).

DesLauriers, A.M. and Carlson, C.F. (1969) *Your Child is Asleep: Early Infantile Autism*. Homewood, IL: Dorsey Press.

Education Committee (2016) *Mental Health and Well-being of Looked-After Children*. London: House of Commons.

Favazza, A.R. (1989) Why patients mutilate themselves. *Hospital and Community Psychiatry* *40*(2): 137–145.

Gerhardt, S. (2004) *Why Love Matters: How Affection Shapes a Baby's Brain*. London: Routledge.

Golding, K. (2008) *Nurturing Attachments: Supporting Children Who Are Fostered or Adopted*. London: Jessica Kingsley.

Gov.uk    https://www.gov.uk/government/publications/immigration-statistics-october-to-december-2016/asylum

Graham-Bermann, S.A. and Levendosky, A.A. (1998) Traumatic stress symptoms in children of battered women. *Journal of Interpersonal Violence 13*(1): 111–128.

Hughes, D. (2006) *Building the Bonds of Attachment*. Lanham, MD: Rowland & Littlefield.

Her Majesty's Stationery Office (HMSO) (1989) The Children Act 1989. London: HMSO. Available at: www.legislation.gov.uk/ukpga/1989/41/contents (accessed 23 February 2018).

Her Majesty's Stationery Office (HMSO) (2002) Adoption and Children Act 2002. London: HMSO.

Lewis, E., Rubin, D.M., O'Reilly, A.L., Luan, X. and Localio, A.R. (2007) The impact of placement stability on behavioral well-being for children in foster care. *Paediatrics 119*(2): 336–344.

Littlechild, B. and Smith, R. (2013) *A Handbook for Interprofessional Practice in the Human Services*. London: Pearson.

MacBeath, J., Galton, M., Steward, S., MacBeath, A. and Page, C. (2006) *The Costs of Inclusion*. London: National Union of Teachers.

Munro, E.R. and Hardy, A. (2006) *Placement Stability: A Review of the Literature*. Loughborough: Centre for Child and Family Research, Loughborough University.

National Institute for Health and Clinical Excellence (NICE) (2008) *Attention Deficit Hyperactivity Disorder: Diagnosis and Management of ADHD in Children, Young People and Adults*. London: NICE.

NHS Health Advisory Service (1995) *Together We Stand: Thematic Review of the Commissioning, Role and Management of Child and Adolescent Mental Health Services*. London: The Stationery Office.

NSPCC (2015) *How Safe Are Our Children?* London: NSPCC.

Rogers, M. (2010) The challenges of working with adoption. *The Psychotherapist 44*: 2–15.

Schore, J.R. and Schore, A.N. (2010) Clinical social work and regulation theory: implications of neurobiological models of attachment. In: Bennett, S. and Nelson J.K. (eds) *Adult Attachment in Clinical Social Work*. New York: Springer, pp. 57–75.

Royal College of Psychiatrists (2010) *Self-Harm, Suicide and Risk: A Summary*. London: Royal College of Psychiatrists.

Royal College of Psychiatrists (2012) *Self-harm in young people: information for parents, carers and anyone who works with young people. Mental Health and Growing Up Factsheet* (March). Available at: www.rcpsych.ac.uk/healthadvice/parentsandyouthinfo/parentscarers/self-harm.aspx (accessed 23 February 2018).

Sampson, O. (1976) Fifty years of dyslexia: a review of the literature, 1925–75 II Practice. *Research in Education, 15*(1): 39–53.

Sanderson, C. (2006) *Counselling Adult Survivors of Child Sexual Abuse*, 3rd edn. London: Jessica Kingsley.

Scottish Intercollegiate Guidelines Network (SIGN) (2007) www.sign.ac.uk/our-guidelines.html

Spiers, T. (2001) *Trauma: A Practitioner's Guide to Counselling*. London: Routledge.

United Nations (1989) Convention on the Rights of the Child. Retrieved 2nd April 2017 from http://www.ohchr.org/EN/ProfessionalInterest/Pages/CRC.aspx

Ward, H. and Skuse, T. (2001) Performance targets and stability of placements for children long looked after away from home. *Children and Society 15*: 333–346.

Webster, C. (2002) *The NHS: A Political History*. Oxford: Oxford University Press.

World Health Organization (WHO) (n.d.) *Health systems*. Available at: www.who.int/topics/health_systems/en (accessed 23 February 2018).

# 27

# SCHOOL AND EDUCATION SETTINGS

## PETER PEARCE, ROS SEWELL AND KAREN CROMARTY

**This chapter will discuss:**

- **The role of counselling within a school setting**
- **The history of school counselling in the UK**
- **Details of some aspects of practice for schools counselling**
- **A current picture of the research on school-based counselling**
- **The many challenges and benefits of counselling provision within these settings.**

## INTRODUCTION

Counselling in schools is a very accessible and acceptable intervention for young people and can play a key, proactive and preventative, early intervention role. It is often a much smaller step to make contact with a school counsellor than to be referred to a service separate from the school, and can mean that many young people who might otherwise not be seen, or who might only be referred when problems have become severe and entrenched, can make use of the service.

Because schools are a universal service, accessing provision in schools can help to overcome any perceived stigma or reluctance to attend mental health services. For these reasons, school-based services such as counselling tend to have a high take up, and there is evidence that young people are more likely to access school-based mental health services when compared with non-school-based ones. (The Mentally Healthy Society: Report of the Taskforce on Mental Health in Society (2015))

In addition to this immediate, on-site response for distressed children and young people, counselling can also offer support, consultation and training to staff in the school system.

A range of different school counselling service models currently operate within the UK, which include external agencies delivering the services (e.g. the local authority, or a charity) and schools employing their own counsellors. These models of provision will each impact upon the service that can be provided within the school, considerations that need to be taken into account to ensure the clarity of the role and the lines of responsibility and reporting. Some services have developed along an individualised approach with a counsellor 'in the school but not of the school', and some have become more system-oriented, seeking to understand and align with the values and priorities of the school. Similarly, some services have developed just to provide a one-to-one counselling service to students and some have sought to offer a whole-school service, which, in addition to one-to-one counselling, might include a drop-in, group and family work, peer support, supervision and counselling skills training for teaching staff, and consultation on safe-guarding and policy development (for more details of peer support initiatives, see Chapter 13: 'Supervision').

These different models might each have their relative merits – for example, at the extremes, a lone, independent practitioner might be particularly vulnerable to a funding crisis, a key 'stakeholder' staff member leaving or getting into conflict with a 'school's culture'. At the other end, an embedded, 'school-owned' service might be in danger of being seen by students as not a safe place to talk.

Whatever structure the counselling service takes in a particular school, it is important that the service becomes widely known and what can be offered is understood. Referrals can come through a variety of sources: from the young person themselves or a peer, through parents or carers or other family members, via outside agencies or through a staff member. A majority of referrals are likely, however, to be initiated because of a staff member's concern about a young person, maybe because they have seen them distressed or withdrawn or because they are concerned about the young person's behaviour. 'Could you see Ahmed? He's very disruptive in class and never does his homework.' Referrals are often co-ordinated through the pastoral care team, with the counsellor expecting the referrer to have spoken to the young person about their concern and sought consent for the counsellor to at least see them for an initial meeting. The counsellor's role is then to offer the opportunity for the young person to decide for themselves whether a 'time to talk' in private is something that they might like to try out. In this way, within school, a timely response to issues as they arise can be offered, which feels a small step for the young person and seeks to minimise stigma and pathologising. In this first session, the counsellor needs to be absolutely clear about the limits of confidentiality, in a way that is clearly understood by the client, and how any need to break this would be brokered. In this first session the client will be helped to understand how counselling is different in some ways from other parts of school life: the client may call the counsellor by their first name rather than 'Sir' or 'Miss', for example, quickly signalling how the relationship being offered may differ from that of other adults in school. One student, recognising the gift in this gesture offered by the counsellor, replied jokingly, 'and you can call me Mr Aziz', so the counsellor did, every time they encountered each other from then on. This first session also provides an opportunity to acknowledge that attendance at counselling is part of school and boundaries need to be maintained, so, for example, the client will be expected to turn up on time for a session and, when it is over, then return to their next lesson.

Frequent reasons for referral include family problems, managing anger, bereavement, peer relationship problems and bullying. These may all first come to light because of changes in the young person's behaviour within school perhaps becoming more disruptive or more withdrawn. The theoretical orientation of the counsellor may to some degree determine how these issues will be responded to and it is important for the counsellor to be able to articulate their practice clearly both to the school and to the young person themselves. However, in order to operate effectively in school, regardless of theoretical orientation, the school counsellor needs to be approachable, adaptable and sensitive to systemic complexities of this setting. The young person's behaviour is perhaps best understood as their way of trying to cope with the problem rather than as the problem itself.

## SCHOOL-BASED COUNSELLING INTERNATIONALLY

Harris, in a scoping report for the British Association for Counselling and Psychotherapy (BACP) (Harris, 2013) estimates that school-based counselling is well established in 62 countries, mandatory in 39 countries as well as in 32 American states, one Australian state, three German states, two UK countries and three Canadian provinces. It is offered across the age span in most of these locations and is in the early stages of development in a further seven countries. Harris identifies that in the majority of countries where school-based counselling is mandatory, it is delivered by experienced teachers with an additional postgraduate level qualification in guidance and counselling or school-based counselling. In the UK, counselling is a profession in its own right.

## HISTORY OF SCHOOL COUNSELLING IN THE UK

School counselling in the UK underwent a period of rapid development throughout the 1960s and 1970s, which was later followed by an equally rapid decline in availability during the 1980s. This rise and fall has been variously attributed to a lack of resources, the belief that the counselling role should be more part of the school's pastoral care team role itself and to the fact that early UK counselling was not embedded sufficiently well into the culture of the school or adequately monitored (Robinson, 1996; Bor et al., 2002; Baginsky, 2004). The Children Act (1989) brought increased recognition of the rights of children and young people and with it greater demands on the pastoral care team role within schools, perhaps becoming instrumental in the reversal of this decline and renewed interest in school counselling as an accessible, acceptable and appropriate means of emotional support for young people (Mabey, 1995). Equally, the change in the devolution of school budgets, under Local Management of Schools (LMS) within the Education Reform Act (1988), gave head teachers and governing bodies in England, Northern Ireland and Wales far greater powers to 'buy in' appropriate and relevant services for their individual schools; many commissioned counselling services in both second-ary and primary school settings.

In 2007, the government of Northern Ireland introduced school counselling in all post-primary schools. In 2008 the Welsh government published its National Strategy for School-Based Counselling Services (following the recommendations of the Clwych Inquiry). By 2009, all secondary schools in Wales had access to school-based services, and in 2013 access to counselling for 11–16-year-olds in Wales became a statutory responsibility. For 2014/15, 89% of the 11,500 children and young people receiving school-based counselling in Wales did not need to be referred on and only 4% were referred to Child and Adolescent Mental Health Services (CAMHS) (Statistics for Wales, 2016). A similar commitment to pro-vide school counselling has been made in Scotland (Public Health Institute of Scotland, 2003) though no clear plan to implement this is in place as yet. In the UK, political recognition both of the scale of distress levels in children and young people and that such difficulties can have continuing serious implications into adulthood is increasing.

The Children and Young People's Mental Health Task Force was set up in 2014 with the aim of identifying and implementing improvements in children and young people's mental health services in the UK. The report of this task force, *Future in Mind* (DoH, 2015) identified that schools would be expected to take a central role in promoting mental health and provid-ing services for children and young people, and identified counselling services as 'a valuable complement to CAMHS'. The Health Select Committee also stated that, 'schools have enor-mous potential to help address emerging mental health issues in children and young people' (2014). The Department for Education's (2016) report, *Counselling in Schools: A Blueprint for the Future*, sets out a 'strong expectation' from government that all schools in the future should provide access to counselling services. It outlines how 'counselling within secondary schools has been shown to bring about significant reductions in psychological distress in the short-term, and helps young people move closer towards their personal goals', although there has been no national funding source to secure this provision as yet.

The Mentally Healthy Society: The Report of the Taskforce on Mental Health in Society (2015) similarly asserts that 'all children should be able to access professional, qualified coun-selling and therapy services in their school or college in age-appropriate form', identifying how 'school-based provision tends to be well-suited to offering the type of lower-level inter-vention that can be hard to access through formal CAMHS, but which can prevent problems subsequently becoming more serious'. This report also identifies that 'School-based provision is highly accessible, avoiding lengthy or complex referral processes, and waits tend to be rela-tively short. School is also where young people already are during the day, and – crucially – is where they say they want to access services: over two-thirds say they would rather see a coun-sellor at their school as opposed to outside.'

## THE BENEFITS AND CHALLENGES

As there are significant differences in the respective professional 'cultures' of education and therapy, it is of importance that roles and expectations are clarified in the setting up of any school counselling service. For example in one setting it was suggested that the counselling team should put up the counselling list and timetable on display in the staff room and that the counselling appointments could be read out in assembly to the whole school as this would help to remind students of their appointments. At another time there were discussions about the counselling team becoming class tutors. Whilst these arrangements may be acceptable to some teachers, the confidentiality issues and the dual roles involved would make it impossible to deliver a confidential counselling service built upon trust. It is important to remember that the culture, ethics and requirements of a counselling service may not be familiar or understood by a school who are taking on counselling as an addition to the school system. Prospective school counsellors, therefore, will need to be able to negotiate the service to fit within the school context.

This is a challenging setting for counsellors and working with young people in schools provides its own difficulties. A counsellor can find themselves encountering a client group who have not elected to have counselling or in some cases don't even know what is being offered. Consequently, they can be met by a range of reactions to the referral, which can affect the young person's ability to engage with the counsellor.

The school's culture and the life experiences of the pupils on roll can also be a challenge to counsellors, and issues may arise that they have not encountered during their training. In some communities, boys find it difficult to talk about their feelings, because they have been brought up to be 'strong' not 'weak'. Some young people from particular ethnic groups are often discouraged from sharing with a 'stranger' what is seen as the family's private business.

The level of engagement in counselling can depend too upon the communication skills and developmental stage of the client. Similarly, in schools, there will be some young people who have learning disabilities that may prohibit them from engaging in counselling as well as their peers.

A counsellor in this setting therefore would be well advised to have a great deal of experience in establishing solid working therapeutic relationships with a wide range of clients before embarking on working with difficult to reach clients with complex issues.

### Case study: Jason

Jason was referred to the counselling service because he had disengaged from school, had few friends and was underachieving academically. I was told that his mum was 'lovely' and that she had thought that counselling might be a good idea when the possibility had been suggested at a parents' evening. I was also informed that Jason had reluctantly agreed to see me, and his teachers found him aggressive and argumentative.

*(Continued)*

(Continued)

When I met Jason our first moments together were awkward. He sat quietly and didn't really want to engage with me. I said that I realised that he hadn't really wanted to have counselling but had agreed, which I didn't think was the same thing. From looking down at the floor this comment seemed to make him look up at me but straight back down again. I struggled to make a connection with him and he clearly showed me that he didn't really want to be there. When he first spoke he used few words and seemed quiet and aggressive in his manner. I said that I wasn't a teacher and that he didn't have to call me 'Miss' and that other people had thought he might benefit from some time to talk. He looked straight at me.

J: 'What would I wanna talk to you for? Why would I wanna talk to anyone in this fucking school? I hate it here … I hate school, I don't wanna fucking talk to no-one. You can report me if you like.'

Th: 'Report you, Jason?'

J: 'I was swearing, Miss.'

Th: 'Oh that … that's okay in here. I think I was listening to the fact that you hate school more than the swearing … I was thinking … you know it must be a long day if you hate it.'

J: 'Yeah, it is.' (laughs)

Th: 'And every day Jason … you have to spend a lot of time at school.'

J: 'That's it innit … that's just it! Your whole life in a place you hate.'

Th: '*Your* whole life in a place you hate.'

J: 'It's a thing you say, innit, "I hate school". But me, I really *do* hate school, It's so boring … M … I was gonna call you Miss then … what's your name?'

Th: 'You're bored, Jason.'

J: 'Yeah, and all the teachers … I hate them as well … They hate me too … I'm always in trouble.'

It was hard to engage Jason and there were moments where I really felt that I managed to feel connected to him, but these moments did not stay. Working with Jason, I always felt as though I needed to strive to establish and maintain a working relationship. Gradually as our therapeutic relationship developed, Jason shared more of himself and his struggle to find his place at home in a family of seven children. Jason said that, although he felt loved by his parents, he didn't feel as though they had the time to listen to him, and I began to realise the place of counselling in his life. He never missed a session and displayed very difficult behaviour in school if a session had to be moved or cancelled for school reasons. In the early counselling sessions, Jason would share stories about his school week and shouted and blamed others for his numerous detentions.

J: 'It's not fair because I put my hand up to say that I didn't understand and he kept saying "Jason put your hand down", "Jason put your hand down", so I'd had enough, right, I just got up and went to the door. This is 'im, "where are you going?" This is me, "I'm bored", this is 'im, "sit down now!" I just ignored 'im and walked out.'

I took my constant struggle to offer consistent acceptance and empathy to supervision and I noticed that Jason began to process in the sessions.

J:   'It was jokes today. He said "have you done your homework?" I said "no" and he said "well what a surprise, Jason" and we both laughed. Then I said "I tried but I couldn't do it". He's offered to help me. I'd like help. It was different today. I usually end up shouting and then he gets cross.'

Th:  'Something was different today, Jason, you didn't end up shouting.'

J:   'Yeah … yeah … it's better really. But it wasn't just me, he was nicer.'

Th:  'He was nicer and you were both different with each other.'

As the sessions developed Jason's focus changed from how fed up he was with school to his struggle to achieve academically. I wondered whether Jason had learning difficulties and whether he was bored and hated all the teachers because he could not keep up in class. As he began to gain an understanding of his experience, he identified this for himself and managed to speak to his teacher about this. Things were put in place to help him to manage school. He was assessed by the educational psychologist and dyslexia was diagnosed, and consequently he was able to negotiate a shorter timetable and some help for dyslexia.

It would be easy to read this case material and to assume that once the learning difficulties had been acknowledged and help was in place that Jason's problems were sorted out. This was not the case – we continued our work together as Jason began to make sense of his experiencing and to find his own way to manage to come to school and to participate in school life whilst still hating attending.

School structures require the whereabouts of students to be known, so a mechanism to inform class teachers of a pupil's absence from class will need to be brokered and schools may require appointments during some 'core subjects' to be avoided altogether. Part of the complexity of working in a school context is the need to respect the confidentiality of the young person whilst also communicating with the pastoral care team about the broader picture. Counsellors will therefore need to find a way to liaise with the pastoral care team and senior management about ongoing work in order to help the school understand the delicate balance between supporting the young person's autonomy, respecting their confidentiality and acknowledging the needs arising from the different duty of care held by the school system.

Learning to communicate in a way that is respectful of the school system and negotiating the differing needs and requirements of the two worlds of counselling and education becomes an essential competency within this setting. Counsellors can work most effectively when integrated with the whole pastoral care response of the school, and also need to find a way to enshrine the independence of the service so that students can remain confident of the difference between their counsellor and other staff members in this system.

Counsellors will need to consult with their external supervisor and line manager about the nature of referrals and about the limits of their competence in this setting. They will need to be familiar with the range of local services for children and young people, and understand how the respective referral processes operate. Reasons for referral on will include seeking more specialist help for a particular issue, for example, post-traumatic stress disorder (PTSD), lack of engagement with the current service being offered, a specific request by the client or their family, and following the counsellor's own assessment of their competence with the issues involved.

Counselling in schools requires careful consideration of the potential impact of an array of additional contextual factors. As has been described, these begin with third-party referral – it's most often initially someone else's concern and they may themselves have other concerns or none, and this referrer may continue to be involved, often expecting 'results' quickly, keen to feed back to the counsellor their views of the issues. There may also be other 'stakeholders' who have a significant influence over whether the young person can continue therapy, and the counselling may be taking place in the very setting in which the issues have arisen. The student and counsellor are highly likely to encounter each other around the building and see each other interacting with others in the school system – in fact some of the other 'characters' in the person's narrative may well also be known to the counsellor. Practical issues may also need careful negotiation, including rooming for the work, how the young person leaves class to come to counselling, which classes are acceptable to leave and who in the system needs to be informed that this is happening. In this setting there is no division between working therapeutically and not, as staff members or students might approach us around the building to connect about a referral and it is important that the counsellor becomes proficient at managing these one-way permeable boundaries to ensure that support for the counselling work continues. The counsellor may also be the only adult who doesn't pick the student up on their uniform, lateness or behaviour as they move around the school, and this sometimes needs sensitive brokering both with a staff member seeking additional adult support and with a student given a window of freedom from the school rules but plunged straight back into them at the end of the session.

## RESEARCH

A review of UK school-based counselling (Cooper, 2013) identifies it as one of the most prevalent forms of psychological therapy for young people in the UK, with approximately 70,000–90,000 cases per year, generally being offered one-to-one supportive therapy. So numbers roughly equivalent to those referred to CAMHS for the same age group. In terms of effectiveness, non-directive supportive therapy is a National Institute for Health and Clinical Excellence (NICE)-recommended intervention for mild depression, and there is developing evidence to suggest that school-based humanistic counselling – a distillation of common school-based counselling practices in the UK – is effective at reducing psychological distress, helping young people achieve their personal goals and is cost-effective (Cooper et al., 2009,

2013; Pybis et al., 2012; Rupani et al., 2012; Banerjee et al., 2014; Pearce et al., 2016) and, whilst there is as yet no clear indication from the UK government that counselling will become part of statutory provision, there is broad political recognition that schools are an excellent place to site a mental health professional in terms of accessibility, timeliness and proactive, preventive interventions, not just in one-to-one counselling input but for the role this might potentially have across the school system.

In terms of current ongoing research in the UK, the ETHOS study, led by staff from Roehampton University in collaboration with Metanoia Institute, the BACP, the London School of Economics (LSE), the National Children's Bureau (NCB), Karen Cromarty Consultancy and the Universities of Manchester, London and Sheffield, and funded by the Economic and Social Research Council (ESRC), is a fully powered randomised controlled trial looking into the benefits of providing professional school-based counsellors to support young people experiencing emotional problems. The ETHOS study involves 18 UK schools and approximately 300 participants aged 13–16 years. It is running between April 2016 and March 2019 and is designed to offer a large-scale investigation into the effectiveness and cost-effectiveness of school-based humanistic counselling.

School-based counselling is evaluated positively by service users and school staff, and is perceived by them as an effective means of bringing about improvements in students' mental health and emotional well-being. School staff and service users also perceive school-based counselling as enhancing young people's capacity to engage with studying and learning. A key strength of school-based counselling is that it is perceived as a highly accessible service and that it increases the extent to which all young people have an independent, supportive professional to talk to about difficulties in their lives. However, there are also several areas for development: increasing the extent to which practice is evidence-informed, greater use of outcome monitoring, ensuring equity of access to young people from black and minority ethnic backgrounds, increasing service user involvement and enhancing levels of integration with other mental health provisions. It is hoped that recent initiatives in the development of competences, e-learning resources and accreditation for counsellors working with young people will help to achieve this.

## Key Learning

- Counselling services can operate successfully in schools.
- There are a variety of problems and difficulties that children and young people talk to school counsellors about.
- The school setting can provide a variety of challenges for counsellors, but by working collaboratively with school staff, these can usually be overcome for the benefit of the young clients.
- Whilst the emerging research in this field is growing and positive, there are still many areas of practice to be explored and evaluated.

## Summary

Working as a counsellor in a school setting can be both stimulating and challenging. The demands of the school setting need to be navigated, but this can often be achieved by working closely with school staff, and within existing school systems and structures. Current research is showing that counselling can have a positive impact on young people's lives, which feels like an investment for the psychological well-being of the future. Overall, school-based counsellors – working with colleagues in the field of child and adolescent mental health – have the potential to contribute to an increasingly comprehensive, integrated and 'young person-centred' system of mental health care.

## Discussion Questions

1. What are the factors to take into account when you as a counsellor are ascertaining whether a client is capable of consent to counselling? Where can guidance be sought in law?
2. How can you as a counsellor maintain the trust of clients within an educational establishment, when you are clearly seen as a member of staff outside of the counselling room?
3. In which ways could a counsellor contribute to the institution, above and beyond their work one-to-one in the counselling room?

Turn to p.451 for possible answers.

## Develop Your Skills

1. What are the important factors you would want noting in a referral form to your counselling service?
2. You have been asked to speak about the counselling service during the school assembly. What information needs to be included in your talk?
3. Devise a document that goes back to the referrer at the end of therapy, which updates them on the current situation without breaking client confidentiality.

Turn to p.452 for possible answers.

## Further Reading

British Association for Counselling and Psychotherapy (BACP) (2011 [2009]) *School-Based Counselling Operating Toolkit*. Lutterworth: BACP and Welsh Assembly Government.

British Association for Counselling and Psychotherapy (BACP) (2014) *The Competences Required to Deliver Effective Humanistic Counselling for Young People. Counsellors' Guide*. Lutterworth: BACP.

Prever, M. (2010) *Counselling and Supporting Children and Young People: A Person-Centred Approach*. London: SAGE.

Smyth, D. (2013) *Person-Centred Therapy with Children and Young People*. London: SAGE.

Kirkbride, R. (2018) *Counselling Young People : A Practitioner Manual*. London : SAGE.

### Online Resources

BACP website: www.bacp.co.uk, especially the BACP Children and Young People Division and the Competences for Working with Children and Young People.

Counselling in School: part of Counselling MindEd (https://www.minded.org.uk)

## REFERENCES

Baginsky, W. (2004) *School Counselling in England, Wales and Northern Ireland: A Review*. London, NSPCC.

Banerjee, R., Weare, K. and Farr, W. (2014) Working with 'Social and Emotional Aspects of Learning' (SEAL): associations with school ethos, pupil social experiences, attendance, and attainment. *British Educational Research Journal 40*(4): 718–742. https://doi.org/10.1002/berj.3114

Bor, R., Ebner-Landy, J., Gill, S. and Brace, C. (2002) *Counselling in Schools*. London: SAGE.

Cooper, M. (2009) Counselling in UK secondary schools: a comprehensive review of audit and evaluation studies. *Counselling and Psychotherapy Research 9*(3): 137–150. https://doi.org/10.1080/14733140903079258.

Cooper, M. (2013) *School-Based Counselling in UK Secondary Schools: A Review and Critical Evaluation*. Glasgow: University of Strathclyde.

Department for Education (DfE) (2016) *Counselling in Schools: A Blueprint for the Future*. London: DfE.

Department of Health (DoH) (2015) *Future in mind: promoting, protecting and improving our children and young people's mental health and wellbeing*. Available at: https://www.gov.uk/

government/uploads/system/uploads/attachment_data/file/414024/Childrens_Mental_Health.pdf (accessed 23 February 2018).

Harris, B. (2013) *International School-Based Counselling: A Review of School-Based Counselling Internationally*. London: BACP and Department of Health.

Health Select Committee Third Report (2014) *Children's and Adolescents' Mental Health and CAMHS*. Mental Health Network NHS Confederation. Publications.parliament.UK

Her Majesty's Stationery Office (HMSO) (1989) Children Act 1989. *Family Law, 11*(6): c.41. Available at: www.legislation.gov.uk/ukpga/1989/41/contents (accessed 26 February 2018).

Mabey, J. S. (1995). *Counselling for Young People*. Buckingham: Open University.

O'Brien, S., Greatley, A. and Meek, L. (2015) *The Mentally Healthy Society: The Report of the Taskforce on Mental Health in Society*. Discussion Paper. The Labour Party, London.

Pearce, P., Sewell, R., Cooper, M., Osman, S., Fugard, A.J.B. and Pybis, J. (2016) Effectiveness of school-based humanistic counselling for psychological distress in young people: pilot randomized controlled trial with follow-up in an ethnically diverse sample. *Psychology and Psychotherapy*. https://doi.org/10.1111/papt.12102.

Public Health Institute of Scotland (2003) *Needs Assessment Report on Child and Adolescent Mental Health*. Edinburgh: Public Health Institute of Scotland.

Pybis, J., Hill, A., Cooper, M. and Cromarty, K. (2012) A comparative analysis of the attitudes of key stakeholder groups to the Welsh Government's school-based counselling strategy. *British Journal of Guidance & Counselling 40*(5): 485–498. https://doi.org/10.1080/030698 85.2012.718736.

Robinson, B.D. (1996) School counsellors in England and Wales, 1965–1995; a flawed innovation? *Pastoral Care in Education 14*(3): 12–19.

Rupani, P., Haughey, N. and Cooper, M. (2012) The impact of school-based counselling on young people's capacity to study and learn. *British Journal of Guidance and Counselling 40*(5): 499–514. https://doi.org/10.1080/03069885.2012.718733.

Statistics for Wales (2016) The Welsh Government. http://gov.wales/statistics-and-research/counselling-children-and-young-people/?lang=en

# APPENDIX

## POSSIBLE ANSWERS

### Chapter 4

#### Discussion questions

1. Keep the explanation very simple. You could say that 'people who worry often think in ways that make them feel frightened. When they feel frightened they want to avoid the things that scare them. We will work together to see if this happens for you by looking at the way you think, how you feel and what you do.'

2. You would need to provide a rationale and explain why this was important and negotiate whether they would be able to undertake this task. The 'diary' could be a paper record, computer log, text or email so the boy can choose the method that he finds most attractive. Check that the diary is achievable, for example, you may agree to record a whole week or the next three negative thoughts. If the boy feels unable to keep the diary, then respect his decision. You will still be able to find out about his thoughts by talking through any situations during your next meeting.

3. Ask the young person to predict what they think would happen if this was true, for example, 'I will get D grades or lower'. Ask them to rate how much they believe this thought on a 1–100 scale. The young person could then record all their school marks over the next week. What actually happened is then compared with what they predicted to test their belief. How much they believed the original thought can then be re-assessed to see whether the experiment had helped them discover any new information that challenged their original belief (e.g. 'I seem to get better marks in history').

4. Socratic questions are designed to encourage self-reflection, with the aim of helping the young person find new information and meanings that challenge their existing thoughts. The therapist adopts an open and curious stance and uses questions to draw the young person's attention to exceptions ('Have there been any times that this didn't happen?'), reflect on different perspectives ('What would your best friend think if this happened to them?') and to consider different meanings ('Are there any other explanations for what has happened?').

## Develop your skills questions

1. For younger children cartoons and thought bubbles can be used to identify and discuss what someone might be thinking; pictures and worksheets can stimulate and emphasise key aspects of the CBT model; games like emotional charades can highlight the different facial and bodily signals associated with different emotions. For older children diagrams and summary sheets (explaining the link between thoughts, feelings and behaviours) provide a useful way of summarising the cognitive model; video clips can be a useful way of presenting ideas and stimulating discussions (e.g. around thinking styles and errors).

2. It is not uncommon for young people to reply to direct questions in such a way. This does not mean that they are unable to identify their thoughts, but suggests that alternative methods might be more productive. You can help them tune into their thoughts by talking about positive or familiar events (e.g. preparing for something they like) or by talking about what a third party could be thinking. With younger children you could describe an event and ask them to write or draw a picture in a blank thought bubble to show what someone might be thinking about it. Alternatively, you may discover a child's thoughts by simply listening very carefully to what they say. Descriptions often include thoughts and assumptions that we are not always very good at noticing.

3. The content of anxious cognitions tend to be about threat ('People are looking at me'), danger ('Everyone will make fun of my new trainers') or an inability to cope ('I won't know what to say if they ask me any questions'). Depressive cognitions tend to be about loss ('Everyone I get to know leaves me'), self-deprecation ('I am sure I'm not as interesting as everyone else') and failure ('I am useless at talking to people').

4. Functional thoughts can be described as 'green thoughts' because they are motivating and encourage you to do things. They are positive ('I can do it'), balanced ('This might be hard but I have done it before') and enabling ('I've got nothing to lose by giving it a try'). Dysfunctional thoughts are 'red thoughts', which stop you from doing things. They are negative ('I will get this wrong'), biased ('I can never get this right') and are disempowering ('There is no point in trying').

# Chapter 6

## Discussion questions

1. In his assessment, John could focus on the relationship that home (mum and family) and school (school staff, culture, ethos, etc.) have with each other. Very often, undercurrents of blame between the systems make it difficult to come together in thinking about change (Dowling and Osborne, 2003). Any small shift in the perspective of any of the key people in Abdi's life will create possibilities to shift from being the 'excluded' one. Blame is a barrier to change.

2. Transitions, especially the transition from primary to secondary schools, are anxiety-provoking for many children and families, even the most resilient. This is even more so for traumatised

children, for whom change can evoke terror and fear. Good practice has shown school staff building links, ensuring that information regarding a child's educational, emotional and behavioural needs is passed on. Many secondary schools provide induction programmes, allowing Year 6 students to visit their new school. In Abdi's case, identifying key named people (such as a Year 7 head of year) or support services (such as a drop-in service or school counsellor) to both mum and Abdi may assist them in identifying helpful people to go to when in need of support. Such communication, seemingly simple, can be technically difficult to carry through. However, it goes a long way towards trying to hold the child in mind in the gap between the primary and secondary school systems.

3. The race, ethnicity and age of John are not mentioned in the case study. If you had an impression or image of him, it may be useful to reflect on it. We generally associate characteristics of benevolence, altruism, thoughtfulness and hopefulness with counsellors. What race, ethnicity and age did you associate with these characteristics? An important aspect of developing self-awareness is to recognise your assumptions and biases. Whilst some theories suggest that your individuality should be kept out of the room, we suggest that self-awareness should be developed to ponder such things as: How might an other see me? What labels might they give me? How might this child see me, my clothes, my haircut, my race, my accent, my age, my class, my ability/disability, and what might their associations be with 'someone like me'?

# Chapter 7

## Discussion questions

1. Rogers (1951) argues that if the person can feel fully accepted, constructive personality change will occur. Unconditional positive regard (UPR) may feel difficult to offer in some settings such as schools because we are used to judging children and young people in terms of achievement and behaviour, so UPR would feel contrary to the prevailing culture. We need to consciously resist the ingrained adult inclination to praise a child for 'being good' and saying 'nice things' and instead allow them to voice negative, potentially shameful feelings without fear of judgement or criticism.

2. Limit-setting ensures a safe and secure environment for children – indeed a child can feel scared if left totally 'free'. Clear boundaries also reduce anxiety for the play therapist. Limits structure, teach self-control and self-responsibility, serve to protect the child, the therapist, the toys and the room, and also help to minimise socially unacceptable behaviour (whilst still demonstrating acknowledgement and acceptance of the feelings that may underlie this behaviour). Whilst there are individual variations in approaches to limit-setting, most play therapists clarify that children are not permitted to hurt themselves or the therapist and that the toys and the room are not damaged on purpose. Adherence to time limits is also important.

3. Children who have restricted messy play opportunities may remain disconnected from their physical selves and may become more inhibited in creative or physical self-expression in later life. Those who engage in lots of pretend role-play may be better able to manage different adult roles with more confidence.

## Chapter 13

### Discussion questions

1. If you find yourself regularly providing, or wanting to provide your answers to your supervisees' practice situations, whose needs are you meeting? This response could be an alert to considering how you are using your own supervision or peer consultation.
2. As a supervisor you have a dual responsibility for the safety and potential well-being of your supervisees and their clients, whilst holding a safe, open working space with your supervisee. Monitoring limits of time, place and role becomes part of this duality.
3. Key elements of a supervision contract:

   - Your membership of a professional body.
   - Your professional liability cover.
   - Time, place, frequency and payment for sessions.
   - Conditions of confidentiality.
   - In what circumstances must confidentiality be broken, how will the client be informed?
   - Name the key professionals and other adults with shared responsibility for the child.
   - Identify the line of management accountability.
   - Stages of a complaints procedure:

     o Mutual discussion to resolve the issue.
     o If no resolution possible, refer the situation to management and/or the appropriate professional body, with the knowledge of each party.

## Chapter 15

### Discussion questions

1. In the process of therapy, children with a history of attachment disruptions are slow to develop meaningful and effective therapeutic relationships with counsellors. When they finally develop these types of relationships, it may be their first time to have such a relationship with anyone. Endings with children with attachment disruptions may likely be characterised by a child's tendency to withdraw, become depressed or angry, or revert to apathy towards the counsellor.
2. Endings with children are different from endings with adults due to developmental stages of life. First, the child's understanding of time is different from an adult's. Second, the context of endings is new to a child. Because of greater experience, an adult is more likely to understand

circumstances such as a therapist moving to another job. Even if a therapist explains the necessity of ending, the child is more likely to interpret the ending as being related to something the child has done or said. These types of interpretations need to be worked through during the final sessions as the child comes to understand that ending of therapy does not mean that there is something wrong with them.

3. A therapist is more effective when endings are addressed at the beginning of the counselling relationship. At first contact, the therapist emphasises the need for parents to share concerns as soon as they develop. The therapist also emphasises the importance of allowing several sessions for endings to occur. If parents are certain about ending, the therapist will ask for at least three to four more sessions for a proper closing to therapy.

4. A therapist's personal history of loss has great impact on the therapist's approach to termination. If a therapist has experienced multiple losses but has not undergone personal therapy, the therapist may transfer these experiences to the counsellor–client relationship.

5. A therapist may be impacted by the structure of endings. The finality of a closing session with no further contact will feel disruptive to some therapists, whilst the tapering of sessions or further contact after therapy will cause some therapists to feel that the relationship is deteriorating, not ending.

# Chapter 16

## Discussion questions

1. Some young people say that being asked about their experiences in a research interview, or on a questionnaire, makes them start to reflect on their lives in a way that they hadn't before, and that this leads to realisations about themselves and what they want, which helps to make positive changes. It may also be that taking part in research makes people feel that they are contributing something positive, helping the researchers and the wider population, and that this helps young people to feel better about themselves.

2. Evaluation can be incorporated in different ways, and to different degrees. As a minimum, completing an outcome measure before and after a period of counselling can provide useful information on change. Using measures at every session gives much more in-depth data, which can be used to give detailed feedback to clients and/or counsellors.

3. Some counsellors may feel that evaluation of outcomes impedes their work with clients. It is important that counsellors feel confident with any evaluation tools before using them with clients, and have the opportunity to discuss and explore their experience of evaluation with a supervisor.

# Chapter 17

## Discussion questions

1.  Simon has a number of rights in this situation. He has a right:

    *   to a say in decisions being made about him, under Article 12 of the UN Convention on the Rights of the Child (1989);
    *   to confidentiality, if of 'sufficient understanding', under the *Gillick* case (1986), confirmed by *Axon* (2006);
    *   to therapeutic privacy, under the *Campbell* case (2004);
    *   to services from the local authority, if deemed to be a 'child in need', under Section 17, Children Act 1989.

2.  The school counsellor's legal position is influenced by safeguarding policy and by employment law, that is:

    *   the local authority has a duty to safeguard and promote the welfare of children, under Section 175, Education Act 2002;
    *   the local authority is required to cooperate with social services in providing services for 'children in need', under the Children Acts 1989 and 2004;
    *   the counsellor is obliged to comply with school and local authority policy with regard to attending safeguarding meetings, under the terms of her contract of employment.

3.  The counsellor has a number of options here, for example:

    *   seek professional guidance from the BACP Ethical Framework and the BACP Information Office;
    *   clarify her professional and therapeutic options, through supervision with a suitable qualified counsellor with experience in working with children and young people;
    *   obtain expert legal advice from her professional indemnity insurance provider, or psychologists protection society;
    *   review school policy on confidentiality and information-sharing with the head teacher, in order to protect school counselling confidentiality as far as possible

# Chapter 18

## Discussion questions

1.  Children and young people have a number of rights in this situation. They have a right to:

    *   a say in decisions being made about them, under Article 12 of the UN Convention on the Rights of the Child (1989);

- confidential access to information and medical treatment on sexual health and counselling;
- depending on their having 'sufficient understanding', if aged under 16;
- on the same basis as an adult if aged 16–17;
- not to be discriminated against in the provision of their rights, under Article 2 of the UN Convention.

2.

- by providing children and young people with full information about their rights, as required by the UN Convention, under Article 42;
- by independent monitoring and evaluation of the referral patterns, outcomes and satisfaction levels of children and young people accessing the service;
- by actively involving children and young people in the management of the service, in ways consistent with their age and understanding.

3.

- differing levels of understanding, leading to more limited entitlement to confidentiality for children, on the *Gillick* principle;
- a heightened balance for *welfare* considerations for children, compared with *autonomy* considerations for young people;
- potentially greater scope for counsellor risk-taking with young people, based on ethically informed practice.

# Chapter 19

## Discussion questions

1. The challenging issues are those that any counsellor could face with a young client: working with risk in terms of psychological holding and self-harm, listening to stories of severe trauma and violence and being 'with' Ishtar, yet keeping self safe. There are also issues of spirituality that may be in line with or against your own belief systems.
2. A transcultural approach would involve listening to and accepting Ishtar's accounts of her experience within a framework of cultural and spiritual material that may be very different to your own.
3. By taking a Deaf Awareness course in the first instance, you will become more aware and knowledgeable in respect of issues that may impact on your young deaf clients and learn more about methods of communication. Further preparation would include courses in BSL, or the sign language of your own country.

## Chapter 23

### Discussion questions

There is some evidence to suggest that abuse and neglect in infancy may damage the developing brain (Gerhardt, 2004). However, more research is needed in this area. In other respects, it is important to remain positive and have an optimistic outlook about the capacity of humans to survive trauma and abuse. Research in this area is inherently flawed in that we can never know how many people were abused in childhood, live full and happy lives and choose never to speak of their experiences. These people are absent from our statistics and what we have therefore may be a skewed sample of children and adults whom we know about because of their struggles. Therapy is the perfect place for distorted thinking to be addressed and for clients to discover what coping strategies work for them. The survivor stories in *Strong at the Broken Places* speak for themselves (Sanford, 1991).

Where intervention is limited to six sessions, therapists have to think strategically about their chosen method. Goal-based interventions may be more realistic than the approach used in the case study. During the contracting stage, clients choose which issues they wish to work on and the counsellor helps to ensure the target is realistic. The principle of 'non-maleficence' should be applied: sometimes it is more harmful to create expectations that cannot be met and therapists must avoid this wherever possible.

- Where other needs are more pressing and counselling may undermine the meeting of these, for example, settling into a new home/school, undertaking examinations.
- Where there is a strong risk that therapy may undermine the legal process and the client's greatest priority is the conviction of the perpetrator.
- Where the client does not want therapy and the referral is driven by others (this depends on the age of the child and their ability to make an informed choice).
- In an ideal world, therapy will take place in a purpose-built environment, equipped with resources to enable the full range of interventions the therapist is skilled to offer. In reality, such places are not always available. Each therapist needs to consider their working environment and how this matches the needs of their clients. Children who have been abused may have a great need to feel safe and to be assured of privacy and guaranteed of no interruptions. They may be more sensitive than others to the stigma attached to counselling and believe that everyone knows what has happened to them. On the other hand, some children who have been abused may feel uncomfortable or even threatened by environments that are too intimate. Therapists should be aware that some places have certain associations/negative connotations and, where possible, seek the client's view about where and when sessions should be held. The counsellor feeling at home should always come second to finding the right environment for the client. This should be thought about as part of the referral and planning process.
- The same principles of confidentiality apply to this client group as any other (see Chapters 17 and 18). Information has to be shared where the therapist is made aware that a child is at risk of

significant harm. It is not unusual for children to disclose new information about abuse during therapy. The counsellor needs to be prepared for this and build into the contract what action would be taken in this event. It is unusual for children (especially older children) to 'accidentally' disclose, especially if it has been made clear to them that such information would have to be passed on. In these situations, the counsellor should empower the client by sharing information about what will happen next and allowing them choices wherever this is possible.

# Chapter 26

## Develop your skills questions

1.  The difficulty that Joan, the grandmother has in empathising with Katy when she lashes out at her is apparent and highlights the difficulties in empathising with children and young people who are raging at you. The support offered to Katy and her grandmother alongside each other is central to the therapy.
2.  This is a difficult issue due to the structure of many organisations offering support and services to children and young people. Some services have drop-in slots or keep a selection of appointments free for young clients.
3.  Points to consider include the client's previous experience of relationships ending prematurely and/or badly. They may have experienced several broken relationships and have deep-rooted feelings of loss. By offering a boundaried counselling relationship and a clear structure leading to the inevitable ending, offering some control and power to the child/young person, for example, in the type of ending they would like to experience, the ending may be reparative.

# Chapter 27

## Discussion questions

1.  Age of client (over 16 generally regarded by law as being competent, unless exceptional circumstances; and unlikely that a 13-year-old would be deemed competent to have the capacity to consent).

    *   Maturity: understanding of consequences of his or her actions.
    *   Whether or not suffering from a mental illness.
    *   Whether the client is under the influence of drugs including alcohol.
    *   Conditions of Gillick competence and Age of Legal Capacity (Scotland) Act.

2.  Attention to detail in contracting with client, for example, reassurance of confidentiality within usual limits of risk.

- Explanation of your role in and around the educational establishment, for example, may need to attend staff meetings or be seen talking to other staff in corridors, and confirm that these conversations are not about the content of the counselling session.
- Note that although clients may know others who attend, you will not confirm their attendance with peers.
- Revisit contract regularly, being actively seeking and open to questions.
- Be sensitive to clients when seeing them around the site – discuss with them in session if you should acknowledge, smile, say hello, etc.
- Some establishments have policies on confidential discussions. Check to see if yours does.
- Consider your attendance at public functions such as prize-givings, awards evenings, open days, etc., and if necessary explain to clients in advance that you may be attending.

3. Prepare regular reports for management that identify current trends in the population on the roll, for example, bullying and substance misuse.

- Support management in the writing of policies and guidelines for specific and relevant issues such as safety online and dealing with self-harming behaviours.
- Support whole-school approaches such as critical incidents (e.g. death of a student or staff member).
- Provide training for staff in areas such as mental health and well-being.
- Provide time in school assemblies or curriculum areas for students, for example, informing about the counselling service, stress management during examination periods, etc.
- Attend open days/evenings to inform students, parents and stakeholders about the counselling service and being able to answer any questions they may have.
- Run peer support programmes.

## Develop your skills questions

1. Not all will be appropriate depending on setting, but you may find it helpful to receive information on the following:

- name and role of referrer;
- date of referral;
- name of client;
- age of client;
- year group/course studied/faculty;
- postal address;
- reason for referral;
- does the client support the referral?
- parental permission (if appropriate) sought (how and when);
- can the information on referral be shared with client?

- any barriers of access for the client?
- how urgent is the referral?
- history (include any other services involved with client and any significant events, e.g. bereavement);
- current health (physical and emotional, and including any knowledge of sleep habits/drugs/ alcohol/food – including energy drinks);
- any known details about relationships (peers/staff/family).

2. Consider including:

- name of client;
- thanks for the referral;
- the appropriateness of the referral (or otherwise);
- that therapy is over;
- that the client found it helpful (if this is so);
- date;
- request that the referrer doesn't discuss directly with client, unless the conversation is initiated by the client.

Do:

- discuss this document with your client;
- agree what can and can't be said;
- regard this as a way of promoting appropriate referrals to your service.

3. You have been asked to speak about the counselling service during the school assembly. What information needs to be included in your talk?

- An introduction to yourself.
- A brief explanation about counselling – what it is, and what it isn't.
- What sort of difficulties counselling could help with.
- Who counselling is for.
- How the students can be referred for counselling sessions in the school.
- Stress the importance of students talking to a staff member if they have a concern for themselves or others.

# INDEX